Hampton-Brown EDGE

Reading, Writing & Language

PROGRAM AUTHORS

David W. Moore

Deborah J. Short

Michael W. Smith

Alfred W. Tatum

Literature Consultant

René Saldaña, Jr.

NATIONAL GEOGRAPHIC LEARNING | CENGAGE Learning

Acknowledgments

Grateful acknowledgment is given to the authors, artists, photographers, museums, publishers, and agents for permission to reprint copyrighted material. Every effort has been made to secure the appropriate permission. If any omissions have been made or if corrections are required, please contact the Publisher.

Photographic Credits

Cover: Standing in Awe of the Aurora, Northwest Territories, Canada, Robert Postma. Photograph © Robert Postma/First Light/Getty Images.

Acknowledgments continue on page 892.

For product information and technology assistance, contact us at
Customer & Sales Support, 888-915-3276

For permission to use material from this text or product, submit all requests online at **www.cengage.com/permissions**
Further permissions questions can be emailed to
permissionrequest@cengage.com

National Geographic Learning | Cengage Learning
1 Lower Ragsdale Drive
Building 1, Suite 200
Monterey, CA 93940

Cengage Learning is a leading provider of customized learning solutions with office locations around the globe, including Singapore, the United Kingdom, Australia, Mexico, Brazil, and Japan. Locate your local office at **www.cengage.com/global**.

Visit National Geographic Learning online at **ngl.cengage.com**
Visit our corporate website at **www.cengage.com**

Printed in the USA.
RR Donnelley, Willard, OH

ISBN: 978-12854-39488

Printed in the United States of America
17 18 19 20 21 22
10 9 8 7 6 5 4

CONTENTS AT A GLANCE

Reviewers

We gratefully acknowledge the many contributions of the following dedicated educators in creating a program that is not only pedagogically sound, but also appealing to and motivating for high school students.

Literature Consultant

Dr. René Saldaña, Jr., Ph.D.
Assistant Professor
Texas Tech University

Dr. Saldaña teaches English and education at the university level and is the author of *The Jumping Tree* (2001) and *Finding Our Way: Stories* (Random House/Wendy Lamb Books, 2003). More recently, several of his stories have appeared in anthologies such as *Face Relations*, *Guys Write for GUYS READ*, *Every Man for Himself*, and *Make Me Over*, and in magazines such as *Boy's Life* and *READ*.

Teacher Reviewers

Felisa Araujo-Rodriguez
English Teacher
Highlands HS
San Antonio, TX

Barbara Barbin
Former HS ESL Teacher
Aldine ISD
Houston, TX

Joseph Berkowitz
ESOL Chairperson
John A. Ferguson Sr. HS
Miami, FL

Dr. LaQuanda Brown-Avery
Instructional Assistant Principal
McNair MS
Decatur, GA

Troy Campbell
Teacher
Lifelong Education Charter
Los Angeles, CA

John Oliver Cox
English Language
Development Teacher
Coronado USD
Coronado, CA

Clairin DeMartini
Reading Coordinator
Clark County SD
Las Vegas, NV

Lori Kite Eli
High School Reading Teacher
Pasadena HS
Pasadena, TX

Debra Elkins
ESOL Teamleader/Teacher
George Bush HS
Fort Bend, IN

Lisa Fretzin
Reading Consultant
Niles North HS
Skokie, IL

Karen H. Gouede
Asst. Principal, ESL
John Browne HS
Flushing, NY

Alison Hyde
ESOL Teacher
Morton Ranch HS
Katy, TX

Patricia James
Reading Specialist
Brevard County
Melbourne Beach, FL

Dr. Anna Leibovich
ESL Teacher
Forest Hills HS
New York, NY

Donna D. Mussulman
Teacher
Belleville West HS
Belleville, IL

Rohini A. Parikh
Educator
Seward Park School
New York, NY

Sally Nan Ruskin
English/Reading Teacher
Braddock SHS
Miami, FL

Pamela Sholly
Teacher
Oceanside USD
Oceanside, CA

Dilmit Singh
Teacher/EL Coordinator
Granada Hills Charter HS
Granada Hills, CA

Amanda E. Stewart
Reading Teacher
Winter Park High School
Winter Park, FL

Beverly Troiano
ESL Teacher
Chicago Discovery Academy
Chicago, IL

Dr. Varavarnee Vaddhanayana
ESOL Coordinator
Clarkston HS
Clarkston, GA

Donna Reese Wallace
Reading Coach
Alternative Education
Orange County
Orlando, FL

Bonnie Woelfel
Reading Specialist
Escondido HS
Escondido, CA

Pian Y. Wong
English Teacher
High School of American Studies
New York, NY

Izumi Yoshioka
English Teacher
Washington Irving HS
New York, NY

Student Reviewers

We also gratefully acknowledge the high school students who read and reviewed selections and tested the Online Coach.

Program Authors

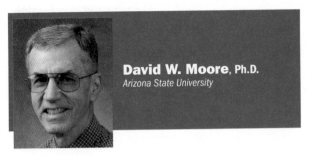

David W. Moore, Ph.D.
Arizona State University

Dr. Moore taught high school in Arizona public schools before becoming a professor of education. He co-chaired the International Reading Association's Commission on Adolescent Literacy and is actively involved with several professional associations. His thirty-year publication record balances research reports, professional articles, book chapters, and books including *Developing Readers and Writers in the Content Areas, Teaching Adolescents Who Struggle with Reading,* and *Principled Practices for Adolescent Literacy.*

Deborah J. Short, Ph.D.
Center for Applied Linguistics

Dr. Short is a co-developer of the research-validated SIOP Model for sheltered instruction. She has directed scores of studies on English Language Learners and published scholarly articles in *TESOL Quarterly, The Journal of Educational Research, Language Teaching Research,* and many others. Dr. Short also co-wrote a policy report: *Double the Work: Challenges and Solutions to Acquiring Language and Academic Literacy for Adolescent English Language Learners.* She has conducted extensive research on secondary level newcomers programs and on long term English language learners.

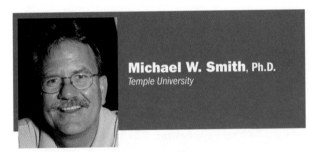

Michael W. Smith, Ph.D.
Temple University

Dr. Michael Smith joined the ranks of college teachers after eleven years teaching high school English. He has won awards for his teaching both at the high school and college level. He contributed to the Common Core State Standards initiative by serving on the Aspects of Text Complexity working group. His research focuses on how readers read and talk about texts and what motivates adolescents' reading and writing both in and out of school. His books include *"Reading Don't Fix No Chevys": Literacy in the Lives of Young Men, Fresh Takes on Teaching Literary Elements: How to Teach What Really Matters About Character, Setting, Point of View, and Theme,* and *Oh, Yeah?! Putting Argument to Work Both in School and Out.*

Alfred W. Tatum, Ph.D.
Northern Illinois University

Dr. Tatum began his career as an eighth-grade teacher and reading specialist. He conducts research on the power of texts and literacy to reshape the life outcomes of striving readers. His research focuses on the literacy development of African American adolescent males. He has served on the National Advisory Reading Committee of the National Assessment of Educational Progress (NAEP). Dr. Tatum's books include *Reading for Their Life: (Re)Building the Textual Lineages of African American Adolescent Males* and *Teaching Reading to Black Adolescent Males: Closing the Achievement Gap.*

Genre Focus
Short Stories

Focus Strategy
Plan and Monitor

THINK AGAIN

EQ ESSENTIAL QUESTION:
What Influences How You Act?

Gum Wall in Pike Place Market, Seattle, Washington, USA, 2009, Jordan Siemens. Photograph ©Jordan Siemens/ Aurora Photos.

WRITING PROJECT

Good Writing Trait
Focus and Unity

Genre Focus
Nonfiction

Focus Strategy
Ask Questions

FAMILY MATTERS

EQ ESSENTIAL QUESTION:
How Do Families Affect Us?

Images of Immigrants in the United States Flag, Immigration Museum, Ellis Island, New York, USA. Photograph ©Kevin Clogstoun/Lonely Planet Images/Getty Images.

WRITING PROJECT

Good Writing Trait
Development of Ideas

UNIT 3

TRUE
SELF

EQ ESSENTIAL QUESTION:
Do We Find or Create Our True Selves?

Kosovar Bosnian Bride, Donje Ljubinje, 2007, Valdrin Xhemaj. Photograph ©Valdrin Xhemaj/epa/Corbis.

WRITING PROJECT

Good Writing Trait
Organization

Genre Focus
Nonfiction

Focus Strategy
Determine Importance

GIVE&TAKE

EQ ESSENTIAL QUESTION:
How Much Should People Help Each Other?

Sisters Helping Each Other Cross a River, Hanoi, Vietnam, Martin Puddy. Photograph ©Martin Puddy/Corbis.

WRITING PROJECT

Good Writing Trait
Voice and Style

Genre Focus
Short Stories

Focus Strategy
Make Connections

FAIR PLAY

 ESSENTIAL QUESTION:
Do People Get What They Deserve?

Boxers Training, Salvador, Bahia, Brazil, David Alan Harvey. Photograph ©David Alan Harvey/Magnum Photos.

Good Writing Trait
Organization

WRITING PROJECT

UNIT 6

Genre Focus
Nonfiction

Focus Strategy
Synthesize

COMING
OF AGE

EQ ESSENTIAL QUESTION:
What Rights and Responsibilities Should Teens Have?

Unit Launch 460
Project: Ad Campaign

How to Read Nonfiction . . . . Structure of Arguments: 464

National Youth Rights Association — **16: The Right Voting Age** . . . . Analyze Viewpoint: . . . . . . ARGUMENT 468
Argument and Evidence

Lee Bowman — **Teen Brains Are Different** . . . . Analyze Text Structure: . . . EXPOSITORY NONFICTION 476
Main Idea and Details

Barbara Bey — **Should Communities Set Teen Curfews?** . . . . Evaluate Evidence . . . MAGAZINE OPINION PIECE 486

Curfews: A National Debate . . . . Analyze Viewpoint: Word Choice . . . COMMENTARY 494

Louise Bohmer Turnbull — **What Does Responsibility Look Like?** . . . . . Evaluate Argument and Reasons . . . . ESSAY 504

Getting a Job . . . . Analyze Author's Tone and Purpose . . . . FUNCTIONAL DOCUMENTS 512

Close Reading
Hara Estroff Marano — **Trashing Teens** . . . . Analyze Viewpoint: Evaluate Argument . INTERVIEW 522

Vocabulary Study
Key Vocabulary 468, 481, 486, 499, 504, 519
Specialized Vocabulary 483
Analogies 501
Multiple-Meaning Words 521

Grammar
Use Indefinite Pronouns 482
Vary Your Sentences 500
Use Compound Sentences 520

Writing About Literature
Response to Literature 481, 499, 519
Letter to the Editor 483
Development of Ideas 501
Expository Essay 521

Teens Covered in Dayglo Paint at a Concert, Austin, Texas, USA, Kitra Cahana. Photograph ©Kitra Cahana/National Geographic Stock.

WRITING PROJECT

Good Writing Trait
Development of Ideas

MAKING IMPRESSIONS

 **ESSENTIAL QUESTION:**
What Do You Do to Make an Impression?

Fourth of July Fireworks Over the Hudson River, New York City, USA, Diane Cook and Len Jenshel. Photograph ©Diane Cook and Len Jenshel/National Geographic Stock.

RESOURCES

Language and Learning Handbook
Language, Learning, Communication

Reading Handbook
Reading, Fluency, Vocabulary

Writing Handbook
Writing Process, Traits, Conventions

Genres at a Glance

Siete Leguas, 1991, Alfredo Arreguín. Oil on canvas, private collection.

Clearing the bark from sticks and arranging it in swirling patterns, 2003, Strijdom van der Merwe. Land art/photo documentation, Kamiyama, Tokushima, Japan.

UNIT 1 SHORT STORIES

 ESSENTIAL QUESTION:

What Influences How You Act?

Think before you act.
—PYTHAGORAS

Through kindness, you can change your fate.
—NGUYES T. NGUYEM

Critical Viewing ▶
Outside a theater in Seattle, Washington, this sticky, ever-expanding wall of gum disgusts some and delights others. What do you think influences people to place gum on this wall?

EQ ESSENTIAL QUESTION:
What Influences How You Act?

Study the Facts
Many things can influence how you act, including certain people. Look at these results from a teen survey about how much celebrities influence teen behavior:

Celebrity Influence

When a celebrity supports not smoking, do teens listen?
Yes — 58%
No — 42%

When a celebrity supports not drinking, do teens listen?
Yes — 54%
No — 46%

When a celebrity supports a product, are you more likely to buy it?
Yes — 18%
No — 25%
Maybe — 57%

Source: 19th Annual *USA Weekend* magazine Teen Survey, 2006

Analyze and Debate
1. Based on this information and on your experience, do you think celebrities are a big influence on teens' behavior?

2. Who do you think are the biggest influences on teens?

Discuss these questions in a group. Explain your opinion and support your ideas with evidence.

EQ ESSENTIAL QUESTION
In this unit, you will explore the **Essential Question** in class through reading, discussion, research, and writing. Keep thinking about the question outside of school, too.

① Plan a Project

Children's Book

In this unit, you will write and publish a children's book about the Essential Question. Decide on the contents of your book, including illustrations. To get started, look at children's books in the school library. Consider

- whether the book is fiction or nonfiction
- how many pages the book has
- how many and what kind of illustrations the book has
- how the author communicates his or her message.

Study Skills Start planning your children's book. Use the forms on myNGconnect.com to plan your time and to prepare the content.

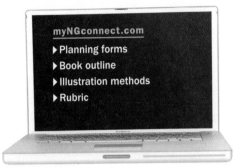

myNGconnect.com
- ▶ Planning forms
- ▶ Book outline
- ▶ Illustration methods
- ▶ Rubric

② Choose More to Read

These readings provide different answers to the Essential Question. Choose a book and online selections to read during the unit.

Facing the Lion: Growing Up Maasai on the African Savanna
by Joseph Lemasolai Lekuton

Lemasolai lives in Kenya and raises cows. When he goes to school, his life changes. He wears new clothes and the teachers call him Joseph. Who is he, Lemasolai or Joseph? How will he choose between his two names and two worlds?

▶ N O N F I C T I O N

Bronx Masquerade
by Nikki Grimes

Wesley writes a poem for his English class. This gives Mr. Ward the idea to create Open Mike Fridays so all the students can share their poetry. For the first time, the students start to share their lives with each other.

▶ N O V E L

Mysteries of Sherlock Holmes
by Sir Arthur Conan Doyle

It is London in the late 1800s. Sherlock Holmes is a clever detective. He finds criminals that even the police cannot catch. Holmes has three mysteries to solve. Join Holmes and his friend Dr. Watson as they follow the clues.

▶ S H O R T   S T O R I E S

myNGconnect.com
- ◎ See more results of the teens and celebrities survey.
- ◎ Read about how some people make sense of life.

USING READING STRATEGIES

When you read fiction or nonfiction, you can use strategies to understand different parts of the text. Reading strategies are tools for thinking that help you interact with the text and take control of your reading comprehension.

Reading Strategy

Reading Strategies

Plan and Monitor	Set a purpose before you read.
	Make predictions and then read on to confirm them.
	Figure out confusing text by rereading or reading on.
Make Connections	Connect what you read with what you have read or experienced.
Visualize	Picture sensory details in your mind.
Make Inferences	Combine what you read with what you know to figure out what the author doesn't say directly.
Synthesize	Bring several ideas together to understand something new.
Ask Questions	Ask about things you don't know. Look for clues in the text.
Determine Importance	Identify and summarize the most important ideas.

◥ **Reading Handbook,** page 647

Now read how one student applied reading strategies with this selection. As you read, pay attention to the reading strategies you use.

DEMO TEXT

PEER PRESSURE: A Little Help from My Friends
by Chris Munroe

Busted!

It happened years ago, but the memory still makes me cringe. It was the last week of eighth grade, and most teachers were letting us goof off until graduation. My favorite teacher, Mrs. Cerda, did not believe in goofing off. She believed in science enrichment projects. I thought the projects were kind of interesting, but everyone else was irritated about the work.

During class, my friend, Karen, grabbed my yearbook. She circled a photo of an unpopular girl and wrote, "Most likely to become a cat lady!" Karen passed the book to Avi who circled another photo and wrote, "Most likely to morph into a crazed werewolf!" He asked me, "What about you, Mr. Science Geek?" Everyone laughed.

Before I read, I can **plan and monitor**. I preview the title and headings. I predict the text will be about "peer pressure."

I remember how I felt in 8th grade. I can **make a connection** to how the class feels about working.

They were my friends, but I was seconds away from getting my own photo circled. I found Mrs. Cerda's picture and scribbled, "Most likely to bore kids to death!" Suddenly, the entire room was silent. My heart started pounding.

"May I see your yearbook, Chris?" Mrs. Cerda asked.

She didn't punish me, but she was hurt and disappointed. That was even worse. Later, I confessed everything to my dad. He said, "I have a fun, new 'enrichment project' for you. It's about peer pressure." It was no fun, but I sure learned a lot.

I can use details to **visualize**, or picture, how Chris feels when Mrs. Cerda is standing behind him.

Under the Influence

Peer pressure happens when people in a group influence individuals in the group to act in a certain way. The pressure isn't necessarily bad. Peers sometimes influence you to make good choices, too.

For example, my friends and I once started a book club to help Avi, who was failing English. We convinced him to read and talk about books together, and it helped him a lot. Last summer, Karen signed up for a baking class. We all teased her, but she persuaded two of us to join. It was the most fun we had all year.

Based on what I read and know, I can **make an inference** that Avi is no longer failing English.

Dealing with negative peer pressure can be difficult, especially for young adults. According to the American Lung Association, more than 3 million American teens smoke, and 25 percent of the 17 and 18 year olds in this report smoke daily. Why would intelligent teens choose such a deadly habit? For some kids, the choice may be influenced by peer pressure. Other reports show there may be connections between peer pressure and crimes like cheating or shoplifting. Sometimes peers can convince you to do things you would never do on your own.

I can **synthesize** the facts here and conclude that older teens started smoking at young ages.

The Power of "No"—and "Yes"

It's tough being the only dissenting member of a group when you don't agree with everyone else. You might get labeled a "loser," "no fun," or even "Mr. Science Geek." What do I do? When I'm in a tricky group situation, I remember the consequences of the "Mrs. Cerda Incident." Then I think of the consequences of the current situation. After all, your friends don't have to live with the consequences of your decisions, but you do.

I can **ask questions** about words or ideas. Clues in the text help me figure out what they mean.

Even in a group, we're all individuals with our own thoughts, ideas, and good judgment. If something doesn't feel right, I say one small but powerful word: "No." The group usually respects it. Occasionally, it makes my friends think about their own decisions, too.

I can **determine importance** by finding the main idea: people should stand up to peer pressure.

Who knows? Maybe I can be the peer who influences people to say "Yes" to something positive. It doesn't hurt to try!

Now let's learn about short stories. One way to find out what makes up a story is to look at a little story like this one. Read "Golden Bay." As you read apply the reading strategies you just reviewed.

DEMO TEXT

Golden Bay

Golden Bay is a new brick apartment building. It is the nicest building in our neighborhood, which is pretty run-down. It is for seniors only. I do not mean high school seniors. I mean old people. Everybody calls the place "Old and Gray" instead of Golden Bay.

Last week, I was hanging out with my friend Boyd, as always. We were passing the building. He stopped and said, "I bet those old people in there have money in their pockets."

"So what?" I asked.

"Claude, you and I are going to get some of that money," he said. I did not like the way he said it, but I didn't say anything.

On Saturday morning, Boyd and I went by Golden Bay again. We were wearing basketball jerseys and holding empty cans that we had wrapped in red and gold paper to match our school colors. We walked right in the lobby.

"It even smells old in here," said Boyd.

"Boyd, we should get out of here," I whispered.

"I thought we were friends," he said. "Friends stick together, don't they?"

"Yeah," I said. I wanted to say something else, but I didn't.

A man's voice growled behind us. "What are you doing here, boys?"

We turned around. The building manager was scowling at us.

"The basketball team needs new uniforms," said Boyd.

"Oh yeah, I heard about that on the news," the man said. "Your school needs money. You kids are going around town with those cans, asking for donations."

"That's right," said Boyd. "That's what we're doing." He poked me with his elbow.

"Yeah, that's right," I said, looking down at my shoes. At that moment, I wished that I could be somewhere else— anywhere else.

"Okay," the man said. "Go ahead and knock on doors."

■ Connect Reading to Your Life

What will Claude do? First, think of all the possible choices he could make.

I think he's going to leave right away.

I don't think so. I think he'll go along with Boyd and get the money.

1. Claude could _____

2. Or _____

3. Or _____

Reading Strategies

▶ Plan and Monitor
· Determine Importance
· Make Inferences
· Ask Questions
· Make Connections
· Synthesize
· Visualize

Now that you have thought about the alternatives, which one do you **predict**, or think, Claude will do based on what you know about him from the story so far? Explain your answer. Also tell what you want to know about Claude that would give you more confidence in your **prediction**.

Now think about Boyd. Based on what you know, what do you predict he will do?

Focus Strategy ▶ Plan and Monitor

You just made educated guesses, or predictions, about the boys. You make predictions all the time. You predict how your teacher will react if you skip class. You predict how a friend will react to a joke. You do this by thinking about what people are like, what they have done before, and what the current situation is like. Sometimes people surprise you, so you need to change your predictions.

Making predictions is a key part of what you do when you **monitor**—or check your understanding—as you read.

■ Your Job as a Reader

When you read, you first figure out what it is you are reading. You look at the title, a little of the text, and maybe the illustrations to figure out that you are reading a story. Then you pay attention to the characters, the setting, and the plot. For example, you learned as much as you could about Claude to predict what he would do. If there were more to this little story, you would then read to find out whether your predictions were accurate.

Academic Vocabulary
- **predict** v., to tell in advance; **prediction** n., a statement of what someone thinks will happen
- **monitor** v., to keep track of or to check

■ Unpack the Thinking Process

Characters

You can tell a lot about the **characters** in a story by paying attention to what they do, say, and think. You probably do this with your friends, too. If you think about what they say—their **dialogue**—and how they act, you get a pretty good idea of what they will do next.

Plot

In many stories, the choices that characters make determine what happens. What happens in a story is called the **plot**. An author selects and arranges the characters' choices and plot events in a logical order, or **sequence**. The first event in "Golden Bay" was that Boyd and Claude passed the apartment building. What was the next event?

Sequence of Events

Event 1	Event 2	Event 3	Event 4
Boyd and Claude pass the apartment building			

In most stories, there is a problem, or **conflict**, that must be solved. (Otherwise, the story would be pretty boring.) What is the conflict in "Golden Bay"?

Setting

Characters make choices because of who they are and the situations they are in. That is why the **setting**—where and when a story takes place—is so important. "Golden Bay" is set in a run-down neighborhood. The boys' high school needs money. The boys do not seem to have much money. Then there is the nice, new apartment building. How might the story be different if Golden Bay were an old, run-down building?

Elements of Literature

character *n.*, a person (or animal) in a story

plot *n.*, the series of events that make up a story

setting *n.*, the time and place of a story

Academic Vocabulary

● **dialogue** *n.*, what the characters say to each other; the characters' words

● **sequence** *n.*, the order in which things happen

● **conflict** *n.*, a problem

Plan and Monitor with Short Stories

Use the elements of short stories—character, plot, and setting—to plan and monitor your reading. Here is a way to make predictions and monitor them.

Prediction Chart

I Notice	I Know	I Predict	Prediction Confirmed?
Claude and Boyd have been friends for a long time.	Good friends usually stick together.	Claude will go along with Boyd.	[ ] yes [ ] no

As you read, keep track and revise your predictions. If you find that you are confused or surprised, take time to **clarify**, or get clear, so you can keep reading.

Try an Experiment

Here are two ways the story might end.

DEMO TEXT *Take 2*

We took the elevator to the top floor and knocked on the first door. An old woman answered. Boyd went into his act, and the woman gave us five dollars. She said, "Good luck to your team! I will be cheering for you."

I wanted to say, "We are not on the team." I almost said it, but I did not.

Boyd laughed when she closed the door, and then I did, too. "It's pretty easy to fool these people, isn't it?" I said.

I felt kind of guilty, but it wasn't enough to stop me from knocking on the next door.

DEMO TEXT *Take 3*

We took the elevator to the top floor and knocked on the first door. An old woman answered. Boyd went into his act, and the woman gave us five dollars. She said, "Good luck to your team! I will be cheering for you."

Boyd laughed when she closed the door, but I just turned around.

"Hey, where are you going?" Boyd asked.

"I'm going home," I explained.

I took the elevator to the lobby and then walked out onto the sidewalk. I started thinking about who my new friends might be.

Think, Pair, Share Think about the characters and setting. Then tell a partner which ending makes more sense to you. Share your ideas with the class.

Academic Vocabulary
- **clarify** *v.*, to make clear and understandable; to get rid of confusion

Monitor Comprehension

1. *Plot/Setting* How can setting influence plot?
2. *Character* What should you pay attention to in order to understand characters?

EQ — What Influences How You Act?
Find out how beliefs can affect people.

Make a Connection

Anticipation Guide Think about some strong beliefs that people have, such as the ones listed in the **Anticipation Guide**. Tell whether you agree or disagree with each statement. Then consider how these beliefs influence people's behavior.

ANTICIPATION GUIDE	Agree or Disagree
1. The number *13* is unlucky.	_____
2. A four-leaf clover is lucky.	_____
3. Hard work always leads to success.	_____
4. You can be anything you want to be.	_____

Learn Key Vocabulary

Study the Words Pronounce each word and learn its meaning. You may also want to look up the definitions in the Glossary.

• Academic Vocabulary

Key Words	Examples
belief (bu-lēf) noun ▶ pages 19, 21, 25	A **belief** is something you think is true. Different people have different **beliefs**. *Synonyms:* opinion, faith; *Antonyms:* uncertainty, doubt
escape (is-kāp) verb ▶ pages 14, 19, 22, 25	To **escape** is to get free. If you are in danger, you try to **escape**. *Synonyms:* get out, flee; *Antonym:* get captured
• **evidence** (e-vu-duns) noun ▶ page 19	When you look for **evidence**, you look for clues or proof that something is true. The police use **evidence** to determine who committed a crime.
experiment (ik-**spair**-u-munt) noun ▶ page 14	An **experiment** is a test or a trial. People do **experiments** to learn about something or to find out whether something works or not. What **experiments** do you do in science class?
failure (fāl-yur) noun ▶ page 16	A **failure** is a bad result. After the heavy rainstorm, we had no electricity because of a power **failure**. *Antonym:* success
misfortune (mis-**for**-chun) noun ▶ pages 24, 27	Has something bad happened to you that you did not expect? If so, you have suffered from **misfortune**. *Synonym:* bad luck
mistaken (mi-**stā**-kun) verb ▶ pages 24, 27	Sometimes people **mistake**, or confuse, sounds. For example, I have **mistaken** a doorbell for a cell phone ring tone. *Synonym:* mixed up
superstition (sü-pur-**sti**-shun) noun ▶ pages 21, 24, 25	A **superstition** is an idea based on fear, not logic. There is a **superstition** that black cats cause bad luck.

Practice the Words Work with a partner. Make a **Vocabulary Study Card** for each Key Vocabulary word. Write the word on one side of a card. On the other side, write its definition and an example sentence. Take turns quizzing each other on the words.

BEFORE READING **The Experiment**

short story by Martin Raim

Reading Strategies

▶ **Plan and Monitor**
- Determine Importance
- Make Inferences
- Ask Questions
- Make Connections
- Synthesize
- Visualize

Analyze Plot and Setting

Every short story has a **plot** and **setting**. The events, or what the characters do, in the story are the plot. The setting is where and when the story takes place. The events of the story are affected by the setting.

Look Into the Text

There was no way out.

The walls of his cell were built of thick cement blocks. The huge door was made of steel. The floor and ceiling were made of concrete, and there were no windows. The only light came from a light bulb that was covered by a metal shield.

There was no way out, or so it seemed to him.

He had volunteered to be part of a scientific experiment and had been put in the cell to test the cleverness of the human mind. The cell was empty, and he was not allowed to take anything into it. But he had been told that there was one way to escape from the cell, and he had three hours to find it.

This paragraph tells about the setting.

These are the first two plot events.

How do the setting and the plot work together?

Focus Strategy ▶ Plan and Monitor

Before you read a story, look it over. As you **preview** the story, try to decide what it is about. Try this strategy with "The Experiment."

HOW TO PREVIEW AND PREDICT

Focus Strategy

1. **Preview the Story** Look at the title, turn the pages of the story, and look at the pictures. Read the first few paragraphs. What do you think this story is about?

2. **Predict** Then, as you are reading, decide, or **predict**, what will happen next in the story. Use a **Prediction Chart** to keep track of your thinking. Note which predictions are logical, or reasonable, and which ones are not.

Prediction Chart

Events in the Plot	My Predictions	Was My Prediction Logical?
The man volunteers for an experiment and has to get out of a cell.	He will look for an opening in the walls.	

The Day I Saw Harry Houdini Escape

September 29, 1915

Today something amazing happened. I was hurrying home when I saw a huge crowd of people staring up at a skyscraper. I looked up and saw a man in a leather straitjacket hanging upside down from the building. It was Harry Houdini.

Harry Houdini tries to struggle out of a straitjacket. The jacket binds his arms tightly to his body.

I had heard of the great Houdini, of course. I had heard that he could escape from anything. I had seen photos of him trying to break out of chains underwater. All his adoring fans believed that he could escape from those terrible traps. But not me. I thought Houdini was great, all right—a great fake.

The crowd began to shout, "Hurry, Houdini! Hurry, Houdini!" He struggled to free himself, bending and twisting his body like a fish caught in a net. His ankles were bound together with thick rope. He looked like a mad man hopelessly trying to get out of the jacket—but within three minutes he had forced it off his body! I cheered wildly with the rest of the crowd.

Tonight, as I write this in my journal, I know that I have changed. I have become one of Houdini's biggest fans. Does this man possess amazing cleverness or some superhuman force? I believe he does. Today, I saw it with my own eyes.

myNGconnect.com

- Read more about Harry Houdini.
- See photos of Houdini's tricks.

The Experiment

by Martin Raim

▲ Critical Viewing: Theme If you could give a title to this painting, what would you call it?

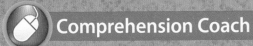

Comprehension Coach

Set a Purpose
A man participates in an experiment.
Find out what happens.

There was no way out.

The walls of his cell were built of thick cement blocks. The huge door was made of steel. The floor and ceiling were made of concrete, and there were no windows. The only light came from a light bulb that was covered by a metal shield.

There was no way out, or so it seemed to him.

He had **volunteered** to be part of a scientific **experiment** and had been put in the cell to test the **cleverness** of the human mind. The cell was empty, and he was not allowed to take anything into it. But he had been told that there was one way to **escape** from the cell, and he had three hours to find it. **1**

He began with the door. It stood before him, huge and gray. The three large hinges on the door were **riveted into** the wall and could not be removed. The door itself seemed too big for the small cell, and for a minute he wondered if it had been put up first and the rest of the cell built around it.

1 Plot and Setting
This three-hour time period is part of the setting. How does it affect the plot?

© Chad Baker

△ Critical Viewing: Setting What is the setting of this work of art? How does it relate to the story?

Key Vocabulary
experiment *n.*, a test or trial to learn about something
escape *v.*, to get free

In Other Words
volunteered agreed, offered
cleverness smartness, intelligence
riveted into attached to, fastened to

Finally he turned away from the door and looked around. He tried pushing against the cement blocks to see if any of them were loose. He searched the floor for a **trap door**. Then he glanced up at the ceiling. The shield! The shield around the light bulb! His mind raced. The metal shield could be used as a tool—the tool he needed! He had found the way to escape! **2**

He moved under the shield and looked closely at it. One good strong pull would free it, he decided. He reached up, grabbed hold of it, and pulled. But the shield stayed attached to the ceiling. He grabbed the shield again, twisting it as he pulled. He felt it rip free, and he fell to the floor **clutching** his treasure.

He had found the way to escape!

The shield was shaped like a cone and had been fastened to the ceiling by three long metal **prongs**. These prongs were sharp. But they were not strong enough to cut through steel or concrete or cement.

He felt a hopelessness creep over him. He could find no use for the shield as a tool. The shield was not what he needed to get out.

Then he had a brilliant idea. True, the metal prongs of the shield could not cut through the steel door or the concrete floor or the cement blocks in the wall. But the prongs might be strong enough to dig out the **mortar** that held the cement blocks in place. He pulled off one of the prongs and scraped hard at the mortar. The mortar crumbled into powder. His idea worked! If he removed enough mortar, he could loosen a couple of the cement blocks, then push them out, and escape!

2 Plot/Predict
What do you think will happen next? Record your prediction on your chart. Read on to see how logical your prediction is.

Monitor Comprehension

Summarize
What does the man need to do? What has he decided to do?

In Other Words
trap door hidden door that covered an opening
clutching holding
prongs strips with pointed ends
mortar building material

He selected two blocks near the door and set to work. The prong dug into the mortar and sent it flying out in a steady stream. The prong was just what he had needed. Now he was sure he would escape. But his hand made a sudden careless twist, and the metal prong broke into two useless pieces.

At first a wave of anger **stunned** him. Then he remembered that the shield had two more prongs. He pulled off another prong and went back to work. He decided he must be more careful—nothing must go wrong. There was still plenty of time left.

Soon he had chipped out four inches of mortar. **3** But the **jagged** edges of the cement blocks had torn the skin off his knuckles. His hands were bleeding from a dozen burning cuts. His back and shoulders hurt from the **strain** of working in one position. The mortar dust blew into his eyes and down his throat. The work dragged on, slower and slower.

Suddenly the second prong broke.

For a minute he welcomed the excuse to stop working. But the thought of **failure** sent him back into action. He pulled off the third and last prong and went to work again. He was a man who did not like to lose—he had to win.

The work dragged on. He **became numb** to the pain in his hands, to the **ache** in his shoulders. His fingers moved **blindly**, and his attack against the mortar grew weaker and weaker.

At last he broke through. He had dug out enough mortar so that now he could see light between the cement blocks. **4**

3 **Access Vocabulary**
What do you think *chipped out* means, based on the text around it? Think about what the man is doing.

4 **Plot/Predict**
What do you think will happen next? Why do you think this will happen? Record your thinking in your chart.

Key Vocabulary
failure *n.*, a bad result

In Other Words
stunned stopped
jagged rough
strain difficulty
became numb did not pay attention
ache pain
blindly without his control

© Brad Holland

◀ Critical Viewing: Effect How do you think the person in this painting feels? What in the painting makes you think that?

With a spurt of new energy he chipped away at the rest of the mortar. Of course there was a way out. He had found it, hadn't he? He had proved that a clever mind could solve any problem. That's how he had done it—with his own cleverness.

At that instant the third prong snapped in his hand.

He stared at the useless pieces. Then in a **blind rage** he slammed his fist against the wall.

In Other Words
blind rage very angry way

Monitor Comprehension

Retell
The man tries his plan. What happens?

Behind him the door of the cell opened slowly. His time had run out. His part of the experiment was over.

He was not allowed to talk about the experiment or about his plan of escape. However, he was sure that he could have escaped. He was convinced that he almost had.

Actually, he had not even come close.

The shield had been put around the light bulb only as a shade for the light. The metal prongs were not meant to be used as a tool.

The man had been clever, but he had let his cleverness **sidetrack him**. If he had not been so quick to use the shield as a tool, if he had not spent all his time chipping out

🔺 Critical Viewing: Plot **What do you think happened in this painting? Explain how this painting relates to the experiment.**

In Other Words
sidetrack him keep him from finding the answer, distract him

the mortar, and if he had not stopped searching the cell, he might have found the real way out. He might have discovered that he could have left the cell as easily as he had entered.

For the huge door had never been locked. **5** ❖

5 Plot and Setting
What did you assume, or suppose, about the setting, based on the text? Why did you make that assumption? Did it make sense for the man to assume the door was locked? Why?

ANALYZE The Experiment

1. **Confirm Prediction** What was the best way to **escape** from the cell?

2. **Vocabulary** How did the man's **belief** affect his ability to escape from the cell? Discuss with a partner.

3. **Analyze Plot and Setting** Work with a partner to list the major plot events in "The Experiment." After you finish, discuss the connection between the plot and the setting.

   1. The man volunteers for an experiment.
   2.
   3.
   4.
   5.

4. **Focus Strategy** **Preview and Predict** Review the **Prediction Chart** you started on page 11. What predictions did you make that were logical? Explain how you made those predictions.

   ↩ Return to the Text

   Reread and Write Imagine that you are the man in the **experiment**. Write a description of how beliefs influenced your actions. Go back into the text to find **evidence**, or supporting details, to support what you say.

Key Vocabulary
belief *n.*, something you think is true
● **evidence** *n.*, proof that something is true

BEFORE READING **Superstitions: The Truth Uncovered**

magazine article by Jamie Kiffel

Reading Strategies

▶ **Plan and Monitor**
· Determine Importance
· Make Inferences
· Ask Questions
· Make Connections
· Synthesize
· Visualize

Analyze Text Features

Magazine articles have **text features** such as main heads, subheads, diagrams, photographs (photos), and captions. These text features help you understand what the article is about. They also show the connection between the ideas.

Look Into the Text

Photos show something in the text.

Everything below the main head tells about the same topic.

SUPERSTITION 1
Ravens predict death.

Where It Came From Ravens are scavengers, so they were often spotted at cemeteries and battlefields—places associated with dying. People started thinking the birds could predict death.

What's the Truth? People who spot ravens could be in for some good luck—not death. According to legend, Vikings sailing the ocean would release captive ravens and follow them toward land. If the birds returned, the sailors knew land was still far away.

Look at the two subheads. What will you learn about the superstition?

Focus Strategy ▶ Plan and Monitor

When you **preview** an article, you look at its text features before you read. Features like heads, diagrams, and photos give you an idea of what the article is about. Then you can **set a purpose**, or goal, for reading. Try this strategy with this magazine article.

HOW TO PREVIEW AND SET A PURPOSE

Focus Strategy

1. **Skim to Preview the Text** First look at the article's title, main heads, and subheads. Then look at its diagrams, photos, and captions. Think about what kind of information the article contains.

2. **Write Questions** Decide what you want to learn from the article. Write questions that you would like to answer.

3. **Set a Purpose** Read to answer your questions.

> **Title:** Superstitions: The Truth Uncovered
> **Main Head:** Superstition 1
> **Subheads:** Where It Came From, What's the Truth?
>
> What are the superstitions?
> Which superstitions do I know?

SUPERSTITIONS:
The Truth Uncovered • by Jamie Kiffel

Connect Across Texts

In "The Experiment," a man's **belief** determines his actions. In this magazine article, find out the truth about some beliefs called **superstitions**.

Some people believe in superstitions to explain **the unexplainable**. Often that means explaining bad luck. Old Mr. Smith's house burned down? He must have forgotten to knock on wood after he said his home **was fireproof**. But where did strange beliefs like this come from, and why did people believe them? Here are the straight facts behind some superstitions.

SUPERSTITION 1
Ravens predict death.

Where It Came From Ravens are **scavengers**, so they were often **spotted** at cemeteries and battlefields—places associated with dying. People started thinking the birds could predict death.

What's the Truth? People who spot ravens could be in for some good luck— not death. According to legend, Vikings sailing the ocean would release **captive ravens** and follow them toward land. If the birds returned, the sailors knew land was still far away. And **tame ravens** are very friendly. "They act like puppies," says Patricia Cole of New York City's Prospect Park Zoo. "They'll sit on your lap, let you scratch their heads, and play tug-of-war!"

The raven became a symbol of death, but some people admire the bird for its intelligence and fearless behavior.

1 Text Features
What do you learn from this photo and the other raven photo that you would not learn if you just read the text?

SUPERSTITION 2
Walking under a ladder is bad luck. 2

Where It Came From In ancient times, people believed that triangles were **sacred**. Walking through a triangle could break the triangle's good powers and let evil things **escape**. In this case, the triangle is formed by the ladder and the ground.

What's the Truth? Triangles aren't sacred. They are just three connected points that, unlike the points of a line, aren't in a row. Math experts such as Professor Albert L. Vitter think of rectangular forms—such as doorways—as two triangles. (Picture a line from one corner of a doorway to its diagonal corner.) According to this notion, when you walk through a doorway you are walking through two triangles. Of course, you know by your own experience that it's perfectly safe to do this!

Triangles in a Doorway

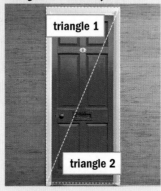

triangle 1

triangle 2

▲ Interpret the Diagram
Explain how a doorway is like two triangles.

2 Text Features/ Preview and Set a Purpose
Look at the photo, the main head, and the sentence under it. What do you think you will learn in this section?

SUPERSTITION 3
Throwing salt over your left shoulder wards off evil.

Where It Came From In the days before refrigeration, salt was very valuable because people used it to preserve meat, fish, and other foods. People worried that evil spirits might try to steal their salt, especially if it spilled. So they tossed salt over their left shoulders into the eyes of any salt-stealing **demons** to stop them.

Key Vocabulary
escape *v.*, to get free

In Other Words
sacred special, holy
wards off evil keeps away evil
demons bad spirits, devils

What's the Truth? Even if there were really demons, throwing salt in their eyes might slow them down for a little while, but it wouldn't stop them. In fact, salt occurs naturally in tears. It and the proteins in tears keep germs away and help prevent eye infections.

Ninety-eight percent of a tear is water. Tears also contain small amounts of sodium chloride, the chemical name for salt.

3 Text Features
What did you learn about salt from reading the caption?

SUPERSTITION 4
Breaking a mirror means trouble.

Where It Came From People used to believe that your reflection was actually your **soul**. So if you broke a mirror, you'd break—and therefore lose—your soul.

What's the Truth? The image in a mirror is **a phenomenon of** light. "When you look at any object in a mirror, what you're actually seeing is reflected light," says Lou Bloomfield, author of *How Things Work: The Physics of Everyday Life.* When you stand in front of a mirror, reflected light from your body bounces off the mirror's surface. That's why you see your reflection.

Reflection in a Mirror

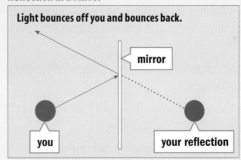

Light bounces off you and bounces back.

mirror

you

your reflection

 Interpret the Diagram When light from your body hits the surface of the mirror, what happens next? What does this action cause you to see in the mirror? **4**

4 Text Features
How does this diagram add meaning to the text? Do you think it is helpful? Explain.

Monitor Comprehension

Explain
Name a superstition described in the article and explain the truth behind it.

In Other Words
soul spirit, inner self
a phenomenon of something that happens with

SUPERSTITION 5
Knocking on wood keeps misfortune away.

Where It Came From People used to believe that gods lived inside trees. If you knocked on wood when you wanted a favor, the tree gods would help you.

What's the Truth? In the past, people may have **mistaken** tree-dwelling insects for gods, says Linda Butler, **an entomologist** at West Virginia University. "Lots of noisy insects live inside trees," she says. "For instance, the larva of the pine sawyer beetle makes a loud gnawing sound when it chews on wood." ❖

wood

larva

The pine sawyer beetle got its name from the sawing noise the larva makes as it chews the wood. **5**

5 Text Features
Do the caption and photo of the larva help you understand the explanation for the superstition? Explain why.

ANALYZE Superstitions: The Truth Uncovered

1. **Explain** Which **superstition** has something to do with demons? Which one has something to do with the soul? Use text evidence to tell the truth behind each one.

2. **Vocabulary** According to the article, what might a superstitious person do to avoid **misfortune**?

3. **Analyze Text Features** Tell a partner which text feature in the article you found most helpful. Explain why.

4. **Focus Strategy Preview and Set a Purpose** Look back at the questions you wrote before you read. Did you learn the answers? What else did you learn that was interesting?

   ⤶ Return to the Text
   Reread and Write What do superstitions cause people to do? Use facts from the text for ideas. Then list each superstition next to what it causes people to do.

Key Vocabulary
   misfortune *n.*, bad luck
   mistaken *v.*, mixed up, confused

In Other Words
   an entomologist a person who studies insects

EQ **What Influences How You Act?**

Critical Thinking

1. **Analyze** Look again at the **Anticipation Guide** on page 10. Do you want to change any of your responses? Discuss your thinking with a group. Be sure to express why you felt you needed to change your responses.

EQ 2. **Compare** In "The Experiment," think about how the man's **belief** influenced his actions. Compare it to how a belief in a **superstition** can influence someone's actions.

3. **Interpret** Which superstition from the article do you think is most powerful? Why?

4. **Speculate** Will the main character in "The Experiment" continue to wonder how he could have **escaped**? Do you think he will ever realize that the door was unlocked? Explain your answer.

EQ 5. **Evaluate** How do beliefs affect people's behavior? Can they be helpful? Support your answer with evidence from the "The Experiment" and "Superstitions."

Write About Literature

Opinion Statement Agree or disagree with this statement: "People make up superstitions when they want to feel in control of something they don't understand." Use examples from both texts to support your response.

Key Vocabulary Review

Oral Review Work with a partner. Use these words to complete the paragraph.

beliefs	experiment	mistaken
escape	failure	superstition
evidence	misfortune	

My friend Dan has many __(1)__ that I don't agree with. When he first saw my new kitten, Midnight, he yelled, "Keep it away! Black cats cause __(2)__. They are bad luck." I had never seen any __(3)__ or proof of that, so I decided to do an __(4)__. I would test Dan's silly __(5)__ by watching what happened when Midnight went near people. At first, Midnight wouldn't cooperate, and I thought the whole thing was going to be a __(6)__. Soon, however, he started walking up to people who passed our front yard. Nobody tried to run away or __(7)__! Nothing bad happened! Dan was __(8)__ about black cats.

Writing Application Think of another example of how a person's belief in a superstition could affect how the person acts. Write a paragraph about it. Use at least four Key Vocabulary words.

Read with Ease: Expression

Assess your reading fluency with the passage in the Reading Handbook, p. 665. Then complete the self-check below.

1. I did/did not use appropriate expression as I read.

2. My words correct per minute: _____.

INTEGRATE THE LANGUAGE ARTS

Write Complete Sentences

Sentences are the building blocks for most writing. In formal English, a sentence expresses a complete idea.

Some people are superstitious.

A sentence needs two parts to be complete. The part called the **subject** tells *whom* or *what* the sentence is about. The complete subject may be one word or several words.

Some people are superstitious.
Superstitions explain bad luck.

The part called the **predicate** tells what the subject *does*, *has*, or *is*. The complete predicate may be one word or several words.

Some people **fear ravens**.
Tame ravens **are very friendly**.

Oral Practice (1–5) Look at the selections you just read. Find five complete sentences and read them to a partner. Ask your partner to tell you the subject and predicate of each sentence.

Writing Practice (6–10) On your paper, use these words in complete sentences.

6. many superstitions
7. are often in cemeteries
8. to break a mirror
9. under ladders
10. the image in a mirror

Ask and Answer Questions

Group Talk Take turns choosing one superstition you just read about. Have others in the group ask you questions about it. Start some questions with *Is*, *Are*, *Can*, and *Will*.

Analyze Plot: Climax

A good story usually has a plot that keeps you guessing about what will happen next. The story often starts when a character has a **problem**. The events build up to the **climax**, or the most exciting part. At the climax, you really want to know how the story will end. Then the final events finish the story.

- The events that lead up to the climax are the **rising action**.
- The events that follow the climax are the **falling action**.
- Any leftover problems are solved at the end, during the story's **resolution**.

The **plot diagram** below shows the plot of "The Experiment." Work with a partner. Copy the diagram onto separate paper and complete the missing events, the climax, and the resolution.

Plot Diagram

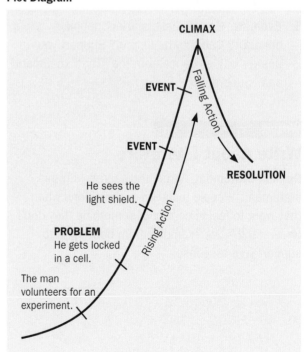

Prefixes

A **prefix** is a word part added at the beginning of a word. It changes the word's meaning. Many English prefixes come from the Latin and Greek languages. The Latin prefix *in-* means "not," so the word *inexact* means "not exact." The Greek prefix *anti-* means "against," so the word *anticruelty* means "against cruelty." Some prefixes also come from earlier versions of the English language. The prefix *mis-* comes from Old English. It means "wrong" or "bad." That's why **misfortune** means "bad luck" and *misunderstood* means "understood wrongly." Copy the words below. Add the prefix *mis-* to each one. Write the meaning of the new word. Sound out the new word, separating the prefix from the root word.

1. behave   **2.** lead   **3.** judge   **4.** adventure

Oral Report

Health: Old Beliefs Many people believe strongly in sayings like *Feed a cold; starve a fever* or *An apple a day keeps the doctor away*. Conduct research to see if there is medical evidence behind these beliefs. Consult with others to formulate a research question to address.

myNGconnect.com
- Find out about apples and other fruits and vegetables.
- Discover the truth behind many old beliefs.

Share your information with the class in a brief oral report. Allow class members to ask questions about your research.

Language and Learning Handbook, page 616

Write a Narrative Paragraph

Narrative writing tells a story. Write a narrative paragraph about a character who has a strong belief.

1 Prewrite

- Write several ideas for interesting characters and their beliefs. Pick one idea to write about.
- Think about the conflict and resolution.
- Choose a setting.
- Think about the order of events in the plot.

Time Line

First   Then   Later   Finally

2 Draft Use your time line to write your paragraph.

3 Revise Reread your narrative. Ask:

- Do I clearly show my character's belief?
- Are the events in the correct order?
- Are the characters interesting and believable?
- Do I develop conflict in the plot?
- Is the conflict resolved by the end of the paragraph?

4 Edit and Proofread Check your paragraph for errors in spelling, punctuation, and grammar. Correct any mistakes.

5 Publish Print your paragraph and share it with a classmate.

Model Narrative Paragraph

The beginning introduces the character and her belief.	Tova was having a terrible time in math class. Her friends told her that she just wasn't good in math, but she strongly believed she could do the work. She *knew* that she could improve her grade. So she decided to work each night with a math tutor. The first night, she stared at the work, but nothing the tutor said made sense. The next night it was the same, and Tova felt discouraged. She thought maybe her friends were right. After several weeks, however, her tutor's explanations started to become clear. By the end of the semester, Tova was getting better grades in math. She was glad that she had believed in herself.
Use time-order words to signal when events happen.	

Writing Handbook, page 698

1

At a Television Station

Television stations broadcast a variety of programs, including news, talk shows, and movies. Television programs are transmitted over cable television lines, satellite systems, or the airwaves to people's television sets.

Jobs in the Television Broadcasting Industry

In television broadcasting, there are several categories of jobs that require specific training, education, and work experience. Employees who work at small stations often perform several jobs.

Job	Responsibilities	Education/Training Required
Camera Operator 1	• Films material for TV series, news events, and documentaries • May work with a news team to film live events on location	• Courses in camera operation at vocational or technical school, junior college, photography institute, or university
Broadcast Technician 2	• Sets up and operates equipment used to transmit programs • Works with cameras, microphones, recorders, and lighting	• Technical school, associate's degree, or college degree with training in broadcast technology or electrical engineering
Reporter 3	• Gathers information from various sources • Analyzes information and prepares news stories • Presents information on air	• College degree in journalism or communication; training in broadcasting from a technical school

2

Write Questions for Research

Learn more about the television broadcasting industry by asking questions and researching answers.

1. Choose a job that interests you from the chart above, or choose another job in the broadcasting industry.
2. Write three questions that you have about the job.
3. Exchange your list of questions with a classmate and work together to answer the questions. Use Internet or library resources to find the answers. Save the information in a professional career portfolio.

3

myNGconnect.com

🔎 **Learn more about the broadcasting industry.**

🔎 **Download a form to evaluate whether you would like to work in this field.**

📑 **Language and Learning Handbook,** page 616

Use Word Parts

Car companies have Web sites where you can "build" the car you would like to own. You start with a plain "base model." Then you add to it.

Some words are built with additions, too. They may have a prefix added at the beginning or a suffix added at the end. These additions change a word's meaning. The Latin prefix *sub-* means "below" or "under." It changes the word *soil* to *subsoil*. If you know that the Greek suffix *-ism* means "the act of," you could figure out that *patriotism* means "the act of being a patriot." If you know that the Old English prefix *mid-* means "middle," you can figure out that *midyear* means "the middle of the year."

Make Meaning from Word Parts

Work with a partner to learn the meaning of some word parts.

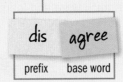

prefix   base word

1. Write each base word, prefix, and suffix on a card.
2. Mix and match cards to make a new word. Check the dictionary to confirm that you made a real word.
3. Have your partner give the meanings of the parts and the whole word.
4. Check the meaning in a dictionary.
5. Listen to each other sound out the new words. Separate the prefixes from the root words you know. Adjust your pronunciation as needed.
6. Switch roles. Continue until you cannot make any more words.

Put the Strategy to Use

Use this strategy to check a word you do not know.

1. Look for a prefix or suffix and cover it.
2. Define the base word.
3. Uncover the prefix or suffix and determine its meaning.
4. Put the meanings of the word parts together to define the whole word.

disagreeable
disagreeable

TRY IT ▶ Read the following passage. Use the strategy described above to write the meaning of the words printed in blue.

▶ I **frequently** go to the mall with my friends. Sometimes we purchase a lot and it's **unmanageable** for us to carry the packages home. When that happens, we **rearrange** our plans. Instead of walking home, we ask our parents to drive us home. They are usually **agreeable** to our plan as long as we did not spend a lot of money.

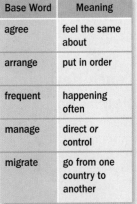

Base Word	Meaning
agree	feel the same about
arrange	put in order
frequent	happening often
manage	direct or control
migrate	go from one country to another

Prefix	Meaning
dis-	not *or* bad
im-, in-	not
mis-	in the wrong way *or* badly
re-	again

Suffix	Meaning
-able, -ible	can be *or* can do
-er	one who does this action
-ion, -tion	condition *or* action
-ly	in the manner of

🦋 Reading Handbook, page 647

EQ What Influences How You Act?

Find out how people get to where they want to go.

Make a Connection

Quickwrite What choices will you have to make about your future in the next few years? Would you like advice from adults to help you decide what to do? Why or why not? Take five minutes to write your ideas. Save your writing.

Learn Key Vocabulary

Study the Words Pronounce each word and learn its meaning. You may also want to look up the definitions in the Glossary.

● Academic Vocabulary

Key Words	Examples
career (ku-**rear**) *noun* ▸ pages 48, 51	You need a lot of training to have a **career** as a doctor or a nurse. *Synonyms*: life's work, profession
comedian (ku-**mē**-dē-un) *noun* ▸ pages 45, 49	A **comedian** is a person who makes people laugh.
● **consent** (kun-**sent**) *noun* ▸ pages 35, 49	When you give your **consent**, you give your approval. *Synonym*: permission
engineer (en-ju-**near**) *noun* ▸ page 35	An **engineer** is a person who plans how to build things like bridges and buildings.
obstacle (**ahb**-sti-kul) *noun* ▸ pages 36, 48, 49	Something that stands in your way, or prevents you from doing something, is an **obstacle**. The lack of money may be an **obstacle** to buying a new car. *Synonym*: problem
● **project** (**prah**-jekt) *noun* ▸ page 35	A school **project** such as a video presentation takes time and planning. *Synonyms*: job, task, assignment
● **react** (rē-**akt**) *verb* ▸ pages 43, 48, 49, 51	To **react** means to act in response to something. How do you **react** when you hear good news? What do you do? *Synonym*: respond
stubborn (**stu**-burn) *adjective* ▸ pages 36, 43	A **stubborn** person is someone who is not willing to change or quit. *Synonym*: strong-willed; *Antonyms*: obedient, flexible

Practice the Words Work with a partner. Make a **Definition Map** for each Key Vocabulary word. Use a dictionary to find other forms of the word.

Definition Map

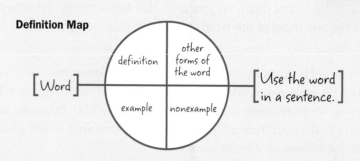

BEFORE READING Building Bridges

short story by Andrea Davis Pinkney

Reading Strategies

▶ **Plan and Monitor**
· Determine Importance
· Make Inferences
· Ask Questions
· Make Connections
· Synthesize
· Visualize

Analyze Character

When you meet new people, you use clues, such as how they look, what they do, and what they say, to figure out what they are like. When you read a story, you can use similar clues to figure out what the **characters** are like.

Look Into the Text

A description shows what the characters look like.

Mama Lil and I had been butting heads ever since I could remember. And the older I got, the more at odds we were.

　　She thought I weighed too much and dressed badly. I thought she smoked too much and overdid it with her fake gold chains. Time after time, she'd asked me, "How you ever gonna land a decent man with them chunky arms and those T-shirts that put your navel on parade? No self-respecting seventeen-year-old should be letting it all hang out like *that*."

Dialogue is what a character says. What does this dialogue show about Mama Lil?

Focus Strategy ▶ Plan and Monitor

When you read, make sure you understand the text. If there is something in the text that confuses you, reread or read on to make it clear, or to **clarify ideas**.

HOW TO CLARIFY IDEAS

Focus Strategy

Suppose you read this text and aren't sure what "at odds" means.

Mama Lil and I had been butting heads ever since I could remember. And the older I got, the more at odds we were.

What can you do?

1. **Reread** The first sentence says, "Mama Lil and I had been butting heads." When people "butt heads," are they in agreement or at odds?

2. **Read On** If you still don't understand, keep reading. You may be able to figure things out.

   YOU WONDER: Why are they at odds?

   READ ON: She thought I weighed too much and dressed badly. I thought she smoked too much and overdid it with her fake gold chains.

How does reading on help you understand how Mama Lil and the girl were "at odds"?

The Writer and Her Inspiration

Andrea Davis Pinkney
(1963–)

Andrea Davis Pinkney works as a publisher in New York City.

Early in her life, **Andrea Davis Pinkney** decided she wanted a career in writing. Part of the reason she made that choice was television.

One of her favorite shows featured Mary Tyler Moore. Moore played the role of a TV journalist in Minneapolis, Minnesota. Ms. Pinkney wanted to be like this character. So she went to college and studied journalism.

Her other favorite TV character was a boy on *The Waltons* who wanted to be a writer. He always had paper with him to write what he saw and experienced. Today, Ms. Pinkney carries a notebook everywhere. She likes to observe people, noting what their lives might be like. Then she uses these ideas for the characters in her stories.

She admits, "I'm a horrible speller. I'm a very bad grammarian. If someone had told me 'because you can't spell and your grammar is awful, you can't write,' I would have given up and not tried. That's not all there is to it. Writing is really about communicating your ideas."

myNGconnect.com

🌐 Read an interview with Andrea Davis Pinkney.

🌐 Find out about TV shows that have had an impact on our culture.

BUILDING
BRIDGES

adapted from a short story by
Andrea Davis Pinkney

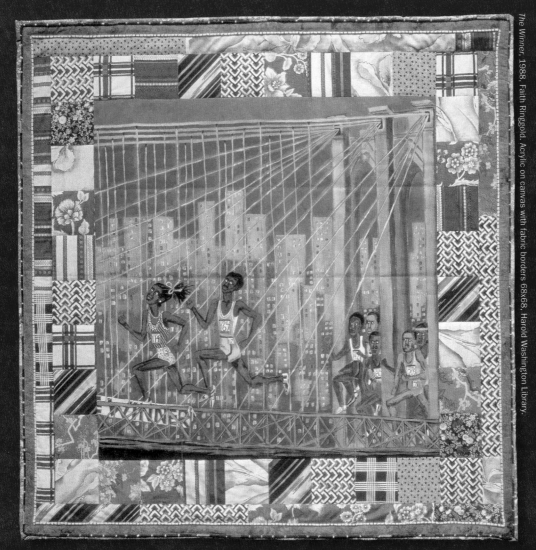

The Winner, 1988, Faith Ringgold. Acrylic on canvas with fabric borders 68x68, Harold Washington Library.

▲ Critical Viewing: Design Think about the shapes, lines, colors, and textures in this painting. How are these elements arranged? Why do you think the artist arranged them that way?

 Comprehension Coach

Bebe and her grandmother are fighting about Bebe's future.
Find out what each one wants.

At first, Mama Lil said it plain and simple: "No." Then, like always, she spoke her full mind. "Bebe, get that backward idea out your head. That grit-work **ain't no** place for you. And besides, I **ain't never heard of no girls to be** doing *that*. You need to be getting yourself a real summer job, something civilized." **1**

Mama Lil pushed her breakfast plate aside and took a final drag on her cigarette. "And don't ask me again about signing that permission paper," she said. "I ain't gonna be the one who allows you to take part in such foolishness."

I leaned back in my kitchen chair, my arms folded tight. The chair's vinyl stuck to my skin, taping itself to the place where my T-shirt scooped down in back. It was as if, like Mama Lil, that chair wanted to hold me in its clutches. **2**

I'd been living with Mama Lil since I was six, when my own mama and daddy were killed in an apartment building fire. Lillian Jones was my mom's mother. Everybody on our street called my grandmother Mama Lil, and that's what I called her, too. Mama Lil and I had been **butting heads** ever since I could remember. And the older I got, the more **at odds we were**.

She thought I weighed too much and dressed badly. I thought she smoked too much and overdid it with her fake gold chains. Time after time, she'd asked me, "How you ever gonna land a decent man with them chunky arms and those T-shirts that put your navel on parade? No self-respecting seventeen-year-old should be letting it all hang out like *that*."

1 Character
What can you tell about Mama Lil, based on what she says to Bebe?

2 Character
What is Bebe like? How do she and Mama Lil get along? How do you know?

In Other Words
ain't no isn't any
ain't never heard of no girls to be have never heard of any girls who are
butting heads disagreeing
at odds we were we disagreed

But then, too, I had a sister-to-sister connection to Mama Lil that not many kids had with their grandmas. I was Mama Lil's only true family, and she was the only real parent I had. If I ever left her, she'd have nobody. And if she passed on, I'd be alone in the world.

For weeks I'd been asking Mama Lil to let me join the youth renovation team. It was a group of kids that had been chosen by city officials to work with **engineers** to help repair the Brooklyn Bridge. The **project** would last the summer and pay good money. It would help me get to college, where I wanted to study engineering.

Untitled (Head #2), 2005, Greg Breda. Acrylic on canvas, Tilford Art Group, Los Angeles.

⬛ Critical Viewing: Character What can you tell about this girl's personality from her face? How is she like Bebe?

But Mama Lil wasn't having it. To her, I was "stooping to do a bunch of low-down mess-work." Truth be told, Mama Lil was scared of something she didn't know. She hardly ever left our neighborhood in Brooklyn. To her, the Brooklyn Bridge was a mystery.

And I think that deep down Mama Lil was afraid something bad would happen to me, the same way it happened to my mama and daddy. **3** Also, Mama Lil couldn't read or write very well. I read most of her mail to her and helped her sign her checks. The two-page **consent** form she had to sign, giving me permission to work on the bridge project, was a challenge to her pride.

3 Character/ Clarify Ideas
What happened to Bebe's mother and father? Reread the fourth paragraph on page 34 if you are not sure.

Key Vocabulary
engineer *n.*, a person who plans how to build things like bridges and buildings
● **project** *n.*, job, task, assignment
● **consent** *n.*, permission

Historical Background
The Brooklyn Bridge connects Brooklyn and Manhattan Island in New York City. It was built in the late 1800s and took more than thirteen years to build. It is still used by thousands of people every day.

Then there was the fact that I would be the only girl working with the bridge crew. "If God had meant you to do a man's work, he would have made you a man," she said.

All these **strikes** stood against me ever getting to work on that bridge. But the biggest **obstacle** of all, the thing that made Mama Lil the most **stubborn**, was my dream of becoming an engineer. Mama Lil didn't fully understand what an engineer was. I'd tried to explain it to her. I'd shown her my sketchbook full of drawings of city structures and machines. But Mama Lil didn't *know* any engineers. She'd never seen one at work.

Ms. 'Tude, 2004, William Pajaud. Oil pastel, private collection, courtesy of M. Hanks Gallery, Santa Monica, California.

▲ Critical Viewing: Character Does this picture match the image of Mama Lil that you have in your imagination? Explain.

And to make matters worse, she'd asked her friends down at Rimley's Beauty Parlor about engineering. They'd convinced her that I was **headed down the wrong path**. "Ain't no black woman doing no engine-ing," she'd said.

"Engin*eering*," I'd corrected.

In some respects, Mama Lil was right. It *was* true that there weren't many black women engineers. I knew from the **get-go** that if I hoped to become an engineer, my road ahead would be lonely and hard. But I wanted to build bridges more than anything. ▪4

4 Character
How do Bebe's thoughts show what she is like?

Monitor Comprehension

Explain
Describe how Bebe sees herself in the future. Tell how Mama Lil sees her. How do you know?

Key Vocabulary
obstacle *n.*, something that prevents you from doing something
stubborn *adj.*, not willing to change or quit

In Other Words
strikes problems
headed down the wrong path making bad choices
get-go beginning

Predict

**Mama Lil and Bebe still can't agree.
What do you think will happen?**

A week passed. A week of Mama Lil and I not speaking about the bridge project, or the permission form. It was due—signed by her—in four days. That's when the renovation was supposed to begin.

On the Saturday night before the project was to start, Mama Lil did something that got me real mad. She brought home a summer job application from Rimley's Beauty Parlor. "Bebe, I went and done you a big favor," she said. **5** "Vernice Rimley needs somebody to sweep hair and clean her sinks. She can't pay you nothing to start, but you'd get a **heap** of training. By next summer you'd be doing perms and manicures, and getting tips on top of a regular salary. And you could even bring your paper tablet. You could draw during your breaks."

Mama Lil put the application down on the coffee table. "Bebe, if you **put your mind to it**, you could be awfully good at doing hair. Give it a chance, child," she urged.

My forehead and upper lip grew moist with the sweat that anger brings on. "Mama Lil," I began, "*look* at me."

But Mama Lil lit a cigarette. She inhaled, then closed her eyes to release a stream of smoke. "I'm enjoying my cig, Bebe," she said. "It tastes better with my eyes closed."

I leaned in the doorway, my anger rising. "Mama Lil, your eyes are *always* closed. *Closed* to seeing me," **6** I said. "I don't want to spend my summer sweeping hair. The bridge is **where my heart's at**, Mama Lil."

She was doing her best to tune me out. "Yeah, that's right," I said, my voice strained with frustration. "Try to make me and my dreams disappear, like your puffs of smoke!"

5 Clarify Ideas
Why would Bebe get "real mad" at a "big favor" Mama Lil does for her?

6 Character/ Clarify Ideas
What does "Closed to seeing me" mean here? How does it describe Bebe's feelings about Mama Lil?

In Other Words
heap lot
put your mind to it decide to try hard
where my heart's at what I really want to do

Bridge Tower, 1929, Glenn O. Coleman. Oil on canvas, Brooklyn Museum of Art, New York, Bequest of Alexander M. Bing, The Bridgeman Art Library.

▲ Critical Viewing: Design How do the colors and lines in this painting suggest the feeling of a busy place?

Mama Lil opened her eyes. They looked weary, and her expression looked pained. She sighed. "Bebe, I'm an old woman. I don't have many of my own dreams to go after." Her voice trailed off to silence. Then her face softened. For the first time ever, I saw Mama Lil's eyes fill with regret. "What little bit of dreaming I got left in me," she said, "I'm putting to you." **7**

Mama Lil let out a heavy breath. Then she admitted what we'd both known all

> **I don't have many of my own dreams to go after.**

along. "Your dreams are the kind that'll take you away from here, Bebe. They'll take you away from your Mama Lil."

I shrugged.

Mama Lil said, "That's an upsetting truth, Bebe. It makes **my heart hurt** every time I think on it."

"Mama Lil, I got to find *my* way," I said slowly. "If that bridge renovation wasn't **tapping on my soul**, I'd go ahead and sweep hair down at Rimley's."

For once, Mama Lil was looking into my face, hearing my words. **8**

"Let me go, Mama Lil. Let me dream," I **pleaded** softly.

Mama Lil sat as still as a statue. I reached into my pocket to find the bridge project consent form. I unfolded it and set it on the coffee table, next to the application from Rimley's. "Mama Lil," I said carefully, "if you don't sign this—if you *won't* sign it—I'll sign it myself. I been helping you sign checks and letters for years now. I can sign your name on this consent form. Nobody will know the difference."

7 Clarify Ideas
Reread Mama Lil's words. What is her message to Bebe? Think about how she uses words. Are the meanings exact, or do they suggest something more?

8 Character
What do Mama Lil's actions tell you about her? How has she changed?

Monitor Comprehension

Confirm Prediction
Was your prediction accurate? If not, why? What happened that you did not expect?

In Other Words
my heart hurt me feel sad
tapping on my soul something I really want to do
pleaded begged

The next morning, I awoke to the smell of ham coming from the kitchen. My clock said 5:36, and the bridge renovation crew was scheduled to meet at 7:00. I threw on my T-shirt and jeans and grabbed my sketchbook.

"Hey, Mama Lil," I said, entering the kitchen.

Mama Lil peered at me over the top of her narrow glasses, glasses she wore only for reading. "Sit, Bebe, your ham's ready," she said. I shrugged and slid into my chair. The hands on the kitchen clock were settling on 6:00.

Mama Lil served both our plates. She sat down across from me and started eating. She was acting like it was any other morning. She chatted on about her late-night comedy show and the pigeons that nested on the ledge of her bedroom window. 9 I was certain she'd **done away with** the consent form for the bridge project, and was doing her best to ignore the whole thing.

I ate in silence. I was wondering if the bridge crew leader would let me onto the project without signed permission. I'd have to leave for the site soon, if I wanted to get there on time. I finished my last bite of ham. Then I said firmly, "Mama Lil, I'm going to the bridge."

"I know, Bebe," she said.

That's when Mama Lil reached into the pocket of her **housedress** and pulled out the consent form. "You gonna need this," she said, sliding the papers across the table.

I unfolded the form, which had become worn and crumpled. But Mama Lil hadn't signed it. It was the same as it had always been.

9 **Character**
Why do you think Mama Lil is acting like this? Give two reasons.

In Other Words
done away with thrown away
housedress simple, comfortable dress

Mama Lil could see the upset pinching at my face.  "Now hold it, Bebe," she said. "Don't be so quick to put on that **down-in-the-mouth** expression."

"But you didn't sign the form, Mama Lil!"

"Calm down, child." Mama Lil's tone was solid. She said, "You're **jumping out the gate too fast**."

10 Language
The author uses familiar words in an unusual way. What does "upset pinching at my face" mean?

Detail of *The Sky's the Limit*, 1995, Emma Amos. 22½ ft. mosaic ceiling, Intermediate School 90, New York City Board of Education, Manhattan.

▲ Critical Viewing: Character Which person in this mosaic could be Bebe? Why?

In Other Words
down-in-the-mouth sad, frowning
jumping out the gate too fast making a quick conclusion

"The project's gonna start without me!" I snapped.

Mama Lil's eyes looked red-tired. "I been up most the night, Bebe," she said. "I been thinking, praying, and trying my best to read that permission paper. They sure got a whole bunch of words on that thing, just to say I'm gonna let you help fix a bridge."

I could feel my whole body fill with relief. Mama Lil said, "I may not know how to read that good. But I *do* know I ain't supposed to sign something I ain't fully read."

The project's gonna start without me!

Mama Lil pushed her glasses up on her nose. They were speckled with dots of grease that had sprung from the hot ham skillet. **11** "Will you help me read the permission paper, Bebe?" she asked. "Will you help me understand what it's saying to me?"

I slid my chair to Mama Lil's side of the table. Together, we read the consent form. When we were done, Mama Lil took a pen from her housedress pocket. She held it awkwardly and signed the form with her crooked handwriting. She gave her signature a good looking-over. Then she folded the form and pressed it into my hand. "Bebe, that bridge is lucky to have you," she said. **12**

I hugged Mama Lil good and hard, then I got up to go. I smiled big, right at her. "Yeah, it is," I said. ❖

11 Clarify Ideas
What does *speckled* mean here? Which words in the sentence help you figure out the meaning?

12 Character
Could you imagine Mama Lil saying this earlier? What does this dialogue show about her character?

Monitor Comprehension

Confirm Prediction
Was your prediction accurate? If not, why? What happened that you did not expect?

ANALYZE Building Bridges

1. **Explain** What caused the disagreement between Bebe and Mama Lil about the bridge? Do you think what happened at the end is realistic? Use evidence from the text to explain your answer.

2. **Vocabulary** Bebe says that Mama Lil is **stubborn**. How can you tell that Bebe is stubborn, too?

3. **Analyze Character** With a partner, find several clues in the story that show what Mama Lil and Bebe are like. Write the clues on a chart.

Type of Clue	Bebe	Mama Lil
What the Character Looks Like		
What the Character Does		
What the Character Says		

4. **Focus Strategy Clarify Ideas** Choose one part of the story where you needed to clarify the meaning of specific words or phrases in order to understand the ideas. Have your partner clarify the ideas in that part. Did your partner understand the text the same way you did?

Return to the Text

Reread and Write Explain why Bebe **reacted** so strongly when Mama Lil said no to her summer plans. Reread the text and list the clues you find. Then write a paragraph to explain Bebe's strong reaction.

Key Vocabulary
• **react** *v.*, to respond

Analyze Text: Memoir

A **memoir** is a writer's personal account of real events that happened in his or her life. Memoirs are nonfiction, but they often have a plot like a short story.

Look Into the Text

Leguizamo tells about himself. He uses a conversational, or friendly, tone.

> I was a nerd in junior high. A really bad nerd. I was seriously out of touch, especially the way I dressed. When you're a poor kid at a poor school, you worry a lot about how you look all the time, how much money you're spending on clothes and all that. I had problems, man. I wore high waters. And my shoes? Forget about it. I had fake sneakers— you know, the kind your mother finds in those big wire bins.

How does the author feel about what he had to wear?

Focus Strategy ▶ Plan and Monitor

While you read, you can **clarify ideas**. If you don't understand a sentence you are reading, try looking at its structure or the way it is built. Then break it into smaller parts, or meaningful chunks. You may also want to read the hard parts more slowly.

Reading Strategies

▶ Plan and Monitor
· Determine Importance
· Make Inferences
· Ask Questions
· Make Connections
· Synthesize
· Visualize

HOW TO CLARIFY IDEAS

Focus Strategy

1. **Break Up the Sentence** Find the main part of the sentence first. Then find how the other parts tell about the main part. Use the punctuation to help see the parts.

> When you're a poor kid at a poor school, you worry a lot about how you look all the time, how much money you're spending on clothes and all that.

2. **Slow Down** Don't race over the text. Slow down to get the meaning.

Connect Across Text
In "Building Bridges," Bebe knows what she wants in life. Read this memoir about what causes a teen to change his life.

THE RIGHT WORDS
AT THE RIGHT TIME

by John Leguizamo

I was a nerd in junior high. A really bad nerd. I was seriously out of touch, especially the way I dressed…

Key Vocabulary
comedian *n.*, a person who makes people laugh

▲ John Leguizamo's family moved from Colombia to the United States when he was four. He grew up to become an award-winning actor, **comedian**, producer, and writer.

When you're a poor kid at a poor school, you worry a lot about how you look all the time, how much money you're spending on clothes and all that. I had problems, man. I wore **high waters**. And my shoes? Forget about it. I had fake sneakers—you know, the kind your mother finds in those big wire bins.

"Hey, John, here's one I like! Go find the one that matches!"

"I found it, Ma, but it's only a three and a half."

"Don't worry. We'll cut out the toes."

So there I am, pants too high, sneakers too tight, underwear without leg holes. I was the **Quasimodo of Jackson Heights**. Then it hits me: this is no way to get girls. So I had my mission then: become cool. **1**

I totally changed. I hung out with the gangsters. Cut class. By the time I got to high school, I was getting in trouble all the time.

What I loved most was **cracking** jokes in school. I liked keeping the kids laughing. Even the teachers laughed sometimes, which was the best part. See, I was still so **out of it** in a way—too cool to hang with

Leguizamo has become a successful comedian and actor. He has been nominated for two Tony Awards for work in theater. He won an Emmy Award in 1999 for work in television.

1 Memoir
What have you learned about the author so far? What do you expect to find out?

In Other Words

high waters pants that were too short
Quasimodo of Jackson Heights strange-looking one in my neighborhood. Quasimodo is a deformed man in *The Hunchback of Notre Dame*, a book by Victor Hugo.

cracking telling
out of it odd, different from everyone else

the nerds, not cool enough to be with the *real* cool guys—I figured my only value was to be funny. I enjoyed people enjoying me.

Anyway, one day during my junior year, I was walking down the hallway, making jokes as usual, when Mr. Zufa, my math teacher, pulled me aside. I got collared by the teachers all the time, so I didn't think much about it. Mr. Zufa looked at me and started talking.

"Listen," he says, "instead of being so **obnoxious** all the time—instead of wasting all that energy in class—why don't you rechannel your hostility and humor into something productive? 2 Have you ever thought about being a comedian?"

I didn't talk back to Mr. Zufa like I usually would have. I was quiet. I probably said something like, "Yeah, cool, man," but for the rest of the day, I couldn't get what he said out of my head.

It started to hit me, like, "Wow, I'm going to be a loser all my life." And I really didn't want to be a loser. I wanted to be somebody. 3

But that one moment Mr. Zufa collared me was the turning point in my life. Everything kind of **converged**, you know? The planets aligned.

But the big change didn't happen overnight.

Eventually, I got into New York University, where I did student films. One of the movies won **a Spielberg Focus Award**, and suddenly my life changed.

2 **Clarify Ideas**
Do you understand what Mr. Zufa is telling Leguizamo? What strategy can you use if you are confused?

3 **Memoir**
What part of Leguizamo's life does he share here?

Leguizamo was voted "Most Talkative" in high school.

Monitor Comprehension

Paraphrase
In your own words, tell what happened to John Leguizamo in high school.

In Other Words
obnoxious annoying
converged came together, worked out
a Spielberg Focus Award an award given by Steven Spielberg, a famous movie director

I got an agent and wound up as a guest villain on *Miami Vice*. That started my **career**.

I've run into Mr. Zufa a bunch of times since high school and told him how his advice turned my life around. And I'm not just saying that. Here's a guy who was able to look beneath all the stuff I pulled in class and find some kind of merit in it, something worth pursuing. How cool is that? ❖

ANALYZE The Right Words at the Right Time

1. **Explain** How did the author **react** to his teacher's advice? Use evidence from the text to explain your answer.

2. **Vocabulary** When Leguizamo was in school, what **obstacles** did he face? What did he do to overcome these obstacles?

3. **Analyze Text: Memoir** With a partner, share the most interesting insight you learned about John Leguizamo.

4. **Focus Strategy** **Clarify Ideas** Look at the last paragraph of the selection. Clarify the ideas in it and then retell it in your own words.

Return to the Text

Reread and Write The author tells about a teacher who influenced his choice of **career**. Reread the memoir to find other things that may have influenced him, too. Write your ideas in a paragraph.

Key Vocabulary
career *n.*, life's work, profession
• **react** *v.*, to respond
obstacle *n.*, something that prevents you from doing something

In Other Words
Miami Vice a popular TV show

EQ What Influences How You Act?

Critical Thinking

EQ 1. **Compare** Review the **Quickwrite** you did on page 30. Would you **react** to advice from adults more as Bebe did or more as John Leguizamo did? Why?

2. **Interpret** John Leguizamo's talk with a teacher was a turning point in his life. Might Bebe's talks with Mama Lil be a turning point in her life? Explain.

3. **Imagine** Both the story and the memoir are set in cities. How would the characters be different if the events took place in the suburbs or in the country? Explain.

4. **Speculate** Do you think John Leguizamo would have listened to Mama Lil's advice? Why or why not? Include evidence from the text in your answer.

EQ 5. **Evaluate** Would Bebe have gone to the bridge without Mama Lil's **consent**? Would John Leguizamo be a **comedian** without his teacher's words? Include evidence from the text in your answer.

Write About Literature

Journal Entry When you read stories and memoirs, you can get ideas about dealing with your own problems. What did you learn about making choices by reading about Bebe and John Leguizamo? Use examples from both texts. Write a journal entry to tell what you learned.

Key Vocabulary Review

Oral Review Work with a partner. Use these words to complete the paragraph. Take turns sounding out the words to help you learn them. If you recognize any prefixes or root words, use them to help you figure out the new words.

career	engineers	react
comedian	obstacles	stubborn
consent	projects	

Darnell wanted his mother's __(1)__ before he joined the army, but she did not __(2)__ well. At first she refused. Darnell told her not to be so __(3)__ . He said that being in the army could be a lifetime __(4)__ because he would learn many skills. He said that __(5)__ in the army build dams and bridges, and that he wanted to work on __(6)__ like that. Darnell's mother said she wanted him to be a __(7)__ and make people laugh. Darnell said there were too many __(8)__ to success in that kind of work.

Writing Application Recall a time you overcame an **obstacle**. Write a paragraph about it. Use at least three Key Vocabulary words.

Read with Ease: Phrasing

Assess your reading fluency with the passage in the Reading Handbook, p. 666. Then complete the self-check below.

1. I did/did not pause appropriately for punctuation and phrases.

2. My words correct per minute: _____ .

Make Subjects and Verbs Agree

The **verb** you use depends on your **subject**. These subjects and verbs go together. All the verbs are **forms of _be_**.

I **am**	We **are**
You **are**	You **are**
He, she, or it **is**	They **are**

Action verbs have two forms in the present:

I **think** of the future. Bebe **thinks** of the future.

Add **-s** to the action verb only when you talk about one other person, place, or thing. Find the subject in each sentence. How does the verb end?

Bebe **helps** Mama Lil read.

Mama Lil **wears** too many gold chains.

She often **disagrees** with Bebe.

Oral Practice (1–5) Choose from each column to make five sentences. Use words more than once.

Example: Mama Lil is scared.

Mama Lil	is	different things.
She	want	scared.
Bebe	are	to be an engineer.
They	hopes	a dreamer.

Written Practice (6–15) Write ten sentences about Bebe and Mama Lil. Start with these sentences and choose the correct verb. Then tell more.

Bebe (live/lives) with Mama Lil. Bebe (dream/ dreams) of building bridges. Her grandmother (want/wants) her to cut hair. Bebe and Mama Lil often (argue/argues). But they (is/are) close.

Ask and Answer Questions

Pair Talk Ask a partner about his or her future job. For example, _What_ happens in an animal clinic? _Who_ works there? _Where_ do the dogs sleep?

Dialect

Dialect is a version of language used by a specific group or in a specific region. Dialect can include special expressions as well as how words are pronounced.

In "Building Bridges," Mama Lil and Bebe speak using dialect. Here are some examples from the story:

- Mama Lil (p. 35): "stooping to do a bunch of low-down mess-work"
- Bebe (p. 39): "tapping on my soul"
- Mama Lil (p. 41): "Don't be so quick to put on that down-in-the mouth expression."
- Mama Lil (p. 41): "You're jumping out the gate too fast."

With a partner, locate these phrases or sentences in "Building Bridges." Use context clues or the glossary on the page to figure out what Mama Lil or Bebe is saying. Then find an example of dialect in "The Right Words at the Right Time."

Source: ©Mark Parisi

Prefixes

A **prefix** is a word part added at the beginning of a word. It changes the word's meaning. The Latin prefix *re-* means "back" or "again." When you **react**, you "act back" at someone or something. The Greek prefix *anti-* means "against." When you are *antiwar*, you are "against war." The prefix *un-*, which comes from Old English, means "not," so *unlikely* means "not likely." Write the meaning of the underlined word.

1. Rewrite the paragraph to correct mistakes.
2. The city council passes antipollution laws.
3. She sold her unwanted clothes at the garage sale.

Career Chart

Social Studies: Career Choices Bebe is interested in engineering. John Leguizamo became a comedian. What kind of **career** is right for you? Gather information about jobs that match your talents and interests.

myNGconnect.com
- Discover what you would be good at.
- Learn about the jobs you are interested in.

Organize your information in a chart. Share it with a classmate who has similar career interests.

📗 **Language and Learning Handbook**, page 616

Write a Short Comparison

Some tests ask you to write a response to literature. The prompt will often name the selection and ask you to think about some part of it.

1 **Unpack the Prompt** Read the prompt and underline the important words.

> **Writing Prompt**
>
> In "Building Bridges," Bebe shows that she is strong enough to do something important. Think about a time when you had to be strong or overcome an obstacle. Write a short essay that compares your experience and Bebe's. Use examples from the story and your life to support your ideas.

2 **Plan Your Response** Compare a personal experience to Bebe's. Use a Venn diagram to help you plan.

Venn Diagram

My moment of strength | Both | Bebe's moment of strength

3 **Draft** When you compare, organize your comparison like this. Add specific ideas from your diagram.

> **Essay Organizer**
>
> In "Building Bridges," Bebe shows she is a strong person when she [tell what Bebe does]. To do this, Bebe has to [tell what Bebe has to do] because [tell why]. In my life, I showed I was strong when [tell what you did]. In order to do this, I had to [tell what you had to do]. My experience is [like/different from] Bebe's because [tell why].

4 **Check Your Work** Reread your draft. Ask:

- Did I respond to the writing prompt?
- Did I give examples to support my ideas?
- Do the subjects and verbs agree?

📗 **Writing Handbook**, page 698

ROLE-PLAY

You can learn a lot about a character or another person by acting as he or she would in a certain situation. This is known as "role-playing." Role-play with another student, pretending to be two characters from one of the selections in this unit. Here is how to do it:

1. PLAN YOUR ROLE-PLAY

Choose the characters you want to be in your role-play. Then each of you should do the following:

- Think about the character you are playing: his or her personality traits, needs, problems, and ways of speaking and moving.
- Think about the characters' relationship: Are they friends? What does each character want from the other? How might their relationship affect how they respond to each other?
- Think of dialogue that sounds like what your character might actually say.

2. PRACTICE YOUR ROLE-PLAY

Work with your partner to do the following:

- Keep your role-play less than five minutes.
- Introduce the situation—the setting, the plot, and the conflict.
- Speak and move in a way that fits the character.

3. DO YOUR ROLE-PLAY

Keep your role-play interesting by doing the following:

- Remain in character at all times—try to "be" that person.
- Do not forget what your character wants in the situation, and try very hard to get it.
- Speak clearly and loudly enough for the audience to understand everything you say.

myNGconnect.com
🔊 Download the rubric.

4. DISCUSS AND RATE THE ROLE-PLAY

Use the rubric to discuss and rate the role-plays, including your own.

ROLE-PLAY RUBRIC

Scale	Content of Role-Play	Student's Preparation	Student's Performance
3 Great	• Made me understand or sympathize with the character in a new way • Was interesting and held my attention throughout	• Understood the character very well • Chose a situation that worked well with the story and the characters	• Used believable movements and speech • Spoke clearly and loudly
2 Good	• Fit my view of the character • Held my interest much of the time	• Understood the character fairly well • Chose a situation that worked fairly well with the story and the characters	• Was fairly believable • Could be heard most of the time
1 Needs Work	• Did not seem like the character at all • Was not very interesting	• Did not seem to understand the character • Did not choose a situation that worked well with the story and the characters	• Was stiff and unbelievable • Could not be heard or understood well

DO IT ▶ Now that you know how to role-play, act out the story and make it believable!

📖 Language and Learning Handbook, page 616

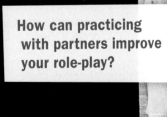

How can practicing with partners improve your role-play?

EQ ## What Influences How You Act?
Find out how easily people can be fooled.

Make a Connection

Brainstorm With a group, brainstorm foolish things that people have believed in that are not true, such as *The moon is made of cheese.* List your responses. Then talk about why people are fooled sometimes.

Learn Key Vocabulary

Study the Words Pronounce each word and learn its meaning. Work with a partner. Repeat the words to each other. Listen to each syllable, and give feedback to correct mistakes. You may also want to look up the definitions in the Glossary.

● Academic Vocabulary

Key Words	Examples
confident (**kon**-fu-dunt) *adjective* ▶ pages 58, 63, 67	When you are **confident,** you feel sure of yourself. For example, if you study, you might feel **confident** that you will do well on a test. *Antonym:* unsure
● **convince** (kun-**vins**) *verb* ▶ pages 65, 66, 67	When people **convince** you of something, they make you believe it. You feel certain that what they say is true. *Synonyms:* win over, persuade
doubt (dowt) *verb* ▶ pages 58, 67	When you **doubt** something, you aren't sure if you believe it. *Synonyms:* question, deny; *Antonym:* be certain
foolish (fü-lish) *adjective* ▶ pages 65, 67	**Foolish** people are not wise. They believe things that are silly or that don't make sense.
nerves (nurvz) *noun* ▶ page 58	Some actors suffer from **nerves** before they go on stage. They feel worried and scared.
shock (shok) *noun* ▶ page 61	People who receive bad news often suffer a great **shock**. *Synonym:* surprise
tragedy (**tra**-ju-dē) *noun* ▶ page 58	The death of a loved one is a **tragedy**. *Synonym:* very sad event; *Antonym:* comedy
worthless (**wurth**-lus) *adjective* ▶ page 65	A smashed remote control is **worthless** because you can't use it or sell it. *Synonym:* useless; *Antonym:* valuable

Practice the Words Work with a partner to put the Key Vocabulary words into groups. For example, *nerves*, *shock*, and *tragedy* are all related to fear. Use a **Category Chart**. What other words can you add to the categories?

Category Chart

Fear	Belief	Sadness	Value
nerves shock			
Lack of Fear	**Disbelief**	**Happiness**	**No Value**
confident			

BEFORE READING The Open Window

short story by Saki

Reading Strategies

▶ Plan and Monitor
· Determine Importance
· Make Inferences
· Ask Questions
· Make Connections
· Synthesize
· Visualize

Analyze Character and Plot

To understand what the **characters** are like in a story, pay attention to their **dialogue**—what they say—and to their actions and how other characters feel about them. The **plot** of the story is often made up of the characters' actions.

Look Into the Text

Framton's action gets the story started. It is an important event in the plot.

Framton Nuttel tried to think of something to talk about with the girl. He also wondered what he would say to the aunt. At his sister's recommendation, he had come to their home in the country to rest and cure his nerves. But he doubted whether this visit with total strangers was going to help him.

"I know how it will be," his sister had said before he left for the country. "You won't speak to anyone down there. Your nerves will be worse than ever from moping."

What do you learn about Framton from his sister's words, or dialogue?

Focus Strategy ▶ Plan and Monitor

As you read, you will see words that you don't know. Sometimes you can skip the word, keep reading, and still understand the story. Other times, you need to figure out the word in order to understand what you are reading. Here's how.

HOW TO CLARIFY VOCABULARY

Focus Strategy

THE TEXT SAYS: "You won't speak to anyone down there. Your nerves will be worse than ever from moping."

YOUR QUESTION: What does moping mean?

1. **Find Context Clues** Look for words that might give you clues to the meaning, such as, "You won't speak to anyone" and "Your nerves will be worse."

2. **Analyze the Clues** Use the clues to determine the meaning of the word.

   YOU THINK: If he won't speak to people and his nerves won't improve, he's probably acting sad or depressed. Maybe moping means acting depressed.

3. **Replace** Use the meaning in the sentence: "Your nerves will be worse than ever from acting depressed." Does that make sense?

The Writer and His Background

Saki
(1870–1916)

Saki wrote short stories, popular novels, and plays. He was also a war reporter.

Saki's real name was Hector Hugh Munro. He was born in the Asian country of Burma, now called Myanmar. When he was a toddler, his mother was killed by a charging cow. His father sent Saki and his older brother and sister to live with relatives in England. They were raised by their grandmother and two very strict aunts.

The aunts had many rules. Saki didn't like the rules, but he had to obey. He was not allowed to play outside very often. The windows in his house were never even opened.

Saki rebelled against this strictness when he grew older. He wrote many short stories about clever youths who trick the mean people in their lives. A lot of his tales have surprise endings.

Fortunately for Saki, his stories were popular and brought him fame and a good income.

myNGconnect.com
- Read more of Saki's work.
- See photos of Myanmar.

THE OPEN WINDOW

ADAPTED FROM A STORY BY SAKI

Drawing Room, 1a Holland Park, 1887, Anna Alma-Tadema. Watercolor. Russell-Cotes Art Gallery and Museum, Bournemouth, UK. The Bridgeman Art Library.

▲ Critical Viewing: Setting Imagine standing in this room and looking out the window. What might you see?

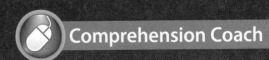
Comprehension Coach

A girl tells a visitor about a great tragedy. Find out what happened.

"My aunt will be down soon, Mr. Nuttel," said the **confident** fifteen-year-old young lady.

Framton Nuttel tried to think of something to talk about with the girl. He also wondered what he would say to the aunt. At his sister's recommendation, he had come to their home in the country to rest and cure his **nerves**. **1** But he **doubted** whether this visit with total strangers was going to help him.

"I know how it will be," his sister had said before he left for the country. "You won't speak to anyone down there. Your nerves will be worse than ever from **moping**. So I'll give you letters of introduction to all the people I know. **2** Some of them are quite nice."

Framton wondered whether Mrs. Sappleton, the girl's aunt, was one of the nice people.

"Do you know many of the people here?" asked the niece. She thought that they had been silent long enough.

Young Girl Painting, 19th century, English School. Watercolor, private collection, The Maas Gallery, London, UK, The Bridgeman Art Library.

△ **Critical Viewing: Character** Which description of the girl in the story could also describe this girl in the painting?

1 Character
What kind of person is Framton Nuttel? How can you tell?

2 Clarify Vocabulary
What do you think "letters of introduction" are? Look for clues in the text. Explain the clues you find.

Key Vocabulary
tragedy *n.*, a very sad event
confident *adj.*, sure of yourself
nerves *n.*, worried and scared feelings
doubt *v.*, to be unsure

In Other Words
moping feeling sorry for yourself

"Hardly anybody," said Framton. "My sister stayed here four years ago. She gave me letters of introduction to some of the people she met."

He said the last sentence unhappily. 3

"Then you don't know about my aunt?" continued the self-assured young lady.

"Only her name and address," he admitted. He wondered whether Mrs. Sappleton was married or **widowed**. Something about the room made him believe she was married.

"Her great tragedy happened three years ago," said the niece. "That would have been after your sister was here."

"Her tragedy?" asked Framton. It was hard to imagine tragedies in this restful place.

Her great tragedy happened three years ago...

"You may wonder why we keep that window wide open on an October afternoon," said the niece. She pointed out a large French window that opened onto a lawn.

"It is quite warm today," said Framton. "But what does that window have to do with her tragedy?"

"On this day three years ago, her husband, her two young brothers, and their little brown dog left through that window to go hunting. They never came back. On the way to their favorite hunting spot, they all drowned. It had been a very wet summer. Places that used to be safe to walk across were not safe. **The marsh gave way** suddenly without warning. Their bodies were never recovered. That was the **dreadful** part of it."

3 Character
How do you think Framton would feel at a party or in a crowded room? Why do you think that?

Monitor Comprehension

Explain
What did the niece say the great tragedy was?

In Other Words
widowed whether her husband was dead
The marsh gave way The ground under them fell in
dreadful horrible, awful

Predict
How will Framton react to the girl's sad story?

ow the girl's voice softened. "Poor aunt always thinks that they will come back some day. She believes they will walk in that window just as they used to do. That is why the window is kept open every evening until the sun goes down." **4**

She continued. "My poor aunt often talks about how her husband went out that day with his white raincoat over his arm. And her youngest brother would sing, 'Bertie, why do you **bound**?' to annoy her. Do you know, sometimes on still, quiet evenings like this, I almost get a creepy feeling that they will walk in through that window . . ."

She stopped with a little shudder. **5**

It was a relief to Framton when the aunt hurried into the room, apologizing for being late.

"I hope Vera has been amusing you?" she said.

"She has been very interesting," said Framton.

"I hope you don't mind the open window," said Mrs. Sappleton. "My husband and brothers will be home soon. They always come in this way. They've been out hunting today. They'll make a muddy mess all over my poor carpets. So like you men, isn't it?"

She continued talking about hunting and birds and ducks. But to Framton it was all purely horrible. He tried hard to change the subject, but his hostess was only partially paying attention to him. Her eyes were looking past him to the open window. It was certainly **an unfortunate coincidence** that his visit was on the day of this tragic anniversary.

4 Character
What do the girl's words tell you about the aunt?

5 Clarify Vocabulary
What does *shudder* mean? Look for clues in the paragraphs above and below.

In Other Words
bound run, jump, leap
an unfortunate coincidence unlucky

"The doctors agree that I need complete rest. I also need to avoid anything that might excite me too much. And I cannot do difficult exercise," announced Framton. He mistakenly thought total strangers would be interested in his medical problems. "But the doctors do not agree about my diet," he continued.

"No?" said Mrs. Sappleton, **in a voice that only replaced a yawn at the last moment**. Then she suddenly brightened up, but not at what Framton was saying.

"Here they are at last!" she cried. "Just in time for tea. They look as if they are muddy up to their eyes!"

Framton shivered slightly and turned toward the niece with a sympathetic look. The child was staring out through the open window with horror in her eyes. In cold **shock** Framton swung around in his seat and looked in the same direction.

Jacques-Emile Blanche, John Singer Sargent (1856–1925). Musée des Beaux-Arts, Rouen, France.

△ **Critical Viewing: Character** What do you think this man is like? How does he seem like Framton?

6 Language
Do you think the hunters really have mud "up to their eyes"? What does the aunt mean by this expression? What effect does the author create by using exclamatory sentences here?

✓
Monitor Comprehension

Confirm Prediction
What did you guess about Framton's reaction? Did your prediction match what happened in the story?

Key Vocabulary
shock *n.*, surprise and fear

In Other Words
in a voice that only replaced a yawn at the last moment almost yawning

Predict

***Why do you think Vera
reacts as she does?***

Three figures were walking across the lawn toward the window. They all carried guns under their arms. And one of them was wearing a white coat. A tired brown **spaniel was at their heels**.

Noiselessly they walked toward the house. Then a hoarse young voice sang out: "I said, Bertie, why do you bound?"

Framton grabbed wildly for his stick and hat. He ran out the door, down the **gravel drive**, and through the front gate. A bicyclist on the road drove into the bushes to avoid hitting him.

"Here we are, my dear," said the man in the white raincoat, coming in through the window. "We're fairly muddy, but most of it's dry. Who was that who rushed out as we came up?"

The False Mirror, 1928, René Magritte. Oil on canvas, The Museum of Modern Art, New York.

▲ Critical Viewing: Effect What feeling do you get when you look at this painting? Why does it make you feel like that?

"A very unusual man," said Mrs. Sappleton. "He could only talk about his illnesses. Then he rushed off without a word when you arrived. It was as if he had seen a ghost." **7**

7 Character and Plot
Why did Framton rush off without a word?

In Other Words
spaniel was at their heels dog was walking
  close beside them
gravel drive driveway covered with little rocks

"It must have been the spaniel," said the niece calmly. "He told me he was terrified of dogs. A pack of wild dogs once chased him into a **cemetery**. And he had to spend the night in a newly dug grave with the creatures **snarling** above him. That would be enough to make anyone frightened."

Wild tales at short notice were her specialty. ❖

ANALYZE The Open Window

1. **Explain** What does Framton do at the end of the story? Why? Include evidence from the text in your answer.

2. **Vocabulary** What does Vera do that proves she is confident?

3. **Analyze Character and Plot** Work with a partner. How would you describe Framton? Vera? Use a chart to record clues from the text that support your descriptions.

Type of Clue	Framton	Vera
What the Character Says		
What the Character Does		

4. **Focus Strategy** **Clarify Vocabulary** Find two or more words in the text that you didn't know or weren't sure about. Ask a partner to clarify the meanings. Do your partner's definitions match yours?

   Return to the Text

   Reread and Write What do you think influences how the niece acts? Reread the text and then write an explanation.

In Other Words
cemetery place where dead people are buried
snarling barking and growling
Wild tales at short notice were her specialty.
She was great at making up stories.

BEFORE READING One in a Million
folk tale

Reading Strategies

▶ **Plan and Monitor**
· Determine Importance
· Make Inferences
· Ask Questions
· Make Connections
· Synthesize
· Visualize

Analyze Cultural Perspectives: Folk Tale

A **folk tale** is a simple story that has been shared and told to many people over the years. Folk tales usually reflect the culture they came from. Folk tales, myths, and legends are stories that often have imaginary beings or try to explain people's beliefs or how something came to be. Such traditional tales are often timeless, passed down from generation to generation.

Look Into the Text

Often, folk tales from a culture feature the same main character.

> Nasruddin Hodja looked at his donkey and frowned. The beast was a bag of bones and had a dirty, shaggy coat. It stood under a tree, dully chewing a clump of grass. "Look at you," Hodja sneered. "You are completely worthless to me. All you do is stand under that tree. You refuse every order I give you!"
>
> The lazy donkey didn't even look at Hodja. It kept chomping away. "That's it!" Hodja cried in frustration. "I'm going to sell you!"
>
> So the next day Hodja led the scrawny creature to the crowded marketplace in the center of the village. He was grateful for the thirty dinars a foolish man offered him for the beast.

The plot involves simple events and problems. What is Hodja's problem?

The setting and events reflect the traditions of the culture.

Focus Strategy ▶ Plan and Monitor

As you read, use context clues to clarify a word or group of words that you don't understand. Try this strategy with the text above.

HOW TO CLARIFY VOCABULARY

Focus Strategy

THE TEXT SAYS:
> "That's it!" Hodja cried in frustration. "I'm going to sell you!"
> So the next day Hodja led the scrawny creature to the crowded marketplace in the center of the village. He was grateful for the thirty dinars a foolish man offered him for the beast.

YOUR QUESTION: What does dinars mean?

1. **Reread** Go back over the words and sentences near the unfamiliar word.

2. **Look for Context Clues** Use the clues to figure out what *dinars* means.

   YOU THINK: Sell and marketplace are clues. Dinars are probably some kind of coins.

3. **Replace** Change *dinars* to the meaning you figured out. "He was grateful for the thirty coins a foolish man offered him for the beast." Does it make sense?

One in a Million
a traditional Middle Eastern tale

Connect Across Texts
In "The Open Window," the girl **convinces** Framton of something. What is Hodja convinced of in this folk tale?

Nasruddin Hodja looked at his donkey and frowned. The beast was **a bag of bones** and had a dirty, shaggy coat. It stood under a tree, **dully chewing a clump of grass**. "Look at you," Hodja sneered. "You are completely **worthless** to me. All you do is stand under that tree. You refuse every order I give you!"

The lazy donkey didn't even look at Hodja. It kept **chomping away**.

"That's it!" Hodja cried in frustration. "I'm going to sell you!"

So the next day Hodja led the scrawny creature to the crowded marketplace in the center of the village. He was grateful for the thirty **dinars** a **foolish** man offered him for the beast. Hodja went on with his business as the buyer led the hopeless creature away. **1**

Later, as Hodja wound his way out of the marketplace, he noticed a crowd of eager shoppers. Curious to see what treasure they were after, Hodja pushed through to the center of the group. He was startled to see his donkey! The beast's new owner was shouting, "Look at this fine animal! Have you ever seen a better donkey? See how clean and strong it is! You will never find a better worker. Who will bid for this exceptional creature?" **2**

The buyers pressed forward eagerly. "What a prize! What a find!" they murmured excitedly. One shopper offered forty dinars for the donkey.

1 Folk Tale
What does the setting tell you about life in this culture?

2 Clarify Vocabulary
What clues help you figure out what *exceptional* means? Read the sentence again, using the definition in place of *exceptional*.

Key Vocabulary
• **convince** *v.*, to make someone believe something
worthless *adj.*, useless
foolish *adj.*, not wise, silly

In Other Words
a bag of bones very thin
dully chewing a clump of grass chewing some grass in a slow, bored way
chomping away eating, chewing
dinars gold coins

Another man offered fifty. A third offered fifty-five!

Puzzlement furrowed Hodja's brow. "I thought that donkey was just an ordinary animal," he said to himself, scratching his scraggly beard. "Was I a fool? It is obviously very special. It's one in a million . . ."

The new owner swept his arm toward the donkey and cried, "How can you **pass up** the chance to own such a magnificent beast? See how the muscles ripple under the smooth, silky coat. Look at those bright, intelligent eyes . . ."

Hodja squeezed his way to the front of the crowd. The man's **flowery words** floated through the warm air, filling Hodja's ears. "Seventy-five dinars once," the man yelled. "Seventy-five dinars twice . . ."

Hodja's skin tingled. He raised his hand excitedly and shouted, "I bid eighty dinars!" **3** ❖

3 Clarify Vocabulary
How can the word *excitedly* help you guess what the word *tingled* means?

ANALYZE One in a Million

1. **Explain** Why does Hodja spend so much money to buy the donkey? Include evidence from the text in your answer.

2. **Vocabulary** How does the donkey's new owner **convince** people that the animal is valuable?

3. **Analyze Cultural Perspectives: Folk Tale** Provide two details you learned about Middle Eastern culture from this folk tale.

4. **Focus Strategy Clarify Vocabulary** Explain what the phrase "one in a million" means. What context clues help clarify its meaning?

   ⤶ Return to the Text

   Reread and Write Imagine you own the donkey and want to sell it. Write an ad to influence people to buy it. Reread the text to find ideas.

In Other Words
Puzzlement furrowed Hodja's brow. Hodja looked confused.
pass up miss, not take
flowery words nice words, nice description

Cultural Background
Nasruddin Hodja is a popular archetype, or certain type of character, in Middle Eastern tales. Sometimes he is a fool, but sometimes he is wise. He is known by different names throughout the Middle East.

EQ What Influences How You Act?

Critical Thinking

EQ 1. Interpret What influenced Framton's behavior? What influenced Hodja's?

2. **Analyze** The sentence, *Wild tales told at short notice were her specialty*, describes the niece in "The Open Window." Does the description also apply to the donkey seller? Explain. Include evidence from the text in your answer.

3. **Compare** Which character do you think is more **foolish**, Framton in "The Open Window" or Hodja in "One in a Million"? Support your answer with evidence from the text.

EQ 4. Imagine Picture yourself in Framton's place. Would you believe the girl's story, or would you **doubt** it? How would you react when the hunters come home?

5. **Speculate** Imagine Framton was in Hodja's place. What would he do? What would Vera do in Hodja's place? Include evidence from the text in your answer.

Write About Literature

Opinion Statement Were the characters in these stories tricked mostly because they were foolish or mostly because they met **confident**, talented liars? Write a paragraph in which you state your opinion and support it with examples from both texts.

Key Vocabulary Review

Oral Review Work with a partner. Use these words to complete the paragraph.

confident	foolish	tragedy
convinced	nerves	worthless
doubted	shock	

I should never have listened to my friend's idea about visiting a spooky old house at midnight. I felt jumpy and thought I could cure my shaky __(1)__ by doing something daring. My friend seemed so __(2)__, so sure he was right, that he __(3)__ me to go with him. When we got to the house, my friend told me about a terrible __(4)__ that had happened there years ago. Even though I __(5)__ that his story was true, my heart began to pound. Then we heard a crash inside the house. I started running away in horror and __(6)__. When my friend began to laugh, I felt silly and __(7)__. Now I know that my friend's idea of fun has no value—it is __(8)__.

Writing Application Write a paragraph about a time when someone was able to **convince** you or a friend to do something. Use at least three Key Vocabulary words.

Read with Ease: Intonation

Assess your reading fluency with the passage in the Reading Handbook, p. 667. Then complete the self-check below.

1. I did/did not raise and lower the tone of my voice as I read.

2. My words correct per minute: _____.

INTEGRATE THE LANGUAGE ARTS

Fix Sentence Fragments

This group of words looks like a sentence. It begins with a capital letter and ends with a period.

Comes to their home to rest.

The group of words looks like a sentence, but it is not complete. It is a **sentence fragment**. The fragment needs a **subject** :

The man comes to their home to rest.

A fragment may need a **verb** .

Fragment: Her husband.
Sentence: Her husband **leaves** .

A fragment may need to become part of another sentence.

Fragment: And never come back.
Sentence: They go hunting and never come back.

Oral Practice (1–5) Look at the selections you just read. Find five complete sentences. Remove the sentence's subject or verb. Say it as a fragment. Ask your partner to change it back into a sentence.

Written Practice (6–10) Number your paper. Label each group of words with **S** for *Sentence* or **F** for *Fragment*. Then rewrite each fragment as a complete sentence.

6. She talks about that day often.
7. Thinks they will return.
8. The window stays open.
9. The man and his sons.
10. Tells wild tales.

Ask and Answer Questions

Question Quiz Make up five questions about "The Open Window" beginning with *Do* ____ ? or *Does* ____ ? Ask a partner your questions. After your partner answers, switch roles.

Compare Settings

The **setting** of a story is where and when it takes place. Setting is a major element of fiction, along with character and plot.

Sometimes authors tell the setting directly—for example, *It was a damp September afternoon in Houston in 1995.*

Other times, they describe the setting and let you imagine it. For example, an author might say, *Car horns blasted and the streets were busy with back-to-school shoppers.* The phrase *back-to-school* suggests September. Cars suggest modern times and a city.

Compare the settings in "The Open Window" and "One in a Million." Look for descriptions in the text that suggest the place and approximate time, such as the year or the season. Take notes. Then discuss these questions with a partner.

- Where and when is each story set? What do the details tell you?
- Which story has a setting that you can picture in your mind? Why do you think you can picture it so well?
- How does the setting of each story affect the plot and characters?

"Think spring."

Source: ©Frank Modell/*The New Yorker*

Suffixes

A **suffix** is a word part added at the end of a word. It changes the word's meaning. The suffix -*less* means "without." The suffix -*ful* means "full of." Read the first two examples on the chart. Then copy the chart and fill in the rest.

WORD	SUFFIX	MEANING
1. worthless	-less	without worth
2. dreadful	-ful	full of dread
3. hopeless		
4. hopeful		
5. doubtful		

Trait: Focus and Unity

When you write, include a **topic sentence** that states the central idea. Make sure your composition is all about that central idea.

Not Focused

> Many folk tales feature a character that is a trickster. One character is Coyote. Coyote appears in many Native American folk tales. In some stories, Coyote and Skunk have trouble with hunting. Anansi the spider is a trickster in some African tales. I read a story about Anansi on the Internet. In other African tales, the trickster is a hare.

Here is how the writer fixed this mistake.

Much Better

> Many folk tales feature a character that is a trickster. One character is Coyote. Coyote appears in many Native American folk tales. Another trickster, Anansi the spider, is in some African tales. In other African tales, the trickster is a hare.

Folk Tales

Social Studies: Trickster Tales The trickster is an archetypal, or common, character that occurs in many types of literature. Hermes, in Greek mythology; Tom Sawyer, from Mark Twain's *The Adventures of Tom Sawyer;* and Puck, in Shakespeare's *A Midsummer Night's Dream,* are all examples of tricksters. Discover folk tales about tricksters. Notice how the characters, settings, and plots are similar to or different from those of "One in a Million." Retell the stories in a small group. Can you think of things that folk tales have in common with modern literature?

myNGconnect.com
- **Learn what a trickster tale is.**
- **Read trickster tales from other cultures.**

📗 **Language and Learning Handbook**, page 616

Read the paragraph below. What is the central idea? Look for it in the topic sentence. Which sentences do not go with the central idea? Rewrite the composition to improve its focus and unity.

> The character of Anansi has different names in different cultures. In Jamaica, he is Annancy and might be a person or a spider. The weather is great in Jamaica. On other Caribbean islands, he is the spider Kompa Nanzi. The Caribbean is south of the United States. Jamaica is in the Caribbean. In the American South, he became a human female, Aunt Nancy.

📗 **Writing Handbook**, page 698

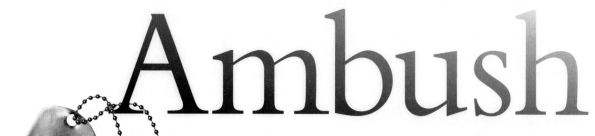

Ambush

BY TIM O'BRIEN

1   When she was nine, my daughter Kathleen asked if I had ever killed anyone. She knew about the war; she knew I'd been a soldier. "You keep writing these war stories," she said, "so I guess you must've killed somebody." It was a difficult moment, but I did what seemed right, which was to say, "Of course not," and then to take her onto my lap and hold her for a while. Someday, I hope, she'll ask again. But here I want to pretend she's a grown-up. I want to tell her exactly what happened, or what I remember happening, and then I want to say to her that as a little girl she was absolutely right. This is why I keep writing war stories:

2   He was a short, slender young man of about twenty. I was afraid of him—afraid of something—and as he passed me on the trail I threw a grenade that exploded at his feet and killed him.

3   Or to go back:

4   Shortly after midnight we moved into the ambush site outside My Khe. The whole **platoon** was there, spread out in the dense brush along the trail, and for five hours nothing at all happened. We were working in two-man teams—one man on guard while the other slept, switching off every two hours—and I remember it was still dark when Kiowa shook me awake for the final watch. The night was foggy and hot. For the first

In Other Words
Ambush Surprise Attack
platoon group of soldiers

Historical Background
The **Vietnam War** took place from 1954-75 throughout Southeast Asia. The government of North Vietnam, supported by China and the Soviet Union, fought to take over the government of South Vietnam, supported by the United States.

few moments I felt lost, not sure about directions, **groping** for my helmet and weapon. I reached out and found three **grenades** and lined them up in front of me; the pins had already been straightened for quick throwing. And then for maybe half an hour I kneeled there and waited. Very gradually, in tiny slivers, dawn began to break through the fog, and from my position in the brush I could see ten or fifteen meters up the trail. The mosquitoes were fierce. I remember slapping at them, wondering if I should wake up Kiowa and ask for some repellent, then thinking it was a bad idea, then looking up and seeing the young man come out of the fog. He wore black clothing and rubber sandals and a gray **ammunition** belt. His shoulders were slightly stooped, his head cocked to the side as if listening for something. He seemed at ease. He carried his weapon in one hand, muzzle down, moving without any hurry up the center of the trail. There was no sound at all—none that I can remember. In a way, it seemed, he was part of the morning fog, or my own imagination, but there was also the reality of what was happening in my stomach.

Over four million of these made and sold every week, Diarmuid Kelley (b.1972). Oil on canvas, private collection, The Bridgeman Art Library.

▲ Critical Viewing: Effect What is the mood, or feeling, of this painting? How does it relate to the mood of the story?

In Other Words
groping searching awkwardly
grenades small bombs
ammunition bullet

I had already pulled the pin on a grenade. I had come up to a **crouch**. It was entirely automatic. I did not hate the young man; I did not see him as the enemy; I did not ponder issues of morality or politics or military duty. I crouched and kept my head low. I tried to swallow whatever was rising from my stomach, which tasted like lemonade, something fruity and sour. I was terrified. There were no thoughts about killing. The grenade was to make him go away—just evaporate—and I leaned back and felt my mind go empty and then felt it fill up again. I had already thrown the grenade before telling myself to throw it. The brush was thick and I had to lob it high, not aiming, and I remember the grenade seeming to freeze above me for an instant, as if a camera had clicked, and I remember ducking down and holding my breath and seeing little wisps of fog rise from the earth. The grenade bounced once and rolled across the trail. I did not hear it, but there must've been a sound, because the young man dropped his weapon and began to run, just two or three quick steps, then he hesitated, **swiveling** to his right, and he glanced down at the grenade and tried to cover his head but never did. It occurred to me then that he was about to die. I wanted to warn him. The grenade made a popping noise—not soft but not loud either—not what I'd expected—and there was a puff of dust and smoke—a small white puff—and the young man seemed to jerk upward as if pulled by invisible wires. He fell on his back. His rubber sandals had been blown off. There was no wind. He lay at the center of the trail, his right leg bent beneath him, his one eye shut, his other eye a huge star-shaped hole.

I did not hate the young man...

In Other Words
crouch low, bent-leg position
swiveling turning

Fallen Timbers/Fallen Time, 1989, David A. Given with Arturo Alonzo Sandoval. Mixed media, National Veterans Art Museum, Chicago Illinois.

▲ Critical Viewing: Effect How is the United States flag used in this piece of art? What effect does this have?

5   It was not a matter of live or die. There was no real **peril**. Almost certainly the young man would have passed by. And it will always be that way.

6   Later, I remember, Kiowa tried to tell me that the man would've died anyway. He told me that it was a good kill, that I was a soldier and this was a war, that I should shape up and stop staring and ask myself what the dead man would've done if things were reversed.

7   None of it mattered. The words seemed far too complicated. All I could do was **gape** at the fact of the young man's body.

8   Even now I haven't finished sorting it out. Sometimes I forgive myself, other times I don't. In the ordinary hours of life I try not to **dwell on** it, but now and then, when I'm reading a newspaper or just sitting alone in a room, I'll look up and see the young man coming out of the morning fog. I'll watch him walk toward me, his shoulders slightly stooped, his head cocked to the side, and he'll pass within a few yards of me and suddenly smile at some secret thought and then continue up the trail to where it bends back into the fog. ❖

In Other Words
peril danger
gape stare
dwell on think a lot about

THINK AGAIN

EQ ESSENTIAL QUESTION:

**What Influences
How You Act?**

myNGconnect.com

⊙ **Download the rubric.**

Present Your Project: Children's Book

It is time to write and publish your children's book about the Essential Question for this unit: What Influences How You Act?

Review and Complete Your Plan

Consider these points as you complete your project:

- How will your children's book address the Essential Question?
- Will your book be fiction or nonfiction?
- What kind of illustrations will you include?

Divide the tasks of writing, illustrating, and publishing.

Create and Publish Your Children's Book

Follow your plan, dividing the tasks among group members. Share the finished book with your classmates.

Evaluate the Children's Books

Use the online rubric to evaluate each of the children's books, including the one that you created.

Reflect on Your Reading

Think back on your reading of the unit selections, including your choice of Edge Library books. Discuss the following with a partner or in a group.

Genre Focus   Compare and contrast the elements of a short story with the features of a memoir. Give examples, using the selections in this unit.

Focus Strategy   Choose a selection in this unit that you think might be difficult for some people to read. Name three strategies that would help someone clarify understanding. Write an explanation of these strategies on a note card and share it with a partner.

EQ Respond to the Essential Question

Throughout this unit, you have been thinking about what influences how people act. Discuss the Essential Question with a group. What have *you* decided? Support your response with evidence from your reading, discussions, research, and writing.

Write a Personal Narrative

Sometimes a new experience changes how we think and act. For this project, you will write about an experience that made you think twice.

Study Personal Narratives

Personal narratives tell stories from your own life. They include real people, places, and events from your own experiences. They also include your thoughts and feelings about those experiences.

❶ Connect Writing to Your Life

You tell personal narratives all the time. You might tell a classmate about events from your summer vacation. You might tell friends about a learning experience or something funny that happened in school.

❷ Understand the Form

Remember, you are not just writing for yourself but for others, too. To communicate the significance of events to your audience, make your narrative interesting to them. You also need to relate a clear sequence of events, so your narrative needs a beginning, a middle, and an end.

Beginning
State the belief that you had at the beginning of the experience. Start with interesting background that briefly explains why you had that belief or how it affected you. Introduce the experience that changed your belief. Establish the **controlling idea** of your narrative.

Middle
Tell about the experience that changed your thinking. Locate scenes and incidents in specific places. Tell what happened in the order that it happened. Share your thoughts and feelings. Use lively details and dialogue.

End
Summarize how the experience changed your thinking. Be sure to state your new belief clearly. Explain how it affects you today.

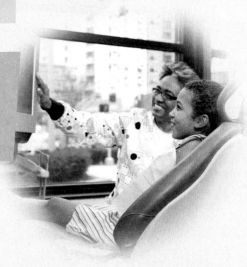

Now look at these parts in action. Read a personal narrative by a professional writer.

❸ Analyze a Professional Model

As you read, look for the three main parts of the story.

Dentists Don't Bite!

by Vicki Tellez

When I was a little girl, I believed the dentist office was so scary that it made my teeth chatter. Don't get me wrong. Dr. Curtis had a kind smile for everyone. "I want to help you smile, too," she'd say. But somehow I didn't see how big, ugly dental tools would do that. *Bzzzrrt!* That was the sound of the drill. It looked like a machine from a science fiction movie. Now would *you* smile if you heard that coming toward you? No wonder I hated every visit.

Then something happened that turned my ideas upside down. Like when you stand on your head and see the world in a whole new way.

One Sunday, I was playing tag outside with my sister Ana. I tripped, banging my mouth on the sidewalk. I was in pain but was not sure what had happened. Ana pointed to the ground. "Your teeth!" she screamed. I looked down and there were my two front teeth.

I grabbed them and ran into the house. My mother stayed calm as she phoned Dr. C. Then she put my teeth into a cup of milk. I'm not joking! Dr. C said it would help. To me, it just seemed strange. But I held the cup on my lap as Mom drove us to Dr. C's office. It was Sunday, but she rushed out to meet us. "I can save those teeth," she said, smiling. As for me, I felt like I'd never smile again. First, Dr. C gave me something so I would not feel any pain. Then, she picked up her tools and set to work. I watched the flash of shiny, metal tools and heard a gentle murmur as Dr. C spoke to me and Mom. "The roots of the teeth will heal. Just you wait and see."

Every week, Dr. C checked how I was doing. Soon, I felt as good as new. So Dr. C saved me from looking silly, and I changed the way I look at going to the dentist. Once, it made my teeth chatter in fear. But now going to the dentist truly makes me smile!

The writer clearly states her **old belief in the beginning.**

The writer gives reasons for her belief and examples of how it affected her.

The middle part tells about the experience that changed the writer's belief.

The writer relates the sequence of events in **chronological order.**

Descriptive details and **dialogue** make the scene come alive.

In the end, how does the narrator's belief change?

Prompt Write a personal narrative about an experience that changed your thinking. Be sure to tell:
- your old belief
- what happened to change your mind
- your thoughts and feelings about the experience
- your new belief

✔Prewrite

Now that you know the basics of personal narratives, plan one of your own. Planning will make it easier for you to write later on. Making a Writing Plan helps you avoid the "blank page blues," when you can't think of anything to say.

❶ Choose Your Topic

Here are two great ways to choose your topic:

- Think about a belief you used to have. What made you change your mind? Would telling about it make a good story?
- Think about a memorable experience in your life. Why do you remember it so clearly? How did it make you think twice?

- When you choose your topic, come up with a question about the topic of your experiences or beliefs. Brainstorm ideas with a partner or in a small group.

❷ Clarify the Audience, Controlling Idea, and Purpose

Who will be reading your story? Knowing your audience will help you decide what language and details to include. Jot down your ideas.

Think about the belief that changed. Write down what your belief was, what happened to change it, and what it is now. This is your controlling idea.

Finally, consider your purpose, or reason, for writing. Is your purpose to entertain readers? To explain something about yourself or share a big idea about life? Jot down your purpose.

❸ Gather Supporting Details

Next, gather details about the experience that changed your belief. Recall what happened, what you thought, and how you felt. Jot down the details.

Then tell your story to a partner. Have your partner take notes and ask questions to

- get more details that are specific, important, and on target
- help you clarify your ideas
- fill in background information.

Prewriting Tip

Ask yourself these questions to find your controlling idea:

- What did I believe at first? Why?
- What event changed my belief?
- How did I feel about the event?
- What do I believe now?

❹ Organize the Details

Use a chart like the one below. In the first part, list background information. In the second, organize details in chronological order, or the order in which they happened. State the change of belief in the third part.

Technology Tip

List the details on your computer screen. Then use Cut and Paste from the Edit menu to move the details around as you need to.

Before: I hated vegetables.	Experience: I tried vegetables.	After: I like vegetables.
looked strange or boring had a soggy texture	the Simon family invited me to dinner Marc's dad grilled vegetables	I became interested in cooking.

❺ Finish Your Writing Plan

To capture your prewriting ideas, make a Writing Plan like the one below. Show which details will go in the beginning, the middle, and the end.

Writing Plan

Topic	learning to eat vegetables
Audience	my teacher and my classmates
Controlling Idea	I hated vegetables until I tried fresh vegetables cooked on a grill.
Purpose	to show how an experience changed my belief
Time Frame	start today; due in a week

Beginning
1. I hated vegetables.
2. I did not like the texture.
3. I did not like the way they looked.

Middle
4. I was visiting my new friend Marc Simon.
5. His family invited me to dinner.
6. His father grilled vegetables from the garden.
7. The vegetables tasted much better than I expected.
(Nice detail. Move this to the middle.)

End
8. I decided that I like vegetables.
9. I became interested in cooking.

Reflect on Your Writing Plan

▶ Will the way you organized the details keep the ideas focused and flowing logically from one idea to the next? Talk it over with a partner.

✔ Write a Draft

Use your Writing Plan as a guide while you write your narrative. It's fine to make mistakes. You can improve your draft later. Just keep writing!

1 Keep Your Ideas Flowing

If you have trouble getting your ideas on paper, try these techniques:

- **Find a Good Place to Write** Choose a quiet, comfortable place where you can think. It may be at home, in class, or in a library.
- **Work on the Middle First** If you have trouble getting started, skip to the middle of your personal narrative. Focusing on the experience that changed your belief may help you decide what background to write.
- **Leave Space and Move On** Sometimes it is hard to think of a word or remember a detail. Don't let this stop the flow of your writing. Just leave a space and move on. Add the missing word or detail later.
- **Use Mental Imagery** Close your eyes and replay the experience in your mind. Jot down details and dialogue.

> I did not want to eat vegetables. The thought of it tied my stomach in knots. Can't think of anything to say. Wait. I remember being at Marc's. The sight of purple potatoes. Weird.

2 Create a Catchy Beginning

How will you engage your readers' attention? Use your personal style and voice to support your purpose for writing. Coming up with a great beginning can help the rest of the writing flow, and it can reveal the unique voice that is you. Here's an example:

OK

> I thought vegetables were awful.

Better

> I used to believe that most vegetables were only good for feeding our pet rabbit.

Technology Tip

Make your text double- or triple-spaced, or as your teacher directs. (Use the Paragraph feature from the Format menu to change line spacing.) Print a copy of your draft to read later. The extra space between lines will give you room to mark changes.

Read this draft to see how the student used the Writing Plan to get ideas down on paper. This first draft does not have to be perfect. As you will see, the student fixed the mistakes later.

The Day I Ate Purple Potatoes

i used to believe that most vegetables were only good for feeding our pet rabbit. I also have a dog, and I used to have a turtle, but it ran away. Not that turtles run. i was a guy who liked meat and potatoes. i used mashed potatoes to hide other veggies Mom sneaked onto my plate. I disliked the strong smell of boiled asparagus. a bowl of mushy beans looked like drowned bugs. salad was boring.

Then, when I was sixteen we moved to Salinas, California next to the Simons' house. Their our neighbors. This was the third time my family had moved. One Sunday, Marc Simon and I were on the patio, doing math homework and laughing at our own jokes.

Mr. and Mrs. Simon were in they're garden. "Would you like to stay for dinner?" Mr. Simon asked. "I have the grill on." Expecting hamburgers. I happily said yes.

Then I saw that he carried a basket of vegetables. He had all the kinds I hated, and some I'd never seen before. Even the potatoes were strange Wow They were purple Who ever heard of purple potatoes But meat wasn't on the menu. Nervously, I watched as Mr. Simon grilled some vegetables and Mrs. Simon made a salad with the rest. "You've never had vegetables like these before," said Marc proudly.

"Its true," I agreed weakly. Imagine how I felt.

Dinner was soon ready. "Here you go," said Mr. Simon, "Dig in." Dig in? I wanted to dig a hole in the yard and bury My dinner. Instead, I took a small bite, then another, and another. What a surprise. The flavors were good. I liked the corn, green beans, and the eggplant. The purple potatoes were moist, buttery, and flavorful.

Today, I still. Eat hamburgers. However, that dinner changed my opinion of vegetables.

Reflect on Your Draft

▶ Did you establish a controlling idea and support it with specific details? Did you relate events in chronological order? Talk it over with a partner.

✓Revise Your Draft

Your first draft is done. Now, polish it. Improve the focus and unity and your choice of supporting details and words. Tighten the organization. Make what was just OK into something much better.

❶ Revise for Focus and Unity

Good writing always has a **focus**—a central or controlling idea. In a personal narrative, the focus is telling the story of an interesting event in the writer's life.

Good writing also has **unity**. That means that all of the parts tell about, or support, the controlling idea. In a personal narrative, unity means that the facts and events, descriptive details, figurative language, and dialogue all go with the controlling idea. They should also be appropriate for your genre, purpose, and audience. Transitions and rhetorical devices can also help unify your writing. Return to your writing plan. Review the purpose of your essay as you revise your writing.

Don't expect to show perfect focus and unity in your first draft. Every writer needs to rewrite. Revising helps you sharpen your focus. Get out a colorful pen or pencil. Allow yourself ten minutes to add transitions and rhetorical devices to focus and unify your writing. Then take out any word, sentence, or even paragraph that doesn't go with your controlling idea.

TRY IT ▶ With a partner, identify the focus of the draft below. Evaluate which parts of the draft do not support or relate to the writer's controlling idea. Discuss how the unity of the draft is better without those parts.

Student Draft

> I used to believe that most vegetables were only good for feeding our pet rabbit. I also have a dog, and I used to have a turtle, but it ran away. Not that turtles run. I'm a guy who liked meat and potatoes. I hated the strong smell of asparagus. A bowl of beans looked like bugs to me. Salad was boring.

Now use the rubric to evaluate the focus and unity of your own draft. What score do you give your draft and why?

Focus and Unity

myNGconnect.com

🔊 Rubric: Focus and Unity

🔊 Evaluate and practice scoring other student narratives.

	How clearly does the writing present a central idea or claim?	How well does everything go together?
4 Wow!	The writing expresses a <u>clear</u> central idea or claim about the topic.	<u>Everything</u> in the writing goes together. • The main idea of each paragraph goes with the central idea or claim of the paper. • The main idea and details within each paragraph are related. • The conclusion is about the central idea or claim.
3 Ahh.	The writing expresses a <u>generally</u> clear central idea or claim about the topic.	<u>Most</u> parts of the writing go together. • The main idea of most paragraphs goes with the central idea or claim of the paper. • In most paragraphs, the main idea and details are related. • Most of the conclusion is about the central idea or claim.
2 Hmm.	The writing includes a topic, but the central idea or claim is <u>not</u> clear.	<u>Some</u> parts of the writing go together. • The main idea of some paragraphs goes with the central idea or claim of the paper. • In some paragraphs, the main idea and details are related. • Some of the conclusion is about the central idea or claim.
1 Huh?	The writing includes many topics and <u>does not</u> express one central idea or claim.	The parts of the writing <u>do not</u> go together. • Few paragraphs have a main idea, or the main idea does not go with the central idea or claim of the paper. • Few paragraphs contain a main idea and related details • None of the conclusion is about the central idea or claim.

❷ Revise Your Draft

You've now evaluated the focus and unity of your own draft. If you scored 3 or lower, how can you improve your work? Use the checklist below to revise your draft.

Revision Checklist

Ask Yourself	Check It Out	How to Make It Better
Is my narrative focused?	If your score is 3 or lower, revise.	☐ If you are telling about more than one belief, focus on just one. ☐ Focus on one belief and one experience that changes it. Cut any others. ☐ If there is no central or controlling idea, add one.
Is my narrative unified?	If your score is 3 or lower, revise.	☐ Remove or replace any sentence or paragraph that is not about the controlling idea. ☐ Add a topic sentence to each paragraph that doesn't have one. ☐ Cut, move, or replace any details that do not really support a paragraph's main idea.
Does my narrative have a beginning, a middle, and an end?	Find and mark the boundaries between these parts.	☐ Add any part that is missing. ☐ Move any paragraph or sentence that is in the wrong part.
Are the supporting details vivid and interesting?	Underline details that appeal to the senses. **Highlight** dialogue. Are there enough of both to bring the experience alive for the reader?	☐ Add sensory details or dialogue.
Will readers be able to follow my narrative?	Read it to someone or ask someone to read it. Ask about any parts that were hard to follow.	☐ Add any missing details. ☐ Add sequence words and phrases.

❧ **Writing Handbook**, p. 698

❸ Conduct a Peer Conference

It helps to get a second opinion when you are revising your draft. Ask a partner
to read your draft and look for

- any part of the draft that is confusing
- any place where something seems to be missing
- anything that the reader doesn't understand.

Then talk with your partner about the draft. Focus on the items in the Revision
Checklist. Use your partner's comments to make your narrative clearer, more
complete, and easier to understand.

❹ Make Revisions

Look at the revisions below and the peer-reviewer conversation on the right.
Notice how the peer reviewer commented and asked questions. Notice how
the writer used the comments and questions to revise.

Revised for Focus and Unity

> I used to believe that most vegetables were only good for
> feeding our pet rabbit. ~~I also have a dog, and I used to have a turtle,~~
> ~~but it ran away. Not that turtles run.~~ I'm a guy who liked meat and
> potatoes. I hated the strong smell of asparagus. A bowl of beans
> looked like bugs to me.

Revised Ending

> Today, I still eat hamburgers. However, that dinner changed
> my opinion of vegetables. I no longer use mashed potatoes to hide
> vegetables. In fact, I'm learning to cook veggies and even make salads.

Peer Conference

Reviewer's Comment:
I think you went off track
in the first paragraph. Your
paper is about vegetables,
not pets, isn't it?

Writer's Answer: Oops!
I see what you mean. I'll
fix that.

Reviewer's Question: I'm
not clear about how your
belief changed. Do you
want to tell more about
how this affected you?

Writer's Answer: You're
right, it's not very specific.
I'll add some details.

**Reflect on
Your Revisions**

▶ Think about the results
of your peer conference.
What are some of your
strengths as a writer?
What are some things
that give you trouble? Ask
your teacher for additional
feedback.

✔ Edit and Proofread Your Draft

Your revision should now be complete. Before you share it with others, find and fix any mistakes that you made.

❶ Capitalize First Words in Sentences and the Pronoun *I*.

Capital letters give important visual clues to readers. Use a capital letter to show where a sentence begins.

> **D**inner was soon ready. **T**he flavors were good.

The personal pronoun *I* also uses a capital letter.

> Today, **I** still eat hamburgers.

TRY IT ▶ Copy the sentences. Fix the four capitalization errors. Use proofreader's marks.

> i wanted to dig a hole in the yard and bury My dinner. instead, i took a small bite, then another, and another. The flavors were good.

❷ Add End Punctuation Correctly

End punctuation makes different kinds of sentences easier to understand.

Use a period at the end of a sentence or a polite command. You should also use a period at the end of a statement that includes a question.

> "Here you go," said Mr. Simon. "Dig in."
> "Would you like to stay for dinner?" he asked.

Use a question mark at the end of a direct question.

> Who ever heard of purple potatoes?

Use an exclamation mark to show strong feeling or surprise

> What a surprise!
> Wow! They were purple!

TRY IT ▶ Copy the sentences. Add the correct end punctuation.

> 1. "Do you eat hamburgers?" I asked Marc
> 2. Wow What kind of vegetable is this

Proofreader's Marks

Use these proofreader's marks to correct capitalization and punctuation errors.

Capitalize:
then i saw the basket.

Do not capitalize:
I laughed at Her jokes.

Add a period.
I like vegetables⊙

Add a question mark:
Can you stay for dinner⌄

Add an exclamation mark.
Oh, I'd love to⌄

Proofreading Tip

If you are unsure of where to place end punctuation in direct quotations, you can refer to a style manual.

❸ Check Your Spelling

Homonyms are words that sound alike but have different meanings and spellings. Spell these homonyms correctly when you proofread.

Homonyms and Their Meanings	Examples
its (pronoun) = belonging to it	I noticed **its** purple color.
it's (contraction) = it is or it has	"**It's** true," I agreed.
their (pronoun) = belonging to them	They were in **their** garden.
there (adverb) = that place or position	Marc was the first friend I made **there**.
they're (contraction) = they are	**They're** our neighbors.

TRY IT ▶ Copy the sentences. Find and fix the two homonym errors.

> It's flavor was unusual, but it really was not too bad. "It's tasty," I told Marc, "and its great that you grew it yourself."

❹ Check Sentences for Completeness

A sentence expresses a complete thought and has a subject and predicate.

Problem	Solution
Sentence is missing a subject. Then moved to Salinas.	**Add the missing subject.** Then we moved to Salinas.
Sentence is missing a verb. I glad about the invitation.	**Add the missing verb.** I was glad about the invitation.
Sentence fragments do not express a complete thought. Mr. Simon. Was in the garden.	**Join the fragments to express a complete thought.** Mr. Simon was in the garden.

TRY IT ▶ Copy the sentences. Find and fix the two incomplete sentences.

> Today, I still. Eat hamburgers. However, I no longer use mashed potatoes. To hide other vegetables.

🔖 **Writing Handbook**, p. 765

Technology Tip

Most word-processing software includes a spell-check feature and a grammar feature. Always use these but know their limits. Spell-checkers cannot find some homonym errors.

Reflect on Your Corrections

Double-check any parts of your paper of which you are unsure. Exchange papers with a partner. Have your partner help with a final check of grammar, capitalization, punctuation, and spelling. Have him or her check for complete sentences and subject-verb agreement. Also have your partner point out words or phrases you may have used incorrectly.

Here is the edited version of "The Day I Ate Purple Potatoes." What improvements did the student writer make?

The Day I Ate Purple Potatoes

I used to believe that most vegetables were only good for feeding our pet rabbit. I was a guy who liked meat and potatoes. I used mashed potatoes to hide the other veggies Mom sneaked onto my plate. I disliked the strong smell of boiled asparagus. A bowl of mushy beans looked like drowned bugs. Salad was boring.

Then, when I was sixteen we moved to Salinas, California next to the Simons' house. They're our neighbors. This was the third time my family had moved. One Sunday, Marc Simon and I were on the patio, doing math homework and laughing at our own jokes.

Mr. and Mrs. Simon were in their garden. "Would you like to stay for dinner?" Mr. Simon asked. "I have the grill on." Expecting hamburgers, I happily said yes.

Then I saw that he carried a basket of vegetables. He had all the kinds I hated, and some I'd never seen before. There were glossy black globes of eggplant, ruby red tomatoes, orange peppers, and neon green beans. Even the potatoes were strange. Wow! They were purple! Who ever heard of purple potatoes? But meat wasn't on the menu. Nervously, I watched as Mr. Simon grilled some vegetables and Mrs. Simon made a salad with the rest. "You've never had vegetables like these before," said Marc proudly.

"It's true," I agreed weakly. My stomach was tying up in knots. I felt panic.

Dinner was soon ready. "Here you go," said Mr. Simon. "Dig in." Dig in? I wanted to dig a hole in the yard and bury my dinner. Instead, I took a small bite, then another, and another. What a surprise. I liked the crunchy, sweet corn, the tender green beans, and the rich taste of eggplant. The purple potatoes were moist, buttery, and flavorful.

Today, I still eat hamburgers. However, that dinner changed my opinion of vegetables. I no longer use mashed potatoes to hide vegetables. In fact, I'm learning to cook veggies and even make salads.

For better focus and unity, the writer deleted all details that did not support the controlling idea.

The writer **capitalized** the first word in each sentence, as well as the pronoun *I*.

The writer used the correct **homonyms**.

The writer fixed the fragments to make a **complete sentence**.

The writer added specific details to make the experience vivid for the reader. The writer also added correct **end punctuation**.

The writer tells how the experience felt. The writer also corrected a **homonym**.

The writer added details to the conclusion to reflect the controlling idea and purpose more fully.

✔ Publish and Present

You are now ready to publish and present your narrative. Print or write a clean copy and share it with your audience. You may also want to present your work in a different way.

Alternative Presentations

Do a Reading Read your narrative to the class. Make it come alive by reading with expression.

1 Introduce your Narrative Tell your audience the subject. For example, you might say, "My narrative tells why I no longer think that _____."

2 Read with Expression Use your tone of voice to show how you felt.

3 Watch Your Pacing Don't rush your presentation. Speak at a pace that is comfortable for your audience. Look up from time to time to see people's reactions. Does anyone look puzzled? If so, slow down.

4 Make Eye Contact Don't hide your face behind paper. Look over the paper at your audience to make eye contact from time to time.

5 Ask for Feedback When you are finished, thank your audience. Then ask for feedback:

- Was the beginning interesting? If not, how could I improve it?
- Was it easy to understand my controlling idea? If not, how could I make it clearer?
- Did the narrative feel complete? If not, what suggestions do you have for strengthening the ending?

Submit Your Writing to a School Newspaper or Magazine Does your school have a newspaper or magazine? If so, you might try to publish your personal narrative in it.

1 Meet the Requirements Find out the rules for submitting writing to the school newspaper or magazine. For example, it may require writing of a certain length. Make the needed changes to your narrative before submitting it.

2 Make Changes to Suit Your Audience Remember that what you publish will have a bigger audience than just your teacher and classmates. If necessary, revise your narrative to make it better suited to the whole school.

3 Meet Deadlines Most publications have a deadline after which they will not accept writings. Be sure to submit your narrative before the deadline.

🔖 **Language and Learning Handbook**, p. 616

Publishing Tip

Format your typed work according to your teacher's guidelines.

If you've handwritten your work, make sure your work is legible and clean.

Reflect on Your Writing

▶ Ask for and use feedback from your audience to evaluate your strengths as a writer.

- What parts of your narrative did your audience like?
- What parts of your narrative did your audience say need improvement?
- What would you like to do better the next time you write? Set a goal for your next writing project.

☑ Save a copy of your work in your portfolio.

How Do Families Affect Us?

In every conceivable manner, the family is the link to our past, the bridge to our future.

—ALEX HALEY

Not having a family made me very self-reliant and independent. If you have nobody to rely on, then you have to do it yourself.

—BEN NIGHTHORSE CAMPBELL

Critical Viewing ▶
At the Ellis Island Immigration Museum in New York, a display of diverse faces greets visitors. What does the display suggest about families in the United States?

FAMILY MATTERS

EQ ESSENTIAL QUESTION:
How Do Families Affect Us?

Study the Facts

Editors of a national teen magazine asked, "How do you feel about your parents?" Here are the results of their survey, based on about 700 responses from teens.

How Teens Feel About Their Parents	
74%	say they get along with their parents
82%	don't think their parents understand what it's like to be a teenager
65%	say their parents don't really know who they are
54%	would not tell their parents if they had a serious problem
77%	lie to their parents if they are doing something their parents would not approve of
88%	say their parents are sometimes an embarrassment
66%	say they will *not* be like their parents when they get older

Source: *Teen People* magazine; June 1, 2003

Analyze and Debate

1. In general, do most teens have a positive feeling about their parents? Which pieces of data support your answer? Which information seems contradictory—or seems to go against other information?

2. Do you think the teens answered all of the questions truthfully?

Talk with a group. Explain your opinions, and support your ideas with examples from your own experience as well as the experiences of people you know or have read about.

EQ ESSENTIAL QUESTION

In this unit, you will explore the **Essential Question** in class through reading, discussion, research, and writing. Keep thinking about the question outside of school, too.

① Plan a Project

Documentary

In this unit, you'll be making a short (three-minute) documentary about a family. Decide if your documentary will be about your own family or another family. To get started, watch a biographical documentary on TV. Notice

- whether the documentary includes interviews
- what kinds of questions are asked during the interviews
- how the documentary includes background information
- whether the documentary is entertaining.

Study Skills Start planning your documentary. Use the forms on myNGconnect.com to help plan your time and to prepare the content.

myNGconnect.com
- ▶ Planning forms
- ▶ Tips for making a documentary
- ▶ Interview forms
- ▶ Rubric

② Choose More to Read

These readings provide different answers to the Essential Question. Choose a book and online selections to read during the unit.

Walking Stars
by Victor Villaseñor

When sixteen-year-old Joseph becomes ill and is hospitalized, his dog Shep goes crazy. This true but amazing story is the first of many in the collection. As the stories show, every family is filled with magic, if we just look hard enough.
▶ NONFICTION

Jane Eyre
by Charlotte Brontë

Jane Eyre has been without a real home most of her life. At eighteen, she finally has one—Thornfield Hall. Soon Jane discovers that the house is full of secrets and lies. What truths will Jane discover there? Explore the influence of Brontë's story on modern literature.
▶ CLASSIC

myNGconnect.com
- 🔽 Read stories about African Americans who trace their family histories.
- 🔽 Explore statistics on family issues.
- 🔽 View online exhibits on genetics, an area of science that explains how parents give some traits to their children.

Finding Miracles
by Julia Alvarez

Milly Kaufman doesn't want anyone to know she was adopted from Latin America. But when Pablo moves to town from Latin America, Milly becomes curious about her own birth. Who were her parents? Why did they leave her in an orphanage?
▶ NOVEL

NONFICTION

You know that there are many different kinds of fictional stories. There are many different kinds of nonfiction, too. Read these four kinds.

DEMO TEXT #1

Last Saturday, my dad needed to take some stuff to the recycling center. I had other plans, but he said I had to go with him. "It will be an education," he explained. Right.

We drove forever and finally turned onto a bumpy dirt road. All of a sudden—the smell! It was horrible. In front of us was a huge mountain of trash—rotting food, used diapers, old furniture, and things I couldn't recognize.

"That's the landfill," my father pointed out. "It's where trash goes when it cannot be recycled."

Gross. I thought of all the times I had complained about having to recycle stuff at home. Smelling that pile of trash, I really started to think. Maybe recycling wasn't so bad.

DEMO TEXT #2

Household waste is a special category of trash. In your home, hazardous waste can include cleaners, paints, and motor oil, all of which can be hazardous to the health of your family and the environment. Here is how to identify and dispose of hazardous waste:

1. **Check labels**. Words such as *warning, caution, toxic,* and *flammable* indicate that the product contains dangerous materials.
2. **Use it up**. Use all of a product so that you don't throw any of it in the trash. Or give leftovers to someone else who needs it.
3. **Dispose of it properly**. Find out if your garbage company has special hazardous material collection days, or find out where you can safely drop off these materials.

DEMO TEXT #3

Every family in the United States should make a serious commitment to recycling. First, private residences are responsible for 60% of what goes into U.S. landfills. Second, landfills are filling up. Many cities and towns no longer have space to store huge amounts of garbage. Finally, reducing waste and recycling will help protect the environment for future generations. Families should work to keep the world a clean and safe place for their children and grandchildren. To learn what your family can do, visit your community's Web site or the U.S. Environmental Protection Agency. Start reducing waste now!

Every year, people in the United States produce millions of tons of trash. In fact, it would take a line of trucks stretching halfway to the moon to carry all the trash that Americans generate annually. Private residences—not businesses—are responsible for more than half of this waste, which includes everything from junk mail to cereal boxes. Much of this trash can be recycled, but sorting items and taking them to the curb or to a recycling center can be inconvenient.

Often, the job falls to one member of the family, and that person may get tired of the job. Some communities have recognized this and encourage families to recycle together.

Waste Generation in the U.S. in 2003
(approximate percentages)

Commercial locations (businesses, schools, hospitals, etc.)

Private residences

60%

40%

Source: U.S. Environmental Protection Agency, 2003

■ Connect Reading to Your Life

Here are some possible titles for the Demo Texts you just read. With a group, match each Demo Text with the best title. Take notes to keep track of people's choices. Choose each title as a group.

I think the title of #1 is "A Saturday Lesson."

Yeah, me too. The writer says he started to think, so I think he learned a lesson.

Demo Text #1	Start Recycling Now!
Demo Text #2	A Saturday Lesson
Demo Text #3	Trash Facts
Demo Text #4	How to Dispose of Hazardous Waste

Focus Strategy ▶ Ask Questions

To figure out which title went with which Demo Text, you probably asked yourself (or your partner) some questions, such as:

- What kind of writing is this? What does it sound like?
- Why did the author write this? What does he or she want me to think?
- What clues in the text help me figure out why the author wrote it?

You ask yourself questions all the time. When a friend tells you some surprising news, you ask questions to find out more. When you see something you have never seen before—such as a new kind of car—you ask questions to find out what it is. When your teacher gives you really difficult homework, you ask why—what is the reason?

Asking questions is an important reading strategy. Experienced readers know that a text isn't always easy to understand (or accurate!) and that asking questions is a good way to both understand and **evaluate** the text.

■ Your Job as a Reader

When you read anything—but especially nonfiction—you must first figure out what it is you are reading. You do this by looking at the title, reading a little of the text, and looking at the illustrations. Your job as a reader is to be active as you read— to question the ideas, the facts, and the author's reason for writing.

■ Unpack the Thinking Process

Ask: Why Did the Author Write It?

When you read the Demo Texts, you may have wondered about the **author's purpose**, or reason, for writing.

There are many different reasons for writing, but here are some of the most common ones. Which Demo Text matches each purpose and type of text?

Author's Purpose	Type of Text	Demo Text #
To narrate	**Narrative**	
To inform or explain	**Expository**	
To argue	**Argument**	
To tell how to do something	**Procedural**	

Elements of Literature

author's purpose *n.*, the reason an author writes a text
narrative *adj.*, that tells a story
expository *adj.*, that informs and explains
argument *n.*, a text or talk intended to persuade
procedural *adj.*, that tells how to do something

Academic Vocabulary

● **evaluate** *v.*, to judge the worth or importance of something; **evaluation** *n.*, the act or process of judging the worth of something

Ask: What Kind of Information Is in the Text?

Once you know what *kind* of nonfiction you're reading, you'll have a better idea of how to approach it. For example:

- You may have figured out that Demo Text #1 is narrative nonfiction because it narrates a real event. The author has carefully chosen details to leave a specific impression of the event. With this kind of nonfiction, you can relax a bit and enjoy it, asking questions only if something is unclear.
- Demo Text #2 is procedural nonfiction. Procedural text gives detailed steps to follow and can include lists of materials. With this kind of nonfiction, you might slow down and even take notes.
- Demo Text #3 is an argument. The purpose is to persuade you, so watch how the author uses language to get you to agree with his or her point of view. Study the author's facts and logic to decide whether you should believe the author or do what he or she says.
- Demo Text #4 is expository nonfiction. Its purpose is to inform or explain. With this kind of nonfiction, you could ask questions to clarify or to figure out what else you would like to learn about the topic.

■ Try an Experiment

Nonfiction texts are all around you. With a group, go on a nonfiction scavenger hunt. Copy the chart below.

Types of Text	Examples	Kinds of Information	Author's Purpose
Narrative			
Expository			
Argument			
Procedural			

1. Discuss where you can find examples of each **category**, or type, of nonfiction, such as procedural nonfiction in a science textbook.
2. Collect as many examples as you can.
3. Ask yourselves: What kind of information does the author include?
4. Determine the author's purpose for writing each one.
5. Share what you find with the rest of the class.

Academic Vocabulary
- **category** *n.*, a group or division in a system of classification; **categorize** *v.*, to classify or put into groups

Monitor Comprehension

Author's Purpose
Give four reasons why authors write nonfiction texts.

EQ How Do Families Affect Us?
Explore the science behind family resemblances.

Make a Connection

KWL Chart Discuss with a group what you know about family resemblances, or similarities. Write your ideas in column 1. In column 2, write what you want to learn about the topic. Then, after reading, use column 3 to list what you learned.

KWL Chart

WHAT I <u>K</u>NOW	WHAT I <u>WANT</u> TO KNOW	WHAT I <u>L</u>EARNED
Everyone in my family has brown eyes.	Do I have brown eyes because my parents have brown eyes?	

Learn Key Vocabulary

Study the Words Pronounce each word and learn its meaning. You may also want to look up the definitions in the Glossary.

● Academic Vocabulary

Key Words	Examples
control (kun-**trōl**) *verb* ▶ page 104	When you **control** something, you have the power to direct or manage it. Who **controls** a team—a player or the coach?
● **extraction** (ik-**strak**-shun) *noun* ▶ pages 113, 114	**Extraction** is the act of removing one thing from another thing. A dentist might perform an **extraction** of a bad tooth. *Synonym:* removal; *Antonym:* addition
inherit (in-**hair**-ut) *verb* ▶ pages 106, 111, 115, 117	We **inherit** things from family members who lived before us. From our parents, we usually **inherit** our appearance. We might **inherit** money and property from a grandparent.
molecule (**mo**-li-kyūl) *noun* ▶ pages 102, 111	A **molecule** is a very small particle or piece of a substance. A **molecule** of water is made up of two hydrogen atoms and one oxygen atom. water molecule — oxygen — hydrogen
● **sequence** (**sē**-kwuns) *noun* ▶ page 102	The alphabet follows a certain **sequence**, or order: *a, b, c,* and so on to *z.*
trait (trāt) *noun* ▶ pages 107, 109, 111, 115	A **trait** is a feature or a certain way that something is. Eye color is one **trait** for a person's appearance. *Synonym:* characteristic
● **transmit** (trans-**mit**) *verb* ▶ page 109	To **transmit** something is to pass it on to someone or something else. My friend **transmits** text messages on her cell phone. *Synonyms:* send, pass on; *Antonym:* receive
● **unique** (yū-**nēk**) *adjective* ▶ pages 105, 115	Something that is **unique** is one of a kind. Each of us has a **unique** set of fingerprints. No one has fingerprints exactly like mine. *Antonym:* common

Practice the Words Work with a partner to write four sentences. Use at least two Key Vocabulary words in each sentence.

Example: The manager <u>controls</u> the <u>sequence</u> of the employee's work.

Reading Strategies

· Plan and Monitor
· Determine Importance
· Make Inferences
▶ **Ask Questions**
· Make Connections
· Synthesize
· Visualize

BEFORE READING Genes: All in the Family
science article by Robert Winston

Analyze Author's Purpose

A **science article** is one kind of **expository nonfiction**. In a science article, the author shares ideas and information about the natural world. The author includes facts—things that can be proved and presents key terms—words you should know about the topic. Authors usually organize science articles with heads and diagrams that explain the ideas.

Look Into the Text

What Is a Gene?

The word *gene* has several meanings, but in essence, a gene is an instruction that tells your body how to work. The instruction is stored as a code in the molecule DNA.

Key terms are included.

This **head** tells what the section is about.

What **details** does the author include to support his purpose of explaining DNA?

Focus Strategy ▶ Ask Questions

As they read, active readers **ask** themselves **questions** to understand what they read or to figure out what is important. Try this strategy with the text above.

Focus Strategy

HOW TO SELF-QUESTION

1. **Ask Questions** Pay attention to ideas the writer spends a lot of time on or calls out with text features and diagrams. Then ask yourself questions about these ideas to be sure you understand them. Ask why the information is important.

2. **Write Your Questions** Remember that questions usually begin with *Who, What, When, Where, Why,* or *How.* Write the page number in case you need to go back.

3. **Answer the Questions** Look for answers in both the text and the visuals. Write the answer next to the question. Include the page number where you found the answer.

Double-Entry Journal

Page/Question	Page/Answer
p. 102: What is DNA?	

The Father of Genetics

It wasn't until 16 years after Gregor Mendel's death that scientists accepted his work in genetics.

Genetics is the study of how traits, such as how tall you are or the color of your eyes, are passed from parent to child. In the 1850s **Gregor Johann Mendel** figured out how this process works. He is considered the "father of genetics."

As a young man, Mendel joined a monastery, which is a place where priests and other religious people live and work. They sent him to a university to study science. Then he returned to the monastery and did his research in the monastery's garden, in the rolling hills of central Europe. He grew and studied pea plants. By recording what traits the "parent" pea plant passed to the "child" pea plant, he proved that parents' traits are passed to their children.

Genetics has come a long way since then. Now scientists are using what they know about genes to do many things, including curing illnesses and making disease-resistant crops.

myNGconnect.com

🔾 Read more about Gregor Mendel.
🔾 Conduct your own experiment.

GENES:
All in the Family

Do you look a little like your mom? Or a lot like your grandfather? Have you ever wondered why? You can blame it all on your genes.

by Robert Winston

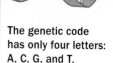

What Is a Gene?

The word *gene* has several meanings, but in essence, a gene is an instruction that tells your body how to work. The instruction is stored as a code in the **molecule DNA.**

DNA Carries Genes

DNA is an amazingly long but ultra-thin molecule. It is shaped like a twisted ladder, the **rungs** of which make up a simple code with only four letters: A, C, G, and T (the letters stand for chemicals in the rungs). **1** A gene is a **segment** of DNA containing a particular **sequence** of letters—a bit like a paragraph in a book. In most genes, the sequence of letters is a code for the sequence of different units (amino acids) in a protein molecule. Genes carry the code for many thousands of different proteins.

Chromosomes Carry DNA

Your DNA has to fit into a tiny space, so it is packed up in **an ingenious** way. Each molecule of DNA is **coiled** to make a thread, the thread is coiled again to make a cord, and so on (just as thin fibers can be wound together to make rope). The end result is a chunky, X-shaped structure called a chromosome. Chromosomes are far too small to see **with the naked eye**—you'd need about 100,000 of them just to fill a period. Even so, each chromosome contains a whopping 7 feet (2 meters) of DNA. **2**

The genetic code has only four letters: A, C, G, and T.

1 Ask Questions
You can use a comparison to ask a question. How is DNA like a ladder?

2 Ask Questions
Ask a question based on what you have just read about how DNA forms a chromosome. Then give the answer.

Key Vocabulary
molecule *n.*, a very small particle or piece of a substance
• **sequence** *n.*, order

In Other Words
DNA *deoxyribonucleic acid*
rungs steps
segment part, section
an ingenious a clever
coiled twisted
with the naked eye without a special tool

Finding DNA in a Cell

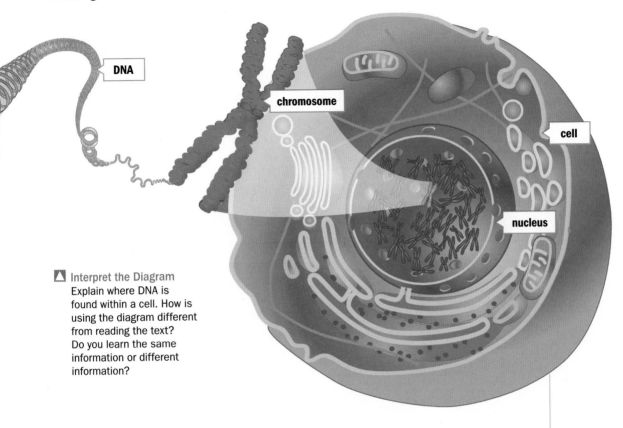

DNA

chromosome

cell

nucleus

▲ Interpret the Diagram
Explain where DNA is
found within a cell. How is
using the diagram different
from reading the text?
Do you learn the same
information or different
information?

Cells Carry Chromosomes

Each cell in your body (with a few exceptions) contains a set of
46 chromosomes **squashed** together inside the cell nucleus. The full
set of 46 chromosomes carries all your genes, so you have a complete
set of genes inside every cell. **3** That's an awful lot of DNA! If you
unraveled all the DNA from every chromosome in every cell in your
body and laid the molecules end to end, your DNA would stretch to
the Sun and back more than 400 times. Yet all the information in
your genes could be stored on a single CD.

3 Ask Questions
Ask yourself a *what*
question about
chromosomes.
Then answer it.

Monitor Comprehension

Explain
Tell how genes are
related to a DNA
molecule. Use the text
and diagram to inform
your answer.

In Other Words
squashed packed

Where Do My Genes Come From? ▮4

Your genes come from your parents, theirs come from their parents, and so on—all the way back to the first living thing that ever existed. Genes are passed down through families, and that's why you probably look a bit like your parents. Physical characteristics, like long eyelashes, red hair, freckles, or blue eyes, run in families because they are **controlled** by genes.

How Parents Pass Along Their Genes

Mother
46 chromosomes per cell

23 are passed to you →

You
46 chromosomes per cell

← 23 are passed to you

Father
46 chromosomes per cell

▲ Interpret the Diagram How many of your chromosomes come from your father? Your mother?

▮4 **Author's Purpose**
What do the text head and the title of the diagram tell you about this section? Why would the author include this information?

Key Vocabulary
control *v.*, to have the power to manage or direct something

Half your genes come from your mother and half come from your father. They were passed on to you in chromosomes carried by **sperm and egg cells**. Sperm and egg cells have only 23 chromosomes each—half the usual amount. When they meet and form **an embryo**, they create a new person with a full set of 46 chromosomes.

You actually have two sets of genes: one set from your mother and another from your father. These two **genomes** give you a mixture of your mother's and father's features—perhaps you have your mother's hair and your father's eyes, for instance. **5**

Every child in a family is different because the parents' genes are shuffled and then divided in two before making each sperm and egg cell. So each child gets a <mark>unique</mark> set of genes (except for identical twins).

What's a Dominant Gene?

Since you have two sets of genes, you have two options for everything. Take eye color, for instance. You get eye-color genes from both parents, but you might get a gene for brown eyes from your mother and one for blue eyes from your father. Sometimes one option **takes priority over** the other—we call it a dominant gene. The brown-eye gene is usually **dominant over** the blue-eye gene, for instance. **6**

5 Access Vocabulary
What clues from the text help you understand the word *genome*? Think about how the word is related to the word *gene*.

6 Author's Purpose
Answer the text head question: "What's a dominant gene?" How does this heading support the author's purpose?

Monitor Comprehension

Explain
Tell two things you learn about genes on pages 104–105.

Key Vocabulary
• **unique** *adj.*, one of a kind

In Other Words
sperm and egg cells the cells from your mother and father that created you
an embryo the early stage of human life
genomes sets of chromosomes
takes priority over is stronger than
dominant over stronger than

Genes that are overpowered by dominant genes are recessive. For a recessive gene to have an effect, you'll need two copies—one from each parent.

Dominant Eye-Color Gene 7

 **+**  **=**

| If one of your parents has blue eyes . . . | . . . and the other has brown eyes | . . . you'll *probably* have brown eyes, too. |

7 Author's Purpose
Explain how the information in this diagram relates to the information in the section.

What Makes Me Male or Female?

Two of your 46 chromosomes are special—they control your sex. These sex chromosomes are shaped like the letters *X* and *Y*. If you have two *X*s, you're a girl. If you have an *X* and a *Y*, you're a boy. In boys, the genes on the X-chromosome have an effect whether or not they are dominant, because there isn't a matching *X* to complement them. This makes boys **especially prone to genetic defects** like color-blindness.

Are You Color-blind?
If you can't see a number in this circle of colored dots, you might be color-blind. Color-blindness is caused by a recessive gene on the X-chromosome. Girls who **inherit** the gene usually have normal vision, but boys become color-blind. Test your family for color-blindness. If you or any of your brothers are color-blind, the gene almost certainly came from your mother. **8**

8 Author's Purpose
State the facts in this paragraph. Why are facts included in science articles?

Key Vocabulary
inherit *v.*, to get things from family members who lived before us

In Other Words
especially prone to genetic defects
more likely to inherit traits

Test Your Genes

Take the genes test. Most of these characteristics can be caused by a single dominant gene.

Cleft Chin
A crease in the bottom of your chin is called a cleft chin.

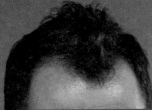

Widow's Peak
A widow's peak is a V-shaped pattern in your hairline, revealed when you brush your hair back.

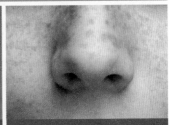

Freckles
Freckles are spots of darker color on your skin. They are more pronounced when you're tanned.

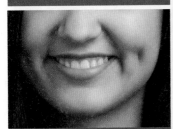

Dimple
A dimple is a small dent that appears in one or both cheeks when you smile.

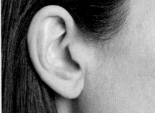

Free Earlobe
If your earlobe hangs free at the bottom, you have the dominant gene; otherwise, you have the recessive gene.

Hand Clasping
When you clasp your hands, which thumb is on top? The way that feels right is partly due to your genes. 9

9 Access Vocabulary
What do you think *clasp* means? Use the photo and caption to help you figure out its meaning.

What Does It Mean?

All your genes come from your parents, so any characteristic caused by a dominant gene will probably also appear in one of your parents. If you can roll your tongue, the chances are that your mother or father can, too. And at least one of your four grandparents will have the dominant **trait**.

Key Vocabulary
trait *n.*, a characteristic, a certain way something is, a feature of something

Monitor Comprehension

Summarize
Name the genetic traits mentioned on pages 106–107. What will you remember about these details?

Do Genes Determine Everything?

Some genes have a very simple and obvious effect. A single gene can make you color-blind or give you red hair, for instance. So you might think there's a gene for each of your characteristics, from the shape of your face to the length of your legs. However, the truth is not so simple. Many, perhaps most, of your characteristics involve lots of genes working together. Your height, your looks, the **texture** of your skin, the sound of your voice, the color of your hair, and so on, probably all depend on the combination of genes you have.

Things get even more complicated when it comes to genes that affect your brain. Genes can certainly have an influence on how smart, **outgoing**, adventurous, or creative you are. But they don't determine your personality—they just influence how it might develop. **10** And so do many other **factors**, such as your family, your friends, the decisions you make in life, and luck. ❖

10 Ask Questions
Stop and ask a question that is different from the section head. Then answer the question based on what you have read.

The gene for red hair is recessive. Only 4% of people carry it.

In Other Words
texture feel
outgoing socially friendly
factors things, conditions

ANALYZE Genes: All in the Family

1. **Paraphrase** Tell two things you learned about genes.
2. **Vocabulary** With a partner, discuss some physical **traits** that parents can **transmit** to their children.
3. **Analyze Author's Purpose** What is the author's purpose in writing this science article? How do features like the heads and the diagrams help the author achieve this purpose?
4. **Focus Strategy Ask Questions** Tell a partner three of the questions you asked yourself during reading. If you found the answers, share them, too.

   ## Return to the Text

   Reread and Write Think of two of your physical traits. Write a journal entry to explain how families affect us. Use facts from the text to support your ideas.

Key Vocabulary
transmit *v.*, to pass on or send

BEFORE READING How to See DNA

science procedure by the
Genetic Science Learning Center

Reading Strategies

· Plan and Monitor
· Determine Importance
· Make Inferences
▶ **Ask Questions**
· Make Connections
· Synthesize
· Visualize

Analyze Author's Purpose

The author's purpose in a **science procedure** is to explain how to do something related to science. This type of writing tells the goal of the procedure, lists materials, and gives step-by-step directions. Always follow the directions closely for a successful project or experiment.

Look Into the Text

You Will Need:

- 1/2 cup green split peas
- 1/8 teaspoon salt
- 1 cup cold water
- blender
- strainer
- measuring cups and spoons
- liquid detergent
- small glass tubes or containers
- meat tenderizer
- rubbing alcohol
- small wooden stir sticks

A materials list tells what you need.

Step

Blender Insanity!

Put the split peas, salt, and cold water in a blender. Put the blender lid in place. Blend on high for 15 seconds. The blender separates the pea cells from each other, so you now have a really thin pea-cell soup.

The text is organized in steps. Why does the author choose this format?

Focus Strategy ▶ Ask Questions

As you read this science procedure, notice what **questions** you are asking yourself. When you are aware of the questions you have, you are more likely to read actively.

HOW TO SELF-QUESTION

Focus Strategy

1. **Record Your Questions** You may ask questions to:
   - clear up confusion: *What does this word mean?*
   - help you keep track of the process: *Why do I need to do this?*
   - recall what you know: *What do I already know about this?*

2. **Find Answers to Your Questions** Read the text and look at the visuals.

3. **Follow Up** Add opinions, comments, or additional questions.

1. **Question:** Why do you blend the peas?
2. **Answer:** to separate the cells from each other
3. **Comment:** I wonder what blended peas would look like.

How to See **DNA**

by the
Genetic Science
Learning Center

Connect Across Texts

You read about DNA in "Genes: All in the Family." In this science procedure, you will discover what DNA looks like.

The **traits** that you **inherit** from your parents are **determined** by DNA. This is true for all living things: The cells of every plant and animal contain DNA **molecules**. DNA carries the genetic information that determines what the plants and animals will look like, among other traits. You may wonder, though: What does DNA look like? Try this activity to find out.

How to See DNA

Purpose: In this activity, you will free DNA from the cells of green split peas. Then you will be able to see what DNA looks like.

You Will Need:
- 1/2 cup green split peas
- 1/8 teaspoon salt
- 1 cup cold water
- blender
- strainer
- measuring cups and spoons
- liquid detergent
- small glass tubes or containers
- meat tenderizer
- rubbing alcohol
- small wooden stir sticks **1**

1 Author's Purpose
Why is the materials list provided at the beginning of this science procedure?

Key Vocabulary

trait *n.*, a certain way something is, a feature of something

inherit *v.*, to get things from family members who lived before us

molecule *n.*, a very small particle or piece of a substance

In Other Words

determined controlled

Step 1

Blender Insanity!

Put the split peas, salt, and cold water in a blender. Put the blender lid in place. Blend on high for 15 seconds. The blender separates the pea cells from each other, so you now have a really thin pea-cell soup.

Step 2

Soapy Peas

Pour the pea mixture through a strainer into a measuring cup. Add 2 tablespoons of liquid detergent to the strained peas. Swirl to mix.

Let the mixture sit for 5–10 minutes. **2**

2 Ask Questions
What questions can you ask and answer to make sure you understand this process? Have you followed the directions as written?

Why Do This?

Each pea cell is surrounded by a membrane, or outer covering. Inside the membrane is a nucleus. The nucleus is protected by another membrane. And inside the nucleus is the DNA.

To see the DNA, you have to break through both membranes. **3** Detergent can handle this task.

A cell's membrane has lipid (fat) molecules with proteins connecting them. When detergent comes near the cell, it captures the lipids and proteins, breaking down the cell membrane and freeing the DNA from the nucleus.

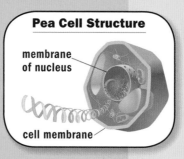

Pea Cell Structure

membrane of nucleus

cell membrane

3 Ask Questions
Ask yourself, "What do I already know about DNA?" How does answering this question help you understand the text better?

Step 3

Enzyme Power

Pour the mixture into the glass containers. Fill each container one-third full. Then, add a **pinch** of meat tenderizer (enzymes) to each container and stir gently. Be careful! If you stir too hard, you'll break up the DNA, making it harder to see.

Why Do This?

You may wonder why you are adding meat tenderizer to the soapy pea mixture.

Meat tenderizer contains enzymes, proteins that help chemical reactions happen more quickly. Without enzymes, your body would **grind to a halt**.

The DNA in the nucleus of a cell is protected by other kinds of proteins. Enzymes cut through those proteins.

Step 4

Alcohol Separation

Tilt your glass container. Slowly pour rubbing alcohol into the container and down the side. It should form a layer on top of the pea mixture. Continue pouring until you have about the same amount of alcohol as pea mixture in the container.

DNA will rise from the layer of pea mixture into the alcohol layer. Use a wooden stick to draw the DNA from the alcohol. After you finish, you will have completed a DNA **extraction**!

Why Does This Happen?

Turn the page and find out...

> **4 Author's Purpose**
> How do the photos help you understand what to do?

Key Vocabulary
- **extraction** *n.*, the act of removing one thing from another thing

In Other Words
pinch little bit
grind to a halt stop suddenly and completely

Monitor Comprehension

Summarize
Briefly tell the steps in this procedure.

Alcohol is **less dense than** water, so it floats on top. Because two separate layers are formed, all of the fats (lipids) and protein that you broke up in Steps 2 and 3, along with the DNA, have to decide: "Hmmm, which layer should I go to?"

Most particles and molecules will stay below the alcohol or dissolve in it. The DNA will float in the alcohol and will not be dissolved. This makes it easy to extract. ❖

ANALYZE How to See DNA

1. **Explain** Why is the alcohol layer on the top? Include evidence from the text in your answer.

2. **Vocabulary** Why do you need enzymes for this DNA **extraction**?

3. **Analyze Author's Purpose** Work with a partner to list the four steps in the procedure. List the step. Explain what you learned in it. Then tell how the step supports the author's purpose.

Step	Information in the step	Support the author's purpose by
1. blend peas, salt, and water in a blender	explains how to separate pea cells	clearly explaining how to get started
2.		

4. **Focus Strategy Ask Questions** Choose two of the questions you asked yourself. Compare them with a partner's questions. How are they similar? How are they different?

Return to the Text

Reread and Write Write a note to the Genetic Science Learning Center. Tell whether the procedure was easy to follow. Support your ideas with examples from the text. Include suggestions for improvement, if you have any.

In Other Words
less dense than not as thick as

EQ How Do Families Affect Us?

Reading
Critical Thinking

1. **Analyze** With your group, complete the **KWL Chart** from page 98. Add and discuss information you learned.

2. **Compare** Both selections present information about DNA. In what ways are the selections similar? How are they different? What did you learn from the science procedure that you could not find out from the science article?

3. **Speculate** We **inherit** our **traits** from our families. Why might it be helpful to know which traits you share with family members?

4. **Infer** How can individuals be **unique** if they get genes from their parents? Use evidence from the selections to support your answer.

EQ 5. **Generalize** Do you think that people who closely resemble a parent physically can also resemble that person in other ways? Support your answer with ideas from the science article.

Writing
Write About Literature

Opinion Paragraph What determines who you are? Do you think that genes are mainly responsible? Look for supporting evidence in both texts and use it to write your paragraph.

Vocabulary
Key Vocabulary Review

Oral Review Work with a partner. Use these words to complete the paragraph.

control	molecule	transmit
extraction	sequence	unique
inherit	traits	

Just as our parents pass along __(1)__ to us, the world's scientists __(2)__, or pass along, knowledge. For example, the scientists who broke the code of the long, twisting DNA __(3)__ gave us a __(4)__, one-of-a-kind gift. A scientist's mission is the careful drawing out or __(5)__ of knowledge from the real world. Scientists direct, or __(6)__, their procedures through an orderly __(7)__ of steps. Because of scientific progress, each generation knows more than the last. We __(8)__ the knowledge that came before us.

Writing Application What do you know about DNA? Write a paragraph about it. Use at least five Key Vocabulary words.

Fluency
Read with Ease: Phrasing

Assess your reading fluency with the passage in the Reading Handbook, p. 668. Then complete the self-check below.

1. I did/did not group words correctly as I read.

2. My words correct per minute: _____.

Grammar

Use Subject Pronouns

A **subject pronoun** is used in the subject of a sentence.

Use **I** when you talk about yourself.

Use **we** when you talk about another person or persons and yourself.

Use **you** when you talk to one or more than one person.

Use **he**, **she**, **it**, and **they** when you talk about other people or things.

How do you know which to use?

Think about the number:

One	he	she	it
More Than One	they	we	

Think about gender:

Male	he
Female	she

Oral Practice (1–5) Say five sentences to a partner about traits you and your family have. Your partner repeats each sentence using a subject pronoun.
Example: <u>Matt and I</u> have blue eyes.
<u>We</u> have blue eyes.

Written Practice (6–10) Fix four more pronouns and rewrite the paragraph. Then add one more sentence about DNA. Use a subject pronoun.

>   **He**
>   Ray has dimples. ~~It~~ smiles like his brother. DNA determines human traits. They is coiled into a thread called a chromosome. A mother has 46 chromosomes. They passes 23 chromosomes to her child. A father has 46 chromosomes. It passes on 23 chromosomes, too. Chromosomes carry information. We determine if you are a girl or a boy.

Poster

Science: The Human Genome Project In 2003, scientists mapped the human genome—the set of genes that human beings share. Conduct some research to learn more about this project. Find out who did the project and what scientists learned from it. Discover why the project is important to everyone.

Organize your ideas on a poster. Share your poster with the class.

myNGconnect.com

- Get the basic facts about genes.
- Find out about the Human Genome Project.
- Watch documentary programs about the project.

▶ **Language and Learning Handbook**, page 616

▶ **Writing Handbook**, page 698

"What ever will we think about now that the genome project is almost complete?"

Source: ©Victoria Roberts/*The New Yorker*

Language Development

Express Likes and Dislikes

Group Share Write something you like to do with family or friends and something you dislike. Discuss your notes with classmates.

Context Clues

Sometimes you can use clues in the text to figure out the meaning of unfamiliar, elaborate, or complex words or phrases.

- **Definition**: A widow's peak is a V-shaped pattern in your hairline. (Signal word: *is*)

- **Appositive Definition**: Each pea cell is surrounded by a membrane, or outer covering. (Signal word: *or* with a comma in front of it)

You can also use context to understand **connotations** of words—the feelings associated with the word. With a partner, find the word *defects* on p. 106. Use context clues to determine whether the word has a positive or negative connotation.

Summarize

One way to learn what is important in an article is to **summarize** it. When you summarize an article, you tell the most important ideas from it. To summarize "How to See DNA" you can:

1. **Identify** the topic, often found in the title of the article.
2. **Locate** the most important information, using key words, headings, and illustrations.
3. **Write** a paragraph. State the topic in your first sentence. In your other sentences, give the key details from the article.
4. **Share** your summary with a partner.

Write an Expository Paragraph

A test prompt may ask you to provide information about a topic and include examples.

1. **Unpack the Prompt** Read the prompt and underline the important words.

> **Writing Prompt**
>
> "Genes: All in the Family" explains how traits are transmitted from parents to children. Write a paragraph to explain the process. Give examples.

2. **Plan Your Response** Use a chart to help you plan.

Genetic Process	Example
parent with dominant trait	Grandma: dimples
+ parent with recessive trait	Grandpa: no dimples
child usually has dominant trait	My mom: has dimples

3. **Draft** Organize the ideas in your chart like this.

Paragraph Organizer

Some inherited traits are dominant. This means that if one parent has [name a dominant trait] and the other parent has [name the recessive trait] , then their child probably has [name the dominant trait] . In my own family, my [name family member] has [name a dominant trait] , which is dominant. My [name another family member] has [name the recessive trait] , a recessive trait. And, sure enough, [name family member] has [name dominant trait] .

4. **Check Your Work** Reread your paragraph. Ask:

- Does my paragraph address the prompt?
- Did I explain the genetic process clearly?
- Do pronouns agree with their antecedents?

Try to correct any mistakes. Show your paragraph to a partner to check for their errors.

▼ Writing Handbook, page 698

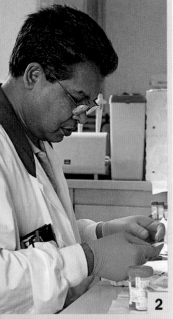

Inside a Medical Laboratory

Employees in medical laboratories perform tests on human skin and bodily fluids to identify and treat diseases. Some lab workers work in hospitals. Others work in doctors' offices and clinics, independent medical labs, and blood banks.

Jobs in Medical Laboratories

Doctors rely on medical test results to make life-or-death decisions. To perform accurate tests, medical labs employ different types of workers. Each position has separate duties and a different level of training.

Job	Responsibilities	Education/Training Required
Medical Laboratory Technician **1**	• Prepares samples of body tissue • Performs routine tests • Uses precision equipment	• High school diploma • One- or two-year training program to pass certification exam
Medical Technologist **2**	• Monitors quality of testing • Interprets and reports test results • Maintains equipment • Supervises other laboratory workers	• College degree in medical technology or a related field • In some states, certificate in medical technology
Clinical Laboratory Director **3**	• Sets rules and standards • Supervises technologists and job quality • Develops and maintains budgets	• College degree • Medical degree and/or Ph.D.

Research the Job Outlook

Analyze the job outlook for one of the medical laboratory jobs above.

1. Prepare a four-column chart with the following heads: Job, Number of Employees in the Industry, Salary, and Job Outlook.

2. Consult the *Occupational Outlook Handbook*. Read about your chosen job.

3. Use the chart to fill in information about your chosen job. Work with a partner to determine if your job has a positive or negative job outlook. Save the information in a professional career portfolio.

myNGconnect.com

🔾 Learn more about the field of medical technology.

🔾 Download a form to evaluate whether you would like to work in this field.

📕 **Language and Learning Handbook,** page 616

Use Context Clues

When you introduce someone, you probably say something like this: "This is Lupita, my cousin from Chicago." You add information so people know who Lupita is.

Written passages also sometimes introduce difficult words by giving extra information. This extra information is one kind of **context clue**. Look at how the extra information in the following sentence explains the word *accolade*.

I often receive accolades, **or praise**, for doing my chores.

Extra information is often separated from the rest of the sentence by punctuation such as commas, dashes, or parentheses. Sometimes words or phrases like *or*, *such as*, or *including* signal context clues.

Explore Words and Context Clues

Work with a partner to use context clues to determine word meaning.

1. Read the passage on the right.

2. Look for context clues to determine meanings for each highlighted word.

3. Check the meaning in a dictionary.

> My bedroom is extremely **cluttered**, or really messy. It is a **cubbyhole**, or a very small space, so I do not have a lot of storage. I am going to have my allowance **revoked**, including my lunch money, if I do not clean everything up.

Put the Strategy to Work

When you see a word you do not know, use this strategy to look for context clues.

1. Look for extra information as clues to a word's meaning.

2. Look for punctuation that separates information from the rest of the sentence.

3. Notice if any words or phrases signal context clues.

TRY IT▶ Read the passage below. Use context clues to write a definition for each word in blue type.

> ▶ I have been keeping my room **immaculate** by doing things such as putting my clothes and books away. My parents have agreed to let me **refurbish**, or redecorate, because of my neatness. I cannot wait to **designate**, or choose, the new paint color.

📖 **Reading Handbook,** page 647

How Do Families Affect Us?
Learn about the impact of family meals.

Make a Connection

Discussion Talk about family meals. Discuss questions like these:

- How often does a family eat dinner together?
- What time does a family usually eat?
- How often is the TV on when a family eats?
- What does a family talk about at dinner?

Use the ideas from your discussion to form generalizations about families and meals.

Learn Key Vocabulary

Study the Words Pronounce each word and learn its meaning. You may also want to look up the definitions in the Glossary.

● Academic Vocabulary

Key Words	Examples
● **appreciate** (u-**prē**-shē-āt) *verb* ▶ pages 134, 135	When you **appreciate** something, you understand that it is good. *Synonyms*: be grateful, value; *Antonyms*: ignore, neglect
● **beneficial** (be-nu-**fi**-shul) *adjective* ▶ page 128	Something that is **beneficial** helps you. Exercise is **beneficial** because it helps you be healthy. *Synonym*: helpful; *Antonym*: harmful
● **bond** (bond) *noun* ▶ page 128	When you have a **bond** with someone, you have a special attachment to that person. *Synonyms*: connection, tie
● **consume** (kun-**süm**) *verb* ▶ pages 126, 129	When you **consume** things, you use them up. When you eat food, you **consume** it. *Antonyms*: save, keep
● **data** (**dā**-tu) *noun* ▶ page 124	**Data** is information that is collected and organized for a topic. According to **data** from the U.S. Census Bureau, 85% of adults age 25 and over completed high school.
● **research** (ri-**surch**) *noun* ▶ pages 126, 135	People do **research** by gathering information. My **research** reveals that my family has lived in this city for seventy-six years. *Synonym*: study
● **survey** (**sur**-vā) *noun* ▶ page 127	When you conduct a **survey**, you ask people questions to find out what they think or do. *Synonym*: poll
united (yū-**nī**-tid) *adjective* ▶ page 124	When a team is **united**, the players work well together. *Synonyms*: joined, combined; *Antonym*: separated

Practice the Words Work with a partner. Make a **Vocabulary Study Card** for each Key Vocabulary word. Write the word on one side of a card. On the other side, write a synonym and an example sentence. Take turns quizzing each other on the words.

Vocabulary Study Card

appreciate

front

be thankful

I appreciate my friends.

back

BEFORE READING Do Family Meals Matter?

research report by Mary Story
and Dianne Neumark-Sztainer

Reading Strategies

- Plan and Monitor
- Determine Importance
- Make Inferences
▶ Ask Questions
- Make Connections
- Synthesize
- Visualize

Analyze Author's Purpose

A **research report** is **expository nonfiction**, or writing that informs. The purpose of a research report is to present and explain the facts that a researcher has gathered about a topic. Often the information is presented in text features, such as charts and graphs.

Look Into the Text

The head identifies the topic.

The report includes numerical data.

Views on Family Meals

Is eating together really becoming less important to the American family? In a study called Project EAT (Eating Among Teens), 98% of the parents said that it was important to eat at least one meal together each day. Sixty-four percent of the adolescents in the study agreed with their parents.

How do the authors use data to explain the information in the report?

Focus Strategy ▶ Ask Questions

Asking questions as you read a research report helps you understand the information. Where you find the answers to your questions is important, however. Are the answers right there in the text, or do you have to look for them?

HOW TO FIND QUESTION-ANSWER RELATIONSHIPS

Focus Strategy

1. **"Right There" Answers** Sometimes you can point to the text and say that the answer to a question is "right there."

   YOU ASK: What percent of teenagers agree that family meals are important?

   ANSWER: "Sixty-four percent of the adolescents in the study agreed…"

2. **"Think and Search" Answers** Sometimes you have to put information together from different parts of the report to find an answer.

   YOU ASK: What are the advantages of eating regular family meals?

   There are answers to this question throughout the report. Keep reading to find them.

Fast Food for Fast Times

Before the 1970s, three of every four meals eaten in the United States were made at home. Today, most of the meals that Americans eat are prepared outside the home, mainly at fast-food restaurants. In 2005, U.S. consumers spent about $163 billion on fast food (compared with $6 billion in 1970).

Restaurants began as a way to serve people who were traveling. Then in 1948, Richard and Maurice McDonald opened a new type of restaurant. They had a small number of items on their menu, but they arranged their kitchen so the workers could make a lot of food really quickly. Their new system was extremely successful. Since then, many different types of fast-food restaurants have copied this idea.

Many people rely on fast food. Thousands of working parents who don't want to cook, adults who need a quick lunch, and over-scheduled teenagers on their way home from school buy meals that are cheap, fast, and filling.

Many social scientists believe that fast food is a sign of the fast-paced culture we live in. Generations ago, families would sit and talk as they ate dinner together. According to Robin Fox, a social scientist at Rutgers University, "Fast food has killed this. We are reduced to sitting alone and shoveling it in. There is no ceremony in it."

Think about how fast food affects your life. Share your thoughts in a small group.

myNGconnect.com

🔍 Get nutrition data on fast foods.
🔍 View information about how fast food is made.

Do Family Meals Matter?

Most people think it is important to be with family on special occasions. But are everyday events, like family meals, important , too?

adapted from a research report by Mary Story and Dianne Neumark-Sztainer

Comprehension Coach

Eating Together

In every human society, people share food. Throughout history, eating together has been like a glue that holds a society together. Studies of human societies clearly show that meals help people feel connected to one another. **1**

Just as sharing food holds societies together, family meals help family members feel **united** and loved. Yet today, families seem too busy to eat together. In fact, it seems that the family meal is becoming less important in our lives. **2**

Most **studies** show that over half of families with children eat dinner together at least five times a week. One-third or less have fewer than three meals together a week.

In one study of 9- to 14-year-olds, 43% of the **adolescents** reported eating dinner with their families every day. Forty percent said they ate with their families most days. Seventeen percent had family meals some or no days.

Family meals are more common among younger children than adolescents. **Data** from a national study of adolescent health showed that about 74% of 12- to 14-year-olds had eaten five or more evening meals with a parent during the previous week. This figure fell to 61% for 15- to 16-year-olds. It dropped to 42% for 17- to 19-year-olds.

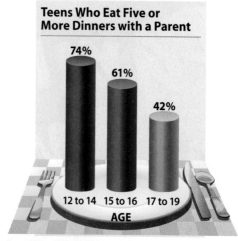

Teens Who Eat Five or More Dinners with a Parent

74% — 12 to 14
61% — 15 to 16
42% — 17 to 19
AGE

Source: U.S. Council of Economic Advisors, May 2000

1 Ask Questions
Stop and ask a question here. Look for the answer as you continue reading.

2 Access Vocabulary
The **connotation** of a word is the feeling associated with the word. Does the word *busy* have a positive or negative connotation here? Why?

◀ Interpret the Graph
Do more 12- to 14-year-olds or 17- to 19-year-olds eat with a parent?

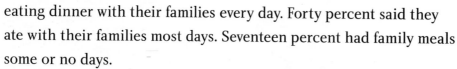

Key Vocabulary
united *adj.*, joined, together
● **data** *n.*, information collected and organized for a topic

In Other Words
studies research projects scientists do
adolescents teens

Views on Family Meals

Is eating together really becoming less important to the American family? In a study called Project EAT (Eating Among Teens), 98% of the parents said that it was important to eat at least one meal together each day. Sixty-four percent of the adolescents in the study agreed with their parents.

Some teens don't care about spending time with their families, but most teens admit they value family meals.

In the project, 79% of teens also said they enjoyed eating meals together with their family. However, family meals were either not important or not enjoyable for 20% to 25% of adolescents. ■3 They gave a variety of reasons, including:

- **indifference** ("It just doesn't matter.")
- lack of time ("Everyone coming and going at different times.")
- arguing and fighting at the dinner table

3 Ask Questions
Reread the question at the top of the section. It has a "Think and Search" answer. Put information together to answer it.

Monitor Comprehension

Summarize
Tell the results of two different studies about family meals.

In Other Words
indifference not caring

Family Meals and Diet 4

In our **research**, we have observed that young people who eat alone or with their friends have the poorest diets. Adolescents who regularly eat meals with their families do better. They usually eat a healthier, **better-balanced** diet.

Gillman and other researchers also studied the diets of adolescents. They compared those who ate family dinners most days to those who ate family dinners never, or only a few days a week. Eating together more often was linked to better eating habits. This included eating more fruits and vegetables, less fried food, and fewer soft drinks. The participants also ate less **saturated and trans fat**. They **consumed** more fiber, calcium, folate, iron, and vitamins. 5

On average, a teen eats fast food twice a week. According to Channel One News Network, thirty-one percent of all the food eaten away from home is from a fast-food restaurant.

4 Author's Purpose
What is the topic of this section? How can you tell?

5 Ask Questions
What do the authors mean by "better eating habits"? Does this question have a "Right There" answer? Why?

Key Vocabulary
- **research** *n.*, the gathering of information
- **consume** *v.*, to use things up, to eat

In Other Words
better-balanced more varied
saturated and trans fat harmful fat

Family Meals and Teen Behavior

Research has shown that young people are most likely to **avoid** problem behavior, such as drug or alcohol use, the more their parents are involved in their lives. Teens who are closer to their parents are more likely to be successful at school. They also have higher educational goals.

A **survey** for the National Center on Addiction and Substance Abuse found that:

- 86% of teens who had dinner with their families five or more nights a week said they had never tried smoking, compared with 65% who had dinner with their families two nights a week or less

- 68% of teens who had dinner with their families five nights a week or more reported never trying alcohol, compared to 47% of teens who ate dinner with their families two nights a week or less

- teens eating a family dinner five or more times a week were almost twice as likely to receive As in school compared to teens who had a family dinner two or fewer times a week (20% vs. 12%) [6]

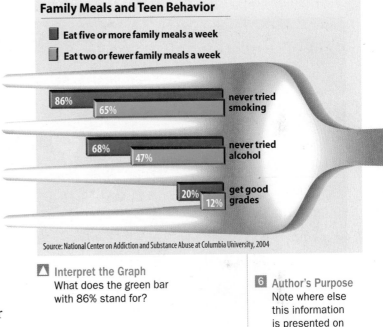

Family Meals and Teen Behavior

■ Eat five or more family meals a week
□ Eat two or fewer family meals a week

86% / 65% — never tried smoking
68% / 47% — never tried alcohol
20% / 12% — get good grades

Source: National Center on Addiction and Substance Abuse at Columbia University, 2004

▲ Interpret the Graph
What does the green bar with 86% stand for?

[6] Author's Purpose
Note where else this information is presented on the page. How does seeing this information in two ways help you understand the author's purpose?

Monitor Comprehension

Explain
Name the benefits teens get from eating with their families.

Key Vocabulary
● **survey** *n.*, a poll

In Other Words
avoid stay away from

In Conclusion

In our culture, the act of sharing meals is an important way to develop and keep strong family **bonds**. Regular family meals are key parts of family life. They may be very **beneficial** in the lives of teens. ❖

Family meals can be home-cooked or take-out food. To encourage family meals, the National Center on Addiction and Substance Abuse began "Family Day—A Day to Eat Dinner with Your Children." Many politicians, organizations, and businesses have helped promote it.

Key Vocabulary
- **bond** *n.*, attachment, connection, tie
- **beneficial** *adj.*, useful, helpful

Cultural Background
You may think fast food is a modern idea, but it's not. There were bread and olive stands in ancient Rome. And the hamburger, which is very popular in today's fast-food industry, was first served in Germany in the 1800s.

ANALYZE Do Family Meals Matter?

1. **Explain** Why does the National Center on Addiction and Substance Abuse urge families to have meals together? Use text evidence to support your answer.

2. **Vocabulary** When teens don't eat with their families, what kinds of foods are they likely to **consume** ?

3. **Analyze Author's Purpose** This report uses text features to organize and present information. With a partner, complete a chart like the one below with an example of each feature.

Feature	Example and Page Number	Purpose
Head		
Data		
Graph or chart		

4. **Focus Strategy Ask Questions** Ask a partner a question about the selection. After your partner answers it, discuss if it is a "Right There" or "Think and Search" answer. Switch roles.

Return to the Text

Reread and Write Answer the question in the title: "Do Family Meals Matter?" Gather evidence from the text to support your answer.

BEFORE READING **Fish Cheeks**

anecdote by Amy Tan

Reading Strategies

- Plan and Monitor
- Determine Importance
- Make Inferences
▶ **Ask Questions**
- Make Connections
- Synthesize
- Visualize

Analyze Author's Purpose

An author usually writes an **anecdote** to tell about an interesting or funny event in a person's life. It is a form of **narrative nonfiction**, writing that tells a story about something that really happened. It is shorter than a memoir and focuses on a single event.

Look Into the Text

The first-person pronouns hint that this is a true story about Tan.

On Christmas Eve, I saw that my mother had outdone herself in creating a strange menu. She was pulling black veins out of the backs of fleshy prawns. The kitchen was littered with appalling mounds of raw food: A slimy rock cod with bulging fish eyes that pleaded not to be thrown into a pan of hot oil. Tofu, which looked like stacked wedges of rubbery white sponges. A bowl soaking dried fungus back to life. A plate of squid, crisscrossed with knife markings so they resembled bicycle tires.

And then they arrived—the minister's family and all my relatives in a clamor of doorbells and rumpled Christmas packages. Robert grunted hello, and I pretended he was not worthy of existence.

Descriptive language gives you a mental picture of the food.

How does Tan make this scene entertaining?

Focus Strategy ▶ Ask Questions

Sometimes as you read, you have **questions** for the author or even for yourself. The answers might not be stated directly in the text. Asking yourself these questions helps you think about what is important in the text.

HOW TO FIND QUESTION-ANSWER RELATIONSHIPS

Focus Strategy

1. **"Author and You" Answers** Unless you can speak to the author and get answers to your questions, you have to use the information in the text to make a logical prediction about the answers.

   YOU ASK: Why does Tan describe the food in so much detail?

   Think about what is happening in the story and how she felt then.

2. **"On Your Own" Answers** Some questions are for just you. The answers are not in the text at all. The answers come completely from your own experiences or feelings.

   YOU ASK: How would I feel about this food?

   Only you can answer that question!

Connect Across Texts

"Do Family Meals Matter?" discusses families eating together. In this anecdote, Amy Tan describes a memorable family meal.

FISH CHEEKS

BY AMY TAN

I fell in love with the minister's son the winter I turned fourteen. He was not Chinese, . . .

▲ The author, Amy Tan, has written numerous books including *The Joy Luck Club*, which was retold in a movie of the same name, and *The Chinese Siamese Cat*, which inspired the children's TV show "Sagwa."

but as white as Mary in the manger. For Christmas I prayed for this blond-haired boy, Robert, and a slim new American nose.

When I found out that my parents had invited the minister's family over for Christmas Eve dinner, I cried. What would Robert think of our **shabby** Chinese Christmas? What would he think of our noisy Chinese relatives who lacked proper American manners? What terrible disappointment would he feel upon seeing not a roasted turkey and sweet potatoes but Chinese food? **1**

On Christmas Eve, I saw that my mother had outdone herself in creating a strange menu. She was pulling black veins out of the backs of fleshy prawns. The kitchen was littered with **appalling** mounds of raw food: A slimy rock cod with bulging fish eyes that **pleaded** not to be thrown into a pan of hot oil. Tofu, which looked like stacked wedges of rubbery white sponges. A bowl soaking dried **fungus** back to life. A plate of squid, crisscrossed with knife markings so they resembled bicycle tires. **2**

prawns or shrimp

tofu

And then they arrived—the minister's family and all my relatives in a clamor of doorbells and rumpled Christmas packages. Robert grunted hello, and I pretended he was not **worthy of existence**. **3**

Dinner threw me deeper into **despair**. My relatives licked the ends of their chopsticks and reached across the table, dipping into the

1 Ask Questions
If you are not sure why Tan cries when she hears about the minister's family, what question can you ask yourself to understand how she feels?

2 Author's Purpose
How do the images in this section add to the humor of the selection?

3 Ask Questions
What question could you ask Tan? Make a logical prediction about the answer.

In Other Words
shabby low-quality
appalling terrible
pleaded begged
fungus mushrooms
worthy of existence important to me
despair hopelessness

dozen or so plates of food. Robert and his family waited patiently for platters to be passed to them. My relatives murmured with pleasure when my mother brought out the whole steamed fish. Robert **grimaced**. Then my father poked his chopsticks just below the fish eye and plucked out the soft meat. "Amy, your favorite," he said, offering me the tender fish cheek. I wanted to disappear.

At the end of the meal my father leaned back and belched loudly, thanking my mother for her fine cooking. "It's a polite Chinese custom, to show you are satisfied," he explained to our astonished guests. Robert was looking down at his plate with a reddened face. The minister managed to muster a quiet burp. I was stunned into silence for the rest of the night. 4

After all the guests had gone, my mother said to me, "You want be same like American girls on the outside." She handed me an early gift. It was a miniskirt in beige tweed. "But inside, you must always be Chinese. You must be proud you different. 5 **You only shame is be ashame.**"

The minister managed to muster a quiet burp.

And even though I didn't agree with her then, I knew that she understood how much I had suffered during the evening's dinner.

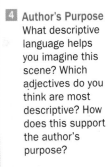

squid

4 Author's Purpose
What descriptive language helps you imagine this scene? Which adjectives do you think are most descriptive? How does this support the author's purpose?

5 Access Vocabulary
Does the word *different* have a positive or negative connotation here? Why?

Monitor Comprehension

In Other Words
grimaced made an unhappy expression
You only shame is be ashame. The only thing you should be embarrassed about is that you are embarrassed.

Paraphrase
Use your own words to describe the advice that Tan's mother gave her after the dinner.

It wasn't until many years later—long after I had gotten over my crush on Robert—that I was able to **appreciate** fully her lesson and the true purpose behind our particular menu. **6** For Christmas Eve that year, she had chosen all my favorite foods. ❖

6 Access Vocabulary
What does "I had gotten over my crush" mean? Use "many years later" as a clue.

ANALYZE Fish Cheeks

1. **Explain** Why did Tan's mother serve her daughter's favorite foods? Use evidence from the text to explain your answer.

2. **Vocabulary** Why didn't Tan **appreciate** the meal when she was 14 years old?

3. **Analyze Author's Purpose** Work with a partner. Take turns reading passages from the anecdote that are funny or memorable to you. Discuss how they support the author's purpose.

4. **Focus Strategy Ask Questions** Ask a partner a question you had for the author and one you had for yourself. Do you agree on the answers? Discuss.

▷ Return to the Text

Reread and Write Imagine that many years have passed. Write a letter from Amy Tan to her mother recalling the meal. Use details from the text in your letter.

About the Writer

Amy Tan (1952–) shares homes in San Francisco and New York City with her husband, one cat, and two dogs. In addition to writing, she also sings with the band Rock Bottom Remainders, which includes novelist Stephen King and columnist Dave Barry.

Key Vocabulary
- **appreciate** *v.*, to understand that something is good, to act grateful for it, to value it

EQ How Do Families Affect Us?

Critical Thinking

1. **Analyze** What should teens **appreciate** about family meals? Give an example from each text.

EQ 2. **Compare** What message about families do the selections "Do Family Meals Matter?" and "Fish Cheeks" have in common? How is the message presented differently in these selections?

3. **Imagine** If you were at the Tan family meal, how would you feel about it?

4. **Speculate** Why do you think the number of teens who eat dinner with their parents at least five times a week drops as teens get older?

EQ 5. **Assess** Look back at "Genes: All in the Family." Which do you think is a more powerful influence on children—genes, or family and cultural customs?

Write About Literature

Critical Review Which type of nonfiction held your interest more—the **research** report or the anecdote? Why? Reread both texts and tell what you liked and didn't like about each one. Use a chart like the one below to collect your thoughts.

	Do Family Meals Matter?	Fish Cheeks
Likes		
Dislikes		

Key Vocabulary Review

Oral Review Work with a partner. Use these words to complete the paragraph.

appreciate	consume	survey
beneficial	data	united
bond	research	

Scientists have done a lot of __(1)__ on people's eating habits. They have statistics, or __(2)__, to prove that there is a __(3)__ or link between good food and good health. People who __(4)__ fast food at every meal are likely to have more health problems than those who eat at home. Fast-food eaters are also likely to miss out on some of the __(5)__ effects of eating fresh fruit and vegetables. A __(6)__ conducted by scientists shows that teens are __(7)__ in their preference for fast food. They may not __(8)__ the benefits of a well-balanced diet.

Writing Application Recall a time when you especially enjoyed a meal with your family. Tell about it in a paragraph. Use at least three Key Vocabulary words.

Read with Ease: Intonation

Assess your reading fluency with the passage in the Reading Handbook, p. 669. Then complete the self-check below.

1. I did/did not make my voice rise and fall as I read.

2. My words correct per minute: _____.

Use Action Verbs in the Present

An **action verb** tells what the subject of a sentence does. An action verb in the present tells what the subject does now or does often.

We **visit** my family on Sundays.
We **eat** dinner with chopsticks.

Add **-s** to the action verb only when you talk about one other person, place, or thing.

Dad **eats**.
My aunt **laughs**.

An action verb can have a **helping verb** and a **main verb**. The helping verbs **can**, **could**, **may**, or **might** come before the main verb.

We **might eat** tofu. I **can cook** tofu in many ways.

Never add **-s** to **can**, **could**, **may**, or **might**.

Oral Practice (1–5) With a partner, take turns saying five sentences about a character's actions in "Fish Cheeks." Use present tense action verbs in your sentences. **Example:** Amy sees the raw food.

Written Practice (6–10) Fix three more verbs and rewrite the paragraph. Add two more sentences about Amy. Use present tense action verbs.

>   wants
>   Amy ~~want~~ to be like other Americans. She think that her family should serve turkey. Her mother mays create a strange menu. Amy wonder what the guests will think.

Express Ideas and Feelings

Pair Talk Tell a partner about a time you shared an important meal with others. What was the occasion? How did you feel about it?

Analyze Descriptive Language

Like Amy Tan in "Fish Cheeks," writers use **descriptive language** to help their readers picture characters, objects, and places. Descriptive details that appeal to the senses support the author's tone and shape the mood of the text. For example, Tan appeals to different senses in her description to make the dinner scene seem more real.

- *Sight*: Relatives dip into the plates.
- *Sound*: Relatives murmur with pleasure.
- *Taste*: Relatives lick their chopsticks.
- *Touch*: Mother is pulling black veins out of fleshy prawns.

With a partner, identify the descriptive details in the following sentences. Discuss which sense or senses each detail appeals to.

1. "The minister's family and all my relatives arrived in a clamor of doorbells."
2. "A slimy rock cod with bulging fish eyes that pleaded not to be thrown into a pan of hot oil."
3. "It was a miniskirt in beige tweed."

Write two sentences of your own with descriptive details about food.

Context Clues

When you see an unfamiliar word or phrase in a text, use the words around it that are familiar to you—the context clues—to figure out what it means. One kind of clue to look for is an **example**:

> Young people are more likely to avoid problem behavior, such as drug or alcohol use, the more their parents are involved in their lives.

Drug and alcohol use are examples that show the meaning of *problem behavior.* The words *such as, including, like,* and *for example* signal an example. Look for example clues in the selections. What words do the clues help you figure out?

Oral Report

Social Studies: Dining Customs Conduct research to learn more about the dining customs of an ethnic group. You may encounter unfamiliar ethnic words or phrases. Sound them out to see if they sound familiar. You can also use context clues to figure them out.

Organize your important details and ideas. Give an oral report to share what you learn. Use formal language because you are speaking to an audience.

myNGconnect.com

- Learn about Chinese dining customs.
- Check out dining traditions and recipes from around the world.

📗 **Language and Learning Handbook,** page 616

Write a Biographical Sketch

A **biographical sketch** is a narrative about a real person. It gives facts about the person's life. Write a short biographical sketch about someone you know.

1 Prewrite What facts do you know about the person's life? Come up with several research questions to ask about important parts of the person's life. Share your questions with a partner or group to help choose the best question. Talk with the person to learn new information. Use a chart to summarize and to keep track of the facts.

Born (where? when?)	Alabama, 1959
Main events in person's life	Joined the navy Lived in Spain Was a radio operator
Skills or talents	Good at repairing things

2 Draft Use the information to write a draft.

3 Revise Reread your draft. Check that you used dates and time words to tell when events took place. Think about how the sentences flow from one to the next. What details might improve it?

Student Writing Model

My father, Morris, was born on a farm in Alabama in 1959. He had an older sister, an older brother, and twin sisters who were younger. All of the children helped on the farm. As teenagers, my dad and his brother kept the farm equipment working. That's how they both got to be so good at repairing things.

My dad was a good student. When he graduated from high school, he joined the navy. There, he became a radio operator.

Before he joined the navy, Morris had never lived anywhere else but Alabama. Seeing so many different places was exciting. Morris's favorite country was Spain, where he lived for a year.

4 Edit and Proofread Reread and check for mistakes in spelling and punctuation. Make sure any quotes from the person are in quotation marks. Make corrections.

5 Publish Read the sketch aloud to a classmate. Then add your writing to a class binder.

📗 **Writing Handbook,** page 698

Interview

Everyone has been influenced by someone, and sharing these life experiences is a great way to get to know a person better. Knowing what questions to ask and how to ask them are important parts of the interview process. Interview a classmate about someone who has been a strong influence in his or her life—someone such as a teacher, a grandparent, or a role model. Here's how to do it:

1. Plan Your Interview

Decide which classmate you would like to interview. Then do the following:

- Write down at least five questions to ask that will prompt details about the person who had influence. Ask the 5W questions: *Who, What, Where, When,* and *Why.*

- Eliminate questions that might make the person uncomfortable or that are too personal.

- Think about whether you want to use formal or informal language. Which style is more appropriate for your interview?

2. Practice Your Interview

Share your questions ahead of time with the person you are interviewing.

- Get feedback about your questions.

- Rewrite any questions that seem vague or confusing. Write questions that you would be able to answer yourself. Use words that are familiar to you.

What can the speaker do to make the interviewee feel more comfortable?

3. Conduct Your Interview

Keep your interview interesting and friendly by doing the following:

- Make the person you are interviewing feel relaxed and comfortable by chatting informally before you start asking the interview questions.
- Maintain eye contact. This helps the interviewee feel that you are interested in everything he or she says.
- Listen actively to the interviewee by taking notes on his or her ideas and responses to your questions. Write down important points while you summarize what he or she says.
- Ask follow-up questions based on the interviewee's responses.
- Speak clearly and acknowledge, verbally or nonverbally, the interviewee's answers.
- When the interview is over, thank the interviewee.

4. Discuss and Rate the Interview

Use the rubric to rate your interview.

Interview Rubric

To Rate the Interview

Scale	Content of Questions	Delivery of Questions	Response to Answers
3 Great	• Questions covered the 5Ws. • Questions were on the topic.	• Made the interviewee feel comfortable. • Asked the questions clearly and with respect.	• Acknowledged answers verbally or nonverbally. • Asked good follow-up questions.
2 Good	• Questions covered most of the 5Ws. • Questions usually were on topic.	• Made the interviewee a little uncomfortable. • Treated the interviewee with respect most of the time.	• Usually acknowledged answers. • Usually asked good follow-up questions.
1 Needs Work	• Questions did not cover most of the 5Ws. • Questions were off the topic.	• Made the interviewee uncomfortable. • Did not treat the interviewee with respect.	• Did not acknowledge answers. • Did not ask good follow-up questions.

DO IT ▶ Now that you know how to conduct an interview, interview a classmate and enjoy getting to know that person better!

📖 Language and Learning Handbook, page 616

myNGconnect.com
🌐 Download the rubric.

How Do Families Affect Us?
Read about how the behavior of parents can make a difference.

Make a Connection

Quickwrite How do parents' ideas affect their children? Take a minute to write about ideas parents have that might affect their children. Then share your ideas with a group.

Learn Key Vocabulary

Study the Words Pronounce each word and learn its meaning. You may also want to look up the definitions in the Glossary.

• Academic Vocabulary

Key Words	Examples
abusive (u-**byū**-siv) *adjective* ▶ page 153	**Abusive** actions are harmful. A factory that pollutes the air and water is **abusive** to the environment. *Synonyms:* cruel, harsh; *Antonym:* helpful
approval (u-**prü**-vul) *noun* ▶ page 145	When you agree with something or think favorably about it, you give it **approval**. "Thumbs up" is a sign of **approval**.
behavior (bi-**hā**-vyur) *noun* ▶ pages 154, 155, 157	How you act is your **behavior**. Students with good **behavior** may be named "Student of the Month." *Synonym:* conduct
• **circumstance** (**sur**-kum-stans) *noun* ▶ page 144	**Circumstance** is how things are or what happens. What **circumstance** might make you late for school?
destiny (**des**-tu-nē) *noun* ▶ page 145	Your **destiny** is what is supposed to happen to you in the future. Is it your **destiny** to become like your parents? *Synonym:* fate
embarrass (im-**bair**-us) *verb* ▶ page 154	If you **embarrass** someone, you make that person feel confused, uneasy, or ashamed. I used to **embarrass** my older brother by hanging around him at school.
• **role** (rōl) *noun* ▶ pages 151, 155	A **role** is a part you play on stage or in real life. What is your **role** in your family?
valuable (**val**-yū-bul) *adjective* ▶ page 153	A gold ring is **valuable**. It has worth. What is the most **valuable** thing you own? *Synonym:* important; *Antonym:* worthless

Practice the Words Work with a partner to complete a **Denotation/Connotation Chart** for each word. Using a dictionary, write the denotation, or definition, of the word in one column. In the next column, tell the word's connotation, or the feelings associated with the word. Write a plus sign (+) for positive feelings or a minus sign (–) for negative feelings.

Denotation/Connotation Chart

Word	Denotation	Connotation (+ or –)
abusive	harmful, cruel	–

Before Reading Only Daughter

memoir by Sandra Cisneros

Reading Strategies

- Plan and Monitor
- Determine Importance
- Make Inferences
- ▶ **Ask Questions**
- Make Connections
- Synthesize
- Visualize

Analyze Author's Purpose

A **memoir** is a type of **narrative nonfiction**. It tells about a certain time in the writer's life and is told in the writer's own words. A memoir usually includes:

- details about important events and people in the writer's life
- why these events and people are important and how they affected the writer

Look Into the Text

Cisneros tells about an event in her life.

Once, several years ago, when I was just starting out my writing career, I was asked to write my own contributor's note for an anthology I was part of. I wrote: "I am the only daughter in a family of six sons. *That* explains everything."

Well, I've thought about that ever since, and yes, it explains a lot to me, but for the reader's sake I should have written: "I am the only daughter in a *Mexican* family of six sons." Or even: "I am the only daughter of a Mexican father and a Mexican-American mother." Or: "I am the only daughter of a working-class family of nine." All of these had everything to do with who I am today.

How might the author's details help her accomplish her purpose?

Focus Strategy ▶ Ask Questions

As you read, you may have **questions** about what the author is trying to tell you. You may wonder why the author is sharing specific information with you. You may even have ideas for how he or she could be clearer.

How to Question the Author

Focus Strategy

1. **Use a Double-Entry Journal** In one column, write your question for the author. Include the page number where you had the question.

2. **Answer Your Question** As you read on, try to answer your question. The answer may be right there, or you may need to think about it and search for it.

3. **Think Beyond the Text** The answer may not be in the text. You could think about what you know from your life as well as the author's life and make a reasonable prediction about the answer.

Double-Entry Journal

Page and Question	Answer
Page 144: I don't understand. What does "I am the only daughter in a family of six sons" explain?	

Sandra Cisneros
(1954–   )

When **Sandra Cisneros** was accepted to the Iowa Writers' Workshop, a famous writing program at the University of Iowa, she was thrilled. Once she got there, though, she felt out of place. All of the other students, it seems, came from wealthy families. She recalls, "My classmates were from the best schools in the country." Cisneros felt alone. She sensed that the other students wouldn't understand what it was like to grow up poor.

She felt even worse the day they studied an author who compared people's houses to their souls. Cisneros grew up in crowded houses in poor neighborhoods in Chicago. It upset her to think that her family's ugly houses were pictures of her soul.

It wasn't long after this, however, that she began to appreciate what set her apart from the other students. In her writing, she started to reveal her background, the people she knew, and the places where she had grown up. In 1984 she published *The House on Mango Street*, which captured life in inner-city Chicago neighborhoods. The book has been hugely successful.

Cisneros may have had a difficult start at the workshop in Iowa, but she learned the most important lesson for a writer: Write what is true to your heart and your soul.

myNGconnect.com

- See Sandra Cisneros's Web site.
- Learn more about *The House on Mango Street*.

Only Daughter

by Sandra Cisneros

Set a Purpose
*Find out how Sandra Cisneros's brothers
and father affected her life.*

Once, **several years ago,** when I was just starting out my writing career, I was asked to write my own contributor's note for an anthology I was part of. I wrote: "I am the only daughter in a family of six sons. *That* explains everything."

Well, I've thought about that ever since, and yes, it explains a lot to me, but for the reader's **sake** I should have written: "I am the only daughter in a *Mexican* family of six sons." Or even: "I am the only daughter of a Mexican father and a Mexican-American mother." Or: "I am the only daughter of a **working-class** family of nine." **1** All of these had everything to do with who I am today.

I was/am the only daughter and *only* a daughter. Being an only daughter in a family of six sons forced me by **circumstance** to spend a lot of time by myself because my brothers felt it beneath them to play with a *girl* in public. But that aloneness, that loneliness, was good for **a would-be writer**—it allowed me time to think and think, to imagine, to read and prepare myself. **2**

Sandra Cisneros was born in Chicago in 1954. She has two older brothers and four younger brothers.

1 Author's Purpose
Who does Cisneros include in her memoir? Why do you think she includes them?

2 Ask Questions
What is Cisneros saying here? How might being alone be good for someone who wants to be a writer?

Key Vocabulary
• **circumstance** *n.*, how things are or what happens

In Other Words
sake understanding
working-class lower-class
a would-be writer someone who wanted to be a writer

Being only a daughter for my father meant my **destiny** would lead me to become someone's wife. That's what he believed. But when I was in fifth grade and shared my plans for college with him, I was sure he understood. I remember my father saying, "*Que bueno, mi'ja,* that's good." That meant a lot to me, especially since my brothers thought the idea **hilarious**. What I didn't realize was that my father thought college was good for girls—for finding a husband. After four years in college and two more in graduate school, and still no husband, my father shakes his head even now and says I wasted all that education.

In retrospect, I'm lucky my father believed daughters were meant for husbands. It meant it didn't matter if I majored in something silly like English. After all, I'd find a nice **professional** eventually, right? This allowed me the liberty to putter about embroidering my little poems and stories without my father interrupting with so much as a "What's that you're writing?"

> ... my father thought college was good for girls —for finding a husband.

But the truth is, I wanted him to interrupt. I wanted my father to understand what it was I was scribbling, to introduce me as "My only daughter, the writer." Not as "This is my only daughter. She teaches." *El maestra*—teacher. Not even *profesora.* **3**

In a sense, everything I have ever written has been for him, to win his **approval** even though I know my father can't read English words, even though my father's only reading includes the brown-ink *Esto* sports magazines from Mexico City and the bloody *¡Alarma!*

3 Author's Purpose
What does the description of the father tell you about the conflict between Cisneros and her father?

Key Vocabulary
destiny *n.*, what is supposed to happen to you in the future; fate
approval *n.*, accepting something as good or correct; a good opinion of something

In Other Words
Que bueno, mi'ja That's good, my daughter (in Spanish)
hilarious very funny
In retrospect Looking back
professional educated man with a good job
profesora professor (in Spanish)

magazines that feature yet another sighting of **La Virgen de Guadalupe** on a tortilla or a wife's revenge on her philandering husband by bashing his skull in with a *molcajete* (a kitchen mortar made of volcanic rock). Or the *fotonovelas*, the little picture paperbacks with tragedy and trauma erupting from the characters' mouths in bubbles. **4**

My father represents, then, the public majority. A public who is disinterested in reading, and yet one whom I am writing about and for, and privately trying to **woo**. **5**

When we were growing up in Chicago, we moved a lot because of my father. He **suffered periodic bouts of nostalgia**. Then we'd have to let go our flat, store the furniture with mother's relatives, load the station wagon with baggage and bologna sandwiches, and head south. To Mexico City.

We came back, of course. To yet another Chicago flat, another Chicago neighborhood, another Catholic school. Each time, my father would seek out the parish priest in order to get a tuition break, and complain or **boast**: "I have seven sons."

> When we were growing up in Chicago, we moved a lot because of my father.

He meant *siete hijos*, seven children, but he translated it as "sons." **6** "I have seven sons." To anyone who would listen. The Sears Roebuck employee who sold us the washing machine. The

4 Author's Purpose/ Ask Questions
Ask yourself a *why* question about the author's purpose for describing what her father likes to read.

5 Ask Questions
What might you ask the author about her writing? Where might you find the answer?

6 Author's Purpose
Why does Cisneros tell this important detail about her life?

In Other Words
La Virgen de Guadalupe a religious figure
woo attract
suffered periodic bouts of nostalgia
  sometimes missed his old home
boast brag, speak proudly

Cultural Background
Fotonovelas are popular graphic novels written in Spanish. Topics include crime, cowboys, romance, and the lives of famous people.

United States and Mexico

 Analyze the Map
About how many
miles is it from
Chicago to Mexico
City? Why do you
think moving back
and forth was
so important to
Cisneros's father?

short-order cook where my father ate his ham-and-eggs breakfasts.
"I have seven sons." As if he deserved a medal from the state.

My papa. He didn't mean anything by that mistranslation, I'm sure.
But somehow I could feel myself being erased. I'd tug my father's
sleeve and whisper: "Not seven sons. Six! And *one daughter*."

Monitor Comprehension

Summarize
Decide the important
details in this section.
Retell them in a few
words.

𝒲hen **my oldest brother** graduated from medical school, he **fulfilled** my father's dream that we study hard and use this— our heads, instead of this—our hands. Even now my father's hands are thick and yellow, stubbed by a history of hammer and nails and twine and coils and springs. "Use this," my father said, tapping his head, "and not this," showing us those hands. He always looked tired when he said it.

Cisneros's success as a writer allowed her to fulfill her dream of owning her own home. She lives in San Antonio, Texas.

In Other Words
fulfilled satisfied

Wasn't college **an investment**? And hadn't I spent all those years in college? And if I didn't marry, what was it all for? Why would anyone go to college and then choose to be poor? Especially someone who had always been poor.

Last year, after ten years of writing professionally, the **financial rewards** started to trickle in. My second National Endowment for the Arts Fellowship. A guest professorship at the University of California, Berkeley. My book, which sold to a major New York publishing house. **7**

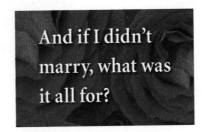

And if I didn't marry, what was it all for?

At Christmas, I flew home to Chicago. The house was **throbbing**, same as always; hot *tamales* and sweet *tamales* hissing in my mother's pressure cooker, and everybody—my mother, six brothers, wives, babies, aunts, cousins—talking too loud and at the same time, like in a Fellini film, because that's just how we are.

I went upstairs to my father's room. One of my stories had just been translated into Spanish and published in an anthology of Chicano writing, and I wanted to show it to him. Ever since he recovered from a stroke two years ago, my father likes to spend his leisure hours horizontally. And that's how I found him, watching a Pedro Infante movie on **Galavision** and eating rice pudding. **8**

There was a glass filled with milk on the bedside table. There were several **vials** of pills and balled Kleenex. And on the floor, one black sock and a plastic urinal that I didn't want to look at but looked at anyway. Pedro Infante was about to burst into song, and my father was laughing. **9**

7 Author's Purpose
Why does the author skip ahead from her youth and tell about her successes?

8 Ask Questions
Think of the details that Cisneros includes here. Question the author about them.

9 Author's Purpose
How do the images in this paragraph help you visualize this scene from the author's life?

In Other Words
an investment something we spent money on because we would get something back
financial rewards money for my hard work
throbbing busy and noisy
Galavision Spanish-language television
vials small bottles

Cultural Background
Pedro Infante Cruz (1917–1957) was a popular Mexican singer and movie star. When Cruz died in a plane crash, the president of Mexico declared a national day of mourning, out of respect for the star.

I'm not sure if it was because my story was translated into Spanish, or because it was published in Mexico, or perhaps because the story dealt with Tepeyac, the *colonia* my father was raised in, but at any rate, my father punched the mute button on his remote control and read my story. **10**

I sat on the bed next to my father and waited. He read it very slowly. As if he were reading each line over and over. He laughed at all the right places and read lines he liked out loud. He pointed and asked questions: "Is this So-and-so?" "Yes," I said. He kept reading.

When he was finally finished, after what seemed like hours, my father looked up and asked: "Where can we get more copies of this for the relatives?" **11**

Of all the wonderful things that happened to me last year, that was the most wonderful. ❖

Cisneros worked on her novel *Caramelo* for almost ten years. The novel was inspired by her father's life. It was published in 2002, in both English and Spanish.

10 Ask Questions
What questions could you ask and answer about this paragraph?

11 Author's Purpose
Cisneros tells exactly what her father does and says as he reads her story. What does she accomplish by including these details?

Monitor Comprehension

Confirm Prediction
Was your prediction correct? What happened that you did not expect?

In Other Words
colonia neighborhood (in Spanish)

ANALYZE Only Daughter

1. **Explain** What made her father's request more wonderful to Cisneros than all the rewards she received that year?

2. **Vocabulary** What **role** did Cisneros's father expect her to play in life? What role did she play?

3. **Analyze Author's Purpose** With a partner, create an author's purpose chart. On the left, list details Cisneros included in her memoir. On the right, tell why she included each detail.

Author's Purpose Chart	
Detail	**Why Included**
1. brothers wouldn't play with her	explains why she spent time alone
2. _____	_____
3. _____	_____

4. **Focus Strategy Ask Questions** What question did you ask that was especially useful to you as a reader? Tell how you answered it and why it was useful.

   Return to the Text
   Reread and Write In general, how does Cisneros's family affect her life? Use facts from the text to support your ideas.

Key Vocabulary
- **role** *n.*, a part you play on stage or in real life

BEFORE READING Calling a Foul

news commentary by Stan Simpson

Reading Strategies

· Plan and Monitor
· Determine Importance
· Make Inferences
▶ Ask Questions
· Make Connections
· Synthesize
· Visualize

Analyze Author's Viewpoint

A **news commentary** explains the author's viewpoint, or the author's ideas and feelings about a current topic. A commentary often includes:

- facts: information that can be proved
- opinions: feelings or beliefs that cannot be proved true or false

By thinking about the author's purpose and the facts the author includes, the reader can often discover the author's viewpoint.

Look Into the Text

These words express the author's viewpoint.

> Bad-behaving parents at sports events have become a painful reality. The stuff that happens after the game is just as shocking. A Connecticut parent spit at a high school basketball coach because he didn't like how the coach was coaching. Referees and coaches have been physically attacked after school games. And it's not unusual for parents to be banned from a game until they can control their emotions.
>
> State high school athletic directors say it is more difficult than ever to attract coaches and game officials.

Do these sentences state facts or opinions?

Focus Strategy ▶ Ask Questions

As you read a news commentary, notice how the author expresses his or her viewpoint. Use this strategy as you **question** the author of "Calling a Foul."

HOW TO QUESTION THE AUTHOR

Focus Strategy

1. **Stop and Ask** What is Stan Simpson trying to say? Are his ideas clear? Does he choose the best words to express his ideas?

   YOU READ: Bad-behaving parents at sports events have become a painful reality.

   YOU ASK: Is the behavior of parents at sports events really painful?

2. **Question the Argument** Notice how the author supports his viewpoint. Does he use facts to justify his opinion?

   YOU READ: Referees and coaches have been physically attacked after school games.

   YOU ASK: Is this a fact or an opinion?
   Does this support his argument that bad-behaving parents are a painful reality?
   Does he have a strong or weak argument?

STAN
SIMPSON

Calling a Foul

Bill Cardarelli was impressed by a high school basketball player. He thought she would be a fine addition to the St. Joseph College women's team he coached.

Then he saw her dad in action as **a spectator**.

"He was absolutely bad-mouthing the coach," Cardarelli recalled. "I mean yelling: 'You don't know how to coach! What are you doing?'"

The kid was no longer that **valuable** to Cardarelli.

"I stopped **recruiting her**," he said. "Because you knew what was **in line for** the next coach to get that guy."

Bad-behaving parents at sports events have become a painful reality.

The stuff that happens after the game is just as shocking. A Connecticut parent spit at a high school basketball coach because he didn't like how the coach was coaching. Referees and coaches have been physically attacked after school games. And it's not unusual for parents to be banned from a game until they can control their emotions. **1**

State high school athletic directors say it is more difficult than ever to attract coaches and game officials. They're not willing to put up with **abusive** parents.

Now there's a bill that would make it a crime to attack a sports official at a game.

Time-out.

Has it really come to this? Do we need a law to remind adults that they should act like grownups at sports events? **2**

"That's a sad **commentary**," said John Shukie, president of the Connecticut Association of Athletic Directors. "It's kind of **an indictment of** where sports have been going in our society. The importance people place

1 Ask Questions
Ask and answer a question about what Simpson is writing.

2 Author's Viewpoint
How do you think the author views this bill? What part of the text makes you think so?

Key Vocabulary
valuable *adj.*, having worth, important
abusive *adj.*, hurtful, cruel, harsh

In Other Words
a spectator someone watching the game
recruiting her trying to get her to join my team
in line for going to happen to
commentary statement about the issue
an indictment of a negative comment about

on winning and losing is greater than ever now."

The small percentage of **overzealous** parents out there has become an unwelcome part of youth athletics. You can't stop these parents. You can only hope to keep them under control. Many want their children to be successful athletes so badly that they don't notice their kids are NOT good enough to get athletic scholarships. It doesn't matter how many trophies their kids won in sports when they were really little. The parents **embarrass** themselves and their kids with their angry performances.

"We have lost our sense of **decorum**," says athletic director June Bernabucci of Hartford. "Parents and all adults have to stop **living vicariously through** their children and their sports activities."

No law in the world will stop a fuming parent from fighting with a coach or an official. **3** But every parent of a student athlete should sign an agreement that outlines consequences for his or her bad **behavior**:

- I will not confront a coach or sports official after a game ends.

- I will not shout insults at other athletes on either team.

- I will not use **profanity**.

- I will sit in the stands, support the team, and pretend that I'm the adult. **4**

Yeah, maybe it's a little childish. But wait until you hear the consequences.

Repeat offenders would be **banned** from games, unless they wear a huge sign: *As a parent, I stink.* ❖

3 Author's Viewpoint
Is this a fact or an opinion? Do you agree? Why or why not?

4 Ask Questions
Ask and answer a question about Simpson's agreement.

Key Vocabulary
embarrass *v.*, to make someone feel confused, uneasy, or ashamed
behavior *n.*, the way a person acts, conduct

In Other Words
overzealous extreme, intense
decorum good behavior
living vicariously through pushing their own dreams on
profanity bad words
banned kept away from

ANALYZE Calling a Foul

1. **Explain** According to the agreement that Simpson proposes, how should parents act at games?

2. **Vocabulary** How might parents with good **behavior** at games affect their kids?

3. **Analyze Author's Viewpoint** What evidence does the author cite to support his viewpoint that bad behavior by parents hurts youth sports?

4. **Focus Strategy Ask Questions** Work with a partner. Compare the questions you asked. Did you and your partner have similar questions and answers?

   ## ↩ Return to the Text
   Reread and Write Reread the text. Picture yourself in the **role** of a parent who gets very intense at high school games. Write a short response to Simpson's commentary.

Key Vocabulary
- **role** *n.*, a part you play on stage or in real life

About the Writer

Stan Simpson (1962–) writes a weekly column for the *Hartford Courant*, a newspaper in Hartford, Connecticut. He also hosts a weekly news radio program. His work addresses a wide range of issues, including education, criminal justice, and local politics.

The National Alliance for Youth Sports is a group that encourages safe sports for young people. About once a week, the group posts a survey question on its Web site. Here are the results for two questions.

What is the biggest problem in youth sports today?

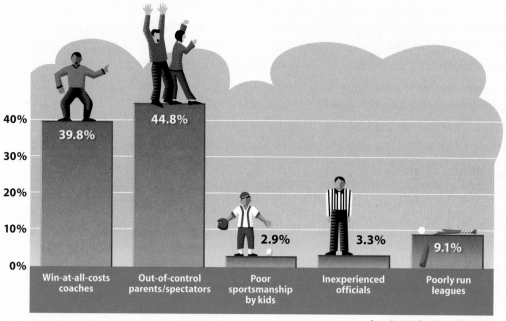

Source: National Alliance for Youth Sports, 2003

Who is at fault for the violence in youth sports?

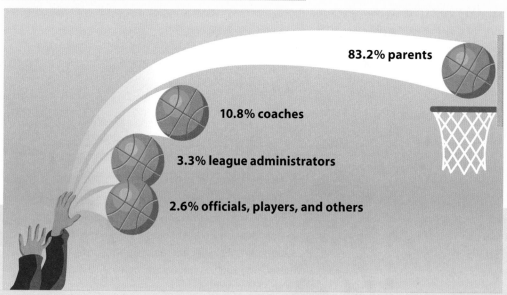

Source: National Alliance for Youth Sports, 2005

EQ How Do Families Affect Us?

Reading

Critical Thinking

EQ 1. Analyze What impacts do parents' **behaviors** have on their children? Support your viewpoints with evidence from the selections.

2. Compare Compare Cisneros's parents to the parents of the high school basketball player. In each case, how do the parents affect their child?

3. Interpret Recall "Do Family Meals Matter?" and "Fish Cheeks." What kind of conversation might Cisneros and her father have at a family dinner?

4. Judge Did you prefer reading the memoir or the commentary? Explain why. Mention specific parts that you enjoyed.

EQ 5. Assess Think about all of the selections you read in this unit. Which do you think has the biggest influence on kids: parents' behavior, their customs, or their genes?

Writing

Write About Literature

Guide for Parents What three things can parents do to support their children in a positive way? List examples from both texts. Then use your list to write a short guide for parents.

> Positive Things Parents Can Do
>
> 1. _____
>
> 2. _____
>
> 3. _____

Vocabulary

Key Vocabulary Review

Oral Review Work with a partner. Use these words to complete the paragraph.

abusive	circumstances	role
approval	destiny	valuable
behavior	embarrass	

I always seem to play a certain __(1)__ in my family. I love to joke and make people laugh. Sometimes my silly way of acting, or __(2)__, makes my parents blush. I __(3)__ them when I joke around in front of their friends. In other __(4)__, they enjoy my humor. My parents never yell at me and are never __(5)__. The most important or __(6)__ thing I could have in my life is their __(7)__ of me. However, it seems to be my fate, or __(8)__, to be the family joker.

Writing Application Describe a situation in which a parent's behavior really helped his or her child. Use at least four Key Vocabulary words.

Fluency

Read with Ease: Expression

Assess your reading fluency with the passage in the Reading Handbook, p. 670. Then complete the self-check below.

1. I did/did not match the sound of my voice to the feelings shown in the passage.

2. My words correct per minute: _____.

Use Verbs to Talk About the Present

The verb **have** has two forms in the present.

> I **have** six brothers. They **have** one daughter.
> She **has** no sisters. He **has** seven children.

The verb **be** has three forms in the present.

> I **am** the only daughter. You **are** his son.
> She **is** one of six children.

Am, **is**, and **are** can also be **helping verbs**. A helping verb can come before a main verb that ends with **-ing**. The helping verb agrees with the subject.

> I **am** studying English. She **is** writing stories.
> We **are** reading them.

Oral Practice (1–5) With a partner, take turns saying the sentences. Choose the correct form of the verb in parentheses.

1. Ms. Cisneros _____ a big family. (have)
2. She _____ writing stories to please her father. (be)
3. I _____ hoping to be a writer, too. (be)
4. My parents _____ a magazine. (have)
5. They _____ going to publish my stories. (be)

Written Practice (6–10) Rewrite the paragraph. Choose the correct present tense form of the verb. Add two more sentences about Sandra Cisneros. Use present tense verbs.

> Sandra Cisneros (have/has) six brothers. Sandra (write/writes) about her relatives. Her father (am reading/is reading) the stories.

Express Needs and Intentions

Act It Out With a partner, role-play a conversation between Sandra Cisneros and her father. Tell each other about something you need and how you plan to get it.

Analyze Style

The words that authors choose and the way they arrange words make up their style of writing. An author's style may change depending on the form, or genre, and the effect he or she wants to have on the readers.

In "Calling a Foul," Stan Simpson gives his viewpoint and wants the reader to share it. His **voice** for this news commentary is to write as if he is speaking to the reader.

- He uses the second-person pronoun *you*.
- He uses an informal **tone** with words and phrases, such as *stuff* and *yeah*.
- He breaks up the paragraphs where he would pause while talking.

Choose one other selection in this unit. Work with a partner. Identify the form and discuss the author's style. Notice

- the author's choice of words, voice, and tone
- how the author arranges the words
- the effect of the style.

Soccer-Parent Coach

"O.K., big cheer here, but nothing that might be construed as pressure. Quiet now, but a supportive quiet. Watch your body language"

Source: ©Kim Warp/*The New Yorker*

Context Clues

Synonyms are words that have about the same meaning as each other. **Antonyms** are opposites. Clues with synonyms and antonyms can help you figure out the meanings of unfamiliar words.

- **Synonym Clue**: Do we need a law to remind <u>adults</u> that they should act *like* <u>grown-ups</u>?

- **Antonym Clue**: Polite parents can <u>come to the game</u>, *but* loud parents should be <u>banned</u>.

Signal words for synonym clues include *as*, *like*, *also*, *too*, and *same*. Antonym clues include *but*, *yet*, *however*, *though*, *instead of*, and *unlike*. Look for these kinds of clues in the selections and identify the words they help you understand.

Flier

Social Studies: Places of Origin Sandra Cisneros's father grew up in an area of Mexico City known as Tepeyac. Find out about an area where someone you know came from. Research to find out interesting details about the place. Make a colorful ad to distribute as a flier. Persuade people to visit by including photos, maps, or drawings. Share your flier with the class.

myNGconnect.com

🔇 **Explore places around the world.**
🔇 **View maps and check out facts.**

🍂 **Language and Learning Handbook,** page 616

Trait: Development of Ideas

A good narrative paragraph begins with an interesting idea that gets the attention of readers and makes them want to keep reading. The details that follow explain and support the idea. Then the paragraph ends with a memorable sentence so the writing feels complete.

Just OK

> For three years, I was too shy to try out for the school musical. This year, the musical is "The Music Man." My grandma loves my singing. She really encouraged me to try out for the musical. I got a part with a solo! I was worried. I just finished my solo, and the audience is clapping and cheering. It wasn't as hard as I thought it would be. I would like to sing in front of an audience again.

Much Better

> I did it. People are clapping for me. I just finished singing, and now the entire audience is cheering for me. For three years, I was too shy to try out for a part in the school musical, but my grandma really encouraged me to try out this year. I got a role with a solo. It wasn't that hard. I can't wait to sing on stage again next year.

Practice

Think of a problem that your family or friends helped you solve. Write a short piece that tells about the problem and its solution. Remember:

- Start your piece with an interesting sentence.
- Use specific descriptive details to expand on the topic.
- End your piece with a strong sentence.

🍂 **Writing Handbook,** page 698

from

The Color of Water

by James McBride

1 It was kill or be killed in my house, and Mommy understood that, in fact created the system. You were **left to your own devices** or so you thought until you **were at your very wits' end**, at which time she would step in and rescue you. I was terrified when it came my turn to go to school. Although P.S. 118 was only eight blocks away, I wasn't allowed to walk there with my **siblings** because kindergarten students were required to ride the bus. On the **ill-fated morning**, Mommy chased me all around the kitchen trying to dress me as my siblings laughed at my terror. "The bus isn't bad," one quipped, "except for the snakes." Another added, "Sometimes the bus never brings you home." **Guffaws** all around.

2 "Be quiet," Mommy said, inspecting my first-day-of school attire. My clothes were clean, but not new. The pants had been Billy's, the shirt was David's, the coat had been passed down from Dennis to Billy to David to Richie to me. It was a gray coat with a fur collar that had literally been chewed up

Comforters, Ron Waddams © 1983, Acrylic on board, courtesy Larren Art Trust, Beaconsfield, England.

In Other Words
left to your own devices on your own
were at your very wits' end couldn't think of anything else to do
siblings brothers and sisters
ill-fated morning morning of my first day
Guffaws Laughter

by somebody. Mommy dusted it off with a whisk broom, set out eight or nine bowls, poured oatmeal in each one, left instructions for the eldest to feed the rest, then ran a comb through my hair. The sensation was like a tractor pulling my curls off. "C'mon," she said, "I'll walk you to the bus stop." Surprise reward. Me and Mommy alone. It was the first time I remember ever being alone with my mother.

3   It became the **high point** of my day, a memory so sweet it is burned into my mind like a tattoo, Mommy walking me to the bus stop and every afternoon picking me up, standing on the corner of New Mexico and 114th Road, clad in a brown coat, her black hair tied in a colorful scarf, watching with the rest of the parents as the yellow school bus swung around the corner and came to a stop with a hiss of air brakes.

> It became the high point of my day...

4   Gradually, as the weeks passed and the terror of going to school **subsided**, I began to notice something about my mother, that she looked nothing like the other kids' mothers. In fact, she looked more like my kindergarten teacher, Mrs. Alexander, who was white. Peering out the window as the bus rounded the corner and the front doors flew open, I noticed that Mommy stood apart from the other mothers, rarely speaking to them. She stood behind them, waiting calmly, hands in her coat pockets, watching intently through the bus windows to see where I was, then smiling and waving as I yelled my greeting to her through the window. She'd quickly grasp my hand as I stepped off the bus, ignoring the stares of the black women as she **whisked** me away.

In Other Words
high point best part
subsided was less powerful, decreased
whisked quickly took

School's Out, 1936, Allan Rohan Crite. Oil on canvas, Smithsonian American Art Museum.

▲ Critical Viewing: Character How do the adults and children in this painting get along? How does the artist illustrate the relationships?

5   One afternoon as we walked home from the bus stop, I asked Mommy why she didn't look like the other mothers.

6   "Because I'm not them," she said.

7   "Who are you?" I asked.

8   "I'm your mother."

9   "Then why don't you look like Rodney's mother, or Pete's mother? How come you don't look like me?"

10   She sighed and shrugged. She'd obviously **been down this road** many times. "I do look like you. I'm your mother. You ask too many questions. Educate your mind. School is important. Forget Rodney and Pete. Forget their mothers. You remember school. Forget everything else. Who cares about Rodney and Pete! When they go one way, you go the other way. Understand? When they go one way, you go the other way. You hear me?"

In Other Words
been down this road answered this question

11   "Yes."

12   "I know what I'm talking about. Don't follow none of them around. You **stick to** your brothers and sisters, that's it. Don't tell nobody your **business** neither!" End of discussion.

13   A couple of weeks later the bus dropped me off and Mommy was not there. I **panicked**. Somewhere in the back of my mind was the memory of her warning me, "You're going to have to

> "You stick to your brothers and sisters, that's it."

learn to walk home by yourself," but that memory blinked like a distant fog light in a stormy sea and it drowned in my panic. I was lost. My house was two blocks away, but it might as well have been ten miles because I had no idea where it was. I stood on the corner and **bit back** my tears. The other parents regarded me sympathetically and asked me my address, but I was afraid to tell them. In my mind was Mommy's warning, drilled into all twelve of us children from the time we could walk: "Never, ever, ever tell your business to nobody," and I shook my head no, I don't know my address. They **departed** one by one, until a sole figure remained, a black father, who stood in front of me with his son, saying, "Don't worry, your mother is coming soon." I ignored him. He was blocking my view, the tears clouding my vision as I tried to peer behind him, looking down the block to see if that familiar brown coat and white face would appear in the distance. It didn't. In fact there wasn't anyone coming at all, except a bunch of kids and they certainly didn't look like Mommy. They were a **motley crew** of girls and boys, ragged, with wild hairdos and unkempt jackets, hooting and making noise, and only when they were almost upon me did I recognize the faces of my elder siblings and my little sister Kathy who trailed behind them. I ran into their arms and collapsed in tears as they gathered around me, laughing. ❖

In Other Words
stick to stay with
business personal information
panicked got very worried and scared
bit back tried to stop
departed left
motley crew mixed group

FAMILY MATTERS

EQ ESSENTIAL QUESTION:

How Do Families Affect Us?

myNGconnect.com

📀 Download the rubric.

Present Your Project: Documentary

It is time to produce your documentary about the Essential Question for this unit: How Do Families Affect Us?

1 Review and Complete Your Plan

Consider these points as you complete your project:

- What parts of the documentary will tell about the Essential Question?
- How will you organize the information in an interesting way?
- How will you edit the documentary so it is short but meaningful?
- Whose point of view does your documentary present?
- Do you think your documentary will appeal to a broad audience, or a specific one?

Discuss your ideas with a friend. Prepare your script. Conduct and record the interviews. Edit the material.

2 Show Your Documentary

Show your documentary to the class. Answer questions from the audience.

3 Evaluate the Documentaries

Use the online rubric to evaluate each of the documentaries, including your own.

Reflect on Your Reading

Think back on your reading of the unit selections, including your choice of Edge Library books. Discuss the following with a partner or in a group.

Genre Focus Compare and contrast the elements in a science article and a memoir. Give examples, using the selections in this unit.

Focus Strategy Choose two questions you asked in this unit. Have your group answer them. Then explain how you uncovered the answers in the text.

EQ Respond to the Essential Question

Throughout this unit, you have been thinking about how families affect us. Discuss the Essential Question with a group. What have *you* decided? Support your response with evidence from your reading, discussions, research, and writing.

Write a News Article

Writing Portfolio

Writing Mode
Informative/Explanatory

Writing Trait Focus
Development of Ideas

What's new in your school? In your neighborhood?
This project gives you a chance to find out and
report back. For this project, you will write a news
article about a school or community event.

Study News Articles

News articles report key facts about real events. They are examples of informative/explanatory writing because they give information. Reporters use third-person pronouns, such as *he*, *she*, and *they*, to tell what happened in an objective way, without expressing their own opinions or feelings.

❶ Connect Writing to Your Life

You have probably read many news articles in your life. Maybe you read them in online newspapers and e-zines. Or maybe you like to read a daily or weekly paper and get your news there. Whatever the source, news articles are a window to the world. They tell you what is happening far away and just down the street.

❷ Understand the Form

News articles keep you informed by answering important questions about events. These questions are called the **5Ws and an H** (or **W/H questions**):

- *Who* is involved?
- *What* happened?
- *When* did it happen?
- *Where* did it happen?
- *Why* did it happen?
- *How* did it happen?

In short paragraphs, news articles present facts in order of importance. The facts are stated objectively, or in a way that does not include the writer's personal opinions or feelings.

Headline
Choose a title that catches the reader's attention.

Lead
Start by introducing the topic of the article. Briefly provide answers to the most important W/H questions.

Body
Develop the article. Support answers to the W/H questions with direct quotations and other details. Arrange details from most important to least important.

Tail
End the article with an interesting quotation or detail.

Now see how these parts come together. Read a news article by a professional writer.

3 Analyze a Professional Model

As you read, look for answers to the W/H questions.

Working Toward Peace, One Square at a Time

Nancy Maes, Special to the Tribune
December 5, 2006

Lots of kids wish grown-ups were more committed to the idea of global peace. Recently, some Chicago-area kids put action behind their wishes.

More than 300 students used colored pens, pieces of fabric , and glue to decorate quilt squares expressing their thoughts and feelings about peace.

The kids, ages 8 to 17, were taking part in the Children's Humanitarian Peace Quilt Program, called "One Peace at a Time." The squares were sewn by local artists into more than thirty quilts and will be sent to children in war-torn Iraq.

Karina R., 13, of Chicago says her quilt square "was based on the physical and emotional barriers that separate people."

"There is a hand reaching toward the ocean, which is the physical barrier that separates us from the children in Iraq, and in the middle of the ocean there is a heart that shows that we care about them. But I put a piece of white cloth over the heart because some of us are afraid to reach out to the children and they may be afraid to let us reach them. The white cloth over the heart is see-through, so even if there is a barrier you can penetrate it."

Alejandro B., 13, of Chicago put a heart in the center of his quilt square and surrounded it with pieces of brightly colored fabrics.

"I picked vivid colors . . . because I wanted to tell the children in Iraq not to focus on the bad things that are happening to them, but to try to think about the positive things in life," he says. "And I wanted to let them know that we are supporting them. The quilts are a small step toward peace."

The quilts will be displayed Dec. 8 to Dec. 10 at "One of a Kind," a show and sale.

The headline gives a hint about the topic of the article.

The opening paragraph, or lead, introduces the topic.

These facts answer the questions **When? Where? Who?**

These facts answer the questions **How? What?**

The body supports the answers to the W/H questions with direct quotations.

Why do you think the writer ended with these facts?

▶**Prompt** Write a news article about a school or community event. Be sure to include:

- a catchy headline and lead
- answers to the W/H questions in order of importance
- direct quotations and other details
- an interesting ending, or tail

✔Prewrite

Writing is easier when you prewrite, or plan ahead. That's especially true when you write an article about a real event. Take time now to make a Writing Plan. It will save you time later when you write.

❶ Choose Your Topic

Use these strategies to find out what interesting events are taking place in your school or neighborhood:

- With a group of classmates, brainstorm a list of school events that recently happened or will soon happen. Think about dances, concerts, parents' nights, field trips, fund-raisers, and other special events.
- Read your community newspaper. What events do you want to know about?
- Interview teachers or neighbors to find out what's new and interesting.

Which event interests you the most? That's the event you should write about.

❷ Clarify the Audience, Topic, and Purpose

Your teacher and classmates are going to be part of your audience. Who else might want to read about the event? Jot down your ideas.

Then, think about the event. What do you want to find out about it? In a news article, you usually want to find the answers to the W/H questions. Jot down a list of questions.

Finally, think about your purpose, or reason, for writing. Is your purpose to inform readers? What other purposes might your news article have?

❸ Gather Quotations and Supporting Details

Next, gather facts and quotations for your news article. Your main source of information will probably be people. Interview people who planned the event or attended it. Ask them your W/H questions. Take notes.

Technology Tip

Tape record your interviews if you can. Take some notes during the interview, but listen to the tape later to verify, or check, the person's actual words.

4 Organize the Details

News articles give information in order of importance. They answer the main W/H questions in the beginning. Make a list like the one below. Decide what your readers will need to know first, next, and so on.

Who?	Student Council
What?	a dance
When?	last Saturday
Where?	high school gym
Why?	raise money for Keisha Kandun and her family

Prewriting Tip

Analyze the organization of news articles in your local newspaper. See how reporters organize details in order of importance. Model your article after theirs.

5 Finish Your Writing Plan

Make a Writing Plan like the one below. Show which details will go in the lead, body, and tail.

Writing Plan

Topic	Rock the House dance
Audience	my teacher and my classmates
Purpose	to tell what happened at an event
Form	news article
Time Frame	five days from today!

Lead
1. The Rock the House dance was held last Saturday.
2. It was in the Central High School gym.
3. The dance raised $2,348 for the Kanduns.
4. The money will go toward rebuilding their house.

Body
5. The student council organized the dance.
6. Lightning hit the Kandun house, which caught fire.
7. The Harlequins played at the dance.

Tail
8. End with a quotation from the guitarist.

Reflect on Your Writing Plan

► Does your plan establish the structure you need for the news article? Do you have enough details and quotations to support the answers to the W/H questions? If not, go back through your notes and see if you can add additional information to your plan.

✔ Write a Draft

Now use your Writing Plan to write a draft. Remember that your first draft doesn't have to be perfect. You'll have a chance to improve it later on.

Technology Tip

If you word process your draft, you can easily move words, sentences, and paragraphs around. Use Cut and Paste from the Edit menu on your computer.

❶ Keep These Ideas in Mind

News writing may be less familiar to you than other kinds of writing. Keep these newspaper style rules and tips in mind as you write:

- **Remember the W/H Questions** Answer these questions as early in the article as possible. If you need more information, go get it.

- **Use Your Quotations** Support facts by letting people speak for themselves. Choose quotations that show emotions or ideas in memorable ways. Set off the quotations with quotation marks.

- **Be Flexible** Get the most important information and the best quotations down on paper. If you need to change the order, change it. After you see things in writing, it may be easier to tell where facts belong.

- **Be Brief** A news article doesn't include all possible information about an event. Don't be afraid to leave out details that seem unimportant after you start writing. Paragraphs in newspapers are often only a sentence or two.

❷ Create a Catchy Headline

It may not seem important, but the headline of a newspaper article is the first thing a reader sees. Think about it: When you read the paper, do you start at the beginning and read each page all the way through? No. You probably skim the headlines until one catches your attention. Here are some tips for writing an attention-grabbing headline:

- Write the headline after you've finished your article.
- Be sure the headline relates to your topic.
- Use active verbs and descriptive nouns.
- Keep the headline short.

OK	Better
Dance Raises Money to Rebuild Home	Fund-raising Dance Raises Roof

❸ Student Model

Read this draft to see how the student used the Writing Plan to get ideas down on paper. The first draft does not have to be perfect. As you will see, the student fixed the mistakes later.

Fund-raising Dance Raises Roof

A dance held last Saturday in Central high school's gym raised $2,348 to help rebuild the home of freshman Keisha Kandun and her family.

Admission to "Rock the House" was $10, all money went to the Kandun family fund. Volunteers also walked the dance floor with donation buckets to collect more money.

The Kanduns are living with Keisha's grandparents until the Kanduns can move into their new house. The whole family attended the dance then they went on stage to thank the crowd. Rebuilding has already begun, and the family hopes to move back in time for the holidays.

"We appreciate the help so much that I cannot even put it into words," said Mary Kandun, Keisha's mother. "We have always loved the school but we never expected this kind of generosity. You should all be proud of you're school for showing so much heart."

The Kanduns' four-bedroom home was empty on August 14 when it caught on fire. Sadly, the family did not have insurance too pay for the cost of rebuilding.

Central High School student council organized the event with some help. The student council also plans to hold a bake sale and a car wash, sponsored by speedy clean inc., to raise more money.

The dance featured the music of the Harlequins.

"It's cool to be able to play for your fellow classmates," said Adam Flynn, who plays guitar for the band. "We wanted to help out Keisha and her family, too."

Reflect on Your Draft

▶ Do you answer all the W/H questions as early as possible but in order of importance? Do you include enough quotations to support the facts? Look over your draft and decide if you need to add or delete details or change the order of your information.

✔ Revise Your Draft

Your first draft is done. Now, polish it. Improve the development of ideas. Make sure your writing is engaging and includes important and interesting details.

❶ Revise for Development of Ideas

Good writing has **well-developed ideas**. It doesn't just contain a list of facts. A good writer **elaborates** on facts by supporting them with specific details like:

- examples
- quotations
- explanations
- descriptions

Don't expect to fully develop all of your ideas in your first draft. Once you have your thoughts on paper, you can easily see which ideas need to be developed. Look for answers to the W/H questions that aren't supported by details.

TRY IT ▶ With a partner, decide which ideas in the draft below need more explanation and support. Add transitions to develop and connect the ideas.

Student Draft

> The Kanduns' four-bedroom home was empty on August 14 when it caught on fire. Sadly, the family did not have insurance too pay for the cost of rebuilding.
>
> Central High School student council organized the event with some help. The student council also plans to hold a bake sale and a car wash, sponsored by speedy clean inc., to raise more money.
>
> The dance featured the music of the Harlequins.

Now use the rubric to evaluate the development of ideas in your own draft.
What score do you give your draft and why?

Development of Ideas

myNGconnect.com

- Rubric: Development of Ideas
- Evaluate and practice scoring other student papers.

	How thoughtful and interesting is the writing?	How well are the ideas explained and supported?
4 Wow!	The writing engages the reader with meaningful ideas or claims and presents them in a way that is interesting and appropriate to the audience, purpose, and type of writing.	**The ideas or claims are fully explained and supported.** • The ideas or claims are well developed with important details, evidence, and/or description. • The writing feels complete, and the reader is satisfied.
3 Ahh.	<u>Most</u> of the writing engages the reader with meaningful ideas or claims and presents them in a way that is interesting and appropriate to the audience, purpose, and type of writing.	<u>Most</u> of the ideas or claims are explained and supported. • Most of the ideas or claims are developed with important details, evidence, and/or description. • The writing feels mostly complete, but the reader still has some questions.
2 Hmm.	<u>Some</u> of the writing engages the reader with meaningful ideas or claims and presents them in a way that is interesting and appropriate to the audience, purpose, and type of writing.	<u>Some</u> of the ideas or claims are explained and supported. • Only some of the ideas or claims are developed. Details, evidence, and/or description are limited or not relevant. • The writing leaves the reader with many questions.
1 Huh?	The writing does <u>not</u> engage the reader. It is not appropriate to the audience, purpose, and type of writing.	The ideas or claims are <u>not</u> explained or supported. The ideas or claims lack details, evidence, and/or description, and the writing leaves the reader unsatisfied.

✔ Revise Your Draft, continued

2 Revise Your Draft

You've now evaluated the development of ideas in your own draft. If you scored 3 or lower, how can you improve your work? Use the checklist below to revise your draft.

Revision Checklist

Ask Yourself	Check It Out	How to Make It Better
Does my article have a catchy headline?	Read the headline. Will it grab the reader's attention?	☐ Rewrite with active verbs and descriptive nouns.
Does the lead of my article answer all or most of the W/H questions?	Underline the answers to the W/H questions in the lead: • Who? • What? • When? • Where? • Why? • How?	☐ Review your notes. Add any missing information.
Does my article have well-developed ideas?	See whether there is an example, explanation, quotation, or description to support the answer to each W/H question.	☐ Review your notes. Add supporting details and quotations where needed.
Are my ideas presented in an objective way with clear transitions between the ideas?	Look at the statements you made to support each idea. Is each statement a fact?	☐ Take out details that express your own opinions or feelings. ☐ Add transitions so your ideas flow clearly.
Is the tail of my article effective?	Read the last few sentences. Are they interesting?	☐ Rewrite or add an interesting detail or quotation.

🢒 **Writing Handbook,** p. 698

❸ Conduct a Peer Conference

Get a second opinion about your article. Ask a partner to read your draft and answer the following questions:

- Was any part of the article confusing?
- Is there any place where something seems to be missing?
- Is there anything you don't understand?

Then talk with your partner about your draft. Focus on the items in the Revision Checklist. Use your partner's comments to make your article clearer, more complete, and easier to understand. Ask your teacher for additional feedback as you revise your draft.

❹ Make Revisions

Look at the revisions below and the peer-reviewer conversation on the right. Notice how the peer reviewer commented and asked questions. Notice how the writer used the comments and questions to revise.

Revised for Development of Ideas

> The dance featured the music of the Harlequins. The members of the band, seniors at Central, donated their time to perform.

Revised Tail

> "It's cool to be able to play for your fellow classmates," said
>
> Adam Flynn, who plays guitar for the band. "We wanted to help out
>
> Keisha and her family, too."
> "The band was awesome," said senior Neil Lukowski, who went to the dance with his girlfriend and several friends. "It was a fun night for a good cause."

Peer Conference

Reviewer's Comment: This paragraph could be better developed. Are the Harlequins a local band? What did they play?

Writer's Answer: Let me check my notes. I have more information about the band I can add.

Reviewer's Comment: The article just stops. Maybe you could work on the ending.

Writer's Answer: Yeah. I have some quotations I didn't use. I can add one that sums things up.

Reflect on Your Revisions

▶ It can be hard to see problems in your own writing. What did you learn from your peer conference?

✔ Edit and Proofread Your Draft

Now that you have revised your article, you are ready to edit and proofread it. Find and fix any mistakes that you made.

❶ Capitalize the Names of Groups

Each main word in the name of a specific organization, business, or agency should begin with a capital letter.

Organization: Girl Scouts of America

Government Agency: Environmental Protection Agency (EPA)

Business: Treetown Hardware Store

TRY IT ▶ Copy the sentence. Fix the three capitalization errors. Use proofreader's marks.

> The student council also plans to hold a bake sale and a car wash, sponsored by speedy clean inc., to raise more money.

❷ Use Semicolons

A semicolon (;) is used to join two complete sentences that are closely related. Using only a comma is incorrect and causes a run-on sentence. So does using nothing at all.

Incorrect	Correct
The dance was a success, everyone enjoyed it.	The dance was a success; everyone enjoyed it.
The dance was a success everyone enjoyed it.	

TRY IT ▶ Copy the sentences. Add semicolons where needed.

> 1. Admission to "Rock the House" was $10, all money went to the fund.
> 2. The whole family attended the dance then they went on stage to thank the crowd.

Proofreader's Marks

Use these proofreader's marks to correct capitalization and punctuation errors.

Capitalize:
A dance was held in Central high school's gym.

Do not capitalize:
The dance was held at the High School.

Insert semicolon:
Many students attended; some parents did, too.

Proofreading Tip

If you are unsure of when to use a semicolon, you can refer to a style manual for help.

❸ Check Your Spelling

Homonyms are words that sound alike but have different meanings and spellings. Watch for these homonyms when you are proofreading.

Homonyms and Their Meanings	Examples
to (preposition) = toward	Mari walked **to** the dance.
too (adverb) = also, in addition	I walked, **too**.
two (number) = 2	George brought **two** dates!
your (possessive adjective) = belonging to you	**Your** donation is appreciated.
you're (contraction) = you are	**You're** doing a good thing!

TRY IT ▶ Copy the sentences. Fix any homonym errors.

> 1. Sadly, the family did not have insurance too pay the cost of rebuilding.
> 2. "You should all be proud of you're school for showing so much heart."

❹ Use Subject Pronouns

Subject pronouns take the place of nouns in the subject of a sentence. Subject pronouns can help to make your writing less repetitive and more complex.

> **Roger** could not attend the dance. **He** was too young.
>
> **A local business** is hosting a car wash. **It** is donating all the money to the Kandun Fund.
>
> **The Harlequins** played at the dance. **They** are a great band.

The subject pronouns are:

Singular	Plural
I	we
you	you
he, she, it	they

TRY IT ▶ Copy the sentence. Use a subject pronoun to make it less repetitive.

> The Kanduns are living with Keisha's grandparents until the Kanduns can move into their new house.

🔖 **Writing Handbook**, p. 742

Reflect on Your Corrections

▶ Look back over your corrections. Do you see a pattern? Do you keep making the same kinds of errors? Make a note to watch for these errors in your writing. After you double-check your work, have a partner look it over one more time. Have you corrected the errors?

5 Edited Student Draft

Here's the student's draft, revised and edited. How did the writer improve it?

Fund-raising Dance Raises Roof

A dance held last Saturday in Central High School's gym raised $2,348 to help rebuild the home of freshman Keisha Kandun and her family.

Admission to "Rock the House" was $10; all money went to the Kandun Family Fund. Volunteers also walked the dance floor with donation buckets to collect more money.

The Kanduns are living with Keisha's grandparents until they can move into their new house. The whole family attended the dance; then they went on stage to thank the crowd. Rebuilding has already begun, and the family hopes to move back in time for the holidays.

"We appreciate the help so much that I cannot even put it into words," said Mary Kandun, Keisha's mother. "We have always loved the school, but we never expected this kind of generosity. You should all be proud of your school for showing so much heart."

The Kanduns' four-bedroom home was empty on August 14 when it caught on fire after being struck by lightning. Sadly, the family did not have enough insurance to pay for the cost of rebuilding. Central High School Student Council organized the event with the help of advisor and English teacher Lois Conrad and Principal David Cordero. The student council also plans to hold a bake sale and a car wash, sponsored by Speedy Clean Inc., to raise more money.

The dance featured the music of the Harlequins. The four members of the band, seniors at Central, donated their time to perform.

"It's cool to be able to play for your fellow classmates," said Adam Flynn, who plays guitar for the band. "We wanted to help out Keisha and her family, too."

"The band was awesome," said senior Neil Lukowski, who went to the dance with his girlfriend and several friends. "It was a fun night for a good cause."

The writer **capitalized** the full name of the organizations.

The writer replaced the comma with a **semicolon**.

The writer used a **pronoun** to make the sentence less repetitive.

The writer added the missing **semicolon** to the sentence.

The writer used the correct **homonyms**.

The writer added more detail about the fire.

The writer **capitalized** the full name of the group and added specific details about who helped them.

The writer **capitalized** the full name of the business.

The writer added more details about the band.

The writer added a quotation to sum everything up.

✔ Publish and Present

Your article is finished! You can now share it with your teacher, classmates, family, and other people, too. You may also want to present your work in a different way.

Alternative Presentations

Submit to the Media News stories appear in many types of media. Here are some ideas of places you might publish your news article so that it is available for the public to read:

1 **School Newspaper** Does your school have a student newspaper? If so, then submit your article for publication to one of the paper's editors or its advisor.

2 **School Web Site** Most school Web sites have a page that describes upcoming or recent events so that visitors know what is happening. Your news article could be perfect for that page. Find out who is in charge of the Web site and ask if you can post your article.

3 **Blog** Short for "Weblog," a blog is a personal Web page where you can post information about anything that touches your life. There are several free blog services on the Internet. Under the direction of your teacher, you might be able to choose one and post your article.

Add Visuals If you publish your article in a newspaper or on a Web site, you may be asked to provide several photos about your topic. If you own a camera or can buy a disposable camera, you can take your own photos. Or, you can ask people you interviewed to contribute their photos. Just be sure to get permission either way. Here are some suggestions for gathering good photos:

1 **Choose Interesting Images** Along with the headline, a photo is the first thing that grabs the reader's attention. Choose interesting photos that give a hint about your topic.

2 **Crop Large Photos** Newspapers have a limited amount of space, so photos are usually small. If the image you want to show is only one part of your photo, you can crop, or cut, it to get a smaller, more focused image.

3 **Write Descriptive Captions** A caption is a small bit of text that is placed beneath or beside a photo. Keep your captions brief but be sure to explain how the photo is related to the article.

📖 **Language and Learning Handbook**, p. 633

Publishing Tip

If your teacher has you publish your article on the Internet, you need to format it to make it easy to read on a computer screen.

When you write for the Web, you do not indent paragraphs. Instead, you leave a space between them.

Reflect on Your Work

▶ **Ask for and use feedback from your audience to evaluate your strengths as a writer.**

• Did your audience like your headline?

• Did your audience feel that your article contained interesting and necessary information?

• What would you like to do better the next time you write? Set a goal for your next writing project.

☑ **Save a copy of your work in your portfolio.**

EQ ESSENTIAL QUESTION:

Do We Find or Create Our True Selves?

People often say that this or that person has not yet found himself. But the self is not something one finds; it is something one creates.

—THOMAS S. SZASZ

When I discover who I am, I'll be free.

—RALPH ELLISON

Critical Viewing ▶
In a remote village in Kosovo, bride Rasima Biljibani is transformed by traditional wedding clothing and face decoration. What does this photo suggest about the bride's true self?

TRUE
SELF

EQ ESSENTIAL QUESTION:
Do We Find or Create Our True Selves?

Study the Cartoon

Some people choose clothes that express who they are as individuals. Others prefer to dress like their friends and peers. Look at the cartoon. Read the caption, and think about what it means. Then answer the questions below.

"It lets me be me."

Analyze and Debate

1. Can people really feel more like themselves when they wear certain clothes?

2. Do most teens choose clothes that express who they are as individuals, or do they choose clothes that make them feel like they belong to a group? In what situations might people use clothing to hide their true selves?

3. Can a person create an identity through his or her choice of clothes?

Talk with a group. Explain your opinion and support your ideas with evidence from your own experience. Listen to the other group members' opinions. Take notes so you can ask questions.

EQ ESSENTIAL QUESTION

In this unit, you will explore the **Essential Question** in class through reading, discussion, research, and writing. Keep thinking about the question outside of school, too.

❶ Plan a Project

Gallery Walk

In this unit, you will create a group project and participate in a gallery walk—a critical review of all group projects. Your product should answer the Essential Question. Consider

- a collection of art or photos, with captions
- a song, poem, story, or other writing
- a video recording of a play or other performance.

Study Skills Start planning your project. Ask each person to say what he or she wants to create. Vote to determine the most popular choice. Elect a group leader who will decide how each group member will contribute. Use the forms on myNGconnect.com to plan your time and to prepare the content.

myNGconnect.com
- ▸ Planning forms
- ▸ Sample gallery walk projects
- ▸ Summary of a gallery walk
- ▸ Scheduler
- ▸ Rubric

❷ Choose More to Read

These readings provide different answers to the Essential Question. Choose a book and online selections to read during the unit.

Stargirl
by Jerry Spinelli

Stargirl is not like other people at her school. She wears weird clothes, dances in the rain, and attracts Leo. The other students think she is different. Eventually, Leo thinks so, too. Can Stargirl change, or will the students accept her for who she is?

▸ NOVEL

Out of War
by Sara Cameron

Colombian children know about violence. Their country has been at war for more than forty years. Some courageous young Colombians take action. They want to restore peace to their country. Juan Elias, Farlis, Beto, Johemir, and Alberto build hope for Colombia's future.

▸ NONFICTION

Dr. Jekyll and Mr. Hyde
by Robert Louis Stevenson

Dr. Jekyll has a secret—a powerful drug that turns him into a monster. By day, he is a kind man. But at night he becomes the awful Edward Hyde. Which is more powerful? Can Jekyll control his dark side, or will his dark side control him? Explore how this classical story influences modern literature.

▸ CLASSIC

myNGconnect.com

- 🌐 Take a personality test to find out about your "true self."
- 🌐 Read about peer pressure.
- 🌐 Find out how well you resist peer pressure.

SHORT STORIES

Many stories are told, or narrated, by one of the characters in the story. Pay attention to who is telling the story. You will then get an idea about what you can believe and what you cannot. Read these monologues, or little speeches, to see how this works.

DEMO TEXT #1

I cannot believe that they grounded me for that. Who do they think they are, anyway? They are SO unfair. So what if I took a few bucks from my mother's purse? She would have given it to me anyway. I just didn't feel like asking.

DEMO TEXT #2

Man, my mom must have really been tired last night. I will admit that my room was a little messy, but she just went crazy when she saw my papers and stuff spread out on the floor. I am not sure why she got so upset—maybe she is really tired. I know her job is pretty demanding. But she should know I always pick up my papers eventually. I just like to spread out and do my homework.

DEMO TEXT #3

I am so stressed, and things at home are not making it any easier for me. Chores, chores, chores—that is all I do. All I hear is "Take your dishes to the sink. Take out the garbage. Bring down your laundry so I can do it." All that for a measly $10 a week allowance. And then every night they ask me whether I have done my homework. My parents are a pain. It is a miracle I have made it this far without having a breakdown.

Connect Reading to Your Life

Reading Strategies
- Plan and Monitor
- Determine Importance
- ▶ **Make Inferences**
- Ask Questions
- Make Connections
- Synthesize
- Visualize

The person telling a story is called the **narrator** . With a partner, decide which narrator in the Demo Texts is the most honest and believable and which is least believable. Think about:

- What makes you believe one narrator over another?
- What makes you suspicious of what a narrator says?
- What do you think the truth of the situation is?

> I think the kid in #3 is pretty believable.

> I don't think so. That guy sounds like he is only thinking about himself.

	Demo Text #	Reasons
Most Believable Character:		
Least Believable Character:		

Focus Strategy ▶ Make Inferences

When you decide a narrator might not be giving you the whole story or telling you the truth about something, you need to figure out that truth for yourself. When you do this, you are making a very important kind of **inference**.

You make these kinds of inferences all the time in your everyday life. For example: Two of your friends get into a disagreement, and they both tell you about it. You probably do not believe *either one* of them entirely. It is the same when you watch TV or a movie. You know that some characters are more believable than others. You have to put things together to figure out what really happened.

Elements of Literature
narrator *n.*, the person who tells a story

Academic Vocabulary
- **inference** *n.*, a good guess based on evidence and knowledge; **infer** *v.*, to make a good guess based on evidence and knowledge

■ Your Job as a Reader

A story with a **first-person** narrator—a story told by one of the characters—has a first-person point of view. With this kind of story, it is important to realize that everything you know about the story comes from that one person. You have to decide just how believable that narrator is. Whenever you think that the narrator is not giving you the whole story, it's your job to figure out what really happened.

■ Unpack the Thinking Process

First-Person Point of View

In your everyday life, there are some things that cause you to believe people and some things that make you question them. For example, if a person is very young, you may **assume** that he or she might not have all the facts. As you read, you should also remember that the narrator might not have all the facts. Reread the Demo Texts.

> **DEMO TEXT #1**
>
> I cannot believe that they grounded me for that. Who do they think they are, anyway? They are SO unfair. So what if I took a few bucks from my mother's purse? She would have given it to me anyway. I just didn't feel like asking.

This narrator is only seeing things from his viewpoint, or **perspective**. You may not believe that his parents are unfair, but you can believe that he took money.

> **DEMO TEXT #2**
>
> Man, my mom must have really been tired last night. I will admit that my room was a little messy, but she just went crazy … I know her job is pretty demanding. But she should know I always pick up my papers eventually…

Whether or not you believe the narrator's view of the conflict, you probably *do* believe that the narrator's mother has a demanding job.

Elements of Literature
first-person *adj.*, referring to a narrator who uses pronouns such as *I* and *me*

Academic Vocabulary
- **assume** *v.*, to think that something is true; to suppose
- **perspective** *n.*, a specific angle from which something is viewed or observed

I am so stressed, and things at home are not making it any easier for me. Chores, chores, chores—that is all I do. All I hear is "Take your dishes to the sink. Take out the garbage. Bring down your laundry so I can do it." All that for a measly $10 a week allowance. And then every night they ask me whether I have done my homework. My parents are a pain. It is a miracle I have made it this far without having a breakdown.

You may not believe that the parents are unreasonable, but you probably *do* believe the list of chores and the amount of the allowance.

Once you have identified some facts that you can be sure of, use what you know about the world to make sense of those facts. When you read a story with a first-person narrator, *your* understanding of the situation might be better than the narrator's. A first-person narrator only knows other characters, the plot, and the setting from his or her point of view.

■ Try an Experiment

Add words and phrases to this monologue to show that the narrator is not believable.

My parents are totally _____ . They want me to study every night—and on the weekends. My dad is always telling me to study hard so that I can get a good job. He says, "_____ ." But school is so _____ ! Everybody I know thinks school _____ . What I really want to do is play my music. I've got a bunch of talent. My guitar teacher said, "_____ ." Why don't my parents leave me alone? All I want to do is play my _____ music.

Dramatize and Discuss Act out your completed monologue for a small group. Listen to other students' monologues. Then answer these questions:

1. Which narrator was most unbelievable?

2. What made you suspicious of what that character said?

Monitor Comprehension

First-Person Point of View Why should you question a first-person narrator's point of view?

PREPARE TO READ

▶ **Heartbeat**
▶ **Zits**
▶ **Behind the Bulk**
▶ **Training Tips**

EQ Do We Find or Create Our True Selves?
Explore whether appearance matters.

Make a Connection

Give Your Opinion Tell a partner whether you agree or disagree with this statement: How you look on the outside shows what you think of yourself. Give reasons to support your opinion.

Learn Key Vocabulary

Study the Words Pronounce each word and learn its meaning. You may also want to look up the definitions in the Glossary.

● Academic Vocabulary

Key Words	Examples
appearance (u-**pear**-uns) *noun* ▶ pages 193, 199, 202	Your **appearance** is the way you look. Changing your hairstyle can completely change your **appearance**.
● **depressed** (di-**prest**) *adjective* ▶ page 192	A **depressed** person is sad. Some people get **depressed** during the dark, cold days of winter. *Synonym:* unhappy; *Antonym:* happy
● **distorted** (di-**stor**-ted) *adjective* ▶ pages 201, 204	A **distorted** image is twisted out of shape and does not appear natural or real. **Distorted** facts do not represent the truth very well.
illusion (i-**lü**-zhun) *noun* ▶ page 193	An **illusion** is an image that doesn't match what is real. When a magician changes flowers into a bird, it is not a real change. It is an **illusion**.
● **normal** (**nor**-mul) *adjective* ▶ page 197	On a **normal**, or ordinary, school day, the first class begins at 8:00 in the morning and the last class ends at 3:00 in the afternoon. *Synonym:* usual; *Antonyms:* odd, unusual
solution (su-**lü**-shun) *noun* ▶ pages 193, 199, 204, 207	A **solution** is the answer to a problem. Better public transportation is one **solution** to traffic problems. *Synonym:* answer; *Antonym:* problem
● **transform** (trans-**form**) *verb* ▶ page 194	When you **transform** something, you change it into something else. You can **transform** a dark room by painting the walls white. *Synonym:* change
weight (wāt) *noun* ▶ pages 192, 201, 207	An object's **weight** tells you how heavy it is. Someone can also lift **weights**, a certain kind of gym equipment, to build muscles.

Practice the Words Work with a partner. Make a **Definition Map** for each Key Vocabulary word. Use a dictionary to find other forms of the word. Take turns listening to each other pronounce the new words. Help each other with any difficult syllables.

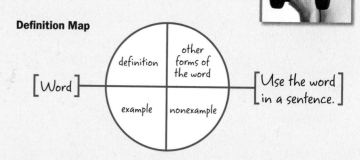

Definition Map

definition / other forms of the word / example / nonexample

[Word] — [Use the word in a sentence.]

BEFORE READING Heartbeat

short story by David Yoo

Reading Strategies

• Plan and Monitor
• Determine Importance
▶ **Make Inferences**
• Ask Questions
• Make Connections
• Synthesize
• Visualize

Analyze Point of View

The narrator is the person who tells the story. A first-person narrator tells the story using *I*, *me*, and *my*. When you read a story with a first-person narrator, you see the characters and events only through the eyes of that character.

Look Into the Text

The narrator uses first-person pronouns when referring to himself.

My nickname's "Heartbeat," because my friends swear that you can actually see the pulse on my bare chest. I've always been skinny. Everyone assumes I'm a weakling because I'm so thin (I prefer "lean and mean" or "wiry"), despite being a three-sport athlete. I decided to do something about it this fall when Sarah, the girl I have a crush on, said "Oh my God…you are so skinny." She was visibly repulsed by my sunken chest as I stepped off the soccer bus after practice. I silently vowed to do everything within my power to become the "after" picture. I was sixteen years old, but looked like I was eleven.

The narrator tells what he thinks and feels. How do you know if it is true?

Focus Strategy ▶ Make Inferences

We **make inferences** every day. Suppose you know that a big project is due. Your friend looks tired. When you ask him about the project, he says, "No big deal. It was easy." His appearance, however, leads you to infer that he stayed up late doing the project. As you read, you make inferences like this, too. Try this strategy with the text above.

HOW TO MAKE INFERENCES

Focus Strategy

1. Look for clues in the text.

YOU READ: Everyone assumes I'm a weakling because I'm so thin (I prefer "lean and mean" or "wiry"), despite being a three-sport athlete.

2. Think about what you know about people like the narrator. What does your experience tell you?

YOU KNOW: Guys, especially athletes, often want to look tough and strong. They can get upset if they don't.

3. Combine what you know with what you read to make an inference.

AND SO: "Heartbeat" is upset about how people think he looks.

David Yoo
(1974–   )

A story could take me fifty hours: forty-eight hours of sitting there thinking and two hours of actual writing. The thinking is the hard part.

David Yoo lives near Boston, Massachusetts.

David Yoo's parents moved to the United States from Korea in the 1960s. Then the family returned to Korea for a few years when Yoo and his sister were young. The children grew up speaking English and Korean. Eventually, both Yoo and his sister became writers. His parents, who are not native English speakers, find it amusing that both their children now write in English for a living.

Most of Yoo's stories are funny. He says, "If readers can laugh, they keep reading." He says that he would never want to write something just to teach a lesson. He also "would never want to read something that sounds like the guy is whining."

Yoo says he writes like this because the books he enjoys reading are funny. He looks for comedy in the movies he sees, too. Looking at the funny side of life helps him write about difficult situations. "Humor is like a protective blanket. It makes it easier to talk about things that otherwise would be too hard to face or write about."

myNGconnect.com

⬤ Visit David Yoo's Web site.
⬤ Read an interview with David Yoo.

HEARTBEAT

by David Yoo

Comprehension Coach

**A boy thinks he is too thin.
Find out what he does to look bigger.**

My nickname's "Heartbeat," because my friends swear that you can actually see the pulse on my bare chest. I've always been skinny. Everyone assumes I'm a weakling because I'm so thin (I prefer "lean and mean" or "**wiry**"), despite being a three-sport athlete. **1** I decided to do something about it this fall when Sarah, the girl I have a crush on, said, "Oh my God . . . you are so skinny." She was visibly repulsed by my sunken chest as I stepped off the soccer bus after practice. I silently vowed to do everything within my power to **become the "after" picture**. I was sixteen years old, but looked like I was eleven.

For the rest of fall, I did countless push-ups and curled free **weights** until I couldn't bend my arms. I got ridiculously strong and defined, but I wasn't gaining **weight**. I wanted to be *thicker*. I didn't care about getting stronger if nobody could tell. I did research, and started lifting heavier weights at lower reps and supplemented my meals with weight-gainer shakes, egg whites, boiled yams, and tubs of cottage cheese. I forced myself to swallow the daily caloric intake equivalent of three overweight men and still wasn't able to increase my mass. (**I have a ridiculously fast metabolism**.) **2** Over Christmas break I cut out all useless movement, like Ping-Pong and staircases because **I'm like a sieve**—the 83 calories in a mini-Snickers bar is moot because I waste 90 chewing it.

I returned to school in January **depressed**, because I was still Heartbeat in everyone's eyes. I constantly weighed myself. At least once an hour, no matter where I was, I'd find a bathroom so I could

1 Inferences
What can you infer about this character based on what he shares so far? Is he concerned about what others think of him? Explain your answer.

2 Access Vocabulary
What clues from the paragraph help you figure out the meaning of *mass*? Give a synonym for this word.

Key Vocabulary
weight *n.*, 1: heavy gym equipment used for exercising 2: how heavy an object is
● **depressed** *adj.*, unhappy, sad

In Other Words
wiry thin, but strong and tough
become the "after" picture look like the strong guy in an advertisement
I have a ridiculously fast metabolism. My body uses up food really fast.
I'm like a sieve food goes right through me

take off my shirt and **flex** in the mirror for a couple of minutes. I was so frustrated that nothing was working—but the frustration didn't last. I was sitting in study hall two weeks ago when Sarah said the magic words: "Have you been working out, Dave? You look bigger." **3** I couldn't tell if she was **being sarcastic**. I went home and inspected myself in the mirror. I did look bigger! But then I realized the reason: I'd accidentally worn *two* T-shirts under my rugby shirt that day. It was just an **illusion**. I was **futilely stuffing my face and religiously pumping iron** and failing to alter my **appearance**, and now I'd stumbled on the simplest **solution** to looking bigger. I felt like I was reborn.

I went to school the next day wearing two T-shirts under my turtleneck. I felt solid. By the end of last week, I was wearing three T-shirts under my rugby shirt. This Monday I tucked four T-shirts under my plaid button-down. It gave me **traps** that didn't exist. My Q-tip–sized shoulders

3 Inferences
How does Dave feel about what Sarah says? Use what you know to infer how Dave feels.

transformed into **NBA-grapefruit deltoids**. I could tell my classmates subtly regarded me differently. It was respect. [4] Sarah gave me a look I'd never seen before, as if she felt . . . *safer* around me. I was walking down the hallway at the end of the day and must have twisted awkwardly because suddenly my zipper literally exploded, and all my T-shirts spilled out of my pants. Luckily, the hallway was empty and I was wearing a belt.

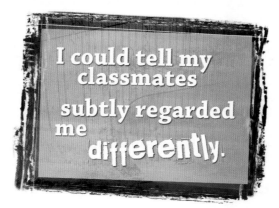

I could tell my classmates subtly regarded me differently.

I realized I had artificially outgrown my clothes. My button-downs were so tight that a few seconds after jamming the extra layers into my pants, the pressure would suddenly bunch the cloth up in random places so it looked like I had a **goiter** on my shoulder or something. I complained to my parents over dinner last night. "I don't fit into anything anymore," I said. "It reflects poorly on you guys. You could get arrested."

"What are you talking about? You look the same as always. You're still my little boy," my dad replied, putting me in a headlock and giving me a noogie. I glared at him.

"I need a new ski jacket," I said. It was true. I could barely clap my hands with all the layers I was wearing. I was getting out of control at this point. The four T-shirts under my wool sweater were smushing my lungs together like a male girdle. It was a small price to pay; nobody called me Heartbeat anymore, I reminded myself. [5]

[4] **Point of View/ Inferences**
Do people really respect Dave more, now that he looks bigger? Why do you think so?

[5] **Point of View/ Inferences**
Is Dave a reliable narrator? Does he really need new clothes? Explain your answer.

Monitor Comprehension

Summarize
Describe the steps that Dave takes to change his appearance. What finally works?

Key Vocabulary
• **transform** *v.*, to change into something else

In Other Words
NBA-grapefruit deltoids large, muscular shoulders like a professional basketball player's
goiter large bump

Predict

Has Dave found a solution to his problem?

After dinner I went to a party. Even though it was winter, I **opted to hang out** on the back porch as much as possible because it was so hot inside. Being indoors was like a sauna, but Sarah was in the basement so I headed that way. We were talking and she noticed that I was dripping with **perspiration**. "You're trembling," she said, touching my shoulder. **6** She thought I was nervous talking to her and probably thought it was cute, but in reality I was on the verge of passing out because I was wearing four tight T-shirts and two long-sleeves under my wool sweater, not to mention the sweatpants tucked into my tube socks to **add heft to my (formerly chicken-legs) quads**. She squeezed my **biceps**.

6 Inferences
Interpret Sarah's reaction. What do her words and actions tell you about how she feels toward Dave?

In Other Words
opted to hang out chose to stay
perspiration sweat
add heft to my (formerly chicken-legs) quads
   make my thin leg muscles look bigger
biceps upper arm muscles

"Jeez, Dave, how many layers are you wearing?" **7**

I couldn't even feel her squeezing them.

"I have to go," I said, excusing myself to another corner of the basement. Everyone was smushed together. It was so hot everyone except me was hanging out in T-shirts and tank tops. I was sopping and delirious and felt **claustrophobic**. My chest was cold because I had four drenched T-shirts underneath my sweater. It looked like I was breaking out with **Ebola** or something. When I coughed, people turned away from me in fear. *Abandon ship, abandon ship!* **8** I had no choice but to take some layers off. I lurched to the bathroom. My arms were ponderously heavy as I pulled off the sweater. Just lifting my arms exhausted me, and I had to stop midway and take a rest by sitting on the edge of the tub, gasping. I slowly peeled off the layers, one at a time. I took off my pants and

7 Inferences
What does Sarah's question tell you about Dave's appearance?

8 Language
When do people abandon, or leave, a ship? What does this reference tell you about Dave's plans?

In Other Words
claustrophobic as if I were stuck in a small space
Ebola a disease

peeled off my sweatpants, too, down to my undies. I dried myself off with a washcloth. My red T-shirt had bled onto the three white Ts because of the sweat, so they now were **faded pink tie-dyes**. I hoisted the bundle of clothes and was shocked at the weight. I jammed them into the closet. I'd retrieve them later, before I left.

I put my sweater back on without anything underneath. After two weeks of constricting my air supply and **range of motion** by wearing upwards of six layers, I was amazed at how much freedom I had with my arms. I felt like dancing for the first time in my life. **9** I suddenly realized what I really looked like at this party: a padded, miserable, and frustrated puffball, burning up in all my layers. All this because I hated my nickname?

I got home and realized I'd left my bundle of wet clothes back at the party. I took this as a sign. My days of wearing extra layers were officially over. Had Sarah fallen for the padded me, she'd be falling for someone else. Besides, winter wasn't going to last forever, and I couldn't just revert back to wearing just one set of clothes like a **normal** human being come spring. The change in my outward appearance would be **the equivalent of a sheared sheep**. From now on, I was going to just be me.

> My days of wearing extra layers were officially over.

That was last night. *I'm not disgustingly thin*, I constantly remind myself. I am wiry. I'm lean and mean. Outside it's snowing again.

9 Inferences
What emotion does Dave feel now? How do you know that?

Key Vocabulary
● **normal** *adj.*, usual, ordinary

In Other Words
faded pink tie-dyes stained with pink spots
range of motion ability to move freely
the equivalent of a sheared sheep just like that of a sheep with its wool cut off

There's a party tonight, and my friends are on their way to pick me up. I don't know what to wear, so I lay out four different outfits on the floor as if they're chalk outlines of people. A car horn honks ten minutes later and I still haven't decided on an outfit. Maybe I'll just wear all of them. ⑩ ❖

10 Inferences
Is Dave joking or serious when he says he'll "wear all of them"? Which clues in the story influence your thinking?

POSTSCRIPT

Zits by Jerry Scott and Jim Borgman

ANALYZE Heartbeat

1. **Confirm Prediction** Does Dave's **solution** work? Explain.

2. **Vocabulary** Do you think Sarah shares Dave's opinion of his own **appearance**? Why do you think so?

3. **Analyze Point of View** Use a chart to record examples of Dave's opinions about what others think of him. Discuss with a partner whether you agree or disagree with Dave. Tell why.

Dave's Opinion	Agree/Disagree	Why
Everyone assumes I'm a weakling.	disagree	He is a three-sport athlete.
I was still Heartbeat in everyone's eyes.		

4. **Focus Strategy Make Inferences** Describe an inference you made about Sarah. Explain what helped you make that inference.

Return to the Text

Reread and Write What do you think Dave discovers about his true self? Reread the story and look for clues. Write a paragraph that explains what Dave discovers about himself.

informative article by Cate Baily

Reading Strategies

- Plan and Monitor
- Determine Importance
▶ **Make Inferences**
- Ask Questions
- Make Connections
- Synthesize
- Visualize

Analyze Point of View

Nonfiction, like fiction, is written from a particular **point of view**. This article uses the **third-person point of view** to tell about another person's experience.

Look Into the Text

These pronouns show third-person point of view.

A third-person narrator can give facts from research.

> Every time he passed a mirror, Craig flexed his muscles. He wanted to look "insanely big—like an action figure."
>
> "When I walked into a room, I wanted heads to turn," he says. People did notice Craig's 225-pound, 5-foot-9-inch frame. But what they didn't see was the physical damage and psychological turmoil going on inside.
>
> The story behind the bulk was five years of steroid abuse and a struggle with muscle dysmorphia. Muscle dysmorphia is a condition in which a person has a distorted image of his or her body. Men with this condition think that they look small and weak, even if they are large and muscular.

The writer uses a quote to tell what the subject, Craig, says and thinks.

Focus Strategy ▶ Make Inferences

When you read, pay attention to all of the information the writer gives. Use one part of the text to **make inferences** about another part.

HOW TO MAKE INFERENCES

Focus Strategy

1. First you read: | He wanted to look "insanely big—like an action figure."

   YOU KNOW: Action figures have big muscles.

   YOU INFER: Craig wanted to have big muscles.

2. Later you read: | The story behind the bulk was five years of steroid abuse and a struggle with muscle dysmorphia.

   YOU REMEMBER: Craig wanted to have big muscles.

3. Put the ideas together.

   YOU INFER: Craig abused steroids and had problems about how he thought about his muscles.

Behind the Bulk

BY CATE BAILY

Connect Across Texts

In "Heartbeat," Dave learns to accept the way he looks. Read this informative article about a young man who tries to build up his body.

Every time he passed a mirror, Craig flexed his muscles. He wanted to look "insanely big—like an action figure."

"When I walked into a room, I wanted **heads to turn**," he says. People did notice Craig's 225-pound, 5-foot 9-inch **frame**. But what they didn't see was the physical damage and **psychological turmoil** going on inside.

The story behind the bulk was five years of **steroid abuse** and a struggle with muscle dysmorphia. Muscle dysmorphia is a condition in which a person has a **distorted** image of his or her body. Men with this condition think that they look small and weak, even if they are large and muscular.

Illegal and Grim

It all started when Craig was 18. Before a summer trip to Orlando, Florida, he was feeling overweight. He wanted to look good, so he resolved to get fit. Running on the treadmill, he slimmed down fast, losing 20 pounds in a month. **1**

But lean wasn't Craig's ideal. "I wanted people to say, 'That guy's huge.'" He lifted **weights** and experimented with steroidal **supplements**, also called dietary supplements. These drugs promise to build muscles. Despite potential risks and unclear effectiveness, they can be bought legally over the counter at many stores.

But what Craig was looking for couldn't be bought in a store. So he turned to anabolic steroids.

Anabolic steroids have some **legitimate** medical uses when taken under a doctor's supervision. But to use steroids for muscle-building in a healthy body is illegal. This didn't

1 Inferences
Do you think Craig ran on the treadmill a lot or a little? Use what you know about weight loss to answer.

Key Vocabulary
- **distorted** *adj.*, twisted out of shape, not representing the truth
- **weight** *n.*, heavy gym equipment used for exercising

In Other Words
heads to turn people to notice me
frame body
psychological turmoil mental confusion
steroid abuse incorrect use of a medical drug
supplements pills
legitimate real, valuable

stop Craig. Neither did the many **grim potential side effects**.

Craig thought he knew exactly what he was getting into. Like 4% of high school seniors and an estimated hundreds of thousands of adults, he took steroids anyway. **2**

Heart Problems

Craig's **appearance** was that important to him. "The scale was my enemy. Every pound meant so much to me," he says.

Craig constantly compared himself to others. He drove his friends and family crazy asking, "Is that guy bigger than me? What about that guy?"

He never had complete satisfaction. "Some days, I'd be **arrogant**, wearing shorts to show off my quads. Other days, I'd be a disaster. On those days, I'd have to wear big, baggy clothes." **3**

Craig's steroid use **escalated** over time. He had begun by taking oral steroids (pills) exclusively. But when he heard that injectable steroids were more effective, he overcame a fear of needles. At his worst, he was injecting three to four times and taking ten pills a day.

The drugs **took their toll**. Craig's hair fell out. Acne popped up all over his back. His face swelled. Then, something even more serious happened: he started having chest pains.

How Weight Training Builds Muscle

Muscle fibers contain long myofibrils, which are made up of strands of protein. When you lift weights, the protein strands get larger. This causes the muscle fibers to expand.

Muscle Before Training

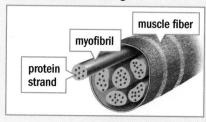

Muscle After Training

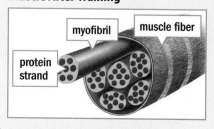

▲ **Interpret the Diagrams** Which part of a muscle fiber gets larger and causes the muscle fiber to expand?

2 Point of View/ Inferences
What information in this paragraph is not part of Craig's story? What do you think the author accomplishes by adding this information?

3 Inferences
Think about what you've read about muscle dysmorphia. Now think about Craig's behavior. What can you infer about muscle dysmorphia?

Key Vocabulary
appearance *n.*, the way someone or something looks

In Other Words
grim potential side effects other bad things the steroids could do to his body
arrogant really proud
escalated increased
took their toll hurt Craig's body

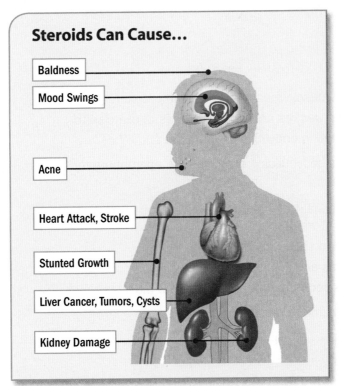

Steroids Can Cause...

- Baldness
- Mood Swings
- Acne
- Heart Attack, Stroke
- Stunted Growth
- Liver Cancer, Tumors, Cysts
- Kidney Damage

▲ Interpret the Diagram Name three problems that steroids can cause.

New Priorities

Craig was having other problems, too. Craig, then 25, was screaming and yelling at his wife a lot. Ultimately, his marriage ended. He lost a **custody battle** over his 1-year-old son, Jake. Craig's wife said that Craig couldn't see their child until he passed a drug test. **4**

That was the moment when everything changed for Craig. He knew he had to quit.

On Father's Day, Craig **went cold turkey**. He knew he needed help, so his parents found him a psychiatrist, who treated him through **the better part of a** year.

Today, Craig's **priorities** have changed. He still wants to be a head-turner, but for a different reason. "Now I'd rather be walking into a room with my son and have people thinking, 'Wow, he's the greatest dad in the world.'"

4 Inferences
How did Craig's wife feel about steroids? How did you infer that?

Monitor Comprehension

Explain
What changed Craig's opinion about using steroids?

In Other Words
custody battle legal fight with his wife
went cold turkey completely quit taking steroids
the better part of a most of the
priorities values

Training Tips

You can stay in shape and build muscle mass naturally, without steroids. Running, riding a bike, and lifting weights are excellent forms of exercise to get or stay fit. If you are interested in bodybuilding, here are some tips:

Check with a doctor. Make sure bodybuilding exercises are appropriate for you.

Lift weights the right way.

- Work with a coach or a personal trainer to figure out how many repetitions ("reps") you should do and at what speed.
- Follow a regular schedule and stick with it.
- Always do warm-up exercises and cool-down exercises.

Eat right. You have to practice good nutrition to build up your muscles.

Get enough rest. Muscles need time to recover from training.

ANALYZE Behind the Bulk

1. **Explain** In what specific ways was Craig affected by taking steroids? Support your answer with evidence from the text.

2. **Vocabulary** Why are steroids a bad **solution** for people who think they look too weak?

3. **Analyze Point of View** Think about how the writer tells Craig's story. How might the facts be **distorted** if Craig had written the article himself? Explain.

4. **Focus Strategy** **Make Inferences** Do you think Craig will ever take steroids again? What clues in the text helped you figure this out?

   Return to the Text
   Reread and Write Why do you think Craig and other athletes take steroids even though the drugs damage their bodies? Look for clues as you reread the article. Write your opinion. Provide at least two reasons.

Key Vocabulary
  solution *n.*, answer to a problem

EQ Do We Find or Create Our True Selves?

Critical Thinking

1. **Compare** Return to the statement you discussed in Make a Connection on page 188. Compare how Dave and Craig would respond to this statement. Use evidence from the text to support your answer.

EQ 2. **Interpret** Do Dave and Craig find their true selves, or do they create their true selves? Explain.

3. **Generalize** Think about all the selections, including the cartoon. How much does what people think about themselves depend on what others think?

4. **Imagine** If you could talk to Dave, what advice would you give him? What advice would you give Craig? Use evidence from the text in your advice.

EQ 5. **Assess** How much does our **appearance** reflect our true selves? Use Dave's and Craig's experiences to help you answer.

Write About Literature

Explanation Why do people worry about how they look to others? Write a short explanation, using examples from both texts.

Key Vocabulary Review

Oral Review Work with a partner. Use these words to complete the paragraph.

appearance	illusion	transform
depressed	normal	weight
distorted	solution	

For some people, it's __(1)__ to be __(2)__ about their looks, or __(3)__. This is a shame, because most of us have a __(4)__ view of how others see us. We may think we should lose __(5)__ or wish we could __(6)__ ourselves overnight into good-looking people. But beauty is just an __(7)__. The reality is that each person is unique and special. Nearly everyone has some attractive qualities. The __(8)__ to the problem is to remind yourself of your good points.

Writing Application Describe a time when you or someone you know was really **depressed** or worried about physical appearance. What happened? Use at least four Key Vocabulary words in your description.

Read with Ease: Intonation

Assess your reading fluency with the passage in the Reading Handbook, p. 671. Then complete the self-check below.

1. I did/did not raise and lower the pitch of my voice as I read.

2. My words correct per minute: _____.

INTEGRATE THE LANGUAGE ARTS

Grammar

Use Verb Tenses

Use the **present tense** to tell about an action that happens now or happens often.

> The boy **checks** himself in the mirror, **flexes** his muscles, and **walks** away.

Use a verb in the **past tense** to show an action that already happened. Past tense verbs often end in **-ed**.

> The boy **checked** himself in the mirror, **flexed** his muscles, and **walked** away.

Some irregular verbs, such as **have** and **be**, have special forms to show past tense:

- **Present:** Dave's friends **have** a nickname for him. Dave **has** the nickname Heartbeat.

  Past: Dave's friends **had** a nickname for him. Dave **had** the nickname Heartbeat.

- **Present:** Dave **is** unhappy. His muscles **are** not big. "I **am** too skinny," he says.

  Past: Dave **was** unhappy. His muscles **were** not big. "I **was** too skinny," he said.

Oral Practice (1–5) Tell a partner what you did last week to stay healthy. Use two or three past tense verbs in each sentence.

Written Practice (6–9) Rewrite each sentence. Change the verbs to the past tense.

6. Dave <u>wants</u> big muscles.
7. He <u>has</u> a plan and <u>follows</u> it.
8. He <u>is</u> fit and strong.
9. He <u>gains</u> no weight, <u>is</u> healthier, and <u>smiles</u> more.

Language Development

Give and Respond to Commands

Role Play With a partner, take turns playing the roles of Dave from "Heartbeat" and one of Dave's friends. The friend tells Dave what exercises to do. Dave responds by doing what the friend tells him.

Literary Analysis

Analyze Point of View

In the **third-person limited point of view**, the narrator focuses on describing the actions, thoughts, and feelings of a single person or character.

In "Behind the Bulk," for example, the narrator quotes Craig and describes his thoughts and feelings. The narrator does not quote Craig's wife, son, or parents or reveal their thoughts and feelings. The narrator tells only Craig's version of events.

With a small group, discuss the questions below to get a better understanding of third-person limited point of view.

- How would the article be different if the narrator told someone else's version of what happened? For example, how would you feel about Craig if you had read his son's version of what happened?

- How would the article be different if the narrator revealed the thoughts and feelings of everyone involved? For example, how would you feel about Craig if you read how his wife and parents felt about his steroid abuse?

"If you put me in your novel, could you give me hair?"

Source: ©Henry Martin/*The New Yorker*

Word Families

Knowing the meaning of one word in a **word family** can help you understand the meaning of another word in the family. For example, you know that **depressed** means "sad" or "unhappy." If you see the word *depression* when reading, you might guess that it means "the state of being sad."

The chart shows words that are related to Key Vocabulary words. Figure out what each related word means. Check your definition in a dictionary.

KEY VOCABULARY	RELATED WORD	DEFINITION
appearance	appear	
solution	solve	
weight	weightless	

Critique

Art: Illustrations Review the illustrations in the short story "Heartbeat." Look at pages 191, 193, 195, and 196. Notice the colors, the images in each illustration, and the background graphics. Form an opinion and make some notes about what you think. Then meet in a small group to discuss the art. Start with these questions:

- Do you like the art? Why or why not?
- How well does the art go with the story?

🔖 **Language and Learning Handbook**, page 616

Trait: Organization

Organization is the order in which you put your ideas—which idea you put first, second, next, and so on. There are many good patterns of organization. The pattern you use depends on your purpose for writing.

One way to organize writing that gives an opinion is to begin with a **claim**, a statement that someone could agree or disagree with. Support the claim with details presented in a logical order, such as from most important to least important.

Just OK

> **Swimming is the best form of exercise.** After you swim, you do not smell like sweat! Swimming is an excellent form of cardiovascular exercise. You can build up all the muscles in your body when you swim a lot. Unlike some high-impact sports, swimming doesn't put stress on your body.

The example below has the details in a logical order. The reader finds out the most important details first. Other details that support the claim, but that are not as important, are at the end of the paragraph.

Much Better

> **Swimming is the best form of exercise.** When you do a lot of swimming, you build up all the muscles in your body. It is an excellent form of cardiovascular exercise. Unlike some high-impact sports, swimming doesn't put stress on your body. Plus, after you swim, you do not smell like sweat!

Practice Choose a topic. Form a statement that makes a claim. List details that will help you defend your claim. Number the details to determine a logical sequence for them. Then write your paragraph.

🔖 **Writing Handbook**, page 698

1

Inside a Health Club

Employees in health clubs help their clients get fit and stay healthy. Some employees lead group classes. Others work with clients individually.

Jobs in the Fitness Industry

Some fitness workers are part-time employees. They travel from one club to another to work. Health clubs hire some full-time workers, too. Here are some of the jobs in health clubs and fitness centers.

Job	Responsibilities	Education/Training Required
Group Exercise Instructor **1**	• Leads exercise classes • Demonstrates types of exercises • Helps participants exercise safely	• Experience with how the class is conducted • Successful audition to teach class
Personal Trainer **2**	• Works individually with clients • Develops personalized fitness plans • Helps clients exercise safely • Keeps records of clients' progress	• High school diploma • Certification in a field of fitness • On-the-job training
Fitness Director **3**	• Develops club's fitness programs • Finds new clients • Coordinates class schedules • Manages budget and staff • Purchases exercise equipment	• College degree in exercise science or physical education • College courses in management and accounting • Experience as a fitness worker

2

Write an E-mail Requesting Information

Request information from a health club or fitness center through e-mail.

1. Choose a job that interests you from the chart above. Visit the Web site of a local fitness center. Find the link to the contact information.

2. Write an e-mail requesting more information about job opportunities for your chosen job. Find out what training and skills are required to work at the facility.

3. Print the facility's response and share it with a partner. Discuss what it would be like to work in a fitness center. Save the information in a professional career portfolio.

3

myNGconnect.com

🔊 Learn more about the fitness industry.

🔊 Download an evaluation form to help you decide if you would like to work in this field.

🖱 **Writing Handbook,** p. 698

Use What You Know

If you look at family photographs, you can probably see how family members look alike. Words belong to families, too. If you look closely at a word you do not recognize at first, you can often find a part within it that you *do* know.

Word families are words that share the same root word. These words share a common origin, often in Greek, Latin, or another language. Here is an example: *My friend has a great book collection.* You may not know the word *collection.* However, you probably know the root word *collect.* You could then guess that *collection* has something to do with collecting things. It means "a group of different but related things."

Use Word Families to Find Meaning

Work with a partner to find familiar parts of words to figure out their meanings.

1. Look at some of the words in the *collect* word family.

2. Discuss what each word may mean.

3. Look up each word in the dictionary.

Words in the Collect Family

collector   collection

collectible   collective

Put the Strategy to Use

When you see a word you do not know, use this strategy to figure out its meaning.

1. Look for a root word. Use the word origin to help you understand the root word's meaning.

2. Identify the other part or parts of the word.

3. Figure out how the part you know fits with the other part or parts.

4. Take a guess at the word's meaning.

TRY IT▶ Explore more word families. Copy and complete the chart below. Think about how the root relates to each of the words in the family.

Word	Root Word	Other Words in the Family
1. dishonest		
2. governor		
3. helpless		
4. knowing		

🔖 Reading Handbook, page 647

EQ **Do We Find or Create Our True Selves?**
Find out about people who put themselves in categories.

Make a Connection

Category Chart When people describe themselves, they often put themselves in categories. Think of some categories that people might put themselves in. Then ask yourself which ones you fit in. Does belonging to a category affect who you are? If so, how?

Category Chart

Category	Do I Belong? (yes/no)
brown-eyed	
oldest child in the family	
athletic	

Learn Key Vocabulary

Study the Words Pronounce each word and learn its meaning. You may also want to look up the definitions in the Glossary.

● Academic Vocabulary

Key Words	Examples
advanced (ud-**vanst**) *adjective* ▶ pages 215, 224	An **advanced** class is more challenging than a beginning class. The students in the **advanced** art class draw very well. *Synonym:* higher level; *Antonym:* beginning
● **category** (**ca**-tu-gor-ē) *noun* ▶ pages 226, 228, 229	All items in the same **category** are similar in some way. *Synonyms:* group, set
poet (**pō**-ut) *noun* ▶ page 215	A **poet** is a person who writes poems.
● **potential** (pu-**ten**-shul) *noun* ▶ page 224	If you have the ability to sing very well, you have the **potential** to be a professional singer in the future. *Synonym:* possibility
program (**prō**-gram) *noun* ▶ pages 219, 224	A **program** is a planned event like a concert or a TV show. What TV **program** is your favorite? *Synonyms:* performance, show
realize (**rē**-u-līz) *verb* ▶ page 220	To **realize** something is to figure it out. A math problem may seem hard, but when you solve it, you **realize** it was easy. *Synonym:* know
serious (**sear**-ē-us) *adjective* ▶ page 223	If you are **serious** about something, you are not joking about it. *Synonyms:* truthful, honest; *Antonyms:* kidding, joking
understand (un-dur-**stand**) *verb* ▶ pages 227, 228	To **understand** something is to know its meaning well. Do you **understand** that math problem, or are you still confused? *Synonym:* comprehend

Practice the Words Work with a partner. Write a question using two Key Vocabulary words. Exchange papers and answer your partner's question using at least one Key Vocabulary word. Continue until you have used all words twice.

Example: Do you think you have the potential to be a poet?
No, my interests do not fit in that category.

BEFORE READING I Go Along

short story by Richard Peck

Reading Strategies
· Plan and Monitor
· Determine Importance
▶ **Make Inferences**
· Ask Questions
· Make Connections
· Synthesize
· Visualize

Analyze Point of View

When you read a story that has a **first-person narrator**, you get a personal view of that story. You only get that one person's **ideas and feelings**, though. The narrator cannot really tell you what other characters think or feel.

Look Into the Text

The narrator uses a first-person pronoun when he refers to himself with other story characters.

Anyway, Mrs. Tibbetts comes into the room for second period, so we all see she's still in school. This is the spring she's pregnant, and there are some people making bets about when she's due. The smart money says she'll make it to Easter, and after that we'll have a sub teaching us. Not that we're too particular about who's up there at the front of the room, not in this class.

The writer makes readers feel as if they are in the room, along with the characters.

Being juniors, we also figure we know all there is to know about sex. We know things about sex no adult ever heard of. Still, the sight of a pregnant English teacher slows us down some. But she's married to Roy Tibbetts, a plumber who was in the service and went to jump school, so that's okay. We see him around town in his truck.

The narrator speaks for all juniors at school. Does he know what they think?

Focus Strategy ▶ Make Inferences

A story never tells you everything you need to know in order to understand it fully. You have to fill in the missing information, or **make inferences**, as you read. Use this strategy with the text above.

HOW TO MAKE INFERENCES

Focus Strategy

1. Notice the details in the text.

2. What information can you add that is not in the text? Write an inference to fill in that information.

3. Think again. Consider if your inference is correct.

4. Keep reading to find more evidence.

1. The text says that: The class is not too particular about who the teacher is.

2. I get the idea that: Not one of the students cares about school.

3. It may not be right because: Maybe only the narrator has this opinion. I'll keep reading to find other details.

Richard Peck
(1934–)

Ironically, it was my students who taught me to be a writer, though I had been hired to teach them.

Peck has written more than thirty books. His work gives a true picture of life as a young adult.

You can find a lot of information about award-winning author **Richard Peck** on the Internet, but you won't find his personal Web site. Peck doesn't have a Web site because he doesn't own a computer. That's because he doesn't like computers. He writes all of his stories using a typewriter.

Peck says that as he writes, he looks across his typewriter and imagines the faces of his readers. His favorite audience is teens. "I certainly don't want to write for myself," he explains.

Peck is a former high school teacher. He didn't think he was making an impact on his students, though. He thought he could reach them by writing stories for them. Peck makes his stories realistic by including characters that seem just like his students.

It took a long time for Richard Peck to become a writer. In fact, he didn't write any fiction until he was thirty-seven years old. Still, he was well prepared when he did. "I was born listening," he explains.

myNGconnect.com
- Read an article about Richard Peck.
- Listen to Richard Peck describe his favorite book.

I Go Along

by Richard Peck

▲ Critical Viewing: Effect What kind of feeling do you get from this landscape? How would you feel if you lived nearby?

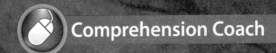
Comprehension Coach

Something unusual happens in class.
Find out what it is.

Anyway, Mrs. Tibbetts comes into the room for second period, so we all see she's still in school. This is the spring she's pregnant, and there are some people making some bets about when she's due. The smart money says she'll make it to Easter, and after that we'll have a sub teaching us. Not that **we're too particular about** who's up there at the front of the room, not in this class.

Being juniors, we also figure we know all there is to know about sex. We know things about sex no adult ever heard of. Still, the sight of a pregnant English teacher slows us down some. But she's married to Roy Tibbetts, a plumber who was in the **service and went to jump school**, so that's okay. We see him around town in his truck. 🔳 1

And right away Darla Craig's hand is up. It's up a lot. She doesn't know any more English than the rest of us, but she likes to talk.

Two Girls 3, 2005, Bekah Ash. Oil on canvas, The Chait Galleries Downtown, Iowa City, Iowa.

1 Point of View
Who is speaking? What part of the text shows that this story has a first-person narrator?

◁ **Critical Viewing: Design**
Notice where the faces are in this painting. What does this design contribute to the general feeling of the painting?

In Other Words
we're too particular about we care
service and went to jump school military and learned to jump out of airplanes with parachutes

"Hey, Mrs. Tibbetts, how come they get to go and we don't?"

She's talking about the first-period people, the **Advanced** English class. Mrs. Tibbetts looks **like Darla's caught her off base**. We never hear what a teacher tells us, but we know this. At least Darla does. ▪2

"I hadn't thought," Mrs. Tibbetts says, rubbing her hand down the small of her back, which may have something to do with being pregnant. So now we're listening, even here in the back row. "For the benefit of those of you who haven't heard," she says, "I'm taking some members of the—other English class over to the college tonight, for a program."

The college in this case is Bascomb College at Bascomb, a thirty-mile trip over an undivided highway.

"We're going to hear a **poet** read from his works."

Somebody halfway back in the room says, "Is he living?" And we all **get a big bang out of this**.

. . . how come they get to go and we don't?

But Mrs. Tibbetts just smiles. "Oh, yes," she says, "he's very much alive."

She reaches for her attendance book, but this sudden thought strikes her. "Would anyone in this class like to go too?" She looks up at us, and you see she's being fair, and nice.

Since it's only the second period of the day, we're all feeling pretty good. Also it's a Tuesday, a terrible TV night. Everybody in the class puts up their hands. I mean everybody. Even Marty Crawshaw, who's already married. And Pink Hohenfield, who's in class today for the first time this month. I put up mine. **I go along.** ▪3

2 Inferences
How does the narrator characterize himself and his classmates? Do you think he is reliable? Explain.

3 Inferences
What does the sentence "I go along" tell you about the narrator? Why do you think the sentence is written in present tense?

Key Vocabulary
advanced *adj.*, more challenging
poet *n.*, person who writes poems

In Other Words
like Darla's caught her off base surprised by Darla's question
get a big bang out of this think this is funny
I go along. I do what everyone else does.

I Go Along **215**

Mrs. Tibbetts looks amazed. She's never seen this many hands up in our class. She's never seen anybody's hand except Darla's. Her eyes get wide. Mrs. Tibbetts has really great eyes, and she doesn't put anything on them. Which is something Darla could learn from.

But then she sees we have to be **putting her on**. So she just says, "Anyone who would like to go, be in the parking lot at five-thirty. And eat first. No eating on the bus."

Mrs. Tibbetts can drive the school bus. Whenever she's taking the advanced class anywhere, she can go to the principal for the keys. She can use the bus anytime she wants to, unless the coach needs it.

Then she opens her attendance book, and we **tune out**. And at five-thirty that night I'm in the parking lot. I have no idea why. **4**

Needless to say, I'm the only one here from second period. Marty Crawshaw and Pink Hohenfield will be out on the access highway about now, at 7-Eleven, sitting on their hoods. Darla couldn't make it either. **Right offhand** I can't think of anybody who wants to ride a school bus thirty miles to see a poet. Including me.

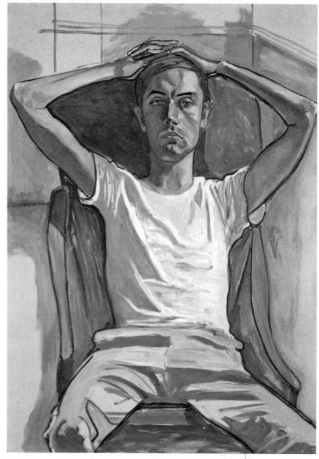

Hartley, 1966, Alice Neel. Oil on canvas, 50x36, National Gallery of Art, Washington, D.C.

 Critical Viewing: Character Look at the boy's expression and the way he is sitting. What can you infer about his character? How would he fit in this story?

4 Inferences
Is the narrator telling the truth when he says he has no idea why he showed up? Explain your answer.

In Other Words
putting her on fooling her, teasing her
tune out stop paying attention
Right offhand At the moment

The Advanced English juniors are milling around behind school. I'm still in my car, and it's almost dark, so nobody sees me.

Then Mrs. Tibbetts wheels the school bus in. She's **got the amber fogs flashing**, and you can see the black letters along the yellow side: CONSOLIDATED SCHOOL DIST. She swings in and hits the brakes, and the doors fly open. The advanced class starts to climb aboard. They're more orderly than us, but they've got their groups too. And a couple of smokers. I'm settling behind my dashboard. The last kid climbs in the bus. **5**

And I seem to be **sprinting across the asphalt**. I'm on the bus, and the door's hissing shut behind me. When I swing past the driver's seat, I don't look at Mrs. Tibbetts, and she doesn't say anything. I wonder where I'm supposed to sit.

They're still milling around in the aisle, but there are plenty of seats. I find an empty double and settle by the window, pulling my ball cap down in front. It doesn't take us long to get out of town, not this town. When we go past 7-Eleven, I'm way down in the seat with my hand **shielding** my face on the window side. Right about then, somebody sits down next to me. I **flinch**.

"Okay?" she says, and I look up, and it's Sharon Willis.

I've got my knee jammed up on the back of the seat ahead of me. I'm bent double, and my hand's over half my face. I'm cool, and it's Sharon Willis.

"Whatever," I say.

"How are you doing, Gene?" **6**

5 Inferences
How does the narrator feel about the advanced class? What part of the text makes you think that?

6 Point of View
What does Sharon tell the reader? Why wasn't this known earlier in the story?

In Other Words
got the amber fogs flashing turned on the yellow lights for driving in fog
sprinting across the asphalt running across the parking lot
shielding covering
flinch move away a little

I'm trying to **be invisible**, and she's calling me by name.

"How do you know me?" I ask her.

She shifts around. "I'm a junior, you're a junior. There are about fifty-three people in our whole year. How could I not?"

Easy, I think, but don't say it. **7** She's got a notebook on her lap. Everybody seems to, except me.

"Do you have to take notes?" I say, because I feel like I'm getting into something here.

"Not really," Sharon says, "but we have to write about it in class tomorrow. **Our impressions.**"

I'm glad I'm not in her class, because I'm not going to have any impressions. Here I am riding the school bus for the **gifted** on a Tuesday night with the major goddess girl in school, who knows my name. I'm going to be clean out of impressions because **my circuits are starting to fail**.

Sharon and I don't turn this into anything. When the bus gets out on the route and Mrs. Tibbetts **puts the pedal to the metal**, we settle back. Sharon's more or less in with a group of the top girls around school. They're not even cheerleaders. They're a notch above that. The rest of them are up and down the aisle, but she stays put. Michelle Burkholder sticks her face down by Sharon's ear and says, "We've got a seat for you back here. Are you coming?" **8**

But Sharon just says, "I'll stay here with Gene." Like it happens every day.

I look out the window a lot. There's still some patchy snow out in the fields, glowing gray. When we get close to the campus of Bascomb College, I think about staying on the bus.

7 Point of View Inferences
Why are Gene's thoughts different from his words? What does that tell you about him as a narrator?

8 Point of View Inferences
What does Gene say about Sharon? Can you trust his words? Why or why not?

In Other Words
be invisible act as if I'm not there
Our impressions. What we think about it.
gifted really smart kids
my circuits are starting to fail I'm too nervous to think clearly
puts the pedal to the metal starts driving fast

On the Bus, 2002, Jo Adang. Oil on canvas, collection of the artist.

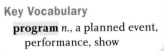 **Critical Viewing: Character** How are these students relating to each other? Explain why you think this.

"Do you want to sit together," Sharon says, "at the **program**?"
I clear my throat. "You go ahead and sit with your people."
"I sit with them all day long," she says. 9

9 Inferences
Why does Sharon continue to sit with Gene? What does this tell you about her?

Monitor Comprehension

Confirm Prediction
Was your prediction correct? Did anything happen that you did not expect? Explain.

Key Vocabulary
program *n.*, a planned event, performance, show

Gene is at the program.
What will he think of it?

At Bascomb College we're up on bleachers in a curtained-off part of the gym. Mrs. Tibbetts says we can sit anywhere we want to, so we get very groupy. I look up, and here I am sitting in these bleachers, like we've gone to **State in the play-offs**. And I'm just naturally here with Sharon Willis.

We're surrounded mainly by college students. The dean of Bascomb College gets up to tell us about the **grant** they got to fund their poetry program. Sharon has her notebook flipped open. I figure it's going to be like a class, so I'm tuning out when the poet comes on.

First of all, he's only in his twenties. Not even a beard, and he's not dressed like a poet. In fact, he's dressed like me: Levi's and Levi's jacket. Big heavy-duty belt buckle. Boots, even. A tall guy, about a hundred and eighty pounds. It's weird, like there could be poets around and you wouldn't **realize** they were there. **10**

But he's **got something.** Every girl leans forward. College girls, even. Michelle Burkholder **bobs up to zap him** with her flash camera.

10 Point of View
How would the last sentence of the paragraph be different from a third-person point of view?

The Student, 2001, Richard Piloco. Oil on canvas, Eleanor Ettinger Gallery, New York.

⚠ **Critical Viewing: Character** What do you think this man is like? What details in the painting make you think so?

Key Vocabulary
realize *v.*, to figure out

In Other Words
State in the play-offs watch our team play in the state tournament
grant money
got something the kind of person that people like
bobs up to zap him jumps up to take a picture of him

He's got a few **loose-leaf** pages in front of him. But he just begins.

"I've written a poem for my wife," he says, "about her."

Then he tells us this poem. I'm waiting for the rhyme, but it's more like talking, about how he wakes up and the sun's bright on the bed and his wife's still asleep. He watches her.

> *"Alone," he says, "I watch you sleep*
> *Before the morning steals you from me,*
> *Before you stir and disappear*
> *Into the day and leave me here*
> *To turn and kiss the warm space*
> *You leave beside me."* **11**

He looks up and people clap. I thought what he said was a little too personal, but I could follow it. Next to me Sharon's made a note. I look down at her page and see it's just an exclamation point. **12**

He tells us a lot of poems, one after another. I mean, he's got poems on everything. He even has one about his truck:

> *"Old buck-toothed, slow-to-start mama,"*

something like that. People laugh, which I guess is okay. He just keeps at it, and he **really jerks us around with his poems**. I mean, you don't know what the next one's going to be about. **13** At one point they bring him a glass of water, and he takes a break. But mainly he keeps going.

11 Inferences
Why does the author include examples of the poems?

12 Inferences/ Language
What does the exclamation point tell you about Sharon's opinion of the poem?

13 Inferences
What does Gene think of the poems? How can you tell?

In Other Words
loose-leaf notebook
really jerks us around with his poems goes quickly from one poem to another

He ends up with one called "High School."

"On my worst nights," he says, "I dream myself back.
I'm the hostage in the row by the radiator, boxed in,
Zit-blasted, and they're popping quizzes at me.
I'm locked in there, looking for words
To talk myself out of being this young
While every girl in the galaxy
Is looking over my head, spotting for a senior.
On my really worst nights it's last period
On a Friday and somebody's fixed the bell
So it won't ring:
   And I've been cut from the team,
   And I've forgotten my locker combination,
   And I'm waiting for something damn it to hell
   To happen." **14**

And the crowd **goes wild**, especially the college people. The poet just gives us a wave and walks over to sit down on the bottom bleacher. **People swarm down** to get him to sign their programs. Except Sharon and I stay where we are.

"That last one wasn't a poem," I tell her. "The others were, but not that one."

She turns to me and smiles. I've never been this close to her before, so I've never seen the color of her eyes.

"Then write a better one," she says.

We sit together again on the ride home.

14 Inferences
What did the poet think of high school? How do you know? Make a list of the words and phrases that support your inference.

In Other Words
hostage prisoner
Zit-blasted with pimples on my face
spotting for trying to find
goes wild acts really excited
People swarm down Everybody rushes down
   from the bleachers

"No, I'm **serious**," I say. "You can't write poems about zits and your locker combination."

"Maybe nobody told the poet that," Sharon says.

"So what are you going to write about him tomorrow?" I'm really curious about this. 15

"I don't know," she says. "I've never heard a poet reading before, not in person. Mrs. Tibbetts shows us tapes of poets reading."

"She doesn't show them to our class."

"What would you do if she did?" Sharon asks.

"Laugh a lot."

The bus settles down on the return trip. I picture all these people going home to do algebra homework, or whatever. When Sharon speaks again, I almost don't hear her.

"You ought to be in this class," she says.

15 Point of View
What does Gene say about this thoughts? Can we believe him?

You can't write poems about zits and your locker combination.

I pull my ball cap down to my nose and lace my fingers behind my head and **kick back** in the seat. Which should be answer enough. 16

"You're as **bright** as anybody on this bus. Brighter than some."

We're rolling on through the night, and I can't believe I'm hearing this. Since it's dark, I take a chance and glance at her. Just the outline of her nose and her chin, maybe a little stubborn.

"How do you know I am?"

"How do you know you're not?" she says. "How will you ever know?"

16 Inferences
Sharon says that Gene should be in the advanced class. What do Gene's actions tell you?

Key Vocabulary
serious *adj.*, not joking

In Other Words
kick back lean back, relax
bright smart, intelligent

But then we're quiet because what else is there to say? And anyway, the evening's over. Mrs. Tibbetts is **braking for the turnoff**, and we're about to get back to normal. And I **get this quick flash of tomorrow**, in second period with Marty and Pink and Darla, and frankly it doesn't look that good. **17** ❖

17 Inferences
Why doesn't tomorrow look very good to Gene?

ANALYZE I Go Along

1. **Confirm Prediction** What does Gene think of the program? Did you predict he would react this way? Explain.

2. **Vocabulary** Do you agree with Sharon that Gene has **potential** as a student in **Advanced** English? Why or why not?

3. **Analyze Point of View** In this story, Gene does not talk directly about his own thoughts and feelings. Why do you think this is? Discuss this question in a small group. Use clues from the story to support your ideas.

4. **Focus Strategy** **Make Inferences** On page 215, Gene says, "I go along." This is also the story title. After the poetry reading and his time with Sharon, do you think Gene will continue to "go along" as he always has? Make an inference and support it with evidence from the text.

   ↪ **Return to the Text**

   Reread and Write What do you think Gene learns about himself from his experience? Write a paragraph, using details from the story to support your view.

Key Vocabulary
- **potential** *n.*, possibility; the ability to do something, given the chance

In Other Words
braking for the turnoff slowing down to turn onto another road
get this quick flash of tomorrow suddenly see a picture of tomorrow in my mind

poem by Langston Hughes

Analyze Structure: Poetry

Poetry is different from prose, or narrative literature such as short stories, in these ways:

- A short story has a narrator. A poem has a speaker.
- In a short story, words are arranged in paragraphs. In a poem, words are arranged in lines.
- Poetry has a musical quality. The rhythm and the sounds of the words are important. You can hear the sounds when you read the poem out loud.

Look Into the Text

A poem is written in lines, not paragraphs.

> The steps from the hill lead down into Harlem
> through a park, then I cross St. Nicholas,
> Eighth Avenue, Seventh, and I come to the Y,
> the Harlem Branch Y, where I take the elevator
> up to my room, sit down, and write this page:
> It's not easy to know what is true for you or me
> at twenty-two, my age. But I guess I'm what
> I feel and see and hear, Harlem, I hear you:

The speaker uses everyday words.

Read these lines out loud. Notice how they sound.

Focus Strategy ▶ Make Inferences

As you read a poem, you can **make inferences** about the speaker, the message, and the audience the speaker is talking to. Use this strategy with the poem above.

HOW TO MAKE INFERENCES

Focus Strategy

1. Reread the lines of the poem above.

2. Collect clues about the speaker, the message, and the audience.

3. Look at all of your clues and think about what you know from your experience. Then make inferences.

Add more clues and inferences to your chart as you read the entire poem.

Inference Chart

	Clues	Inferences
Speaker	· Lives at the Harlem Branch Y · Is 22	Maybe he doesn't have much money since he lives at the Y.
Message	· It's not easy to know what is true.	
Audience		

Connect Across Texts

In "I Go Along," Gene thinks about how people fit in at school. In this poem, the speaker also thinks about **categories** of people.

Theme for
English B
by Langston Hughes

The instructor said,

> *Go home and write*
>
> *a page tonight.*
>
> *And let that page come out of you —*
>
5 > *Then, it will be true.*

I wonder if it's that simple?

I am twenty-two, colored, born in Winston-Salem.

I went to school there, then Durham, then here

to this college on the hill above Harlem.

10 I am the only colored student in my class.

The steps from the hill lead down into Harlem,

through a park, then I cross St. Nicholas,

Eighth Avenue, Seventh, and I come to the Y,

the Harlem Branch Y, where I take the elevator

15 up to my room, sit down, and write this page:

It's not easy to know what is true for you or me **1**

at twenty-two, my age. But I guess I'm what

1 Inferences
Who is the audience of this poem? What clues tell you this? Record your ideas in your chart.

Key Vocabulary
- **category** *n.*, a group of items that are similar in some way

The Savoy Ballroom was an exciting dance spot in Harlem, New York, from the 1920s to the 1950s.

I feel and see and hear, Harlem, I hear you:

hear you, hear me — we two — you, me, talk on this page.

20 (I hear New York, too.) Me — who? **2**

Well, I like to eat, sleep, drink, and be in love.

I like to work, read, learn, and understand life.

I like a pipe for a Christmas present,

or records — Bessie, bop, or Bach.

25 I guess being colored doesn't make me *not* like

the same things other folks like who are other races.

So will my page be colored that I write?

Being me, it will not be white.

But it will be

30 a part of you, instructor.

You are white —

yet a part of me, as I am a part of you.

That's American.

Sometimes perhaps you don't want to be a part of me.

35 Nor do I often want to be a part of you. **3**

2 Poetry
Read lines 18–20 aloud with a partner. Pause after a comma, a colon, a period, or a dash. What do you notice about the way the words sound?

3 Poetry/Inferences
The word *often* is an important clue to the speaker's meaning. Record it in your chart. Then make an inference about its importance.

Key Vocabulary
understand *v.*, to know the meaning of something well

Musical Background
Bessie is Bessie Smith, an American jazz singer of the 1920s and '30s. *Bop*, also called bebop, is a form of jazz that started in the 1940s. Johann Sebastian *Bach* was a composer of classical music.

But we are, that's true!

As I learn from you,

I guess you learn from me —

although you're older — and white —

40   and somewhat more free. **4**

This is my page for English B. ❖

4 Inferences
What does the speaker think of the instructor? How can you tell?

ANALYZE Theme for English B

1. **Summarize** What **categories** does the speaker say that he belongs to? Which category does he think is the most important? How do you know?

2. **Vocabulary** What does the speaker want the instructor to **understand** about his life?

3. **Analyze Structure: Poetry** Tell two ways this poem is different from a short story.

4. **Focus Strategy Make Inferences** What does the speaker think is "American"? What clues suggest this?

Return to the Text

Reread and Write Look back at the poem. Write a paragraph to describe the speaker's true self. Do you think he found it or created it?

About the Writer

Langston Hughes (1902–1967) was one of the most important African American writers of the twentieth century. Famous for his poetry, Hughes was also a successful journalist, playwright, author, and speaker.

EQ **Do We Find or Create Our True Selves?**

Reading

Critical Thinking

EQ **1. Analyze** Return to the chart you completed on page 210. How has your thinking about the **categories** changed based on your reading? Explain.

2. Compare Suppose that Gene and the speaker of "Theme for English B" were having a conversation about the impact of categories. How would their ideas compare? Support your response with evidence from the text.

3. Speculate How do you think the instructor would respond to "Theme for English B"? What clues from the text support your response?

4. Draw Conclusions Imagine that Gene reads "Theme for English B" in his English class. Would he like it as much as the poems he heard at the poetry reading? Why do you think so?

EQ **5. Assess** Is it useful or important to put yourself into categories? Use what you learned from the story and the poem to help you answer.

Writing

Write About Literature

Opinion Statement The people and things around us have a big impact on who we are. Do you agree or disagree? Write your opinion. Support it with examples from both texts. Gather text evidence in a chart.

I Go Along	Theme for English B

Vocabulary

Key Vocabulary Review

Oral Review Work with a partner. Use these words to complete the paragraph.

advanced	potential	serious
category	program	understanding
poet	realize	

What skills do you need to be a writer or __(1)__ ? You may think you need high-level, or __(2)__ , language skills. You may think you must be a __(3)__ person. However, there is no single __(4)__ , or group, to which all poets belong. In fact, almost everyone has the ability, or __(5)__ , to write poetry. You might see people from different backgrounds perform in a poetry __(6)__ . The one thing poets share is a basic knowledge, or __(7)__ , of how words can affect people. When you __(8)__ that you have a message to share, you can write poetry, too.

Writing Application Think of a group that you are part of, such as a family, an ethnic group, or an organization. Write a journal entry telling about yourself as a member of this group. Use at least three Key Vocabulary words.

Fluency

Read with Ease: Phrasing

Assess your reading fluency with the passage in the Reading Handbook, p. 672. Then complete the self-check below.

1. I did/did not pause appropriately for punctuation and phrases.

2. My words correct per minute: _____ .

Use Verb Tenses

A verb in the **present tense** shows that the action happens now or happens often. A verb in the **past tense** shows that the action already happened.

Irregular verbs have special forms to show past tense. For example:

Present: I **go** along, but nobody **sees** me. I **sit** on the bus and **say** nothing.

Past: I **went** along, but nobody **saw** me. I **sat** on the bus and **said** nothing.

Use the **future tense** to tell about an action that has not happened yet. Use **will** before the main verb to tell about the future.

I **will hear** a poet. He **will walk** to the podium, **read** his poems, and **answer** questions.

Remember: If two or more verbs are used in the same sentence, all verbs must be in the same tense.

Oral Practice (1–5) Find five sentences in the selections. Tell a partner whether the verb tells about the present, the past, or the future. Then find an example of parallel structure on pages 222–223.

Written Practice (6–8) Rewrite each sentence. Change the verb to the tense in parentheses.

6. The poet speaks to the students. (future)
7. Sharon sat with me. (present)
8. I will go with the advanced class. (past)

Make and Respond to Requests

Role Play With a partner, take turns playing the roles of Mrs. Tibbetts and one of the students in the class. The student asks the teacher about going on a field trip. The teacher responds to the request.

Analyze Style

Authors choose language that will express their ideas and feelings. The language they use creates a particular **style** and has a certain effect on readers. Authors can change their style to have a different effect—to make a story funny, exciting, or serious.

To keep readers interested, authors can repeat important words and phrases, use a combination of long and short sentences, or use incomplete sentences to give the language an informal sound. Look at this example from "I Go Along":

> Mrs. Tibbetts has really great eyes, and she doesn't put anything on them. Which is something Darla could learn from.

The second sentence is incomplete—it sounds the way someone might talk. This style makes it sound as if the narrator is talking to you.

With a small group, discuss the author's style in "I Go Along." Choose a passage. Look for repeated words and phrases. Look at the variety of sentences. Discuss how the author's style affects you as a reader.

"I thought it had a pretty good story and interesting characters, but I really didn't like the font."

Source: ©David Sipress/The New Yorker

Latin and Greek Roots

The word *audience* comes from the Latin word *aud*, which means "to hear." An audience hears a performance. The word **program** comes from the Greek word *gram*, which means "letter" or "written." Performers often follow a written program.

Knowing these roots can help you learn more words in English. Find the root in each word, guess the word's meaning, and confirm in a dictionary.

WORD	POSSIBLE MEANING	DEFINITION
audible		
audiobook		
monogram		

Evaluation

Music: Styles Listen to the music of Bessie Smith or Johann Sebastian Bach, or to bop-style jazz, and write your impressions.

1 **Find the Music** Choose one type of music. Go to the library or search the Internet to find it.

2 **Listen** Play the music and think about what you hear. Do you like it? What does it make you think of? Would you want to listen to more music like it? Listen again and write your ideas.

3 **Present Your Evaluation** Look at your notes and decide what you will share. Share the music and your ideas about it with your group.

🔖 **Language and Learning Handbook**, page 616

Write a Comparison/Contrast Piece

Write a short piece to compare and contrast the speaker in one of the poems from "I Go Along" with the speaker in "Theme for English B." Tell how they are alike and how they are different.

1 **Prewrite** Read the poems again. Think about what the speakers are like. Use a Venn diagram to record new information about the ways in which the speakers are alike and different.

Venn Diagram

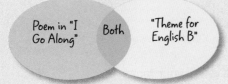

2 **Draft** Use specific ideas from your diagram to write your draft.

> The speaker in the "I Go Along" poem is having nightmares about his high school days, but the speaker in "Theme for English B" is writing for a college class.

This word shows a comparison.

3 **Revise** Exchange papers with a partner. Look for examples that support the ideas. Decide what changes to make.

4 **Edit and Proofread** Reread. Ask:
- Did I use verb tenses correctly?
- Is my spelling correct?

5 **Publish** Print a copy. Share it with a classmate.

🔖 **Writing Handbook**, page 698

Retell a Story

Do you know anyone who tells stories in a way that makes you see the action as if you are there? That person probably gives interesting details and speaks with enthusiasm. You can try retelling one of the stories in this unit to your classmates. Here is how:

1. Plan Your Retelling of a Story

Choose the story you want to retell. Then do the following:

- Think about which parts of the story you liked the most.
- Make notes about the characters, setting, events in the plot, and the order in which they happen.
- Choose words that precisely explain the action, the problem, and the characters.
- Add details that support the main events of the story.

2. Practice Retelling a Story

Use your notes to tell the story to a partner.

- Establish the setting at the beginning.
- Briefly describe the characters.
- Relate the main events in the plot. Lead up to the conflict of the story clearly. Include the parts you liked the most!
- Don't go on and on—make your story short but interesting.

3. Retell the Story

Now tell the story to a group.

- Establish eye contact with your audience.
- Let your enthusiasm show in the tone of your voice, your facial expressions, and your gestures.
- Use your notes as little as possible.
- Speak clearly and loudly in a way the audience will understand.

4. Discuss and Rate the Retelling of a Story

Use the rubric to discuss and rate the story retellings, including your own. As you listen to a retelling, take notes to summarize the main ideas. This will help you be prepared to ask questions about the story. Also listen closely for descriptions or definitions that help you understand unfamiliar words or phrases.

Retelling a Story Rubric

Scale	Content of Story	Student's Preparation	Student's Performance
3 Great	• Covered all the important parts • Details were interesting and related to the important elements of the story	• Seemed to know the story well	• Made me very interested in the story • Spoke clearly
2 Good	• Seemed somewhat accurate • Details were somewhat interesting and mostly related to the important elements of the story	• Seemed familiar with the story	• Made me somewhat interested in the story • Could be heard and understood most of the time
1 Needs Work	• Missed or confused important points in the story • Had little or no details and/or details were not related to the important elements of the story	• Did not seem very familiar with the story	• Did not hold my interest • Could not be heard well

DO IT ▶ Now that you know how to retell a story, go do it—have fun sharing it with your audience!

🔊 Language and Learning Handbook, page 616

How are these students planning their retellings?

myNGconnect.com
🔊 Download the rubric.

PREPARE TO READ

▶ The Pale Mare
▶ My Horse, Fly Like a Bird
▶ Caged Bird

 EQ **Do We Find or Create Our True Selves?**
Discover some struggles that people must face about their identity.

Make a Connection

Quickwrite What do you want more than anything? What could keep you from that dream? Take five minutes to write about these ideas.

Learn Key Vocabulary

Study the Words Pronounce each word and learn its meaning. You may also want to look up the definitions in the Glossary.

• Academic Vocabulary

Key Words	Examples
claim (klām) verb ▶ pages 252, 257	If you **claim** something, you say you have the right to it. If you win a contest, you **claim** the prize. *Synonyms:* demand, take
freedom (frē-dum) noun ▶ pages 252, 254, 255, 257	If you have **freedom**, then you can do, say, or be whatever you want. *Synonym:* liberty
• **goal** (gōl) noun ▶ page 252	When you set a **goal** for yourself, you know what you want to do. *Synonyms:* purpose, aim
ideals (ī-dē-ulz) noun ▶ page 242	**Ideals** are ideas about the right way to live or act. If you believe in treating people fairly, then fairness is one of your **ideals**. *Synonyms:* values, beliefs
implore (im-**plor**) verb ▶ page 241	To **implore** is to beg. I **implore** you not to tell this secret. *Synonyms:* urge, plead
roots (rüts) noun ▶ page 244	Your **roots** are your connections, or ties, to your family or the place you come from. **Roots** are also the part of a plant that is under the ground.
struggle (stru-gul) verb, noun ▶ pages 241, 250	The men **struggle**, or work very hard, to lift the heavy boxes. [*verb*] It is a **struggle** to finish the test in 30 minutes. [*noun*]
• **tradition** (tru-di-shun) noun ▶ page 238	A **tradition** is something people believe or do. People follow **traditions** for years. It is an American **tradition** to watch fireworks on the Fourth of July.

Practice the Words With a partner, complete a **Key Vocabulary Chart** for the Key Vocabulary words.

Key Vocabulary Chart

Word	Synonym(s)	Definition	Sentence or Picture
claim	demand	to say you have the right to something	I claimed the prize I had won.

BEFORE READING **The Pale Mare**

short story by Marian Flandrick Bray

Reading Strategies

- Plan and Monitor
- Determine Importance
▶ Make Inferences
- Ask Questions
- Make Connections
- Synthesize
- Visualize

Analyze Point of View

A **first-person narrator** is one of the characters in the story. The narrator tells the story from his or her own viewpoint or perspective. As a reader, you cannot know how other characters really feel about things, so you should question how much you can trust the narrator.

Look Into the Text

The narrator uses first-person pronouns when she refers to herself.

Strong words tell us about the narrator and how she is feeling.

I sigh. My expertise isn't what he needs. Any fool can take orders. It's not complicated to yell "Four chicken burritos, one green sauce, three red, two large Cokes, two medium 7Ups." No, it's not my expertise in serving food that my precious parents want to preserve. It's that damn tradition again, our *familia* thing, the one that leads to *la raza*, the bigger picture of our people, who we are as Latin Americans. At least that's how Papa and Mama see it. But I don't see things just that way. Not anymore.

Does the narrator think her parents see things the same way she does?

Focus Strategy ▶ Make Inferences

As you read a story, use clues in the text to **make inferences** about characters and events. Notice the kinds of words the writer uses to give the information, as well as what the information is. Try this strategy to find and track clues as you read.

HOW TO MAKE INFERENCES

Focus Strategy

1. Read the text. Notice *what* the narrator says, as well as *how* she says it.

> No, it's not my expertise in serving food that my precious parents want to preserve. It's that damn tradition again, our *familia* thing, the one that leads to *la raza*.

2. Think about your own experience. Use it to make an inference.

Sometimes when I'm angry, I am sarcastic and say the opposite of what I mean. I don't think the narrator means her parents are precious. She's angry at them.

3. Write your ideas on a self-stick note and put it next to the text.

She's angry.

4. Read on. Notice how your ideas about the narrator change as you read through the story.

Marian Flandrick Bray
(1957–)

Marian Flandrick Bray began writing when she was in high school. "I really started in ninth grade, when I wrote a short story about a racehorse," she recalls. "After that, I just kept writing."

Over time, these writings have added up. Bray has published nineteen books and more than two hundred articles and short stories. Horses have been a part of many of these works.

In "The Pale Mare," Bray talks about the Mexican rodeo, or *charreada*. There are many events like this in East Los Angeles, where she grew up.

Seeing the horses get roped by the *charros*, or cowboys, reminded her of what it sometimes feels like to be a girl in Hispanic culture. "I saw the connection between the oppression of females in the Hispanic culture (which I grew up in) and these mares in the event."

myNGconnect.com

◯ **Read an interview with Marian Flandrick Bray.**
◯ **View art that shows *charreadas*.**

The
PALE MARE

by Marian Flandrick Bray

Siete Leguas, 1991, Alfredo Arreguín. Oil on canvas, private collection.

▲ Critical Viewing: Design Notice the shapes and patterns in this painting. What do they make you think of?

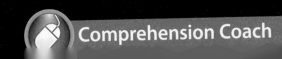
Comprehension Coach

Set a Purpose

Consuela's parents want her to follow the traditions of their culture. Find out how Consuela feels about this.

"But why?" I ask again, even though I know what he'll say. "Because it's tradition."

He always says that. My papa. He's not a tall man, but he has much height in the soaring ways of our family and **la raza**, too.

Papa leans against the shiny side of our vendor truck with the black script that announces *Diaz Family Food*. The heavy smell of grease and corn hangs over us like a banner, an invisible proclamation: tradition.

Our family as always is at the *charreada*, the Mexican-style rodeo, to sell tamales, burritos, refried beans, and sweet bread. The real stuff. Not the Taco Bell version. **1**

I try **a different angle**. After all, I'm good in geometry. "Papa, it's just this one, small weekend. Rafael can help."

My cousin. He helped last year when I had my appendix out. I wonder briefly if I have another body part to give out.

"Consuela," says Papa, then he bends over a sack of pinto beans. He lifts the fifty pounds as easy as my tiny baby sister and continues, "This is the final *charreada* and it is gonna be huge. I need your help. Not Rafael who goofs around."

I sigh. My **expertise** isn't what he needs. Any fool can take orders. It's not complicated to yell, "Four chicken burritos, one green sauce, three red, two large Cokes, two medium 7Ups." No, it's not my expertise in serving food that my precious parents want to preserve. It's that damn tradition again, our **familia** thing, the one that leads to *la raza*, the bigger picture of our people, who we are as Latin **2**

1 Inferences
Consuela makes several comments about tradition. Do you think she is proud of her culture? Write your ideas.

2 Point of View
Which words in this paragraph show that the story is written from a first-person point of view?

Key Vocabulary
• **tradition** *n.*, a belief or a way of doing things

In Other Words
la raza our culture (Spanish term)
a different angle another way
expertise ability to do the job
familia family (in Spanish)

Curbside Cuisine, 2005, Wayne Healy. Acrylic on canvas, 48x48, courtesy of Patricia Correia Gallery, Santa Monica, California.

◀ Critical Viewing: Setting
How do the details in this picture of a food truck help you understand the story?

Americans. At least that's how Papa and Mama see it. But I don't see things just that way. Not anymore.

Papa goes into the house with the beans, for Mama to soak, then cook. I see my **exit** and in the dusk **fling myself** down the street, fast, furious, flying.

Kids play on the street, kicking soccer balls and riding bikes, rushing about like wasps from a knocked-down nest. As usual, it's the boys playing outside, with the rare girl running alongside until she can be gathered back into her house. **3**

Papa is disgusted with my long walks. For once Mama tells him to let me be. She knows that I will explode like a star going nova if I am to stay home always.

3 Inferences
Which words in this paragraph help you make an inference about how Consuela feels about how boys and girls are treated in her culture?

In Other Words
exit chance to leave
fling myself run

Science Background
When some large stars get very old, they can explode in a bright flash. This explosion is called a supernova.

Phoenix Rising, 2004, Paul Botello. Acrylic on canvas, 72x36,
courtesy of Patricia Correia Gallery, Santa Monica, California.

▲ Critical Viewing: Effect What do the images in this painting make you think of?
How might Consuela identify with the girl in the picture?

Each of my strides jars a different, recent memory. **4** Earlier this week at school, my teacher exclaiming over my work in physics, "Excellent work, Consuela. I'll write a letter of recommendation for you. You should really apply to Cal Tech and MIT. You're coming to the weekend astronomy camp, right?" My heart sang. The stars. For the last two years, they are all I've wanted to do: Study them, chart their fierce light, listen to them, learn what they are saying. Stars do talk—really—with radio waves for words. But when I got home from school, **an eclipse was on**.

Parents, on the dark side: "You will not go to any camp. Isn't school during the week enough? You have to help us with the business."

Me, trying to remain calm in the light: "What about Manuel?" My brother, older by a year.

Parents, astonishment: "He has football practice."

"So what! I'm getting top honors in science! He's playing junior varsity football!"

More genuine astonishment: "But he's the son." Meaning, of course, I'm only the daughter, only a girl. Maybe they don't mean to, but they're **banishing me to the dark**. I can't let that happen. **5**

Later Mama tried to soothe me. "**M'ija**, it's because we love you. We want you to be happy with a nice boy, to have a family."

"Are you saying being an astronomer and being happy with a nice boy **are not compatible**?"

She *was* saying that with her hands that touched my hair, with her liquid Spanish murmuring, with her eyes that lingered on my face, **imploring** me to stop **struggling** in this foolish manner. **6**

In Other Words
an eclipse was on it was like the light of the sun was being covered
banishing me to the dark making me do what I don't want to do
M'ija My daughter (in Spanish)
are not compatible do not go together

4 Access Vocabulary
Do you know what the multiple-meaning word *jars* means in this case? If not, look for clues.

5 Inferences
What feelings does Consuela have about the situation? How do you know? Support your answer with evidence from the text.

6 Point of View
On this page, the story is told in flashbacks, or memories, from Consuela. Words like *memory* and *earlier* help us understand this. Choose a sentence or two from the page and write it the way a third-person omniscient narrator would write it.

Monitor Comprehension

Summarize
What do Consuela's parents want for her? What does Consuela want for herself?

Predict

How will Consuela feel at the charreada this year?

I cross busy Lincoln Avenue and head up Rio Hondo Road, past the earth dam. The oil hills, scrubby with ugly bushes, prickled with **derricks**, bunch up on one side, then unfurl into the familiar, sandy, flattened flood plain.

The night is clear, rare in smoggy L.A. My science class is at this moment zooming away from L.A. for a weekend at Joshua Tree. They will observe the breathtaking stars from the desert floor.

A sob shakes my lungs. I didn't even know I was crying, but tears drip down my chin and onto my shirt collar. Why didn't I just go, like my friend Mia suggested? Because I have these stupid **ideals**, like honesty. **7**

I find that, as suddenly as I started, I've stopped crying. The wind, fresh and sharp, brings the hot scent of **livestock**, dirt, and human sweat.

The *charreada*.

The grounds are quiet. The arena is smooth as a flour tortilla. Many of the *charros'* horses are stabled here in tidy, low barns, including the one belonging to *Tío* Jesús, Papa's brother. *Tío* Jesús's horse is an Andalusian, the color of very ripe plums. **8**

The **stock pens** are on the far side, closest to the flood control, the **citified** riverbed that captures the water and hurries it to the sea, thirty miles away. Some of the water rushes from the San Gabriel Mountains, ten miles away, a dark stain in the north sky. The flood control is a hundred miles long, mountains to ocean. I've ridden this nearby stretch a million times, along its sandy path on my uncle's

7 Inferences
What does Consuela say about her ideals? Write what this tells you about her view of herself.

8 Inferences
Notice how Consuela describes the area where the rodeo takes place. Do you think she likes or dislikes it? What makes you think that?

Key Vocabulary
ideals *n.*, ideas about the right way to live or act

In Other Words
derricks oil-drilling towers
livestock horses and cattle
charros' cowboys' (in Spanish)
Tío Uncle (in Spanish)
stock pens places where the animals are kept
citified concrete, cement

Mexican rodeo, 20th century, folk art on wooden sheet/The Art Archive/Superstock

▲ **Critical Viewing: Setting** If you were at the *charreada* in this picture, what sounds would you hear? What else would you notice?

serious but kindly horse. Horses in the city—it sounds funny—the *charros*, they wouldn't have it any other way. Like my family. Life has to be a certain way. Their way.

Not for me, though. Sorry, Papa, Mama. Your world isn't my world. It's not that I'm trying to pretend my Mexican blood doesn't **course** through my veins, it just means that my blood is calling to different things. That isn't wrong or bad.

Is it?

Mama, Papa, they just don't get it.

Or maybe they do. Perhaps that scares them. **9**

9 Inferences
Note how Consuela is feeling here. How do you know?

In Other Words
course go, flow

I climb the sturdy metal pipe **corral**. I bypass the cattle, lumpy beasts dozing like logs in a stream, dull, empty of life, cut off from their **roots**, and head out to the edge of the corrals.

I've been going to *charreadas* since I was a baby. The smell of dirt and animals was often **overlaid** by the stronger scent of greasy bean burritos, but I'd always sniff and sniff until the odor of hot horses and freshly shaken alfalfa flakes overtook me. When I was really little I'd clap my hands and crow, "*Char, char*." I'd play I was a *charro* and swing astride the nearest fence, imagining I rode the finest horses— a Paso Fino, slate gray with white banners for a mane and tail, or a chestnut Andalusian, lifting his hooves high in the Spanish walk. The horse and I always moved as one—a **seamless centaur**. **10**

What happened? Why did I change?

No moon tonight. My science class is observing stars tonight, because a moonless night shows the stars the best. Starlight. I wish I could hold the light of those distant fires in my hands, bright and smooth as a sea stone, or maybe poured into a bowl and drunk like intoxicating tequila, only better.

The barns glow in the orange fog lights. Inside the stalls darkness swells, with an occasional flash of animal life. I hurry around them.

10 Point of View
In this flashback, Consuela tells how she felt about the *charreada* when she was younger. What part of the text makes you think she is a reliable narrator?

There Is Such a Place #62, 2002, Armand Vallée. Oil 12x16, collection of the artist.

🔺 Critical Viewing: Design What takes up the most space in this painting? What part of the story does it remind you of?

Key Vocabulary
roots *n.*, ties to family or the place you come from; part of a plant that is under the ground

In Other Words
corral fence around the place where the horses and cattle are kept
overlaid covered up
seamless centaur creature that is half human and half horse

Farthest from the main arena is the mares' pen. I lean on the rails. The mares **shy** nervously, young wiry things, most of them rented for the weekend from slaughterhouses. By Sunday night, they'll be off to the slaughterhouse stockyards. I never used to think about them. I mean, what was the point?

The last few months, though, I found I couldn't watch the **horse-tripping**. I'd busy myself in our truck, chopping chilis, slicing onions, refilling the Coke machine, anything. But even when I'd turn away from watching the *piales en el lienzo* and *mangana a caballo*, *charros* performing their artistic ropework with

> # I never used to think about them.

the mares their targets, my stomach would still be tightened up because I knew how the mares would look when **snared**. 🔢 If the *charro* does it right, the mare rolls on her shoulder, landing hard, but gets up, shaken, bruised, but walking. If he doesn't throw her correctly, she falls very hard and sometimes can't get up.

Don't get me wrong. Working the magic of the rope is hard, clever work. *Charros* are artists, as much as any writer, painter, singer, or astronomer. *Tío* Jesús trains and trains and he still screws up, snaring a mare wrong, crashing her spectacularly in a wild somersault, so she lands on her head. Sometimes the mares are so injured that the men who rented the mares started a "you broke 'em, you keep 'em" policy. If the horse is so damaged that she can't be loaded and trailered to the slaughterhouse, then they make you keep her.

🔢 **Inferences**
How does Consuela feel about the female horses, the mares? What text clue helped you make this inference?

In Other Words
shy move
horse-tripping event in which the cowboys catch a horse around the legs with a rope
piales en el lienzo and *mangana a caballo* roping events (Spanish terms)
snared caught

I swing my leg over the top pipe and perch on the cold metal. One mare, pale as eggshells, whirls, ears up, like antennae, watching me. If she were a girl, she'd look like Fai, the Chinese girl in my class, also in the science club. Fai works long hours in her parents' Chinese **takeout**. Some nights, she's told me, she doesn't get to bed until two a.m. and then she has to get up at six to make it to school. Fai has deep smudges under her eyes and this little mare would, too, I bet, if horses got bags under their eyes. 🔢

I slip off the corral. Every head flings up, wild forelocks toss between pointed ears, and tension bolts up every leg. All senses lock on me, the intruder.

Carmen, 1994, Angeline Kyba. Oil on canvas, Galeria Café Des Artistes, Puerto Vallarta, Mexico.

In Other Words
takeout fast-food restaurant

12 **Inferences**
Write how Consuela feels about Fai. How do you know that?

◀ **Critical Viewing: Character**
How does this picture compare to the picture you have in your mind of Consuela?

Monitor Comprehension

Explain
Tell how Consuela's opinion about *charreadas* has changed.

Predict
Consuela is with the horses.
What will she do?

"Sorry," I whisper. Several mares whirl at my words and spin away across the pen to the far side. My little Chinese mare is brave. She continues to stare at me. She blinks her large, dark eyes. She shakes her neck and paws the ground with a dainty oval hoof, her gaze never shifting from my face.

Tomorrow will be different. She will burst, terrified, out of the chute. A *charro* will spur his pampered, well-groomed horse after this waif. He will snare her. He will throw her to the ground. Yes, artistically. But the ground is hard whether the rope is tossed prettily or not. In all fairness, I have to ask, is it any worse than roping calves, or goats? No. But it **clutches at** me with a tightness I can't ignore. I just know that I don't want to see her tomorrow frantically scrambling on her hind legs, trying to **scale** the arena's smooth walls, then spinning around the arena for any escape only to be slammed into the ground. **13**

I edge away along the fence line. The wind is cooler, tinged with sage and damp dirt. If I was at Joshua Tree I'd train my **telescope** near the Hercules **constellation** and study M-13, a cluster of stars so dense that if you lived on a planet nearby, night would never fall. There the sky would always be filled with brilliant starlight, clusters of stars like bunches of heavy grapes, plump, white, shining.

Never would there be night. How would that change a human's life? Change a mare's life?

13 Point of View/ Inferences
What do Consuela's thoughts tell you about her? How does the first-person point of view help make Consuela's thoughts clear?

In Other Words
clutches at bothers
scale climb
telescope tool for looking at stars
constellation group of stars

Sol y Sombra, 2003, John Farnsworth. Oil on canvas, private collection.

▲ Critical Viewing: Observations If you were in this picture, would you feel comfortable or uncomfortable? How do you think Consuela would feel? Explain.

I **unlatch** the gate. A packed dirt path leads one way to the arena. Another path, softer, less used, flickers up to the riverbed. I shove the gate wide.

I think the pale mare will realize she'll need to keep going north on the riverbed to the mountains beyond the city, to a place where there is no night for her. **14**

The mares **skitter** from me like bugs over a pond as I walk toward them. The starlit mare is farthest away from me, but she locks onto my gaze, telescoping the distance between us, until we are closer than **any binary star system**. I close in. With a quiet dignity, she suddenly folds, turns, and walks calmly out of the open gate. The other mares see her outside and trot in circles, confused. Silly things. I raise my arms, shooing them out after the pale mare.

The remaining horses rush for the gate like the tail of **a comet**, fine, fiery. In the lead, the pale mare trots, her tail streaming ribbons. She passes under a fog light, an alien creature, then under another and another, until she is herself again, galloping away from the grounds, traveling light.

"That's right," I say admiringly. "Don't even look back." I turn and fade away into the night as shouts from security erupt from a nearby barn. The image of the starlit mare glows before me. Maybe

Don't even look back.

I won't mind as much working tomorrow because in this darkness I'm beginning to see the path the stars have laid down for me. **15** I hurry back home, my step lighter than it has been in a long time. ❖

14 Inferences
What does Consuela mean by the words "a place where there is no night for her"?

15 Inferences
What path does Consuela see for herself? How do you know?

Monitor Comprehension

Confirm Prediction
What clues did you use to make your prediction? If your prediction was not logical, look for clues that would have led to a more logical one.

In Other Words

unlatch open
skitter run away
any binary star system two stars that circle around each other
a comet an object that flies through space

My Horse, Fly Like a Bird

by Virginia Driving Hawk Sneve
adapted from a Lakota warrior's song to his horse

My horse, fly like a bird
To carry me far
From the arrows of my enemies, **16**
And I will tie red ribbons
To your streaming hair.

16 Inferences
How does the phrase "arrows of my enemies" suggest Native American history? What can you infer about the culture and the historical period in which this poem is set?

ANALYZE The Pale Mare

1. **Explain** What happens at the end of the story? What does Consuela do? How do you feel about what she does?

2. **Vocabulary** What is the reason for Consuela's **struggle** with her parents?

3. **Analyze Point of View** How did writing the story in the first-person point of view shape the content of the story? How might the story have been different if told using a third-person point of view? Discuss the questions with a partner.

4. **Focus Strategy Make Inferences** Why do you think Consuela's views of the *charreada* have changed so much since she was a child?

Return to the Text

Reread and Write Do you think Consuela finds or creates her true self? Reread the text. Then write your opinion. Support it with ideas from the text.

BEFORE READING **Caged Bird**

poem by Maya Angelou

Reading Strategies

- Plan and Monitor
- Determine Importance
▶ **Make Inferences**
- Ask Questions
- Make Connections
- Synthesize
- Visualize

Analyze Structure: Poetry

There are many different elements of poetry.

- **rhyme**: similar sounds at the ends of two or more words, such as *bird* and *heard*
- **rhythm**: a pattern of beats, or accents, that gives the poem a certain sound
- **symbol**: something that represents something other than itself, such as a dove as a symbol of peace
- **figurative language: simile** and **metaphor** compare two unlike things
- **allegory:** a type of extended metaphor in which each object or person represents an object or person outside the work

Look Into the Text

In this poem, the caged bird is a **symbol**.

line
> The caged bird sings
> with a fearful trill
> of things unknown
> but longed for still
> and his tune is heard
> on the distant hill
> for the caged bird
> sings of freedom.

stanza

Each line has four or five beats.

Which words rhyme with *trill*?

Compare the structure of this poem with "My Horse, Fly Like a Bird" on p. 250.

Focus Strategy ▶ Make Inferences

Writers can use symbols to represent ideas. Just as you can **make inferences** about events and characters in a story, you can **make inferences** about what the symbols stand for.

HOW TO MAKE INFERENCES

Focus Strategy

1. Many parts of a poem can be symbolic. Start with the title. Also notice the people, places, or things in the poem.

   YOU NOTICE: *This poem is called "Caged Bird." I'd better pay attention to the cages. What do they make me think of?*

2. Think about your own experience. Learn more about the poet's experience.

   YOU THINK: *Cages make me think of jail.*
   Maya Angelou writes about what holds people back.

3. Put the ideas together to make an inference. What can you infer about the cage? Check to see if other details support your inference.

Connect Across Texts
In "The Pale Mare," Consuela's **goal** is to have the **freedom** to be who she really is. What does this poem say about freedom?

CAGED BIRD

by Maya Angelou

A free bird leaps
on the back of the wind
and floats downstream
till the current ends
5   and dips his wing
in the orange sun rays
and dares to claim the sky. **1**

1 Poetry/Inferences
What things could be symbols in these lines? How do you know? What might they mean?

Key Vocabulary
- **goal** *n.*, a purpose
  freedom *n.*, the power to do, say, or be whatever you want
  claim *v.*, to say you have the right to something

In Other Words
current wind

But a bird that stalks
down his narrow cage
10 can seldom see through
his bars of rage **2**
his wings are clipped and
his feet are tied
so he opens his throat to sing.

15 The caged bird sings
with a fearful trill
of things unknown
but longed for still
and his tune is heard
20 on the distant hill
for the caged bird
sings of freedom.

The free bird thinks of another breeze
and the trade winds soft through the sighing trees
25 and the fat worms waiting on a dawn-bright lawn
and he names the sky his own. **3**

But a caged bird stands on the grave of dreams
his shadow shouts on a nightmare scream
his wings are clipped and his feet are tied
30 so he opens his throat to sing.

2 Poetry/Inferences
What word does
the poet use to
describe the bars
on the bird cage?
What might the
bars be a
symbol of?

3 Poetry
Which words
rhyme in this
stanza?

In Other Words
rage anger
trill sound, song
longed for wanted

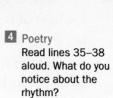

The caged bird sings
with a fearful trill
of things unknown
but longed for still
35 and his tune is heard
on the distant hill
for the caged bird
sings of freedom. **4**

4 Poetry
Read lines 35–38
aloud. What do you
notice about the
rhythm?

ANALYZE Caged Bird

1. **Summarize** Tell how the poem's speaker feels about being free and about being caged. Support your viewpoint with evidence from the poem.

2. **Vocabulary** Why does the caged bird sing only of **freedom**?

3. **Analyze Structure: Poetry** Read the fifth stanza aloud with a partner. Does the caged bird really stand on a grave? Discuss with your partner.

4. **Focus Strategy Make Inferences** What do you think the cage in this poem is a symbol of? Use the figurative language in the poem to support your opinion.

    Return to the Text
    Reread and Write Write a paragraph that compares and contrasts the two birds in this poem. What images does the poet use to show the difference between the birds?

About the Writer

Maya Angelou (1928–) is an important voice in modern American literature. She is an activist, an actor, and an award-winning writer of poetry and prose. She has written about what holds people back, and how people overcome challenges.

EQ Do We Find or Create Our True Selves?

Reading

Critical Thinking

1. **Analyze** What does Consuela want more than anything? What is keeping her from her dream?

2. **Compare** How is Consuela like the caged bird? How is she like the free bird?

3. **Interpret** Consuela's favorite subject is astronomy. What is astronomy a symbol of in the story? Explain your thinking.

4. **Imagine** How do you think Consuela would respond if she read "Caged Bird" in school? Why do you think this?

EQ 5. **Assess** Think about the selections in this unit. What are some "cages" that people are in? Who makes the cages? Is everyone able to break free? Explain your answers.

Writing

Write About Literature

Cause-and-Effect Paragraph What happens when people have as much **freedom** as they want? Use examples from the selections. Organize your thoughts in a chart. Then write a paragraph.

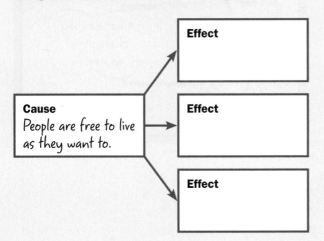

Vocabulary

Key Vocabulary Review

Oral Review Work with a partner. Use these words to complete the paragraph.

claim	ideals	struggles
freedom	implore	traditions
goal	roots	

> Consuela fights, or __(1)__ , against her family __(2)__ , the way her family does things. She appreciates her Mexican ties, or __(3)__ , but her ideas of right and wrong—her __(4)__ , are different from those of her parents. Her parents beg and __(5)__ her to stop fighting for her liberty and __(6)__ . Her hopes and dreams are simple, though. Her __(7)__ is to study astronomy. One day she may be able to __(8)__ this dream for her own.

Writing Application Tell about a difficult time you had with a friend or family member. What was the solution? Use at least three of the Key Vocabulary words in your answer.

Fluency

Read with Ease: Expression

Assess your reading fluency with the passage in the Reading Handbook, p. 673. Then complete the self-check below.

1. I did/did not express feelings as I read.

2. My words correct per minute: _____ .

Grammar

Use Subject and Object Pronouns

A **noun** can be a subject or an object in a sentence.

Consuela likes **science**.
subject   object

Pronouns can take the place of nouns. Use a **subject pronoun** to replace the subject. Use an **object pronoun** to replace the object.

Consuela likes **school**.
She likes **it**.

Subject Pronouns	I	we
	you	they
	he, she, it	
Object Pronouns	me	us
	you	them
	him, her, it	

Oral Practice (1–5) With a partner, read each sentence. Choose the correct pronoun.

1. Consuela arrives. (She/They) sees the corral.
2. The horses move. (They/Them) are nervous.
3. Consuela waves. The horses see (she/her).
4. Consuela goes to the gate. She opens (them/it).
5. Guards see Consuela. (They/He) chase her.

Written Practice (6–10) Rewrite the paragraph. Use the correct pronouns.

Consuela studies the stars. __(6)__ plans to go to astronomy camp. "My friends and __(7)__ will go together," Consuela says. Papa does not allow __(8)__ to go. "Papa loves my brother and __(9)__," thinks Consuela. "I wish he treated __(10)__ fairly."

Language Development

Give Directions

Pair Talk Consuela takes long walks around her neighborhood. Think of a favorite place in your neighborhood. Tell a partner how to get there. Have your partner draw a map to show that he or she understands and can follow the directions.

Literary Analysis

Analyze Point of View

Stories can be written from first-person or third-person point of view. Some stories have an **omniscient** narrator.

Omniscient means "all knowing." An omniscient narrator

- sees everything that happens, everywhere in the story
- tells what each character thinks and feels
- uses third-person pronouns to tell the story.

If "The Pale Mare" had an omniscient narrator, it might have begun:

> Consuela did not want to work. She really wanted to go to Joshua Tree.
> "But why?" she asked Papa again and again.
> Papa needed her help. "When will she understand that family is more important than this trip?" he wondered.

Work with a partner. Continue Consuela's story from the point of view of an omniscient narrator. Tell what will happen after Consuela lets the horses go free.

What can my characters do next?

Word Families

Word families are groups of words that are related by meaning. For example, **freedom** and *free* are in the same word family. This word family has its origins in Old English. Sometimes, knowing the meaning of one word in a family can help you understand what a related word means.

claim		claimant
to say you have the right to something	▶	a person who claims the right to something

Use a dictionary to find other words that belong to the word families for *freedom* and *claim*. Predict, then confirm, the meanings of the new words.

Dramatic Reading

Drama With a group, take turns reading "Caged Bird."

1 Assign each person a stanza.

2 Practice reading your part. What kind of voice will you use? When will you pause? Think about the rhythm of the lines.

3 Take turns reading. Notice how others say their lines. Discuss what each person does well.

🔖 **Language and Learning Handbook**, page 616

Write a Response to Literature

A test may ask you to write a personal response to a story or poem you have read.

1 **Unpack the Prompt** Read the prompt and underline the important words.

> **Writing Task**
> Write a personal response to the short story "The Pale Mare." Give specific examples from the story in your response.

2 **Plan Your Response** Pick one topic to write about, such as:

- the ideas in the text
- the characters
- how the story is written
- how the story relates to your life

Make a list of the three or four most important points you want to make about that topic.

3 **Draft** Organize your response like this. Explain each of your points as much as possible.

> **Organizer**
>
> I [liked/disliked] "The Pale Mare" very much because [tell why you liked or disliked the selection]. One thing I especially [liked/disliked] about the story was [tell what you liked or disliked]. I [liked/disliked] this because [explain why]. Another thing I [liked/disliked] about the story was [tell another thing]. I [liked/disliked] this because it made me feel [explain your reaction]. Overall, [restate or clarify your reason for your overall response].

4 **Check Your Work** Reread your response. Ask:

- Does it address the writing prompt?
- Did I give examples to support my ideas?
- Did I use pronouns correctly?

🔖 **Writing Handbook**, page 698

From Outliers

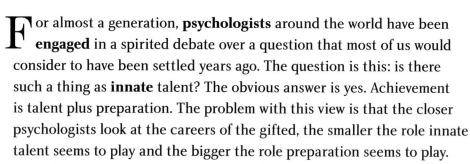

by Malcolm Gladwell

1   For almost a generation, **psychologists** around the world have been **engaged** in a spirited debate over a question that most of us would consider to have been settled years ago. The question is this: is there such a thing as **innate** talent? The obvious answer is yes. Achievement is talent plus preparation. The problem with this view is that the closer psychologists look at the careers of the gifted, the smaller the role innate talent seems to play and the bigger the role preparation seems to play.

2   **Exhibit A in** the talent argument is a study done in the early 1990s by the psychologist K. Anders Ericsson and two colleagues at Berlin's elite Academy of Music. With the help of the Academy's professors, they divided the school's violinists into three groups. In the first group were the stars, the students with the **potential** to become world-class soloists. In the second were those judged to be merely "good." In the third were students who were unlikely to ever play professionally and who intended to be music teachers in the public school system. All of the violinists were then asked the same question: over the course of your entire career, ever since you first picked up the violin, how many hours have you practiced?

3   Everyone from all three groups started playing at roughly the same age, around five years old. In those first few years, everyone practiced roughly the same amount, about two or three hours a week. But when the students were around the age of eight, real differences started to

---

Key Vocabulary
- **potential** *n.*, possibility; the ability to do something, given the chance

In Other Words
Outliers People Who Do Extraordinary Things
psychologists behavior experts
engaged involved
innate natural or inborn
Exhibit A in The first piece of evidence related to

emerge. The students who would end up the best in their class began to practice more than everyone else: six hours a week by age nine, eight hours a week by age twelve, sixteen hours a week by age fourteen, and up and up, until by the age of twenty they were practicing—that is, purposefully and single-mindedly playing their instruments with the intent to get better—well over thirty hours a week. In fact, by the age of twenty, the **elite** performers had each totaled ten thousand hours of practice. By contrast, the merely good students had totaled eight thousand hours, and the future music teachers had totaled just over four thousand hours.

4   Ericsson and his colleagues then compared amateur pianists with professional pianists. The same pattern emerged. The amateurs never practiced more than about three hours a week over the course of their childhood, and by the age of twenty they had totaled two thousand hours of practice. The professionals, on the other hand, steadily increased their practice time every year, until by the age of twenty they, like the violinists, had reached ten thousand hours.

5   **The striking thing** about Ericsson's study is that he and his colleagues couldn't find any "naturals," musicians who **floated effortlessly to** the top while practicing a fraction of the time their peers did.

In Other Words
elite top, best
The striking thing What was amazing
floated effortlessly to made no effort but reached

Nor could they find any "grinds," people who worked harder than everyone else, yet just didn't have what it takes to break the top ranks. Their research suggested that once a musician has enough ability to get into a top music school, the thing that distinguishes one performer from another is how hard he or she works. That's it. And what's more, the people at the very top don't work just harder or even much harder than everyone else. They work much, *much* harder.

6   The idea that excellence at performing a complex task requires a critical minimum level of practice surfaces again and again in studies of expertise. In fact, researchers have settled on what they believe is the magic number for true expertise: ten thousand hours.

7   "The emerging picture from such studies is that ten thousand hours of practice is required to achieve the level of mastery associated with being a world-class expert—in anything," writes the **neurologist** Daniel Levitin. "In study after study, of **composers**, basketball players, fiction writers, ice skaters, concert pianists, chess players, master criminals, and what have you, this number comes up again and again. Of course, this doesn't address why some people get more out of their practice sessions than others do. But no one has yet found a case in which true world-class expertise was accomplished in less time. It seems that it takes the brain this long to **assimilate** all that it needs to know to achieve true mastery."

...the magic number for true expertise: ten thousand hours.

8   This is true even of people we think of as prodigies. Mozart, for example, famously started writing music at six. But, writes the psychologist Michael Howe in his book *Genius Explained*,

9   by the standards of mature composers, Mozart's early works are not outstanding. The earliest pieces were all probably written down by his father, and perhaps improved in the process. Many of Wolfgang's childhood compositions, such as the first seven of his concertos for

In Other Words
neurologist brain doctor
composers people who write music
assimilate put together, combine

piano and orchestra, are largely arrangements of works by other composers. Of those concertos that only contain music original to Mozart, the earliest that is now regarded as a masterwork (No. 9, K. 271) was not composed until he was twenty-one: by that time Mozart had already been composing concertos for ten years.

10 The music critic Harold Schonberg goes further: Mozart, he argues, actually "developed late," since he didn't produce his greatest work until he had been composing for more than twenty years.

11 To become a chess **grandmaster** also seems to take about ten years. (Only the legendary Bobby Fischer got to that elite level in less than that amount of time: it took him nine years.) And what's ten years? Well, it's roughly how long it takes to put in ten thousand hours of hard practice. Ten thousand hours is the magic number of greatness.

12 Even Mozart—the greatest musical **prodigy** of all time— **couldn't hit his stride** until he had his ten thousand hours in. Practice isn't the thing you do once you're good. It's the thing you do that makes you good.

13 The other interesting thing about that ten thousand hours, of course, is that ten thousand hours is an *enormous* amount of time. It's all but impossible to reach that number all by yourself by the time you're a young adult. You have to have parents who encourage and support you. You can't be poor, because if you have to hold down a part-time job on the side to help make ends meet, there won't be time left in the day to practice enough. In fact, most people can reach that number only if they get into some kind of special program—like a hockey all-star squad—or if they get some kind of extraordinary opportunity that gives them a chance to put in those hours. ❖

TRUE SELF

EQ ESSENTIAL QUESTION:

Do We Find or Create Our True Selves?

myNGconnect.com

🔊 Download the rubric.

EDGE LIBRARY

Present Your Project: Gallery Walk

It is time to present your group project about the Essential Question for this unit: Do We Find or Create Our True Selves?

1 Review and Complete Your Plan

Consider these points as you complete your project:

- How well does your project answer the Essential Question?
- How will your group represent its project during the gallery walk?

As a group, decide how you will display your project so everyone can evaluate it. Assign a group member to answer questions.

2 Take the Gallery Walk

Display your work in the gallery. Walk around and look at the other groups' projects. Ask questions. Take notes on how each project deals with the Essential Question.

3 Evaluate the Projects

Use the online rubric to evaluate each group project, including your own.

Reflect on Your Reading

Think back on your reading of the unit selections, including your choice of Edge Library books. Discuss the following with a partner or in a group.

Genre Focus Compare and contrast the point of view in two short stories from this unit. If you were to rewrite one of the selections, would you choose the same point of view or a different one? Explain, giving examples.

Focus Strategy Think about your favorite character in this unit. Tell what he or she is like. Then look back at the selection and notice which details about the character are in the text and which you inferred. Discuss why you made the inferences that you made.

EQ Respond to the Essential Question

Throughout this unit, you have been thinking about whether people find or create their true selves. Discuss the Essential Question with a group. What have *you* decided? Support your response with evidence from your reading, discussions, research, and writing.

Write a Short Story

SUB TOTAL

Writing Portfolio

People sometimes disagree, or misunderstand each other. For this project, you will write a short story about an everyday conflict.

Study Short Stories

Short stories are narratives about imaginary people, places, and events. Writers use vivid details and dialogue to bring the characters and conflict to life.

❶ Connect Writing to Your Life

Even the most imaginative stories don't come out of thin air. Did you ever have a little brother or sister ask you to "make up" a story? You probably got your ideas from your own life and the lives of people you know or have read about. While telling stories is fun, writing them down is a way to keep them forever and still share them with many other people.

❷ Understand the Form

A short story usually has two or more characters, including a protagonist, or main character, and an antagonist. In most short stories, the protagonist faces a conflict, or struggle.

That conflict can lead to one complication after another. This sequence of events, or the plot, rises to a climax, which is a turning point or exciting part of the story. After that, the conflict gets resolved one way or another.

Plot Diagram

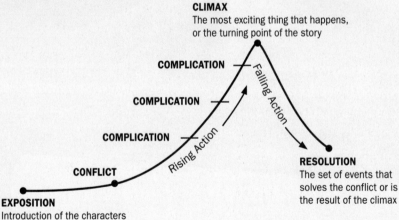

CLIMAX
The most exciting thing that happens, or the turning point of the story

COMPLICATION

COMPLICATION

COMPLICATION

Rising Action

Falling Action

CONFLICT

EXPOSITION
Introduction of the characters and setting. Sometimes presents the central conflict, or problem

RESOLUTION
The set of events that solves the conflict or is the result of the climax

Now read a short story by a professional writer. Using the plot diagram and the margin notes, identify the conflict and analyze the development of the plot.

❸ Analyze a Professional Model

As you read, look for the rising and falling action.

I'll Just Wait

by Jerome McKinnon

She said she'd meet me in City Park at 5:30. I'm pretty sure, because I wrote it down in my notebook, the one I use for my raps and other important stuff, the one that nobody else sees. Anyway, I don't forget things. Maybe Tracy does, though. It's 5:45, and she is nowhere to be seen.

I could call her, but I don't have her number. I could look for her in the rest of the park, but then she could show up and I wouldn't even know. I could call her name, but I would just sound like an idiot, my high-pitched voice yelling her name. It's bad enough I'm sitting out on this park bench like a billboard advertising loneliness. I feel foolish. Should I stay or go?

I'll just wait. The problem is that I'm not a patient guy. I'm always twitching and tapping. My mom says it's like I always have some place else I'd like to be.

Today, however, I'll just wait. But what if Tracy was only joking? I run new raps through my head, just to keep busy, but my rhymes never stay in my head. So I start pounding out beats with my hands and feet, clapping and stomping the rhythm of waiting. I keep a steady low thump with one foot. My hands flap like wings, quick and precise. I drop my head and let my lips mouth the words.

Music pours out of me. I've recited every lyric I know, but the words keep coming, a little loud, but I don't care. Suddenly, I hear another voice.

It hits my ear like a bell, a crystal clear voice right out of a music video, singing in perfect pitch and rhythm over my beats. I stop. Tracy stops. We look at each other and laugh.

"Six thirty, " she says through a smile. "I'm right on time."

I smile back. For the first time in my life, I'm not just waiting.

The first paragraph introduces the characters, setting, and conflict. What is the conflict?

The writer adds a complication.

How does the character's description of his choices build tension?

Vivid details show the effects of the conflict.

The story action rises to a climax, or turning point.

How is the conflict resolved?

▶ **Prompt** Write a short story about a conflict between two people. Be sure to tell:

- what the conflict is
- what the characters and the setting are like
- how the conflict affects the characters
- how the conflict is resolved

✔ Prewrite

You have studied a professional writer's short story. Now write one of your own. Making a Writing Plan is a little like listing all the ingredients that go into a great meal. Each story element is special and adds its own "flavor."

❶ Choose the Conflict

To zero in on an idea for your story, try the following ideas:

- Use your own life as inspiration. What conflicts have you had with another person? What steps did you take to peacefully resolve the conflict?
- Imagine that you lived in another place or time. What conflict would you face as a result?
- Use a Plot Diagram like the one on p. 250 to help you brainstorm ideas.

❷ Clarify the Audience, Theme, and Purpose

Good writers know who is reading their work. Will young children, students in another school, or published writers read your short story? Understanding each group can help you determine your word choices and style.

Think of what your story is mostly about. This is its **theme**, or message. For example, the message of "I'll Just Wait" is that what we think and worry about isn't always so.

Finally, decide why you are writing this story. Is it to share something you have learned? To entertain? Make sure the details you include serve your purpose.

❸ Gather Supporting Details

Now gather details about the story's characters, conflict, and setting. Use these details to create the mood and tone of your story. See how one writer used a freewrite to describe the elements of a possible story.

> My story will be based on a conflict I had with a neighbor. I'll call this character Mr. Lee. He wouldn't let me into his store because he said teenagers cause trouble. I'll make the main character a teenager called Jack. He'll resolve the conflict by proving himself to Mr. Lee.

Prewriting Tip

Gather details based on the elements of a short story, but don't worry about coming up with just the right title, character names, and other minor details. For now, use whatever comes to mind, and revise it later.

❹ Organize the Plot

After you gather your supporting details, organize them. A well-organized story has a clear structure. It's easy for readers to follow because events and details flow well from one part of the story to another. Here is how the writer organized the events and details of the story about Jack and Mr. Lee.

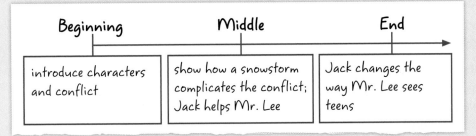

Technology Tip

Use a boldface font for labels such as Beginning, Middle, and End. This will help you keep track of the sections and what should go in each.

❺ Finish Your Writing Plan

Make a Writing Plan like the one below to capture all the planning you have done. Show which details will go in the beginning, the middle, and the end.

Writing Plan

Title	"Actions Speak Louder"
Audience	my classmates and teacher
Theme	sometimes you have to prove yourself
Purpose	to entertain
Time Frame	start today; due in 5 days
Beginning	introduce characters and conflict: teens, kids not allowed in Mr. Lee's store; use dialogue; describe the setting
Middle	snowstorm makes things worse for both characters Jack clears snow to help Mr. Lee
End	Mr. Lee changes his rule Jack is allowed into the store from now on

Reflect on Your Plan

▶ Is the way you organized the details well suited to the narrative form, audience, theme, and purpose? Talk it over with a partner.

✔ Write a Draft

Now you are ready to write your first draft. Don't worry about making everything perfect at this stage. Just follow your Writing Plan and get your ideas down on paper. You can make changes to your narrative later.

Drafting Tip

As you write your draft, jot down any ideas for illustrations or photos that could go with your story.

❶ Getting Ideas Out, Getting Ideas Down

Even the best writers sometimes feel "blocked." Use these techniques to get ideas out of your head and down on the page.

- **Look Again** Take another look at your Writing Plan. Could you define your theme more clearly? Are important details missing from the characters or plot? Have you thought about what sensory details will help set the mood or tone of your story?

- **Role Play** Bring ideas to life by asking friends to help you role-play your story's characters. Give your friends a brief description of each character and the conflict. Then, let your imaginations fill in the blanks. Think of ways to develop the plot so that it will hold the reader's attention. For example, use an unexpected turn of events to surprise your audience. You may also want to use dialogue to help move the plot along.

- **Freewrite** Sometimes writers get stuck trying to write a perfect first sentence. If you're stuck, just start writing about your characters and your idea and don't stop for five minutes. Don't think about punctuation or complete sentences. Write what comes to mind. Then, read what you wrote, and underline or circle the ideas, descriptions, or phrases you like and can use in your story.

See how this writer revisited the prewriting stage to get more ideas flowing.

Beginning

introduce characters and conflict
describe store, weather
Mr. Lee tells Jack to read the sign "No teens or other kids allowed"

Middle

snowstorm makes things worse for both characters
Jack hates walking in the snow
snow blocks door to Mr. Lee's store
Jack helps Mr. Lee

📖 **Writing Handbook**, p. 700

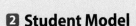

❷ Student Model

Read this draft to see how the student used the Writing Plan to get ideas down on paper. This first draft does not have to be perfect. The student revised it later.

Actions Speak Louder

I heard his harsh voice as the door slammed shut on the snowstorm outside. read the sign, Jack, said Mr. Lee, who owned the corner convenience store. He pointed to a hand-written sign on the door. "no teens or other kids allowed without an adult."

"teens aren't kids," I retorted. "we're adults."

"actions speak louder than words," he replies. Then he is giving me a wink. "say hi to your dad for me." He and Dad worked together at the factory until it closed down.

The snow got worse as I stepped outside. Thanks to Mr. Lee's sign, I had to shiver all the way to the big supermarket several blocks farther. By the time I left the supermarket, I could barely see through the heavy snow. I felt angry at Mr. Lee for makeing me hike through this messy winter storm.

As I passed Mr. Lee's store again, I saw that a snowplow had pushed a huge pile of snow against the store's door. Mr. Lee was stuck inside. Serves him right, I thought. Then I realized how childish that was.

I raced home and put away the groceries. I'll be right back I called to Dad as I grabbed a shovel and headed out into the storm. I got to Mr. Lee's. Then customers were flowing in and out of the store over the newly cleared sidewalk. That's because before that I had set to work carveing a path out of the snowy mountain. Some of the customers were friends from school. Karen from science class stopped in. The snow was cold. The flow slowed (the flow of people, that is). Mr. Lee tapped on the window and wave me inside.

"Who told you to do that?" he asked.

"You do," I said and smiled broadly.

Mr. Lee paused. He smiled and said, "well, I guess I did."

Reflect on Your Draft

▶ Did you introduce your characters and setting in the beginning? Does the order of events make sense? Do events build to a climax? Is the conflict resolved?

3.29

✔ Revise Your Draft

Your short story is starting to take shape. Read it carefully, and ask yourself these questions: Does my story have characters, a setting, and a plot? What is the conflict? What is the resolution? Have I used language and details to set the tone of the story? Now, improve your story.

❶ Revise for Organization

A reader's understanding of a short story depends on its **organization**. In a well-organized story, ideas about the characters, conflict, plot, and other details progress in a logical way. Sometimes the events are presented chronologically, or in the order in which they happen. Other times a writer uses flashbacks, or starts in the present and goes back in time to describe an event that led up to the present. Either way, the order of events must make sense.

In addition, organized writers make effective use of transitional devices to contribute a sense of completeness to their writing. In other words, an organized story doesn't start, stop, get lost, and start up again. Instead, it uses transition words like *soon, the next day, however, instead,* and so on to blend the paragraphs and keep the story rolling along.

TRY IT ▶ Evaluate the drafts below. Which one is better organized? Discuss them with a partner, using the rubric to decide.

Draft 1

> I got to Mr. Lee's. Then customers were flowing in and out of the store over the newly cleared sidewalk. That's because before that I had set to work carving a path out of the snowy mountain. Some of the customers were friends from school. Karen from science class stopped in. The snow was cold. The flow slowed (the flow of people, that is). Mr. Lee tapped on the window and wave me inside.

Draft 2

> When I got to Mr. Lee's, I set to work carving a path out of the snowy mountain. Soon, customers were flowing in and out of the store over the newly cleared sidewalk.
>
> When the flow of people slowed, Mr. Lee tapped on the window and waved me inside.

🞃 **Writing Handbook,** p. 708

Now use the rubric to evaluate the organization of your own draft. What score would you give your draft and why?

Organization

myNGconnect.com
- Rubric: Organization
- Evaluate and practice scoring other student short stories.

	Does the writing have a clear structure, and is it appropriate for the writer's audience, purpose, and type of writing?	How smoothly do the ideas flow together?
4 Wow!	**The writing has a structure that is clear and appropriate for the writer's audience, purpose, and type of writing.**	**The ideas progress in a smooth and orderly way.** • The introduction is strong. • The ideas flow well from paragraph to paragraph. • The ideas in each paragraph flow well from one sentence to the next. • Effective transitions connect ideas. • The conclusion is strong.
3 Ahh.	**The writing has a structure that is generally clear and appropriate for the writer's audience, purpose, and type of writing.**	**Most of the ideas progress in a smooth and orderly way.** • The introduction is adequate. • Most of the ideas flow well from paragraph to paragraph. • Most ideas in each paragraph flow from one sentence to the next. • Effective transitions connect most of the ideas. • The conclusion is adequate.
2 Hmm.	**The structure of the writing is not clear or not appropriate for the writer's audience, purpose, and type of writing.**	**Some of the ideas progress in a smooth and orderly way.** • The introduction is weak. • Some of the ideas flow well from paragraph to paragraph. • Some ideas in each paragraph flow from one sentence to the next. • Transitions connect some ideas. • The conclusion is weak.
1 Huh?	**The writing is not clear or organized.**	**Few or none of the ideas progress in a smooth and orderly way.**

✔ Revise Your Draft, continued

❷ Revise Your Draft

You've now evaluated the organization of your own draft. If you scored 3 or lower, how can you improve your work? Use the checklist below to revise your draft.

Revision Checklist

Ask Yourself	Check It Out	How to Make It Better
Does my story have a clear structure that supports my purpose?	Underline sentences that introduce the characters, the setting, and the conflict.	☐ At the beginning of the story, introduce the protagonist and the antagonist. Clearly state the conflict. ☐ Cut, move, or replace paragraphs that do not fit or have a clear purpose.
Are the ideas and events clearly connected? Does the story move forward smoothly?	If your score is 3 or lower, look at the techniques you used to organize the events.	☐ Move sentences or paragraphs around to tell about events chronologically, in flashbacks, or in another logical order. ☐ Add transitions to clearly connect ideas and actions between sentences and between paragraphs.
Does my story have rising and falling action?	Underline the climax and the resolution.	☐ Add complications that lead to the climax. ☐ Rewrite the ending so the resolution is clear.
Are the characters lively and believable? Will readers care about them? Is the setting vivid?	Underline dialogue and descriptions.	☐ Provide details that show how the main character felt. ☐ Add descriptive detail from your personal experience to make characters and setting seem as real as possible.

📖 **Writing Handbook**, p. 698

3 Conduct a Peer Conference

A peer conference gives you the opportunity to present your work to a reader for the first time. Ask a partner to read your draft and look for

- any part of the draft that is confusing
- any place where something seems to be missing
- anything that the reader doesn't understand.

Discuss your draft with your partner. Focus on the items in the Revision Checklist. Use your partner's comments to improve the organization of your story.

4 Make Revisions

Read the revisions below and the peer-reviewer conversation on the right. Notice the questions the peer reviewer asked and the revisions that were made. How does the writer respond to the reviewer's ideas?

Draft 1

> When I got to Mr. Lee's, I set to work carving a path out of the snowy mountain. Soon, customers were flowing in and out of the store over the newly cleared sidewalk.
>
> ~~Some of the customers were my friends from school. Even Karen~~ ℓ ~~from my science class stopped in.~~ ℓ
>
> ~~It sure was cold.~~ ℓ When the flow slowed, Mr. Lee tapped on the window and waved me inside.

Draft 2

> "Who told you to do that?" he asked.
>
> "You did," I said and smiled broadly. ⌃ "Actions speak louder than words, remember?"
>
> Mr. Lee paused then began to laugh. He walked over to the door. Then he removed the sign.

Peer Conference

Reviewer's Comment: I'm not sure why you include who the customers were. What does that have to do with the theme?

Writer's Answer: You're right! Those details aren't important. I'll delete them to keep the events and ideas connected.

Reviewer's Question: What did Mr. Lee tell Jack to do? I don't get it.

Writer's Answer: He gave Jack the idea when he said "Actions speak louder than words." I'll have Jack remind him of that.

Reflect on Your Revisions

▶ Think about your peer conference. What did you learn from it about your writing for this assignment? What did you learn that you can apply to other writing assignments?

✔ Edit and Proofread Your Draft

Now that you have a revised draft, it is time to polish it for presentation to your readers. Find and fix any mistakes that you made.

❶ Capitalize Quotations Correctly

Capitalize the first word in a direct quotation.

> **"Read** the sign, Jack," said Mr. Lee.
>
> He smiled and said, **"Well,** I guess I did."

TRY IT ▶ Copy the sentence. Fix the two capitalization errors. Use proofreader's marks.

> "teens aren't kids," I retorted. "we're adults."

❷ Use Quotation Marks Correctly

Put quotation marks (" ") around the exact words that characters speak. Do not use quotation marks when you describe what characters said.

Use the comma before someone's exact words. Use the comma after someone's exact words if the sentence continues.

> **Quotations:** He said, **"**No teens or other kids are allowed.**"**
>
> **"**Teens aren't kids,**"** I said.

> **Description:** I said that teens aren't kids.

TRY IT ▶ Copy the sentences. Add any necessary quotation marks and commas. Delete quotation marks that aren't necessary.

> 1. Read the sign, Jack he said.
> 2. I said that "I would clear the snow away."
> 3. "Who told" you to do that? he asked.

Proofreader's Marks

Use these proofreader's marks to correct capitalization and punctuation errors.

Capitalize:
read the sign.

Do not capitalize:
I hurried Home.

Add quotation marks:
ᵛActions speak louder than words,ᵛhe replied.

Add comma:
Jack͜come here.

Delete comma:
The man͵who owns͵the store is Mr. Lee.

Proofreading Tip ▶

If you are unsure of how to use quotations marks and commas in dialogue, refer to a style manual for help.

---

3 Check Your Spelling

Follow these guidelines for making sure you spell words with prefixes or suffixes correctly.

Adding prefixes usually does not change the spelling of the base word.

Prefix	Base Word	New Word
un-	fair	unfair
re-	move	remove

When adding a suffix that begins with a vowel, drop the final e from a base word that ends with e.

Base Word	Suffix	New Word
make	-ing	making
race	-ed	raced

TRY IT ▶ Copy the sentences. Find and fix the two affix spelling errors.

1. Mr. Lee remmoved the sign.
2. I raceed home.

4 Use Correct Verb Tense in Quotations

Use the past tense of a verb to tell about an action that happened in the past.

He **pointed** to the sign on the door.

However, you do not need to change the verb tense in directly quoted speech.

Incorrect	Correct
"Actions **spoke** louder than words," he **replied**.	"Actions **speak** louder than words," he **replied**.
"I **was** right back!" I **told** Dad.	"I **will be** right back!" I **told** Dad.

🔖 **Writing Handbook**, p. 749

Technology Tip

Be sure to use the Spell-checker in your word-processing program, but be aware that it is not perfect. Make sure you know the rules of correct spelling so you can choose the correct spelling from among the computer's suggestions.

Reflect on Your Corrections

▶ Which of these editing and proofreading skills do you find most challenging? Make a note of the ones you find most difficult, and work with a friend to help you fix them on future writing assignments.

⑤ Edited Student Draft

Here's the student's draft, revised and edited. How did the writer improve it?

Actions Speak Louder

I heard his harsh voice as the door slammed shut on the snowstorm outside. "Read the sign, Jack," said Mr. Lee, who owned the corner convenience store. He pointed to a handwritten sign on the door. "No teens or other kids allowed without an adult."

"Teens aren't kids," I retorted. "We're adults."

"Actions speak louder than words," he replied. Then he gave me a wink. "Say hi to your dad for me." He and Dad worked together at the factory until it closed down.

The snow got worse as I stepped outside. Thanks to Mr. Lee's sign, I had to shiver all the way to the big supermarket several blocks farther. By the time I left the supermarket, I could barely see through the heavy snow. I felt angry at Mr. Lee for making me hike through this messy winter storm.

As I passed Mr. Lee's store again, I saw that a snowplow had pushed a huge pile of snow against the store's door. Mr. Lee was stuck inside. Serves him right, I thought. Then I realized how childish that was.

I raced home and put away the groceries. "I'll be right back," I called to Dad as I grabbed a shovel and headed out into the storm. When I got to Mr. Lee's, I set to work carving a path out of the snowy mountain. Soon, customers were flowing in and out of the store over the newly cleared sidewalk.

When the flow of people slowed, Mr. Lee tapped on the window and waved me inside. "Who told you to do that?" he asked.

"You did," I said and smiled broadly. "Actions speak louder than words, remember?"

Mr. Lee paused. Then he removed the sign. He smiled and said, "Well, I guess I did."

The writer added **quotation marks** and a **comma** to direct speech.

The writer capitalized the first word in **direct quotations**.

The writer fixed **spelling** errors in three suffixes.

The writer moved sentences around and added transitions that connected ideas. The writer also deleted details that did not serve the story's purpose.

The writer added **dialogue** to clarify the theme and used the **correct verb tense** in the quotation.

✔ Publish and Present

Congratulations! You have prewritten, drafted, revised, and edited your own short story. Now you're ready to publish and present it to an audience. You may also want to present your work in a different way.

Alternative Presentations

Record a Reading of Your Story Gather a group of students to help you record a reading of your story.

1 Plan the Recording Format Decide how you will record it. Will you make an audio or videotape recording, copy it onto a compact disc to share with others, or create an audio file that can be uploaded onto a Web site? Be sure to check with your teacher to see what recording equipment is available. Follow school rules about sharing your work.

2 Cast the Characters Assign roles to yourself and other students. You will need one student to read aloud each character's dialogue, plus one more reader to narrate the part in between. Make photocopies of your story. Ask the readers to highlight the lines they will read aloud.

3 Rehearse Start with a "cold reading." This is when the actors read aloud a text together for the first time. Don't worry if you occasionally make mistakes, such as reading the wrong line or skipping a line. Practice a few more times and you'll soon know each line by heart.

4 Perform You can keep your copies of the story in front of you even as you perform. But don't hide behind them! Remember, people will be listening to, and perhaps viewing, your recorded performance. Read with expression, and vary the tone of your voice.

Present Your Process Authors are often asked how they develop their books. Exchange stories with a partner. Then interview each other about your own writing process.

1 Review Each Step Ask questions about each step in the writing process. Which step did your partner most enjoy? Which was most difficult? How is this like or unlike your experience?

2 Listen Carefully Listen closely to your partner's responses before you ask another question. He or she may say something that you can learn from.

3 Ask About the Theme Find out more about your partner by asking him or her about the theme. Why is this idea important? What else would the author like readers to know about the inspiration for the story?

🔖 **Language and Learning Handbook,** p. 616

Presenting Tip

Before you record your story, make a practice tape. Read your story aloud, and record your practice reading. Listen to the practice tape to hear what you need to fix.

Reflect on Your Final Work

▶ Think back on your experience in the writing process.

- Which step in the process was easiest?
- Which was most difficult?
- What one thing would you most like to change about your finished story?
- What will you do differently next time?

☑ Save a copy of your work in your portfolio.

EQ ESSENTIAL QUESTION:

How Much Should People Help Each Other?

The point is not to pay back kindness, but to pass it on.

—JULIA ALVAREZ

If you give what you do not need, it is not giving.

—MOTHER TERESA

Critical Viewing ▶
Two sisters help each other cross a muddy river in Hanoi, Vietnam. In their traditional *ao dai* gowns, they form a vision of grace and kindness. Is it possible to be too helpful?

GIVE & TAKE

ESSENTIAL QUESTION:
How Much Should People Help Each Other?

Study the Facts

According to government reports, more than 65% of high school students volunteer in their communities, helping individuals or organizations in need. In a national survey, teens gave the following responses to questions about volunteering:

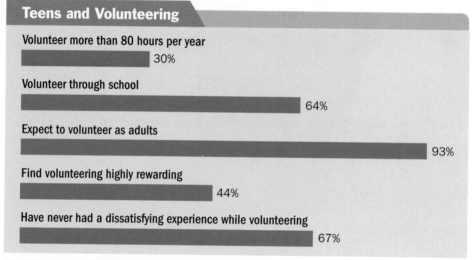

Teens and Volunteering

Volunteer more than 80 hours per year
30%

Volunteer through school
64%

Expect to volunteer as adults
93%

Find volunteering highly rewarding
44%

Have never had a dissatisfying experience while volunteering
67%

Source: *USA Weekend* magazine; April 24, 2005

Analyze and Debate

1. Do the results of this survey surprise you? Why do you think teens choose to volunteer?

2. Do you agree with the survey results, based on what you know?

Talk about the survey data and discuss the questions in a group. Give reasons for your answers.

ESSENTIAL QUESTION

In this unit, you will explore the **Essential Question** in class through reading, discussion, research, and writing. Keep thinking about the question outside of school, too.

① Plan a Project

Multimedia Presentation

In this unit, you will give a multimedia presentation about the Essential Question. Find media, such as photos, film clips, and audio files, that support your ideas. To get started, do an Internet search using the key words *volunteer opportunities* and *teens*. Look for

- the kinds of opportunities that are available
- organizations that need volunteers
- the benefits of volunteering
- any qualifications required of volunteers.

Study Skills Start planning your multimedia presentation. Use the forms on myNGconnect.com to plan your time and to prepare the content.

myNGconnect.com
▸ Planning forms
▸ Scheduler
▸ Rubric

② Choose More to Read

These readings provide different answers to the Essential Question. Choose a book and online selections to read during the unit.

The Forbidden Schoolhouse
by Suzanne Jurmain

In 1833, Prudence Crandall opened a school for African American girls. Although the community was against her, Prudence began teaching her students. The struggle was harder than she could have imagined. Was the right to an education really worth fighting for?

▸ NONFICTION

The Ch'i-lin Purse
retold by Linda Fang

Have you ever helped a stranger? Or been asked for help by someone you did not know? This collection of Chinese folk tales includes clever characters who often help strangers. Each story shows how one person's act of kindness can change another person's life forever. Explore how stories like folk tales and myths influence modern literature.

▸ FOLK TALES

Of Sound Mind
by Jean Ferris

Theo wants to follow his dreams and go away to college. But his mother, father, and younger brother are deaf. How can he leave when his family needs him so much? Then he meets Ivy. Can Ivy show Theo how to give to others without giving up everything he wants?

▸ NOVEL

myNGconnect.com

🔄 **Explore opportunities for youth volunteers.**
🔄 **Read stories about people who have volunteered.**
🔄 **Respond to message board postings about volunteering.**

There are all kinds of nonfiction, and they all give information—a lot of information. Read this article and begin to make sense of a lot of information. Ask your teacher or a classmate to help clarify new words or ideas.

DEMO TEXT

Injury Spoils Tiger Win

BANVILLE — The Banville Tigers continued their march toward the county championship Friday with a 21–14 win over Stilton, but victory came at a price. Tiger quarterback Antwon Trease was sacked in the second quarter, sustaining severe leg and knee injuries. After the game, Coach Fred Wilson said, "We don't know how serious the injuries are yet. Antwon could be out for the rest of the season."

Antwon could be out for the rest of the season.

Tiger quarterback Antwon Trease was injured in the second quarter. Trainers had to carry him from the field on a stretcher.

Seesaw Battle

For three quarters, Banville and Stilton traded the lead. Banville scored first on a 22-yard pass from Trease to Cory Stern. Stilton answered in the last seconds of the first quarter, scoring from the 2-yard-line to cap a 72-yard march. At the end of the game, with 32 seconds left and the score tied 14–14, Banville had the ball on the Stilton 35-yard line. After Ted Peterson ran for 5 yards, reserve quarterback Sam Yamamoto launched a pass deep for Jake Jackson. Jackson caught the ball and ran for the game-winning touchdown.

Disaster Strikes

When Trease dropped back to pass late in the second quarter, Stilton swarmed through the pass protection and sacked Trease for a 7-yard loss. Trease did not get up.

Too Dangerous?

After the game, concerned parents gathered to discuss Trease's injuries and how to keep other players safe. District statistics show that sports injuries are a growing problem.

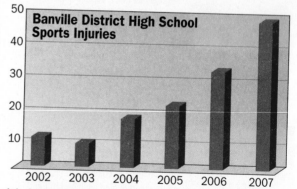

Banville District High School Sports Injuries

Injuries in high school sports are increasing in Banville Unified School District.

■ Connect Reading to Your Life

You probably don't remember every detail about the article, even though you read it only a minute ago. But you probably remember a few things. Rate these statements as true or false. Just go from your memory. Don't look back at the article.

Reading Strategies

- Plan and Monitor
- ▶ **Determine Importance**
- Make Inferences
- Ask Questions
- Make Connections
- Synthesize
- Visualize

	True or False
1. Antwon was injured in the game.	
2. The Tigers did not win the football game.	
3. Injuries among high school players in the district are on the rise.	
4. Each team was in the lead at some point during the game.	

Compare your answers with a partner's, and then confirm your understanding by checking the article. Discuss how the different features in the article helped you figure out the answers.

Focus Strategy ▶ Determine Importance

You probably rated most or all of the statements correctly because you paid attention to what was important in the article. And how did you do *that*? The text helped you. There were clear signposts pointing to what was important:

- a headline
- other heads
- a photo
- a graph

All these things gave you important information at a glance.

It's just like when you go to a new store. You pay attention to big or colorful signs that tell you where you need to go, but you don't remember every single thing that you pass along the way.

■ Your Job as a Reader

Experienced readers know that they can't pay attention to everything. What *do* you pay attention to then? It's your job as a reader to figure that out. Usually, you pay attention to what the author says is important—which you can tell by the signposts in the text—and to why you are reading in the first place.

■ Unpack the Thinking Process

Let's take a closer look at how you knew what was important in the news article.

Text Features

People who write, edit, and design articles for newspapers, magazines, and textbooks help you know what is most important about the text. They use tools called text features. Find each of these text features in "Injury Spoils Tiger Win."

Purpose of Text Features

Text Feature	Purpose
Headline (Title)	Describes or hints at the main idea
Photo	Illustrates people, places, or events
Information Graphic	**Summarizes** information or adds new information to support the main idea
Section Heads	Tell the main idea of a section, or part
Paragraphs	Tell one main idea each
Display Quote	Shows an important statement in a noticeable way

Use text features before, during, and after reading to help you determine what is important and how the ideas are connected.

- **Before Reading:** Scan the heads and graphics for an idea of what the reading is about. Use the information you gather to set your purpose for reading.

- **During Reading:** Turn each head into a question, and read that section to answer the question. Really read the captions under the photos and other information graphics as you go. These can summarize information in the text or add important information.

- **After Reading:** Review the key ideas by scanning the heads again and skimming the text. This will help you summarize the text and remember the most important information. Also notice how the author uses text features to develop ideas and draw connections between sections of the text.

Academic Vocabulary

- **summarize** v., to briefly give the main points; to sum up;
  summary n., a short statement that gives the main points

Text Structures

Writers not only use text features to show you what's important, they also organize their ideas in a certain way to help the reader. For example, in biographies and autobiographies, writers often organize information in time, or **chronological**, order. The Demo Text also does this, with one exception. In news articles, the most important event is first, followed by the events that lead up to it, mostly in chronological order.

■ Try an Experiment

Read this brief article.

DEMO TEXT #2

When Nikki Kubicek was a kid, she loved to watch her older sister play for the Park Valley softball team. Four years ago, Kubicek joined the team herself. She has become one of the best hitters in the team's history. The 5-foot-2 powerhouse has set 9 school records, including most runs batted in during a tournament (2), highest season batting average (.555), and most stolen bases in a tournament (6). Last week, Kubicek was named the team's Player of the Year for the second time. At the award dinner on Saturday night, Kubicek basked in compliments. "She gives all she has in every game," Coach Santos said. "Many great players have played for this team," Kubicek said. "It's a great feeling to be among them."

With a small group, add text features to the article to show what is important and to strengthen the development of ideas.

1. Brainstorm a headline for the article.

2. Consider how the ideas are developed. Determine where to break the text to make logical sections. Create a head for each section.

3. Choose a display quote.

4. Sketch an information graphic or a photo.

Debrief Now compare your text features with another group's. **Justify**, or explain, how each of your features helps the reader determine what is important and strengthens the development of ideas.

Monitor Comprehension

Elements of Literature
chronological *adj.*, arranged according to the order in which events happened

Academic Vocabulary
• **justify** *v.*, to give a good reason for something; **justification** *n.*, a good reason or explanation

Text Features What are the main reasons for having different text features?

How Much Should People Help Each Other?
Read about helpful and harmful relationships.

Make a Connection

Think, Pair, Share Would you tell lies to protect people you love? Would you solve their problems rather than your own? Think about these questions. Then discuss them with a partner. Share your ideas with the class.

Learn Key Vocabulary

Study the Words Pronounce each word and learn its meaning. You may also want to look up the definitions in the Glossary.

• Academic Vocabulary

Key Words	Examples
agony (**a**-gu-nē) *noun* ▶ pages 298, 300	To be in **agony** is to experience great suffering. *Synonym:* pain
avoid (u-**void**) *verb* ▶ pages 290, 295	Do you try to **avoid**, or stay away from, unhealthy foods? *Antonyms:* find, get
consequence (**kon**-su-kwens) *noun* ▶ pages 291, 301	A **consequence** is something that happens as a result of some action. *Synonyms:* result, effect; *Antonym:* cause
dependent (di-**pen**-dunt) *adjective* ▶ page 293	If you need someone to help you most of the time, you are **dependent** on that person. Children are **dependent** on their parents for food and housing.
• **enable** (i-**nā**-bul) *verb* ▶ pages 290	To **enable** a person to do something is to help make it possible. Parents who pay for their son's college **enable** him to succeed.
relationship (ri-**lā**-shun-ship) *noun* ▶ pages 293, 295, 297, 300, 301	A **relationship** tells how people or things are connected to each other. Marriage is one kind of **relationship**. Friendship is another.
rescue (**res**-kyū) *verb* ▶ page 290	To save a person from harm is to **rescue** him or her. If you fall into a lake, you may need someone to **rescue** you. *Synonym:* save
responsibility (ri-spon-su-**bi**-lu-tē) *noun* ▶ pages 290, 301	A **responsibility** is something that a person must do. The **responsibility** of a student is to go to school, study, and learn. *Synonym:* job, duty, obligation

Practice the Words Work with a partner. Make a **Definition Map** for each Key Vocabulary word. Use a dictionary to find other forms of the word.

Definition Map

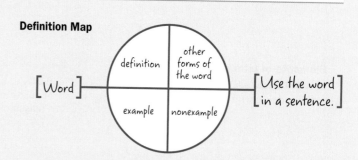

BEFORE READING Enabling or Disabling?

informational text by Sandra R. Arbetter

Reading Strategies

- Plan and Monitor
▶ Determine Importance
- Make Inferences
- Ask Questions
- Make Connections
- Synthesize
- Visualize

Analyze Development of Ideas

Text features help you understand the information in nonfiction texts. These text features are central to how the author develops ideas and clearly presents them to readers.

- The title tells what the selection is about.
- A section head tells the main idea of an entire section.
- Each paragraph tells about a single idea.
- Visuals, like diagrams, give extra information or explain the text.

Look Into the Text

The section head is a clue to the main idea.

The Enabler

Jerry had a hectic week, so hectic that he didn't have time to study for Friday's social studies test...

"Ma," he said, "please call me in sick. If I don't get some extra time to study I'm going to flunk."

So Mom called him in sick on Friday, and he got a C when he took the test on Monday. Jerry gave her a big hug and called her his chief helper. Another description would also fit: his chief enabler. If that sounds like a compliment, it's not.

What details support the main idea that Mom is Jerry's enabler?

Focus Strategy ▶ Determine Importance

You can't always remember all the details in informational text, but you want to remember the **main ideas**. Try this strategy with the text above.

Focus Strategy

HOW TO UNCOVER MAIN IDEAS IN NONFICTION

1. **Form a Question** Turn the section head into a question.

Section head:	Question:
The Enabler	What is an enabler?

2. **Make a Web** Write your question in the center.

3. **List Details** Look for information to answer your question. For example, list details about how Jerry's mother helps him.

4. **Write a Main Idea Statement** Look at the question again. Review the details. Write one sentence that answers the question. That is the main idea.

An enabler helps people avoid responsibilities.

Web

She rescues him from difficulties.   She lies for him.

What is an enabler?

Miss Goodanswer's Advice for Teens

How Hannah Can Help

Dear Miss Goodanswer,

I really want to help my best friend. A few months ago, she found out that her boyfriend was cheating on her, so she stopped seeing him. Now he says he has changed. He wants to date her again.

I know he is lying. He will break her heart again. The last time they stopped dating, I didn't want her to feel so alone. I called her every night. She cried for hours. I felt so bad for her. I couldn't tell her to face the fact that he is a jerk. I actually told her to go back to him.

I do not want her to go through all of this again. It was too hard the first time. How can I keep my friend from making the same mistake again?

—Hannah Helpful

Dear Hannah Helpful,

My advice is first to realize that you are part of the problem here! You need to step back and let your friend learn her own lessons. Support her, but do not call her every night.

Be honest, too. Tell her how you feel. Explain why you think it would be a mistake for her to date her former boyfriend. Tell her why you think he is lying. Explain that it hurts you to see your friend in pain.

Then let your friend decide what to do.

Suppose she decides to go out with him again. And suppose the same thing happens. Let her make the choice. You are not helping by being so involved.

I know it's hard to see your friend make mistakes. But remember that you can't control her.

—Miss Goodanswer

myNGconnect.com

🔵 Read an online teen advice column.
🔵 View an animated advice column.

Enabling or Disabling?

by Sandra R. Arbetter

Most people think helping others is a good thing, but is it? Is it possible to help too much?

 Comprehension Coach

The Enabler

Jerry had a **hectic** week, so hectic that he didn't have time to study for Friday's social studies test. Basketball practice on Monday and Tuesday, a game on Wednesday, and his girlfriend's birthday on Thursday. But he didn't waste time worrying. He was sure his mom would be willing to help him out.

"Ma," he said, "please call me in sick. If I don't get some extra time to study I'm going to **flunk**."

So Mom called him in sick on Friday, and he got a C when he took the test on Monday. Jerry gave her a big hug and called her his chief helper. Another description would also fit: his chief enabler. **1** If that sounds like a compliment, it's not.

Jerry's mom **enabled** him to **postpone taking** the test and get a passing grade on it. But she also enabled him to **avoid** his **responsibilities**. She enabled him to think he could lie and get away with it. And she enabled him to depend on other people to **rescue** him from a difficult situation.

Parents may enable their children to avoid responsibilities by "helping" too much. Young people may not learn how to do things themselves, such as completing homework, solving problems, or making decisions.

1 Access Vocabulary
Based on what you have read so far, what do you think is the difference between an *enabler* and a *helper*?

Key Vocabulary
- **enable** *v.*, to help make something possible
- **avoid** *v.*, to stay away from
- **responsibility** *n.*, job, duty
- **rescue** *v.*, to save someone from harm

In Other Words
hectic busy
flunk fail the test
postpone taking wait until later to take

Alcoholism—and Beyond 2

Enabling is a term that's been used for a long time as it relates to **alcoholism**. The term refers to family and friends who **smooth the way** for alcoholics so that they never have to face the **consequences** of their behavior. The term *enabler* has been broadened to include anyone who enables a person to continue with destructive behavior.

In the family of an alcoholic, a spouse, a parent, or even a child can enable the alcoholic to continue drinking. That's one reason alcoholism is often called a family disease. Enablers hardly ever realize that they are doing harm. They are just trying to help.

Let's say the father is an alcoholic and the mother is an enabler. She may see her husband as the **culprit** and herself as **a martyr**, acting selflessly to save the family.

When her husband has had too much to drink the night before and can't get up for work, she calls in to the office to say he is sick. When he's sprawled out on the sofa in a drunken haze, she tells the children that he's tired from a hard day at work. When he's too drunk to attend a family birthday party, she tells the relative he's loaded down with work. **3**

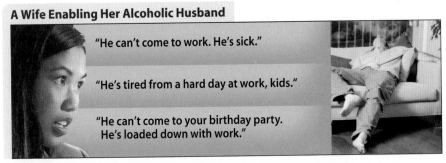

A Wife Enabling Her Alcoholic Husband

"He can't come to work. He's sick."

"He's tired from a hard day at work, kids."

"He can't come to your birthday party. He's loaded down with work."

⚠ **Interpret the Visual** What is the relationship between these people? Why is the woman saying these things?

Key Vocabulary
consequence *n.*, the result of some action

In Other Words
alcoholism a disease that causes someone to drink too much alcohol like beer or wine
smooth the way make it easy
culprit one who does something wrong
a martyr the one who suffers

---

2 Development of Ideas
Turn this section head into a question. Read on to find details on this page to answer your question. Write your ideas on your web.

3 Identify Main Ideas
What details show that this woman enables her husband to continue drinking?

Monitor Comprehension

Paraphrase
In your own words, tell what an enabler does.

The children in an alcoholic family may act as enablers by pretending the drinking isn't happening.

"My dad is an alcoholic," says 13-year-old Jenny. "One night he got so drunk he punched my brother and would have **socked** my mother, too, but he tripped and fell on the floor and passed out. No one in the family paid attention. They acted as though it weren't happening." **4**

Enablers Often . . .

- feel safest when giving help to someone else

- feel responsible for other people's actions and feelings

- feel **guilty** and anxious when someone they love has a problem

- think they MUST solve that person's problem

- try to help others instead of themselves

- stop everything to help save someone in need

- feel angry and upset if their solutions don't fix the problem

- feel worse about other people's problems than about their own problems

- refuse to accept painful facts about someone they love. **5**

4 Development of Ideas/Identify Main Ideas
What information on this page helps answer your section question? Review all the details and write a main idea for this section.

5 Development of Ideas
Why do you think this checklist is included in this informational text?

In Other Words
socked hit
guilty responsible, at fault

Two-Way Street

What's in all this for the enabler? For one thing, it ensures that the other person will stay emotionally **dependent** on the enabler. But a strange thing can happen. The enabler can become dependent too. The **relationship** can work like this: Janey enabled her boyfriend Frank to take unfair advantage of his **asthma**. Whenever he was upset, he'd start **wheezing**, so Janey felt she could never disagree with him. If he wanted to go to the movies, that's where they went, even if Janey had seen the film already. If Frank wanted pizza, then pizza it was, **no matter how Janey's mouth watered for** a burger. 6

Janey also tried to keep others from upsetting Frank. When they were with friends, she worried that someone would say something that could send Frank into an asthma attack. She felt she had to control the conversation and the

6 Development of Ideas
Turn the section head into a question. Has the author provided any details yet that help you answer your question? What details, if any, has the author given?

Monitor Comprehension

Describe
Use evidence from the text to tell what characteristics of an enabler Janey has.

Key Vocabulary
dependent *adj.*, needing help most of the time
relationship *n.*, the way that people are connected to each other

In Other Words
asthma disease that sometimes made it difficult for him to breathe
wheezing trying to get his breath
no matter how Janey's mouth watered for even if Janey really wanted to eat

entertainment so he'd stay happy and healthy. She felt personally responsible for his well-being, and took pride in every day that passed without a wheeze.

Her self-esteem was dependent on how Frank felt. If he felt good, so did she. If he was unhappy, so was she. He depended on her to enable him to control others with his asthma.

However, Janey was equally dependent on Frank. She had become what **psychologists** call a *codependent*, a person who focuses on another person rather than on himself or herself. **7** Janey's enabling let her **sidestep** unpleasant feelings about Frank's behavior. Such feelings can be a normal part of facing problems, making mistakes, and growing up.

7 Access Vocabulary
The prefix *co-* means "with" or "together." How does this help you understand what *codependent* means?

Codependent Relationship

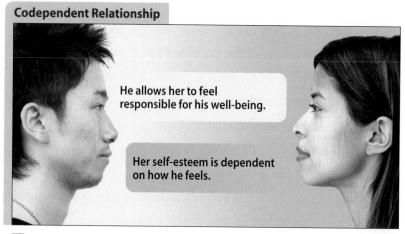

He allows her to feel responsible for his well-being.

Her self-esteem is dependent on how he feels.

▲ Interpret the Visual Explain how these two people are codependent. **8**

8 Development of Ideas/Identify Main Ideas
Review the ideas and information in the visual and the entire section. What is the main idea of "Two-Way Street"?

Some of the nicest people are enablers. In fact, the problem is that they are too nice. They do too much, too soon, too often. When it comes to helping other people, sometimes less is more. ❖

In Other Words

psychologists professionals who study the way people act and think
sidestep not think about, not pay attention to

ANALYZE Enabling or Disabling?

1. **Explain** In what important way are Jerry's mom and Janey alike? Cite text evidence. How does their behavior affect their **relationships**?

2. **Vocabulary** Is it a mistake to help loved ones **avoid** their responsibilities? Why or why not?

3. **Analyze Development of Ideas** Find a visual in the informational text. Is it easier to understand the information through the text or through the visual aid? Explain what it contributes to the text.

4. **Focus Strategy Determine Importance** Study the webs you made for this selection. What was the main idea of each section? What were the details that supported it? Complete this outline and use it to construct the main idea of the entire selection with a partner.

> I. The Enabler
>   A. The Main Idea
>
>   B. Details
>   1.
>   2.
>   3.

Return to the Text

Reread and Write Using what you now know about enablers, write a journal entry to describe how much people should help each other. Reread the text to find examples that support your ideas.

BEFORE READING This I Believe

essay by Isabel Allende

Reading Strategies

• Plan and Monitor
▶ Determine Importance
• Make Inferences
• Ask Questions
• Make Connections
• Synthesize
• Visualize

Analyze Development of Ideas

A writer of nonfiction uses many text features, such as headings, photos, and captions, to present and develop his or her ideas. Look at the photos to see what the text is about. Read the photo captions, too. They may give important details that are not in the text.

Look Into the Text

Allende writes about Paula, the woman in this photo.

Paula was living in Madrid, Spain, when she became sick from a rare blood disease. Allende was by her daughter's side until Paula died.

What facts do you learn from the caption?

Focus Strategy ▶ Determine Importance

When you read nonfiction, look for the **main ideas**, or the most important ideas, in the selection. The author may not state them directly, so you may need to use clues to determine what they are. Like section heads, the title may be a clue. The **supporting details** in the text also may be clues.

HOW TO RELATE MAIN IDEAS AND SUPPORTING DETAILS

Focus Strategy

1. **Turn the Title into a Question** This will guide you as you look for clues about the main ideas.

2. **Look for Supporting Details** Find ideas and information in the text and in the photos and captions. Record what you find.

3. **Determine the Main Ideas** Look at your notes. How do the details answer your question? Write one or two sentences to sum up the important ideas.

Main Idea and Details Chart

Title: "This I Believe"
What does the author believe?

Detail:

Detail:

Detail:

Main Ideas:

Connect Across Texts
You learned about harmful **relationships** in "Enabling or Disabling?"
In this essay, Isabel Allende writes about a beautiful relationship.

This I Believe

by Isabel Allende

I have lived my life with passion and in a hurry, trying to accomplish too many things. I never had time to think about my beliefs until my 28-year-old daughter Paula fell ill . . .

Key Vocabulary
relationship *n.*, the way that people are connected to each other

▲ Isabel Allende was a journalist in Chile but left the country in 1975 after her uncle, the president, was killed. Since then, she has written many short stories, articles, and novels.

She was **in a coma** for a year and I took care of her at home, until she died in my arms in December of 1992.

During that year of **agony** and the following year of **grieving**, everything stopped for me. There was nothing to do—just cry and remember. However, in that experience I discovered there is consistency in my beliefs, my writing and the way I lead my life. I have not changed: I am still the same girl I was fifty years ago, and the same young woman I was in the 1970s. I still lust for life. I am still **ferociously** independent. I still crave justice. And I fall madly in love easily.

Paralyzed and silent in her bed, my daughter Paula taught me a lesson that is now **my mantra**: You only have what you give. It's by spending yourself that you become rich.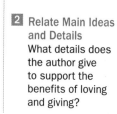

Paula was living in Madrid, Spain, when she became sick from a rare blood disease. Allende was by her daughter's side until Paula died.

Paula led a life of service. She worked as a volunteer helping women and children eight hours a day, six days a week. She never had any money, but she needed very little. When she died she had nothing and she needed nothing.

During her illness I had to let go of everything: her laughter, her voice, her grace, her beauty, her company and finally her spirit. When she died I thought I had lost everything. But then I realized I still had the love I had given her. I don't even know if she was able to receive that love. She could not respond in any way—her eyes were **somber** pools that reflected no light. But I was full of love and that love keeps growing, and multiplying, and giving fruit.

1 **Development of Ideas**
What information has the author presented so far that helps you answer the guiding question, "What does the author believe?"

2 Relate Main Ideas and Details
What details does the author give to support the benefits of loving and giving?

Key Vocabulary
agony *n.*, great suffering and worry

In Other Words
in a coma not aware and not moving
grieving being very sad and missing her
ferociously very, extremely
Paralyzed Not able to move
my mantra what I try to do, my motto
somber dark and sad

The pain of losing my child meant I had to **throw overboard all excess baggage** and keep only what is essential. Because of Paula, I don't **cling** to anything anymore. Now I like to give much more than to receive. I am happier when I love than when I am loved. I adore my husband, my son, my grandchildren, my mother, my dog, and frankly I don't know if they even like me. But who cares? Loving them is my joy. **3**

I don't cling to anything anymore.

Give, give, give—what is the point of having experience,

Desperate for a story to tell her sick daughter, Allende wrote a letter that became a best-selling memoir, *Paula*. Allende remembers, "I was not thinking of publishing. My only goal was to survive." **4**

3 Development of Ideas
How does the display quote help to strengthen the author's development of ideas?

4 Development of Ideas
What information does the caption add? Why did the author decide to write about her daughter?

Monitor Comprehension

Paraphrase
What happened that changed Allende's life? How did her life change?

In Other Words
throw overboard all excess baggage get rid of things I didn't need
cling hold on tightly

knowledge or talent if I don't give it away? Of having stories if I don't tell them to others? Of having wealth if I don't share it? I don't intend to be cremated with any of it! It is in giving that I connect with others, with the world, and with the divine.

It is in giving that I feel the spirit of my daughter inside me, like a soft presence. ❖

ANALYZE This I Believe

1. **Explain** According to this essay, what makes Allende happiest?

2. **Vocabulary** How would you describe the **relationship** between the author and her daughter?

3. **Analyze Development of Ideas** What information do you get from the photos and captions that is not in the text?

4. **Focus Strategy Determine Importance** Study the notes in your **Main Idea and Details Chart**. Write a few sentences that state the main ideas of the essay.

◗ Return to the Text

Reread and Write What did the author learn—during and after her year of **agony**—about people helping others? Reread the essay to find three examples of what she learned. Write a brief explanation.

About the Writer

Isabel Allende (1942–) shares her writings with millions of readers around the world. "I think of my writing as a humble offering that I put out there with an open heart and a sense of wonder. With some luck, maybe someone will accept the offering and give me a few hours of his or her time so that we can share a story."

EQ ## How Much Should People Help Each Other?

Critical Thinking

EQ **1. Analyze** Based on what you just read in both selections, when do you think it is a good idea to help other people? Explain.

2. Compare Compare Isabel Allende's **relationship** with her daughter to Jerry's relationship with his mother in "Enabling or Disabling?" How are the relationships alike? How are they different? Support your answer with evidence from the texts.

3. Interpret Isabel Allende says, "You only have what you give. It's by spending yourself that you become rich." What do you think she means?

4. Judge What do you think of Allende's decision to "give, give, give"?

EQ **5. Synthesize** How can someone tell if he or she is actually helping someone or if he or she is an "enabler"? Do you think Allende would call herself an enabler? Use evidence from the text in your answer.

Write About Literature

Journal Entry What kind of help should parents give their teenagers? What kind of help should parents not give? Gather evidence from both texts in a **T Chart**. Then write a journal entry explaining your beliefs.

T Chart

How Parents Can Help	How Parents Should Not Help

Key Vocabulary Review

Oral Review Work with a partner. Use these words to complete the paragraph.

agony	dependent	rescue
avoided	enable	responsibilities
consequences	relationship	

I have a good __(1)__ with my parents. They help me, but they also remind me that I have many __(2)__ , or duties. "Children cannot remain __(3)__ on their parents forever," they always say. "We cannot __(4)__ you from the __(5)__ every time you make a bad choice." Once I __(6)__ my work on a science project for weeks. The night before it was due, I was in __(7)__ , worrying about my failing grade. "I cannot help you now," my mother said. "It's too late. If I __(8)__ you to succeed without your doing the work yourself, you will never learn to do the right thing."

Writing Application Recall a time when you or a friend had to take **responsibility** and accept the **consequences** for certain actions. Write a paragraph about it. Use at least three Key Vocabulary words.

Read with Ease: Phrasing

Assess your reading fluency with the passage in the Reading Handbook, p. 674. Then complete the self-check below.

1. I did/did not group words properly as I read.

2. My words correct per minute: _____ .

Grammar
Show Possession

Use possessive adjectives and possessive pronouns to show who owns something.

	Possessive Adjectives	Possessive Pronouns
One Owner	my your his, her, its	mine yours his, hers
More Than One Owner	our your their	ours yours theirs

A **possessive adjective** always comes before a noun.

This is **her** problem. It is not **my** problem.

A **possessive pronoun** can replace a possessive adjective and a noun.

This is **her** problem. This is **hers**.
It is not **my** problem. It is not **mine**.

Oral Practice (1–5) Tell a partner about ways people help each other. Use at least five possessive words.

Written Practice (6–10) Complete each sentence with the correct possessive word.

6. Parents want to help _____ children.
7. These are your responsibilities. These responsibilities are _____.
8. The mother helps _____ son.
9. The father gives advice to _____ daughter.
10. Janey has a boyfriend. Frank is _____ boyfriend.

Language Development
Describe an Experience

Group Talk Describe something that happened to two characters on TV. Tell what they experienced and how it affected their relationship. Give plenty of specific details.

Literary Analysis
Analyze Style

Authors choose their words carefully. First they think about their topic, their purpose, and their audience. Then they choose the language, or **voice**, that will best express their ideas. This choice of language is the writer's **style**.

Some authors want their writing to be familiar, like spoken language. They use an everyday tone with words and phrases such as those in the beginning of "Enabling or Disabling?"

> He was sure his mom would be able to help him out.

Sometimes authors want readers to stop and think, so they use words in unusual ways. Authors can use words to shock or surprise their readers, too. Or their style might include descriptive words and imagery to help readers picture ideas in their minds.

Notice Allende's voice, tone, and word choice in "This I Believe." Choose two sentences to discuss. Explain how the author's words affect you.

Source: ©Fran/CartoonStock, Ltd.

Multiple-Meaning Words

Many English words have more than one meaning. In the dictionary, these meanings are numbered.

date *verb* **1.** to mark with the day or date **2.** to go out on romantic meetings

Since *date* is always spelled the same, the best way to figure out the correct meaning is to study the context clues near the word. Which meaning of *date* is used in Hannah's letter on page 288?

Look up each word below in a dictionary and list its meanings. Then find the word on page 290 and tell which meaning applies.

1. waste   **2.** grade   **3.** lie

Poster

Social Studies: Support Groups Everyone struggles with a problem on occasion. Many local and online groups help people with tough problems. Find out what one support group does and how the group helps people. Then make a poster of the information you learn. Share it with your class.

myNGconnect.com

- Learn about an organization that helps people overcome substance abuse.
- Find an organization that helps people with cancer.
- Learn how families can deal with diabetes.

📎 **Language and Learning Handbook**, page 616

📎 **Writing Handbook**, page 698

Write a Paragraph to Express an Idea

Think of a good way to help your community. Write a paragraph to express your idea.

1 Prewrite Use a **Main Idea and Details Chart** to plan your paragraph. Start with an idea, or topic. State this main idea in a topic sentence. Then add details and brainstorm some questions to ask: Why is this a good way to help the community? Who needs this help? How could people make it happen? Share your questions with a partner or a small group. Pick the strongest question or detail to research.

Main Idea and Details Chart

Main Idea: Visiting senior citizens is a good way to help your town.
Detail:
Detail:
Detail:

2 Draft Use your chart to draft your paragraph.

> The best way to help your town is to visit senior citizens. Many of them have lost their loved ones. Visitors give them something to look forward to each week. Also, making friends with older people can really broaden your horizons. Be sure to make time for this useful community service.

3 Revise Reread your paragraph. Ask yourself:

- Does the paragraph clearly express my idea?
- Do the details support the main idea?

4 Edit and Proofread Check your work. Did you use possessive words correctly?

5 Publish Put your paragraph in a class binder. Ask a librarian to display it in the library.

📎 **Writing Handbook**, page 698

Inside a Mental Health Center

Mental health professionals care for people who suffer from a range of mental and emotional illnesses. These may include personality disorders, substance abuse problems, and emotional stress. Mental health professionals often work as a team. They use hospital services and community resources to assist patients.

Jobs in the Mental Health Profession

A mental health center or clinic needs a variety of people who treat specific mental and emotional problems while offering health care support. Each job requires specific training, education, and work experience.

Job	Responsibilities	Education/Training Required
Psychiatric Aide **1**	• Helps patients dress, bathe, and eat • Helps patients participate in social activities • Observes patients and reports behavior to other team members	• High school diploma or equivalent • On-the-job training
Social Worker **2**	• Counsels patients and advises them and their family members about social services • Coordinates care with other team members • Plans rehabilitation programs	• College degree in social work or psychology • Master's degree
Psychiatrist **3**	• Diagnoses and treats mental illness • Prescribes medications and other treatments • Admits patients to hospitals or treats them when they visit hospitals	• Degree from medical school • Four years of postgraduate residency or hospital training • Board certification in psychiatry

Research a Career

Find out what a career as a mental health professional would be like.

1. Choose the job that interests you most from the chart above.
2. List three to five questions you have about the job.
3. Consult at least two career information Web sites to answer your questions.
4. Write a summary of what you have learned. Share your findings with other classmates who are interested in the same career. Save the information in a professional career portfolio.

myNGconnect.com

🔊 Learn more about the mental health profession.

🔊 Download a form to evaluate whether you would like to work in this field.

◤ **Language and Learning Handbook**, page 616

Access Words During Reading

When you read, you may not understand some parts of the text. Use this set of strategies to help you access the meaning of unfamiliar words as you read.

Use Strategies During Reading

1. What unfamiliar word should I figure out in order to understand the selection?

2. Have I seen this word before? What do I know about it already?

    Now do I understand the word well enough to continue?

3. Does this part of the selection help me understand the word? Do other parts of the selection help me understand the word?

    Now do I understand the word well enough to continue?

4. Do any parts of the word help me understand it?

    Now do I understand the word well enough to continue?

5. Who or what can help me understand the word right away?

    If I still don't understand the word, I'll note it and come back to it later.

Put the Strategy to Work

TRY IT▶ Read the following passage and apply the five steps above. Then answer the question.

▶ Earth's atmosphere has five layers. The troposphere, the layer right above the earth's surface, is where meteorological events happen. The next layer, or stratosphere, is where jets fly to avoid the meteorological events. The mesosphere is where meteors burn up. Space shuttles orbit in the thermosphere, the thin fourth layer. The exosphere, the fifth layer, meets outer space.

What layer do jets fly in and why? Which strategies did you use to help you answer the question?

🦪 **Reading Handbook,** page 647

PREPARE TO READ

▶ Brother Ray
▶ Hard Times
▶ Power of the Powerless: A Brother's Lesson

EQ How Much Should People Help Each Other?
Learn what families do for each other in special situations.

Make a Connection

Quickwrite Think about a time when you took care of a family member such as a baby brother, an older grandparent, or an ill parent. How did you feel about it? Take a few minutes to write your response.

Learn Key Vocabulary

Study the Words Pronounce each word and learn its meaning. You may also want to look up the definitions in the Glossary.

● Academic Vocabulary

Key Words	Examples
advice (ud-**vīs**) *noun* ▶ pages 310, 315, 322, 323	When you ask a friend for **advice**, you want ideas on how to solve a problem. *Synonym:* suggestions
● **communicate** (ku-**myū**-nu-kāt) *verb* ▶ page 313	Some deaf people **communicate** by using hand signs to express their ideas. *Synonym:* talk
condition (kun-**di**-shun) *noun* ▶ page 318	A person with a medical **condition** has a problem with his or her health. *Synonyms:* situation, problem
disabilities (dis-u-**bi**-lu-tēz) *noun* ▶ pages 315, 317, 322, 323, 325	**Disabilities** can limit what a person does or how the person does things. Some people with physical **disabilities** use wheelchairs to move around.
discipline (**di**-su-plun) *noun* ▶ pages 311, 315	**Discipline** is training that shows people or animals how to behave. Punishment can be one form of **discipline**.
hero (**hear**-ō) *noun* ▶ pages 318, 322, 323	When you admire someone a lot, that person is your **hero**. A firefighter who saves someone's life is also a **hero**.
outlook (**owt**-look) *noun* ▶ page 311	Your **outlook** is your opinion or point of view. A difficult job can be fun when you have a positive **outlook** about it.
presence (**pre**-zuns) *noun* ▶ page 321	Sometimes you can feel a person's **presence** even if he or she is not really there. *Synonyms:* being, spirit; *Antonym:* absence

Practice the Words Work with a partner to complete a **Key Vocabulary Chart** for the Key Vocabulary words. Share your chart with another pair. Check each other's work.

Key Vocabulary Chart

Word	Synonym(s)	Definition	Sentence or Picture
advice	help, tips	a recommendation for how to do something	My mom gives me advice on how to do the laundry.

BEFORE READING Brother Ray

autobiography by Ray Charles and David Ritz

Reading Strategies
· Plan and Monitor
▶ **Determine Importance**
· Make Inferences
· Ask Questions
· Make Connections
· Synthesize
· Visualize

Analyze Text Structure: Chronology

In an **autobiography**, the writer tells his or her own life story. The writer often tells about events in the order they happened. This structure is called **chronological order**, or time order. Use a sequence chain to record when events happen in this selection.

Look Into the Text

Time-order words and phrases tell when events happen.

> Mama always wanted me to learn things. Even though she didn't have much education herself, she taught me all she knew—the numbers, the alphabet, the way to spell, how to add and subtract. So when I started going blind, she began to look into schools for me. I was the only blind person in Greenville; people just didn't know what to do with me.
>
> Mama sought out advice. She asked Miss Lad who worked at the post office. She talked to the banker and to Mr. Reams who owned the general store. Soon everyone in town learned about my plight.

Ray starts going blind.　Mama looks for schools and asks advice.　Everyone finds out about Ray's problem.

Sequence Chain

Focus Strategy ▶ Determine Importance

A good way to think about what is important is to **summarize** it. When you summarize a passage that you read, state only the most important ideas. Leave out less important details, and don't give your own opinion. Try this strategy with the first paragraph above.

HOW TO SUMMARIZE NONFICTION

Focus Strategy

1. **Identify the Topic** What is the paragraph mostly about? Notice the words *learn*, *education*, *taught*, and *schools*. The topic is Ray's education.

2. **Find the Important Information** What is the most important idea about Ray's education? What less important details can you leave out?

3. **Summarize the Paragraph** In your own words, tell about the topic and important information.

4. **Avoid Opinions** Because this is a summary and not a critique, do not include your own opinion here.

   Ray's mother wanted him to get a good education, but no one in town knew how to teach a blind boy.

Ray Charles
(1930–2004)

I never wanted to be famous. I only wanted to be great.

Few people have influenced American music as much as **Ray Charles**. His nickname was "The Genius."

Charles grew up in a small town in Florida. At the age of seven he became blind. Later, when he was sent to a school for the blind, he learned things that would greatly affect how he would live his life.

He learned how to read and type Braille, a language that uses small raised dots, or bumps, on paper for the letters of the alphabet. Readers feel the words with their fingers, instead of using their eyes to see them. He learned how to play the piano and the clarinet. He also heard different kinds of music that he'd never heard before—from classical and big band to country-western.

While he was still a teen, Ray Charles began earning money by playing music. He started out by playing with other musicians in small clubs. Soon he was blending different musical styles into a new style called *soul*. People who came to the clubs loved this new sound. By the 1950s, he had become very popular.

Charles's career lasted for more than fifty years. He received twelve Grammy Awards and earned a place in the Rock and Roll Hall of Fame. But Ray Charles was humble, as he revealed in a 1993 *Rolling Stone* interview. "When people call me a genius or a legend, they're just showing the ultimate respect for my music. I know very well that I'm far from a genius. I'm just a guy who does a lot of things in music pretty well."

myNGconnect.com

🔊 Listen to excerpts of Ray Charles's hit songs.
🔊 Visit the artist's official Web site.

Brother Ray

Ray Charles's Own Story

by Ray Charles and David Ritz

Comprehension Coach

Mama always wanted me to learn things. Even though she didn't have much education herself, she taught me all she knew—the numbers, the alphabet, the way to spell, how to add and subtract. So when I started going blind, she began to look into schools for me. I was the only blind person in Greenville; people just didn't know what to do with me.

Mama **sought out advice**. She asked Miss Lad who worked at the post office. She talked to the banker and to Mr. Reams who owned the general store. Soon everyone in town learned about my **plight**.

It was the white folks who told Mama about the State School for the Blind in St. Augustine.

It didn't take her long to decide. I was going to have to go to school and live in St. Augustine. **1**

Mama knew what was best, though, and she insisted that I get some education in one form or another. She couldn't see me growing up without knowing how to read or write. She understood that one day I'd have to be on my own.

My own reaction to leaving was a big fat NO. Didn't want to leave Mama. That simple. Going blind was one thing; I was getting used to that. But leaving her was something else. She was all I knew. She was **my whole world**.

1 Analyze Structure: Chronology
Put this event in your own words and write it on your sequence chain.

⚠ **Interpret the Map** Use the compass rose on this map to tell which direction St. Augustine is from Greenville.

Key Vocabulary
advice *n.*, ideas about how to solve a problem; suggestions

In Other Words
sought out asked other people for
plight problem
my whole world the most important person in my life

No matter. Mama told me I was leaving, so I was leaving. End of discussion. I had a couple of months to get used to that idea, and during this last period at home I was treated the same as a normal child. Fact is, I was made to do the same **chores** I had done when I could see. **2**

Mama was a country woman with a whole lot of common sense. She understood what most of our neighbors didn't—that I shouldn't **grow dependent on** anyone except myself. "One of these days I **ain't gonna** be here," she kept **hammering inside my head**. Meanwhile, she had me scrub floors, chop wood, wash clothes, and play outside like all the other kids. She made sure I could wash and dress myself. And her **discipline** didn't stop just **'cause** I was blind. She wasn't about to let me get away with any foolishness.

Some of the neighbors gave Mama a hard time. They got on her case when they saw me working out back or helping her in the house. **3**

In 2004, a movie was released about Ray Charles. This photo shows the moviemakers' re-creation of Charles's childhood home. It includes a traditional African bottle tree, which people believed kept evil away.

"He's blind," Mama told them, "but he ain't stupid. He's lost his sight, but he ain't lost his mind."

So you can imagine how strong Mama had to be—and how intelligent—to fight against this **outlook** and allow me to go out on my own. And she did all this even with the other folks looking down on her.

2 Analyze Structure: Chronology
What words does the author use in this paragraph to show when the events happened?

3 Access Vocabulary/ Summarize
What does "got on her case" mean? How did the neighbors treat Mama?

Key Vocabulary
discipline *n.*, training on how to behave
outlook *n.*, point of view, opinion

In Other Words
chores jobs at home
grow dependent on need
ain't gonna am not going to
hammering inside my head repeating
'cause because

Not only did she make me help around the house, she made certain that I did the job right.

One day, for instance, she told me to scrub and mop the floor. I thought I might as well get off easy, so I skipped the scrubbing part. I just **sloshed** some water around the floor and mopped up.

Mama came back and **blew a fuse**; I mean, she was smoking with anger. ■4 Made me do the whole thing over again, from **scratch**. That hurt. But I do believe I learned something **'bout** doing a job right. ■5

The woman never let me get away with anything just 'cause I was blind. I was treated like I was normal. I acted like I was normal. And I wound up doing exactly the same things normal people do.

Take my bicycle. Somehow—I can't remember the exact circumstances—I was given one. Couldn't have been much older than ten or eleven. Riding was something I learned to do quickly. I loved the feeling of motion, and being blind wasn't gonna stop me from enjoying the bike.

Now most mamas would die rather than let a blind child scoot around on a bike. And at first I know Mama was scared for me. She had to be. But she let me do it. She let me find out for myself. She let me stray, little by little, further and further away from her. ■6 And once she saw I was capable of **maneuvering** this bike, she became less afraid.

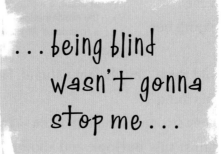

... being blind wasn't gonna stop me ...

■4 Language
How is the description "smoking with anger" related to the figure of speech "blew a fuse"? What do they tell you about Mama's reaction?

■5 Summarize
What is this section mostly about? What is important to remember?

■6 Access Vocabulary/ Summarize
What does "little by little" mean? Tell how Mama let Ray ride the bike.

Monitor Comprehension

Explain
How did things change for Ray after he became blind? For Mama?

In Other Words
sloshed poured
blew a fuse got very angry
scratch the beginning
'bout about
maneuvering using, riding

"I'm not always gonna be with you."

Those were Mama's words, and I can't tell you how many times she must have said them to me. Still, they didn't start meaning anything until I was fifteen and she was gone.

I can't remember who gave me the news at school. I heard the words, and suddenly a series of shocks attacked my brain. A big lump formed in the middle of my throat and just stayed there. Like a rock.

They told me I was going home, and I went. Even after I arrived in Greenville, the lump didn't budge. I couldn't eat; food seemed to expand in my throat; I couldn't sleep; I couldn't **communicate** with anyone. 7

Folks started worrying about me. No one knew what to do. I was **a zombie**. I had real trouble, and all I could keep thinking was why, why couldn't I kiss her again? 8

Ray Charles lost the most important person in his life when his mom died of a heart attack. She was thirty-two years old.

7 Analyze Structure: Chronology/ Summarize
Summarize what happened and add it to your sequence chain.

8 Main Idea and Details/ Summarize
Summarize the important idea in this paragraph. Then summarize the less important details.

Key Vocabulary
• **communicate** *v.*, to talk

In Other Words
a zombie acting as if I couldn't think or feel

Then a woman came to me. She was known in Greenville as Ma Beck. Ma Beck was **the salt of the earth**, and when it came to matters of the heart and soul, she knew her business. She let me have it:

"Boy, don't you remember what your mama told you? Well, you better. You better remember what your mama said. Your mama wouldn't want you acting this way. No, she wouldn't. You know the things she tried to teach you. You've been acting like a crazy boy, and, if she was here, she wouldn't **put up with** it. So stop acting like a crazy boy. Stop feeling sorry for yourself. Your mama spent her whole life preparing you for this here day. You know what she taught you. You know what she told you. You **gotta** carry on. That's all there is to it. That's what she'd want. And that's what you gotta do. You gotta carry on, **RC**." 9 10

That did it.

I knew that I had to have faith in myself; I had to start **buying my own line**.

Now I'm able to do what I want, when I want. I've been that way since Mama died. ❖

9 Language
Ray Charles uses the expression "let me have it" to mean "attacked me with words." How do you think Ma Beck felt when she talked to Ray?

10 Summarize
What are the important ideas in Ma Beck's advice?

Ray Charles was a highly successful musician. His music has inspired many people, including numerous other musicians.

Monitor Comprehension

Explain
How did Ray react to the news about Mama?

In Other Words
the salt of the earth very special
put up with allow
gotta have got to
RC Ray Charles
buying my own line believing my own words

Hard Times
by Ray Charles

My mother told me
'fore she passed away
Said, "Son when I'm gone,
Don't forget to pray
'Cause there'll be hard times,
Hard times.
Who knows better than I?"

Well, I soon found out
Just what she meant
When I had to pawn my clothes
Just to pay the rent
Talkin' 'bout hard times,
Hard times.
Who knows better than I?

ANALYZE Brother Ray

1. **Explain** In what ways was Ray Charles's mother the most important person in his life? Use evidence from the text to explain your answer.

2. **Vocabulary** Why did Charles's mother believe that education and **discipline** were especially important for her son? Tell how you know.

3. **Analyze Text Structure: Chronology** Review your **Sequence Chain** with a partner. Do you agree about the events and their sequence?

4. **Focus Strategy Determine Importance** Decide what this selection is mostly about and which information is most important. Put these ideas in your own words.

⤴ Return to the Text
Reread and Write What **advice** might Ray Charles give to parents about helping their children with **disabilities**? Reread the text to find at least two of his ideas.

Key Vocabulary
disabilities *n.*, problems that can limit what a person does

In Other Words
'fore before
pawn my clothes trade my clothes for money
Talkin' Talking

memoir by Christopher de Vinck

Reading Strategies

- Plan and Monitor
▶ **Determine Importance**
- Make Inferences
- Ask Questions
- Make Connections
- Synthesize
- Visualize

Analyze Text Structure: Chronology

Authors often use **chronological order** to tell about the events in a person's life. Sometimes they tell an event out of sequence to make the story more interesting or to add context. A change in the sequence is a time shift.

Look Into the Text

A past-tense verb shows that the story begins in the past.

    I grew up in the house where my brother was on his back in his bed for almost 33 years, in the same corner of his room, under the same window, beside the same yellow walls. Oliver was blind, mute. His legs were twisted. He didn't have the strength to lift his head nor the intelligence to learn anything.

This time-order word shows a shift to the present.

    Today I am an English teacher, and each time I introduce my class to the play about Helen Keller, "The Miracle Worker," I tell my students about Oliver. One day, during my first year teaching, a boy in the last row raised his hand and said, "Oh, Mr. de Vinck. You mean he was a vegetable."

How can you tell that there is another time shift in the story?

Focus Strategy ▶ Determine Importance

As you read nonfiction, determine what is important so you can remember it. One way to do this is to stop and **summarize** each paragraph. This will make it easier to summarize the entire selection.

HOW TO SUMMARIZE NONFICTION

Focus Strategy

1. **Identify the Topic** Look at the title and the first paragraph for clues to what the selection is mostly about.

2. **Stop and Think** As you read, pause after each paragraph to determine what is most important to know about the topic.

3. **Record Your Ideas** Write the important information in a **Summary Planner**. Leave out less important details.

4. **Summarize the Selection** Review your notes. Then "add them up" to state what is most important about the topic.

Summary Planner

Title: _____

Topic: _____

> **Paragraph 1:**
> The author's brother was helpless.

+

> **Paragraph 2:**

+

[and so on, until the end of the selection]

=

Summary of Selection: _____

Power of the Powerless: A Brother's Lesson

by Christopher de Vinck

Connect Across Texts

In "Brother Ray," Ray Charles tells what happened when he became blind. In this memoir, de Vinck tells about a boy with many **disabilities**.

I grew up in the house where my brother was on his back in his bed for almost 33 years, in the same corner of his room, under the same window, beside the same yellow walls. Oliver was blind, **mute**. His legs were twisted. He didn't have the strength to lift his head nor the intelligence to learn anything.

Today I am an English teacher, and each time I introduce my class to the play about **Helen Keller**, "The Miracle Worker," I tell my students about Oliver. One day, during my first year teaching, a boy in the last row raised his hand and said, "Oh, Mr. de Vinck. You mean he was **a vegetable**." **1**

I **stammered** for a few seconds. My family and I fed Oliver. We changed his diapers, hung his clothes and bed linen on the basement line in winter, and spread them out white and clean on the lawn in the summer. I always liked to watch the grasshoppers jump on the pillowcases.

We bathed Oliver. Tickled his chest to make him laugh. Sometimes we left the radio on in his room. We pulled the shade down over his bed in the morning to keep the sun from burning his tender skin. We listened to him laugh as we watched television downstairs. **2**

1 Language
De Vinck repeats the boy's slang, or informal words. What is your reaction to his use of the slang word *vegetable* here?

2 Summarize
What important information does the author present about his brother and his family? Write it in your planner.

Key Vocabulary
disabilities *n.*, problems that can limit what a person does

In Other Words
mute not able to speak
Helen Keller a famous blind and deaf woman
a vegetable someone who can't move or talk (slang)
stammered was not able to speak clearly

We listened to him rock his arms up and down to make the bed squeak. We listened to him cough in the middle of the night.

"Well, I guess you could call him a vegetable. I called him Oliver, my brother. You would have liked him."

One October day in 1946, when my mother was pregnant with Oliver, her second son, she **was overcome by fumes** from a leaking coal-burning stove. My oldest brother was sleeping in his crib, which was quite high off the ground so the gas didn't affect him. My father pulled them outside, where my mother **revived** quickly. **3**

On April 20, 1947, Oliver was born. A healthy looking, plump, beautiful boy. One afternoon, a few months later, my mother brought Oliver to a window. She held him there in the sun, the bright good sun, and there Oliver looked and looked directly into the sunlight, which was the first moment my mother realized that Oliver was blind. My parents, the true **heroes** of this story, learned, with the passing months, that blindness was only part of the problem. So they brought Oliver to Mt. Sinai Hospital in New York for tests to determine the extent of his **condition**. **4**

The doctor said that he wanted to make it very clear to both my mother and father that there was absolutely nothing that could be done for Oliver. He didn't want my parents to **grasp at false hope**.

> # I called him Oliver, my brother. You would have liked him.

3 Analyze Structure: Chronology/ Summarize
What important time-order words tell you that this paragraph is about the past? Retell what happened.

4 Main Idea/ Summarize
What ideas and information in this paragraph are most important to know? Summarize them.

Key Vocabulary
hero *n.*, someone whom others admire; someone who acts with courage to help others
condition *n.*, a problem with a person's health

In Other Words
was overcome by fumes lost consciousness because of the strong gas
revived woke up and felt better
grasp at false hope hope for something that would not happen

Mother and Child, 2003, Anne Rothenstein. Oil on board, private collection, England & Co. Gallery, London, The Bridgeman Art Library.

 Critical Viewing: Character How do you think the mother in this painting feels about her child? Explain how this relates to Oliver's mother.

"You could place him in an institution," he said. "But," my parents replied, "he is our son. We will take Oliver home of course." The good doctor answered, "Then take him home and love him." **5**

5 Summarize
What is the important information in this paragraph? Summarize it

Monitor Comprehension

Explain
What caused Oliver's disabilities? How did his parents react to his condition?

Patterned Landscape, 1999, Anne Rothenstein. Oil on canvas, private collection, England & Co. Gallery, London, The Bridgeman Art Library.

▲ **Critical Viewing: Design** Notice the colors and patterns in this painting. How do they make you feel? How does that feeling compare with the feeling of Oliver's home?

Oliver grew to the size of a 10-year-old. He had a big chest, a large head. His hands and feet were those of a 5-year-old, small and soft. We'd wrap a box of baby cereal for him at Christmas and place it under the tree; pat his head with a damp cloth in the middle of a July heat wave. His baptismal certificate hung on the wall above his head. A bishop came to the house and **confirmed** him. 6

6 **Summarize**
What is important in this paragraph?

Even now, years after his death from pneumonia on March 12, 1980, Oliver still remains the weakest, most helpless human being I ever met, and yet he was one of the most powerful human beings

In Other Words
confirmed performed a religious ceremony for

I ever met. **7** He could do absolutely nothing except breathe, sleep, eat, and yet he was responsible for action, love, courage, insight. When I was small my mother would say, "Isn't it wonderful that you can see?" And once she said, "When you go to heaven, Oliver will run to you, **embrace** you, and the first thing he will say is 'Thank you.'" I remember, too, my mother explaining to me that we were blessed with Oliver in ways that were not clear to her at first.

So often parents are faced with a child who is severely retarded, but who is also **hyperactive**, demanding or wild, who needs constant care. So many people have little choice but to place their child in an institution. We were fortunate that Oliver didn't need us to be in his room all day. He never knew what his condition was. We were blessed with his **presence**, a true presence of peace.

When I was in my early 20s I met a girl and fell in love. After a few months I brought her home to meet my family. When my mother went to the kitchen to prepare dinner, I asked the girl, "Would you like to see Oliver?" for I had told her about my brother. "No," she answered.

Soon after, I met Roe, a lovely girl. She asked me the names of my brothers and sisters. She loved children. I thought she was wonderful. I brought her home after a few months to meet my family. Soon it was time for me to feed Oliver. I remember **sheepishly asking** Roe if she'd like to see him. "Sure," she said. **8**

> We were blessed with his presence, a true presence of peace.

7 Analyze Structure: Chronology
What time-order phrases show that the author has shifted to the present?

8 Analyze Structure: Chronology
What time-order words and phrases help you follow the sequence of events on this page?

Monitor Comprehension

Explain
How did Oliver's presence help his family?

Key Vocabulary
presence *n.*, the fact or feeling that someone is there

In Other Words
embrace hug
hyperactive overly active
sheepishly asking feeling unsure as I asked

I sat at Oliver's bedside as Roe watched over my shoulder. I gave him his first spoonful, his second. "Can I do that?" Roe asked with ease, with freedom, with compassion, so I gave her the bowl and she fed Oliver one spoonful at a time.

The power of the powerless. Which girl would you marry? Today Roe and I have three children. **9** ❖

9 Summarize
What important ideas are in the last paragraph? Write them in your planner.

ANALYZE Power of the Powerless

1. **Explain** Who is Roe and what is her relationship to Oliver? Include evidence from the text to support your answer.

2. **Vocabulary** Why does the author describe his parents as **heroes**?

3. **Analyze Text Structure: Chronology** Find one place in the text where the author shifts from past to present time or from present to past time. Work with a partner. Describe the time shift and explain why it occurs.

4. **Focus Strategy Determine Importance** Complete your **Summary Planner**. Share your summary of the selection with a partner. Compare to see if you agree about the main ideas.

↩ Return to the Text

Reread and Write What **advice** might Christopher de Vinck give to parents about helping their children with **disabilities**? Reread the text to find at least two of his ideas.

Key Vocabulary
advice *n.*, ideas about how to solve a problem; suggestions

About the Writer

Christopher de Vinck (1951–) has been a high school English teacher and administrator in New Jersey for more than twenty-five years. This memoir was published in 1985. Many people, including President Ronald Reagan and Pope John Paul II, thanked de Vinck for his inspiring words.

EQ How Much Should People Help Each Other?

Critical Thinking

EQ 1. Compare In what ways do you think Ray Charles's mother and Oliver's parents had similar ideas about how much people should help each other? Explain.

2. Analyze Christopher de Vinck says that his parents are **heroes**. Do you think the mother of Ray Charles was also a hero? Why or why not?

3. Interpret What does Christopher de Vinck mean by the "power of the powerless"?

4. Judge What do you think about how Christopher de Vinck chose his wife? Was this a good way to decide whom to marry? Why or why not?

EQ 5. Speculate Can family members of people with **disabilities** be enablers? Defend your answer with reference to all of the selections you have read so far in this unit.

Write About Literature

Summary Paragraph Both Ray Charles and Christopher de Vinck got important **advice** from their mothers. Write a paragraph that summarizes what each mother taught her son. Gather examples for your paragraph in a **T Chart**:

T Chart

Charles's Mother	de Vinck's Mother

Remember, you do not need to include your personal opinions in a summary, as you would in a critique or an evaluation. Focus on the author's main ideas.

Key Vocabulary Review

Oral Review Work with a partner. Use these words to complete the paragraph.

advice	disabilities	outlook
communicate	discipline	presence
condition	hero	

My Uncle Lester is my __(1)__ , the person I admire most in the world. About a year ago, he lost his legs and hurt his spine in a car accident. Now he has many __(2)__ . At first, he was very sad and angry to have such a serious health __(3)__ . For months he did not want to __(4)__ with his family or friends. Then his daughter reminded him of the rules and strict __(5)__ he had used to make her behave as a child. She gave her father a suggestion, or __(6)__ : "Dad, now it is your turn to work hard and stop feeling sorry for yourself." Uncle Lester listened. He changed his __(7)__ and studied to become a computer programmer. Today, his being, or __(8)__ , makes the whole family feel lucky and proud.

Writing Application Recall a time when you gave or received good advice. Use three Key Vocabulary words to write a paragraph about this event.

Read with Ease: Expression

Assess your reading fluency with the passage in the Reading Handbook, p. 675. Then complete the self-check below.

1. I did/did not use my voice to express feeling.

2. My words correct per minute: _____ .

INTEGRATE THE LANGUAGE ARTS

Use Prepositions Correctly

Prepositions show how things relate. Some prepositions show location:

on the piano	**under** the lights
at the concert	**next to** Ray
in the audience	**behind** the chair

Some prepositions show direction. They come at the beginning of a <u>phrase</u>.

Ray walked **across** the stage.

I went **to** my seat.

Other prepositions just connect ideas in a <u>phrase</u>:

Ray sang a song **from** his heart.

The song was **in** memory **of** his mother.

Ray sang it **with** love **for** her.

Oral Practice (1–5) Say each sentence to a partner. Choose the correct preposition.

1. Ray lived (in/for) Greenville.
2. He lived (with/to) his mother.
3. Later Ray went (to/across) a special school.
4. It was a school (at/for) blind students.
5. Ray traveled (on/across) Florida to get there.

Written Practice (6–10) Add prepositions to this paragraph to describe the photo at the right. Choose from among these prepositions: *on, in, to, at, with, under, next to.*

Mama sat __(6)__ the chair. She looked __(7)__ Ray and put her hand __(8)__ his face. They talked __(9)__ each other. Ray was glad to be __(10)__ her.

Describe People and Places

Group Talk Describe a person and a place in "Brother Ray" or "Power of the Powerless." Your group makes a sketch to show what they "see."

Compare Literature and Film

Novels and short stories have inspired many popular films. So have nonfiction texts.

Work with a group. Think of a movie that was inspired by a book or something else you've read. Use the discussion questions below to explain the differences between written stories and their filmed versions. Be sure to use language related to literature and film to strengthen your understanding of new vocabulary.

- What information and ideas are included in the text but not in the movie? Why do you think the filmmakers left out some information?

- How do elements in the movie, such as music and the actors' voices and expressions, change the way you feel about the events?

- Did watching the movie and reading the book help you understand the theme of the story?

- Did the visuals help you understand the dialogue?

The motion picture *Ray*, released in 2004, was based on Ray Charles's memoir. In this scene from the movie, Ray's mother, Aretha Robinson (played by Sharon Warren), talks with young Ray (played by C.J. Sanders).

Vocabulary Study

Context Clues

When you don't know what a word means, you can look for **context clues** nearby. Read these sentences from "Brother Ray." Find them in the text. Tell the meaning of each underlined word. Explain the context clues you used to figure it out.

1. "I acted like I was normal. And I <u>wound up</u> doing exactly the same things normal people do." p. 312

2. "Now most mamas would die rather than let a blind child <u>scoot</u> around on a bike." p. 312

3. "A big lump formed in the middle of my throat and just stayed there… Even after I arrived in Greenville, the lump didn't <u>budge</u>." p. 313

Research/Speaking

Slide Show

History: Biographies Like Ray Charles, many people have overcome **disabilities** . Research and choose a person to learn about. Gather ideas from several sources, and check to make sure that each source is reliable. Organize your research into a computer slide show. Pretend you are the person's personal narrator. Tell why the person is famous and how the person overcame his or her disability. Present your slide show to the class.

myNGconnect.com

- 🔎 **Learn about famous people in history.**
- 🔎 **Read about contemporary people.**

📙 **Language and Learning Handbook,** page 616

Writing on Demand

Write a Personal Essay

A test may ask you to write a paragraph about someone who is important to you.

① Unpack the Prompt Read the writing prompt and underline the important words.

> **Writing Prompt**
>
> One definition of *hero* is "someone who is greatly admired." What person is a hero to you? Write a paragraph about a personal hero. Include reasons and examples to support your choice.

② Plan Your Response Choose a person to write about. Think of how this person fits the prompt's definition. Use a **Cluster Diagram** to help you plan.

Cluster Diagram

③ Draft Organize your paragraph like this. Add specific ideas from your diagram.

Essay Organizer

My personal hero is [tell who your hero is]. [He/she] fits the definition of a hero because [tell your first reason]. For example, [give an example]. Another reason for my choice is [tell your second reason]. A good example is [give your second example]. No one else I know is as brave and helpful as [repeat your hero's name].

④ Check Your Work Reread your paragraph. Ask:

- Does my hero fit the definition in the prompt?
- Did I give good reasons and examples of why the person is a hero?
- Did I use prepositions correctly?

📙 **Writing Handbook,** page 698

Oral Report

Do you want to inform people about a great organization that helps people? An oral report is your chance to let your classmates know about such an organization. In an oral report, you present information about a subject and take questions from your listeners. Here is how to give an oral report:

1. Plan Your Oral Report

Choose a service organization to tell your audience about. Then do the following:

- List questions your audience might ask, and answer them.
- Make notes for your report. Have two or three important points to make, and give facts and examples to develop each point.
- Think of descriptive language to use to describe the organization's work.
- Consider using multimedia to support your talk.

2. Practice Your Oral Report

Review what you will say several times before your presentation.

- Become familiar with your notes so that you do not need to refer to them too often.
- Make sure you speak in the amount of time you are given.
- Practice your report and ask a friend to give positive feedback.
- If you include visuals, practice using them.

3. Give Your Oral Report

As you give your oral report, keep your presentation interesting and lively by doing the following:

- Make eye contact with individuals in your audience.
- Speak clearly and loudly enough for the audience to understand.
- Be sure to clearly state your opinion, or thesis, about how this organization benefits people, and support your argument with details.
- Glance at your notes if necessary, but do not read from them.

myNGconnect.com
🔾 **Download the rubric.**

4. Discuss and Rate the Oral Report

Use the rubric to discuss and rate the oral reports, including your own. As you listen to the reports, take notes that summarize the speaker's ideas so you are prepared to ask questions later.

Oral Report Rubric

Scale	Content of the Oral Report	Student's Preparation	Student's Performance
3 Great	• Thoroughly covered the subject with a lot of good information. • Taught me something and made me want to know more about the organization.	• Presented a clear, well-focused view of the organization. • Chose many good examples and other support.	• Spoke clearly and was easy to follow. • Responded very well to the questions and comments.
2 Good	• Covered the subject somewhat. • Taught me a little bit about the organization.	• Presented a reasonably clear view of the organization. • Included some helpful examples and other support.	• Spoke clearly most of the time and was usually easy to follow. • Responded somewhat well to the questions and comments.
1 Needs Work	• Did not cover the organization very well. • Did not teach me anything.	• Presented a disorganized view of the subject. • Did not include much supporting information.	• Was hard to hear and understand. • Did not respond well to the questions and comments.

DO IT ▶ When you are finished preparing and practicing, give your oral report, and be informative!

📖 Language and Learning Handbook, page 616

How could this speaker improve her presentation?

How Much Should People Help Each Other?

Read about people who can barely survive on their own.

Make a Connection

Discussion Look at this cartoon. Work with a group to discuss what it means. Then talk about how you feel about the topic. Maybe you can share a time when you encountered someone who was experiencing hardship. How did you act? Did it teach you to respect them and their hardships? Give reasons for your opinions.

Source: ©Mike Baldwin/CartoonStock, Ltd.

Learn Key Vocabulary

Study the Words Pronounce each word and learn its meaning. You may also want to look up the definitions in the Glossary.

• Academic Vocabulary

Key Words	Examples
arrange (u-**rānj**) *verb* ▶ page 334	Do you **arrange** for a ride to school or does the bus pick you up? *Synonym:* organize
destruction (di-**struk**-shun) *noun* ▶ pages 339, 341	The hurricane caused **destruction** all along the coast. Houses were destroyed for miles around. *Synonyms:* ruin, wreckage; *Antonyms:* creation, construction
dignity (**dig**-nu-tē) *noun* ▶ pages 336, 337, 340, 341, 342	A person who has **dignity** has self-respect. *Synonym:* pride; *Antonym:* shame
guardian (**gar**-dē-un) *noun* ▶ page 334	A **guardian** is a person who is responsible for someone else. A grandparent may become the **guardian** for a child whose parents die.
• **intervene** (in-tur-**vēn**) *verb* ▶ page 339	If you **intervene** in someone's life, you get involved. When should you **intervene** to help someone in trouble? *Synonym:* step in; *Antonym:* ignore
• **survive** (sur-**vīv**) *verb* ▶ pages 337, 339	If someone **survives** a bad storm, the person is still alive when the storm has ended. *Synonyms:* live, last; *Antonym:* die
veteran (**ve**-tu-run) *noun* ▶ pages 333, 342	A **veteran** is someone who was once in the military, such as the army or navy.
willingly (**wi**-ling-lē) *adverb* ▶ page 334	If no one is forcing you to do something, then you are doing it **willingly**. *Antonym:* unwillingly

Practice the Words Work with a partner. Make a **Vocabulary Study Card** for each Key Vocabulary word. Write the word on one side of a card. On the other side, write its definition, a synonym or antonym, and an example sentence. Then take turns quizzing each other on the words.

BEFORE READING He Was No Bum

eulogy by Bob Greene

Reading Strategies

· Plan and Monitor
▶ Determine Importance
· Make Inferences
· Ask Questions
· Make Connections
· Synthesize
· Visualize

Analyze Text Structure: Chronology

The author's purpose in writing a eulogy (yū-lu-jē) is to honor the memory of someone who has died. Often, the writer tells about events in **chronological order**. When events are told in chronological order, they are told in the order in which they happened.

Look Into the Text

How does this eulogy start?

A bum died. That's what it seemed like. They found his body in a flophouse on West Madison Street, Chicago's Skid Row. White male, approximately fifty-five years old. A bum died.

They didn't know.

He was no bum. And his story… well, let his story tell itself.

Tells the name of the person the eulogy honors

The man's name was Arthur Joseph Kelly. Growing up, he wanted to be a firefighter. When he was a child he would go to the firehouse at Aberdeen and Washington, the home of Engine 34. His two sisters would go with him sometimes. The firefighters were nice to the kids. This was back in the days when the neighborhood was all right.

Tells his life story from childhood

As you read, use a **time line** to keep track of events in Arthur Joseph Kelly's life.

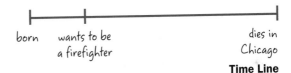

born   wants to be a firefighter   dies in Chicago

Time Line

Focus Strategy ▶ Determine Importance

When a friend tells you a story, you may understand it better if you hear details that mean something to you. For example, if a friend tells you about a movie, you use your experience of movies to help you understand your friend's story. As you read, your personal connections to the topic help you understand the text.

HOW TO DETERMINE WHAT'S IMPORTANT

Focus Strategy

1. **Identify the Topic** Note what the author is talking about.

2. **Find Important Details** Write the ideas and information that are most important to know about the topic.

3. **Make Personal Connections** Relate the details to experiences in your personal life. Making connections between your own life and details in the text, clarifies the text and makes it more memorable.

This selection is mostly about:

The most important details are:

One detail I can relate to is:

Post-Traumatic Stress Disorder

Post-traumatic stress disorder, or PTSD, is a mental condition that can result from a life-threatening experience. Someone can get PTSD after being in a war or a serious accident. Until recent times, PTSD was called shell shock, and people thought it was only caused by wartime experience. People who are in a natural disaster or who are violently attacked can also suffer from PTSD.

People with PTSD often have nightmares and flashbacks about the experience. They can have difficulty sleeping. They also can feel as if they don't fit in with other people anymore. These symptoms can make it very difficult for people with PTSD to lead a normal life.

PTSD can lead to alcohol and drug abuse. People with PTSD often have family problems. They may not be able to get and keep a job. Some people have even lost their homes as a result of their problems.

Men, women, and children of all ages can suffer from the disorder. About 30% of the men and women who have been in war zones suffer from PTSD. About 8% of men and 20% of women who witness life-threatening events will develop PTSD, and roughly 30% of these people will suffer with it throughout their entire lifetime.

myNGconnect.com

◐ **Read more about PTSD.**
◐ **Learn about a veteran with PTSD.**

HE WAS NO BUM

by Bob Greene

Comprehension Coach

A bum died. That's what it seemed like. They found his body in a **flophouse** on West Madison Street, Chicago's Skid Row. White male, approximately fifty-five years old. A bum died.

They didn't know.

He was no bum. And his story . . . well, let his story tell itself.

The man's name was Arthur Joseph Kelly. Growing up, he wanted to be a firefighter. When he was a child he would go to the firehouse at Aberdeen and Washington, the home of Engine 34. His two sisters would go with him sometimes. The firefighters were nice to the kids. This was back in the days when the neighborhood was all right.

Arthur Joseph Kelly became a teenager, and then a man, and he never quite had what it takes to be a firefighter. He didn't make it. **1** He did make it into the Army. He was a private in World War II, **serving in the European Theater of Operations. 2** He didn't make out too well. He suffered from shell shock. It messed him up pretty badly.

1 **Determine Importance**
What important information do you learn about Kelly? Why is this important? Explain.

2 **Analyze Text Structure: Chronology**
What can you add to your time line based on this information?

◀ Patch worn on Chicago Fire Department uniforms

▲ Army identification tags, or "dog tags"

In Other Words
flophouse run-down apartment
serving in the European Theater of Operations involved in the fighting in Europe

An elevated train system, known as the "L," connects different neighborhoods in Chicago.

He was placed in a series of military hospitals, and then, when the war was over, in **veterans'** hospitals. Whatever had happened to him in the service wasn't getting any better. He would be released from a hospital, and he would go back to the old neighborhood in Chicago, and suddenly the "L" train would come rumbling overhead and Arthur Joseph Kelly would dive to the ground. Some people laughed at him. He didn't want to do it. A loud noise and he would drop.

He walked away from a veterans' hospital in 1954. **3** He decided that he had to live in the real world. But he was in no condition to do that. He tried for a while, and then he went back to the only place that he remembered as being a place of happiness.

He went back to the fire station at Aberdeen and Washington.

Key Vocabulary
veteran *n.*, someone who was in the armed forces

3 Analyze Text Structure: Chronology
What events have happened in Kelly's life so far? Add them to your time line.

Monitor Comprehension

Explain
Who was Arthur J. Kelly? What was his connection to a Chicago fire station?

Some of the men of Engine 34 remembered Arthur Joseph Kelly from when he was a boy. They remembered him as a bright-eyed child wanting to be a firefighter. And now they saw him as a shell-shocked war veteran.

They took him in.

They fed and clothed him and gave him a place to sleep and let him be one of them. He wasn't a firefighter, of course, but he lived in the firehouse, and he had the firefighters as his friends. The military people didn't know what to do with **his veterans' benefits**, so some of the firefighters went to the Exchange National Bank and **arranged** for the benefit money to be paid to a special account. The firefighters of Engine 34 **took it upon themselves** to become Arthur Joseph Kelly's **conservator** and **guardian**. ▪4

The years went by. Some of the firefighters were transferred, and some retired, and some died. But there was always at least one firefighter at the station who would take responsibility for Arthur Joseph Kelly. The firefighters didn't ask for anything in return, but Kelly would **stoke the furnace** and clean up and help out as much as he could. There were maybe a dozen firefighters over the years who became his special guardians—the ones who would deal with the bank and the military, and who would make sure that no harm came to Kelly. For a long time it was the Sullivan brothers; when they left Engine 34, another firefighter **willingly** took over, and then another. ▪5

▪4 **Determine Importance**
What details do you learn here? What connections can you make between Arthur and someone you have known?

▪5 **Analyze Text Structure: Chronology**
Stop and add these events to your time line.

Key Vocabulary
arrange *v.*, to organize
guardian *n.*, a person who is responsible for someone else
willingly *adv.*, without being forced

In Other Words
his veterans' benefits the money and services he got from the government for his time in the army
took it upon themselves agreed
conservator protector
stoke the furnace put fuel in the heater

Firefighters, like those mentioned in the eulogy, are often very close. Many of them work 24-hour shifts. Coworkers become like a second family.

Once Arthur Joseph Kelly went to a Cubs game. A car **backfired**. He hit the ground. There was some snickering. But an older man, who had been in the service himself and was familiar with shell shock, helped Kelly up and said, "That's all right, fellow. You'll be all right." After that, Kelly stayed close to the firehouse.

His mind and his nerves were not good. The firefighters had to remind him to bathe, and to change clothes, and to eat properly. They did it, for twenty years and more, without anyone asking. 6 "He's **an easygoing** fellow," one of them said. "He doesn't harm anybody. It's not so hard for us to take care of him."

Then the firehouse closed down. The firefighters were transferred to another station house, at Laflin and Madison. Arthur Joseph Kelly went with them, but it wasn't the same. It wasn't the firehouse he had loved as a child. He didn't want to live there.

6 Analyze Text Structure: Chronology How long did Kelly stay at the firehouse? Use evidence from the text to explain your answer.

In Other Words
backfired made a loud, exploding noise
an easygoing a likeable

Cultural Background
Cubs is the nickname for Chicago's Major League Baseball team. The team has been playing at Wrigley Field in Chicago for more than 90 years.

So the last firefighter to take care of him—George Grant, a fifty-one-year-old father of eight—found Arthur Joseph Kelly a place to live. It wasn't much—it was the room on Madison Street—but every month Grant would take care of the financial arrangements with the bank, and would go to Madison Street to give money to a lady who ran a tavern near Kelly's room. **7** The understanding was that she would give Kelly his meals at the tavern. No liquor. The firefighters didn't want Kelly to end up as a Madison Street **wino**.

When a firefighter dies, his or her coworkers may wear special uniforms and perform a traditional ceremony at the funeral.

"The firemen had started taking care of **Art** way before I even got on the force," Grant said. "I just happened to be the last in a long line of men who took care of him. I didn't mind."

When Arthur Joseph Kelly was found dead in his room, they thought he was a bum. But they should have been at the funeral.

Arthur Joseph Kelly was buried with **dignity**. He was carried to his grave by uniformed firefighters. They were **his pallbearers**. **8**

7 Analyze Text Structure: Chronology/ Determine Importance
Why was George Grant an important person in Kelly's life? Add the information to your time line.

8 Author's Purpose
What does the author accomplish by ending with the story of Kelly's funeral?

Key Vocabulary
dignity *n.*, self-respect

In Other Words
wino drunk, alcoholic
Art Arthur Joseph Kelly
his pallbearers the ones who carried his coffin

Most of the firefighters were not even born when, as a boy, Kelly had started hanging around the firehouse. But they were there at the end. The firefighters never let Kelly live like a bum. They didn't let him die like one, either. ❖

ANALYZE He Was No Bum

1. **Confirm Predictions** How did the firefighters at Engine 34 treat Kelly? Give details. Was that what you had predicted?

2. **Vocabulary** In what ways did the firefighters help Kelly live with **dignity**?

3. **Analyze Text Structure: Chronology** Use your completed time line to briefly tell the events described in the eulogy.

4. **Focus Strategy** **Determine Importance** Name one detail from the eulogy that you connected with something in your personal life. Explain how making that connection helped you better understand the selection.

🔄 Return to the Text

Reread and Write Think about how the firefighters helped Kelly **survive**. Reread the text to find details of what they did. Then write an e-mail message to the firefighters to tell how you feel about their work for Kelly.

Key Vocabulary
● **survive** *v.*, to live, to last

About the Writer

Bob Greene (1947–) got his start in publishing when he was only seventeen years old and a newspaper printed a funny story he had written. Greene wrote columns for Chicago newspapers for thirty-one years. Today, he writes books about families and the pressures of modern life.

Reading Strategies

• Plan and Monitor
▶ Determine Importance
• Make Inferences
• Ask Questions
• Make Connections
• Synthesize
• Visualize

Analyze Language: Simile and Metaphor

As you read, look for **figurative language**—words that mean something different from their literal, or exact, meanings. Figurative language creates images in imaginative ways. Often, it makes comparisons between things that are not really alike. Two types of figurative language are **similes** and **metaphors**.

- Similes use *like* or *as* to compare two things that are not alike. The simile "Fog drops like a heavy curtain" compares fog to a curtain.
- Metaphors often suggest that one thing *is* another. The metaphor "A curtain of fog drops over the hills" says that the curtain is made of fog. An extended metaphor in which each element symbolizes something outside the poem is called an **allegory**.

Look Into the Text

when i watch you
in your old man's shoes
with the little toe cut out
sitting, waiting for your mind
like next week's grocery
i say
when i watch you
you wet brown bag of a woman
who used to be the best looking gal in georgia

This **simile** compares the woman's mind with "next week's grocery."

What two things does this **metaphor** compare?

Focus Strategy ▶ Determine Importance

Poets typically try to pack a lot of feeling into a few words. One way to understand a poem is to unpack it—to select the images you find most striking and explain what they make you think of and feel.

HOW TO DETERMINE WHAT'S IMPORTANT

Focus Strategy

1. **Record Text** In one column of a **T Chart**, write the words or phrases that are meaningful to you.

2. **Note Its Meaning** In the other column, write why the details are meaningful.

T Chart

Text from the Poem	Why Text Is Meaningful
wet brown bag of a woman	This compares the woman to an old used lunch bag that someone throws away. This comparison makes me depressed.

Connect Across Texts

In "He Was No Bum," firefighters **intervened** to help Arthur Joseph Kelly **survive**. Who helps a needy woman in this poem?

miss rosie

by Lucille Clifton

when i watch you [1]
wrapped up like garbage
sitting, surrounded by the smell
of too old potato peels
5   or
when i watch you
in your old man's shoes
with the little toe cut out
sitting, waiting for your mind
10 like next week's grocery [2]
i say
when i watch you
you wet brown bag of a woman
who used to be the best looking gal in georgia
15 used to be called the Georgia Rose
i stand up
through your destruction
i stand up

Old Woman, 2005, Maia Stefana Oprea. Acrylics, watercolor and ink, private collection of Ortansa Van Der Wateren, London.

▲ **Critical Viewing: Design** Study the lines in this painting. How do they add to the work? Compare the feeling of the art to the feeling of the poem.

1 **Poetry**
Sometimes poets don't follow punctuation or spelling rules. What rule does the poet break in this poem?

2 **Simile and Metaphor/ Determine Importance**
What figurative language does the speaker use here? What do you learn about Miss Rosie from this comparison?

Key Vocabulary
• **intervene** *v.*, to get involved
• **survive** *v.*, to live, to last
  destruction *n.*, ruin, wreckage

In Other Words
peels skins
the Georgia Rose a beautiful woman whom everyone loves

All that may be needed is that the injustice in the world be mentioned so that nobody can ever say, "Nobody told me."

—Lucille Clifton

ANALYZE miss rosie

1. **Interpret** What does it mean to "stand up" for someone? In what way does the speaker "stand up" for the woman? Use evidence from the poem to explain your answer.

2. **Vocabulary** How does the poem's title give **dignity** to the old woman?

3. **Analyze Language: Simile and Metaphor** With a partner, discuss the figurative language in the poem. What do you learn about Miss Rosie from the comparisons?

4. **Focus Strategy** **Determine Importance** With which detail in the poem did you make a personal connection? Explain.

Return to the Text

Reread and Write Reread the poem and visualize, or imagine seeing, Miss Rosie on the street. How would you react to her? Would you want to help her? Write a journal entry with your ideas.

About the Writer

Lucille Clifton (1936–2010) was an award-winning poet and novelist. Her work was often about trying to overcome mistakes from the past. She also served as a Distinguished Professor at St. Mary's College in Maryland.

Key Vocabulary
dignity *n.*, self-respect

EQ How Much Should People Help Each Other?

Reading
Critical Thinking

EQ **1. Analyze** Look at the cartoon on page 328 again. What new ideas do you have about how much people should help the homeless?

2. Compare Across Texts Both selections show a different view of someone who might be considered "a bum." Explain how the selections give **dignity** to Arthur Joseph Kelly and Miss Rosie.

3. Speculate How do you think Kelly's presence in the firehouse affected the firefighters? How might his presence have helped them?

4. Synthesize Read Lucille Clifton's quote on page 340 again. Explain how it applies to both selections.

EQ **5. Judge** Some people give money to homeless people on the street. Based on what you read about Kelly and Miss Rosie, do you think this is helpful? Why or why not?

Writing
Write About Literature

Opinion Statement Is it a mistake to judge people by their looks or actions when you do not know their personal histories? Write your opinion. Support it with examples from both texts.

	Looks / Actions	Personal History
Arthur Joseph Kelly		
Miss Rosie		

Vocabulary
Key Vocabulary Review

Oral Review Work with a partner. Use these words to complete the paragraph.

arranged	guardians	veteran
destruction	intervene	willingly
dignity	survive	

My two cousins were homeless after a hurricane caused the __(1)__ of their house. They were lucky to __(2)__ the terrible storm. Their father is a __(3)__ of the war in Iraq and is in the hospital. He is a proud man. He feared he would lose his __(4)__ if he asked anyone for help. My parents decided to __(5)__ . They __(6)__ for my cousins to live in our home until their father got out of the hospital. Because they are taking care of my cousins for a while, my parents became their __(7)__ . My parents are helping __(8)__ because they believe that family members should help each other.

Writing Application Think of a scene of **destruction** from a photograph, the news, or real life. Write a paragraph to describe the scene. Use at least four Key Vocabulary words.

Fluency
Read with Ease: Intonation

Assess your reading fluency with the passage in the Reading Handbook, p. 676. Then complete the self-check below.

1. I did/did not raise and lower the pitch of my voice.

2. My words correct per minute: _____ .

Use the Correct Pronoun

A pronoun takes the place of a **noun**. The pronoun you use depends on the noun it replaces. To choose the correct pronoun, ask yourself:

- Does the noun name a male or a female?
- Does the noun name one or more than one?
- Is the pronoun the **subject** or the **object** in the sentence? Study these examples:

The **boy** has plans. **He** wants to be a fireman.

A **girl** visits the firehouse. Everyone likes **her**.

The **firehouse** is in Chicago. **It** is old.

The **firefighters** help. **They** protect Arthur.

Oral Practice (1–5) With a partner, take turns using each pair of words below in sentences. Your sentences should tell about "He Was No Bum."
Example: *Arthur went to war. War changed him.*

Arthur, him	the Sullivan brothers, they
a war veteran, he	firehouse, it
firefighters, them	

Written Practice (6–10) Choose the correct pronouns and rewrite the paragraph. Add two more sentences about Arthur. Use pronouns.

Arthur served in World War II. (He/It) suffered from shell shock. The military hospital helped Arthur. (It/They) was a safe place. Firefighters welcomed Arthur. They remembered (he/him).

Describe Events

Group Talk Think about the funeral of Arthur Joseph Kelly. Give specific details to describe what happened at the funeral. Express your ideas about why the firefighters held the funeral as they did. Use words like **veteran** and **dignity**.

Analyze Repetition and Alliteration

Writers often choose words for the way they sound. Sometimes they repeat a word or group of words. Such **repetition** can help make an important point.

Notice the repetition in these lines from Langston Hughes's "Theme for English B":

> I feel and see and hear, Harlem, I hear you:
> hear you, hear me—we too—you, me, talk on this page.

Writers also repeat the beginning sounds of words. This is called **alliteration**. Notice the repeated *h* sound in the example above.

Work with a partner. Discuss these questions:

- In "He Was No Bum," what sentence does the author repeat in the first paragraph? What important point does this make?
- What lines are repeated in "miss rosie"? Why do you think the author repeats these lines?
- Say the third line of "miss rosie" aloud. What sound is repeated? What effect does it have?
- What beginning sound is repeated in the words of the newspaper headline below?

Multiple-Meaning Words

Multiple-meaning words are words that have more than one meaning. In the dictionary, these meanings are numbered.

service *noun* **1.** a helpful action; assistance **2.** any branch of the armed forces

The best way to figure out the appropriate meaning of *service* is to use context clues. Which meaning is used on page 333? Name the words near *service* that helped you figure out its meaning.

Find each word in a dictionary and list its meanings. Then find the word on page 332 or 333. Use context clues to determine which meaning applies.

1. body   **2.** private   **3.** station

Extemporaneous Talk

Government: Helping Veterans U.S. veterans receive benefits from the government. Today, many veterans coming back from war can get treatment for post-traumatic stress disorder. Research to learn more.

Take notes with information you want to share. Don't write your speech. Just use your notes to give an informal talk—an extemporaneous speech—to your group.

myNGconnect.com

- 🔗 Find out how the government helps homeless veterans.
- 🔗 Learn about job training for veterans.
- 🔗 Read about special programs for veterans.

📖 **Language and Learning Handbook**, page 616

Trait: Voice and Style

Writers make decisions about their **voice** and **style**.

- Voice is the language, tone, and word choice that makes the writing uniquely yours.
- Style is how you use words and sentences to address your audience and purpose. You would use a different style for a note to a friend than for an essay.

The following is the first paragraph of a student's news article. Does the writer use a unique voice and sentences that are appropriate for a news article?

Just OK

> This teenager, Janell Jefferson, thinks all kids should know how to ride bikes. Her mom, Teresa Jefferson, owns the bike shop, Wheels in Motion, across the street from King Middle School. Janell and her mom fixed up a ton of bikes and gave them to an after-school program at the school. Janell thinks it would be cool to give more bikes to more kids so they could learn to ride them.

Much Better

> Teenager Janell Jefferson thinks every kid should know how to ride a bike. Her mother, Teresa Jefferson, owns the bike shop, Wheels in Motion, across the street from King Middle School. Janell and her mom fixed up twenty-five bikes for the after-school program at the school. The generous teen says, "My goal is to help as many kids as possible to learn to ride a bike."

Revise the following paragraph to express your own voice. Use a style that is appropriate for a news article.

> This high school kid Juan Hinojosa knows a lot about making computer games. He goes to a club after school and thought it would be cool to teach some of the little kids there how to make a computer game. So now he's teaching them. Juan wants to see if some company might buy the game when they're done. If a company buys it, he would use the money for new computers for the club.

After you rewrite the article, check your work. Did you use your own voice? Is the style appropriate for the audience and genre? Make revisions if necessary.

📖 **Writing Handbook**, page 698

from Household Words

by Barbara Kingsolver

1   I was headed home with my mind on things; I can't even say what they were. It was an afternoon not very long ago, and probably I was ticking through the **routine sacrament** of my day—locating every member of my family at that moment and organizing how we would all come together for dinner and what I would feed us—when my thoughts were bluntly interrupted. A woman was being attacked fifty feet away from me. My heart thumped and then seemed to stop for good and then thumped hard again as I watched what was happening. The woman was slight, probably no taller than my older daughter, but she was my age. Her attacker, a much taller man, had no weapon but was hitting her on the head and face with his fists and open hands, screaming, calling her **vile** names right out in the open. She ducked, in the way any animal would, to save the more fragile bones of her face. She tried to turn her back on him, but he pursued her, smacking at her relentlessly with the flat of his hand and shouting angrily that she was trash, she was nothing, she should get away from him. And she was trying, but she couldn't. I felt my body freeze as they approached. They came very close, maybe ten feet away or even less, and then they moved on past us. I say *us* because I wasn't alone here: I was in a crowd of several dozen people, all **within earshot**. Maybe there were closer to a hundred of us; I'm not sure. Unbelievably, most weren't even looking. And then I did my own unbelievable thing: I left. I moved forward toward my home and family and left that battered woman behind.

In Other Words
routine sacrament most important
  spiritual activity
vile very bad, horrible
within earshot close enough to hear

2   I did and I didn't leave her behind, because I'm still thinking and now writing about this scene, **reviling** my own **cowardice**. Reader, can you believe I did what I did? Does it seem certain that I am heartless?

3   Let me give some more details of the scene, not because I hope to be forgiven. I ask only that all of us try to find ourselves in this weird landscape. It was the United States of America. I was at a busy intersection, in a car. The woman had the leathery, lined face and tattered-looking hair of a person who lives her whole life outdoors beneath the sun. So did her attacker. Both of them wore the clothes that make for an instantly recognizable uniform: shirts and pants weathered by hard daily wear to a neutral color and texture. Her possessions, and his, were stuffed into two bulky backpacks that leaned against a signpost in a median dividing six lanes of city traffic. I was in the middle lane of traffic on one side. All of the other people in this crowd were also in automobiles, on either side of me, opposite me, ahead and behind, most of them with their windows rolled up, listening to the radio or talking on cell phones. From what I could tell, no one else was watching this woman get beaten up and chased across three, then six, then nine separate lanes of traffic in the intersecting streets. I considered how I could get out of my car (should I leave it **idling**? lock it? what?) and run toward this woman and man, shouting at him to stop, begging the other drivers to use their phones to call the police.

Magical, plainpicture/neuebildanstalt/Dott.

⚠ **Critical Viewing: Effect** Why do you think the artist chose to cover part of the woman's face? What effect does it have on the feeling you get from the art?

> ## Reader, can you believe I did what I did?

In Other Words
reviling harshly judging
cowardice lack of bravery
idling running

And then, after I had turned over this scenario in my mind for eight or nine seconds, the light changed and every car but mine began to move, and I had to think instead about the honking horns, the blocked traffic, the public **nuisance** I was about to become, and all the people who would shake their heads at my do-gooder foolishness and inform me that I should stay away from these rough-looking characters because this was obviously a domestic dispute.

4   But that could not have been true. It was not domestic. *Domestic* means "of the home," and these people had no home. That was the problem—theirs, mine, everybody's. These people were beneath or somehow outside the laws that govern civil behavior between citizens of our country. They were homeless.

5   In his poem "Death of a Hired Man," Robert Frost captured in just a few words the most perfect definition of home I've ever read:

6   *Home is the place where, when you have to go there,*
They have to take you in.

7   I wish I could ever have been so **succinct**. I've spent hundreds of pages, even whole novels, trying to explain what home means to me. Sometimes I think it's the only thing I ever write about. Home is place, geography, and psyche; it's a matter of survival and safety, a **condition** of attachment and self-definition. It's where you learn from your parents and repeat to your children all the stories of what it means to belong to the place and people **of your ken**. It's a place of safety—and that is one of the most real and pressing issues for those who must live without it. For homeless women and men, the probability of being sexually assaulted or physically attacked is so great that it's a matter not of *if* but of *when*. Homelessness is the loss first of community and finally of the self. It seems **fatuous** that I could spend so much time contemplating the **subtle nuances** of home (let alone buy a magazine devoted to home remodeling

---

Key Vocabulary
condition *n.*, situation

In Other Words
nuisance problem
succinct exact
of your ken you know
fatuous foolish
subtle nuances small details

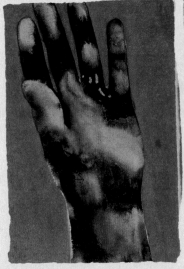
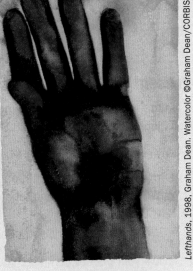

Lefthands, 1998, Graham Dean. Watercolor ©Graham Dean/CORBIS

⚠ Critical Viewing: Effect What do you notice about the two hands in this painting? What do you think the author of the essay would notice about them?

or decor) when there are people near me—sometimes only a few feet away from me—who don't have one, can't get one, aren't even in the picture.

8   I wish I could go back to that afternoon that haunts me and do what I know I should have done: get out of my car, make a scene, stop traffic, stop a violent man if I could. Home is the place where, when you have to go there, they have to take you in. My car might have been the place she had to go, with no other earthly alternatives left to her, and so it may be that I have to take her in, take that risk, get **criticized or tainted** by the communicable disease of **shame** that is homelessness. In some sense she did come in, for she is still with me. I **rehearse** a different scene in my mind. If I meet her again I hope I can be ready.

9   It's a **tenuous** satisfaction that comes from rationalizing problems away or **banning them from** the sidewalk. Another clean definition I admire, as succinct as Frost's for the complexities of home, is Dr. Martin Luther King Jr.'s explanation of peace: True peace, he said, is not merely the absence of tension. It's the **presence** of justice. ❖

Key Vocabulary
presence *n.*, being, the fact or feeling that something is there

In Other Words
criticized or tainted judged or dirtied
shame embarrassment and disgrace
rehearse replay
tenuous weak
banning them from not allowing them on

GIVE & TAKE

EQ **ESSENTIAL QUESTION:**
How Much Should People Help Each Other?

myNGconnect.com

⚙ **Download the rubric.**

EDGE LIBRARY

Present Your Project: Multimedia Presentation

It is time to complete your multimedia presentation about the Essential Question for this unit: How Much Should People Help Each Other?

1 Review and Complete Your Plan

- How does your presentation answer the Essential Question?
- What media—graphics, photos, film clips, audio files—can you include?
- What equipment will you need to present the different media?

Follow your plan to complete your presentation. Then practice it before you present it to the class.

2 Give Your Multimedia Presentation

Make sure your audience can see and hear your presentation. Speak clearly. Be prepared to answer questions. As you give your presentation, be sure to clearly describe the information you're presenting in your various media. Also, use vocabulary related to the media to express your understanding of new words and concepts.

3 Evaluate the Multimedia Presentations

Use the online rubric to evaluate each multimedia presentation, including your own. Be sure to watch and listen. Use the speaker's words along with the visuals shown to make guesses, or inferences, about the presentation's meaning.

Reflect on Your Reading

Think back on your reading of the unit selections, including your choice of Edge Library books. Discuss the following with a partner or in a group.

Genre Focus Choose a nonfiction selection. Name and give examples of its text features. Then suggest two specific text features you would add if you were the editor.

Focus Strategy Summarize your favorite reading selection in this unit. Then tell which details in that selection were the most important to you and how you determined this.

EQ Respond to the Essential Question

Throughout this unit, you have been thinking about how much people should help each other. Discuss the Essential Question with a group. What have *you* decided? Support your response with evidence from your reading, discussions, research, and writing.

Write a Problem-Solution Essay

We all face problems in our lives. Some problems require simple solutions. Others are more complex. For this project, you will write an essay about a problem in your community or in the world.

Study Problem-Solution Essays

Problem-solution essays tell readers about a problem. They also give one or more ways to solve the problem and tell why the solutions are practical.

❶ Connect Writing to Your Life

You find solutions to problems nearly every day. If you forget to bring your lunch to school, you buy it in the cafeteria. If you do not have enough money to buy lunch, you borrow some from a friend. No matter what size the problem is, finding a solution involves the same process. This project will help you develop this process.

❷ Understand the Form

A problem-solution essay has several purposes:

- to inform the reader about the problem
- to explain one or more possible solutions and why they make sense
- to address readers' concerns or explain why other solutions are not as good

To write a good problem-solution essay, you must include these parts:

1. Problem	Clearly state the problem. Give important background information. Explain its causes and effects. Tell why it is a problem. This is called making a **claim**.
2. Solution	Explain your solution. Claim why it makes sense, and acknowledge possible **counterclaims**, or arguments that people might have against the solution. If you have more than one solution, explain each one.
3. Evidence	Give facts, statistics, expert opinions, examples, and other data to show why your solution is a good one. This information can also give more details about the seriousness of the problem. Explain, if possible, why other solutions are not as good.
4. Conclusion	Summarize your argument. Restate the problem and solution in a way that sounds logical and objective.

Now look at how these parts work together.
Read a problem-solution essay by a professional writer.

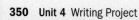

❸ Analyze a Professional Model

As you read, look for the important parts of a problem-solution essay.

Poison in the Yard

by Mary Kong-Thao

Many people like lush, green lawns. They want grass that looks beautiful and feels soft to sit and walk on. Unfortunately, growing the perfect lawn can also be dangerous. Pesticides, or poisonous chemicals, are being used by more and more people. This has increased the risk people and animals have of being harmed by these poisons.

> This paragraph makes a claim that introduces the **problem**.

Nearly 78 million households in the United States use pesticides. They use them to prevent weeds from growing on their lawns and in their gardens. They also use them to keep plants and flowers looking healthy.

Unfortunately, many pesticides can also cause harm. If wild animals and family pets eat plants sprayed with pesticides, they can become ill or die. Pesticides soak through the grass and drip into our water supply. They float in the air and end up in our food. Some pesticides can cause cancer, nervous system damage, and birth defects.

> These paragraphs give causes and effects of the problem. A **statistic** shows the size of the problem.

How can we care for our lawns and gardens and protect our health? The answer is organic, or natural, alternatives. Examples are using mulch to control weeds and wearing soybean oil as mosquito repellant.

> The writer uses a **question** as a transition.
>
> This paragraph offers a **solution**.

Some people might think that pesticide alternatives cost more than regular pesticides. However, pesicide-free methods can actually save money. For example, in 1996, California cotton farmers stopped using pesticides. Instead, they planted their crops near alfalfa fields, which naturally contain a large amount of insects that keep cotton from being hurt by other insects. These farmers saved the money they would have spent on pesticides. Their cotton crops were just as large as those of farmers who still used pesticides.

> This paragraph addresses a possible objection to the solution and gives an **example** as evidence that the solution works.

It is not always easy to make changes. However, if we each used just one alternative method to pesticides, the environment would become much safer for people and animals.

> The concluding paragraph restates the problem and solution in a clear, logical way.

> **Prompt** Write a problem-solution essay about a problem you see in the world or in your community. Be sure to:
> - define the problem
> - list causes and effects of the problem
> - suggest a solution and support it with evidence
> - address possible counterclaims about the solution
> - conclude with a logical summary

✔ Prewrite

Now that you have seen an example of a problem-solution essay, plan one of your own. Planning will make it easier for you to write later on. Making a Writing Plan helps you gather everything you need to write a clear, well-organized essay.

❶ Choose Your Topic

Write about a problem you care about. Here are some ways to think of a topic:

- Sit quietly and think. What problems do you face? What do you care about? What bothers you?
- Think about a global issue. Look for a specific situation to focus on.

❷ Clarify the Audience, Controlling Idea, and Purpose

Who will read your essay? You will need to write in a style that is clear and appropriate to your audience. What language can you use to explain your idea to them? Write down your notes about your audience.

What do you want the audience to understand about the problem? That is your **controlling idea**. Jot it down.

Why do you want to write about this topic? The reason is your purpose for writing. Take notes about your purpose.

❸ Gather Supporting Details

You can find details about your topic in many ways. Gather details that will address both the problem and the solution. Make sure you find support for your essay from reliable sources. Try to locate information that presents more than one viewpoint on the issue. This way you will be able to see all aspects of the problem.

❹ Organize the Details

Organize your details in a logical order:

- problem (include background information)
- causes and effects of the problem (include evidence)
- solution and why it makes sense (include evidence)
- possible counterclaims or objections

> **Prewriting Tip**
>
> Ask yourself the following questions about your sources:
>
> - Who wrote the information I am using?
> - Will my audience consider these sources reliable?
> - Are there real facts and data I can use, not just opinions?

❺ Finish Your Writing Plan

Make a Writing Plan using an outline like the one below. Put your details in the order you want them to appear in your essay.

Technology Tip

Use the Outline feature in a word-processing program to help create your plan. Choose Bullets and Numbering from the Format menu to use the Outline feature.

Writing Plan

Topic	bullying in schools
Audience	my teacher, my parents, and my classmates
Controlling Idea	bullying is harmful and needs to be stopped
Purpose	to give a solution to the problem of bullying
Time Frame	one week from today

I. Problem and background. Bullying in schools
  A. can be hitting, name-calling, exclusion, e-mail harassment
  B. 15–20% of students are victims
  C. 15–20% of students are bullies

II. Causes.
  A. trouble at home
  B. student not doing well in school
  C. rejection
  D. popularity

III. Effects.
  A. hampers ability to learn
  B. depression, loneliness, insecurity

IV. Solution. Communication among teachers, administrators, students, parents
  A. zero-tolerance policies (sometimes harsh, punish wrong kids?)
  B. support for teachers
  C. notify parents
  D. talk with children, encourage them to report

V. Why it makes sense.
  A. Norway study gives proof
  B. Hillsboro's successful zero-tolerance policy

VI. Conclusion. Members of community should start communicating

Reflect on Your Writing Plan

▶ Do you have an idea or two for each main part of your essay? If not, look for more ideas.

✔ Write a Draft

After you finish your Writing Plan, you can start your draft. Remember that it is OK to make mistakes now. Just get your thoughts on paper. You will have chances to improve the writing later.

❶ Keep These Ideas in Mind

You will rely mostly on your Writing Plan as you write your draft. However, you will want to keep these other tips in mind:

- **Give Yourself Plenty of Time** You will need to think about some of your ideas. You may need to research background information and supporting details.

- **Grab Your Reader Right Away** Begin with an interesting fact or tell a story. State the problem clearly. What do your readers know? What do they need to know? Why does the problem matter? Show your readers.

- **Put Your Ideas into Words** You are writing about an issue that you care about. This is your chance to educate others. Be direct. Use an objective tone that makes your readers trust your argument.

❷ Use Evidence for Support

Your end goal when writing a problem-solution essay is to prove your claim. In order to do this, you need to provide evidence that supports both the problem and the solution. Here are some useful kinds of evidence:

- **Facts** are statements that are proven to be true.
- **Statistics** are specific measurements and numbers.
- **Expert opinions** are the beliefs of people who know a lot about the topic.

> **Technology Tip**
>
> Copy your outline into a separate document. Delete the numbers and letters. Turn the list into a draft. Make each line a complete sentence. Combine sentences into paragraphs.

OK

> Lots of students are victims of some type of bullying. Many students admit to being bullies, too.

Better

> Studies show that 15–20 percent of students are victims of some type of bullying. Surprisingly, the same number of students are reported as being bullies.

❸ Student Model

See how the student used the Writing Plan to get ideas down. The draft does not have to be perfect. The student will revise and fix the mistakes later.

Bullying: How Can We Stop It?

We see it in popular movies and on TV. It is also a problem that many students face in real life. What a bummer! Bullying has become a totally huge problem at Lincoln high school. Bullying is also a problem in schools all across the United states. Bullying harms both the victim and the bully. More seriously, bullying affects students school experience.

Bullying comes in many forms. It can take the form of throwing punchs, name-calling, exclusion, and some students even get harassed on the Internet. Studyes show that 15–20 percent of students are victims of some type of bullying. Surprisingly, the same number of student's are reported as being bullies.

What makes a student become a bully? There are many reasons. Bullys may have trouble at home. Bullies may be failing in school. Or bullies do not feel accepted by their schoolmates. Some bullies even become bullies because they want to feel more popular. In the end, bullies hurt others to feel better about themselves.

Bullying has serious consequences for the victims, too. It's negative effects can impair a students ability to learn. Victims are also more likely to become depressed, lonely, and insecure. These feelings can stay with victims well into their adult lifes.

Schools can adopt a "zero tolerance" policy. Punishing all bullies equally, no matter what the offense or the circumstances, may seem unfair. It is better, however, to have one strict rule that everyone must follow than to have unclear limits.

Teachers, administrators, parents, and students must communicate with each other. Administrators should provide assistance to teachers who have bullies in their class. Parents should talk with their children about what goes on at school. Students should be encouraged to report bullying.

These measures do work. A study of these combined practices in norway showed that they reduced bullying in a school by 50 percent. Closer to home, in hillsboro, the school district's new zero-tolerance policy has helped prevent many additional bullying attacks.

While there are many causes of bullying, it is also a problem that can be solved. Anyone who disagrees is being ridiculous.

Reflect on Your Draft

▶ Did you follow your outline to write your draft? Did it help you cover the main parts of a problem-solution essay?

✔ Revise Your Draft

Your first draft is done. Now, you need to polish it. Improve the voice and style so that it is appropriate for your purpose and audience. Make the tone neutral and objective. Make your writing flow with varied sentence structure and word choice.

❶ Revise for Voice and Style

When you speak, you have a **voice**. The same is true when you write. Your writing voice is determined by the following traits:

- your tone
- your word choice
- your sentence structure

Your **tone** shows how you feel about your topic. Depending on what you are writing, the tone can be serious, friendly, questioning, or persuasive. In a problem-solution essay, however, you should keep your tone as neutral as possible. You want the facts to speak for themselves.

The **word choice** and **sentence structure** you use make up your **style**. Do you use mostly big or little words? Are your sentences long or short? Good writers use a variety of words and sentences to make their writing style more interesting and meaningful for their audience. They also choose a style that is appropriate to the audience and genre. For instance, if the audience is a group of younger students, the writer would probably use simpler words and shorter sentences. If the audience is the school board, the writer would use a more formal, business-like style.

When you look over your draft, see if you notice any patterns in your writing. Is there some word or phrase you keep using? Is there a common sentence structure in your writing? Once you notice these patterns, you can decide if they work with the audience and purpose of your essay.

TRY IT ▶ With a partner, decide how the tone and style of the draft below could be improved.

Student Draft

> We see it in popular movies and on TV. It is also a problem that many students face in real life. What a bummer! Bullying has become a totally huge problem at Lincoln high school. Bullying is also a problem in schools all across the United States. Bullying harms both the victim and the bully. More seriously, bullying affects students school experience.

Now use this rubric to evaluate the voice and style of your own draft. What score do you give your draft and why? With a partner, evaluate the voice and style of the Student Model on p. 355. Decide together how to score the model for each of the descriptions in the rubric. Point out specific details in the model that led you to score it that way.

Voice and Style

myNGconnect.com

- Rubric: Voice and Style
- Evaluate and practice scoring other student essays.

	Does the writing have a clear voice and is it the best style for the type of writing?	Is the language interesting and are the words and sentences appropriate for the purpose, audience, and type of writing?
4 Wow!	The writing <u>fully</u> engages the reader with its individual voice. The writing style is best for the type of writing.	The words and sentences are interesting and appropriate to the purpose and audience. • The words are precise and engaging. • The sentences are varied and flow together smoothly.
3 Ahh.	<u>Most</u> of the writing engages the reader with an individual voice. The writing style is mostly best for the type of writing.	<u>Most</u> of the words and sentences are interesting and appropriate to the purpose and audience. • Most words are precise and engaging. • Most sentences are varied and flow together.
2 Hmm.	<u>Some</u> of the writing engages the reader, but it has no individual voice and the style is not best for the writing type.	<u>Some</u> of the words and sentences are interesting and appropriate to the purpose and audience. • Some words are precise and engaging. • Some sentences are varied, but the flow could be smoother.
1 Huh?	The writing does <u>not</u> engage the reader.	<u>Few or none</u> of the words and sentences are appropriate to the purpose and audience. • The words are often vague and dull. • The sentences lack variety and do not flow together.

❷ Revise Your Draft

You have now evaluated the voice and style of your own draft. If you scored 3 or lower, how can you improve your work? Use the checklist below to revise your draft.

Revision Checklist

Ask Yourself	Check It Out	How to Make It Better
Do I use a voice that makes my argument sound believable?	If your score is 3 or lower, revise.	☐ Read your essay aloud. Listen for any language that sounds too informal or emotional instead of factual.
Does the tone stay the same?	If your score is 3 or lower, revise.	☐ Read your essay aloud. Listen for changes in tone. ☐ Choose new words that make the tone consistent.
Does the style fit the audience?	If your score is 3 or lower, revise.	☐ Look for words that your audience may not relate to.
Do I use transitions and varied sentence structure to make my writing flow?	If your score is 3 or lower, revise.	☐ Add transitional words, phrases, and sentences. ☐ Make sure sentences are varied to add rhythm to your writing.
Do I state the problem clearly? Do I give enough background information, along with causes and effects?	Read your essay to someone else. See if you provide enough information for your classmate to understand the problem.	☐ Research more background information about the problem, including more causes and effects.
Do I support my solution with enough evidence?	Read your essay to someone else. See if the solution seems believable to the person.	☐ Research more evidence to support your solution.
Do I end my essay with a clear summary of the problem and solution?	Read the end of your essay. See if it sums up your argument logically and objectively.	☐ Elaborate or trim to make the conclusion concrete and to the point.

📔 **Writing Handbook,** p. 698

❸ Conduct a Peer Conference

It helps to get advice from others when you are revising your draft. Ask a partner to read your draft and look for

- a clear problem
- one or more effects
- one or more causes
- a clear solution
- evidence to support the solution
- a counterclaim and response
- a strong conclusion

Talk with your partner about your draft. Focus on the items in the Revision Checklist. Revise your draft using your partner's feedback as a guide.

❹ Make Revisions

Look at the revisions below and the peer-reviewer conversation on the right. Notice how the peer reviewer commented and asked questions. Notice how the writer used the comments and questions to revise.

Revised for Voice and Style

> We see it in popular movies and on TV. ^but^ It is also a problem that many students face in real life. ~~What a bummer!~~ Bullying has become a ~~totally huge problem~~ ^major issue^ at Lincoln high school, ^as well as at^ ~~Bullying is also a problem in~~ schools all across the United states. ~~Bullying~~ ^Physical and verbal teasing^ harms both the victim and the bully. More seriously, bullying affects students school experience.

Revised Ending

> While there are many causes of bullying, ^from anger to low self-esteem,^ it is also a problem that can be solved. ~~Anyone who disagrees is being ridiculous.~~ With clear rules and communication, we can hold bullies responsible for their actions while helping them change their behavior.

Peer Conference

Reviewer's Comment: Could you vary the sentence length? Also, some of the language seems too informal, and you repeat *problem* and *bullying* a lot.

Writer's Answer: You're right. I'll work on the tone and combine sentences to fix the repetition.

Reviewer's Comment: Can you be more specific and less emotional?

Writer's Answer: Yes. I'll probably get my point across better if I include facts instead of insults!

Reflect on Your Revisions

▶ A partner can help you take a good look at your essay and may see things you missed. What did your partner find? Were you surprised?

✓ Edit and Proofread Your Draft

Your revision is complete. Now you need to find and fix any mistakes you made.

❶ Capitalize the Names of Places

Capitalize all main words in the names of specific places, such as countries, cities, states, and buildings.

> **Country:** South Africa; Republic of South Africa
> **City and State:** Los Angeles, California
> **Buildings:** Sears Tower; King High School

Do not capitalize the names of nonspecific places.

> a high school   a skyscraper   a village

TRY IT ▶ Copy the sentences. Fix the five capitalization errors. Use proofreader's marks.

> 1. Bullying has become a major issue at Lincoln high school.
> 2. A study in norway showed how to reduce bullying.
> 3. We can help make our High School safer for everyone.

❷ Use Apostrophes Correctly

An apostrophe has two different purposes:

- It represents a missing letter or letters in a contraction.
  can**'t** (cannot)   she**'ll** (she will)   didn**'t** (did not)
- It is used with the letter s to show possession.
  Marco**'s** book   the school**'s** policy   the girl**'s** class

There are two important rules to remember when using apostrophes:

- The apostrophe goes after the final s of a plural word.
  the twin**s'** school   the three bullie**s'** detention
- An apostrophe is only used with the pronoun *it* when forming the contraction *it is*.
  It**'s** not fun to get picked on.

TRY IT ▶ Copy the sentences. Add or remove apostrophes where needed.

> 1. Bullying affects students school experience.
> 2. The same number of student's are reported as being bullies.
> 3. It's clear that bullying causes it's victims major stress.

Proofreader's Marks

Use the proofreader's marks to correct errors.

Capitalize:
I live in hillsboro.

Do not capitalize:
The Town has 1,500 people.

Add apostrophe:
He'll go with you

Delete apostrophe:
The dog wagged it's tail.

Proofreading Tip

If you are unsure of where to place an apostrophe, you can refer to a style manual for help.

❸ Check Your Spelling

To make them plural, add -es to nouns that end with the letters *ch*, *s*, *sh*, *x*, and *z*.

> bus, buses   wish, wishes

If a noun ends in a consonant + *y*, change the *y* to *i* and add -es.

> baby, babies   daisy, daisies

For some nouns that end in *f* or *fe*, change the *f* or *fe* to *v* and add -es.

> leaf, leaves   wife, wives

TRY IT ▶ Copy the sentences. Find and fix the spelling errors.

> 1. Bullying can take the form of throwing punchs.
> 2. Bullys may have trouble at home.
> 3. These feelings can stay with victims well into their adult lifes.

❹ Use Parallel Structure

When you list a series of things, actions, or ideas in a sentence, they must be parallel in form. Each word, phrase, or clause in the series must have the same function or word pattern. For example, do not mix nouns with verbs.

Incorrect: Administrators must communicate with **teachers**, **students**, and **talk to parents**.

Correct: Administrators must communicate with **teachers**, **students**, and **parents**.

or

Administrators must **communicate with** teachers, **listen to** students, and **talk to** parents.

Also, do not mix words or phrases with independent clauses.

Incorrect: Bullying can take the form of **throwing punches**, **name-calling**, **exclusion**, and **some students even get harassed on the Internet**.

Correct: Bullying can take the form of **throwing punches**, **name-calling**, **exclusion**, and **even Internet harassment**.

TRY IT ▶ Copy the sentence. Rewrite it, giving it parallel structure.

> Bullying can cause physical injuries, stress, result in poor grades, and it often leads to depression.

Writing Handbook, p. 698

Reflect on Your Corrections

▶ Remember these tips whenever you write. Use them for all kinds of writing. The more you practice, the better you will be!

Here is the student's draft, revised and edited. How did the writer improve it?

Bullying: How Can We Stop It?

We see it in popular movies and on TV, but it is also a problem that many students face in real life. Bullying has become a major issue at Lincoln High School, as well as at schools all across the United States. Physical and verbal teasing harm both the victim and the bully. More seriously, bullying affects students' school experience.

Bullying comes in many forms. It can take the form of throwing punches, name-calling, exclusion, and even Internet harassment. Studies show that 15–20 percent of students are victims of some type of bullying. Surprisingly, the same number of students are reported as being bullies.

What makes a student become a bully? There are many reasons. Bullies may have trouble at home. They may be failing in school. Or they do not feel accepted by their schoolmates. Some even become bullies because they want to feel more popular. In the end, bullies hurt others to feel better about themselves.

Bullying has serious consequences for the victims, too. Its negative effects impair a student's ability to learn. Victims are also more likely to become depressed, lonely, and insecure. These feelings can stay with victims well into their adult lives.

How can we stop bullying? Schools can adopt a "zero tolerance" policy. Punishing all bullies equally, no matter what the offense or the circumstances are, may seem unfair. It is easier, however, to have one strict rule that everyone must follow than to have unclear limits.

Additionally, teachers, administrators, parents, and students must communicate with each other. Administrators should provide assistance to teachers who have bullies in their class. Parents should talk with their children about what goes on at school, and students should be encouraged to report bullying.

These measures do work. A study of these combined practices in Norway showed that they reduced bullying in a school by 50 percent. Closer to home, in Hillsboro, the school district's new zero-tolerance policy has helped prevent many additional bullying attacks.

While there are many causes of bullying, from anger to low self-esteem, it is also a problem that can be solved. With clear rules and communication, we can hold bullies responsible for their actions while helping them change their behavior.

The writer fixed **capitalization errors**, removed informal language, and created sentence variety. The writer also added an **apostrophe**.

The writer corrected the **plural noun error**, removed an **apostrophe**, and made the sentence structure **parallel**.

The writer corrected the **plural noun error**.

The writer removed an incorrect **apostrophe** and added a missing one. The writer also corrected the **plural noun error**.

The writer added a **question** and a **transition** word to connect ideas.

The writer fixed **capitalization errors** and added an **apostrophe**.

The writer summarized the argument clearly and objectively.

✔ Publish and Present

Print your essay or write a clean copy for publication or presentation.
Give an audience a chance to hear your solution to the problem. You may
also want to present your work in a different way.

Alternative Presentations

Do a Reading Read your problem-solution essay aloud to your class. Follow
these tips for a good presentation:

1 Read with Expression Use the tone of your voice to keep your audience's
attention.

2 Watch Your Pacing Don't read too fast. Pause after important points and
let your words sink in.

3 Make Eye Contact Glance down at your essay, but keep your head up and
your eyes on people in your audience as much as possible. Doing so will
make them feel like you are speaking directly to them.

4 Ask for Feedback When you are finished, thank your audience. Then ask
your audience for suggestions on how you might improve your technique.
Also ask whether your controlling idea was clearly stated and well-supported
with evidence. Did you address concerns and counterclaims?

Publish in a Newspaper Submit your essay to a newspaper. Many papers
publish short essays from readers. Your local paper or school paper might
accept yours.

1 Find a Publication Look for newspapers in your school or community.

2 Check the Guidelines Many publications have guidelines for writers.
Ask for them if you can't find any.

3 Send Your Work Mail or e-mail your work. Include a way for the publisher
to contact you. Ask for feedback on your work.

📖 **Language and Learning Handbook**, p. 616

Publishing Tip

Format your typed work
according to your teacher's
guidelines.

If you've handwritten your
work, make sure your work
is legible and clean.

Listening Tip

Listen carefully when
others present their
essays. Take notes to
summarize the speaker's
ideas. Listen closely
for descriptions or
definitions that will help
you understand unfamiliar
words or phrases. If
you don't understand
something, use your
notes to ask questions.

Before you give feedback,
think about whether
the report's style and
organization helped
illustrate the meaning
and purpose.

**Reflect on
Your Work**

▶ Ask for and use feedback
from your audience to
evaluate your strengths
as a writer.

• Did your audience
  understand the problem
  and your solution?

• Did your essay make the
  audience agree with your
  argument?

• What would you like to
  do better the next time
  you write? Set a goal for
  your next writing project.

☑ Save a copy of
  your work in your
  portfolio.

EQ ESSENTIAL QUESTION:

Do People Get What They Deserve?

The rain falls on the just and the unjust.

—HOPI PROVERB

Injustice anywhere is a threat to justice everywhere.

—MARTIN LUTHER KING, JR.

Critical Viewing
Boxers practice together at a community center in Salvador, Brazil. In boxing, opponents are matched in weight and ability to help ensure fair play. But do athletes like these men always get what they deserve?

FAIR
PLAY

EQ ESSENTIAL QUESTION:
Do People Get What They Deserve?

Study the Cartoon
Does everyone play fair? Who decides what is fair? Look at the cartoon:

"How would you feel if the mouse did that to you?"

Analyze and Debate
1. How do rules and laws protect people from being treated unfairly? Do laws protect everyone equally?

2. Is there ever a time when someone should not be punished for doing something harmful or against the law?

Talk with a group. Explain your opinions and support your ideas with evidence from your own knowledge, experience, and observations.

EQ ESSENTIAL QUESTION

In this unit, you will explore the **Essential Question** in class through reading, discussion, research, and writing. Keep thinking about the question outside of school, too.

① Plan a Project

Comic Book or Graphic Novel

In this unit, you will be producing a comic book or graphic novel about the Essential Question. Choose a subject, create characters, and develop a plot. To get started, read some comic books and graphic novels about heroes, real and mythical. Look for

- the types of characters and how they are shown
- how the plot develops
- how the writer makes the story interesting.

Study Skills Start planning your comic book or graphic novel. Use the forms on myNGconnect.com to plan your time and to prepare the content.

myNGconnect.com
▸ Planning forms
▸ Scheduler
▸ Examples of comic books
▸ The basics of graphic novels
▸ Rubric

② Choose More to Read

These readings provide different answers to the Essential Question. Choose a book and online selections to read during the unit.

Cesar Chavez: Fighting for Farmworkers
by Eric Braun

Cesar Chavez was a farmworker in California in the 1950s. Farmworkers were not treated fairly. Chavez decided it was time for a change. He risked his life to create that change and became one of the greatest leaders in the history of the United States.

▸ NONFICTION

Emako Blue
by Brenda Woods

Emako had it all. She was kind. She had a beautiful singing voice. She was going to be famous. But Emako died before her dreams came true. Her friends are left alone to mourn her death. Together they share memories of Emako, the girl who was supposed to be a star.

▸ NOVEL

Dracula
by Bram Stoker

Jonathan Harker visits Count Dracula at the count's mysterious castle in Transylvania. There, he discovers that Count Dracula is a vampire. Can Jonathan stop Dracula from hurting innocent people, or will he become another victim? Explore how the classic story of Dracula continues to influence modern literature.

▸ CLASSIC

myNGconnect.com

🔊 View presentations on preventing youth violence.
🔊 Read about fairness in the U.S. criminal justice system.

Short stories are about more than characters, setting, and plot. Read "Final Cut" to understand theme in stories. After reading, summarize the story with a partner. Write a list of several possible themes, or messages, for the story.

FINAL CUT

Rachel had to admit it: she was looking forward to the final project for English. They could choose any book and any project. Mr. Hill, Rachel's teacher, explained that he wanted them to work in pairs. That made it even better. But Rachel's feelings changed quickly. Mr. Hill came up to her and said, "Rachel, I want you to work with Jane."

Jane! Rachel looked over at her. She had mousy brown hair, wore goofy outfits, and never spoke. Rachel heard one of her friends laugh. "This project is ruined," thought Rachel.

Jane walked over to Rachel's desk and just stood there. "Oh, sit down," Rachel finally said. Jane slumped into a chair and didn't say anything. "OK," Rachel sighed. "Do you have any ideas?"

"I thought we could do a film," Jane said.

"Yeah, right," thought Rachel. "How?"

Jane continued, "I've been kind of playing around with making films for a while. I could show you." They agreed to meet later.

After school, Rachel and her friends were at the library, talking. Rachel didn't even notice when Jane got there. One of her friends made things worse by saying, "Rachel, your new friend is here."

Once they were settled at the library, things changed. Jane took out a laptop and started a film clip. "This one is about dreams," she said about her first film, which was amazing. "And this one is about my mom." Rachel choked back tears. The short clip was a good-bye to Jane's mother, who had died recently. Rachel asked, "Can you teach me how to do this?" Jane answered, "Yeah, I can."

After that, Rachel spent all her free time with Jane. She learned about the camera and about editing. She also learned about her friends. They were mad that she was not spending time with them. Every time they saw Jane, one was sure to say "Nice outfit" and laugh.

Finally, it was project day. Jane let Rachel set up their clip. They had spent hours on it. When it was done, no one said a word. Then Mr. Hill started to clap. Everyone joined in, although Rachel noticed that her friends were not clapping quite as hard as the other kids in the class.

After class, Rachel's friends met her at the door. "So now you can get back to normal and drop that geek." Jane was packing up. Rachel looked hard at the girls and turned without saying a word. She started to help Jane with the equipment. Jane flashed her a little smile. Then Rachel asked Jane, "Want to get some coffee after school?"

Connect Reading to Your Life

Imagine that the author of "Final Cut" is an advice columnist. How would the author respond to the following e-mail?

I have no friends at school. Kids make fun of my clothes, my hair, my music. Most of the time I don't care. I love my music. The music teacher lets me practice piano during lunch. He wants me to join the jazz band, but I'm not going to do it. The idea of spending more time at school makes me sick. I practice piano four or five hours every day after school. When I do it, I'm happy. Then the next day comes and I have to go back to school. I hate it. What should I do?

Sour Note in Cincinnati

Share your ideas with a partner. Remember to answer as if you were the author of "Final Cut."

Reading Strategies

· Plan and Monitor
· Determine Importance
· Make Inferences
· Ask Questions
▶ Make Connections
· Synthesize
· Visualize

Focus Strategy ▶ Make Connections

The advice you gave depended on your understanding of "Final Cut" and your understanding of high school. In fact, to understand the story you had to make connections between what you know from life and what you read in the story. You make connections all the time. If you are watching a reality show on TV and you think:

- "I'd never do that," you are making a connection between the show and your life.

- "I can't believe people are willing to act that way," you are making a connection between what you know of the world and what you are watching.

- "This reminds me of that other show," you are making a connection between one show and another.

Your Job as a Reader

One of your jobs as a reader is to make connections to find the author's point. Have you ever listened to a friend and said, "You're telling me this because … ?" You were trying to figure out the point. In a similar way, you also look for the point in short stories. As you read, talk to the author in the same way as you talk to your friends. Think: "You're telling me this because … ?"

■ Unpack the Thinking Process

Theme

The **theme**, or point, in a story is an idea that comes from the story and that can be applied to new situations. That is how you were able to guess what the author of "Final Cut" would say to Sour Note in Cincinnati. The story was about Rachel and Jane, but its ideas could be applied to other situations.

Different readers might disagree about a story's theme, but it is important to recognize that the theme of the story goes beyond the details of character, setting, and plot. To understand theme, you need to make connections to the characters, the conflict, and the **consequences** of the characters' actions.

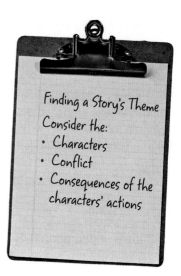

Finding a Story's Theme

Consider the:
• Characters
• Conflict
• Consequences of the characters' actions

Character

To understand the theme of "Final Cut," for example, you must have some sense of what kind of people the characters are. Look back at the story. The author tells very little about Rachel's friends. You don't even know their names. You probably have a pretty good idea of what they are like, though, because you probably have met people like them in your own life.

Conflict

You also have to make connections to understand the story's conflict. For example, the author doesn't say what Rachel was thinking and feeling when her friends made fun of Jane. To understand, you have to apply what you know about what it means to be popular or unpopular in school.

Elements of Literature
theme *n.*, a story's important message about life

Academic Vocabulary
• **consequence** *n.*, an effect, or what happens as a result of something; **consequent** *adj.*, following as a result

Consequences

The story also doesn't explain directly the consequences of Rachel's decisions. You have to apply what you know about the excitement of learning new things. To understand the consequences of Rachel's actions—inviting Jane for coffee in front of her friends—you have to apply what you know about people like Rachel's friends.

- You may personally know some people like that.
- You may have seen people like that around school.
- You may have seen a movie or read another story that has similar characters.

You also have to apply what you know about friendships, what you know about the world, and what you have learned from reading or watching other stories to understand how the story would continue.

■ Try an Experiment

Pretend the story ended this way:

DEMO TEXT *Take 2*

After class, Rachel's friends gathered at the door. "Now that that's over, you can get back to normal and drop that geek." Jane was in the back of the room, packing up equipment. Rachel smiled at the girls and went back into the classroom. She started to help with the equipment. Jane flashed her a little smile. Rachel smiled back. "After school, maybe you and I and the others," she nodded her head in the direction of the other girls, "could go to the mall. We could maybe help you pick out some new clothes." Jane responded quickly, "That would be just great. Without my mom, I haven't really felt much like shopping."

Think, Pair, Share Answer these questions with a partner, and then share your responses with the class.

1. Based on this new ending, how would your advice to Sour Note in Cincinnati change?

2. How is the theme of the original "Final Cut" different from the theme of the story with the new ending?

Monitor Comprehension

Theme What is a theme? Does a story have only one? Explain.

EQ **Do People Get What They Deserve?**
Find out how people deal with bullies.

Make a Connection

Anticipation Guide Think about how it feels when someone bullies you. Then tell whether you agree or disagree with these statements.

ANTICIPATION GUIDE   Agree or Disagree

1. People should always stand up to bullies. _____

2. Bullies are unhappy people. _____

3. It's better to be bullied than to be a bully yourself. _____

Learn Key Vocabulary

Study the Words Pronounce each word and learn its meaning. You may also want to look up the definitions in the Glossary.

● Academic Vocabulary

Key Words	Examples
● **attitude** (a-tu-tüd) *noun* ▶ pages 380, 383, 386, 391, 392	Your **attitude** is the way you feel about something or the way you look at the world. If someone "has **attitude**," he or she has unfriendly or negative feelings about something. *Synonyms:* view, outlook
bully (boo-lē) *noun; verb* ▶ pages 376, 378, 380, 385, 389, 391, 393	A **bully** is a person who is repeatedly mean to others, especially if they are weaker. **Bullies** often scare or hurt other people. [*noun*] To **bully** someone is to threaten that person. [*verb*]
● **challenge** (cha-lunj) *verb* ▶ pages 376, 383	To **challenge** people is to try to get them to do something difficult or to compete with you. Has anyone ever **challenged** you to run ten miles? *Synonym:* dare
confront (kun-**frunt**) *verb* ▶ pages 377, 390, 391	To **confront** means to meet someone face-to-face to discuss a problem, or to face a difficult situation. Your teacher may **confront** a student who is late to class. *Antonym:* ignore
intimidate (in-**ti**-mu-dāt) *verb* ▶ pages 383, 388, 391	People who **intimidate** us make us feel unimportant or afraid. What kind of person might **intimidate** you? *Synonyms:* threaten, frighten
reform (ri-form) *verb* ▶ page 390	To **reform** is to change for the better. When criminals **reform**, they do not commit crimes.
● **revelation** (re-vu-lā-shun) *noun* ▶ pages 389	A **revelation** is something that is revealed, or made known. Suppose you discovered that you could play golf really well. Would that **revelation** surprise you? *Antonym:* secret
sympathetic (sim-pu-**the**-tik) *adjective* ▶ pages 379, 393	A **sympathetic** person understands the feelings of others and is kind. When you are upset, a **sympathetic** friend can make you feel better. *Synonyms:* understanding, caring; *Antonyms:* unfeeling, uncaring

Practice the Words Work with a partner to write four sentences. Use at least two Key Vocabulary words in each sentence.

Example: Someone with a <u>sympathetic</u> <u>attitude</u> is caring and helpful.

BEFORE READING Jump Away

short story by René Saldaña, Jr.

Reading Strategies

• Plan and Monitor
• Determine Importance
• Make Inferences
• Ask Questions
▶ **Make Connections**
• Synthesize
• Visualize

Analyze Theme

Most stories have a **topic**. The topic is what the story is about, such as *teenagers*. Stories also have a **theme**. The theme is the author's message about the topic, such as *teenagers are very clever*.

Authors don't usually tell you the theme. You have to figure it out. As you read, take notes about the characters' thoughts, words, and actions. Consider the end of the story, too. Use these clues to identify the theme.

Look Into the Text

Fenny's thoughts show that he is afraid of Mike, a bully.

Fenny wasn't scared that way. He wasn't bothered by heights. That's not why he was clinging to the bridge railing. He just didn't want to go in before Mike said so. That'd mean certain trouble for him at school. Today was their turn. Six or seven of them, all the oddballs on campus, challenged to jump from Jensen's Bridge to prove themselves to Mike and the rest of his crew of strong-arms.

What do Mike's actions show about bullies?

Focus Strategy ▶ Make Connections

The text you read becomes more meaningful when you connect it to your own life, to things you have read, and to the world around you.

HOW TO MAKE CONNECTIONS

Focus Strategy

Take notes about the characters as you read. Then use this strategy to make connections.

- **Text to Self** If a character note reminds you of your own life, write *T-S* next to it. Explain how the connection helped you understand the text.

- **Text to Text** If a character note reminds you of another story, poem, book, or other text you have read, write *T-T* next to it. Name the other text. Explain how the connection helped you understand the text.

- **Text to World** If a character note relates to problems or issues in the world, write *T-W* next to it. Explain how the connection helped you understand the text.

Character Notes

1. Fenny clung to the metal railing. T-S

I remember being on a high bridge. I held onto the railing as I looked down below.

The Writer and How He Works

René Saldaña, Jr.
(1968–   )

It's the revision part of writing that I enjoy most, because that's where I get to tell the story as cleanly and as clearly as possible.

Saldaña grew up in Texas. He teaches in the College of Education at Texas Tech University.

René Saldaña, Jr., says that he uses himself as a model for his characters. "I think there's a part of me in each of my characters," he explains, "both good and bad characters, positive and negative."

Saldaña also looks outside of himself for story ideas. He says, "I usually carry a journal, and when the spirit moves, I write. I listen to people quite a bit; even folks who aren't talking to me, I listen to. I jot down what they say that sounds interesting."

"I do a lot of sitting around thinking, staring out into a distance. I read a bunch, and watch television a bunch, too." He says that watching TV is research. His wife doesn't agree with this. Saldaña says,

"She thinks I watch too much TV. We don't have cable because I'd be watching even more!"

The idea for the story "Jump Away" came from another story Saldaña wrote. In "The Dive," a girl named Melly wants to jump off a bridge that all the boys in town jump from. She wants to prove she is as tough as they are. Saldaña says, "I asked myself, Who would be among the [boy] jumpers? And why would he do such a crazy thing as to jump from a bridge into a river?" The answers became the story "Jump Away."

myNGconnect.com

Check out a writers' group and see how writers work together.
Look through a magazine published just for writers.

JUMP AWAY

by René Saldaña, Jr.

Comprehension Coach

Fenny clung to the metal railing behind him. The cement ledge under him was hot on his bare feet. He looked at the river fifteen feet below and nodded. Easy enough, he thought. **1** Not scary like in all those movies where the manly-man hero's walking across a rotting wooden bridge, way above a rushing river, in search of the **ever-elusive treasure**. Then someone else, the **sidekick or the sarcastic native guide**, says, "Whatever you do, don't look down." And always, always, the "hero" (who it turns out is afraid of heights) does look down and freezes stiff or makes some kind of "fraidycat" remark that usually makes audiences laugh. **2**

Fenny wasn't scared that way. He wasn't bothered by heights. That's not why he was clinging to the bridge railing. He just didn't want to go in before Mike said so. That'd mean certain trouble for him at school. Today was their turn. Six or seven of them, all the **oddballs** on campus, **challenged** to jump from Jensen's Bridge to prove themselves to Mike and the rest of his crew of **strong-arms**.

Fenny looked upriver, some hundred fifty yards, and saw two people. Fishing, he figured. Fenny couldn't see the rods

Oglethorpe Bridge, 2005, Rani Garner. Oil on canvas, collection of the artist.

△ **Critical Viewing: Setting** What is this place like? How would this painting change if Fenny and Mike were on the bridge?

1 Make Connections
Have you or anyone you've known ever been in a similar situation? If so, explain how it helps you understand Fenny's situation.

2 Language
What do the quotation marks around the word *hero* tell you? Is the author using the word in a serious or a sarcastic way? Explain. Is this "hero" brave or fearful?

Key Vocabulary
bully *n.*, a person who is repeatedly mean to others
● **challenge** *v.*, to try to get someone to do something difficult; to dare someone

In Other Words
ever-elusive treasure treasure he can never find
sidekick or the sarcastic native guide partner or the local guide who laughs at him
oddballs strange kids
strong-arms bullies, mean classmates

themselves, much less the lines. How the two sat and held out their arms, their reeling in and casting motions, told him that's what they were up to.

"Any of you want to back out?" asked Mike. He was also hanging on to the rail, several jumpers to Fenny's left. Mike swung out, holding on with one hand. He looked at the rest of them, a smile on his face, but a **glare** too. Mike had been in charge at school of recruiting the "next batch." That's what he called those who he felt needed to show they were real men, "not the skinny **punks** I think you really are." At school this last week, Mike and his boys had surrounded the would-be jumpers one at a time and told them, "Jump, or **be jumped**." **3** Every one of the boys Mike <mark>confronted</mark> during the past week showed up today. "Any of you girls want to back out? It's okay if you do. Not all of us have to be man enough. How about you, Femmy? You look a bit shaky." He laughed.

ANY OF YOU GIRLS WANT TO BACK OUT?

Fenny said, "It's *Fenny*. Don't worry about me. I'm jumping. I'm just waiting for the word." **4** He let go with one hand to brush back his hair.

Mike **humphed**. "And the rest of you punks? What's it going to be? Any of you others wanna back out?"

No one said anything.

Fenny wasn't afraid, but even so he really didn't want to jump. No, really he did. But on his own terms. Not forced like what Mike was doing to them here. He wanted to go when he wanted. Better yet, he would've liked to have been fishing instead, like the two people

3 Access Vocabulary
What does "would-be jumpers" mean? Use other words in the sentence as clues.

4 Theme/Make Connections
Make a character note to record what Fenny's words tell you about him. What T-S, T-T, or T-W connection can you make to this?

Key Vocabulary
confront *v.*, to meet someone face-to-face about a problem or to face a difficult situation

In Other Words
glare mean look
punks worthless guys
be jumped get beat up, get hurt
humphed made a noise to show that he didn't care

upriver. He looked at them again. He saw one of them standing up, looking in their direction. It was a girl **with her hand cupped over her eyes**. She was wearing a sleeveless shirt and her arms looked pinkish to Fenny. The day was good for fishing. It was warm enough, almost no current to speak of.

Fenny pulled a stick of gum from his shorts pocket. What am I doing here? he thought. What do I care what Mike thinks about me? Fenny remembered a story he'd read recently in class. It was about a boy who's been challenged to dive fifty feet from a ledge into a pool of water at the base of a waterfall. The boy in the story doesn't dive. Instead he **treks** back down to the base where the others, a girl included, **figure him for a wimp**. Easy for a kid to do in a story, Fenny thought. He doesn't have to worry about a very real **thug** like Mike, whose very real fists mean very real bruises and black eyes and a bloody nose. **5**

"Last chance," said Mike.

▲ Critical Viewing: Character Do you think this picture shows a bully or someone who is being bullied? Explain your ideas.

5 Theme/Make Connections
How does Fenny feel about **bullies**? What clue does this give you about the story's theme? How do you connect with this? Make a character note.

Monitor Comprehension

Summarize
How does Fenny react to the bully?

In Other Words
with her hand cupped over her eyes shading her eyes with her hand
treks walks
figure him for a wimp think he is a coward or weak guy
thug mean guy

Fenny considered climbing back over the railing, walking down to the riverbank, up to the people fishing, and asking, "**How're they biting**?" Maybe sitting down beside one of them and saying, "What about you giving me a turn?" Then casting his line and lazy-lazy reeling it back in. No matter **nothing was biting**. The sun on his face and arms would be good. But then he'd remember Monday was just around the corner. Everyone at school would know he hadn't jumped. He'd get beaten up, or worse. Mike or someone else would pull his pants down around his ankles and shove him down in the hall between periods. Everyone would laugh. The girls would giggle at his skinny legs, point at his tight white underpants while he tried covering himself with one hand and with the other try to pull his pants up. Not one **sympathetic** girl in the bunch. Not one who would come up to him after to say, "Listen, Fenny, these guys are jerks blah blah blah." Nope, just laughing. 6

Forget the fishing, he thought. "So, what? Are we jumping or are you **yapping**?" Fenny said. He turned and looked at Mike. When Fenny saw Mike's ugly stare, he knew that even if he jumped today, he'd still be *Femmy* at school. Mike would still be the jerk who pushed him around. It's not like we'll be best of friends come Monday, he thought.

"Whoa," Mike said, "anxious, are we? Just **hold your horses**, Femmy. It'll happen soon enough. I just need to try to scare the rest of your buddies. One of them, at least one of them, will back down if we wait up here long enough. Right? 7 Who's first to back out? It's

6 Theme/Make Connections
Do you think Fenny's worries are justified? Explain your answer based on the text, as well as connections you can make with your own life, your reading, or what you know about the world.

7 Theme/Make Connections
What do Mike's words tell you about him? What does this remind you of in your life? Make a character note.

Key Vocabulary
sympathetic *adj.*, kind, understanding, caring

In Other Words
How're they biting? Are you catching any fish?
nothing was biting they were not catching fish
yapping talking
hold your horses wait

not going to be Femmy by the sound of him. So who's it going to be? How about you, Ritchie? No? You? Or you?" Mike went down the line, calling each of the boys by name, waiting six or seven seconds, all the time staring at them. Not one of them **backed down**, though.

"Impressive. Okay, then, on the count of three. Ready? On my three. One," said Mike.

To heck with it, Fenny thought. I'm going in early, on my own. Mike or no Mike.

"Two." Right before he called three, Fenny said, "Three," and jumped, toes pointed right at the water. **8** He took a breath and kept his eyes open. It looked to him like the fishing girl was looking their way. Fenny stiffened and **cut** right into the water, no problem. He breathed hard out of his nose **on impact**. Then he was under, **murky** and green down there. He heard the others' muffled screams, then the **gurgling of them breaking the water**. Fenny went all the way down, down far enough to feel the slimy bottom of the river oozing between his toes. His eyes were open the whole way, bulging from the pressure and stinging from keeping them open.

He pushed himself off the river bottom and shot up and out of the water. The others swam to the bank. Mike was already out and shaking himself off. Then a couple joined him. Then the rest. All of them looking for a place to lie down. Fenny took his time, though, flipped over and swam on his back. **9**

OKAY, THEN, ON THE COUNT OF THREE. READY?

8 Theme
What does Fenny do? What does this action suggest about his **attitude** toward **bullies**?

9 Theme/Make Connections
How does Fenny act? What does this remind you of? Make a character note.

Key Vocabulary
attitude *n.*, **1**: a way of feeling about or looking at the world **2**: unfriendly or negative feelings toward someone or something

In Other Words
backed down gave up
cut went, dived
on impact when he hit the water
murky dark
gurgling of them breaking the water sound they made when they went into the water

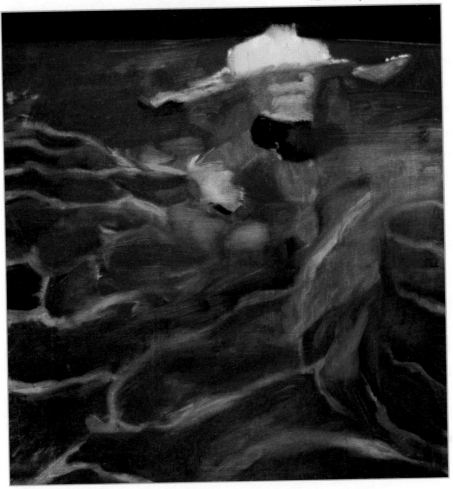

▲ Critical Viewing: Design Look at the colors, lines, and shapes in this painting. How do these elements give the feeling of being underwater?

"Couldn't wait, could you?" Mike screamed. **10**

Fenny swung his arm up over his body in a perfect **arc** and sliced his hand into the water. He reached way, way down and felt the river bottom with his knuckles under him. He'd almost reached the edge.

10 Theme/Make Connections
What do Mike's sarcastic words show you about him? What connection do you make to this?

In Other Words
arc curve

He stood up, water up to his knees pushing against him. He saw the others, everyone except for Mike, lying down in the sun. Mike glared at him. "I said go on three. My three. Not two, not two and a half. And definitely not your three. That too difficult a plan for you?" See, things hadn't changed much. Mike was still a jerk.

"Easy enough plan. Your three, not mine. You were just taking **your sweet time**, though. Like you were having a hard time figuring what came after two."

Fenny saw the others **tilt their heads up and in his direction**. One or two of them leaned up on an elbow. Mike inched his way up to Fenny with his chest sticking out, his slicked-back hair shining in the sun. "What'd you say?" Now the two were up on each other, face to face, breathing heavy. "I know you just didn't speak **out of turn**. And I know you didn't just say what I think I heard you say. Right?"

Fenny was quiet.

Then he said, "No, you heard me right."

The speed of what happened next **caught Fenny off guard**. But it didn't surprise him. Mike's fist caught him full on the left side of his face, right on the cheekbone, and Fenny was down on the ground.

"You know," said Mike, "you diving today, it doesn't change anything."

Of course it doesn't, thought Fenny. Why would it? ❖

Wrestlers, circa '99, Peter Harrap. Oil on canvas, private collection, The Bridgeman Art Library.

▲ **Critical Viewing: Effect** What is the mood, or feeling, of the painting? Does it match the mood of the story? Explain.

🔢 **Theme/Make Connections** Why isn't Fenny surprised by Mike's reaction? Does this change what you thought the theme of the story was? Why or why not? Make a T-S, T-T, or T-W connection.

Monitor Comprehension

Confirm Prediction Did you think the ending would be like this? Why or why not?

ANALYZE Jump Away

1. **Summarize** Tell how Fenny responds when Mike **challenges** him to jump into the river.

2. **Vocabulary** What will Fenny's **attitude** be the next time he runs into a guy like Mike?

3. **Analyze Theme** Look back at your character notes. What do you think is the theme, or message, of the story? Compare your idea with a partner's.

4. **Focus Strategy Make Connections** What T-S, T-T, or T-W connection can you make to the theme of this story? How does this help you better understand "Jump Away"?

Return to the Text

Reread and Write Why does Mike **intimidate** Fenny and the other kids? Look for evidence in the story. Then write your answer.

Key Vocabulary
intimidate *v.*, to make someone feel unimportant or afraid

personal narrative by Laila Ali

Analyze Theme

Narrative writing tells a story. Every narrative—whether fiction or nonfiction—has a message or **theme**. The first clue to discovering the theme is often the title. Other clues come from how the people in the narrative solve problems and how they change.

Look Into the Text

The title hints at the story problem and the theme.

SHOWDOWN WITH BIG EVA

I saw my sophomore year as a new beginning. I was looking forward to going to a new high school and was happy to be starting out fresh…

My older sister, Hana, and my best friend, Alice, had been going to Hamilton High, where they seemed to be having fun. I knew there were cliques, but I figured I'd find my own place.

I was at Alice's house a month before school started when I felt the first twinge of trouble. Alice was on the phone with a girl reputed to be the roughest sister at Hamilton. For some reason this girl had attitude about me and was talking mess. She was telling Alice how she had every intention of kicking my butt. "If she's talking about me," I said, "let her say it to me."

What problem does Laila face?

Focus Strategy ▶ Make Connections

As you read "Showdown with Big Eva," think about the connections you make with the text. Some of these connections may just be interesting. Other connections may help you understand the text better.

HOW TO MAKE CONNECTIONS

Focus Strategy

1. Review the three kinds of connections.

   • **Text to Self** Connect the text to your own life and experiences.
   • **Text to Text** Connect the text to other things you have read.
   • **Text to World** Connect the text to problems and issues in the world.

2. Use a chart to track connections. Explain how the connections help you. For example, they might help you understand the characters' feelings better, keep you interested in the text, or make you want to learn more.

Text to Self Connections	The text says …	This reminds me of …	This helps me understand the text better because …

Connect Across Texts

In "Jump Away," Fenny figures out how he will deal with a threat from Mike. In this personal narrative, a student tells how she dealt with a **bully**.

SHOWDOWN WITH BIG EVA

by Laila Ali

I saw my sophomore year as a new beginning. I was looking forward to going to a new high school and was happy to be starting out fresh . . .

Key Vocabulary

bully *n.*, a person who is repeatedly mean to others

▲ The author, Laila Ali, became a professional boxer like her famous father, Muhammad Ali.

I even got a new hairdo, a short cut that made me feel more mature. It was a clean look; I was looking for a clean start.

My older sister, Hana, and my best friend, Alice, had been going to Hamilton High, where they seemed to be having fun. I knew there were cliques, but I figured I'd find my own place.

I was at Alice's house a month before school started when I felt the first twinge of trouble. Alice was on the phone with a girl **reputed** to be the roughest sister at Hamilton. For some reason this girl had **attitude** about me and was **talking mess**. She was telling Alice how she had every intention of kicking my butt. "If she's talking about me," I said, "let her say it to me."

I got on the phone.

"I hear you think you're **all that**," said the girl I'll call Big Eva.

"I don't think anything."

"Well, don't think you can just stroll over to Hamilton and be cool. Because you can't. I don't want you there. If you show up that first day, I'll **whup you**." 🔲 1

"Tell you what," I said, "not only will I show up that first day, but I'll personally come over and introduce myself to you. That way you don't have to go looking for me."

"You don't know who you talking to."

"I **ain't** talking to anyone." And with that, I hung the phone up in her ear.

Hana Ali (left), Muhammad Ali, and Laila. This photo was taken many years after Hana and Laila met Big Eva.

1 Make Connections What connection can you make to the text here? Explain it in your chart.

Key Vocabulary
- **attitude** *n.*, **1**: a way of feeling about or looking at the world **2**: unfriendly or negative feelings toward someone or something

In Other Words
reputed known, said
talking mess saying bad things about me
all that really great
whup you hit you, beat you up
ain't am not

When the first day of school came around, I was ready. Because Hana had preceded me at Hamilton, no one quite knew what to make of me. Hana was sweet; I was fire. Hana was friendly; I was **reserved**. **I gave off a don't-mess-with-me vibe.** And I wasn't interested in joining any clique. I've always gone my own way. **2** Alice and Hana were my only friends—and that was enough. In fact, I was with Alice and Hana when I had my first "encounter." We were heading toward the school's main entrance.

A group of seven or eight tough-looking girls were hanging out on the steps. They all had attitudes. The biggest among them had a deep cut across her face. I wouldn't call her pretty.

"That's Big Eva," whispered Alice. I had figured as much.

I walked over to Big Eva and stood right in front of her, toe to toe.

"I'm Laila."

I walked over to Big Eva and stood right in front of her...

Big Eva started rolling her neck, chewing gum and scowling like she wanted to fight. I still didn't know why and I didn't care. I wasn't budging. **3**

"I told you I'd introduce myself," I said. "So here I am."

"Girl," she said, "you don't know who you're messing with."

Her girls **closed ranks** and started moving in on me. I still didn't budge. That's when the bell rang.

"After school," said Big Eva. "I'll be looking for you."

"I'll save you the trouble. I'll meet you right here."

Word got out. The whole school was **buzzing with anticipation**.

In Other Words
reserved quiet
I gave off a don't-mess-with-me vibe. People thought that they should stay away from me.
closed ranks stepped close together
buzzing with anticipation excited

Big Eva, who wouldn't back down, and Laila Ali, who wouldn't be **intimidated**, were going head to head.

When the final bell rang at 3:30, I was back on the steps, waiting for Big Eva, with a crowd gathering round. Everyone wanted action, and I was ready for *whatever*. When Eva didn't show up, I was half-relieved, half-disappointed. I started walking to Taco Bell, and a large group walked with me. After a few steps, I looked across the street and saw Big Eva and her girls, heading for the same place. A large group also trailed them. It was a scene straight out of **Grease**.

...I was ready for *whatever.*

When we got to Taco Bell, I ordered, then found a seat on one side of the restaurant. Eva's gang sat on the other. **4** I wasn't sure what she wanted to do, but I was going to let her make the first move because she was the one who had the problem with me.

Hana, Alice, and I sat there for a good half hour. By then the place was packed with Hamilton students waiting for a **brawl**. I felt a hundred eyes on me, but I just sat and ate my taco. When I was finished, I got up, slowly walked past Eva's table and, without saying a word, dumped my garbage in the trash. Eva kept rolling her neck, but she never made a move. Nothing happened—until the next day.

I was in the girls' room when Big Eva showed up. "**You're all show and no go**," she said.

"Fine," I said. "Let's go."

She shoved me hard. I shoved her back harder. **5** And just as we were about to **get cracking**, a teacher walked through the door. A few seconds later we were sitting in the principal's office.

4 Make Connections
Think about restaurants you know that are like this one. How does this connection help you picture the scene in the narrative?

5 Theme/Make Connections
How does Laila deal with her problem here? Have you or a friend of yours ever been in a situation like this? If so, did you or your friend deal with it the way Laila did? Explain.

Key Vocabulary
intimidate *v.*, to make someone feel unimportant or afraid

In Other Words
Grease a musical about teens in the 1950s
brawl fight
You're all show and no go You talk a lot, but you don't do anything
get cracking really start fighting

The principal started a long speech about the **futility** of fighting. I interrupted her.

"Look," I said directly to Big Eva, "I'm not interested in fighting. I never was. I just wasn't about to be **bullied**. What makes you think you can go around here bullying everybody?"

I expected Eva to start talking more mess. Instead, something amazing happened. Big Eva started crying. I mean, big tears. Maybe it was because the door was closed and we were alone in that office; maybe because she'd been holding it in so long; or maybe because she sensed that I wasn't really angry at her. Whatever the reason, in between tears she **let loose** all the reasons she'd been acting the bully. All her tears and fears came spilling out—how she hated being overweight, how she felt ugly inside, how she never got any attention at home, how the only way she beat back bad feelings was by intimidating others, how deep down she really hated herself and the **ugly front she had created** to scare off the world. 🔲6

I was shocked by Big Eva's gut-honest **revelations**. And also moved—so moved that I shed a few tears myself. I knew she was being honest; I could feel all the hurt this girl had suffered. I even put my arms around her and let her cry in my arms—both of us sobbing. Two girls who twenty minutes earlier were ready to fight were now acting like long-lost sisters. It was crazy, but in its own way, it was beautiful.

Laila uses her fighting spirit in her boxing. In 2002, she won a best female athlete award from Black Entertainment Television.

6 Theme
How does Big Eva change here? Is Laila's problem solved? How does Big Eva's change help you understand the theme of the story?

✓
Monitor Comprehension

Retell
How did Laila react to Big Eva's revelations?

Key Vocabulary
  bully *v.*, to threaten
 • **revelation** *n.*, something that is revealed, or made known

In Other Words
futility uselessness
let loose started to talk about
ugly front she had created mean way she acted

I'm not saying Big Eva **reformed** and joined the Girl Scouts, but **the chip was off her shoulder**. From that day on, Big Eva and I were cool. ❖

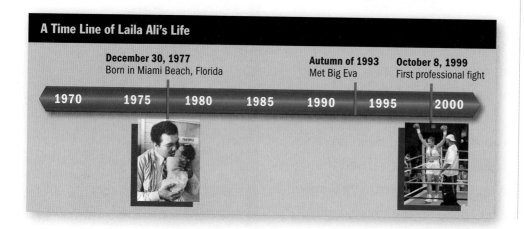

A Time Line of Laila Ali's Life

December 30, 1977
Born in Miami Beach, Florida

Autumn of 1993
Met Big Eva

October 8, 1999
First professional fight

1970   1975   1980   1985   1990   1995   2000

ANALYZE Showdown with Big Eva

1. **Summarize** How does Big Eva feel about herself and her life?
2. **Vocabulary** What would have happened if Laila had not **confronted** Big Eva?
3. **Analyze Theme** Discuss how Laila and Big Eva change and how they solve their problem. Use these ideas to describe the theme, or message, of this narrative.
4. **Focus Strategy Make Connections** Describe an incident you know about that is similar to what happens in this narrative. How did knowing about this incident help you understand "Showdown with Big Eva"?

🔖 **Return to the Text**
Reread and Write Imagine you are Big Eva. Do you think people get what they deserve? Reread the text and then write your thoughts.

Key Vocabulary
reform *v.*, to change for the better
confront *v.*, to meet someone face-to-face about a problem or to face a difficult situation

In Other Words
the chip was off her shoulder she wasn't so angry anymore

EQ **Do People Get What They Deserve?**

Reading

Critical Thinking

1. **Analyze** Look back at the **Anticipation Guide** on page 372. Now that you have read both selections, how would you complete the guide?

EQ 2. **Compare** Does Fenny get what he deserves in "Jump Away"? Does Mike? Compare their situation with what happens to Laila and Eva in "Showdown with Big Eva."

3. **Interpret** Do you think it was easy to **intimidate** Laila Ali? Would it be easy to intimidate Fenny? Use evidence from the texts to explain.

EQ 4. **Speculate** At the end of "Jump Away," Fenny considers whether it was worth it to **confront** Mike. Think about what he concludes. What do you think Laila would say about his conclusion? Explain your answer.

5. **Draw Conclusions** Why do you think some people support **bullies** and others like Laila Ali stand up to them? Discuss your ideas with a partner.

Writing

Write About Literature

Opinion Statement The selections present different views of how a bully reacts when confronted. Which narrative do you think is more realistic? Why? Use examples from both texts to write a paragraph stating your opinion.

Vocabulary

Key Vocabulary Review

Oral Review Work with a partner. Use these words to complete the paragraph.

attitude	confront	revelation
bully	intimidated	sympathetic
challenged	reform	

Last Monday the biggest, toughest __(1)__ in school __(2)__ me to a fight at the end of the day. He looked scary and really __(3)__ me. I found my brother at lunch and asked him what to do. My brother was kind and very __(4)__ to my situation. His feeling, or __(5)__, was that it is never a good idea to __(6)__ a bully. He said it's not cowardly to avoid a fight you can't win. The bully won't __(7)__ in the end. My brother is a strong guy, so I was surprised. His answer came as a __(8)__ to me.

Writing Application Write a paragraph to describe a situation in which your **attitude** toward someone changed. Use at least three Key Vocabulary words.

Fluency

Read with Ease: Phrasing

Assess your reading fluency with the passage in the Reading Handbook, p. 677. Then complete the self-check below.

1. I did/did not effectively group words together.

2. My words correct per minute: _____.

Use Adjectives to Elaborate

Adjectives are describing words. Use adjectives to elaborate, or tell more, about people, places, things, ideas, and feelings. Some adjectives describe the way someone or something looks, sounds, smells, tastes, or feels.

Eva is **big** and **tall**. She makes a **loud**, **snapping** sound with her gum. The gum makes her breath smell **sweet** and **fruity**.

Use adjectives to make your writing more interesting. Choose lively, descriptive adjectives to elaborate. Which sentence below provides the most detail?

She has a cut across her face.
She has a **big** cut across her face.
She has a **deep**, **jagged** cut across her face.

Oral Practice (1–5) With a partner, look at the pictures in the selections you just read. Describe one of the pictures in five sentences. Use at least one adjective in each sentence.

Written Practice (6–10) Use adjectives to add details to the paragraph below.

    I will never forget the day I accidentally knocked the school bully's lunch tray to the floor. I felt __(6)__ when I saw what I had done. He was a __(7)__ guy. "Sorry," I said in a __(8)__ voice. He had a __(9)__ look on his face. So I felt __(10)__ when he smiled and said, "Don't worry about it."

Ask for and Give Information

Interview a Classmate Think of three questions to ask about a hobby. Start your questions with words such as *when, where, what, who, how, are, were, can, do,* or *did*. Then answer your partner's interview questions.

Analyze Mood and Tone

The **mood** of a piece of writing is the feeling you get when you read it. For instance, a story might make you feel happy or nervous. A writer chooses words that create a certain mood. Look at how "Jump Away" begins:

> Fenny clung to the metal railing behind him.

Notice that Fenny doesn't just touch the railing or hold onto it. He *clings* to it. And the railing is *behind* him, which creates a feeling of fear. The mood would be different if the story began this way: *Fenny rested his hands gently on the railing in front of him.*

The **tone** of a story is the author's **attitude** toward the characters and the topic. For example, an author's attitude might be serious, cheerful, or admiring. An author's words reveal his or her attitude.

Think about the mood and tone of "Jump Away." Discuss these questions with a partner:

- How does the story make you feel? What words does the author use to create the mood?

- What is the author's attitude about bullies? How can you tell? Be specific.

"There's an awful lot of anger there."

Source: ©Edward Koren/*The New Yorker*

Vocabulary Study

Relate Words

One strategy to learn new words is to put them in groups, or categories. The web below shows words related to things that **bullies** do. Add to the web. Use a thesaurus to find **synonyms**, or words with similar meanings.

intimidate   confront

things that
bullies do

Then create a web of words that describe nice people. Start with **sympathetic**.

Listening/Speaking

Dramatization

With a partner, dramatize "Showdown with Big Eva."

1. **Practice** Reread the narrative. Choose a scene and your roles. Make up dialogue as you practice acting out the scene.

2. **Write the Dialogue** Pick the best dialogue. Write what each person says.

3. **Perform** Tell the audience which scene you will be dramatizing. Then perform it.

4. **Ask for Reactions** Invite members of the audience to tell how they liked your performance.

▼ **Language and Learning Handbook**, page 616

Writing

Write an Expressive Paragraph

In **expressive writing**, writers share their thoughts and feelings about a topic. Write an expressive paragraph about bullies. Tell what you think and feel about them.

1. **Prewrite** Recall experiences you may have had with bullies or things you have heard about them. How do those recollections make you feel? Capture your feelings in a chart. Use sarcasm as the bully would use it. Put quotes around the word or phrase to indicate the sarcasm.

Chart About Bullies

My Experiences	My Feelings
A bully intimidated my friend last year.	anger fear

2. **Draft** Use your chart as a guide to write your paragraph. Write from your own point of view. Use the pronouns *I* and *me*.

3. **Revise** Read your paragraph. Ask:
   - Does my paragraph express my thoughts and feelings about the topic?
   - Did I use the pronouns *I* and *me*?

4. **Edit and Proofread** Correct any errors in spelling, punctuation, and grammar.

5. **Publish** Rewrite neatly or print a clean copy of your paragraph. Share it in a small group.

Model Expressive Paragraph

> I hate bullies. Last year, at my old school, there was a bully who intimidated my friend. Whenever she would come near us, anger bubbled up inside me. I wanted to shout, "What right do you have to treat other people like that?" Sometimes I felt ashamed because I didn't have the courage to stop the bully. The truth is, I'm afraid that the bully will bother me next. Yet I know that most bullies are insecure inside. That's why they try to hurt other people. It makes them feel superior.

These pronouns show that the text is from the writer's point of view.

What feelings and thoughts does the writer express here?

▼ **Writing Handbook**, page 698

Inside a School

Educators are mainly responsible for teaching students while considering the individual needs and abilities of each person. The educational staff may also work with parents and the community to provide educational support, training, and programs outside of school.

Jobs in Schools

Working in a school requires many skills and abilities. School educators tend to be people who enjoy helping young people from diverse backgrounds. Each educator position calls for specific education and training.

1

2

Job	Responsibilities	Education/Training Required
Teacher Assistant 1	• Helps teachers with instructional and clerical tasks • Assists students with special needs • Keeps records	• High school diploma, some college education, or a certification program • On-the-job training
Teacher 2	• Helps students learn and apply concepts in different subjects • Helps prepare students for college or future careers • Meets with parents and staff to assess and discuss a student's performance	• College degree • Teacher training program that includes practice teaching • Teaching license from the state board of education
Principal 3	• Supervises staff members • Establishes programs and procedures • Interacts with parents and community organizations	• Master's degree or Ph.D. in education administration • State license as school administrator • On-the-job training

Write a Letter of Invitation

Invite a staff member to talk to your class about his or her job. You might consider inviting the school's librarian, reading specialist, school counselor, or any of the jobs listed above.

1. Plan a business letter inviting a staff member to address your class.
2. Suggest a few major areas for the talk in the letter, such as training, responsibilities, and advice.
3. Write your letter using the form recommended by your teacher. Then read your letter aloud to the class. Save the information in a professional career portfolio.

3

myNGconnect.com

🔵 Learn more about school jobs.
🔵 Download a form to evaluate whether you would like to work in this field.
🔵 Download a model business letter.

📖 **Writing Handbook, page 698**

Make Word Connections

A tiny poodle doesn't look much like a big, shaggy sheepdog. However, you recognize both as dogs. Even if you see a type of dog you have never seen before, you know it is a dog. You relate it to others you know and put it in the "dog" category in your mind.

You can learn more about new words by relating them to words you already know. Take the word *amble*. You look it up in the dictionary and learn that it means to walk at a slow, easy pace. You relate it to other words that describe walking speed, such as *stroll* and *skip*. You would likely conclude that *amble* is slower than *walk* but faster than *plod*.

Explore Word Relationships

Using an *array* is one way to organize word relationships. Work with a partner on the following activity.

1. Copy the array frames below onto a piece of paper.

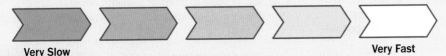

Very Slow   Very Fast

2. Read the words related to *walking* in the box.

3. Create an array of these words. Put the word that means the slowest kind of walking in the far left frame. Put the word that means the fastest kind of walking in the far right frame. These words are **antonyms**, or words with opposite meanings.

4. Fill in the other frames with words that mean walking from slower to faster. The words in the middle are **synonyms**, or words whose meanings are almost the same.

5. Use the dictionary as needed to help you place each word in order.

> **Words Related to Walking**
> - amble
> - stride
> - race
> - march
> - stroll

Put the Strategy to Use

When you learn a new word, relate it to others you know.

1. Identify the new word and determine its meaning. Use a dictionary if necessary.

2. Think of other words you know that are similar.

3. Create an array of those words by putting them in a logical order.

TRY IT▶ Read the sentence below. Use strategies, including looking in a dictionary, to define the words in blue type. Then create an array for each of those words.

When Reynaldo told his joke, his **boisterous** uncle would **guffaw merrily**.

▼ Reading Handbook, page 647

PREPARE TO READ
▶ Fear
▶ Violence Hits Home

EQ ## Do People Get What They Deserve?
Find out how people respond to violence in their communities.

Make a Connection

Quickwrite Think of people you know or have heard of who help improve their communities. Based on what you know, explain what kind of work is likely to be rewarded. Do these people get what they deserve?

Learn Key Vocabulary

Study the Words Pronounce each word and learn its meaning. You may also want to look up the definitions in the Glossary.

● Academic Vocabulary

Key Words	Examples
defiant (di-**fī**-unt) *adjective* ▶ page 406	A **defiant** person tries to go against, or oppose, power or authority. Are you **defiant** when someone tries to make you do something you don't want to do? *Antonym:* obedient
intruder (in-**trüd**-ur) *noun* ▶ pages 404, 407, 409, 415	An **intruder** is someone who enters a place where he or she should not be. For example, an **intruder** might break into a house to steal something. *Antonym:* guest
● **motivate** (**mō**-tu-vāt) *verb* ▶ pages 412, 414, 415	Prizes and money can **motivate** people, or give them a reason, to work hard. *Synonym:* inspire; *Antonym:* discourage
● **positive** (**po**-zu-tiv) *adjective* ▶ page 409	What are the **positive**, or good, things in your life? *Synonyms:* helpful, favorable; *Antonyms:* bad, negative
● **reaction** (rē-**ak**-shun) *noun* ▶ page 411	A **reaction** is what you think or do because of something else. To cry is a natural **reaction** to pain.
● **response** (ri-**spons**) *noun* ▶ pages 407, 415	A **response** is an answer or a reply. You can give a **response** to many things, such as a question, an invitation, or a short story.
revenge (ri-**venj**) *noun* ▶ page 410	When you take **revenge**, you hurt someone who has hurt you. *Antonym:* forgiveness
violence (**vī**-luns) *noun* ▶ pages 409, 415	**Violence** is physical action that is very rough, harmful, and mean. Someone uses **violence** to injure another person. *Antonym:* peace

Practice the Words Work with a partner to complete an **Expanded Meaning Map** for each of the Key Vocabulary words.

Expanded Meaning Map

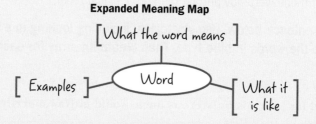

BEFORE READING Fear

short story by Terry Trueman

Reading Strategies

· Plan and Monitor
· Determine Importance
· Make Inferences
· Ask Questions
▶ **Make Connections**
· Synthesize
· Visualize

Analyze Theme

The **theme** is the main message of a story. One way to uncover the theme is to look for clues in the title, the setting, and the thoughts and actions of the characters. Pay attention to the problems that the characters face and how they solve those problems. Put the clues together to determine the theme.

Look Into the Text

Notice details about the setting.

> Alphonso "Zo" Driggers is fourteen years old. He is taller than a lot of kids his age in the neighborhood, taller and thinner. He has lived in the same place since he was born. Two weeks ago, his mother, who lives alone with Zo in their small clapboard house, finally decided to install security bars on the windows and expensive security doors on both the front and back.

What clue here suggests a problem the characters might face?

Focus Strategy ▶ Make Connections

As you read, think about how the story **connects** to your own life, to other things you have read, and to the world around you. Then determine how the connection is useful for understanding the text.

HOW TO MAKE CONNECTIONS

Focus Strategy

Read the text aloud with a partner. Share your connections and ideas.

> Alphonso "Zo" Driggers is fourteen years old.

ONE PERSON THINKS: That kid's name reminds me of a character on some old TV show.

ANOTHER PERSON THINKS: I'm two years older than that kid.

Discuss with your partner how your connections help you understand the story. Connections that help you picture the setting, the characters, and the plot are the most helpful.

Terry Trueman
(1949–)

I've always been the guy least likely to deserve, much less achieve, success.

Terry Trueman lives in Spokane, Washington, with his wife and two sons.

From his speedboat and 1976 Corvette Stingray sports car, **Terry Trueman**'s life is full of excitement. Similarly, his stories are often fast-paced and filled with adventure.

Yet Trueman's writing often raises the kinds of questions that make people stop and think. What does it mean to be human? How do people make difficult choices?

When his son was born with cerebral palsy, a condition that causes brain damage, Trueman couldn't believe it. As he slowly came to accept his son's situation, he wrote his first novel. The book, *Stuck in Neutral*, is told from the point of view of a fourteen-year-old boy with cerebral palsy. It won a Michael L. Printz Award for Excellence in Young Adult Literature.

"It was a surprise. I had hoped it would find an audience. And I knew it was pretty good. But you never really know what will happen."

To date, Trueman has published four novels and many short stories. Trueman says about the future, "I feel now that anything I get from my life from this point forward is just gravy. I'm not planning ahead at all."

myNGconnect.com

Read an interview with Terry Trueman.
Visit Terry Trueman's Web site.

Fear
by Terry Trueman

▲ Critical Viewing: Effect What feeling does this painting suggest to you? Why?

 Comprehension Coach

Alphonso "Zo" Driggers is fourteen years old. He is taller than a lot of kids his age in the neighborhood, taller and thinner. He has lived in the same place since he was born. Two weeks ago, his mother, who lives alone with Zo in their small **clapboard** house, finally decided to install security bars on the windows and expensive security doors on both the front and back. Their house has been **burglarized** four times in the last three and a half years, the last time, three weeks ago, while both Zo and his mom were sleeping. **1**

That night, the burglars came in, stole the twenty-five-inch flat-screen color TV Zo's mother had purchased just six weeks before (the fourth TV in as many years), a portable CD player, and even some jewelry from the small blue jewelry box Zo's mother keeps on the top of her headboard, only a few feet away from where she was sleeping.

Zo's father is not around. He never has been. Zo has not seen his dad for quite a while, the last time being Christmas three years ago, when his father had shown up unexpectedly, drunk and acting stupid. Zo's mother had only let Zo's dad stay for a few minutes, then he had left. His dad had not brought Zo any gifts, but he had slipped him a ten-dollar bill on his way out the door. At the time, Zo thought that he would never spend that money, that he'd keep it forever to remind him of his dad. But the **lure** of candy and of buying popcorn for all his friends at the school

1 Theme
What is it like in Zo's neighborhood? What problem do Zo and his mother face?

In Other Words
clapboard wooden
burglarized robbed, broken into
lure attraction, appeal

popcorn sale had proven too much of a temptation to resist—soon the **ten was ancient history**, just like Zo's dad.

It is a school night, a Tuesday, in early February. Zo's mother, who works as a checker in a grocery store, has an evening shift—something that doesn't happen very often. Zo is home alone. For the most part, he doesn't mind. He has some schoolwork to do, but with his mom gone, he turns on MTV and watches videos. It's a dark night; a winter breeze is blowing along the street outside—not cold, but not warm either. There is a dark feeling to the evening. **2**

Zo gets a bowl of ice cream and sits down on the couch. An older video is playing. As he lifts a soupspoon of ice cream toward his mouth, a big bite of Rocky Road, suddenly Zo hears something. It's a **very distinctive** sound, and he recognizes it instantly. Somebody outside is messing with the window in the **spare** bedroom at the back of the house, the room that his mother uses for sewing.

Zo freezes. He quietly lowers the spoon back into the bowl and sets it on the table in front of him. Moving as silently as he can, he tiptoes over to the hall closet where his aluminum baseball bat leans against the wall just inside the door. He quietly pulls the

Somebody outside is messing with the window . . .

bat out and grips it. His mother doesn't own any guns. **3**

There are more sounds from the back of the house; Zo can now hear the window squeak as it is pushed up and open. The door to

2 Make Connections
What does the author's description of the dark winter night remind you of? How does this connection help you understand the story?

3 Theme
What happens at Zo's house? How does he react to this problem?

In Other Words
ten was ancient history ten dollars was gone
very distinctive one-of-a-kind
spare extra

that room is closed, but it's a weak door, loosely hanging on old hinges. There is over an inch of space between the bottom of the door and the floor.

Zo moves silently down the hall, avoiding spots where he knows the floor **creaks**. He edges his way along the wall, so that whoever is out there won't see his footsteps in the light, which shines into the darkened room from beneath the door.

Suddenly, Zo hears a whispered voice from outside.

"She's got bars up!" the voice says.

"I can see that, man, pull **'em outta** the way."

"You pull 'em; they're strong."

Zo hears a slight creaking sound and a soft grunt. Then more creaking and another grunt, then **quiet cursing**. There is silence for several moments. Zo hopes and prays that they have gone away. Maybe the bars were too much, maybe they . . .

"HEY, ALPO!" a voice calls from the back door, several feet to the east of the window where they have been trying to break in. "Open up this door. We need to get something."

Zo hears a mean laugh, low and cold. "Yeah, Al-phon-zooo," comes a second voice, **higher pitched** than the first. "Open up."

 Critical Viewing: Setting
If you were in the room in this picture, what would you see? How would you feel? How does it compare to Zo's house?

Monitor Comprehension

Describe
Describe the frightening situation that Zo is in.

In Other Words
creaks makes noise
'em outta them out of
quiet cursing someone saying bad words in a low voice
higher pitched sounding higher

Zo slides down the wall against which he's been leaning. He pulls his knees up to his chest and forms a small ball there on the floor. He's frozen with fear. His legs **are rubber**, his armpits drip sweat, and his palms are soaked as he tries to grip the taped handle of the baseball bat. His arms **turn to lead**; he wonders how he'll ever find the strength to even stand up, much less to swing the bat hard enough to do any damage to anybody. He knows there are at least two of them out there; they might have weapons. They seem to know him and how afraid he is.

A terrible **uncontrollable quivering** grips his body. As he looks across the room at the telephone, he wonders if he could crawl that far and call for help. But lots of times the police don't come into this neighborhood at this time of night unless they have to, and when they do come, it's almost always too late, almost always after a crime has already been committed. **4**

One of the voices outside seems to read his mind. "Don't be thinking about calling the police, Alpo—the police don't care about you. Besides, you go phoning the cops, can't handle your own stuff, you know that's weak. The word gets out that you bring the police around, you know—that's weak, Alpo!"

The other voice laughs again. "You know that's the truth, Alpo," he says, pauses a second, then laughs again, an angry, horrible laugh, then says, mean and low, "Open up this damn door!"

There is a vague familiarity to the voices. Where has Zo heard them before? It could be anywhere, the 7-Eleven or the nearby

4 Theme/Make Connections What does this description of Zo's situation remind you of? How does it help you connect with the story's theme? Discuss this with a partner.

In Other Words
are rubber feel weak
turn to lead feel very heavy
uncontrollable quivering shaking that he can't stop
There is a vague familiarity to the voices. The voices sound a little familiar.

playground with its rusted hoops and metal nets. It could be anywhere and it could be anyone. How can he make them go away? How can he save himself? He's too afraid to even think.

Fear. Zo hates his fear. He forces himself to his feet and walks, almost **in a trance**, toward the back door of the house. He stands at the door, tears rolling down his face as he reaches his hand toward the bolt lock, ready to twist it open. His fingers touch the metal handle. It's cold. In the grip of his **terror**, he can't think of anything else to do.

Le Crieur, 2002, Steven Spazuk. Soot on paper, collection of the artist.

◀ Critical Viewing: Effect
How does this art make you feel? Compare that feeling to how the story is making you feel. Which helps you better relate to what is happening to Zo? Explain.

In another second, he could turn the lock and these **intruders** would come in. Zo feels such shame **at his cowardice**; he knows he is a coward. He pauses and tries to catch a breath. Thinking about his shame, he realizes and **flashes** in an instant, "I'd rather be dead than this afraid." 5

5 Theme/Character
What change does Zo go through here? What makes him change?

Key Vocabulary
intruder *n.*, someone who goes where he or she should not go

In Other Words
in a trance as if he were dreaming
terror fear
at his cowardice because he is afraid
flashes understands

"I said open this door, Alpo! We know you, and you're not **gonna** stop us. Open up now, and we won't hurt you. You make us get mean and we'll get you, maybe tonight, maybe tomorrow, but trust me, Alpo, we'll get you."

Zo whispers to himself again, "I'd rather be dead than this afraid." He takes another deep breath and pulls his hand back from the lock. "I'd rather be dead than this afraid." Something happens inside his chest—somehow he is able to breathe again, able to think. And now he feels angry. "I'd rather be dead," he whispers.

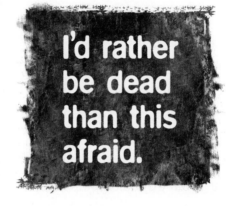

"We'll get you, Alpo!" the voice says again, full of hate and **menace**.

"You might," Zo answers back, surprised by the strength of his voice.

"No 'might,' we will!" The voice is cold and **murderous**.

"You think I don't know you?" Zo says. "You think I can't find out who you are?"

"So what?" one of the voices answers. "You can't do anything!" They both laugh.

"Can't, huh?" Zo snaps back.

The first voice speaks again, another mean laugh in his words. "Oh right, you're all tough and bad, huh?" They laugh again.

Zo pauses for another second, takes another deep breath and speaks low and angrily. "I will call the cops. I'll tell them a couple losers are trying to rob us—I'll tell them that you **threatened** me, said you're gonna kill me. **6** Everyone in the neighborhood will

6 Theme
How is Zo solving his problem?

In Other Words
gonna going to
menace desire to harm Zo
murderous full of hate, full of a wish to kill
threatened said you were going to hurt

know that you're the kind of guys who try to scare a kid who's home all alone. Is that what you want? Is that how you're gonna build up **your rep**? Anything happens to me, the cops will find you. You think you're bad enough to handle that?" Zo pauses a moment to let his questions sink in, now he laughs his own mean laugh. "I don't think so! You say another word, I'll call 'em. **Period.**"

There is a long moment of silence. The voices from outside are quiet. Finally one of them speaks, the meanness gone. "The cops don't care about you, boy—"

Zo interrupts loudly, his voice strong and **defiant**. "They care about guys like *you!*" he snaps back. "I let you in here, let you steal our stuff while I sit here like a little baby, hell, I might as well be dead anyways. But if I call the cops, get them after you—you'll be the ones who are scared! If you think I'm lying, count ten seconds and listen for sirens—I'm gonna call **911** right now!"

Zo hears another moment of silence, then, just outside the door, a hushed, hurried whispering.

Finally the first voice speaks again. "All right, Alpo, hold on, take it easy. Forget about it. Just keep the cops out of this, okay? Just **chill**. We were just playing with you anyway—relax, you know, don't worry about anything Alpo, just—"

Zo interrupts, "My name is Zo, not Alpo!"

▲ Critical Viewing: Design
How might this scene be different during the day? How might it be different if viewed from the other side of the fence?

Key Vocabulary
defiant *adj.*, going against or trying to oppose power or authority; not obedient

In Other Words
your rep your reputation, what people think about you
Period. And that's it.
911 the emergency services number
chill be calm, relax

Zo waits for a **response**, but in the next moment he hears only the sound of the chain-link fence rattling as the strangers leap over it and then run away into the darkness.

Walking back to the couch, he sits back down and glances at his bowl of ice cream—it hasn't even melted too badly yet. As he picks it up, he smiles to himself. "That's Zo, not Alpo! My name is Zo!" **7** ❖

7 Theme
How does Zo feel now? Tell why, and explain how this change in Zo helps you understand the theme.

ANALYZE Fear

1. **Confirm Prediction** Did you correctly predict what would happen, or did the ending surprise you? Use evidence from the story to explain your answer.

2. **Vocabulary** What caused the **intruders** to change their plans?

3. **Analyze Theme** Work with a partner to discuss the clues to the theme. What was the problem? How did the characters solve it? Write a sentence that states the theme.

4. **Focus Strategy** **Make Connections** What movie, song, or other story does "Fear" remind you of? Tell why. Explain how this connection helps you understand the story.

Return to the Text

Reread and Write Suppose Zo goes to school the next day and talks with a friend about this incident. Reread the text. Then write what you think Zo and his friend would say about whether or not the intruders got what they deserved.

Key Vocabulary
- **response** *n.*, an answer or a reply

magazine article by Denise Rinaldo

Analyze Development of Ideas

Many writers include text features that help readers see the development of ideas. These features may also make the text more interesting. Here are some features you might find:

• heads and subheads that divide the text into parts
• text that is printed in easy-to-read columns
• colorful diagrams or charts
• photos with informative captions

Look Into the Text

The color and style of the section heads are different from the other text.

A Bad Situation

Growing up in Oakland, California, Antonio Bibb knew about violence. His community has been plagued by murders, battles between gangs, and robberies. So when Antonio heard about an anti-violence program for high school students

called Teens on Target, he was intrigued...

He also wanted to show others that he was on the side of peace. "Pretty much every adult on my dad's side of the family has been in jail, including my dad," Antonio says. "Even when I was young, people were starting to judge me and categorize me because of that."

Notice how the text is set in two long, narrow columns. How do columns help readers?

Focus Strategy ▶ Make Connections

As you read this article, **make connections** to yourself, to other texts, and to the world. Think about how the connection adds to your understanding of the article.

HOW TO MAKE CONNECTIONS

Focus Strategy

1. **Identify** As you read, stop when something in the article makes you think of something else.

2. **Evaluate** Does the connection help you understand the events? If so, write it down. Tell what you connect to and why you make the connection.

3. **Label** Tell what kind of connection it is: *T-S* (text to self), *T-T* (text to text), or *T-W* (text to world).

Connections Chart

When I read	I make the connection
about Antonio living in a community with violence	with Zo in "Fear" because he also lives in a dangerous neighborhood. T–T

Violence Hits Home

by Denise Rinaldo

Connect Across Texts

In "Fear," Zo faces **intruders** who are trying to break into his house. In this magazine article, a teen struggles against **violence** in his own community.

A Bad Situation

Growing up in Oakland, California, Antonio Bibb knew about violence. His community **has been plagued by** murders, battles between gangs, and robberies. So when Antonio heard about an anti-violence program for high school students called Teens on Target, he was **intrigued**. He was in the seventh grade at the time, but promised himself that when he got to high school, he'd join the group.

Antonio knew lots of kids who had lost family members to violence. He felt lucky he hadn't, and he wanted to do something **positive**. "I felt like there was no way to stop violence, but I hoped I might be able to change things a bit," Antonio, now 18, says. **1**

He also wanted to show others that he was on the side of peace. "Pretty much every adult on my dad's side of the family has been in jail, including my dad," Antonio says. "Even when I was young, people were starting to judge me and categorize me because of that."

Positive Start

In his freshman year, Antonio joined Teens on Target. By tenth grade, he was doing well in school and had become a leader in the program. He got to travel to Maryland for an anti-violence conference. "It was more than **an extracurricular activity to me**," Antonio says. "I really felt like I was helping to stop younger kids from making the same mistakes adults in their families might be making."

1 Make Connections
Think of something you have wanted to change. Explain how this connection helps you understand Antonio.

Key Vocabulary
intruder *n.*, someone who goes where he or she should not go
violence *n.*, physical action that is very rough, harmful, and mean
• **positive** *adj.*, good, helpful, favorable

In Other Words
has been plagued by has had many
intrigued very interested
an extracurricular activity to me something I did outside of school

Antonio stands on the street where his uncle was killed. "I kept thinking of my little cousin growing up without a father," the teen says.

Then, one day during his junior year, Antonio received terrible news. Antonio's Uncle Michael, with whom he had been extremely close, was shot and killed on a street, **in a case of mistaken identity**.

"My father told me and I didn't believe it," Antonio says. "It didn't really **sink in** until I flipped on the news and I saw another one of my uncles on the air talking about it."

Antonio says that he walked through the next several months feeling a combination of disbelief and sadness. His family was **in turmoil**. "They were broken," he says. **2** Sometimes, Antonio had thoughts of **revenge** —of turning to violence himself and **tracking down** his uncle's killer. "I kept thinking of my little cousin growing up without a father," he says.

2 Access Vocabulary
Broken has several meanings—it is a multiple-meaning word. Tell what it means here and then give another definition of it.

Key Vocabulary
revenge *n.*, the act of hurting someone who has hurt you

In Other Words
in a case of mistaken identity by a killer who thought the uncle was someone else
sink in seem real
in turmoil upset and confused
tracking down finding

Teen in Turmoil

Experts say Antonio's **reaction** was normal for a teen who has lost a close family member to violence.

"Revenge fantasies are common," says Kenneth J. Doka, a professor of psychology at the College of New Rochelle in New York and an expert in **grief** and dying. "The key, of course, is helping people not act out on those feelings."

Thanks to his work with Teens on Target, Antonio understood that and did not seek revenge. The memory of his uncle, who Antonio says was "a very powerful and positive man," also helped.

In the fall of his senior year, Antonio was starting to feel like his old self. Then, tragedy struck again. "I lost my best friend in a gang-related shooting," he says. Antonio **snapped** back into revenge mode, and this time it was worse.

"I was ready to quit Teens on Target," he says. "I felt like I had to get back at somebody. There was no reason for my uncle and my friend to die, and I was going to do something about it."

After his best friend was killed, Antonio really struggled with thoughts of revenge.

3 Development of Ideas
What do you learn from this photo and caption?

Monitor Comprehension

Explain
Why did Antonio want to leave Teens on Target?

Key Vocabulary
• **reaction** *n.*, what you think or do because of something else

In Other Words
grief deep sadness
snapped went

To the Rescue

Who kept Antonio from **snapping**? A woman named Teresa Shartell. Teresa is the Teens on Target program coordinator with whom Antonio had been working since his freshman year. She was his teacher, counselor, and friend.

"Teresa reminded me that lots of kids we work with were going through the same situation I was, and that now I was in an even better position to **motivate** them," Antonio says. "She said they'd see how I was reacting to my situation and that would really help them out."

Antonio says he "took what Teresa said and **ran with it**. I realized that we're all going to go through pain. It's what you choose to do with it that makes you the person you are."

The teen **threw himself into his work** with Teens on Target with more passion than ever. He also **vowed to serve as an inspiration for** his now-fatherless cousin. "A lot of kids turn to violence because they see it at school and at home; they don't have strong role models," Antonio says. "I'm trying to be that role model for my cousin." **4**

4 Make Connections
What connection can you make here? Explain how it helps you understand the text.

Teresa Shartell (right) helped Antonio channel his anger over losing his uncle and friend into helping others keep the peace.

Key Vocabulary
- **motivate** *v.*, to give reason to, to inspire, to stimulate

In Other Words
snapping doing the wrong thing
ran with it really used it, really applied it
threw himself into his work decided to work intensely
vowed to serve as an inspiration for promised to act the right way to help

Root Causes

WHAT CAUSES VIOLENCE? HOW CAN VIOLENCE BE AVOIDED?

FEAR. If someone is afraid to walk down a street, he or she may carry a weapon for protection. A better idea is to talk to someone like a parent, teacher, or counselor who can help resolve a tense situation peacefully.

STEREOTYPING. Violence can result when people are judged by their looks, dress, or whom they hang out with. A better idea is to get to know people before you decide how you feel about them.

BAD ROLE MODELS. If kids grow up surrounded by violence, they're going to **emulate** it. Providing positive role models and teaching kids to act peacefully can prevent future violence. **5**

A Life's Work

Antonio plans to **devote** his life to the fight against violence. That includes making sure as few people as possible have to go through the kind of losses he's experienced. One of his goals is to reduce the number of guns on the street. "If it hadn't been so easy to get guns, I think my uncle would still be living," Antonio says. **6**

Now a high school graduate, Antonio has continued to work with Teens on Target and is shopping around for a college to attend. "My life is pretty blessed right now," he says. "I'm doing

5 Development of Ideas
What information does this feature provide? Paraphrase the points.

6 Make Connections
What connection can you make between Antonio's statement about guns and the experiences he has had in his life?

Monitor Comprehension

Summarize
How did Teresa help Antonio?

exactly what I want to do." Antonio is used to giving advice to kids. "Be a leader. Stop following everyone else," he says. "It doesn't matter if you can't buy the stuff you think is cool from movies and videos—**some Phat Farm or some Sean John** or whatever it is. Just be yourself. The more you shine for yourself, the more you can shine in front of everybody else." ❖

ANALYZE Violence Hits Home

1. **Summarize** What is Antonio's advice to kids?

2. **Vocabulary** Explain what **motivates** Antonio to stay involved with Teens on Target. Tell what happened to him as a result of his involvement.

3. **Analyze Development of Ideas** Which text features made it easier for you to understand the development of ideas in the article? Tell why.

4. **Focus Strategy Make Connections** Whom does Antonio remind you of? Explain how this adds to your understanding of the article.

   ### Return to the Text

   Reread and Write Write an e-mail message to Antonio telling him how the article helped you think about people getting or not getting what they deserve. Reread the text for details.

In Other Words
some Phat Farm or some Sean John popular clothes or shoes

EQ Do People Get What They Deserve?

Critical Thinking

1. **Interpret** Look back at what you wrote in the **Quickwrite** on page 396. If Zo and Antonio read your **response**, what do you think they would say?

EQ 2. **Analyze** Do the **intruders** get what they deserve in "Fear"? Explain your answer.

3. **Compare** How are the settings in these selections similar? How are they different?

4. **Speculate** What advice might Antonio give someone like Zo if they spoke after an encounter with intruders?

EQ 5. **Generalize** Do you think people who commit **violence** get what they deserve in time? Use ideas from the two selections as you explain your answer.

Write About Literature

Letter to the Editor Should groups like Teens on Target receive money from the government? Write your opinion in a letter to the editor of a school or local newspaper. Support your views with information from both texts.

Key Vocabulary Review

Oral Review Work with a partner. Use these words to complete the paragraph.

defiant	positive	revenge
intruders	reactions	violence
motivate	response	

> When __(1)__ broke into our youth center and vandalized our computers, there were lots of different __(2)__ among teens in the neighborhood. Some people felt that we should find out who did it and take __(3)__ . Others thought that this was the wrong __(4)__ . It would only lead to ugly behavior or __(5)__ . I agreed with them. I wanted us to do something more __(6)__ and helpful. I said that we might be able to use this incident to push or __(7)__ the city to help us fight crime in our neighborhood. I said we should work within the law. We shouldn't become another group of angry, __(8)__ youths.

Writing Application Describe a situation in which you **motivated** someone or someone motivated you. Use at least four Key Vocabulary words in your paragraph.

Read with Ease: Intonation

Assess your reading fluency with the passage in the Reading Handbook, p. 678. Then complete the self-check below.

1. I did/did not make my voice rise and fall as I read aloud.

2. My words correct per minute: _____ .

Grammar

Use Adjectives Correctly

To compare two people, places, or things, add **-er** to one-syllable adjectives.

The boy is **tall** and **thin**. Zo is **taller** and **thinner**.

To compare three or more people, places, or things, add **-est** to one-syllable adjectives.

They bought four **new** TVs. This one is the **newest**.

For adjectives of three or more syllables, use **more** instead of **-er** and **most** instead of **-est**.

One sound is **more threatening** than the other. Which noise sounds the **most distinctive**?

Some two-syllable adjectives take **-er** and **-est**. Others take **more** and **most**.

The threats are **scarier** than the noises, so Zo is **more frightened** than before.

A few adjectives that compare have special forms.

Zo thinks candy is a **good** snack, but popcorn is **better**. He thinks ice cream is the **best** snack of all.

Oral Practice (1–5) With a partner, say five sentences comparing Zo to the burglars. **Example**: *The man seems tough, but Zo is tougher.*

Written Practice (6–8) Rewrite each sentence. Use an adjective to make a comparison.

6. One man is _____ than the other. (intimidating)
7. He is the _____ kid in the neighborhood. (tall)
8. Feeling brave is _____ than feeling scared. (good)

Language Development

Engage in Conversation

Pair Talk What was the scariest part of the story "Fear"? Share your ideas and listen to what your partner says. Do you agree or disagree? Summarize your reasons and respond thoughtfully to your partner's ideas.

Literary Analysis

Analyze Suspense

Some stories have **suspense**—a feeling of uncertainty or excitement about what will happen next. In this example from "Fear," Zo hears a noise on a dark night:

> Somebody outside is messing with the window in the spare bedroom at the back of the house, ...

The author creates suspense by putting Zo in a dangerous situation. He keeps the suspense going by making the danger come closer: *Zo hears a mean laugh, low and cold.*

Authors use other devices—besides putting characters in danger—to create suspense. For example, characters can face a struggle, be in a contest, or have to make an important decision.

With a small group, discuss these questions:

• What was the most suspenseful moment in "Fear"? What language did the author use to make it suspenseful?

• How did the author structure the text in "Fear" to make it suspenseful?

What about this photo suggests suspense? How or why?

Relate Words

If two words are **synonyms**, they have about the same meaning. Two words that are **antonyms** have opposite meanings. Use print and digital thesauruses to find a synonym and an antonym for each word below.

1. expensive
2. sadness
3. prevent
4. strength

Many analogies are based on pairs of synonyms or antonyms. For example, *big* is to *large* as *small* is to *tiny*. When you have completed your chart, use it to write an analogy.

Review

Literature: Graphic Novels Talk with your school librarian to get a list of recommended graphic novels. Choose a graphic novel to review. Think about:

- if the characters, plot, and art are interesting
- whether you like the graphic novel and why

Try to look at other forms of the graphic novel. Watch a film based on the novel. Listen to a book on tape. Using a variety of media can help you understand the story better and also give you context clues to figure out any difficult words.

Draft your ideas. Use these notes to deliver your review to the class. Act as the story's narrator.

🢓 **Language and Learning Handbook**, page 616

Write a Character Sketch

A test may ask you to write about a character. A character sketch describes what a character is like using specific details and examples.

1 Unpack the Prompt Underline important words.

> **Writing Prompt**
> Write a character sketch of Zo in "Fear." Give your general impression of the character. Support it with examples from the story.

2 Plan Your Response What kind of person do you think Zo is? List details.

Zo	
Age/Physical Build:	14, tall and thin
Family/Home:	lives with his mom in a neighborhood with crime
Feelings:	feels like a coward sometimes; feels ashamed of himself for being afraid of bad guys
Actions:	confronts some intruders; makes them go away
Personality Traits:	smart, brave, strong

3 Draft Begin your sketch with a main idea that tells your general impression of Zo. Then refer to your list. Tell which details from the story give you that impression and why. Conclude your character sketch by restating your idea about Zo.

4 Check Your Work Reread your character sketch. Ask:

- Does my sketch address the prompt?
- Did I include details from the selection?
- Did I use adjectives to elaborate my writing?

🢓 **Writing Handbook**, page 698

PANeL DiSCUSSiON

Do people get what they deserve? A great way to hear different points of view on any issue is to hold a panel discussion, in which each group member speaks about a different part of an issue or topic. When you share thoughts and listen to others' thoughts, you encourage respect for other people and their points of view. Here is how you can do it.

1. Plan Your Panel Discussion

Discuss the question "Do people get what they deserve?" with a group of four or five people:

- As a team, plan how you will discuss and share ideas, and make rules for how you will make decisions.
- Have one person prepare a short response to the question with examples from personal experiences, another person with examples from world events, and another person with examples from movies, books, or television.
- Have each panelist make notes about what he or she will say, listing a basic main idea and good supporting information.
- Decide who will be the moderator, or the person who introduces the speakers and takes questions from the audience afterward.

How can you keep the discussion lively?

2. Practice Your Panel Discussion

Work together to make the presentations go smoothly.

- The moderator practices introducing each speaker and directing questions.
- Panelists make sure their responses can be delivered in the set time and practice building on or clarifying the ideas of the previous speaker.
- Give helpful suggestions as you listen to each other practice. If you have information that would clarify a panel member's point, share it with him or her.

3. Hold Your Panel Discussion

The panelists should sit at a table in the front of the room in the order in which they will speak. The moderator should sit in the center.

- Speak with emotion and energy, especially since you are seated.
- Make eye contact with individuals in the audience.
- Listen carefully and respectfully to the rest of the group. If a panel member says something that confuses you, ask him or her to clarify meaning.

4. Discuss and Rate the Panel Discussion

Use the rubric to discuss and rate the discussions, including your own. Consider each response's style and structure. Ask yourself whether the style helped communicate meaning and purpose. Then ask yourself whether the structure supported the meaning and purpose.

Panel Discussion Rubric

Scale	Content of Panel Discussion	Participant's Preparation	Participant's Delivery
3 Great	• Thoroughly covered the topic with many good examples • Presented several interesting viewpoints	• Seemed to know a lot about the topic • Was very smooth in presentation and transitions	• Was clear and easy to follow • Handled the questions and comments very well
2 Good	• Gave some good coverage to the topic with some good examples • Presented some different viewpoints	• Seemed somewhat informed about the topic • Was fairly smooth in presentation and transitions	• Was somewhat clear and easy to follow • Responded to questions and comments fairly well
1 Needs Work	• Gave only some coverage to the topic • Presenters repeated each other	• Did not seem familiar with the topic • Seemed unrehearsed in presentation and transitions	• Was hard to hear and understand • Did not respond to questions and comments well

DO IT ▶ Now that you know how to conduct a panel discussion, go do it—keep it engaging and lively!

🔖 Language and Learning Handbook, page 616

myNGconnect.com
🔄 Download the rubric.

PREPARE TO READ

EQ Do People Get What They Deserve?
Find out what happens to people who insult others.

Make a Connection

Discussion In a small group, discuss these questions:

- How does it feel to be insulted? How do people usually respond to an insult?
- When have you ever insulted anyone? Did you pretend that you were just kidding or teasing?

Learn Key Vocabulary

Study the Words Pronounce each word and learn its meaning. You may also want to look up the definitions in the Glossary.

● Academic Vocabulary

Key Words	Examples
● **assume** (u-**süm**) *verb* ▶ pages 435, 436, 437	When you **assume** something, you think that it is true. Do you **assume** that you will take exams at school? *Synonyms:* believe, expect; *Antonym:* not know
compromise (**kom**-pru-mīz) *noun* ▶ page 426	In a **compromise**, each side gets something it wants and gives up something it wants. To end a fight, you can make a **compromise.** *Synonym:* deal
existence (ig-**zis**-tuns) *noun* ▶ page 431	**Existence** means the state of living or being. Does your **existence** depend on food and water? *Synonym:* life; *Antonym:* death
ignore (ig-**nor**) *verb* ▶ page 428	When you **ignore** something, you pay no attention to it. Usually it is best to **ignore** bullies. *Synonym:* disregard; *Antonym:* notice
inconvenient (in-kun-**vē**-nyunt) *adjective* ▶ page 428, 439	Something that is **inconvenient** happens at a bad time or is a hassle. When you're in a hurry, it is **inconvenient** to help your little sister get ready for school. *Synonym:* troublesome
insult (in-**sult**) *verb* ▶ pages 433, 437, 439	You **insult** someone when you are rude and say or do something mean to that person. *Synonyms:* hurt, offend; *Antonym:* praise
ridiculous (ru-di-**kyu**-lus) *adjective* ▶ page 425	Something that is **ridiculous** is silly or foolish. Do dogs wearing sunglasses look **ridiculous**? *Synonym:* crazy; *Antonym:* serious
value (**val**-yū) *verb* ▶ page 431	When something is important to you, you **value** it. You might **value** a good friend or your school. *Synonym:* care about

Practice the Words Work with a partner. Make a **Vocabulary Study Card** for each Key Vocabulary word. Write the word on the front. Write its definition, a synonym or antonym, and an example sentence on the back. Take turns quizzing each other on the words.

Vocabulary Study Card

compromise

front

an agreement that solves a problem; a trade-off

The politicians agreed to a compromise and stopped arguing.

back

BEFORE READING Abuela Invents the Zero

short story by Judith Ortiz Cofer

Reading Strategies

- Plan and Monitor
- Determine Importance
- Make Inferences
- Ask Questions
- ▶ **Make Connections**
- Synthesize
- Visualize

Analyze Theme

The **theme** is the message of a story. Often, a story has more than one theme. To find the theme, look for clues in the title and the story elements:

- The **title** may tell the topic. The theme may explore this topic.
- The **setting** and **plot** help you understand the characters.
- Understanding the **characters** brings you closer to the author's message. That's because the theme is usually related to what the characters experience, what they learn, or how they change.

Look Into the Text

Notice that Abuela's words are similar to the title, "Abuela Invents the Zero."

The setting is the United States. Think about how Abuela might feel on her first visit.

"You made me feel like a zero, like a nothing," she says in Spanish, *un cero, nada.* She is trembling, an angry little old woman lost in a heavy winter coat that belongs to my mother. And I end up being sent to my room, like I was a child, to think about my grandmother's idea of math.

It all began with Abuela coming up from the Island for a visit. It was her first time in the United States. My mother and father paid her way here so that she wouldn't die without seeing snow. If you asked me, and nobody has, the dirty slush in this city is not worth the price of a ticket. But I guess she deserves some kind of award for having had ten kids and survived to tell about it.

How might Abuela's experience relate to the theme?

Focus Strategy ▶ Make Connections

As you read, **make connections** with the story. The connections you make will help you understand the story. Notice how your connections change as you continue to read. Try this strategy with the text above.

Focus Strategy

HOW TO MAKE CONNECTIONS

1. **Use a Double-Entry Journal** Copy the passage that reminds you of something. Include the page number. Write a comment explaining the connection.

2. **Follow Up on Your Comments** As you read more of the story, think about your comments. You may want to add new ideas based on what you learn in the story.

Double-Entry Journal

Passage and Page	Comment
"If you asked me, and nobody has, ..." p. 424	I understand this because I often feel like no one cares about my opinion.

The Writer and Her Experience

Judith Ortiz Cofer
(1952–)

When my abuela sat us down to tell a story, we learned something from it, even though we always laughed. That was her way of teaching.

Judith Ortiz Cofer is a professor of English and creative writing at the University of Georgia.

Judith Ortiz Cofer was born in Puerto Rico. When she was only two, her family moved to the United States. Yet she often visited Puerto Rico and stayed with her grandmother.

Cofer describes her grandmother as "a powerful person in our family." When her grandmother died, Cofer felt as if part of her own life had been lost. "She had very little formal education," Cofer says of her grandmother, "but she could silence an entire room when she said, 'Tengo un cuento' or 'I have a story to tell.' And we would all sit around

like children and listen."

Cofer herself began telling stories at an early age. "I used to try to impress my father, who was hard to impress, by telling him stories. I used to pretend to be a boy and a warrior. Then I'd tell my father war stories that he liked."

Now Cofer says, "Most of the stories in my work date back to times when I would sit around at my grandmother's house and listen."

myNGconnect.com

🔊 Visit Judith Ortiz Cofer's Web site.
🔊 Learn more about storytelling.

Abuela Invents the Zero

by Judith Ortiz Cofer

Doña Rosita Morillo, 1944. Frida Kahlo. Oil on canvas mounted on masonite, Fundación Dolores Olmedo, Mexico City, D.F., Mexico.

▲ Critical Viewing: Character Does this woman seem "lost in thought"? What could she be thinking about?

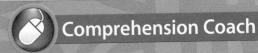
Comprehension Coach

"You made me feel like a zero, like a nothing," she says in Spanish, *un cero, nada.* She is trembling, an angry little old woman lost in a heavy winter coat that belongs to my mother. And I end up being sent to my room, like I was a child, to think about my grandmother's idea of math. **1**

It all began with **Abuela** coming up from **the Island** for a visit. It was her first time in the United States. My mother and father paid her way here so that she wouldn't die without seeing snow. If you asked me, and nobody has, the dirty **slush** in this city is not worth the price of a ticket. But I guess she deserves some kind of award for

1 Theme/Character
What have you learned about the characters so far? What clues might these ideas give to the story's theme?

©Rafael Lopez/theispot.com

◁ **Critical Viewing: Design**
What colors do you notice in this painting? Where are the brightest colors? How do colors direct you to look at certain shapes in the painting?

In Other Words
Abuela Grandmother (in Spanish)
the Island Puerto Rico
slush wet snow

Geography Background
Puerto Rico is an island in the Caribbean, near the Dominican Republic and Haiti. Puerto Rico has a warm, tropical climate.

having had ten kids and survived to tell about it. My mother is the youngest of the bunch. Right up to the time when we're supposed to pick up the old lady at the airport, my mother is telling me stories about how hard times were for **la familia** on **la isla**. *La abuela* worked night and day to support them after their father died of a heart attack. I'd die of a heart attack too if I had a troop like that to support. I had seen her only three or four times in my entire life, whenever we would go for somebody's funeral. I was born here and I have lived in this building all my life. **2** But then Mami says, "Connie, please be nice to Abuela. She doesn't have too many years left. Do you promise me, Constancia?" When she uses my full name, I know she means business. So I say, "Sure." Why wouldn't I be nice? I'm not a monster, after all.

> I'm not **a monster,** after all.

So we go to **Kennedy** to get *la abuela*. She is the last to come out of the airplane, on the arm of the cabin attendant, all wrapped up in a black shawl. He hands her over to my parents like she was a package sent airmail. It is January, two feet of snow on the ground, and she's wearing a shawl over a thin black dress. That's just the start.

Once home, she refuses to let my mother buy her a coat because it's a waste of money for the two weeks she'll be in *el Polo Norte*, as she calls New Jersey, the North Pole. **3** So since she's only four feet eleven inches tall, she walks around in my mother's big black coat looking **ridiculous**. I try to walk far behind them in public so that

2 Make Connections
Describe a person you know who seems like Connie. Make an entry in your journal to explain how this helps you understand what is going on in the story so far.

3 Language
Why do you think the author includes Spanish words like *el Polo Norte*?

Key Vocabulary
ridiculous *adj.*, silly, foolish

In Other Words
la familia the family (in Spanish)
la isla the island (in Spanish)
Kennedy John F. Kennedy International Airport

no one will think we're together. I plan to stay very busy the whole time she's with us so that I won't be asked to take her anywhere, but my plan is ruined when my mother comes down with the flu and Abuela absolutely *has* to attend Sunday mass or her soul will be eternally damned. She's more Catholic than the Pope. My father decides that he should stay home with my mother and that I should escort *la abuela* to church. He tells me this on Saturday night as I'm getting ready to go out to the mall with my friends.

"No way," I say.

I go for the car keys on the kitchen table: he usually leaves them there for me on Friday and Saturday nights. He beats me to them.

"No way," he says, **pocketing them** and grinning at me.

Needless to say, we come to a **compromise** very quickly. I do have a responsibility to Sandra and Anita, who don't drive yet. There is a Harley-Davidson fashion show at Brookline Square that we *cannot* miss.

"The mass in Spanish is at ten sharp tomorrow morning, *entiendes*?" My father is dangling the car keys in front of my nose and pulling them back when I try to reach for them. He's really enjoying himself.

"I understand. Ten o'clock. I'm out of here." I pry his fingers off the key ring. **4** He knows that I'm late, so he makes it just a little difficult. Then he laughs. I run out of our apartment before he changes his mind. I have no idea **what I'm getting myself into**.

4 Access Vocabulary
What do you think *pry* means? Think about what is happening in the story and use other words, such as *his fingers off*, as clues.

Monitor Comprehension

Paraphrase
Tell what Connie thinks about her grandmother.

Sunday morning I have to walk two blocks on dirty snow to retrieve the car. I warm it up for Abuela as instructed by my parents, and drive it to the front of our building. My father walks her by the hand in baby steps on the slippery snow. The sight of her little head with a bun on top of it sticking out of that huge coat makes me want to run back into my room and get under the covers. I just hope that nobody I know sees us together. **5** I'm dreaming, of course. The mass is packed with people from our block. It's a **holy day of obligation** and everyone I ever met is there.

I have to help her climb the steps, and she stops to take a deep breath after each one, then I lead her down the aisle so that everybody can see me with my bizarre grandmother. If I were a good Catholic, I'm sure I'd get **some purgatory time taken off for my sacrifice.** She is walking as slow as **Captain Cousteau** exploring the bottom of the sea, looking around, taking her sweet time. Finally she chooses a pew, but she wants to sit in the *other* end. It's like she had a spot picked out for some unknown reason,

5 Make Connections
When have you felt like this? In your journal, tell how this adds to your understanding.

Grandmother, 1983, James E. Corley. Oil painting, collection of the artist.

◄ Critical Viewing: Design
How do you think the woman in this painting feels? What is it about the painting that makes you think that?

In Other Words
holy day of obligation special religious day
some purgatory time taken off for my sacrifice less punishment for the bad things I've done since I'm being good now
Captain Cousteau Jacques Cousteau, a famous ocean explorer and researcher

Cultural Background
Mass is a religious service in the Catholic Church and some other Christian churches. At mass, people pray, listen to holy readings, and participate in traditional ceremonies.

and although it's the most **inconvenient** seat in the house, that's where she has to sit. So we squeeze by all the people already sitting there, saying, "Excuse me, please, *con permiso*, pardon me," getting annoyed looks the whole way. By the time we settle in, I'm drenched in sweat. I keep my head down like I'm praying so as not to see or be seen. She is praying loud, in Spanish, and singing hymns at the top of her creaky voice. **6**

I **ignore** her when she gets up with a hundred other people to go **take communion**. I'm actually praying hard now—that this will all be over soon. But the next time I look up, I see a black coat dragging around and around the church, stopping here and there so a little gray head can peek out like a periscope on a submarine. There are giggles in the church, and even the priest has frozen in the middle of a blessing, his hands above his head like he is about to lead the congregation in **a set of jumping jacks**.

I realize to my horror that my grandmother is lost. She can't find her way back to the pew. I am so embarrassed that even though the woman next to me is **shooting daggers at me with her eyes**, I just can't move to go get her. I put my hands over my face like I'm praying, but it's really to hide my **burning cheeks**. I would like for her to disappear. I just know that on Monday my friends, and my enemies, in the barrio will have a lot of senile-grandmother jokes to tell in front of me. **7** I am frozen to my seat. **8** So the same woman who wants me dead on the spot does it for me. She makes a big deal out of getting up and hurrying to get Abuela.

6 Theme/Character
How does Connie feel about her situation? How does Abuela feel? What clue does this scene give you about the theme of the story?

7 Access Vocabulary
Use the context to determine the meaning of the word *barrio*, which comes from a Spanish word.

8 Theme/Character
What do you learn about Connie from her reaction?

Key Vocabulary
inconvenient *adj.*, troublesome
ignore *v.*, to pay no attention to something

In Other Words
take communion to the front of the church for a special part of the church service
a set of jumping jacks some exercises
shooting daggers at me with her eyes looking at me in a really angry way
burning cheeks embarrassment

Portrait with Eyes Closed, 2004, Yolanda Gonzalez. Acrylic on canvas, private collection.

▲ **Critical Viewing: Character** How are Connie and the girl in this painting alike? What does this girl's facial expression remind you of? Explain.

The rest of the mass is a blur. All I know is that my grandmother kneels the whole time with her hands over *her* face. She doesn't speak to me on the way home, and she doesn't let me help her walk, even though she almost falls a couple of times. 🔳9

When we get to the apartment, my parents are at the kitchen table, where my mother is trying to eat some soup. They can see right away that something is wrong. Then Abuela points her finger at me like a judge passing a sentence on a criminal. She says in Spanish, "You made me feel like a zero, like a nothing." Then she goes to her room.

I try to explain what happened. "I don't understand why she's so upset. She just got lost and wandered around for a while," I tell them. But it **sounds lame**, even to my own ears. My mother gives me a look that makes me **cringe** and goes into Abuela's room to get her version of the story. She comes out with tears in her eyes.

"Your grandmother says to tell you that of all the hurtful things you can do to a person, the worst is to make them feel as if they are worth nothing." 🔳10

I can feel myself **shrinking** right there in front of her. But I can't bring myself to tell my mother that I think I understand how I made Abuela feel. I might be sent into the old lady's room to apologize, and it's not easy to admit you've been a jerk—at least, not right away with everybody watching. 🔳11 So I just sit there not saying anything.

> You made me feel like a
> **zero...**

9 Make Connections/ Theme
What do Abuela's actions remind you of? How does this connection help you understand the story and its theme? Make a note about it in your journal.

10 Theme
How does this sentence relate to the story's title? Explain.

11 Access Vocabulary
The word *apologize* contains the Greek root *logos*, meaning "speech" or "word." What does the word *apologize* mean here?

In Other Words
The rest of the mass is a blur. I don't remember the rest of the service.
sounds lame doesn't sound good, is a weak excuse
cringe feel terrible inside
shrinking getting smaller

My mother looks at me for a long time, like she feels sorry for me. Then she says, "You should know, Constancia, that if it wasn't for this old woman whose **existence** you don't seem to **value**, you and I would not be here."

That's when *I'm* sent to *my* room to consider a number I hadn't thought much about—until today. ⓬ ❖

⓬ Theme
Has Connie changed? Why do you think that?

ANALYZE Abuela Invents the Zero

1. **Confirm Prediction** Did you predict what would happen at church? What happened that you did not expect?

2. **Vocabulary** Does Connie **value** Abuela? Explain your answer.

3. **Analyze Theme** Think about what Connie and Abuela experienced. Share ideas with a partner. Work together to write a sentence that states the theme, or message, of the story.

4. **Focus Strategy Make Connections** How does Connie's relationship with Abuela compare to your relationships with family or friends? Explain how such comparisons add to your understanding of the story.

🔁 **Return to the Text**

Reread and Write Write a note to Abuela about people getting what they deserve. Look back at the text to find details that support your ideas.

Key Vocabulary
existence *n.*, the state of living or being, life
value *v.*, to believe that something is important or has worth

Before Reading Karate

personal narrative by Huynh Quang Nhuong

Reading Strategies

- Plan and Monitor
- Determine Importance
- Make Inferences
- Ask Questions
▶ **Make Connections**
- Synthesize
- Visualize

Analyze Language: Irony

Using words to express something different from the true meaning of the words is **irony**. An ironic word or phrase sometimes appears in quotation marks. **Situational irony** is when the outcome of an event is different from what was expected. **Verbal irony** is when what is said is the opposite of what is meant. One way that writers indicate that they are using verbal irony is to put a word or set of words in quotation marks.

Look Into the Text

Notice how the author describes the situation.

> My grandmother had married a man whom she loved with all her heart, but who was totally different from her. My grandfather was very shy. He never laughed loudly, and he always spoke very softly. And physically he was not as strong as my grandmother. But he excused his lack of physical strength by saying that he was a "scholar."
>
> About three months after their marriage, my grandparents were in a restaurant. A rascal began to insult my grandfather because he looked weak and had a pretty wife. At first he just made insulting remarks, such as "Hey! Wet chicken! This is no place for a weakling!"

How would you expect a weak man to react to the insult? How would you expect the wife to react?

Focus Strategy ▶ Make Connections

Make connections between what you already know about a topic and what you read about it. Try this strategy with the selection.

HOW TO MAKE CONNECTIONS

Focus Strategy

1. **Before Reading** Look at the title of this selection. Use a **Connections Chart** to record what you already know about karate.

2. **During Reading** As you read, keep in mind what you already know about karate. Explain the connections between the text and your prior knowledge. Tell how these connections help you understand the text better.

3. **After Reading** Think about all the connections you made. How did they affect your reading of the story?

Connections Chart

What I already know about karate:

Connections I Make	How My Prior Knowledge Helps Me Understand
p. 433: I've seen karate movies where people start insulting others and then they start to fight.	I can imagine what might happen between these people in the story.

Karate
by Huynh Quang Nhuong

Connect Across Texts

In "Abuela Invents the Zero," Connie is unkind to her grandmother. In this personal narrative, find out what happens when someone is unkind to the author's grandfather.

My grandmother had married a man whom she loved with all her heart, but who was totally different from her. My grandfather was very shy. He never laughed loudly, and he always spoke very softly. And physically he was not as strong as my grandmother. But he excused his lack of physical strength by saying that he was a "**scholar**."

About three months after their marriage, my grandparents were in a restaurant. A **rascal** began to **insult** my grandfather because he looked weak and had a pretty wife. At first he just made insulting remarks, such as, "Hey! Wet chicken! This is no place for a weakling!"

This story takes place in a restaurant in Vietnam, the country where the author was born and grew up.

◄ Analyze the Visuals
What information about the story do you learn from this globe and photo?

Key Vocabulary
insult *v.*, to say or do something mean to someone

In Other Words
scholar person who studies a lot
rascal mean person

Vocabulary Note
The word *karate* comes from a Japanese word meaning "empty hand." Karate is a form of self-defense. The word is no longer treated as a foreign word in English, but instead has become part of the English language.

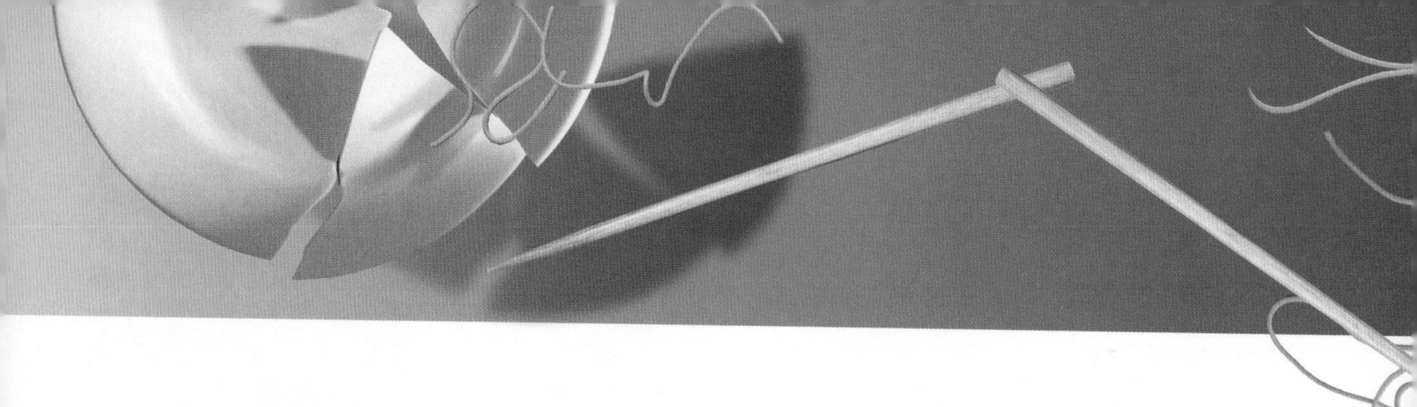

My grandfather wanted to leave the restaurant even though he and my grandmother had not yet finished their meal. But my grandmother pulled his shirtsleeve and signaled him to remain seated. She continued to eat. She looked as if nothing had happened.

Tired of yelling insults without any result, the rascal got up from his table and moved over to my grandparents' table. He grabbed my grandfather's chopsticks. My grandmother immediately **wrested** the chopsticks from him and struck the rascal on his cheekbone with her elbow. **1** The blow was so quick and powerful that he lost his balance and fell on the floor. Instead of finishing him off, as any street fighter would do, my grandmother let the rascal recover from the blow. But as soon as he got up again, he kicked over

> She looked as if nothing had happened.

the table between him and my grandmother. Food and drink flew all over the place. Before he could do anything else, my grandmother kicked him on the chin. The kick was so **swift** that my grandfather didn't even see it. He only heard a heavy thud. Then he saw the rascal tumble backward and collapse on the ground. **2**

1 Irony
What is ironic about this situation? Tell why it is ironic.

2 Make Connections
How does what you already know about karate help you understand this scene? Explain on your Connections Chart.

In Other Words
wrested pulled, grabbed
swift quick

All the onlookers were surprised and delighted, especially the owner of the restaurant. Apparently the rascal, one of the best karate fighters of our area, came to his restaurant every day and left without paying for his food or drink. **3** The owner was too afraid to confront him.

While the rascal's friends tried to **revive him**, everyone else surrounded my grandmother. They asked her who had taught her karate. She said, "Who else? My husband!"

After the fight at the restaurant people **assumed** that my grandfather knew karate very well, but refused to use it for fear of killing someone. In reality, my grandmother had received special training in karate from my great-great uncle from the time she was eight years old.

3 **Make Connections**
Compare the rascal with other fighters. Explain on your chart how this helps your understanding.

What is **karate?**

Karate is a form of self-defense that developed long ago in Asia. Traditionally, karate students do not use any weapons. They use their arms and legs to hit and kick opponents.

Key Vocabulary
- **assume** *v.*, to think that something is true

In Other Words
revive him wake him up

✔ **Monitor Comprehension**

Infer Why did the author's grandmother say her husband had taught her karate? Use evidence from the text to support your inference.

Anyway, after that incident, my grandfather never had to worry again. Any time he had some business downtown, people treated him very well. And whenever anyone happened to bump into him on the street, they bowed to my grandfather in a very respectful way. **4** ❖

4 Irony
People seemed to be afraid of the grandfather. Why is that ironic?

ANALYZE Karate

1. **Explain** Why was the restaurant owner afraid to confront the rascal? Use evidence from the text to support your answer.

2. **Vocabulary** What did the rascal **assume** about the author's grandparents?

3. **Analyze Language: Irony** Describe the ironic situation in the narrative. Explain what made it ironic.

4. **Focus Strategy Make Connections** Look back at your **Connections Chart**. Choose one connection and tell a partner how that connection helped you understand the text better and how it made the information more meaningful.

Return to the Text

Reread and Write Did the rascal get what he deserved? Reread the text to find reasons to support your response. Then write a journal entry to express your opinion.

About the Writer

Huynh Quang Nhuong (1946–2001) grew up in a village in Vietnam that was surrounded by rice fields, mountains, and jungle. He moved to the United States to get treatment for a paralyzing injury he got during the Vietnam War. While living in the United States, he wrote two books about his experiences growing up in Southeast Asia.

EQ Do People Get What They Deserve?

Critical Thinking

1. **Analyze** In "Abuela Invents the Zero," what lesson does Connie learn from her grandmother? What lesson did you learn from the grandmother in "Karate"?

2. **Interpret** What theme do "Abuela Invents the Zero" and "Karate" share?

3. **Compare** Think about how Laila Ali responds to Big Eva in "Showdown with Big Eva." Compare Laila's response with the grandmother's response to the rascal in "Karate." How are they alike? How are they different?

4. **Judge** Did Connie get what she deserved, or was she treated too harshly? What about the rascal, the grandmother, and the grandfather? Use evidence from the texts to defend your answers to a group.

EQ 5. **Speculate** Would Connie or the rascal believe they got what they deserved? Which one would be more likely to think so? Support your answer with evidence from the texts.

Write About Literature

Letter of Advice How would you advise a good friend to respond to an **insult**? Write a letter to your friend. Support your views with examples from both texts. If you include irony in your letter, use quotation marks to draw attention to any ironic remarks.

Key Vocabulary Review

Oral Review Work with a partner. Use these words to complete the paragraph.

assumed	ignored	ridiculous
compromise	inconvenient	value
existence	insulted	

> Every August, my family spent a week at the beach. I __(1)__ we would go this year, too. However, my brother accused me of not paying attention to his life, or __(2)__ . He said that I __(3)__ the fact that he would be away at college. He explained that it would be troublesome or __(4)__ for him to travel a thousand miles to the beach. In fact, he __(5)__ me by calling me foolish and __(6)__ . Dad came along and settled our argument. He suggested a __(7)__ . The family could go to the beach early in June, before my brother left for school. We all agreed, because we love the ocean and __(8)__ any time we can spend there.

Writing Application Describe a situation in which you **assumed** something but were wrong. Include irony. Use quotation marks to draw attention to an ironic remark. Use at least three Key Vocabulary words in your paragraph.

Read with Ease: Expression

Assess your reading fluency with the passage in the Reading Handbook, p. 679. Then complete the self-check below.

1. I did/did not match the sound of my voice to what I was reading.

2. My words correct per minute: _____ .

Use Adverbs Correctly

An **adverb** is a describing word. Adverbs often end in **-ly**. Adverbs can tell *how*, *when*, or *where*.

- An **adverb** can describe a verb.

  My grandfather speaks **quietly**. (how)

  My grandmother **quickly** kicked the rascal. (when)

  He fell **down**. (where)

- An **adverb** can also describe an adjective or another adverb.

  She is **very** angry.

  She walks **really** slowly.

- Some **adverbs** compare actions. Use **more** or **-er** to compare two actions. Use **most** or **-est** to compare three or more actions.

  He strikes **fast**. She strikes **faster**.

  They kick **quickly**. I kick the **most quickly** of all.

Oral Practice (1–5) With a partner, take turns forming sentences about "Karate." Use an adverb in each sentence: *very, loudly, away, softly, never*.

Written Practice (6–10) Fix four more adverbs below and rewrite the paragraph. Then, add one more sentence with an adverb.

more powerfully

Grandmother fought ~~powerful~~ than Grandfather. A rascal yelled loud. Grandfather sat quiet. Grandmother struck most quickly than the rascal. Everyone was surprised, but particular the rascal.

Define and Explain

Pair Talk Tell a classmate about a game or sport you know well. Explain the rules of the game and how it is played. Describe where the game takes place and what equipment the players use.

Panel Discussion

Social Studies: Human Relations Explore this question: *Is violence ever appropriate or necessary?*

1. **Prepare Your Ideas** Think about your own knowledge or experiences that relate to the question. Clarify your opinions. Think of supporting examples or facts. Take notes and organize your ideas.

2. **Conduct the Discussion** The class will be arranged in panel groups. Each group will have a chance to discuss the topic in front of the audience. When you are on the panel, wait patiently for your turn. Then state your views clearly and present supporting information. When you are in the audience, listen attentively and respectfully. Someone else's experience may be funny to you, but not to others. Look at the rest of the class. Are they laughing? Use these context clues to decide what response is appropriate.

3. **Ask Questions** Audience members can ask questions after each panel presents its ideas.

▶ **Language and Learning Handbook**, page 616

Source: ©Charles Barsotti/*The New Yorker*

Antonyms

Antonyms are words that mean the opposite or nearly the opposite of each other. For instance, the opposite of **insult** is *praise*. Some antonyms are formed just by adding a prefix such as *un-*, *in-*, or *ir-*. Here is an example:

- convenient—happens at a good time
- **inconvenient**—happens at a bad time

Use a thesaurus or dictionary to find an antonym for each word below. Note the antonyms formed by adding prefixes.

1. known   **3.** responsible   **5.** friendly

2. weak   **4.** stingy   **6.** active

Analyze Flashback

A **flashback** is a break in the action of a story. The author takes the reader back in time to tell about something that already happened. It is usually used to give the reader background information about a character or an event.

Sometimes, the author tells almost an entire story in flashback. "Abuela Invents the Zero" begins in present time. Then the author introduces a flashback. *It all began with Abuela coming up from the Island for a visit.* Then the author returns to the present at the end.

With a partner, trace the time shifts in "Abuela Invents the Zero." Locate when the author goes from present to past and then back to the present.

Trait: Organization

When you write, think about your topic and how you will organize the information about that topic. **Chronological order** is a good way to organize a story to show how one event leads to another.

Use **transitions** to show how events relate to each other. A transition may be a single word or a group of words. Usually, it comes at the beginning or the end of a sentence.

Transitions can tell when something happens:

- As soon as he arrived, …
- Finally, …

Transitions also can show other relationships:

- Because she did not earn much money, …
- … even though she was happy there.

Just OK

> Tran wanted to move to a big city. He did not have much money. He worked hard. He was able to move to New York City.

Much Better

> Tran wanted to move to a big city when he graduated. He did not have much money, though. He worked hard for three years. Then, in 2004, he finally was able to move to New York City.

Practice Use the sentences below to write a paragraph that follows chronological order. Add transitions to show how events relate to each other. Combine sentences and add details.

Tran arrived in New York City in June.
He saved money by staying at a friend's apartment.
He found a job as a store clerk.
The job did not pay very much.
He became the assistant manager in November.
He earned more money.
He got his own apartment in January.

🔖 **Writing Handbook,** page 698

Why We Must Never Forget

BY NORMAN Y. MINETA

February 15, 1992

1   I am proud to join you here today. Very proud. . . . The fact that our nation—the United States of America—has now apologized to us for our **internment** fifty years ago tells me how much this nation has changed, and that the changes have been for the better. With those changes have come understanding, reflection, and the recognition that basic human rights either apply to us all—or they belong to no one. *However*, there is no escaping another truth: that the **specter** of racism is lurking in us all. . . .

2   It was here in California and the West Coast fifty years ago that our life as a community was forever transformed by an attack that struck at the heart of the U.S. Constitution. This was an attack not of our making. But three thousand miles away in Washington, D.C., the government of the United States—our government—decided that Americans of Japanese ancestry were a categorical threat to the United States.

3   No matter that these threats were unproven, or that we were either American citizens or permanent resident aliens. All were **tarred** with the same indiscriminate brush of racial hatred and fear.

4   We were all scared, those of us who were alive at the time. The entire world was at war. The United States had been brought into this war—the Second World War—after the Empire of Japan had attacked Pearl Harbor, Hawaii, on December 7, 1941. One of the first **casualties** of that attack was faith and trust within our American nation.

5   America quickly saw little value in distinguishing between the attackers that Sunday morning and loyal Japanese Americans who were every bit as much the target of that dawn air raid in Hawaii. All too much effort was invested, instead, in **expedience**. And the search was on for **scapegoats**. . . .

In Other Words
internment imprisonment
specter danger
tarred painted
casualties losses
expedience fast action
scapegoats people to blame

Historical Background
During World War II, U.S. citizens of Japanese ancestry were unfairly forced to live in internment camps. In 1988, Congressman Norman Y. Mineta helped pass a bill requiring the U.S. government to apologize.

6   One by one, Japanese American communities along the West Coast disappeared: removed into stark, barren camps scattered throughout some of the most inhospitable regions of the United States. The myth that this forced relocation was being done for our protection was a lie exposed by the first sight of camp guard towers with their machine guns pointed in at us, instead of out.

7   Tens of thousands of us spent up to four long years in these camps. The vast majority of us cooperated with our government, determined to prove our loyalty **in the long run** by sacrificing peacefully **in the short run** our most basic rights as Americans. And we served this country well. Far above and beyond **the call of duty**. . . .

> *One by one, Japanese American communities along the West Coast disappeared…*

8   Internment drained and **crippled** many Japanese American families. Homes, farms, and businesses were lost. Lives were ruined. . . .

9   The result was that once the war had ended and the camps were closed, we tried to forget the internment.

10   Parents never spoke of it to their children. But here there was an inescapable contradiction: How can you prove your loyalty once and for all, as we had tried to do, if you allow personal justice denied to stand silently in a specter of shame? The answer is, you can't.

Manzanar Internment Camp, Manzanar, California, circa 1943, Bill Manbo. Photograph, Takao Bill Manbo.

In Other Words
in the long run over time
in the short run at that moment
the call of duty what was expected
crippled permanently harmed

11 And the lesson I learned was that wronged individuals must stand up and fight for their rights if our nation is to be true to its principles, without exception. That's what our successful effort to **redress** the internment was meant to do.

Dorothea Lange, 1942.

U.S. Army medic Ted Miyata (right) was sent home in 1942 to help his mother (left) prepare for internment.

Paul Kitagaki, Jr., 2007.

Miyata's daughter stands where her grandmother and father were photographed sixty-five years before.

12 For me, that ten-year struggle in Congress won back for us our **dignity**. In the Civil Liberties Act of 1988 . . . it says, and I quote:

13 *The Congress recognizes that, as described by the Commission on Wartime Relocation and Internment of Civilians, a grave injustice was done to both citizens and permanent resident aliens of Japanese ancestry by the evacuation, relocation, and internment of civilians during World War II.*

14 *As the Commission documents, these actions were carried out without adequate security reasons and without any acts of **espionage or sabotage** documented by the Commission, and were* **motivated** *largely by racial prejudice, wartime **hysteria**, and a failure of political leadership.*

15 *The excluded individuals of Japanese ancestry suffered enormous damages, both material and intangible, all of which resulted in significant human suffering for which appropriate **compensation** has not been made.*

16 *For these fundamental violations of the basic civil liberties and constitutional rights of these individuals of Japanese ancestry, the Congress apologizes on behalf of the Nation.*

Key Vocabulary
- **motivate** *v.*, to give reason; to inspire; to stimulate

In Other Words
redress provide compensation for
dignity self-worth
espionage or sabotage spying or disloyalty
hysteria panic
compensation payment

17   That last sentence means more to me than perhaps any other in law, for it represents everything that our government is designed to do when it works at its best. And today, fifty years after **Executive Order 9066** was signed, the successful effort to redress that wrong stands as a reminder of what ultimate accountability can and should mean in the United States.

Dorothea Lange, 1942.

Paul Kitagaki, Jr., 2006.

Labeled with identification tags, Fumiko Hayashida and baby Natalie leave their farm.

Sixty-four years later, mother and daughter stand at their Washington farm.

18   It should mean truth. It should mean justice. And it should mean universality of the rights guaranteed by the U.S. Constitution.

19   But today, we must remain vigilant to ensure that these truths hold true for our children and grandchildren. The most recent wave of **Japan-bashing and America-bashing** holds for us a special danger. Those who prefer not to learn from the mistakes of the past, those who prefer **a jingoism** of hate, those who prefer to seek scapegoats continue to pose a threat.

20   The war in the Middle East last year demonstrated how genuine a concern this is for every minority community. In 1942, Japanese Americans were threatened and interned. But in 1991, when Arab Americans were threatened, there were voices within government and without to **bear witness**. We helped stop history from repeating itself.

21   None of us can predict who might next fall target to hysteria, racism, and weak political leadership. But with our strength of conviction and witness to history, I do believe that we can ensure that such a tragedy as our internment never befalls anyone ever again here in the United States. ❖

Today a monument marks the spot where the Manzanar Internment Camps were.
Manzanar National Historic Site/Park and Recreation

In Other Words
Executive Order 9066 the law that ordered the Japanese internment
Japan-bashing and America-bashing cruel comments about Japan and America
a jingoism an extreme culture
bear witness call attention to it

FAIR PLAY

EQ **ESSENTIAL QUESTION:**

Do People Get
What They Deserve?

myNGconnect.com

🌐 **Download the rubric.**

EDGE LIBRARY

Present Your Project: Comic Book or Graphic Novel

It is time to complete your comic book or graphic novel about the Essential Question for this unit: Do People Get What They Deserve?

1 Review and Complete Your Plan

Consider these points as you complete your project:

- How does your comic book or graphic novel address the Essential Question?
- Does each panel of your comic book or graphic novel show an important action or tell something about a character?
- How can you build suspense throughout the story?
- Did watching or listening to other forms of graphic novels (film, audio book) help you to develop the language and themes of your story?

2 Publish Your Comic Book or Graphic Novel

Make copies of your comic book or graphic novel. Exchange copies with classmates.

3 Evaluate the Comic Books and Graphic Novels

Use the online rubric to evaluate each of the comic books or graphic novels, including your own.

Reflect on Your Reading

Think back on your reading of the unit selections, including your choice of Edge Library books. Discuss the following with a partner or in a group.

Genre Focus Which selection had the most meaningful theme for you? Tell the theme and explain why it is meaningful to you.

Focus Strategy Choose one of the selections from this unit. Explain two of the connections you made to it. How did these connections affect your experience of the text?

EQ Respond to the Essential Question

Throughout this unit, you have been thinking about whether people get what they deserve. Discuss the Essential Question with a group. What have *you* decided? Support your response with evidence from your reading, discussions, research, and writing.

Write a Description of a Process

What are you good at? Can you describe how to bake bread or train a dog? Can you explain how an airplane or a smoke detector works? For this project, you will describe a process.

Study a Description of a Process

Process descriptions explain how to do something or how something works. Writing a good description of a process is like looking under the hood of a car, identifying all the parts, and knowing just what they do.

1 Connect Writing to Your Life

You probably describe processes more often than you realize. You may have explained how to get from school to your house or how to shoot a 3-point hoop. You rely on process descriptions, too, such as learning a new computer skill. This project builds on your skill for describing a process you know well.

2 Understand the Form

Remember, you are helping others to figure out how something works or to learn how to do something. That's why there's even a process for successfully describing a process! Remember to follow the directions on the flow chart closely to make sure your description is accurate. Just follow the steps on this flow chart:

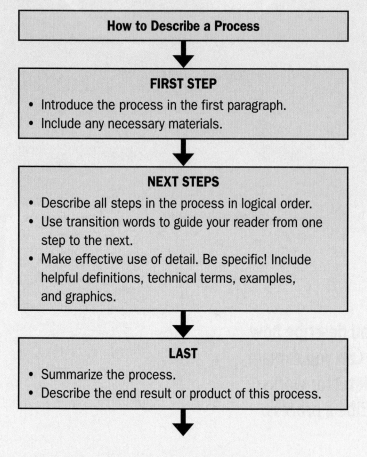

Now look at these parts in action. Read a description of a process by a professional writer.

As you read, try to picture the process that the writer describes.

How a Smoke Detector Works

Every year in the United States, more than 5,000 people die in home fires. Yet most of those lives could have been saved by a simple device: the smoke detector. Smoke detectors are low-cost, easy to install, and are often available free at your local fire department. Add the proper batteries and you're all set. But how does a smoke detector work? Let's look at a photoelectric smoke detector and find out.

Inside a photoelectric smoke detector is a little space called a sensing chamber. The sensing chamber houses a light source and a part called a photocell. The photocell stores an electrical current.

From the moment you put the batteries into the smoke detector and attach it to a ceiling, its parts set to work. The light source sends out a beam of light. The photocell keeps its electrical current going.

Then, if smoke gets into the sensing chamber and blocks the light beam, the light will bounce off the smoke and scatter. As a result, not as much light touches the photocell. Next, the photocell reacts to the loss of light by making an electrical current. This in turn makes the electric current flow right to the alarm. Finally, the alarm turns on and makes a sound so loud you can't ignore it—even if you had been fast asleep!

Of course, the most important part of the process depends on you. Now that you know just how smoke detectors work and how affordable they are, why not set up smoke detectors in your home today? Just think of the lives you'll save.

The writer introduces the process by making a clear statement of the **topic** and the **purpose**.

The writer describes the process step by step, in logical order.

The writer uses **transition words and phrases** to make the order clear.

The writer restates the process and its benefits.

The writer includes a visual aid to support the text and help readers understand the process.

How does this graphic diagram help the reader understand the process?

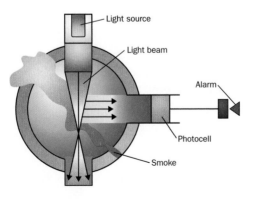

Light source
Light beam
Alarm
Photocell
Smoke

▶ **Prompt** Write a description of how something works or is done. Be sure to tell:

- the benefits of the process
- what materials are needed
- what the steps are, in order
- the end result or product

✓ Prewrite

Now that you have seen a good description of a process, plan one of your own. Planning will make it easier to write later on. Making a Writing Plan helps you describe the process from start to finish.

❶ Choose Your Topic

Here are some ways to help you choose your topic:

- Make a list of activities you know how to do well.
- Make notes about times others asked you to explain something.
- In a small group, brainstorm a list of things that would be helpful to teach other students.

❷ Clarify the Audience, Controlling Idea, and Purpose

Knowing your audience will help you decide on the language to use and information to include. Who might have a special interest in learning about the process you describe? What would they already know about the topic? What details must you make sure to explain?

Consider the **controlling idea**, or main point, you want to make about the process. Why is it useful or fun to know? Write down your controlling idea.

Your purpose for writing a process description is to inform and explain. Make sure each step and detail you include is focused on this purpose.

❸ Gather Supporting Details

Think about the steps involved in your process and any needed supplies. Decide whether you need to research additional background to explain the topic clearly. Consider whether you would like to include photos, drawings, charts, or other graphics in your description. Jot down notes to check your understanding of the process.

Prewriting Tip

To identify the audience and controlling idea, ask yourself these questions:

Audience
- Who am I writing for?
- How will the audience affect the language I choose?
- What information does this audience need?

Controlling idea
- What is the main thing I want to say about the process?
- How will this controlling idea affect the details I include?

---

4 Organize the Details

The next step is to organize the details. You can use a flow chart like the one on page 424 to put the steps in the order in which they are to be performed.

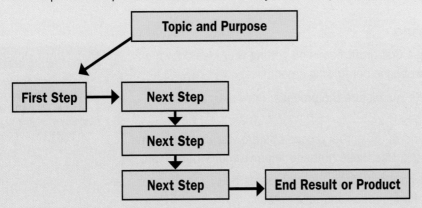

Technology Tip

Use the graphic tools of your computer to make a flow chart, complete with arrows.

You can list one step in each box. Then use your mouse to click on a box, hold down on the mouse, and drag the box wherever you need to place it. Move the boxes around until they are in logical order.

5 Finish Your Writing Plan

Use your prewriting ideas to make a Writing Plan like the one below.

Writing Plan

Topic	how to train a dog to pick things up
Audience	my teacher, classmates, pet owners
Controlling Idea	it can be a big help around the house
Purpose	to show someone how to do this
Time Frame	due ten days from today

First

My mom broke her leg, couldn't bend, I taught our dog to pick things up.

Things you need: dog treats and a glove or other object.

Next

Put glove on the floor and tell the dog to get it.

First, just get the dog to look at it.

As soon as it does, give it a treat and a lot of praise.

Then add something, like it has to take a few steps toward the glove. Don't give a treat until it does.

Then hold back the treat until the dog actually touches the glove.

Encourage the dog with praise.

Use the same process for getting the dog to bring it to you.

Last

Now you know how to train a dog.

Reflect on Your Plan

▶ Did you organize the details in a way that will clearly convey each step in the process? Talk it over with a partner.

✔ Write a Draft

Now use your Writing Plan to write your description of a process. It's OK to make mistakes. You can improve your draft later.

❶ Keep Your Ideas Flowing

Remember that you are writing a first draft. Focus on getting your ideas down on paper. Try these ideas if your writing is not flowing smoothly.

- **Draw the Process** To help you picture the process, draw diagrams or sketches of the steps.
- **Perform the Process** Perform the actual process before you write about it. Ask a partner to take notes. Use those notes to improve your Writing Plan.
- **Discuss It** Tell someone how to perform the process as he or she tries to follow what you say. Ask for feedback and take notes.
- **Skip the Hard Part** If you have trouble writing one part of your process description, skip it and move on to another. Come back to that part later.

❷ Use Transitions

How will you get your paragraphs to flow when you have so many details to include? Let transitions come to your rescue! Transitions are words and phrases that show the connection between ideas. In a process description, transitions:

- clarify the sequence of events (*first, next, finally*)
- help readers picture the process (*in front, toward, nearest*)
- show how details are alike or different (*also, either, instead, unlike, however*).

Good transitions guide readers along and show how ideas relate to each other. Here's an example:

Without Transitions

> The dog has learned to look at the object. Make a change. Don't give the treat right away. Use the treat to motion the dog toward the glove. Repeat the command, "Get!" The dog moves forward. Give it a treat.

With Transitions

> After the dog has learned to look at the object, make a change. This time, instead of giving the treat right away, use the treat to motion the dog toward the glove as you repeat the command, "Get!" When the dog moves forward, give it a treat.

> **Drafting Tip**
>
> Leave extra space between lines as you write or type. Then you will have plenty of space to make changes to your draft later.

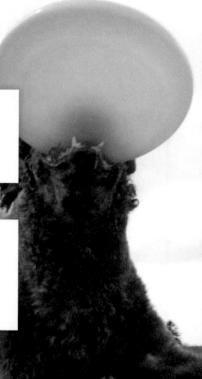

3 Student Model

Notice how the student followed the Writing Plan to develop a draft. As you can see, it isn't perfect. That's fine. The student improved the draft later.

How to Train a Dog to Get Things for You

Last july mom broke her leg. She had to wear a cast and could not bend. So I trained our dog samson, who is part labrador and part french poodle, to retrieve things and carry them to mom. Samson learned quick because it seemed like a game, and mom found it helpful. You can train your dog to pick things up, too.

Get the dog to pay attention to the glove. There are things you have to do to make this happen. Different things like before you even get started you will need to get a bunch of stuff, for rewards for the dog. And a glove or other household object that your dog can use for practice. And then you teach it to look at the glove. Put the glove on the ground and call out "Get!" as you point to it.

When the dog looks at the glove give it a treat. Pat and praise your dog, too.

The dog has learned to look at the object. Make a change. Don't give the treat right away. Use the treat to motion the dog toward the glove. Repeat the command, "Get!" The dog moves forward. Give it a treat.

Have the dog touch the glove with its nose. The dog picks up the glove. The dog should carry the glove to you.

That's all I know, I guess.

Reflect on Your Draft

▶ Reflect on the process that you used to write your draft. What worked well for you? What will you do differently next time?

✔ Revise Your Draft

Once your first draft is done, you need to polish your writing. Check to see if you need to improve the organization.

❶ Revise for Organization

One thing that all good process descriptions have in common is **organization**. A well-organized description has a clear structure that is appropriate for the writer's purpose. It includes all the steps, and provides enough detail for readers to carry out the process themselves. This includes listing any materials the reader might need. A good description of a process also uses specific terms and defines them.

The paragraphs and sentences of a clear description are carefully organized as well. A good writer uses transition words and phrases, such as *before you get started, first, next, finally,* and so on to guide readers smoothly from idea to idea. Just as one step in a staircase leads to the next, a well-written process description takes readers from one step of the process to the next in logical order.

TRY IT ▶ With a partner, evaluate the organization of the draft below. Is it well organized, poorly organized, or somewhere in between? Explain.

Student Draft

> Get the dog to pay attention to the glove. There are things you have to do to make this happen. Different things like before you even get started you will need to get a bunch of stuff, for rewards for the dog. And a glove or other household object that your dog can use for practice. And then you teach it to look at the glove. Put the glove on the ground and call out "Get!" as you point to it.

Now use the rubric to evaluate the organization of your own draft. What score would you give your draft and why?

Organization

	Does the writing have a clear structure, and is it appropriate for the writer's audience, purpose, and type of writing?	How smoothly do the ideas flow together?
4 Wow!	The writing has a structure that is <u>clear</u> and appropriate for the writer's audience, purpose, and type of writing.	The ideas progress in a smooth and orderly way. • The introduction is strong. • The ideas flow well from paragraph to paragraph. • The ideas in each paragraph flow well from one sentence to the next. • Effective transitions connect ideas. • The conclusion is strong.
3 Ahh.	The writing has a structure that is <u>generally</u> clear and appropriate for the writer's audience, purpose, and type of writing.	<u>Most</u> of the ideas progress in a smooth and orderly way. • The introduction is adequate. • Most of the ideas flow well from paragraph to paragraph. • Most ideas in each paragraph flow from one sentence to the next. • Effective transitions connect most of the ideas. • The conclusion is adequate.
2 Hmm.	The structure of the writing is <u>not</u> clear or <u>not</u> appropriate for the writer's audience, purpose, and type of writing.	<u>Some</u> of the ideas progress in a smooth and orderly way. • The introduction is weak. • Some of the ideas flow well from paragraph to paragraph. • Some ideas in each paragraph flow from one sentence to the next. • Transitions connect some ideas. • The conclusion is weak.
1 Huh?	The writing is not clear or organized.	<u>Few or none</u> of the ideas progress in a smooth and orderly way.

myNGconnect.com

⬟ Rubric: Organization

⬟ Evaluate and practice scoring other student process descriptions.

❷ Revise Your Draft

You have now evaluated the organization of your own draft. If you scored
3 or lower, how can you improve your work? Use the checklist below to revise
your draft.

Revision Checklist

Ask Yourself	Check It Out	How to Make It Better
Is the order of my process description correct and clear?	If your score is 3 or lower, revise.	☐ Move any sentence or paragraph that is in the wrong order. ☐ Add any steps that are missing.
Did I achieve smoothness with transition words and phrases?	If your score is 3 or lower, revise.	☐ Add transition words to lead readers smoothly through the process.
Will my readers be able to follow what I say?	Read your draft to someone, or ask him or her to read it. Ask about any parts in the process that were hard to follow.	☐ Rewrite sentences that are vague or confusing. Use specific words and details.
Do I need to define or explain any terms?	Underline terms that might need definitions or explanations.	☐ Add definitions or explanations of terms that readers may find unfamiliar or need to have clarified.
Would examples or graphics make the steps or details clearer?	Underline steps or details that might benefit from a verbal or visual illustration.	☐ Add examples or illustrations to make the steps or details clearer.
Have I ended with a summary of the process and clearly stated what the end-result or product should be?	Read the ending. See if it sums up the steps and identifies the final product.	☐ Rewrite or add to the ending, if necessary.

🔖 **Writing Handbook**, p. 698

❸ Conduct a Peer Conference

With a partner, hold a peer conference. Read each other's drafts. Look for these areas that need improvement:

- anything that seems to be missing
- anything that seems like it does not belong
- anything that is hard to follow or understand

Focus on the items in the Revision Checklist. Use your partner's comments to improve the organization of your description of a process and make it clearer.

❹ Make Revisions

Look at the revisions below and the peer-reviewer comments on the right. Notice how the peer reviewer asked questions and made comments to help the writer. The writer then used the questions and comments to revise the first draft.

Revised for Organization

> First, ~~Get~~ the dog to pay attention to the glove. There are things you have to do to make this happen. Different things like before you even get started, you will need ~~to get a bunch of stuff, for~~ dog treats to give as rewards ~~for the dog.~~ And a glove or other household object that your dog can use for practice. ~~And then you teach it to look at the glove.~~ Put the glove on the ground and call out "Get!" as you point to it.

Revised Ending

> Have the dog touch the glove with its nose. The dog picks up the glove. The dog should carry the glove to you.
>
> ~~That's all I know, I guess.~~ I have used this process to train Samson to retrieve the newspaper, Mom's slippers, and other items, and, just for fun, a flying disc. Yes, I did it, and you can do it, too.

Peer Conference

Reviewer's Question: I'm having trouble figuring out what happens when. I'm also not sure what materials I need.

Writer's Answer: I'll add specific details and move sentences around to put the steps in order.

Reviewer's Question: The ending seems abrupt, as if you'd suddenly lost interest.

Writer's Answer: I'll revise, using examples to summarize the process. I'll add a personal touch, too.

Reflect on Your Revisions

▶ Think about the different things you did in revising your process description. Which were the most helpful? Which will you do when you revise in the future?

✓ Edit and Proofread Your Draft

Now that your revision is complete, find and correct any mistakes that you made.

1 Capitalize Proper Nouns and Adjectives

Proper nouns name specific persons, places, and things. They are always capitalized. Common nouns, which are general, are not capitalized.

Common	Proper Nouns
mom	Mom
month	July

Capitalize proper adjectives, which are made from proper nouns.

Proper Noun	Proper Adjective
France	French

TRY IT ▶ Copy the sentences. Fix the capitalization errors. Use proofreader's marks.

> 1. I told mom I could train our Dog, samson.
> 2. The dog is part french poodle.

2 Punctuate Introductory Words and Clauses Correctly

Some words and phrases introduce sentences. These words and phrases are not complete sentences and should be followed by a comma.

Place a comma after introductory words such as yes, *no*, *first*, and *next*, and adverbs such as *happily* and *unfortunately*.

Yes, I did it.

Honestly, the process works.

Place a comma after long or introductory clauses.

After the dog has learned to look at the object, make a change.

Before you get started, gather these materials.

TRY IT ▶ Copy the sentences. Add commas wherever needed.

> 1. Instead of giving the treat right away wait a moment.
> 2. Unfortunately dogs can't talk.

Proofreading Tip

If you are unsure about whether a noun or an adjective should be capitalized or not, look it up in a style manual to see if there is a similar example.

Proofreader's Marks

Use proofreader's marks to correct capitalization and punctuation errors.

Capitalize:
Last july, mom broke her leg.

Do not capitalize:
My Mom broke her leg.

Add a comma:
Yes I trained our dog.

First look at the dog.

❸ Check Your Spelling

Follow these rules for spelling *ie* and *ei*:

Rule	Examples
Use *i* before *e* except after *c*	believe friend
For a long *a* or *ar* sound, use *ei*	weight their
For a long *e* sound after *c* use *ei*	ceiling perceive

Memorize these exceptions to the rules: *weird, either, neither, seize, leisure.*

TRY IT ▶ Copy the sentences. Find and fix the two spelling errors.

> 1. Reward the dog when you recieve the glove.
> 2. I taught Samson to retreive things.

❹ Use Adjectives and Adverbs Correctly

Usually, the adjective comes before the noun it describes. But a predicate adjective appears in the predicate and still describes the noun in the subject.

Samson is a **large** dog. He is **friendly**, too.

An adjective is never plural, even if the noun it describes is plural.

Many **hungry** dogs enjoy treats. I trained all the **smart** dogs.

Don't use an adjective when you need an adverb. Never use an adverb after a linking verb.

Incorrect	Correct
Samson learned **quick**.	Samson learned **quickly**.
I am **patiently**.	I am **patient**.

TRY IT ▶ Copy the sentences. Rewrite these sentences using the correct adjectives or adverbs.

> 1. We have two beautifully dogs.
> 2. She was carefully and trained her dog slow.

🔖 **Writing Handbook**, p. 757

Technology Tip

The Spell-checker on your computer can help you identify spelling errors. Some online dictionaries also let you hear how a word is pronounced.

Reflect on Your Corrections

▶Exchange papers with a partner. Have your partner help with a final check of capitalization, punctuation, spelling, and sentences.

5 Edited Student Draft

Here is the edited version of the process description. How did the writer improve it?

How to Train a Dog to Get Things for You

Last July, Mom broke her leg. She had to wear a cast and could not bend. So I trained our dog Samson, who is part Labrador and part French poodle, to retrieve things and carry them to Mom. Samson learned quickly because it seemed like a game, and Mom found it helpful. You can train your dog to pick things up, too.

Before you get started, you will need dog treats to give as rewards and a glove or other household object that your dog can use for practice. Honestly, you may also need patience!

First, get the dog to pay attention to the glove. Put the glove on the ground and call out "Get!" as you point to it. When the dog looks at the glove, give it a treat. Pat and praise your dog, too.

After the dog has learned to look at the object, make a change. This time, instead of giving the treat right away, use the treat to motion the dog toward the glove as you repeat the command, "Get!" When the dog moves forward, give it a treat.

Each time the dog learns a new step, use the treat to teach it the next step. Have the dog touch the glove with its nose, then pick up the glove in its teeth, and finally, carry the glove to you.

I have used this process to train Samson to retrieve the newspaper, Mom's slippers, and other items, and, just for fun, a flying disc. Yes, I did it, and you can do it, too.

The writer corrected errors in the **capitalization** of proper nouns and adjectives.

The writer fixed a **spelling** error and changed an incorrect adjective to an **adverb**.

The writer placed a **comma** after each introductory word and clause.

The writer organized sentences in this paragraph to put the steps in logical order and better connect ideas.

The writer used **transitions** to guide the reader through the process.

The writer ended with sentences that sum up the benefits of the process and signal that the description is complete.

✔ Publish and Present

Print or type a final version of your process description. Share it with others so they can learn from you. You may also want to present your work in a different way.

Alternative Presentations

Give a Demonstration Can your process be demonstrated in class? If so, read your process description aloud while a classmate demonstrates the steps.

1 **Bring the Right Materials** Depending on the process, you may need tools, ingredients, supplies, or special equipment. Check with your teacher first.

2 **Pass Out Copies** Hand out copies of your process description to your teacher and your classmates. That way they can follow along as they watch the demonstration.

3 **Read the Steps Slowly** Give your assistant enough time to follow what you are saying and show each step.

4 **Get Feedback** Ask your assistant to describe any problems he or she had. Get feedback from your other classmates, too. Make improvements based on the feedback.

Give a Computer Presentation You might also use computer software to create a computer presentation.

1 **Organize Your Presentation** Use computer presentation software to present your process description. When you create your presentation, it will be made up of a series of slides. Decide how you will organize the process description and what you will put on each slide.

2 **Choose Your Visuals** Add visuals to your presentation. Decide whether you will create colorful graphs and charts, find photos, or use art to illustrate the process. In addition to slides, you can print out handouts for your audience.

3 **Practice Your Presentation** Practice in front of a friend or family member. This will help you see if you need to make changes, such as improve an illustration, speak with more expression, or have a volunteer help you give the presentation.

4 **Present Your Work** Remember, you are now an expert on this process! Have fun, and come prepared to answer any questions your audience may have.

📗 **Language and Learning Handbook**, p. 616

Presenting Tip

If you are using visuals such as charts with your demonstration, make sure you give listeners time to enjoy the visuals.

Reflect on Your Work

▶ Use feedback from your audience to evaluate your strengths as a writer. You might ask your readers these questions:

• Was my process description useful to you?

• What parts of it were clear?

• What parts need improvement? Why?

Based on the answers you receive, decide what you would like to do better the next time you write.

 Save a copy of your work in your portfolio.

EQ **ESSENTIAL QUESTION:**

What Rights and Responsibilities Should Teens Have?

A youth is to be regarded with respect.
—CONFUCIUS

Good sense comes only with age.
—IRISH PROVERB

Critical Viewing ▶
Covered in bright paint, teens dance at a concert in Austin, Texas. Teens are known for going to extremes, so should their rights and responsibilities be limited?

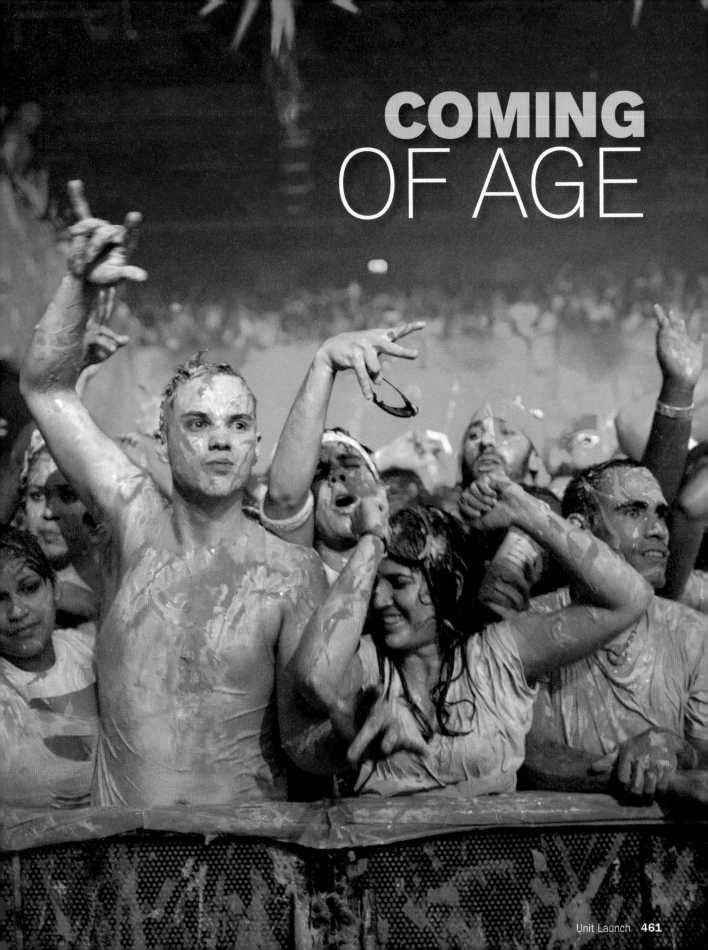

COMING OF AGE

EQ ESSENTIAL QUESTION:
What Rights and Responsibilities Should Teens Have?

Study the Photograph
In many states, school officials can search a student's locker if they think it contains drugs, weapons, or other objects that are not allowed. Do you know what the policy is in your state? At your school? Look at the photograph.

Should principals and other school officials have the right to search student lockers?

Take a Position
1. How does a school's right to search lockers affect students' rights?

2. What rights to privacy should students have? What responsibilities should go along with those rights? What should students do if they see illegal activities at school?

Talk with a group. Explain your opinions and support your ideas with evidence from your own knowledge, experience, and observations.

EQ ESSENTIAL QUESTION
In this unit, you will explore the **Essential Question** in class through reading, discussion, research, and writing. Keep thinking about the question outside of school, too.

① Plan a Project

Ad Campaign

In this unit, you will work with a group to create an ad campaign that relates to the Essential Question. Your ad campaign will focus on a social or cultural issue of interest to teens, such as lowering the voting age or putting parental warning labels on music.

Team Work Have each team member look at ads in different media. Share and compare your findings. Once everyone has contributed, hold a vote to decide what type of campaign you will create. Pick a campaign manager to lead the campaign.

Study Skills Start planning your ad campaign. Use the forms on myNGconnect.com to plan your time and to prepare the content.

myNGconnect.com
- ▶ Planning forms
- ▶ Scheduler
- ▶ Tips for creating an effective PSA
- ▶ Rubric

② Choose More to Read

These readings provide different answers to the Essential Question. Choose a book and online selections to read during the unit.

Thura's Diary
by Thura Al-Windawi

On March 20, 2003, the United States and its allies bombed Iraq. Life changed overnight for 19-year-old Thura Al-Windawi. Thura watched helplessly as friends and family fled from Baghdad. As bombs exploded all around, she kept a diary to record the horrifying events.

▶ NONFICTION

Ties That Bind, Ties That Break
by Lensey Namioka

Ailin lives in China in 1911. It is Chinese tradition for girls to have their feet bound. But Ailin is independent and knows she will never be free if her feet are bound. She chooses freedom, but it has a high price. Ailin thinks she made the right choice. Did she?

▶ NOVEL

Crazy Loco
by David Rice

Harry's grandfather is a rabbit killer. Loco is a dog who thinks he can drive. *Crazy Loco* is a collection of humorous stories about family, friends, and finding yourself. And sometimes they are about being a little crazy.

▶ SHORT STORIES

myNGconnect.com
- 🔗 Find out more about the youth rights movement.
- 🔗 Read about youth who speak out for their rights.
- 🔗 Read what one organization says about teens' rights at school.

Writers of persuasive nonfiction want to convince readers to agree with their position, or viewpoint. Read this passage. Decide whether you agree with the author's viewpoint on school uniforms.

DEMO TEXT #1

Support School Uniforms Now!

Our school district should adopt a uniform policy for all schools. Last year I saw one student making fun of another student's old clothes. They got into a fight. Both were suspended from school. I thought to myself, "If we wore school uniforms, this would never have happened."

Dr. Donald Philpot, a professor at our local college, led a study of middle and high schools last year. This study proved that school uniforms are good for students. Schools with a uniform policy had a 40% decrease in fights over two years. Schools without uniforms had a small increase in fights.

The average cost of uniforms for one student is $175 per year, according to clothing sellers. Some families spend ten times that amount on back-to-school clothes every August! This is a fact some students brag about.

A school uniform policy would have three more benefits. First, it would keep expenses lower for all families. Second, it would keep wealthier students from acting superior because their families can afford to spend a lot of money on their clothes. Third, it would keep students whose families are not wealthy from feeling embarrassed about their clothes.

It seems that many people are already aware of the benefits of uniforms. Dr. Philpot's survey showed that 72% of students and 82% of parents are in favor of school uniforms. During a recent interview, Dr. Philpot said, "People know that school uniforms reduce fighting, keep students from worrying about fashion trends, and create a level playing field for those who can't afford expensive, trendy clothes."

It's clear that requiring uniforms reduces violence at school and keeps students from caring too much about unimportant things like fashion. Adopting a uniform policy is a healthy step. Everyone has a responsibility to help make schools safe. Call or write the district superintendent to show your support.

■ Connect Reading to Your Life

What is the author's position? Do you agree or disagree with the author's viewpoint? Take a vote.

Now think about why you voted the way you did. List your three reasons.

Reading Strategies

· Plan and Monitor
· Determine Importance
· Make Inferences
· Ask Questions
· Make Connections
▶ **Synthesize**
· Visualize

Schools that make students wear uniforms have less fighting.

It's a free country. People should be able to wear what they want.

I agree with the author because ...	I disagree with the author because ...
1.	1.
2.	2.
3.	3.

Focus Strategy ▶ Sythesize

As you decided whether you agreed with the author, you thought about the **evidence** the author gave. Then you thought about which evidence was most meaningful. Anytime you bring together different ideas, you are synthesizing.

You do this often in life. Think about a time when you made a big decision, such as which after-school job to apply for. What information did you consider?

- what the job paid
- the hours you would need to work
- whether you would be good at that job

You considered these things (and probably more), decided how important each one was, and then concluded what to do. Whatever the choice—what to eat, when to study, or whom to go out with—you synthesize to decide what to do or think.

■ Your Job as a Reader

When you read persuasive nonfiction, first recognize that the author is trying to persuade you to agree with his or her viewpoint. Your job as a reader is to consider the author's ideas and decide whether you agree with his or her position. For example, you may have synthesized all of the author's evidence and still had a different opinion about school uniforms.

Academic Vocabulary

• **evidence** *n.*, information that supports or proves a point; **evident** *adj.*, clearly seen, apparent

■ Unpack the Thinking Process

Reading persuasive nonfiction can be a challenge, because you need to figure out how the writer is trying to persuade you.

Structure of Arguments

All persuasive writing starts with a **claim**. Claims are statements that give the writer's position, or the point a writer is trying to make. What claim does the author make in the Demo Text?

Good writers then support their claims with strong, relevant **evidence**.

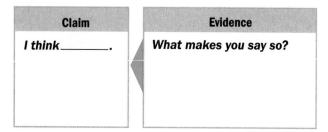

Claim	Evidence
I think _____.	*What makes you say so?*

Types of Evidence

Evidence is the information that helps writers prove their claim. Evidence comes in many forms. Which of these are used in the Demo Text?

Kinds of Evidence	
Facts	Dates, names of people and places, other things that can be proved
Statistics	Measurements and numbers
Quotations	Exact words from interviews or documents
Expert Opinions	Ideas from people who know a lot about the topic
Personal Memoirs	Stories the author tells about his or her experience with the topic

Synthesize

Once you've read an author's claim and considered the supporting evidence, figure out whether you agree with the author's position. Does all of the evidence add up to a convincing argument?

Elements of Literature

claim *n.*, a statement that defines an idea as true or false, right or wrong, good or bad

■ Try an Experiment

Read this persuasive text.

No School Uniforms!

Mandatory school uniforms may sound like a good idea, but I think it's a bad policy. My cousin goes to a school where they require school uniforms. And guess what? Kids still find things to tease each other about.

It would be much better to have students wear different things and to learn how to accept one another. When students become adults and enter the real world, they will have to learn to deal with differences. It just makes sense that they should learn this behavior in school.

School uniforms won't necessarily save families money, either. According to a survey I read in the local paper, about 50% of families don't buy brand-name clothes in the first place. Some families in the survey actually spent more when a school uniform policy was put in place. For example, one family used to spend around $400.00 for their two kids at the start of each school year. They reported that the uniforms cost them more than $500.00.

Finally, school uniforms prevent students from expressing their individual beliefs and personalities. Agnes Levin, a local teen counselor, was recently interviewed about school uniforms. "Making everyone dress the same is terrible," she said. "It destroys students' individuality and spirit."

It's easy to see how mandatory uniforms can prevent students from learning proper behavior, can cost families more money, and can suppress students' personalities. Take action against requiring school uniforms at our school! Contact the district superintendent to make it known that you oppose school uniforms.

Think, Pair, Share Answer these questions with a partner.

1. What is the author's claim?

2. What evidence does the author use to support the claim?

3. Is the author's evidence convincing? Why or why not? Explain your thinking.

4. What group of readers would most likely be influenced by the author's argument? Students? Parents? School administrators? Explain your answer.

Now take another vote about school uniforms. Did you change your mind?

Monitor Comprehension

Persuasion How do authors try to convince readers to agree with their viewpoint? What should readers do before deciding if they agree?

EQ **What Rights and Responsibilities Should Teens Have?**
Decide whether teens are mature enough to vote.

Make a Connection

Quickwrite At what age should U.S. citizens be allowed to vote? Why do you think that is an appropriate age? Take about five minutes to write your answer. Include any facts you know.

Learn Key Vocabulary

Study the Words Pronounce each word and learn its meaning. You may also want to look up the definitions in the Glossary.

● Academic Vocabulary

Key Words	Examples
● **establish** (i-**sta**-blish) *verb* ▶ page 478	When you **establish** a bank account or an e-mail account, you set it up so that you can start to use it. *Synonym*: create; *Antonym*: get rid of
● **generation** (je-nu-**rā**-shun) *noun* ▶ page 473	A **generation** is a group of people who are born and who live around the same time. Grandparents, parents, and children form three **generations**.
judgment (**juj**-munt) *noun* ▶ pages 475, 477	**Judgment** is the ability to use what you know to make a decision. A person who has good **judgment** thinks carefully before deciding something. *Synonym*: evaluation
● **mature** (mu-**choor**) *adjective* ▶ pages 473, 477, 480, 481	A **mature** person is someone who acts grown up. People become physically **mature** at different ages. *Antonyms*: immature, babyish
● **participate** (par-**ti**-su-pāt) *verb* ▶ page 472	To **participate** is to take part. What sports do you **participate** in at school? *Synonyms*: share, do
politics (**pah**-lu-tiks) *noun* ▶ pages 474, 481	When you discuss **politics**, you talk about the government and what people think about it.
qualified (**kwah**-lu-fīd) *adjective* ▶ pages 474, 475	If you are well-trained and prepared for a job, then you are **qualified** for it. We hired a **qualified** plumber to fix the broken water pipe. *Synonyms*: skilled, experienced
vote (vōt) *verb* ▶ pages 473, 475, 481	To **vote** is to make your choice in an election. If you could **vote**, who would you want for president?

Practice the Words Work with a partner. Make a **Definition Map** for each Key Vocabulary word. Use a dictionary to find other forms of the word.

Definition Map

[Word] — (definition / other forms of the word / example / nonexample) — [Use the word in a sentence.]

16: The Right Voting Age

persuasive argument by the
National Youth Rights Association

Reading Strategies

· Plan and Monitor
· Determine Importance
· Make Inferences
· Ask Questions
· Make Connections
▶ Synthesize
· Visualize

Analyze Viewpoint: Argument and Evidence

A writer who has a strong opinion about a topic can write a **persuasive argument** to express that viewpoint. In an argument, the writer states a claim and supports it with **evidence**: facts or data. Using this evidence, the writer tries to persuade readers to agree with his or her claim. The writer may also use several persuasive techniques, such as appealing to readers' emotions, setting up and solving an unrealistic problem, or trying to scare readers into agreement.

Look Into the Text

This head states the writer's claim.

What other facts support the writer's claim?

☑ Youths Need the Right to Vote

The National Academies, scientists who write reports for the government, state that 80% of 16- and 17-year-olds work before graduation. The *Houston Chronicle* reports that 61% of teenagers work during the school year. Taxes are taken from these teens' paychecks. But these teens have no say about the ways that tax money is spent.

The writer uses data to support the argument.

What is the emotional impact of the phrase "have no say"?

Focus Strategy ▶ Synthesize

When you read an argument, look at the evidence the writer uses to support his or her claim. Think about what you know. Then **draw conclusions**, or develop judgments, about the evidence. This is one thing you do when you **synthesize** information, or combine ideas and information to form new understandings.

HOW TO DRAW CONCLUSIONS

Try this strategy as you read the text above.

1. Identify the writer's claim. Record the evidence that supports the claim. Note if it is factual evidence.

2. Analyze the evidence. What does your experience tell you? Are the sources reliable? A reliable source is objective or respects facts.

3. Does the evidence support the writer's claim? Is it relevant? That is, is it related to the claim the writer makes?

Focus Strategy

Evidence Chart

1. **Evidence:**
   Most teens work and pay taxes. They can't choose how taxes are spent. (facts from text)

   +

2. **What I Know:**
   The data sources are reliable. The facts about taxes are true. (experience)

   =

3. **Conclusion:**
   This evidence is reliable and relevant.

When the Voting Age Changed

The 26th Amendment to the Constitution was passed in 1971, toward the end of the Vietnam War. This period was a troubled time in the United States. Groups of people protested against the war by speaking out in public.

There were many protests about the draft—military service required by law. Nearly all males 18 years or older qualified for the draft. Many young men between 18 and 21 years old fought in Vietnam.

At that time, U.S. citizens could not vote until they were 21 years old. Some people thought it was unfair that an 18-year-old had the responsibility of serving in the military but did not have the right to vote.

After much discussion, Congress lowered the national voting age to 18 years. The 26th Amendment to the Constitution set the minimum age for voting in both state and national elections. It was ratified, or approved, in July 1971. Because of this amendment, about eleven million more people were able to vote in the 1972 election (although not all of them actually voted).

Before 1971, only ten states allowed people younger than 21 to vote. What many people do not realize is that the 26th Amendment allows each state to lower the voting age even more, if it wants—to 17 or even 16 years of age.

myNGconnect.com

- Learn more about the 26th Amendment.
- Find out more about youth protests against the war in Vietnam.

16: The Right Voting Age

adapted from an article by the National Youth Rights Association

According to the current United States law, citizens can vote when they are 18 years old. Teens may wonder why they have to wait so long. This article suggests lowering the voting age to 16. See if you agree.

 Comprehension Coach

According to the National Youth Rights Association, young people should be empowered to participate in the democratic process starting at the age of 16. Lowering the voting age is an idea whose time has come.

☑ Youths Need the Right to Vote

The National Academies, scientists who write reports for the government, state that 80% of 16- and 17-year-olds work before graduation. The *Houston Chronicle* reports that 61% of teenagers work during the school year. Taxes are taken from these teens' paychecks. But these teens have no say about the ways that tax money is spent.

Youths also give part of their pay to Social Security. But today's adults are deciding how young people's Social Security money should be saved. **1** So, youths can't control whether or not their

1 Argument and Evidence What evidence have you read so far that supports the writer's claim?

Members of "Students Against Vanishing Ecosystems," or "S.A.V.E.," help bring awareness to environmental issues. Clubs like S.A.V.E. let teenagers express their views and make a difference.

Key Vocabulary
• **participate** *v.*, to take part in an activity or event

money will be there for them when they're older and they really need it.

Young people have strong views about the environment. But they have no voice in determining the leaders who must protect it.

As students, youths are most directly impacted by education policy. They have the best perspective to determine what changes are needed. But they can't **vote** on these changes.

☑ Youths Have the Maturity Needed to Vote

Youths become physically **mature** at an earlier age. *Newsday* reports that the average age **of puberty** has declined. In the **mid-1800s**, it was 16½. In 1900, it was 15. Today, the average age of puberty is about 12. **2**

Today's youths are smarter than previous **generations**. Experts cited in *The New York Times* assert that the explosion of television, video games, computer communication, and particularly the Internet, sharpen youths'

abilities to think, analyze, and solve problems. Studies begun by Professor James Flynn show that **IQ** scores grew by 17 points from 1947 to 2001.

Teens are already treated like adults. For example, 16-year-olds can drive legally in many states. Also, young people can be tried for serious crimes as adults. In some states, this can happen at age 16. Sometimes the age is even younger. As a result, the *Jones Law Review* reports that the number

Driver's License Age Requirements

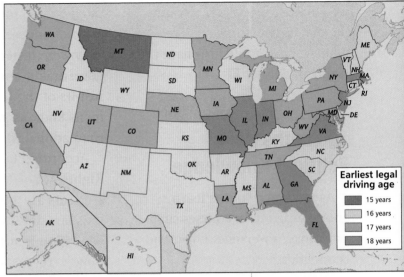

Source: Federal Highway Administration; U.S. Dept. of Transportation, 2004

▲ Analyze the Map
In how many states is the legal driving age less than 17 years?

2 Argument and Evidence/Draw Conclusions
Does the information in this paragraph support the writer's claim? Add this information to your chart.

Monitor Comprehension

Paraphrase
According to this writer, why should teens have the right to vote?

Key Vocabulary
vote *v.*, to make choices in elections
● **mature** *adj.*, like a grown-up
● **generation** *n.*, a group of people who are born and who live around the same time

In Other Words
of puberty when people become physically mature
mid-1800s middle of the 1800s
IQ Intelligence Quotient. A person's IQ is a score from a special test designed to measure intelligence.

of juveniles in adult prisons grew 47% in just five years. If young people can be punished like adults, they should also have the rights of adults. **3**

☑ Youths Have Political Knowledge

As students, youths learn about **politics** in courses such as history, government, law, and economics.

Young people are learning more about politics than adults.

For example, some teens participated in the "We the People" education program. Then they were tested in the areas of government and politics. The results of the testing showed that teens knew as much as or more than adults. **4**

According to the Voting Rights Act of 1965, high school students are **qualified** to vote. This law states that a sixth-grade education is **sufficient** for voting. If most 16-year-olds have a tenth-grade education, then they are definitely qualified to vote.

3 Argument and Evidence/Draw Conclusions
Does the evidence in this paragraph support the author's claim? Is the evidence relevant? Is it strong enough to add support to the author's claim?

4 Argument and Evidence/Draw Conclusions
Does the evidence support the writer's claim? What does your experience tell you about the evidence? Add to your chart.

Knowledge of Current Government and Politics

Test Item	CORRECT RESPONSES	
	Teens	Adults
What political office is held by [name of vice president]?	94%	74%
Who determines if a law is constitutional: the president, the Congress, or the Supreme Court?	97%	66%
How much of a majority is required for the Senate and House of Representatives to override a presidential veto?	84%	34%
Which party had the most members in the House in 2004? **5**	79%	68%
Which party is more conservative than the other at the national level?	81%	57%

Source: We the People Survey, Center for Civic Education, 2003; American National Election Studies, 1991

5 Access Vocabulary
What is the meaning of *party* in this case? Use a dictionary to check the definition of this multiple-meaning word.

⚠ Interpret the Chart For which question was there the biggest difference between the responses of teens and adults?

Key Vocabulary
politics *n.*, the government and what people think about it
qualified *adj.*, well-trained and prepared

In Other Words
sufficient enough

✓ Youths Want the Right to Vote

The Washington Post surveyed teens about their views. Seventy-three percent of teens had an interest in politics. Ninety-five percent of these teens viewed voting in a presidential election as important.

Teens support a lower voting age. *Education Week* reported on young people who participated in a mock election in Minneapolis. Seventy-three percent of them supported a voting age of 16. 6

Teens will vote—and vote smart—if they are given the right. ❖

6 Argument and Evidence/Draw Conclusions Notice the pieces of evidence presented on this page. Are the sources reliable? Which evidence on this page is most relevant?

ANALYZE 16: The Right Voting Age

1. **Explain** According to the author, in what ways are teenagers **qualified** to **vote**?

2. **Vocabulary** Do you think 16- and 17-year-olds would use good **judgment** if they were allowed to vote? Use evidence from the article and your own experience to answer.

3. **Analyze Viewpoint: Argument and Evidence** What evidence does the writer give to prove that teens are already treated like adults?

4. **Focus Strategy Synthesize** Does the evidence in this article support the writer's claim? Explain your answer.

⤺ Return to the Text

Reread and Write Does the National Youth Rights Association have a strong enough argument to keep fighting for teens' voting rights? Reread the text to find evidence for your ideas. Then write a comment for the association's Web site.

Key Vocabulary
judgment *n.*, the ability to make good decisions

BEFORE READING Teen Brains Are Different

expository nonfiction by Lee Bowman

Reading Strategies

· Plan and Monitor
· Determine Importance
· Make Inferences
· Ask Questions
· Make Connections
▶ Synthesize
· Visualize

Analyze Text Structure: Main Idea and Details

When a writer wants to give information, he or she may begin with the **main idea** and then organize the rest of the writing with **details** that tell about the main idea. You often see this **text structure** for expository nonfiction.

Look Into the Text

This is the main idea of the selection.

The latest brain research strongly shows that teen brains are very different from adult brains. In teens, parts of the brain related to emotions, judgment, and "thinking ahead" are not fully operating. This is one reason why teens show less maturity and control than adults.

This detail supports the main idea.

Dr. Ruben Gur is a professor of psychology who studies brain behavior. He points out that impulse control comes last to the brain and is often the first to leave as people age.

As you read, use a **Main Idea Chart** to keep track of the details that support the main idea of the selection.

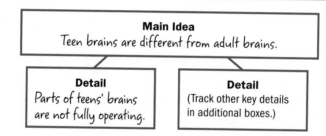

Main Idea
Teen brains are different from adult brains.

Detail
Parts of teens' brains are not fully operating.

Detail
(Track other key details in additional boxes.)

Main Idea Chart

Focus Strategy ▶ Synthesize

We **draw conclusions** every day. Imagine that you see people running from a building. The people look scared. You smell smoke. You decide that the building is on fire. In the same way, you draw conclusions when you read.

HOW TO DRAW CONCLUSIONS

Focus Strategy

Try this strategy with the text above.

1. Notice the details.

> In teens, parts of the brain related to emotions, judgment, and "thinking ahead" are not fully operating.

2. Think about what you know.

Sometimes I blurt things out and then later regret what I said. Maybe it's because the emotional part of my brain is developing.

3. Decide what you believe.

Teens don't always use good judgment because their brains are still developing.

Teen Brains Are Different

by Lee Bowman

Connect Across Texts

The National Youth Rights Association uses evidence to support its claim that teens are **mature** and ready for responsibilities. This expository nonfiction presents research to support another view.

Have you ever seen a movie in which a teenager got trapped inside an adult body? Maybe you think the teen can really think and act like an adult. The answer may surprise you.

Teen and Adult Brains

The latest brain research strongly shows that teen brains are very different from adult brains. In teens, parts of the brain related to emotions, **judgment**, and "thinking ahead" are not fully operating. This is one reason why teens show less maturity and control than adults.

Dr. Ruben Gur is a professor of psychology who studies brain behavior. He points out that **impulse control** comes last to the brain and is often the first to leave as people **age**. **1**

How the Brain Matures

Until recently, most brain experts thought that the brain stopped growing by the time a person was about 18 months old. They also thought that the brain **had almost all of its neurons** by age three.

In fact, **the brain's gray matter** has a final period of growth around

According to research, teenagers cannot control their emotions and behavior as well as adults because teens' brains are still growing.

1 Main Idea and Details
What is this article mostly about? What important detail does this paragraph tell? Add this detail to your chart.

◄ Analyze the Photo
Does the photo provide meaningful evidence opposing the claim that teens are mature? Explain.

Key Vocabulary
- **mature** *adj.*, like a grown-up
  judgment *n.*, the ability to make good decisions

In Other Words
impulse control being able to think before acting
age get older
had almost all of its neurons was almost developed
the brain's gray matter part of the brain

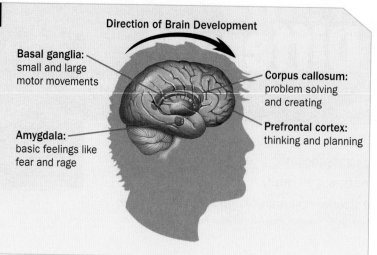

Inside a Teen Brain

Direction of Brain Development

The brain grows rapidly before birth and for the first few years of life. A second growth spurt starts around age 12. It lasts through the teen years, when the brain develops gradually from back to front.

Basal ganglia: small and large motor movements

Amygdala: basic feelings like fear and rage

Corpus callosum: problem solving and creating

Prefrontal cortex: thinking and planning

▲ Interpret the Diagram According to this diagram, which part of the brain develops last?

the ages of 11 to 13. This occurs in the front of the brain, an important area for thinking and planning.

These new brain cells do not start working right away, though. It seems to take most of the teen years for them to link to the rest of the brain and to **establish** millions of connections. Only then do the cells allow their owners to think and behave like adults.

At the same time, **adolescent hormones** activate other areas of the brain. The flow of hormones especially affects the amygdala.

This is a simple part of the brain that controls basic feelings like fear and rage.

Different Responses

The result is that teens look at things differently than adults. In a recent study, Deborah Yurgelun-Todd of Harvard Medical School and McClean Hospital noted how teens and adults respond differently to the same pictures. The **subjects** were shown photos of people who looked afraid. The adults named the correct emotion, but the teens seldom did. **2**

2 Draw Conclusions
Why do you think teens did poorly on this test? Use details from the text, the diagram, and from your own experience to explain.

Key Vocabulary
• **establish** *v.*, to set up, to create

In Other Words
adolescent hormones natural chemicals in teens' bodies
subjects teens and adults in the study

Cultural Background
Many medical terms and names of body parts come from Greek and Latin root words. For example, *amygdala* comes from a Greek root that means "almond." Scientists use this word because this part of the brain has the shape of an almond.

Yurgelun-Todd and her team repeated the test. This time they **scanned** the subjects' brains. They discovered that the adults and teens used different parts of the brain. Adults used both the advanced front part and the **more primitive** amygdala to process what they had seen. Younger teens used only the amygdala. Older teens **showed a shift toward using** the front part of the brain.

Yurgelun-Todd says that teens may be physically mature. But that does not mean that they can make evaluations as well as adults. "Good judgment is learned," she adds. "But you can't learn it if you don't have the necessary hardware."

Brain Hardware: Use It or Lose It

The development of teen brains involves a process called *myelinization*. During this process, layers of fat cover wire-like nerve fibers that connect parts of the brain. Over time, this helps the brain operate in a more precise and efficient way. It doesn't just affect thinking and problem solving, though. It also impacts body movement and mastery of skills, from throwing a baseball to playing a horn.

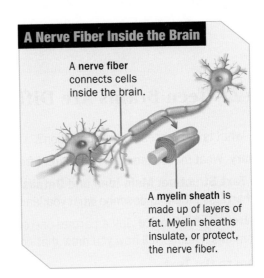

A Nerve Fiber Inside the Brain

A **nerve fiber** connects cells inside the brain.

A **myelin sheath** is made up of layers of fat. Myelin sheaths insulate, or protect, the nerve fiber.

If you don't use your brain cells, they die off. Brain cells that aren't being used don't hook up to other parts of the brain and usually get killed off. "If they're not on the network, they die and their place is taken up with **cerebral fluid**. This goes on well beyond age eighteen," said Dr. David Fassler, a psychiatrist at the University of Vermont.

3 **Main Idea and Details**
Add this detail about *myelinization* to your chart. How does the detail support the main idea of the article?

◁ **Analyze the Diagram**
If a myelin sheath is damaged, what might happen?

Monitor Comprehension

Explain
In Yurgelun-Todd's test, why did young teens use only the amygdala? How does using only the amygdala affect a teen's judgment-making abilities?

Dr. Jay Giedd studies brains at the National Institute of Mental Health. He thinks the new understanding of teen brains "argues for doing a lot of things as a teenager. You are **hardwiring** your brain in adolescence," Dr. Giedd says. "Do you want to hardwire it for sports and playing music and doing mathematics, or for lying on the couch in front of the television?" 4 ❖

4 Draw Conclusions Based on information from Dr. Jay Giedd and others, what would happen to the brain of a teenager who spends a lot of time watching television?

ANALYZE Teen Brains Are Different

1. **Explain** What is the process of myelinization?

2. **Vocabulary** What makes teen brains different from **mature** brains?

3. **Analyze Text Structure: Main Idea and Details** What details did you collect in your chart? Use them to describe what you learned in this selection.

4. **Focus Strategy Synthesize** Tell a partner one conclusion you made about teens from this reading. Tell how you drew that conclusion.

   ↩ **Return to the Text**

   Reread and Write Based on what you just learned about teen brains, name three rights and responsibilities that younger teens (13- to 15-year-olds) should *not* have. Use facts from the selection to support your ideas.

In Other Words
hardwiring setting up permanent patterns for

EQ What Rights and Responsibilities Should Teens Have?

Critical Thinking

EQ **1. Analyze** Are 16-year-olds **mature** enough to **vote**? Use information from both articles to support your answer.

2. Compare In your opinion, which of the two selections has more relevant and convincing evidence? Tell why you think so.

3. Interpret Do you think watching TV will increase or decrease a teen's IQ? Use information from the articles to explain.

4. Draw Conclusions Each selection uses facts about the physical maturity of teens as evidence to support its ideas. Compare the facts. Draw conclusions about whether the evidence each author provides is relevant and reliable.

EQ **5. Synthesize** Based on what you read in the two selections, do you think the driving age should be raised in your state? Support your opinion with evidence from the selections.

Write About Literature

Analysis What characteristics do you think make someone a good voter? For example, does a person have to know a lot about **politics**? Write a short analysis explaining your answer. Be sure to have introductory and concluding paragraphs, and include examples and specific quotations from both texts.

Key Vocabulary Review

Oral Review Work with a partner. Use these words to complete the paragraph.

established	mature	qualified
generation	participate	vote
judgment	politics	

From 1900 to 1920, an entire __(1)__ of women fought for the right to __(2)__. Many of the women worked, paid taxes, and even owned property. They certainly were old enough, or __(3)__ enough, to vote. However, they were not considered responsible enough to __(4)__, or take part, in __(5)__. In the women's opinion, or __(6)__, they were just as __(7)__ to vote as the men were. Finally, the government passed the Nineteenth Amendment to the Constitution. This law __(8)__ women's right to vote.

Writing Application Describe an important issue in politics that you think the government should work on. Use at least three Key Vocabulary words.

Read with Ease: Intonation

Assess your reading fluency with the passage in the Reading Handbook, p. 680. Then complete the self-check below.

1. My voice did/did not sound natural.

2. My words correct per minute: _____.

Grammar

Use Indefinite Pronouns

Use an **indefinite pronoun** when you are not talking about specific persons, places, or things.

Does **anyone** know about teen brain growth?

The verb you use depends on the indefinite pronoun.

- These indefinite pronouns are always singular. Use a **singular verb** with them.

anybody	everyone	somebody	no one
anything	everything	something	nothing

Something causes brain development.

- These indefinite pronouns are always plural. Use a **plural verb** with them.

both	few	many	several

Many of the researchers **agree**.

- These indefinite pronouns can be singular or plural.

all	any	most	none	some

All of the research **is happening** now. **All** of the researchers **are working** fast.

Oral Practice (1–5) Say the sentences with a partner. Use *everything, anything, everyone, no one,* or *all.*

1. Do you know _____ about teen brain research?
2. I don't know _____, only some things.
3. _____ should learn about brain growth.
4. _____ of the researchers agree about teen brains.
5. _____ thinks teen brains are like adult brains.

Written Practice (6–10) Start a paragraph with: *Adult and teen brains are not the same.* Add five more sentences. Use indefinite pronouns.

Language Development

Make Comparisons

Group Talk Discuss and compare adult and teen brains. How are they different?

Literary Analysis

Evaluate the Author's Purpose and Viewpoint

The **purpose** of a persuasive text is to persuade readers to think or take action. Usually, the author has an agenda, or goal. For example, what do you think is the agenda of the National Youth Rights Association in their selection "16: The Right Voting Age"?

An author of a persuasive text chooses facts that illustrate his or her **viewpoint**. The author may ignore facts that show other viewpoints. Sometimes, though, authors mention different viewpoints and give reasons why the evidence supporting them is not relevant and/or reliable.

Authors often write specifically for an intended audience. The text may include information that will interest the audience. It may also include claims that the intended audience is likely to agree with.

With a group, read another persuasive text:

- an editorial from a newspaper
- a speech by a politician
- a news commentary on a political topic

Identify the author's purpose, viewpoint, and intended audience. Tell how they affect the text.

Source: ©Harley L. Schwadron/CartoonStock, Ltd.

Specialized Vocabulary

Many of the Key Vocabulary words in this lesson relate to a specific area of study: government. This makes them specialized vocabulary words. Here are some more words that relate to the same topic:

amendment	elect	poll
branch	party	primary

Use a dictionary to learn about these words.

- What is the part of speech?
- How many meanings does the word have?
- Which meaning fits the government context?

Evaluate a Public Service Announcement

Communications A public service announcement, or PSA, is like an ad, but it does not advertise a product. Some PSAs tell about safety issues such as wearing seatbelts or drinking alcohol responsibly. Choose one PSA to evaluate. Who is the intended audience? Does the PSA present reliable facts? Is it effective? Share the PSA and your ideas about it.

myNGconnect.com

- View PSAs about teen rights.
- Look at announcements about drug abuse.
- View PSAs on respect and understanding.

📖 **Language and Learning Handbook**, page 616

Write a Letter to the Editor

When people have a strong opinion on a topic, they can express it in a letter to a newspaper editor. Using the model, write a letter that states whether the voting age should be lowered to sixteen years.

1 **Prewrite** Decide which side of the issue you support. Choose evidence that supports your claim and that isn't arguable. Organize your ideas.

2 **Draft** Write your letter. Clearly explain how the evidence supports your claim.

3 **Revise** Reread your letter. Does it state your claim clearly? Is the claim supported with relevant and reliable evidence?

4 **Edit and Proofread** Check for spelling errors. Use a dictionary if you are unsure about a word.

5 **Publish** Use the Internet to find the e-mail address of a local news organization. Then e-mail your letter to that organization.

📖 **Writing Handbook**, page 698

Model Letter to the Editor

Dear Editor:

The Constitution should be changed to make the voting age sixteen. Many teens today have part-time or full-time jobs. They pay taxes, but they can't vote on how the money is spent.

During the 1700s, England taxed the American colonies but did not let them vote. The colonists went to war against England and won.

Before 1920, many women in the United States worked and paid taxes but could not vote. That year, the Constitution was changed to allow women to vote.

Today's 16- and 17-year-olds are in the same situation as the colonists and as women before 1920. The law should be changed so they can vote. History supports this change.

Sincerely,

Doug Smith

The writer states his claim at the beginning.

The writer includes facts.

The writer links the historical facts to his claim.

Inside the Postal Service

The United States Postal Service is responsible for delivering letters, bills, packages, and other mail to individuals and businesses throughout the world. Many postal employees work in post offices or mail processing centers. Mail carriers deliver mail to homes and businesses.

Jobs in the Postal Service

Postal service workers provide a variety of services to the public. They are classified as full-time and part-time employees or casuals (employees hired only during busy times of the year). Postal inspectors require special knowledge and training.

Job	Responsibilities	Education/Training Required
Postal Service Clerk **1**	• Assists customers at post office • Determines postage rates for letters and packages • Handles claims for damaged packages	• Minimum age 18 • U.S. citizen or legal resident • Basic English language skills
Mail Carrier **2**	• Sorts mail at post office for delivery • Delivers mail and collects mail from homes and businesses • Collects money for postal fees and leaves notices for mail being held at the post office	• Minimum age 18 • U.S. citizen or legal resident • Basic English language skills • Written exam • Driver's license and road test
Postal Inspector **3**	• Helps enforce U.S. postal service laws • Arrests offenders and works with attorneys to investigate and prepare postal cases for court	• U.S. citizen between ages 21 and 36 • College degree • Good physical condition • Driver's license

Write a Job Summary

Visit the official United States Postal Service Web site to learn more about jobs in the U.S. Postal Service.

1. Research available jobs at the United States Postal Service.

2. Choose a job that sounds interesting and write a job summary. Include the job title and requirements in your summary.

3. Present your summary to the class. Save the information in a professional career portfolio.

myNGconnect.com

🔊 Learn more about jobs in the U.S. Postal Service.

🔊 Download a form to evaluate whether you would like to work in this field.

🔊 Download a job summary form.

📖 **Language and Learning Handbook,** page 616

Build Word Knowledge

If you have an e-mail account, you know what a user profile is. It is a collection of information that identifies the name, location, and other details about the user.

Words have "profiles," too. You can find many details about a word in a **dictionary**. You can learn its meaning. You can learn how to pronounce it, its part of speech, and what language it came into modern English from.

Collect Information About Words

Work with a partner. Use the dictionary entry below and the key to gather information about the words *fraudulent* and *freckle*.

Key	
ME	Middle English (an old version of English)
L	Latin
fr.	from
ȯ	pronounced like the *a* in *saw*
ə	pronounced like *uh*
'	accented syllable
n.	noun
adj.	adjective
adv.	adverb

fraudulent • freeway

fraud·u·lent (frȯ' jə lənt), *adj.*: based on or done by fraud or trickery; deceitful. [ME *fraude* fr. L *fraud*-] –fraud' u · lent · ness, *n.* –fraud' u · lent · ly, *adv.*

freck·le (fre' kəl), *n.*: small brown spot in skin. [ME *frekel* of Scandinavian origin] –freck' ly, *adj.*

1. What does *fraudulent* mean?
2. How many syllables does each word have?
3. What part of speech is each word?
4. How do you pronounce the first syllable of each word?
5. What languages did each word come into modern English from? What were the original languages?
6. What is the noun form of this word?

Put the Strategy to Use

Use a dictionary to gather information about a word. Use the key at the front of your dictionary to understand the symbols.

1. Identify the word's pronunciation and its part of speech.
2. Check the word's meaning.
3. Trace the word's history.
4. Note what other parts of speech can be made from the word.

TRY IT ▶ Work with a partner to create dictionary entries for the following words: *accentuate, aspect, compute, derive, factor, significant.* Follow the steps above to make sure all of the information about the word is included.

▶ Reading Handbook, page 647

PREPARE TO READ

EQ | What Rights and Responsibilities Should Teens Have?
Learn what people think about teen curfews.

Make a Connection

Discussion Some cities have curfews for teens. These laws say teens must stay off the streets at certain times, such as from midnight until 6:00 a.m. With a group, discuss reasons for and against teen curfews.

Learn Key Vocabulary

Study the Words Pronounce each word and learn its meaning. You may also want to look up the definitions in the Glossary.

• Academic Vocabulary

Key Words	Examples
accountable (u-**kown**-tu-bul) *adjective* ▶ page 492	If you are **accountable**, you are responsible for something. Who is **accountable** for the grades you get in school?
• **authority** (u-**thor**-u-tē) *noun* ▶ pages 493, 499	**Authority** is power over others. The police have the **authority** to arrest people who break the law.
• **discrimination** (dis-kri-mu-**nā**-shun) *noun* ▶ page 498	**Discrimination** is treating people unfairly because of what they look like or believe in. *Synonym:* prejudice
impose (im-**pōz**) *verb* ▶ pages 490, 495, 499	When parents **impose** rules, they are setting rules that their children must follow. *Synonyms:* establish, apply; *Antonym:* cancel
neglect (ni-**glekt**) *noun* ▶ page 490	**Neglect** means a lack of care and attention. If you don't take care of plants, they can die from **neglect**. *Antonyms:* care, attention
• **prohibit** (prō-**hi**-but) *verb* ▶ page 495	To **prohibit** is to keep people from doing something. *Synonym:* prevent; *Antonym:* allow
restriction (ri-**strik**-shun) *noun* ▶ page 490	A **restriction** is something that limits activity. A leash is a **restriction** on a dog's freedom. *Synonym:* limit
• **violate** (**vī**-u-lāt) *verb* ▶ page 496	If you **violate** a law, you break it. *Synonym:* go against; *Antonym:* follow

Practice the Words Work with a partner. Make a **Definition Map** for each Key Vocabulary word. Use a dictionary to find other forms of the word.

Definition Map

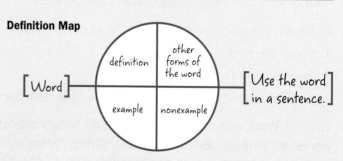

magazine opinion piece by Barbara Bey

Reading Strategies
- Plan and Monitor
- Determine Importance
- Make Inferences
- Ask Questions
- Make Connections
▶ Synthesize
- Visualize

Evaluate Evidence

When writers want to persuade others to a viewpoint, they state a claim and then substantiate, or give evidence to prove, or support, their claim. The evidence could be

- background information about the topic
- an account of an event
- quotes from authorities
- facts, including data from surveys or research.

It is the reader's responsibility to decide if the evidence is relevant, or related to the claim being made, and if the evidence is sufficient, or strong enough, to support it.

Look Into the Text

The heading introduces the writer's viewpoint: that curfews are important.

The Importance of Curfews

Once upon a time, parents weren't afraid to set guidelines or impose restrictions on their children's behavior. They understood that loving their children required setting limits and saying no.

That time is gone. Too many of today's parents just don't want to be responsible for their children.

An account of an event

A case in point: A parent dropped a 12-year-old child off in downtown Orlando at 8 o'clock one morning. At 2 o'clock the following morning, the child was still downtown. That's neglect, plain and simple.

What is the first evidence the writer offers in support of her viewpoint?

Focus Strategy ▶ Synthesize

When you read two arguments on the same topic, examine the evidence different writers use. Evaluate the evidence and think about how writers use emotional appeals or faulty logic to support their claims. Compare the claims, too. Comparing across texts is one way to **synthesize** information. Use a chart to keep track.

Focus Strategy

HOW TO COMPARE ARGUMENTS

Begin your comparison with this selection.

1. Read the text.

2. Identify the claim.

3. List the evidence. Decide if the evidence is relevant. Also consider whether it is sufficient to support the writer's claim.

Comparison Chart

Title: "Should Communities Set Teen Curfews?"

The Claim: Curfews for teens are important.

The Evidence:
1. Parents are not responsible—one parent left a child alone all night—not sure this supports the argument.

Curfews: A Brief History

In the Middle Ages, most towns were built of wood and straw, and people used fire for heat and light. If residents forgot to put out their fires at night, they might accidentally set the town on fire. That's how curfews got started. Every night a curfew bell rang to remind villagers to put out their fires. The word *curfew* comes from the French word meaning "cover fire."

In the United States, curfews specifically for young people were introduced in the early 1900s. In many small towns, a curfew bell signaled to teenagers and children that it was time to go home.

Over the next several decades, the use of curfews declined. More teens were working, and many people felt that curfews were not practical.

During the 1980s, though, violence increased in many neighborhoods of the United States. Some people blamed teens for the increase in crime, and towns began to enforce teen curfews. This trend continued through the 1990s.

myNGconnect.com

○ Learn more about life in the Middle Ages.
○ Find out about teen curfews in the United States.

Should Communities Set

Teen Curfews?

by Barbara Bey

The Importance of Curfews

Once upon a time, parents weren't afraid to set guidelines or **impose** **restrictions** on their children's behavior. They understood that loving their children required setting limits and saying no.

That time is gone. Too many of today's parents just don't want to be responsible for their children.

A case in point: A parent dropped a 12-year-old child off in downtown Orlando at 8 o'clock one morning. At 2 o'clock the following morning, the child was still downtown. That's **neglect**, plain and simple.

Since parents won't parent their children, someone or some **entity** must try to save the youngsters from themselves—and others. If that means imposing a curfew, I say so be it. **1**

1 Evidence/Compare Arguments
What evidence does the writer give in this section? Does it substantiate, or prove, why curfews are important? Is there enough evidence to substantiate the writer's claim? Record this information in your chart.

Curfew Laws in Five U.S. Cities in 2006

City	Age	Weekday Times	Weekend Times
Orlando, FL	under 18	12:00 am – 6:00 am	12:00 am – 6:00 am
Austin, TX	under 17	11:00 pm – 6:00 am	12:30 am – 6:00 am
Washington, D.C.	under 17	11:00 pm – 6:00 am	12:01 am – 6:00 am
Chicago, IL	under 17	10:30 pm – 6:00 am	11:30 pm – 6:00 am
San Francisco, CA	under 14	12:00 am – 5:00 am	12:00 am – 5:00 am

▲ Interpret the Chart Would a 15-year-old in San Francisco be breaking the curfew at 12:30 a.m. on a Sunday morning?

Key Vocabulary
- **impose** v., to establish, to apply
- **restriction** n., something that limits activity
- **neglect** n., a lack of care and attention

In Other Words
entity group, organization

Enforcing the Curfew

Since 1994, Orlando has **banned** anyone under 18 from a downtown area from midnight until 6:00 a.m. every night. **First-time violators** are asked to leave the downtown area. Repeat offenders are cited for trespassing or held in the auditorium of police headquarters until their parents or guardians pick them up. **2**

There are, of course, exceptions to the rules. If kids are with their parents, traveling on Interstate 4 through the downtown area, working, or responding to an emergency, they're within the law.

Kids who are going to or from an event sponsored by a civic, school, or religious organization are also exempted from the rules.

So far, I think the curfew is working. The downtown area is safer for kids. Kids aren't being harassed. **3** In fact, the curfew hasn't caused much trouble at all.

The police are doing a very good job. They've been taught how to deal with situations and problems without **becoming confrontational**. They issue warnings and give kids a certain amount of time to leave. If the kids won't go, police officers pick them up and call their parents.

Teens at school-sponsored events like games are within the law, even if the event ends late at night.

2 Evidence
Why do you think the author includes this information about Orlando?

3 Evidence/Compare Arguments
Record this evidence in your chart. Is it reliable? Explain.

Monitor Comprehension

Explain
According to the author, what does a curfew do that parents do not do?

In Other Words
banned not allowed
First-time violators People who break the law for the first time
becoming confrontational causing a fight

Some of these parents are being charged with neglect. Others are encouraged to take parenting classes to learn how to set limits. Whatever happens, parents of kids who are picked up are being forced to be **accountable**.

Some people say that any curfew **puts young people under house arrest**. But we all have restrictions on us. We can't trespass. We can't **loiter** in certain places. If we do, we're subject to arrest. These laws are already on the books.

Helping Parents to Parent

Sure, I wish we didn't have to impose curfews. It's certainly a sad state of affairs. It would be a better solution by far if parents asserted control of their children. But today's parents don't seem to understand the difference between a parent and a buddy. Too many parents want their children to like them.

Used to be, parents could say no and, if their children didn't happen to like them at that moment or that week, the parents **held their ground**. They survived.

Used to be, when young people were out of the house at 2 o'clock in the morning, they were with their parents or another responsible adult. Once upon a time, **chaperoned** group activities ended at 11:00 p.m. and those out on dates had to be home by midnight.

Today, there are too many parents who are simply not equipped to be parents. It's sad but true that their **offspring** are getting into lots of trouble. They are prey to the deviants out on the streets who give them drugs and alcohol, even force them into prostitution. **4**

City Officials' Opinions About Curfews

- not effective at fighting crime
- somewhat effective
- very effective

4%   50%   46%

Source: National League of Cities, 2003

▲ **Interpret the Graph**
How do most city officials feel about curfews?

4 **Evidence/Compare Arguments**
What evidence does the writer give here? Does it seem reliable? Add the information to your chart.

Key Vocabulary
accountable *adj.*, responsible

In Other Words
puts young people under house arrest is like locking teens in their homes
loiter hang around without a reason
held their ground kept their decision
chaperoned supervised
offspring children

If a legally imposed curfew can save these kids from that kind of fate, I welcome it.

Used to be, we didn't have to worry so much about our kids. Used to be, but not anymore. ❖

ANALYZE Should Communities Set Teen Curfews?

1. **Summarize** Sum up the author's stated evidence for thinking teen curfews are a good thing.

2. **Vocabulary** Do you agree that most parents do not use their **authority** over their teenagers appropriately? Use evidence from the text and your own experience to answer.

3. **Evaluate Evidence** What kind of evidence does the author use most? Do you think the evidence is relevant?

4. **Focus Strategy Compare Arguments** Look at your list of evidence. Is the evidence reliable? Is it sufficient to support the author's claim? How might this author's claim be supported by another writer?

↩ Return to the Text

Reread and Write Reread the text. What is the author's attitude about most parents? How does this influence her argument? Support your analysis with evidence from the text. Do you think the author would give teens more rights or fewer rights? Why?

Key Vocabulary
• **authority** *n.*, power over others

Reading Strategies

· Plan and Monitor
· Determine Importance
· Make Inferences
· Ask Questions
· Make Connections
▶ Synthesize
· Visualize

Analyze Viewpoint: Word Choice

One way writers try to convince you to agree with their opinion is through their word choice. They may use loaded words—words that make you feel angry, proud, afraid, or guilty, for example. Loaded words favor, or support, just the writer's side of an argument.

Look Into the Text

The writer uses loaded words to describe the curfew laws.

What curfews will do is wreak havoc with the constitutional right to freedom of movement. Curfew laws punish the innocent instead of the guilty. They put law-abiding teenagers under house arrest every night of the week. But it's not because they have done anything wrong. It is because of the crimes committed by others.

What emotion do you feel after reading this?

Focus Strategy ▶ Synthesize

You just read "Should Communities Set Teen Curfews?" Think about that writer's argument as you read the next selection, "Curfews: A National Debate." Compare the texts. Think about the different arguments.

HOW TO COMPARE ARGUMENTS

Focus Strategy

1. Review the Comparison Chart you began on page 487. As you read, add the claim and evidence from the second selection to the chart.

2. After you read, compare your notes for both selections. Think about
   - how the claims are different
   - which evidence seems more reliable
   - how well each writer uses evidence to support the claim.

3. Think about your own opinion of each article.

Comparison Chart

Title: "Curfews: A National Debate"
The Claim: Curfews for teens are bad.
The Evidence: 1. against constitutional right to freedom

Curfews:
A National Debate

Connect Across Texts

You read arguments in favor of curfews in "Should Communities Set Teen Curfews?" Read the opposite point of view in this persuasive commentary.

In the summer of 1995, the District of Columbia passed a law **imposing** a curfew on teenagers. The law requires everyone under the age of 17 to be home by 11:00 p.m. on weekdays and midnight on weekends. Then they have to stay put until 6:00 a.m. the next morning. The law also **prohibits** drivers under 18 from driving in the District after midnight. Teenagers face punishment if caught in public after curfew. Their parents could be **prosecuted** as well.

In passing this law, Washington, D.C., joined what has become a trend. According to a report in the *American Journal of Police*, 146 of the country's 200 major cities impose curfews of some sort on minors. That's almost 75% of the cities.

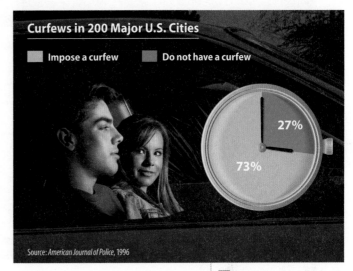

Curfews in 200 Major U.S. Cities

■ Impose a curfew   ■ Do not have a curfew

27%

73%

Source: *American Journal of Police*, 1996

▲ **Interpret the Graph**
What percent of the 200 major U.S. cities have curfews?

Key Vocabulary
• **impose** *v.*, to establish, to apply
• **prohibit** *v.*, to keep people from doing something, to prevent

In Other Words
prosecuted charged by police with breaking the law

Curfews are one of many **misguided** anti-crime strategies. Laws like these **divert** attention from the real causes of crime. **1** The fact is that such laws are **empty political gestures**. They will do nothing to make our streets safer. It is absurd to think that any teenager who is selling drugs or carrying a gun would rush home at 11:00 p.m. to avoid <u>violating</u> curfew. Or that this same teenager won't have a false **ID**. **2**

1 Word Choice
What loaded words does the writer use? Explain how the words make you feel about the topic.

2 Compare Arguments
What evidence does the writer give against having curfews? Is it reliable? Is it relevant and meaningful? Add this information to your chart.

Juvenile Violent Crime

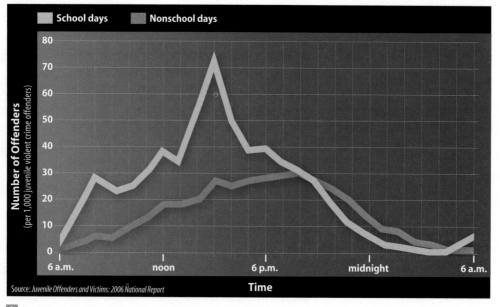

Source: *Juvenile Offenders and Victims: 2006 National Report*

⬛ **Interpret the Graph** At what time during a school day is juvenile crime most likely to occur?

Certainly any crime that would be committed after midnight can just as easily be committed earlier. In fact, the most active period for juvenile crimes is from noon to 6:00 p.m. on school days.

What curfews will do is **wreak havoc with** the constitutional right to freedom of movement. Curfew laws punish the innocent instead of

Key Vocabulary
• **violate** *v.*, to go against

In Other Words
misguided incorrect, unwise
divert shift
empty political gestures passed so the government looks as if it is being helpful
ID identification card
wreak havoc with ruin, destroy

the guilty. They put law-abiding teenagers under house arrest every night of the week. But it's not because they have done anything wrong. It is because of the crimes committed by others.

Curfews criminalize normal and otherwise lawful behavior. Teenagers can't walk the dog or go for an early morning run during curfew hours. Curfew laws **usurp** the rights of parents to raise their children as they think best. It becomes a crime for parents to allow their teenagers to go to the theater or a jazz club. This law **injects** the government where it doesn't belong. **3**

There is also no evidence that curfews work. In Houston, a curfew was introduced, and youth crime went down by 22%. But in New York, where no curfew exists, youth crime went down 30%. In Detroit and New Orleans, youth crime increased after curfews were introduced. And in San Francisco, youth crime went down after a curfew was **repealed**.

3 Compare Arguments
What evidence does the writer give in this paragraph? Is it relevant and meaningful? Add this information to your comparison chart.

Crime and Curfews

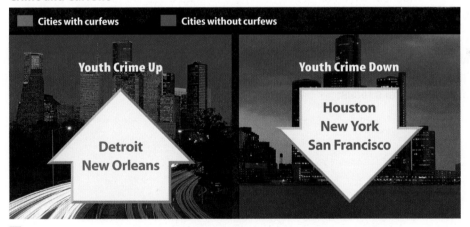

Interpret the Graphic Which cities have curfews? Does crime always go down when a city has a curfew? How can you tell?

Monitor Comprehension

Explain
According to the writer, why don't curfew laws work? Does the writer use meaningful evidence or loaded words to support the claim?

In Other Words
usurp take away
injects puts
repealed removed

Curfews also **squander** police resources that should be used to fight real crime. That is why many police chiefs oppose them.

And inevitably, curfews result in **discrimination**. Studies have consistently found that curfew laws are **disproportionately** enforced in minority communities. **4**

In sum, while curfews may give the appearance of bold action, in reality they do far more harm than good. ❖

4 Word Choice
What emotions do you feel after reading these paragraphs? What words help to generate those emotions?

ANALYZE Curfews: A National Debate

1. **Explain** What does the writer believe that teen curfews do? Explain.

2. **Vocabulary** According to the writer, how could curfews result in **discrimination**?

3. **Analyze Viewpoint: Word Choice** How do you think the writer wanted you to feel about the topic? List five loaded words the author used to make you feel this way.

4. **Focus Strategy Compare Arguments** Look at your notes. Compare the writers' claim and evidence. Which selection has more reliable evidence to support the claim?

   Return to the Text

   Reread and Write Does this writer focus more on teen rights or teen responsibilities? Review the text and write a few sentences to tell why you think this is the writer's focus.

Key Vocabulary
• **discrimination** *n.*, treating people unfairly

In Other Words
squander waste
disproportionately unfairly

EQ What Rights and Responsibilities Should Teens Have?

Reading

Critical Thinking

1. **Analyze** Why do some people in **authority**, such as police chiefs and city officials, want curfews while others in authority oppose curfews? Support your answer with evidence from the texts.

2. **Compare** According to these two articles, how do curfews affect crime rates? Compare the arguments. Does either article have sufficient, reliable evidence to support its claim about the effect of curfews on crime? Explain.

3. **Interpret** Do you think most parents believe that communities should **impose** curfews? Give reasons for your opinion.

4. **Assess** Which article do you agree with? Why? Support your answer with evidence from the texts.

EQ 5. **Synthesize** According to these writers, what are the rights and responsibilities of teens?

Writing

Write About Literature

Argument Do you think teen curfews are a good idea? Write a paragraph in which you state a claim and support it with evidence. Try to include evidence that is reliable, relevant, and sufficient. Use words that appeal to emotions. Before writing, create a Cause-and-Effect chart, and record what you already know about problems and benefits that teen curfews can cause.

Vocabulary

Key Vocabulary Review

Oral Review Work with a partner. Use these words to complete the paragraph.

accountable	impose	restrictions
authorities	neglect	violate
discrimination	prohibit	

The police and other __(1)__ in a major city decided to __(2)__ some __(3)__ on people walking their dogs. The rules __(4)__ people from letting their dogs run free. People who __(5)__, or break, the rules will have to pay a fine. If officials see a dog off a leash, they will assume that no one is taking care of the dog and that it is in danger of __(6)__. They will take the dog to an animal shelter. Officials want dog owners to be __(7)__ for their dogs' behavior. Dog owners argue that the new rules are an example of __(8)__, because they only apply to dogs and not to any other pets.

Writing Application If you were a city official, would you support or oppose teen curfews? Use at least three Key Vocabulary words in your answer.

Fluency

Read with Ease: Expression

Assess your reading fluency with the passage in the Reading Handbook, p. 681. Then complete the self-check below.

1. I did/did not use my voice to express feelings.

2. My words correct per minute: _____.

INTEGRATE THE LANGUAGE ARTS

Vary Your Sentences

A **simple sentence** has one `subject` and one `verb`. Usually, the subject comes before the verb.

Our `city` `has` a curfew.

When you vary your sentences, you make them different from each other, and your writing is more interesting. Here are some ways to vary sentences.

1. Change the word order. Use the `verb` before the `subject`.

   Rarely `are` teens out late at night.

2. Use different types of sentences. The first example below uses only statements. The second example uses questions and exclamations as well. Which is more interesting?

   Teens in my city were getting into trouble. The city set a curfew. Now we all go home by 10 p.m.

   Teens in my city were getting into trouble. What did the city do? It set a curfew, and guess who's home by 10 p.m.!

Oral Practice (1–5) With a partner, make up five sentences about a photo in "Should Communities Set Teen Curfews?" Use different types of sentences.

Written Practice (6–10) Start a paragraph with the sentence below. Add five sentences with more details. Vary your sentences.

   My friends and I like to stay out late.

Express Opinions

Pair Talk Tell a partner how you feel about teen curfews. Use words such as *I think*, *In my opinion*, and *I believe*.

Analyze Persuasive Techniques

Advertisers use techniques to persuade people to buy products or services. Sometimes the ads can be deceptive, or misleading. Ads may

- make claims or promises—for instance, that a product can make you taller or thinner
- quote studies or surveys that make claims seem more credible, or believable
- quote famous people who use the product, or quote experts who say the product works
- use comparisons to show how a product works—for instance, to show how two different kinds of toothpaste clean teeth
- use words or pictures to help viewers imagine having a better life if they used that product
- use exciting background music or visual techniques to generate excitement
- distract viewers with information that is not essential.

1 Choose an ad on TV or in print.

2 Analyze how the ad tries to persuade people to buy something.

3 Describe the ad to your class and discuss the persuasive techniques it uses. Do you think the ad is effective? Do you think it is deceptive? Explain.

"I've hired this musician to play a sad melody while I give you a sob story why I didn't do my homework. It's actually quite effective."

Source: ©Jerry King/CartoonStock, Ltd.

Analogies

An **analogy** is a comparison between two pairs of things. Analogies can show many different relationships, such as objects and their use, or ideas and their opposites. Example:

> Arm is to body as branch is to tree.

To understand an analogy, figure out the relationship in the one pair: arm is to body (relationship = part to whole). The other pair has the same relationship. If you know that an arm is part of the body, you can infer that a branch is part of a tree.

Work with a partner to complete each analogy. Then write a new one.

1. Pencil is to writing as phone is to _____ .

2. Police are to uniforms as actors are to _____ .

Cause-and-Effect Essay

Civics: Current Affairs Curfew laws are just one of the issues that affect communities and teens. Brainstorm other issues that deal with the rights of teens in the community, such as the legal driving age. Choose one issue to research. Then write a short cause-and-effect essay about the issue. Identify a cause (for example, a teen curfew law). Explain its effect (keeps young people safe).

myNGconnect.com

- Explore free speech rights.
- Read about school dress codes.
- Learn about drug tests and student searches.

Writing Handbook, page 698

Language and Learning Handbook, page 616

Trait: Development of Ideas

If you have a strong opinion about an issue, you can write a persuasive argument to tell people about it. You might even persuade people to change rules or laws.

When you write a persuasive argument, include a controlling idea, or **claim** that clearly states your viewpoint. Then give evidence that supports it. Use facts, data, and other reliable evidence to support your claim. Use transitions, such as *however* and *in addition*, to show how the information is related. Choose words that persuade.

Just OK

> I disagree with the school board's decision to cut the music program. I like playing the drums. Some of my friends play musical instruments. Our school used to have a really good music program. Some of our students receive college scholarships to study music.

Much Better

> Our school must not cut its music program. Last month the school board said there wasn't enough money for it. However, the school owns the instruments, so the program doesn't really cost much. Last year the school actually made $1,000 from concerts. In addition, the students benefit—last year, 28% of our music students received college scholarships. The music program should not be cut.

Practice Think of a local law or school policy that you strongly agree or disagree with. Write a persuasive argument to convince others to see the issue as you do. Remember:

- Express your opinion in a sentence.
- Include evidence to support your claim.
- Present evidence in a logical order.
- Use transitions to join the ideas.
- Use persuasive language such as *must not*.

Writing Handbook, page 698

Persuasive Speech

Think about an idea or issue you feel strongly about. Present your opinion and try to convince the audience that your ideas and opinions are worth listening to.

1. Plan Your Speech

Select a topic you have a strong opinion about.

- Write your claim in a carefully worded statement of opinion.
- Do research to find facts and examples that support your claim. Be sure to use reliable sources. Take notes. Make sure the evidence you find is relevant to your argument and that it is accurate.
- Think of opposing arguments that you can mention and argue against. Find sources to support these opinions as well.
- Make graphics or find photos as support.

Structure, or organize, your speech in a way that gets your point across to your audience.

2. Practice Your Speech

Use your notes and practice your speech for a friend.

- Begin by clearly stating your claim.
- Use persuasive words like *must* and *should*. Speak with a convincing tone. Your tone should fit your topic: A light, funny tone matches a humorous subject, while a formal tone matches a serious topic.
- Accurately state your evidence and use effective transitions.
- Display your graphics or photos.
- End with a powerful conclusion.

Notice this speaker's good posture, facial expression, and relaxed position.

3. Give Your Speech

Persuade your audience!

- Make eye contact with individuals in your audience.
- Stay on topic.
- Speak clearly and loudly so that others can understand you.

4. Discuss and Rate the Speech

Use the rubric to discuss and rate the speeches, including your own. As your teacher directs, read or listen to famous speeches to see what rhetorical devices and structures those speakers use. Think about the speakers' main and supporting ideas. Do you clearly understand the speech's main idea? Did the supporting ideas persuade you to change your mind or make you care about the speaker's beliefs? Ask yourself whether the speech's style and structure supported its meaning and purpose. As you read or listen, note what elements of the speech make it effective.

Persuasive Speech Rubric

Scale	Content of Speech	Speaker's Preparation	Speaker's Delivery
3 Great	• Changed my mind/made me care • Was powerful and effective	• Used effective support • Order made sense all of the time	• Grabbed my attention • Showed commitment to the opinion
2 Good	• Was interesting most of the time • Had some effect on my feelings	• Had a few good supporting facts • Order made sense most of the time	• Held my attention • Seemed to believe in the opinion
1 Needs Work	• Was not very interesting • Didn't make me think	• Support was weak or off the topic • Order made no sense	• Did not hold my attention • Did not seem to care much about the subject

DO IT ▶ Now that you know how to deliver a persuasive speech, go develop your own!

📖 Language and Learning Handbook, page 616

myNGconnect.com
🔊 Download the rubric.

EQ What Rights and Responsibilities Should Teens Have?

Read about the reality of adult responsibilities.

Make a Connection

Anticipation Guide Think about what it would be like to get a job, earn a salary, pay your bills, and live on your own. Tell if you agree or disagree with these statements in the **Anticipation Guide**.

ANTICIPATION GUIDE	Agree or Disagree
1. You don't have to finish high school to get a good-paying job.	_____
2. Teens should have the same responsibilities as adults.	_____
3. You aren't mature if you still live at home.	_____

Learn Key Vocabulary

Study the Words Pronounce each word and learn its meaning. You may also want to look up the definitions in the Glossary.

• Academic Vocabulary

Key Words	Examples
afford (u-**ford**) *verb* ▶ page 509	To **afford** something is to have enough money to pay for it. Gwen had two jobs in order to **afford** her bills.
dropout (**drop**-owt) *noun* ▶ pages 508, 511, 519	A **dropout** is someone who quits school before graduating. Most high school **dropouts** have a hard time getting a good job.
experience (ik-**spear**-ē-uns) *noun* ▶ pages 513, 518, 519	**Experience** is something you have done or skills you have practiced. An after-school job can give you work **experience**. *Synonym:* skill
• **income** (**in**-kum) *noun* ▶ page 509	**Income** is the money you earn. Rudy's only **income** was the money he earned washing cars on Saturdays. *Synonyms:* earnings, salary; *Antonym:* expenses
independent (in-du-**pen**-dunt) *adjective* ▶ pages 511, 519	If you are **independent**, you are on your own. You earn money, buy food, pay rent, and take care of yourself. *Antonym:* dependent
position (pu-**zi**-shun) *noun* ▶ pages 508, 511, 513, 518, 521	A **position** is a specific job. You could be hired to fill the **position** of assistant manager. *Synonym:* role
reality (rē-a-lu-tē) *noun* ▶ pages 508, 513	**Reality** is the sum of everything that is real or factual. *Antonym:* fantasy
reckless (**re**-klus) *adjective* ▶ page 510	A **reckless** person takes foolish risks. **Reckless** drivers often cause car accidents. *Synonyms:* careless, bold; *Antonym:* careful

Practice the Words With a partner, make a **Vocabulary Study Card** for each Key Vocabulary word. Write the word on one side. On the other side, write its definition, a synonym or antonym, and an example sentence. Quiz each other.

BEFORE READING What Does Responsibility Look Like?

persuasive essay by Louise Bohmer Turnbull

Reading Strategies

- Plan and Monitor
- Determine Importance
- Make Inferences
- Ask Questions
- Make Connections
▶ Synthesize
- Visualize

Evaluate Argument and Reasons

When persuasive writers state a claim, they also provide **reasons**. Reasons explain why the reader should believe the claim. Writers support their reasons with evidence. Sometimes writers also include a **counterclaim**, or opposing view. Then they explain why the counterclaim is incorrect.

Look Into the Text

The writer begins with a counterclaim and then presents her argument.

Your plans, you say, are to find a job, get a place of your own, and live your own life. These are understandable goals, but completely unattainable for a 16-year-old dropout.

The writer gives reasons why the goals are very hard to reach.

Buy a copy of today's newspaper and turn to the help-wanted section. Circle the jobs for which you qualify. Notice that high-paying positions require college degrees. Other employers want a high school graduate or GED equivalent. Few bosses will hire those under 18 except as babysitters, ushers, dog-walkers, clerks, or fast-food workers. These jobs pay minimum wage with no benefits and little chance for advancement.

Why does it make sense that dropouts have few job opportunities?

Focus Strategy ▶ Synthesize

A **generalization** is a statement that applies to more than one situation. When you read, you **form generalizations**. You take ideas from the text, together with your personal knowledge, and form an idea that applies to many situations.

HOW TO FORM GENERALIZATIONS

Focus Strategy

1. Read the second paragraph above. Note details that are about the same idea: jobs and education.

2. Add examples about this idea from your own experience or knowledge.

3. Make a generalization that seems true for the author's examples and your examples.

4. Read on and use the chart to form more generalizations.

Generalization Chart

Details in Text:
High-paying jobs require college degrees. Other jobs require a high school diploma or GED.

My Experience:
When I applied for a job that paid more than minimum wage, I was rejected because I hadn't graduated from high school yet.

Generalization:
When you have a diploma, you can get a higher-paying job.

A Successful Start

Warren Hardie is the president of a large company that makes equipment for bowling alleys around the world. In this interview, he talks about his first job and what makes people successful.

When Warren Hardie was nine years old, he earned $2.00 per hour working for a geologist.

Q: What important lessons did you learn in your first job that have helped you succeed?

A: Anyone who works earns my respect. You have to work to make money. Responsibility, detail, and quality are all important to success.

Q: Which of those lessons were the most important to your success?

A: I learned the value of having a strong work ethic [the desire to work hard] and of paying close attention to detail.

Q: Have you seen how *not* having those job skills had negative effects on others?

A: Absolutely. Those with a strong work ethic can be successful in school, job, community, and life. Those without a desire to work will struggle to succeed. Work is good. Hard work is better.

Q: What advice would you give to someone starting his or her first job?

A: Do your best. Be reliable. Be honest. Help your coworkers.

myNGconnect.com

Read more "Famous First Jobs" interviews.
View career profile videos.

What Does Responsibility Look Like?

by Louise Bohmer Turnbull

Comprehension Coach

Louise Bohmer Turnbull taught teens for many years. She knows about the problems and frustrations they face on the way to adulthood and offers some advice.

The Harsh Realities

Many teenagers are tired of their adolescent roles. They want freedom from rules, curfews, counselors. And parents. They are eager to quit school and begin their adult life. **1** But how many teenagers really understand what it takes to be an adult? How many really understand the **harsh realities** of responsibility? My advice to teenagers who feel ready to be on their own has not changed.

1 Access Vocabulary
The word *eager* comes from the Latin word *acer*, which means "sharp." Define *eager* and explain how it relates to its origins.

Jobs

Your plans, you say, are to find a job, get a place of your own, and live your own life. These are understandable goals, but completely **unattainable** for a 16-year-old **dropout**.

Buy a copy of today's newspaper and turn to the help-wanted section. Circle the jobs for which you qualify. Notice that high-paying **positions** require college degrees. Other employers want a high school graduate or **GED** equivalent. Few bosses will hire those under 18 except as babysitters, ushers, dog-walkers, clerks, or fast-food workers. These jobs pay **minimum wage** with no benefits and little chance for advancement.

Teens under 18 can get jobs in places such as restaurants and clothing stores, but these jobs usually pay minimum wage.

Key Vocabulary

reality *n.*, the sum of everything real

dropout *n.*, a person who quits school before graduating

position *n.*, a specific job

In Other Words

harsh very difficult, hard

unattainable impossible to reach

GED General Educational Development. People can take a test to get a GED diploma instead of a high school diploma.

minimum wage the least amount per hour

As far as living your own life, your employer will demand that you dress appropriately, be on time, and work the hours and days he or she chooses. You must be courteous even if the customer is rude. You cannot talk back or **your low-paying job is toast**. **2**

If you earn $6.15 an hour and work 40 hours a week, you'll make $1,066 a month. After federal and state taxes are taken out, you'll receive $975.91.

Living Expenses

Now turn to the apartment rental section. In some areas, for about $450 a month, you can rent a studio apartment. That's just a sofa bed in one all-purpose room plus **kitchenette** and bath. Unfurnished one-bedroom apartments begin at about $500. You'll really have to stretch your remaining money ($400 to $475) if you want food, furniture, electricity, a TV, a phone, transportation to your job, cosmetics, clothing, and **incidentals**. Good luck. **3**

2 Argument and Reasons
What is the counterclaim at the beginning of the paragraph? What reasons does the writer give to dispute the counterclaim?

3 Form Generalizations
Use the text to form a generalization about monthly expenses. Add it to your chart.

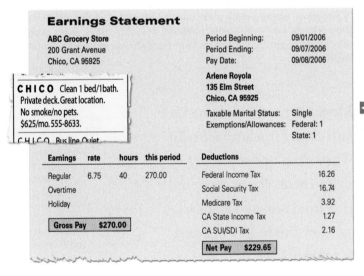

Earnings Statement

ABC Grocery Store
200 Grant Avenue
Chico, CA 95925

Period Beginning: 09/01/2006
Period Ending: 09/07/2006
Pay Date: 09/08/2006

Arlene Royola
135 Elm Street
Chico, CA 95925

Taxable Marital Status: Single
Exemptions/Allowances: Federal: 1
State: 1

CHICO Clean 1 bed/1bath.
Private deck. Great location.
No smoke/no pets.
$625/mo. 555-8633.

CHICO Bus line. Quiet.

Earnings	rate	hours	this period	Deductions	
Regular	6.75	40	270.00	Federal Income Tax	16.26
Overtime				Social Security Tax	16.74
Holiday				Medicare Tax	3.92
				CA State Income Tax	1.27
Gross Pay	**$270.00**			CA SUI/SDI Tax	2.16
				Net Pay	**$229.65**

 Interpret the Paycheck Stub How much is this teen's net pay, or **income**, for one week? How many paychecks will it take for her to **afford** a one-bedroom apartment in Chico?

Monitor Comprehension

Explain
According to the author, what kinds of jobs are available to high school dropouts? About how much could they earn each month?

Key Vocabulary
- **income** *n.*, money that you earn
  afford *v.*, to have enough money for something

In Other Words
your low-paying job is toast you will be fired from your low-paying job
kitchenette a very small kitchen
incidentals other things

In addition, landlords demand **references**. They also want first and last months' rent and a hefty damage deposit before you move in. Many will not rent to minors unless a responsible adult guarantees payment. Property owners often **dictate** the hours you can play your TV and radio or entertain guests. **4**

4 Form Generalizations
Use the text to form a generalization about landlords and teenage tenants. Add it to your chart.

Another option you've mentioned is living in your car while you earned enough money to afford a real place. Where will you park? Police patrol public areas. Storekeepers don't want you in their spaces, and homeowners will not tolerate strangers in front of their houses overnight. The long, leisurely showers you enjoy will be impossible in an automobile, as will clean clothing, home-cooked meals, and nestling down in a warm, comfortable bed.

On TV programs, young people often have apartments like this one from the show *Friends*, with new, stylish furniture. In reality, many young people can only afford to get used furniture from thrift stores, yard sales, friends, or relatives.

You've mentioned an even more **reckless** alternative: joining the homeless. My friend Alan has worked with them for many years. To him, their lives seem like utter misery. They sleep under bridges or in building entrances until the police **evict them**. Plastic bags and cardboard boxes are their only protection from rain and cold. All of their possessions are in grocery carts. They live in fear of being robbed of what little they have by other **vagrants**. **5**

5 Argument and Reasons
What reason does the author give to support her claim that joining the homeless is a bad idea? What evidence does she use to support her reason?

Key Vocabulary
reckless *adj.*, taking foolish risks

In Other Words
references reports from other people about what you are like
dictate set
evict them make them leave
vagrants people without homes and jobs

Often, the homeless are beaten, stabbed, or shot. Getting enough to eat is difficult. Bathing and clean clothes are luxuries. For any kind of income, teenagers sometimes resort to selling drugs or to prostitution. Hardly happy choices. **6**

Believe me, teenager, you are lucky. There are many worse things than school, curfews, counseling, and parents. ❖

6 Form Generalizations
What generalization can you make with this information? Add it to your chart.

ANALYZE What Does Responsibility Look Like?

1. **Summarize** According to this author, why might high school **dropouts** find it difficult to be **independent**? Include evidence from the text in your answer.

2. **Vocabulary** Why do you think most high-paying **positions** require a college degree? Do you think this is fair or unfair? Why?

3. **Evaluate Argument and Reasons** The writer reports teens' ideas of how to become independent. List those ideas and the problem the author points out about each one. Discuss whether the author's reasons make you believe her argument.

Teens' Ideas	Problem
Find a job	Low pay
Get an apartment	

4. **Focus Strategy Form Generalizations** Review your **Generalization Chart**. Use it to make a generalization about what responsibility looks like.

Return to the Text
Reread and Write Do you agree with the generalizations the author makes about teens and responsibility? Reread and look for details to respond to. Then write a brief response to the essay.

Key Vocabulary
independent *adj.*, on your own

BEFORE READING **Getting a Job**
functional documents

Reading Strategies
- Plan and Monitor
- Determine Importance
- Make Inferences
- Ask Questions
- Make Connections
▶ **Synthesize**
- Visualize

Analyze Author's Tone and Purpose

An author chooses words to set a **tone** that reflects his or her attitude toward the topic and audience. When you write an e-mail to a friend, you use informal words that create a friendly tone. When you write a report for school, you use formal language for a serious tone. The tone also depends on your intent, or **purpose**, for writing. This selection contains various documents written by different people. Each document has a different purpose and a different tone.

Look Into the Text

The **greeting** of this cover letter shows a respectful, serious tone.

> Dear Sir or Madam:
>
> I was very interested to see your advertisement in yesterday's *Daily Gazette*. I am interested in a career in hotel and restaurant management and would like the opportunity to work in a restaurant like yours.
>
> Although I cannot work full-time right now, I hope that you will still consider me for a job. I have been working for more than a year as a server during the dinner shift. My current position has given me a chance to acquire excellent serving skills and I am eager to develop them more.

These words express the writer's **formal** tone and purpose.

Which words here show the writer's polite and serious tone?

Focus Strategy ▶ Synthesize

As you read different types of documents, you can **make generalizations** about the information in each type and the reason people use that kind of document. You can generalize about the writer's attitude, or tone, too.

HOW TO FORM GENERALIZATIONS
Focus Strategy

1. **Identify the Document** Tell what type of document it is.

2. **Note Details** Look for important details that show why the writer is writing. Notice what kind of information is in the document. Think about the writer's choice of words and the overall tone.

3. **Generalize** What information does that type of document always have? What tone does it always have?

Generalization Chart

Type of Document	Details About This Document	Generalization
Cover letter	• what job the writer wants • what experience he or she has • polite tone	Cover letters should be polite and should give details about what job you want and what experience you've had.

Getting a Job

> (817) 462-3426. Ask for Larry. Experienced only.
>
> **RESTAURANT**
> F/T Servers needed for downtown restaurant in Lander's Hotel. Dinner shift. Exp req'd. Fax resume and cover to (817) 555-2408 or email landers@towntalk.com
>
> **NOW HIRING**

187 Meadow Road
Grapevine, TX 76051
March 6, 2014

Dear Sir or Madam:

I was very interested to see your advertisement in yesterday's *Daily Gazette*. I am interested in a career in hotel and restaurant management and would like the opportunity to work in a restaurant like yours.

Although I cannot work full-time right now, I hope that you will still consider me for a job. I have been working for more than a year as a server during the dinner shift. My current **position** has given me a chance to acquire excellent serving skills, and I am eager to develop them more.

I would also value the **experience** of working with your management team and hope that you would consider training me to work with them eventually. **1**

My resume and a letter of recommendation are attached for your consideration.

Sincerely,

Ken Wauneka

Ken Wauneka

1 Form Generalizations
Based on this sample, what types of information should cover letters include? What tone should they have?

◀ Analyze the Cover Letter/ Word Choice
What words does Ken use to persuade the people at the restaurant that he should work there?

Key Vocabulary
reality *n.*, the sum of everything real
position *n.*, a specific job
experience *n.*, something you have done, or skills you have learned

Cultural Background
The word *resume* is French. It is often spelled *résumé*, but you may see it without the accents in newspaper ads.

KEN WAUNEKA
187 Meadow Road
Grapevine, TX 76051
(817) 555-3965

Position Desired: *Part-Time Server*

• Dependable • Intelligent • Honest • Hardworking **2**

Career Goal:

Hotel and restaurant management

Paid Work Experience:

Server, Jan. 2013–present
• Work dinner shifts part-time at Green Creek Cafe.

Dishwasher, Busser, Sept. 2012–Dec. 2012
• Worked at El Rancho Restaurant after school and
  on weekends.

Kitchen Helper, Summers 2010–2012
• Helped clean and **run errands** in my uncle's restaurant,
  The Desert Diner.

Education:

Will graduate from high school in June 2014.

References:

• *Rita Sando*, Green Creek Cafe manager   (817) 555-4861
• *Lee Wauneka*, owner of The Desert Diner   (817) 555-2699

2 Author's Tone
and Purpose
Why do you think
Ken includes these
descriptive words
at the top of his
resume? What tone
do they create?

◁ Interpret
the Resume
What jobs has
Ken had? What
other information
does he include
that would help
him get a job as
a server?

In Other Words
run errands do small jobs to help

Cultural Background
Every business and area of work has its own
jargon, or special vocabulary. Jargon includes
words used in a particular way. In the workplace,
a *shift* is the full period of time someone works.
A *busser* is a worker who sets and clears tables.

GREEN CREEK CAFE

64 Baylord Street
Grapevine, TX 76051
(817) 555-4861

March 1, 2014

To Whom It May Concern:

I manage the restaurant where Ken Wauneka has been working. He handles a large section of the restaurant during the dinner shift. I am impressed by his skills as a server during this busy, demanding time.

Ken is not only an excellent server, but he has also **mastered** many other duties, such as assisting the cook and **bussing tables**. Ken is a great team player. He always helps his coworkers during **a crunch**.

We will be sorry to lose Ken, but we know that his goal is to become a manager at an establishment like yours. I think Ken would make a great addition to your staff and I highly recommend him. **3**

Sincerely yours,

Rita Sando

Rita Sando
Manager

3 Author's Tone and Purpose
What is the tone of this letter? What words express this tone? Why does this kind of document have this tone?

◀ **Analyze the Letter of Recommendation/ Details**
What details does Ms. Sando include about Ken that might persuade someone to hire him?

Monitor Comprehension

Describe
What job is Ken trying to get? What does he do to try to get it?

In Other Words
mastered learned
bussing tables clearing away dirty dishes and setting tables
a crunch the busy times

Lander's

HOTEL AND RESTAURANT

JOB APPLICATION

Date _March 10, 2014_

Tell us about yourself.

Name _Ken Wauneka_

Street Address _187 Meadow Road_　　　　Apt. _____

City _Grapevine_

State _Texas_　　　　　　　Zip _76051_

Phone _(817) 555-3965_

What position are you applying for? _server_

What hours and shifts are you interested in?

O Full-time　　　O Breakfast shift

☑ Part-time　　　O Lunch shift

　　　　　　　　☑ Dinner shift

Have you worked in a restaurant before?

☑ Yes　　　　　O No

If Yes, turn to page 2 of this application and describe where you worked and what you did. Begin with your most recent position. **4**

4 Form Generalizations What kinds of information do job applications ask for? Explain why an employer needs or wants that information.

— Page 1 —

Position/Duties:

I am a part-time dinner waiter at Green Creek
Cafe. I tell customers about the daily specials
and take and deliver their orders. At the end
of each shift, I help set up the dining room for
the next day.

Position/Duties:

I started as a dishwasher at El Rancho Restaurant.
When I was promoted to busser, I helped clear
and set tables.

Position/Duties:

I was a Kitchen helper at The Desert Diner.
I cleaned equipment, swept the floors, and
ran errands for the cooks. **5**

When can you start work? __March 24, 2014__

— Page 2 —

5 Author's Tone
and Purpose
What is the
tone of Ken's
responses on the
job application?
Does his tone
support his
purpose? Explain.

◀ Analyze the
Job Application/
Details
What kind of
information is on
page 2 of the
application that
is not on Ken's
resume?

Monitor Comprehension

Summarize
Tell briefly about
Ken's jobs, past or
present, that make
him qualified to work
at Lander's.

Ken,

Ms. Park called from Lander's Restaurant.
She said she enjoyed interviewing you.
She called your references, and
she wants you to start on Saturday!
Congratulations! Call her back
at 555-2408.

—Mom

◀ **Analyze the Note/
Inference**
What can you infer
from what Ken's
mom says in
this note?

ANALYZE Getting a Job

1. **Summarize** What steps does Ken follow to get a **position** at Lander's Restaurant?

2. **Vocabulary** How does Ken's **experience** lead to his new job?

3. **Analyze Author's Tone and Purpose** With a partner, compare and contrast the tone and purpose of the cover letter with the tone and purpose of the letter of recommendation. Describe the tone of each document using one word. What specific words and phrase create this tone?

4. **Focus Strategy Form Generalizations** Review your **Generalization Chart**. Work with a partner to make a generalization about what you need to do to get a job. Pay attention to the context of the situation. When the interviewer asks you a question, do think it would be appropriate to respond with sarcasm?

◀ Return to the Text

Reread and Write Imagine that you worked with Ken at one of his jobs. Write a letter of recommendation for Ken, using his resume and job application for reference. Include information that shows how responsible Ken is. Choose appropriate details from the text.

EQ What Rights and Responsibilities Should Teens Have?

Critical Thinking

1. **Compare** Return to the **Anticipation Guide** you completed on page 504. What details from the two selections made you change your opinions or keep the opinions you had?

2. **Analyze** Is getting a part-time job like Ken's a good step toward being **independent**? Look back at "What Does Responsibility Look Like?" before you respond.

3. **Assess** What are some of the biggest challenges that a high school **dropout** faces? Include examples from the selections.

4. **Speculate** Suppose Ken's best friend wants to quit school to take a full-time job. What points could Ken make to persuade his friend to change his mind?

EQ 5. **Synthesize** Should teens be given the rights and responsibilities of adults? Use information from all of the selections in this unit to support your answer.

Write About Literature

Letter of Persuasion Think of a job that you might want to apply for. Write a cover letter to an imaginary employer persuading that person to hire you. Analyze the demands of the job and explain that you have those qualities. Mention your **experience** and skills in that area of work. Use an appropriate tone for your letter. Consult "Getting a Job" for a model of this type of writing.

Key Vocabulary Review

Oral Review Work with a partner. Use these words to complete the paragraph.

afford	income	reality
dropout	independent	reckless
experience	position	

When I was 16 years old, I got a part-time __(1)__ working in a warehouse. There, I got a lot of practice, or __(2)__ , driving a forklift. I was always careful, never __(3)__ . After two years, I graduated from high school. I did not want to be a high school __(4)__ . For two years, I saved all of my __(5)__ to buy a car. Finally, I could __(6)__ to get my own apartment. Soon I was on my own, completely __(7)__ . After paying all my own expenses for a few months, though, I learned the harsh __(8)__ of being an adult!

Writing Application If you were a parent, would you encourage your teenager to take a part-time job? Use at least four Key Vocabulary words in your answer.

Read with Ease: Phrasing

Assess your reading fluency with the passage in the Reading Handbook, p. 682. Then complete the self-check below.

1. I did/did not group words together properly.

2. My words correct per minute: _____ .

INTEGRATE THE LANGUAGE ARTS

Grammar

Use Compound Sentences

A **clause** is a group of words that has a **subject** and a **verb**. Some clauses are complete sentences.

I **wear** a uniform at work.

A **compound sentence** has two clauses that are complete sentences joined by a **conjunction**. The words **and**, **but**, and **or** are conjunctions. Use a comma (,) before the conjunction.

- Use **and** to join two ideas that are alike.

  I know a lot about my job, **and** I do it well.

- Use **but** to join two ideas that are different.

  I like to cook, **but** I don't like to clean up.

- Use **or** to show a choice between two ideas.

  I can work in the kitchen, **or** I can wait on tables.

Oral Practice (1–5) With a partner, say five sentences about working at a job. Take turns adding **and**, **but**, or **or**, and another sentence to make a compound sentence.

Written Practice (6–10) Combine the simple sentences to make a compound sentence. Use **and**, **but**, or **or**.

6. Lisa has to get a job. She cannot pay her rent.
7. She had an interview. The store called back.
8. The hours fit her schedule. The pay is good.
9. The store is far away. She doesn't have a car.
10. She can take a taxi. She can take the subway.

Language Development

Persuade

Role Play Work with a partner. Imagine one of you wants to move out and live independently. Use ideas from the selections and words like *must*, *have to*, and *should* to persuade each other not to do it.

Literary Analysis

Evaluate Functional Documents

Suppose you are writing a resume using a word processing program. You want to set up the text so it fits on one page, but you can't remember how. You click the Help button for directions.

A help system is a functional document that tells how to do something. The information should be clear and easy to follow. Often, the steps are numbered. If any information is out of order, unclear, or missing, then the document could be useless.

A cover letter, a resume, a business letter, and a job application are also functional documents. In each type of document, the text follows a logical sequence. A letter, for example, includes the sender's address, the date, a greeting, the body of the letter, the closing, and the signature.

Look at each of the functional documents in this unit. With a group, discuss each document.

- What are the features of the document?
- In what order is the information presented?
- Why do you think it is presented in that order?
- Is it a logical order, or would you present the information in a different order? Explain.

Source: ©Anna Gawrys/CartoonStock, Ltd.

Multiple-Meaning Words

Many words in English have an everyday meaning and a special meaning in a career field. For example:

shift *noun* **1.** a move from one place to another **2.** a time period for work

Which meaning of *shift* is used on page 513? Now look up these words in a dictionary and write their meanings. Find the words on pages 513 and 515. Tell which meaning is used.

1. position   **2.** server   **3.** staff

Technical Documents

Social Studies: Technical Documents Technical documents such as computer manuals, how-to guides, and repair manuals give information you might need at work.

Find a technical document at the library, on the Internet, or at home. Meet with a group to share and discuss the document. Explain what the document tells you how to do. Summarize the instructions. If possible, demonstrate the procedure. If you have trouble understanding certain words or concepts, use different forms of the technical manual. For instance, a CD-ROM might have more illustrations than the printed manual. Check against each one to learn and understand the difficult sections.

▼ **Language and Learning Handbook**, page 616

Write an Expository Essay

A test may ask you to write a short essay. A writing prompt will give you a specific topic.

❶ Unpack the Prompt Read the prompt and underline the important words.

> **Writing Prompt**
> What job interests you most? What is it about this job that appeals to you? Write a short essay that describes the job and how you could get it.

❷ Plan Your Response Use an outline to organize your ideas about the topic.

> Ideal Job: _____
> I. Why the job interests me
>   [Details]
> II. What the job involves
>   [Details]
> III. What I must do to get the job
>   [Details]

❸ Draft Organize your short essay as shown. Add specific ideas from your outline.

Organizer

> My ideal job is [name the job]. I have always wanted to work at this job because [explain why this job interests you]. Another reason is that [give other reasons the job interests you].
>
> This job would require me to [explain exactly what you would do on the job]. To get the job, I would have to [list the things you would have to do to qualify, such as passing a training course]. I would really like to try for this job because [explain again briefly why the job is important to you].

❹ ❺ Check and Evaluate Your Work Reread your writing. Ask:

- Did I address the writing prompt?
- Are my ideas well organized?

▼ **Writing Handbook**, page 698

Teen sports fans cheer at a cricket match in Sri Lanka.

Trashing Teens

An Interview with Psychologist Robert Epstein

by Hara Estroff Marano

1   *Psychologist Robert Epstein spoke to* Psychology Today's *Hara Estroff Marano about the legal and emotional constraints on American youth.*

2   **Q.**   Why do you believe that adolescence is an artificial extension of childhood?

3   **A.**   In every mammalian species, immediately upon reaching **puberty**, animals function as adults, often having offspring. We call our offspring "children" well past puberty. The trend started a hundred years ago and now extends childhood well into the 20s. The age at which Americans reach adulthood is increasing—30 is the new 20—and most Americans now believe a person isn't an adult until age 26.

4   The whole culture **collaborates** in artificially extending childhood, primarily through the school system and **restrictions** on **labor**. The two systems evolved together in the late 19th-century; the advocates of **compulsory**-education laws also pushed for child-labor laws, restricting the ways young people could work, in part to protect them from the abuses of the new factories. The juvenile justice system came into being at the same time. All of these systems isolate teens from adults, often in problematic ways.

Key Vocabulary
- **restriction** *n.*, something that limits activity

In Other Words
puberty physical maturity
collaborates works together
labor work
compulsory required

5   Our current education system was created in the late 1800s and early 1900s, and was modeled after the new factories of the industrial revolution. Public schools, set up to supply the factories with a skilled labor force, **crammed** education into a relatively small number of years. We have tried to pack more and more in while extending schooling up to age 24 or 25, for some segments of the population. In general, such an approach still reflects factory thinking—get your education now and get it efficiently, in classrooms in **lockstep** fashion. Unfortunately, most people learn in those classrooms to hate education for the rest of their lives.

6   **Q.** What are some likely consequences of extending one's childhood?

7   **A.** Imagine what it would feel like—or think back to what it felt like—when your body and mind are telling you you're an adult while the adults around you keep insisting you're a child. This infantilization makes many young people angry or depressed, with their distress carrying over into their families and contributing to our high divorce rate. It's hard to keep a marriage together when there is constant conflict with teens.

8   We have completely isolated young people from adults and created a peer culture. We stick them in school and keep them from working in any meaningful way, and if they do something wrong we put them in a pen with other "children." In most **nonindustrialized societies**, young people are integrated into adult society as soon as they are capable, and there is no sign of teen **turmoil**. Many cultures do not even have a term for adolescence. But we not only created this stage of life: We declared it inevitable. In 1904, American psychologist G. Stanley Hall said it was programmed by evolution. He was wrong.

We have completely isolated young people from adults. . .

In Other Words
crammed packed
lockstep exactly the same
nonindustrialized societies places where most people farm or hunt for survival
turmoil confusion or trouble

Historical Background
The industrial revolution was the process of change from a farm-based economy to a factory-based economy that took place in England in the 1700s and then spread throughout most of the world.

9   **Q.** You believe in the inherent competence of teens. What's your evidence?

10   **A.** Dumas and I worked out what makes an adult an adult. We came up with 14 areas of competency—such as interpersonal skills, handling responsibility, leadership—and administered tests to adults and teens in several cities around the country. We found that teens were as competent or nearly as competent as adults in all 14 areas. But when adults estimate how teens will score, their estimates are dramatically below what the teens actually score.

11   Other long-standing data show that teens are at least as competent as adults. IQ is a **quotient** that indicates where you stand relative to other people your age; that stays stable. But raw scores of intelligence peak around age 14-15 and shrink thereafter. Scores on virtually all tests of memory peak between ages 13 and 15. Perceptual abilities all peak at that age. Brain size peaks at 14. Incidental memory—what you remember by accident, and not due to **mnemonics**—is remarkably good in early to mid teens and practically nonexistent by the '50s and '60s.

12   **Q.** If teens are so competent, why do they not show it?

13   **A.** What teens do is a small fraction of what they are capable of doing. If you mistreat or restrict them, performance suffers and is extremely misleading. The teens put before us as examples by, say, the music

A teenager plays the steel drums during the 2012 London Olympics.

In Other Words
competence ability
quotient number from a formula
mnemonics memory tricks

industry tend to be highly incompetent. Teens encourage each other to perform incompetently. One of the anthems of modern pop, "Smells Like Teen Spirit" by Nirvana, is all about how we need to behave like we're stupid.

14 Teens in America are in touch with their peers on average 65 hours a week, compared to about four hours a week in preindustrial cultures. In this country, teens learn virtually everything they know from other teens, who are in turn highly influenced by certain aggressive industries. This makes no sense. Teens should be learning from the people they are about to become. When young people exit the education system and are dumped into the real world, they have no idea what's going on and have to spend considerable time figuring it out.

15 **Q.** What can be done?

16 **A.** I believe that young people should have more options— the option to work, marry, own property, sign contracts, start businesses, make decisions about health care, live on their own—every right, privilege, or responsibility an adult has. I advocate a competency-based system that focuses on the abilities of the individual. For some it will mean more time in school combined with work, for others it will mean that at age 13 or 15 they can set up an Internet business. Others will enter the workforce and become some sort of **apprentice**. The **exploitative factories** are long gone; competent young people deserve the chance to compete where it counts, and many will surprise us. ❖

I believe that young people should have more options...

In Other Words

apprentice assistant who is learning from an expert

exploitative factories workplaces that took advantage of young people

COMING OF AGE

myNGconnect.com

🔍 **Download the rubric.**

EDGE LIBRARY

Present Your Project: Ad Campaign

It is time to create your ad campaign related to the Essential Question for this unit: What Rights and Responsibilities Should Teens Have?

1 Review and Complete Your Plan

Consider these points as you complete your project:

- How will your ad campaign address the Essential Question?
- What language and images will be persuasive to teens?
- How can you make your ad more effective?

Work with your group to complete the ad campaign.

2 Show Your Ad Campaign

Display your ad campaign for the class. Ask for your classmates' reactions to it.

3 Evaluate the Ad Campaigns

Use the online rubric to evaluate each of the ad campaigns, including your own.

Reflect on Your Reading

Think back on your reading of the unit selections, including your choice of Edge Library books. Discuss the following with a partner or in a group.

Genre Focus   What was the most persuasive selection in this unit? What made it more persuasive than the other selections? Give specific examples.

Focus Strategy   With your partner or group, list some of the conclusions and generalizations you made in this unit about teen responsibilities.

EQ Respond to the Essential Question

Throughout this unit, you have been thinking about what rights and responsibilities teens should have. Discuss the Essential Question with a group. What have *you* decided? Support your response with evidence from your reading, discussions, research, and writing.

Write a Persuasive Essay

Writing Portfolio

How do you get your younger brother to mow the lawn for you? You persuade him. This project gives you a chance to see how convincing you can be as you write a persuasive essay.

Study Persuasive Essays

Writers of persuasive essays are trying to convince their readers to agree with them and to perform a particular action. TV commercials, magazine ads, and letters to the editor are all kinds of persuasive writing.

❶ Connect Writing to Your Life

You probably try to persuade other people often. You might try to talk your friends into going to the movies instead of watching TV. You might persuade your family to go to your favorite restaurant for dinner. This project builds on your persuasive powers.

❷ Understand the Form

The **controlling idea** of a persuasive essay is the argument, or **claim**. Usually, the argument is either *for* or *against* some type of issue. Like other kinds of essays, a persuasive essay has an introduction, a body, and a conclusion. A strong persuasive essay must also contain the following parts:

1. Claim	Introduce the issue by giving some background information. Then, state your opinion of the issue.
2. Reasons	List several reasons to support your argument. Why do you think your opinion is correct?
3. Evidence	Give facts, statistics, expert opinions, and examples that illustrate each reason. How do you prove that your reasons are good ones?
4. Counterclaim	Think of what someone on the opposite side of the issue might say. Why isn't your opinion correct? Why aren't your reasons good ones?
5. Rebuttal	Tell why the counter-argument is incorrect. What reasons can you give? What evidence can you show?
6. Call to Action	Restate your argument. What do you want your readers to do?

Now look at how these parts come together. Read a persuasive essay by a professional writer.

❸ Analyze a Professional Model

As you read, look for the important parts of a persuasive essay.

Girls Only? Boys Only?

by Andrea Brown

For a long time, U.S. public schools could not have all-girl or all-boy classes. That was the law. In late 2006, however, the government relaxed that law. Now public schools can have single-gender classrooms. This change is worth a try for many reasons.

First, tests show that girls' brains develop differently from boys' brains. For example, girls tend to develop language skills earlier than boys. Boys, on the other hand, tend to understand spatial relationships (the ways objects relate and fit together) earlier than girls. The difference in development partly explains why boys seem to prefer picture books about how things work, while girls seem to prefer storybooks.

Second, many girls approach schoolwork differently from boys. In general, girls like teamwork. They prefer to work with their classmates. In contrast, boys like competition. They tend to like to compete against other students in class. Girls are also more likely than boys to ask adults for help when they need it.

Third, studies suggest that both boys and girls can succeed in single-gender classrooms. The students may feel more relaxed and confident, too. They are not as worried about giving wrong answers or looking foolish.

Critics of the single-gender classroom are afraid of stereotyping. They believe that it is wrong to say that all boys prefer one thing and all girls prefer another. They fear that teachers may mistakenly encourage girls to do well in reading and writing but not in math and science. These fears are unfounded. All that schools need to do is assign female teachers to all-girl classrooms and male teachers to all-boy classrooms. Girls will then get to see women teaching math and science, and boys will get to see men enjoying literature.

Single-gender classrooms may not be right for every student. However, parents whose children go to public school should have the right to make that choice. I urge you to support your school district in developing that choice.

The writer gives background information about the **issue** and clearly states her **claim**.

The writer gives three reasons to support her claim. She illustrates each reason with examples.

The writer states a **counterclaim** and gives a rebuttal.

At the end, the writer includes a **call to action** that tells readers what to do.

> **Prompt** Write a persuasive essay on an issue about which you have strong feelings. Be sure to:
>
> • tell what the issue is and give your argument
> • give reasons and support them with evidence
> • answer at least one counterclaim
> • tell readers what action to take

✓ Prewrite

Now that you know the basics of a persuasive essay, you are ready to plan one of your own. A good Writing Plan will help you as you draft your essay.

❶ Choose Your Topic

These activities will help you find and choose your topic:

- Complete this sentence five different ways: "The world (or our school or community) would be a better place if _____."

- With friends and family, brainstorm responses to these questions: What important issues do you care about? What change could you or I make to improve the world?

> **Technology Tip**
>
> Look on the Web sites of well-known news organizations or newspapers. This will give you a good idea of current issues that are on the mind of the public.

❷ Clarify the Audience, Controlling Idea, and Purpose

Who are your readers? What background do they need to understand your topic? What opinions do they already have? Jot down your ideas.

Then, write down your argument, or **controlling idea**. Fit it into one of these sentences: "We should do X" or "We should not do Z."

Finally, think about your purpose. What do you want your audience to believe? What do you want your audience to do? Take notes on your ideas.

❸ Develop Reasons and Gather Evidence

Your next step is to think of reasons and gather evidence to support your claim. Here are some helpful suggestions:

- Brainstorm a list of reasons you think your claim is right.

- Interview other students to get their opinions and reasons. When students disagree, make careful note of their reasons.

- Research the topic. Note anything that can be used as evidence. Use reliable sources that present information on both sides of the argument.

- Predict objections to your claim. Use evidence to make effective counterclaims.

- Keep track of the new information you find in a Five-Ws Chart. You can use your notes to help you organize your essay.

> **Prewriting Tip**
>
> Think about the following questions as you research evidence:
>
> • Who wrote this evidence?
> • Will my audience think my sources are reliable?
> • Is this information fact or opinion?

❦ **Language and Learning Handbook,** p. 611

4 Organize Your Reasons

Organize your reasons to support your argument. Build up to a strong finish by putting reasons in order of importance. You can accomplish this by deciding which of your facts and ideas are strongest. This will make it easier to organize a stronger argument. Start with a good reason; then move to a better one. End with your best reason.

5 Finish Your Writing Plan

Use your prewriting ideas to make a Writing Plan like the one below. Remember to list your reasons in order of importance.

Writing Plan

Topic	cell phones in schools
Audience	my classmates, the principal
Controlling Idea or Claim	cell phones are helpful and should be allowed in school
Purpose	to persuade students to sign a petition to allow cell phones in school
Time Frame	one week; start today
Reason 1 Cell phones save time.	**Evidence** I used my phone to borrow a book I needed for class.
Reason 2 Cell phones keep us in touch with our family.	**Evidence** I use my cell phone to let my mom know where I am.
Reason 3 Cell phones help keep us safe.	**Evidence** My friend used her phone to call for help when she fell.
Counterclaim	Some kids use phones to cheat.
Rebuttal	Most of us use our phone for good reasons and should not be unfairly punished.
Call to Action	Sign the petition.

Reflect on Your Writing Plan

▶ Will your reasons be persuasive to your audience? Talk over your plan with a partner.

✔ Write a Draft

Now that you have finished your Writing Plan, use it as a guide as you write your draft. Don't try to create a perfect essay. You can improve it later.

Technology Tip

Save your first draft under two different file names. The second name might simply be "persuasive.essay.2." That way, you have a backup file if you decide you like the first version of a paragraph better.

❶ Use Persuasive Techniques

Capture the attention of your readers with a strong yet creative opening paragraph. Make your argument by using a variety of sentence structures and vivid language. In a persuasive essay, you want to get your audience on your side. There are three techniques you can use to form a convincing argument:

- **Logical Appeal** This technique involves the use of evidence such as facts, statistics, and examples to support your claim.

  > A recent poll of teen cell phone users shows that 87 percent believe their cell phones greatly help them save time and manage their busy schedules.

- **Emotional Appeal** This technique involves the use of strong words that appeal to the audience's needs, values, and attitudes.

  > Taking away our cell phones is the same as taking away our basic rights as human beings! We should not be treated like second-class citizens!

- **Ethical Appeal** This technique involves convincing the audience that you are fair, honest, and well-informed about the issue.

  > Some kids do use their phones for the wrong reasons, and I believe they should be punished. But, I don't think it is fair to punish the rest of us by taking away our phones.

❷ Write a Strong Conclusion

You want your conclusion to be memorable. A good way to end an essay is to quote somebody. The quotation does not have to be from a famous person, but it should relate specifically to the issue.

OK

> In conclusion, we should keep cell phones in our schools because they save time, keep us in touch with our family, and help keep us safe.

Better

> Cell phones are important tools. Students should be allowed to keep them in school. As Matt Murray, the senior class president put it, "Cell phones are a miracle technology." Don't let them take away this miracle.

❸ Student Model

Read this draft to see how the student used the Writing Plan to get ideas down on paper. Remember that this first draft does not have to be perfect. Later, you will see how the student fixed the mistakes.

The Right to Life, Liberty, and Cell Phones?

If you use a cell phone, could you get by without it all day? If our school administration has its way, you will have to. In case you haven't heard, the administration is thinking of baning cell phones in school. I think that stoping students from using their phones is wrong.

We need our phones in school to save us time. For example, yesterday I accidentally left the textbook Social Studies In Action at home. I called my friend Jonas. He left his copy with our teacher. I was able to use it in class. Thanks to my cell phone, I didn't have to go all the way home to get the book. I saved time by calling instead.

Cell phones also help us keep in touch with our family. My mom has asked me to keep my cell phone with me at all times. That way we can keep in touch if one of us is going to be late. I can call her. She can call me. Cell phones give us both peace of mind.

Most important of all, cell phones help keep us safe. If you are walking home from school and something goes wrong, you can call your parents or the police.

I know that some kids use their phones for the wrong reasons. They call each other to cheat on tests. They text message each other instead of paying attention in class. That kind of behavior is wrong. The rest of us should not be punished for the mistakes these kids make.

Cell phones are important tools. Students should be allowed to keep them in school. As Matt Murray, the senior class president put it, "Cell phones are a miracle technology." Don't let them take away this miracle.

Reflect on Your Draft

▶ Think about the process that you used to write your draft. Which parts of the drafting process were hardest? How can you make those parts easier next time?

✔ Revise Your Draft

Your first draft is done. Now you need to polish it. Have you included your audience's viewpoint? Have you stated your position clearly? Does your writing hold the interest of your readers?

❶ Revise for Development of Ideas

Good writing has **well-developed ideas**. It doesn't just contain a list of ideas. A good writer **elaborates** on, or fully explains, ideas and makes them more interesting by supporting them with specific details.

In a persuasive essay, a writer elaborates on a claim by supporting it with reasons. The reasons are, in turn, supported by evidence, such as the following:

- facts
- statistics
- expert opinions
- examples

Don't expect to fully develop all of your ideas in your first draft. As you read your draft, you may notice that some of your reasons need more support. You may need to go back and consider the whole range of information on the topic to select stronger evidence for your claims. It's also important to consider the different views on the topic. Make sure the views expressed are accurate and honest.

TRY IT ▶ With a partner, decide which reason in the draft below needs more evidence to support it.

Student Draft

> We need our phones in school to save us time. For example, yesterday I accidentally left the textbook Social Studies In Action at home. I called my friend Jonas. He left his copy with our teacher. I was able to use it in class. Thanks to my cell phone, I didn't have to go all the way home to get the book. I saved time by calling instead.
>
> Cell phones also help us keep in touch with our family. My mom has asked me to keep my cell phone with me at all times. That way we can keep in touch if one of us is going to be late. I can call her. She can call me. Cell phones give us both peace of mind.
>
> Most important of all, cell phones help keep us safe. If you are walking home from school and something goes wrong, you can call your parents or the police.

Now use the rubric to evaluate the development of ideas in your own draft. What score do you give your draft and why?

Development of Ideas

myNGconnect.com
- Rubric: Development of Ideas
- Evaluate and practice scoring other student essays.

	How thoughtful and interesting is the writing?	How well are the ideas or claims explained and supported?
4 Wow!	The writing engages the reader with meaningful ideas or claims and presents them in a way that is interesting and appropriate to the audience, purpose, and type of writing.	The ideas or claims are fully explained and supported. • The ideas or claims are well developed with important details, evidence, and/or description. • The writing feels complete, and the reader is satisfied.
3 Ahh.	<u>Most</u> of the writing engages the reader with meaningful ideas or claims and presents them in a way that is interesting and appropriate to the audience, purpose, and type of writing.	<u>Most</u> of the ideas or claims are explained and supported. • Most of the ideas or claims are developed with important details, evidence, and/or description. • The writing feels mostly complete, but the reader still has some questions.
2 Hmm.	<u>Some</u> of the writing engages the reader with meaningful ideas or claims and presents them in a way that is interesting and appropriate to the audience, purpose, and type of writing.	<u>Some</u> of the ideas or claims are explained and supported. • Only some of the ideas or claims are developed. Details, evidence, and/or description are limited or not relevant. • The writing leaves the reader with many questions.
1 Huh?	The writing does <u>not</u> engage the reader. It is not appropriate to the audience, purpose, and type of writing.	The ideas or claims are <u>not</u> explained or supported. The ideas or claims lack details, evidence, and/or description, and the writing leaves the reader unsatisfied.

✔ Revise Your Draft, continued

❷ Revise Your Draft

You have now evaluated the development of ideas in your own draft. If your score is 3 or lower, how can you improve your work? Use the checklist below to revise your draft.

Revision Checklist

Ask Yourself	Check It Out	How to Make It Better
Do I clearly state my claim on the issue?	Read your first paragraph. Do you state your claim in it?	☐ End the paragraph by stating your claim.
Do I give interesting and realistic reasons to support my claim?	Reread the body of your persuasive essay. Underline the reasons for your claim.	☐ Make each reason the main idea of a separate body paragraph.
Does my writing engage the readers?	Read the draft to someone, or ask someone to read it. Ask for feedback.	☐ Revise any sentences that do not present ideas in an engaging way. ☐ Add a logical, emotional, or ethical appeal.
Have I developed my reasons with convincing evidence?	Do you provide one type of evidence for each reason?	☐ Research the issue to find more evidence for your reasons. ☐ Add the evidence to your draft.
Do I include at least one counterclaim and a rebuttal?	Underline parts where you gave the opinion of people who disagree with you. Also underline your response.	☐ Add the missing counterclaim ☐ Add the missing rebuttal.
Did I restate the claim and include a call to action?	Read your conclusion. Does it tell the reader to do something?	☐ Add a sentence that tells readers what action to take.

🖢 **Writing Handbook**, p. 698

❸ Conduct a Peer Conference

Having another pair of eyes read your work can make a big difference. Ask a partner to read your draft and look for the following:

- any confusing parts
- places where something is out of order or missing
- reasons that are not backed up with evidence
- an organized structure appropriate for the audience and for the purpose and context of the argument

Then talk with your partner about the draft. Discuss the items in the Revision Checklist. Revise your essay based on your partner's comments.

❹ Make Revisions

Look at the revisions below and the peer-reviewer conversation on the right. Notice how the reviewer asked questions and made comments. Notice how the writer used the questions and comments to revise.

Revised for Development of Ideas

> Most important of all, cell phones help keep us safe. If you are walking home from school and something goes wrong, you can call your parents or the police. *I have a friend named Oksana who was once very glad that she had her cell phone with her when she fell on the ice and broke her ankle. It was dark outside, and no one was around. How long would she have lain on the sidewalk alone if she didn't have her phone with her?*

Revised Ending

> Cell phones are important tools. We should be allowed to keep them in school. As Matt Murray, the senior class president put it, "Cell phones are a miracle technology." Don't let them take away this miracle.
> *Please sign the petition outside the cafeteria to show the administration how important this is to you.*

Peer Conference

Reviewer's Comment: I don't see any evidence to support your third reason.

Writer's Answer: You're right. I need to add an example.

Reviewer's Comment: I like the quotation at the end. But I don't know what you want the reader to do.

Writer's Answer: I said what shouldn't happen, but I didn't say what should happen. I'll add a sentence.

Reflect on Your Revisions

▶ What did your partner like and dislike about your essay? What are your strengths and weaknesses as a writer?

✔ Edit and Proofread Your Draft

Before you share your revised essay, read it over one more time. Find and fix any mistakes that you made.

Proofreading Tip

If you are unsure about which words to capitalize in a title, refer to a style manual for more examples.

❶ Capitalize the Titles of Publications

The main words in the titles of books, chapters, magazines, newspapers, and articles should always be capitalized. Do not capitalize small words such as *a*, *an*, *the*, and *of*. The first word in a title should also be capitalized, even if it's not a main word.

> **Book:** *The Communication Explosion*
>
> **Magazine:** *The Journal of Telecommunications*
>
> **Article:** "Why I Love My Cell Phone"

TRY IT ▶ Copy the sentences. Fix the capitalization errors. Use proofreader's marks.

> Yesterday I accidentally left the textbook Social Studies In Action at home. I needed to read Chapter 8, "the Industrial Revolution."

Proofreader's Marks

Use proofreader's marks to correct errors.

Capitalize:
Black Warrior review publishes fiction and nonfiction.

Do not capitalize:
Have you read *Suddenly Lost in Words* e-zine?

Add italics:
ital I love to listen to Car Talk on Saturdays.

Add underlining:
He'd rather watch Meet the Press. u/s

❷ Use Italics and Underlining

Use *italics* and underlining to set apart a word or words from the rest of the text. If you are writing something on the computer, you can use either method. If you are writing something by hand, however, you should use underlining.

The titles of works that are not part of another, larger work are usually italicized or underlined, including:

- books
- magazines and journals
- newspapers
- movies and plays
- TV and radio programs
- paintings and sculptures

TRY IT ▶ Copy the sentences. Add underlining or italics where needed.

> 1. Did you see the piece about schools and cell phones on Good Morning America?
> 2. No, but I did read an article about teens and cell phones in USA Today.

3 Check Your Spelling

When you add a suffix to certain words, you need to double the final consonant of the root word. Double the consonant when the suffix begins with a vowel and 1.) the root word has only one syllable and ends in a single consonant (other than *w, x, y,* or *z*) preceded by a single vowel; or 2.) when the suffix begins with a vowel and the root word's accent is on the final syllable.

Base Word	Suffix	New Word
sip	**-ing**	sipping
refer	**-ing**	referring
occur	**-ing**	occurring

Technology Tip
If you write on a computer, use the Spell-checker. It will always catch words that need the double consonant but don't have it.

TRY IT ▶ Copy the sentences. Find and fix the two spelling errors.

> The school is thinking of baning cell phones in school. I think that stoping students from using their phones is wrong.

4 Form Compound Sentences

Compound sentences can help add variety to the sentence length in your writing. If you have two short sentences that are closely related, you can show that relationship by adding a coordinating conjunction.

Coordinating Conjunction	Function	Example
and	joins two similar ideas together	I love my cell phone, **and** I use it all the time.
but	joins two contrasting ideas	I have a cell phone, **but** I hardly ever use it.
or	joins two alternative ideas	You can call me on the phone, **or** you can send me an e-mail.

When you join two sentences with a coordinating conjunction, be sure to place a comma before the conjunction.

TRY IT ▶ Copy each pair of sentences and form a compound sentence.

> 1. I called my friend Jonas. He left his copy with our teacher.
> 2. That kind of behavior is wrong. The rest of us should not be punished for the mistakes these kids make.

Reflect on Your Corrections
▶ Read over your essay one more time to check for mistakes. Make a list of your problem areas so you can focus on them when you edit and proofread in the future.

5 Edited Student Draft

Here's the student's draft, revised and edited. How did the writer improve it?

The Right to Life, Liberty, and Cell Phones?

If you use a cell phone, could you get by without it all day? If our school administration has its way, you will have to. In case you haven't heard, the administration is thinking of banning cell phones in school. I think that stopping students from using their phones is wrong.

The writer fixed the spelling errors.

We need our phones in school to save us time. For example, yesterday I accidentally left *Social Studies in Action*, a book that I need for class, at home. I called my friend Jonas, and he left his copy with our teacher. I was able to use it in class. Thanks to my cell phone, I didn't have to go all the way home to get the book. I saved time by calling instead.

The writer fixed the capitalization error and put the title in italics.

The writer created a compound sentence.

Cell phones also help us keep in touch with our family. My mom has asked me to keep my cell phone with me at all times. That way we can keep in touch if one of us is going to be late. I can call her, or she can call me. Cell phones give us both peace of mind.

The writer created a compound sentence.

Most important of all, cell phones help keep us safe. If you are walking home from school and something goes wrong, you can call your parents or the police. I have a friend named Oksana who was once very glad that she had her cell phone with her when she fell on the ice and broke her ankle. It was dark outside, and no one was around. How long would she have lain on the sidewalk alone if she didn't have her phone with her?

The writer added an example as evidence to support the third reason.

I know that some kids use their phones for the wrong reasons. They call each other to cheat on tests. They text message each other instead of paying attention in class. That kind of behavior is wrong, but the rest of us should not be punished for the mistakes these kids make.

The writer created a compound sentence.

Cell phones are important tools, and students should be allowed to keep them in school. Please sign the petition outside the cafeteria to show the administration how important this is to you. As Matt Murray, the senior class president put it, "Cell phones are a miracle technology." Don't let them take away this miracle.

The writer added a call to action in the last paragraph.

✔ Publish and Present

Print out your essay or write a clean copy by hand. Share your opinion with others. You have something to say. You may also want to present your work in a different way.

Alternative Presentations

Record an Audiobook Work with your classmates to create an audiobook of your persuasive essays.

1 List the Essays and Arrange Them in Order Type up a list of all the essay titles. As a group, decide in what order the essays should be presented. Consider clustering together essays about the same subject. Use your finished list as a table of contents.

2 Record Each Essay Each of you should read your essay aloud into a tape or digital recorder. Relax and read with expression.

3 Make and Share Copies Make copies of your audiobook. Create a front and back cover for your tape or CD case. Pass the copies out to your friends and family.

4 Get Feedback Invite your listeners to tell you what they think about the audiobook. What are their favorite essays? Which ones changed their minds about an issue? Have listeners compare your persuasive speech to a famous speech they have heard. Did you use any of the same techniques?

Publish a Magazine You and your classmates could also publish a magazine.

1 Create a Table of Contents Group your essays in a logical order. Give the magazine a catchy title.

2 Design and Print Your Magazine Use a desktop publishing program to lay out your magazine on a computer. Add suitable clip art or other visuals. Make sure you credit any art that someone else created.

3 Distribute Your Magazine Pass out your magazine throughout the school. Distribute it in the community, too. Include an e-mail address at school where readers can write to give you feedback.

Explore Other Perspectives Team up with a classmate who wrote about your topic from a different perspective. Take turns reading your essays to the class. Have your classmates compare the ideas presented in each essay and evaluate the evidence used to support those ideas.

🐚 **Language and Learning Handbook**, p. 616

Publishing Tip

Format your typed work according to your teacher's guidelines.

If you've handwritten your work, be sure your work is legible and clean.

Analyzing Speeches

Have listeners compare the persuasive speeches in the class collection to a famous speech they have heard. Did the class use any of the same devices, such as anecdotes or repeated phrases? Did the class collection use structures such as question/answer format or repetition? Share famous speeches and explain the techniques used.

Reflect on Your Work

▶ **Ask for and use feedback from your audience to evaluate your strengths as a writer.**

• Did your essay make the audience feel like taking action? Did it change anyone's opinion?

• What did your audience think was the strongest point of your essay? What did they think was the weakest point?

• What would you like to do better the next time you write? Set a goal for your next writing project.

✓ Save a copy of your work in your portfolio.

EQ ESSENTIAL QUESTION:

What Do You Do to Make an Impression?

Never let pride be your guiding principle.
Let your accomplishments speak for you.

—MORGAN FREEMAN

A thousand words will not leave so deep
an impression as one deed.

—HENRIK IBSEN

Critical Viewing
A young couple enjoys Fourth of July fireworks from an abandoned railroad platform in New York City, United States. They have found something rare in America's largest city—space. In what other ways might this experience be making an impression on them?

MAKING IMPRESSIONS

EQ ESSENTIAL QUESTION:
What Do You Do to Make an Impression?

Study the Facts
People start to form an impression of you the moment they meet you. What do you think they notice? Look at these facts:

Making Impressions

People form a first impression in about four minutes.

- First they notice your eye contact and body language as well as appearance and clothing.

- Then they notice how you speak—your tone, how fast you talk, how loudly you speak, and how you pronounce your words.

- Finally, they listen to *what* you say.

When people listen to you,

- 7% of what they learn comes from the words you use

- 38% of what they learn comes from the sound of your voice

- 55% of what they learn comes from your body language and facial expressions.

Source: Connie Glaser, "First Impressions," *bizjournals*; January 23, 2006

Analyze and Discuss

1. What can you do to make a positive impression on the people you meet? When is it most important to make a positive impression?

2. How much can you really control what people think of you?

Discuss these questions with a group. Explain your opinions and support your statements with examples and evidence from your own experience.

EQ ESSENTIAL QUESTION
In this unit, you will explore the **Essential Question** in class through reading, discussion, research, and writing. Keep thinking about the question outside of school, too.

1 Plan a Project

Skit

In this unit, you will write and perform a skit, or short play, about the Essential Question. To get started, read other scripts and notice the setting, the characters, and the dialogue.

Study Skills Pick a group and group director. Have each group member contribute ideas for dialogue, characters, and the setting. Use the forms on myNGconnect.com to plan your time and to prepare the content.

Team Work Join in, share information, and listen to other team members' ideas. Make plans and important decisions as a group.

myNGconnect.com
▸ Planning forms
▸ Sample scripts
▸ Scheduler
▸ Rubric

2 Choose More to Read

These readings provide different answers to the Essential Question. Choose a book and online selections to read during the unit. Afterwards, compare the theme or message of the book you read to a classical, traditional, or mythical story you have read.

The Code: The 5 Secrets of Teen Success
by Mawi Asgedom

As a teenager, Mawi Asgedom was a shy refugee from Ethiopia. Then he discovered a way to take control of his life. Asgedom built a better future for himself. Now he can help you build one, too. What are you waiting for?

▸ NONFICTION

The Friends
by Rosa Guy

Everything seems to be going wrong for Phyllisia. Her classmates hate her. Her father and sister do not seem to care about her. And Phyllisia's mother has an awful secret. Phyllisia needs a friend. Edith is nice, but she's poor and unpopular. Should Phyllisia be Edith's friend?

▸ NOVEL

Novio Boy
by Gary Soto

Rudy has a date with an older girl! He wants to impress her, but he needs help. Rudy's friend Alex and his Uncle Juan tell him what to do. His mom lends him money. Will Rudy survive his first date?

▸ DRAMA

myNGconnect.com
◗ Try some games that "break the ice," or help people get to know each other.
◗ Read about rules of etiquette, or how to behave in certain situations.
◗ Find out how to make a good first impression when applying for a job.

Plays are stories brought to life by actors. Read this short script. Bring it to life in your mind as you read. Then read the script aloud with two classmates. Clarify any unfamiliar words or ideas and summarize the action.

DEMO TEXT

Gone!

Act 1

A shopping mall parking garage.

OLIVIA. [*holding several shopping bags*] Do you see that guy over there? Does he look familiar to you?

STACY. [*searching the pockets of her jeans*] Where's the car? Isn't this where we parked?

OLIVIA. Maybe it was on a different level. He looks so familiar.

STACY. No. It was here. I'm sure it was here.

OLIVIA. Press the remote on the key. The alarm will beep. That guy is so cute.

STACY. The key! Where's the key? Olivia, I don't have the key!

OLIVIA. Maybe he's in a band or—what do you mean you don't have the key?

STACY. I left it in the car! I didn't lock the car! The key was in it!

OLIVIA. What? Oh—he's looking this way.

STACY. It's your fault. You kept saying we had to get to the mall before our friends left.

OLIVIA. It's my fault? Let me refresh your memory—I was not driving the car.

HANK. [*walks up*] Hi. Are you having some trouble? Can I help?

STACY. My car—it must have been stolen. I don't know what to do.

HANK. Do you have an alarm? I would think security would have heard—

OLIVIA. [*sets shopping bags down and fixes her hair*] She didn't set the alarm. She didn't even lock the car. She left the key in it!

HANK. Ouch. That doesn't sound good.

OLIVIA. Can you believe she would do that? My name's Olivia, by the way.

STACY. What am I going to do? My parents—my parents—what am I going to do?

■ Connect Reading to Your Life

Let your imagination go to work on "Gone!" Think about ways that "Gone!" is similar to stories and situations in other stories you have read. Picture the characters, the setting, and the action. You may want to close your eyes.

- What do you think Stacy, Olivia, and Hank each look like?
- Where does the action take place? What is happening around the characters?
- What impression does Olivia want to make?

How did you manage to answer these questions? Not all of the answers are in the text. You used your imagination to fill in the blanks. You staged the **drama** in the theater of your mind!

Focus Strategy ▶ Visualize

Think about sitting in a restaurant. The people in the booth behind you are having an argument. You cannot see them, but you can hear them. As you listen to their conversation, you begin to form ideas about them. In your mind, you create the following:

- what they look like
- their ages
- how they feel toward each other

You have no information except what they are saying. Your imagination creates a **mental** picture, or **image**, of the people. Reading drama requires that you use your imagination, too. When you read drama, you have mainly the characters' words to work with. From these words you can "see" what is going on.

■ Your Job as a Reader

When you read drama, the words on the page are only part of the experience. Your job as a reader is to complete the story in your mind.

- Slow down. Think about what the characters say.
- Build the set. Imagine all the details on stage.
- Choose the cast. Select actors to play the characters in your mind. You might think of professional actors, or you might cast people you know.
- Be the director. Imagine how the actors move and speak.

Elements of Literature
drama *n.*, plays—or stories that are acted out—for theater, radio, or television

Academic Vocabulary
- **mental** *adj.*, existing in the mind
- **image** *n.*, a picture

■ Unpack the Thinking Process

Onstage, actors make the characters in a drama real. They move, they speak, and they **interact** according to the script. They perform on a set that someone designed.

There are no real-life actors or sets in a script. All you have when you read a play is **dialogue**, the words that characters speak, and stage directions, or short descriptions of the set and the action. From those words you learn everything the **playwright** has to say about the characters, the setting, and the plot.

Characters and Plot

At the heart of any story are characters and a **conflict**. That's true for short stories and plays. The difference is in how the author tells you. Look at the way a writer might introduce the conflict in a short story.

> Suddenly, Stacy realized why she didn't have the key. "I left it in the car!" she cried. "I didn't lock the car! The key was in it!" In an instant, she pictured the scene at home when she told her parents what had happened. How could she face them?

In the script, or dramatic version, you learn about the conflict only through what Stacy says.

Setting and Stage Directions

If "Gone!" had been a short story, it might have started like this:

> Stacy and Olivia walked into the dimly lighted parking garage carrying their shopping bags. As usual, Olivia was lively and talkative, while Stacy was serious and quiet.

Notice how much the writer tells the reader about the setting and the characters' actions in the short story version. The playwright leaves more to the reader's imagination.

Elements of Literature

dialogue *n.*, the words that characters in a play speak
playwright *n.*, a person who writes a play
conflict *n.*, the problem or struggle that drives a story's plot

Academic Vocabulary

● **interact** *v.*, to say and do things with other people; **interactive** *adj.*, allowing people or things to act with one another

■ Try an Experiment

Drama is meant to be performed. When the actors portray the characters, they bring them to life. Each performance is different.

DEMO TEXT

Act 2

The shopping mall parking garage, twenty minutes later.

STACY. [*to Hank*] Thanks for all your help.

HANK. I didn't really do much.

STACY. You called the police.

HANK. That's nothing.

STACY. You calmed me down, and that was something.

OLIVIA. Hello? Remember me? Olivia? [*to Hank*] Did I mention that my friends call me Liv 'cause I'm full of life?

HANK. [*to Stacy*] Maybe I could give you a ride home. What do you say?

How do you think the play will end? In a group, create a script for the ending of the play. Add details to continue the theme and mood of Act 1 and Act 2 in the script.

- Brainstorm possible endings. One way to get the ideas flowing is to role-play.
- Recall stories you have read (coming-of-age stories, rags-to-riches stories, romances) and think about how those types of stories ended.
- Choose the ending that the group likes best.
- Write the script for your ending, based on your notes.
- Assign roles and choose a director.
- Rehearse the complete act and present it to your classmates.

Debrief After each group has presented, compare and analyze performances.

1. How were the various portrayals of Olivia similar and different?

2. How did watching the performance of the play compare with reading the script silently?

3. Which ending did you like best? Explain how the actors made that ending believable.

4. Which ending was the most appropriate for the style of the play?

5. Describe the functions of the script, the actors, and the director.

Monitor Comprehension

Drama How are plays and short stories similar? In what ways are they different?

Like drama, most poetry is meant to be read aloud. Listen to the rhythm and the sounds of the words in this poem. Then think about how looking at the painting of the moon affects your experience of reading the poem.

Night Sky, Gansovsky Vladislav/Getty Images

DEMO TEXT

Impressions

We think we know each other, you and I,
But we don't really, even though we try.
I look at you, and you look back at me,
But it's our own ideas we really see.
I talk to you. You listen carefully.
And yet it is yourself you hear, not me.

What comes between us, keeping us apart,
So we don't know each other's mind and heart?
We think we know each other, you and I.
But, like the moon shining in the night sky,
We use our bright and sunlit side to hide
The true selves that reside on our dark side.

■ Connect Reading to Your Life

Perhaps you don't think poetry has much to do with your life. Think about your favorite song. You probably know all the words by heart.

The words of a song, or song lyrics, are a type of poetry. Both are meant to be heard, and both say a lot in a few words. Song lyrics also follow patterns, just as many poems do. They often have **verses**, lines that **rhyme**, and lines that repeat.

■ Your Job as a Reader

Slow down when you read a poem. Listen to the "music," or rhythm, of the words. See the images. Feel the emotions of the poem. Look at images that accompany the poem. Compare and contrast the feelings that the poem and the images inspire in you. Your job as a reader is to get involved in the poem. Poetry is meant to cause you to think *and* feel.

Elements of Literature
verse *n.*, a group of lines in a poem or a song
rhyme *v.*, to repeat the final sounds of two or more words, as in the words *hide* and *side*

■ Unpack the Thinking Process

Experienced readers know that there are many **aspects** to poetry. Poems are not just words—those words are carefully chosen and arranged in a certain way.

Look at the Form

Poets choose different forms, or ways to organize their poems. Some poets divide poems into **stanzas** and follow patterns of line length. Others choose a loose **structure**, arranging words in a loose flow. A poet can even arrange words in a shape—for example, a poem about a swan with lines arranged in the shape of a swan.

Listen to the Sound

Appreciating the sounds in a poem draws you into a deeper experience with the poem. It helps you visualize the images and understand the meaning. Here are some devices that poets use to create sound:

- Rhythm, or beat. Try tapping or snapping your fingers as you read a rhythmic poem, as you might do with a song.
- Rhyme, or the repetition of sounds at the ends of two or more lines. Find the rhymes in "Impressions" on page 550.

Visualize the Language

Poets communicate ideas by choosing specific words. Sometimes they use **metaphors** or **similes** , which are kinds of comparisons, to help readers understand their ideas. In "Impressions," the poet compares "you and I" to the moon. Reread the last three lines of the poem. What is the poet saying?

■ Try an Experiment

To get a feeling for the importance of each word in a poem, try changing the words in "Impressions." With a partner, read the first line of the poem. Change one word in that line. Move to the next line and do the same thing.

After you have changed one word in each line, read the new poem. How are the sounds and images different? How is the meaning different?

Write a short original poem. Try a variety of techniques (such as rhyme) and a variety of forms (such as stanzas or shapes).

Monitor Comprehension

Poetry Name three aspects of poetry.

Elements of Literature

stanza *n.*, a section, or verse, of a poem

metaphor *n.*, a comparison between two unlike things

simile *n.*, a comparison between two unlike things that uses *like* or *as*

Academic Vocabulary

- **aspect** *n.*, a particular feature
- **structure** *n.*, the way in which something is organized or put together

EQ **What Do You Do to Make an Impression?**
Read about teens who are nervous on a first date.

Make a Connection

Brainstorm In a small group, discuss new or awkward social situations, such as a first date. What do people do to make a good impression? List your ideas.

Learn Key Vocabulary

Study the Words Pronounce each word and learn its meaning. You may also want to look up the definitions in the Glossary.

● Academic Vocabulary

Key Words	Examples
compliment (**kom**-plu-munt) noun ▸ pages 563, 566, 571	When someone gives you a **compliment**, they say something nice about you. How do you feel when you receive a **compliment**? *Synonym*: praise; *Antonym*: criticism
conceal (kun-**sēl**) verb ▸ pages 563, 570, 571	When you **conceal** your feelings, you keep them secret or hide them. *Antonyms*: show, reveal
elegance (**e**-li-guns) noun ▸ page 556	To have **elegance** is to have high quality, beauty, and style. *Synonym*: good taste
nervous (**nur**-vus) adjective ▸ page 562	When you feel **nervous** about something, you feel worried and uneasy about it. Do you feel **nervous** when you have to speak in front of the class? *Synonyms*: tense, restless; *Antonym*: calm
overprotective (ō-vur-pru-**tek**-tiv) adjective ▸ page 560	When parents are **overprotective**, they are too concerned about their children's health or safety. These parents often will not let their children try new things because they are afraid their children will get hurt.
personality (pur-su-**na**-lu-tē) noun ▸ pages 564, 566	**Personality** refers to a person's characteristics and behavior. Who do you know with a friendly **personality**?
● **reveal** (ri-**vēl**) verb ▸ pages 558, 571	When you **reveal** your feelings, you show them or make them known. *Antonyms*: conceal, hide
romantic (rō-**man**-tik) adjective ▸ pages 556, 571	**Romantic** means filled with love. A bouquet of flowers is a **romantic** gift to give to someone you love.

Practice the Words Work with a partner to make a **Web of Examples** for each Key Vocabulary word. Study the model before you begin.

Web of Examples

Your hair looks good today.

Cool shoes!

Great job on that paper.

compliments

BEFORE READING Novio Boy: Scene 7, Part 1

play by Gary Soto

Reading Strategies

- Plan and Monitor
- Determine Importance
- Make Inferences
- Ask Questions
- Make Connections
- Synthesize
▶ Visualize

Compare Representations: Script and Performance

A **play** is a story that actors perform. Plays have **dramatic elements**, such as:

- **scenes** or **acts**: parts of the play
- **dialogue**: the words the actors speak
- **stage directions**: instructions for the characters and the appearance of the stage

A live performance differs from a script. When you read a play, you create mental images of what you might see on stage. When you watch a play performance, the dialogue is the same, but you experience the play the way the director, actors, and set designer imagine it.

Look Into the Text

The character's name shows who says the dialogue.

Stage directions are in brackets. These tell the actors what to do or how to say their lines.

PATRICIA. No, Rudy. It's just a very fine restaurant. And look, cloth napkins. How fancy!

RUDY. [*studies napkins*] Looks like a diaper.

PATRICIA. Rudy, you're so silly.

[JUAN *starts playing his guitar and singing.* RUDY *and* PATRICIA *listen. Silly song, perhaps* "Tort y Frijoles."]

PATRICIA. He's really talented.

RUDY. He's OK.

WAITER. [*approaches with glasses of water*] Our special for the day is . . .

Compare the script with the production. How did the director and set designer show that the scene takes place in a "very fine restaurant"?

Focus Strategy ▶ Visualize

When you read a play, try to picture, or **visualize**, the scenes to bring them to life. Directors and actors visualize the play when they study a script before they start to rehearse for a production. Then, they try to bring the play to life on stage in the way they imagine it. When you read a play, you get to imagine things they way you see them in your own mind.

HOW TO FORM MENTAL IMAGES

Focus Strategy

1. **Find Clues** Look for words in the dialogue and stage directions that help you understand the characters and events. For example, "How fancy!" and "studies napkins."

2. **Visualize** Stop and concentrate on the descriptive words. Use the written words to create mental pictures.

3. **Sketch** Draw the pictures to show what is happening.

Gary Soto
(1952–)

Gary Soto lives in
Berkeley, California.

In the play *Novio Boy*, a young man faces one of life's most exciting moments—his first date. "I recall the intensity of being in love with a girl in high school," says writer **Gary Soto**. "I would have run my car into a wall for her. But lucky for me, my mode of transportation was my feet."

As it turned out, it was romance that started Soto's literary career. "I proposed to someone. I said, 'Will you marry me?' And she said, 'No.' I was feeling really, really bad, so I turned to poetry." Soto was inspired by what he read, and he decided, "I wanted to do this thing called *writing poetry*. In turn, in my early thirties, I discovered prose as well and wrote a couple of personal essay collections."

Since then, Soto has written many works of poetry, fiction, and drama. A lot of his ideas come from his own experiences as a Mexican American teen in Fresno, California. His stories speak to the teens of today. He says, "I think we are all the same. We might change in dress, we might change in dance or music, and we might change in [trends like] skateboarding."

Soto goes on to say that people of different times and places share more than they may realize. "We like to eat, we like to love, we like to enjoy our free time and friendship. These things don't change, no matter what."

myNGconnect.com

🔘 Visit Gary Soto's Web site.
🔘 Listen to an interview with Gary Soto.

Novio Boy

Scene 7, Part 1

Tres Besos, 2005, Joe Ray. Acrylic on canvas board, private collection.

by Gary Soto

In this play, Rudy, a high school freshman, has a big date with Patricia, a junior. In preparation, Rudy made notes of romantic things to say, got money from his mother and Uncle Juan, and even earned extra cash by selling apples with his friend Alex.

CHARACTERS

RUDY ninth grader, small, sweet, funny
ALEX ninth grader, big, awkward but wise
PATRICIA eleventh grader, tall, romantic
RUDY'S MOTHER mid-thirties, attractive and perky
UNCLE JUAN a Chicano loafer; looks like a hippie
ESTELA friend of Rudy's mother
OLD MAN crusty, but a good guy
WAITER quick and efficient

Comprehension Coach

Set a Purpose
Rudy takes Patricia to a fancy restaurant.
Find out what happens at the beginning of their date.

Lights come up on restaurant. A WAITER is setting a table. WAITER turns when he hears the sound of a guitar playing. JUAN enters.

JUAN. You won't be disappointed. I'll **wow** the crowd.

[JUAN approaches an empty table and with a pretend microphone he asks, "What do you think, friend?" He responds for the invisible friend, "Wow." Repeats this several times, all of the invisible couples saying, "Wow."]

JUAN. Yeah, I'm going to wow the place.

WAITER. You don't have to please me. It's the boss. She expects you to bring in a crowd.

[JUAN sits on a stool, places the guitar on his knee, and strums. He tunes the guitar. He eyes the salsa and chips on a table and begins to help himself. When the WAITER returns with flowers for a table, JUAN returns quickly to his stool.]

*[RUDY and PATRICIA walk into the restaurant. RUDY is awed by the **elegance** of the restaurant. With his back to his date, he takes out his wallet and counts his money. He puts the wallet back quickly when he sees the WAITER approaching.]* **1**

WAITER. *[looking up happily]* **Mademoiselle** and **monsieur**. Please take this seat by the window. *[pulls chair out for PATRICIA]*

PATRICIA. *[sniffs the flower on the table]* It's so **romantic**. So sophisticated, so charming, so . . . And look, a guitarist!

[RUDY sees that it's his UNCLE JUAN, who waves at him. RUDY shakes his head at his UNCLE, as if to say, Don't say anything.] **2**

PATRICIA. It's a **discriminating** restaurant.

RUDY. Do they discriminate against Latinos? If so, **I ain't** going to eat here. We'll go **grub** at Pollo Loco instead.

PATRICIA. No, Rudy. It's just a very fine restaurant. And look, cloth napkins. How fancy!

RUDY. *[studies napkins]* Looks like a diaper.

1 Mental Images
Visualize the scene. If you were playing Rudy, what would you need to do here? Explain why.

2 Mental Images
What words help you visualize what Juan and Rudy are doing? Make a sketch to show your mental image of this scene. How does doing the sketch help you better understand?

Key Vocabulary
elegance *n.*, high quality, beauty, and style
romantic *adj.*, filled with love, sweetness, and flirtation

In Other Words
wow amaze, impress
Mademoiselle Miss (in French)
monsieur sir (in French)
discriminating fancy
ain't am not
grub eat

3 Compare Representations How well do the actors in this production represent the characters as they are described in the Cast of Characters on page 555?

Students from San Antonio, Texas, appear in this 2006 production of *Novio Boy.*

PATRICIA. Rudy, you're so silly.

[JUAN *starts playing his guitar and singing.* RUDY *and* PATRICIA *listen. Silly song, perhaps "Tort y Frijoles."*]

PATRICIA. He's really talented.

RUDY. He's OK.

WAITER. [*approaches with glasses of water*] Our special for the day is . . .

[*A "mooooo" sounds.*]

WAITER. [*continuing*] . . . tender veal. We have spotted cow, brown cow, black-and-white cow, and—

[*The mooing sounds again.*]

WAITER. I'll be back to get your order. I have to see about something in the kitchen. [*leaves, pulling meat cleaver from belt*]

PATRICIA. The food's really . . .

[*moo again*]

PATRICIA. . . . fresh.

RUDY. Sounds like it's still alive. [*notices her jewelry*] That's a cute cat pin.

PATRICIA. I got it when I was eight. That's when we got my cat.

RUDY. What's your cat's name?

PATRICIA. Novio Boy.

RUDY. Novio Boy? You mean, like "sweetheart boy"? **4**

PATRICIA. [*nods her head*] Lots of girl cats find him adorable. You want to see a picture of him?

RUDY. Sure. **5**

4 Dialogue
Whose dialogue **reveals** the meaning of the title of the play? Why do you think the author chose this title?

5 Compare Representations
Compare and contrast the staging of the play in the photo versus the information in the script. Does the photo reveal anything about the scene that the script does not? Explain.

Key Vocabulary
• **reveal** *v.*, to show, to make known

Cultural Background
Spanglish is a form of speech that mixes Spanish and English words. *Novio Boy* is an example of Spanglish. It combines the Spanish word *novio*, meaning "sweetheart," with the English word *boy*.

[PATRICIA *pulls a picture from her purse and shows it to him.*]

RUDY. And what happened to his ear? It's gone.

PATRICIA. He had a fight with another cat. He's small but he's **valiant**, kind of like you.

RUDY. I'm against fighting.

PATRICIA. That's great!

RUDY. Mostly because when I fight I get beat up.

[RUDY *sits and smiles.* WAITER *approaches.*]

WAITER. Have you two decided? The steaks are grade A choice, and the hamburger is fresh ground round, premium grade. Of course, you can have chicken. We can fix it up in some enchiladas, **caldo**, or a taco.

RUDY. I'll pass on the **gallina**.

PATRICIA. [*picks up menu*] I'm **gonna** have the Texas burger with jalapeño cheese. Jumbo fries, a chocolate milkshake, a Caesar salad with garlic dressing. And a large homemade root beer.

[RUDY **grimaces at** *the prices on the menu.*]

RUDY. [*muttering to himself*] Four dollars for fries?

PATRICIA. What are you having?

RUDY. I think I'm going to order just a little bit. [*to* WAITER] Crackers and a small diet soda with no ice. I'm wrestling this year and I have to watch my weight.

[WAITER *writes on his pad and leaves.*]

PATRICIA. Same here. I mean, I'm not wrestling, but I have to watch my weight.

RUDY. No way. You look great.

[PATRICIA **blushes**. *Pause.*]

6 Characterization
What does Patricia's dialogue show about her feelings for Rudy?

Monitor Comprehension

Summarize
Use your own words to tell about the first part of the date.

In Other Words
valiant brave
caldo clear soup, broth (in Spanish)
gallina chicken (in Spanish)
gonna going to
grimaces at makes a face about
blushes turns red from embarrassment

PATRICIA. Guess what?

RUDY. You got your driver's permit?

PATRICIA. How did you know? My dad's going to let me start driving next month. Right now he lets me start up the car in the morning.

RUDY. I'm fourteen, and my mom lets me start up the dryer. [*pause*] What's your mom like? She nice?

PATRICIA. Tall. Taller than my dad, just about an inch or so. She's pretty nice. But, you know, she's kind of **overprotective**. She thinks I'm at the library right now.

RUDY. She does?

PATRICIA. She doesn't like me **seeing** boys.

RUDY. Maybe if you told her I'm a freshman it would be all right. If she comes, I can jump in a high chair.

PATRICIA. Maybe, but probably not. She thinks boys are trouble.

RUDY. Am I trouble?

PATRICIA. [*smiling*] 'Course not.
7 As sweet as you are, how could you be trouble? I mean, you're nicer than most boys, and not stupid, either. [*scoots her chair closer to* RUDY] I can see that there is something behind your eyes. 8

RUDY. You can?

PATRICIA. Sure. Your eyes . . . they tell me that you're . . . daring.

RUDY. Daring?

PATRICIA. Intelligent.

RUDY. Intelligent?

PATRICIA. Loyal.

RUDY. Loyal, too? You can see that in my eyes?

PATRICIA. It's all there.

RUDY. Can you see if I got *ojos mocosos*?

PATRICIA. Rudy, you're silly.

[*As they talk, an* OLD MAN *whom* RUDY *met while he was selling apples enters. He looks about as the* WAITER

7 **Language**
Soto writes some of the dialogue in the way that people really talk. What does Patricia mean when she says *'Course*?

8 **Mental Images**
Picture how Patricia looks and what she does here. Describe what her facial expressions should look like and what kinds of hand and body gestures she should use.

Key Vocabulary
overprotective *adj.*, too concerned about someone's safety or health

In Other Words
seeing dating
ojos mocosos stuff in my eyes (in Spanish)

leads him toward a table. He sees RUDY *and stops.*]

WAITER. [*leaves*] Take any seat, sir.

OLD MAN. [*searching his memory*] Hey, you're that **fella** who sold me the apples, no?

[RUDY, *shocked, shakes hands with the* OLD MAN.]

RUDY. Yeah, that's me.

OLD MAN. You told me I should treat myself to nice things?

RUDY. [*nervously*] Yeah, that's what I said.

OLD MAN. [*bends down and whispers loudly to* RUDY] She's kind of cute. Do you think you can **fix me up** with her mom?

PATRICIA. Well, actually, my mom is married. [*brightly*] But I'm sure that if she were single, she'd have her eyes on someone like you.

OLD MAN. That's good to know. Well, I'm going to have a seat and get a bite to eat. [*loudly, to* JUAN] Say, young man, do you know that one that goes "Ay, ay, ay"?

[RUDY *grimaces.* OLD MAN *finds his seat.*]

PATRICIA. How do you know him?

RUDY. Well, he's one of my . . . clients.

OLD MAN. [*very loudly*] Those were really good apples that you sold me. The Eve apples were really tasty. [*mumbles and then falls silent*]

[PATRICIA *gives a baffled look and then stands up when her beeper goes off.*]

PATRICIA. My beeper! It's my friend Alicia. Rudy, I'm going to make a call. Be back in a second. **9**

RUDY. Sure.

[*When* PATRICIA *is* **out of earshot**, RUDY *speaks to* JUAN.]

RUDY. *Tío*, what are you doing here?

JUAN. It's my new job. What a cosmic coincidence!

9 Plot
What is happening now in the plot? Whose words reveal this information?

In Other Words
fella guy
fix me up get me a date
out of earshot far enough away that she can't hear
Tío Uncle (in Spanish)

RUDY. You're making me **nervous**.

JUAN. Hey, she's a good-looking girl. A little older.

RUDY. Yeah, older. You ever go out with an older woman, **unc**? 10

JUAN. All the time. And even tall girls. I once went out with a girl with a two-foot vertical jump. Don't sweat it, Rudy. [*dips into his pocket for crumpled dollar bills*] Here, dude, this might help out.

RUDY. Thanks, unc.

[JUAN *steps forward, stage center.*]

JUAN. [*to audience*] Yeah, I've had a few girlfriends hang on my arm. It must have been my Chicano magnetism. It sure wasn't my wallet. [*Brings out wallet; accordion plastic picture holder falls out.*] Yeah, I've lost a lot of them. [*He picks up the folder, and looks at the photos as he **reminisces**.*] There was Teresa, Monica, Laura, Cha-Cha from Dinuba. Then there was Rachel, the violinist. Every time I complained that I didn't have any money, she started pretending to play the violin. And, let's see, there's Veronica and Cindy and Estela and, *híjole*, I forgot all about Gaby, that go-go dancer who danced on TV. [*wiggles his hips*] Then I went out with the twins, Jessica and Jennifer—that was fun, until we played tag-team wrestling and they beat me up. Then there was Lupe and Lupe's cousin, Smiley. [*gives big smile; pause*] I guess I got around, and [*looks behind one photo*] *mira*, I got ten dollars stuck behind Sara! I should have stuck with her, my good-luck girl.

[JUAN *returns to his stool when* PATRICIA *returns.*]

RUDY. I requested a song for you.

[JUAN *begins to sing, "Nothing in my wallet but a little crushed Lifesaver!"*]

RUDY. Uncle!—I mean, you! Something quiet.

[JUAN *begins to strum a softer, more romantic song.*] 11

10 Characterization
What do you learn about Rudy's relationship with his uncle from the dialogue?

11 Mental Images
Draw a sketch to show this part of the scene. How does this help you understand what is happening?

Monitor Comprehension

Describe
Tell about the old man's personality. Tell about Juan's personality.

Key Vocabulary
nervous *adj.*, restless, anxious, worried

In Other Words
unc uncle
reminisces thinks about them
híjole hey, gosh (in Spanish)
mira look (in Spanish)

[WAITER *returns with their order.* PATRICIA's *eyes widen and* RUDY *holds up one of his crackers.* WAITER *leaves after* **a *"bon appétit."*** PATRICIA *cuts the hamburger in two and offers a part to* RUDY, *who shakes his head.*]

PATRICIA. Don't be silly! Help yourself. Have some fries. Sounds weird, but I like my fries with mustard.

RUDY. Yeah? Me, too. [*begins to eat* PATRICIA's *fries*] You ever put potato chips in your sandwich and then smash the sandwich?

PATRICIA. All the time. I like the way it sounds when the chips break up.

[*They eat.*]

RUDY. [*clearing his throat*] I like your hair. You know, my mom cuts hair for a living.

PATRICIA. Really?

[RUDY *pulls a notepad from his pocket and holds it in his lap to read it.*]

RUDY. Yeah, you have gorgeously mature and exciting hair. Your mouth is big, like a fashion model's mouth. Your eyelashes blow in the wind. You smell good.

[*Smiling,* RUDY *folds the notepad and puts it back into his pocket.* PATRICIA *smiles at these* **compliments**. *They eat silently.* ALEX's *face appears at the window wearing sunglasses.* ALEX *enters restaurant, slipping a dollar bill to the* WAITER.]

12 Mental Images
What does Rudy take from his pocket and **conceal** on his lap during the dialogue? Sketch this scene.

Key Vocabulary
conceal *v.*, to keep something secret or to hide something
compliment *n.*, something nice that someone says about another person

In Other Words
a "bon appétit" saying "enjoy your meal" (in French)

ALEX. A table near those two. [*sits down, then notices the OLD MAN, who is looking at him curiously*]

OLD MAN. Say, you're the one who sold me the apples, no? [*pointing to RUDY*] With your friend there, no?

[*ALEX hides behind menu, trying to ignore the OLD MAN.*]

OLD MAN. Your friend has got a nice girl there . . . Her mom is married. No use in asking.

[*PATRICIA gets up and stands by JUAN as he strums the guitar very lightly. She snaps her fingers to the music. RUDY, wiping his mouth, excuses himself to go to ALEX's table.*]

RUDY. [*whispering*] ¡Híjole! Pat is **pigging out** and I'm pecking on crackers like a parrot. 🔟

ALEX. And the old dude is here.

RUDY. He took our advice.

OLD MAN. [*mumbling*] Yeah, you're nice boys. Good advice. Tasty apples! And the girl's mother is married. No use in asking.

[RUDY *and* ALEX *force a smile.*]

RUDY. And don't look, but Uncle's playing the guitar. It's his new job.

ALEX. *Your* uncle? Your *Tío* Juan-Juan?

[UNCLE *waves to* ALEX, *who returns his friendly wave.*]

ALEX. So how's it going?

RUDY. I don't know. I read from some notes that I wrote down.

ALEX. Forget the notes. **Speak from your heart.** What did you tell her?

RUDY. First I told her I liked her hair.

ALEX. Good.

RUDY. Then I said she has a big mouth, but a good one, a big mouth like a fashion model's.

ALEX. **Give off** that subject, homes. Talk about her **personality**. Girls like to hear about stuff like that.

RUDY. [*looks around nervously, then addresses his friend*] Alex.

🔟 **Mental Images**
Sketch where all five characters are and what they are doing. Add thought bubbles to show what each one is thinking.

Key Vocabulary
personality *n.*, a person's characteristics and behavior

In Other Words
pigging out eating a lot of food
Speak from your heart. Tell her what you feel.
Give off Forget about

ALEX. [*mocking*] Rudy.

RUDY. Her mom doesn't know she's with me.

ALEX. So?

RUDY. So, maybe her mom might find out and hit me.

ALEX. That's why you have feet. Run if you see her. I'll keep an eye out. [*reaches into his pocket*] Here, man. You can pay me back later.

[ALEX *stuffs a wad of money into* RUDY's *shirt pocket.* RUDY *smiles and gives his best friend a* **low five**.]

RUDY. You're the best, Alex.

ALEX. OK, get back in there. Turn on the charm. Don't worry about her mom. [*pause*] But if her dad shows up, then you run. I got my bike outside. ❖

14 **Compare Representations** Notice the props and costumes in the photo of this student production. How did the director use props and costuming to support the script? How do these things help support the playwright's dialogue? What do they add to a production?

Monitor Comprehension

Inference
Why did Alex come into the restaurant?

In Other Words
low five hand slap to say "thanks"

ANALYZE Novio Boy: Scene 7, Part 1

1. **Explain** How does Rudy feel about this date? How do Juan and Alex contribute to this feeling? Use the stage directions and lines of dialogue to support your answers.

2. **Vocabulary** How is Rudy's **personality** different from Patricia's? How is it similar?

3. **Compare Representations: Script and Performance** Reread parts of the play aloud with a group. Discuss how hearing the words spoken is different from reading them silently.

4. **Focus Strategy Form Mental Images** Sketch what happens at the end of this selection. How does sketching help you understand what's happening?

Return to the Text

Reread and Write Reread the text to find details about Patricia. Then pretend you are Rudy and write more **compliments** that will help you make a good impression on Patricia.

Part 2 of this scene from _Novio Boy_ begins on page 579.

BEFORE READING Oranges

poem by Gary Soto

Reading Strategies

• Plan and Monitor
• Determine Importance
• Make Inferences
• Ask Questions
• Make Connections
• Synthesize
▶ Visualize

Analyze Elements of Poetry

A **narrative poem** tells a story. Like other stories, narrative poems have characters, a setting, a plot, and a theme. The character who tells the story is the **speaker**.

Look Into the Text

What do you learn about the speaker?

> The first time I walked
> With a girl, I was twelve,
> Cold, and weighted down
> With two oranges in my jacket.
> December. Frost cracking
> Beneath my steps, my breath
> Before me, then gone,
> As I walked toward
> Her house, …

Can you describe the story's setting?

Focus Strategy ▶ Visualize

As you read a narrative poem, **visualize**—or create mental pictures of—the characters, setting, and events in the plot.

HOW TO FORM MENTAL IMAGES

Focus Strategy

1. **Focus on Descriptive Details** Look for words that help you picture the characters, setting, and events in your mind. For example, in the first four lines, you find out that the boy is twelve, he's cold, and he's wearing a jacket with oranges in the pockets. Create a mental picture of this.

2. **Sketch the Events** Sketch the image of each event. Make a storyboard—a series of drawings like a comic strip. This will help you think about the details and track the plot.

Storyboard

Connect Across Texts

In Part 1 of Novio Boy, *you read about the beginning of Rudy and Patricia's date. Read about another first date in this narrative poem.*

Oranges
by Gary Soto

The first time I walked
With a girl, I was twelve,
Cold, and weighted down
With two oranges in my jacket.
5 December. Frost cracking
Beneath my steps, my breath
Before me, then gone,
As I walked toward
Her house, the one whose
10 Porch light burned yellow
Night and day, in any weather.
A dog barked at me, until
She came out pulling
At her gloves, face bright
15 With rouge. I smiled,
Touched her shoulder, and led
Her down the street, across
A used car lot and a line
Of newly planted trees,

Classic Tiles Composition II, 2001, Ger Stallenberg. Oil on canvas, private collection, the Netherlands.

▲ Critical Viewing: Effect How does the mood in this painting relate to the poem? How is it different from the poem?

In Other Words
rouge blush, red makeup

20 Until we were breathing
Before a drugstore. We
Entered, the tiny bell
Bringing a saleslady
Down a narrow aisle of goods. **1**

25 I turned to the candies
Tiered like bleachers, **2**
And asked what she wanted—
Light in her eyes, a smile
Starting at the corners

30 Of her mouth. I fingered
A nickel in my pocket,
And when she lifted a chocolate
That cost a dime,
I didn't say anything.

35 I took the nickel from
My pocket, then an orange,
And set them quietly on
The counter. When I looked up,
The lady's eyes met mine,

40 And held them, knowing
Very well what it was all
About. **3**

Outside,
A few cars hissing past,

1 Elements of Poetry/Mental Images
What is the setting for this part of the story? Who are the three characters? Sketch the scene in your storyboard.

2 Figurative Language/Mental Images
Notice the phrase "tiered like bleachers." How does that simile help you visualize the cultural setting of the poem?

3 Mental Images
Visualize this scene between the speaker and the saleslady. Sketch it in your storyboard.

In Other Words
Tiered Placed, Arranged
fingered felt

45 Fog hanging like old
Coats between the trees.
I took my girl's hand
In mine for two blocks,
Then released it to let
50 Her unwrap the chocolate.
I peeled my orange
That was so bright against
    The gray of December
That, from some distance,
55 Someone might have thought
I was making a fire in my hands. **4** ❖

4 Mental Images
Picture the final event in the poem. Sketch it in your storyboard.

ANALYZE Oranges

1. **Explain** What is the speaker referring to when he talks about "a fire in my hands"?

2. **Vocabulary** In the drugstore, what does the boy want to **conceal** from the girl?

3. **Analyze Elements of Poetry** Discuss the poem with a partner. What theme, or message, does the poem convey about first dates?

4. **Focus Strategy** **Form Mental Images** Share your storyboard with a partner. Compare the images that you visualized. Use your storyboard to retell the narrative.

↩ Return to the Text

Reread and Write Look at your storyboard and read the poem again. Write captions for the pictures you drew. Show them to a partner and discuss whether the boy made a good impression on his date.

Key Vocabulary
conceal *v.*, to keep something secret or to hide something

EQ What Do You Do to Make an Impression?

Reading
Critical Thinking

EQ 1. Analyze With your group, go back to your **Brainstorm** list from page 552. Which ideas for making a good impression did Rudy follow? Which ideas should he have followed?

2. Compare What event do both *Novio Boy* and "Oranges" describe? Which selection uses descriptive words to create a mood and tell a story? Which one **reveals** characters and events through dialogue? Support your answer with examples from the selections.

3. Interpret Why do the boys in the selections try to **conceal** things from the girls? How do you think the girls would react if they knew these things?

4. Generalize Which date do you think is more **romantic**—the one in *Novio Boy* or the one in "Oranges"? Are first dates usually romantic? Explain your answer.

EQ 5. Assess Do you think it is a good idea to be yourself on a first date? Why or why not? Support your answer with examples from *Novio Boy* or "Oranges."

Writing
Write About Literature

Opinion Statement Do you think someone should spend a lot of money to impress a date? Write your opinion in a paragraph, supporting it with your own experiences and examples from both texts.

Self	Novio Boy	Oranges

Vocabulary
Key Vocabulary Review

Oral Review Work with a partner. Use these words to complete the paragraph.

compliments	nervous	reveal
conceal	overprotective	romantic
elegance	personality	

I have played the guitar for five years, but I have to tell, or __(1)__, a secret: I still get scared and __(2)__ when I perform. People say I am quiet and shy when they describe my __(3)__. My mother worries and is __(4)__ of me. One day I was invited to play the guitar in the beautiful home of a friend. The house was furnished with great style and __(5)__, and the people were beautifully dressed. I could barely __(6)__ my fear of playing for this audience, but I overcame it and played two Spanish love songs. Afterward, I received many __(7)__. "Those love songs were so __(8)__!" one woman said. "You played with so much feeling!"

Writing Application Think of a time when you received a **compliment** or gave someone else a compliment. Write a paragraph telling about it. Use at least three Key Vocabulary words.

Fluency
Read with Ease: Expression

Assess your reading fluency with the passage in the Reading Handbook, p. 683. Then complete the self-check below.

1. I did/did not use my voice to express feelings.

2. My words correct per minute: _____.

Grammar

Use Complex Sentences

A **complex sentence** has one independent, or main, clause and at least one dependent clause.

A **main clause** expresses a complete idea. It can stand alone as a sentence.

The restaurant is crowded.

A **dependent clause** is not a complete idea. It needs the main clause to make sense.

The restaurant is crowded because the food is good.

The first word in a dependent clause is a **subordinate conjunction**. Words like **because**, **since**, **when**, **after**, and **although** are subordinate conjunctions. They help show how the two parts of a sentence are related.

Rudy asks Patricia to dinner **because** he likes her.

They go to a good restaurant **although** Rudy doesn't have a lot of money.

Oral Practice (1–5) With a partner, talk about the play. Say a sentence followed by **because**, **since**, **when**, **after**, or **although**. Have your partner finish the sentence.

Written Practice (6–10) Use the conjunction and add a clause to make a complex sentence.

6. Rudy is surprised. (when)
7. Rudy recognizes Uncle Juan. (although)
8. Patricia orders a lot to eat. (because)
9. The waiter brings the food. (after)
10. Rudy takes out his notepad. (since)

Language Development

Engage in Discussion

Group Talk Do you think Rudy is making a good impression on Patricia? Listen to what others have to say and ask them questions. Share your ideas and opinions, too.

Literary Analysis

Compare Themes

Drama and poetry are two different **genres**, or types of literature. A play has a **theme**, or message, and so does a narrative poem. The author's choice of genre affects how the theme is expressed.

A **play** is meant to be performed by actors who say the dialogue and act out the story. Therefore, the theme is frequently revealed through dialogue and action.

Word choice is especially important in **poetry**. Poets often choose words because of the images they create or because they have a particular sound. A poet chooses words carefully to express his or her theme. Each word matters because a poem often uses so few words to express an idea.

Working in a group, compare the themes of *Novio Boy* and "Oranges." Then discuss how the theme is developed in each genre (drama or narrative poetry). Compare that development. Start with these questions:

- What is the theme of the play and the theme of the poem?
- Can you tell more about the theme from descriptions or from dialogue and action?

Idioms

An **idiom** is a group of words that, together, mean something different from what the words mean by themselves. You can use context clues to figure out the meaning of an idiom.

Work with a small group to figure out the meaning of each underlined idiom.

1. Rudy watches to see if Patricia's parents come into the restaurant. He keeps an eye out for them.
2. Rudy's mom always knows what he is doing. She has eyes in the back of her head.
3. Patricia ordered a big meal, but she couldn't finish it. Her eyes were bigger than her stomach.

Choral Reading

Literature: Poetry Form two groups and read "Oranges" aloud. Decide how to alternate lines.

Practice before the reading. Here are some tips:

- Think about what the words mean. Read with feeling and with understanding.
- Pronounce each word clearly.
- Follow the rhythm of the poem by paying attention to punctuation and line breaks.

Stand when your group reads its lines. Then listen attentively when the other group reads.

🔖 **Language and Learning Handbook**, page 616

Write a Script

A **script** is the written text of a play. It contains the characters' dialogue and stage directions that describe the setting and the characters' actions. Imagine a couple on their first date. Write a script for a brief scene from the date.

❶ **Prewrite** Try acting out the scene. Determine:
- Who are the characters?
- Where do they go? What is it like there?
- What do the characters say and do?

❷ **Draft** Write down what you acted out. Begin by describing the setting in the first set of stage directions. Write the characters' names and their dialogue. Include stage directions that tell the actors what to do.

❸ **Revise** Read your script. Ask yourself:
- Is my script written in the correct form? Does the dialogue sound like real people talking?
- Do the stage directions clearly tell the actors what to do?

Model Script

> *Mario's pizza shop on a Saturday night. Loud music blasts out of speakers. Sixteen-year-old Marcus and fifteen-year-old Anna enter.*
>
> **MARCUS.** [*covers one ear and shouts over the music*] There's nowhere to sit. I guess we should have come earlier.
>
> **ANNA.** [*pointing*] We could sit at the counter.
>
> **MARCUS.** What? I can't hear you.
>
> **ANNA.** [*shouts, but as she is talking the music suddenly stops*] I said we could sit at the counter!
>
> [*Everyone looks up to see who is talking so loudly. Anna looks embarrassed.*]

Stage directions describe the setting and the characters' actions.

A **character's name** shows who is speaking the dialogue.

❹ **Edit and Proofread** Correct any errors in spelling, punctuation, and grammar.

❺ **Publish** Share your script in a small group. Act out the scene with a partner.

🔖 **Writing Handbook**, page 698

1

2

Inside a Restaurant

People who work in restaurants prepare and serve food to customers. Small restaurants may have just a few workers. Large restaurants may hire many workers to make sure customers receive good food and service.

Jobs in Restaurants

Restaurants offer many job opportunities for young people who can work part-time as cashiers and food servers. Tips make up a major part of a server's income.

Job	Responsibilities	Education/Training Required
Cashier **1**	• Totals bills and processes different forms of payment • Checks money in register against receipts	• Basic math skills • On-the-job training
Server **2**	• Explains menus, takes orders, and serves food • May prepare some food items for customers • Places orders and calculates bills	• Experience as food server preferred • Basic math skills • On-the-job training
Chef **3**	• Creates recipes; measures, mixes, and cooks ingredients • Directs other kitchen workers • Orders food supplies and plans menus	• Vocational school program, cooking school, or college degree in culinary arts • Apprenticeship or internship training • On-the-job training

Fill Out a Job Application

You will need to fill out a job application for most restaurant jobs. Practice filling out a typical application.

1. Have the required information you will need to complete the application: your personal contact information and Social Security number, the names of three responsible adults you can use as references, and your education and job history.

2. Fill out the application neatly. Use blue or black ink.

3. Trade your completed application with a partner. Check each other's work for accuracy. Save your application in a professional career portfolio.

myNGconnect.com

◉ Learn more about restaurant jobs.
◉ Download a form to evaluate whether you would like to work in this field.
◉ Download an application form.

3

Interpret Non-Literal Language

You know the words *bite* and *tongue*. What does the following sentence mean?

> Becca has to **bite her tongue** whenever Alex offers his silly opinions during debates.

The phrase in blue type means something different from the meaning of each of its words. Phrases like this are called **idioms**, and you will often encounter them in everyday speech. Becca does not *really* bite her tongue. "Bite her tongue" is an idiom that means to remain quiet even if you want to talk.

You can use **context clues** to figure out the meaning of an idiom. In this example, the word "silly" suggests that Becca disagrees with Alex's opinions and would like to argue with him. You can also form a mental picture of the idiom. Doing so, you see biting your tongue stops you from speaking. You could then guess the meaning of the idiom.

Understand Idioms

Work with a partner. Match each highlighted idiom below with its meaning from the choices in the box. Use a dictionary as necessary.

1. Before her debate, Tiffany had practiced a lot and was sure she would win. She was **as cool as a cucumber**.
2. Sanji thought the debate would be **a piece of cake** because he had won the last one.
3. When the bell rang, Brad knew he had **to wrap it up** so he could leave.
4. No other debate team in the state can **hold a candle to** the All-Star Champs.

A. come close to

B. calm

C. to finish

D. very easy

Put the Strategy to Use

When you see an idiom, try one or more of these strategies to figure out its meaning.

1. Look for context clues.
2. Form a mental picture of the puzzling phrase.
3. Guess the meaning from the context and the mental picture.
4. Look up the idiom online, in a dictionary, or ask someone.

TRY IT ▶ Read the sentences below, and use the strategy above to figure out the meaning of the idioms in blue type.

> ▶ Earl tried to forget his argument with Devonte. It was **water under the bridge**. But Earl decided he would never **go out on a limb** and try to help Devonte again. From now on, Devonte would have to **face the music** and deal with things on his own.

🔖 **Reading Handbook,** page 647

575

EQ ## What Do You Do to Make an Impression?
Read about people who gain confidence in themselves.

Make a Connection

Discussion With a small group, read aloud the quotations about confidence. Discuss what you think each quotation means and how it applies to your own life.

> You have to expect things of yourself before you can do them.
> —Michael Jordan
>
> Nobody can make you feel inferior without your consent.
> —Eleanor Roosevelt

Learn Key Vocabulary

Study the Words Pronounce each word and learn its meaning. You may also want to look up the definitions in the Glossary.

• Academic Vocabulary

Key Words	Examples
ashamed (u-shāmd) *adjective* ▶ page 584	When you feel guilty or embarrassed about something, you feel **ashamed**. *Antonym:* proud
conscious (kon-shus) *adjective* ▶ page 583	When you are **conscious** of something, you feel its presence, or you know something is happening. We were **conscious** of the cell phone ringing in the quiet movie theater. *Synonym:* aware
desire (di-zīr) *noun* ▶ pages 589, 590, 591	A **desire** is something you want strongly. My **desire** is to travel to Africa one day. *Synonym:* wish
flirt (flurt) *verb* ▶ pages 585, 591	To **flirt** is to act as if you are attracted to someone, or like that person. Dan likes to **flirt** with all the girls, but he is not serious about any of them.
horizon (hu-rī-zun) *noun* ▶ page 589	The **horizon** is the line where the sky and earth seem to meet.
privacy (prī-vu-sē) *noun* ▶ pages 584, 591	**Privacy** means being away from others or keeping information about yourself secret from others. It is hard to have **privacy** when you share a room with two sisters. *Antonym:* openness
recover (ri-ku-vur) *verb* ▶ page 581	When you **recover** from something, you return to the original state, or how you normally are. *Synonyms:* restore, get back
• **reluctant** (ri-luk-tunt) *adjective* ▶ pages 587, 589	When you feel **reluctant** about doing something, you feel unsure and unwilling to do it. *Synonym:* uncertain; *Antonyms:* eager, willing

Practice the Words Work with a partner. Make a **Vocabulary Study Card** for each Key Vocabulary word. On one side, write the word. On the other side, write its definition, a synonym or antonym, and an example sentence. Take turns quizzing each other on the words.

Reading Strategies

- Plan and Monitor
- Determine Importance
- Make Inferences
- Ask Questions
- Make Connections
- Synthesize
▶ **Visualize**

Analyze Structure: Script

In a short story, the author can write descriptive paragraphs to tell about the **characters** and events in the **plot**. In a play, the playwright or dramatist chooses which scenes to include and uses the structure of the play, including **dialogue** and **stage directions** to reveal details about the characters and plot.

> ### Look Into the Text
>
> These stage directions tell what the characters are doing and give clues about their personalities.
>
> [RUDY, *straightening the collar of his shirt, returns to the table;* PATRICIA *hurries to the table as well.*]
>
> **PATRICIA.** Is he a friend of yours?
>
> **RUDY.** Kind of. [*pause*] Patricia, you got a … complex personality. I mean, you're not stuck-up. You're willing to go out with a boy who …
>
> **PATRICIA.** What?
>
> **RUDY.** [*shyly*] Never mind.
>
> **PATRICIA.** Come on, tell me.
>
> **RUDY.** Who still has his G.I. Joes.
>
> **PATRICIA.** You're cute! [*pause*] You know, I saw you play baseball before.

What do you learn about the characters in this dialogue?

Focus Strategy ▶ Visualize

Sensory images are details that help you experience a piece of writing through all five senses: sight, sound, smell, taste, touch. In a play or movie, analyze what impact visual and sound effects may have.

Focus Strategy

HOW TO IDENTIFY SENSORY IMAGES

1. Look for words that tell how things look, sound, smell, taste, and feel. Notice the words that Rudy uses in this excerpt to talk about baseball.

   > **RUDY.** … You got to grip the bat like you mean it, kick at the dirt in the batting box, stare at the pitcher like you hate him, and do this. [*spitting into palms*]… you got to … put some black shine under your eyes, polish your mitt …

2. Imagine this scene that Rudy describes. What do you see, hear, smell, taste, and touch?

My Response to the Text	
I see: boy holding bat, kicking dirt, staring, spitting, black shine under eyes, shiny mitt	**I smell:** dirt, polish, leather mitt
	I taste: my sour mouth, slightly dry
I hear: shoe kicking dirt, spitting sound	**I feel:** hands gripping bat, foot kicking dirt

Gaining Confidence Through Theater
from KCET *Life and Times* TV Show

"I learned that anything is possible. That's how it changed my life," says Sayda Trujillo.

Karla Diaz and Sayda Trujillo were students in Los Angeles. They were both bored with school and did not have great hopes for the future. Then Karla saw an ad for a drama project called the Community Arts Partnership. The project was led by college students and teachers from the California Institute of the Arts.

Sayda and Karla began studying acting and other theater skills after school—and they both found something they loved. At first, they were not close friends. Then their friendship grew as they learned how to work together on stage and behind the scenes.

Karla says, "It's a really demanding program in terms of the stuff that you learn. You're ready to step out to do anything."

Sayda says, "After a few years of being here, I felt even my work at school was better. When things were bad, I always felt like I had this."

Both Karla and Sayda decided to go to college to study drama. Sayda is the first one in her family to go to college and the first one to go into the arts.

Karla and Sayda have come a long way from being bored students. They have returned to the program to teach a new generation of students. Recently, they wrote and produced a play together. Sayda says, "[This drama program has] given me this gift, this power, this confidence, to believe that I can do anything and go anywhere as long as I really want it."

myNGconnect.com

- Learn more about Karla and Sayda's experiences.
- Read about other afterschool and weekend arts programs around the nation.

Novio Boy

Scene 7, *Part 2*

Tres Besos, 2005, Joe Ray. Acrylic on canvas board, private collection.

by Gary Soto

Patricia and Rudy are in a restaurant on their first date. At the end of Part 1, Patricia was listening to the musician while Rudy was talking with his friend Alex. Now they are both returning to their seats.

Comprehension Coach

Set a Purpose

Rudy and Patricia are still on their date. Find out what happens.

[RUDY, *straightening the collar of his shirt, returns to the table;* PATRICIA *hurries to the table as well.*]

PATRICIA. Is he a friend of yours?

RUDY. Kind of. [*pause*] Patricia, you got a . . . complex personality. I mean, you're not stuck-up. You're willing to go out with a boy who . . .

PATRICIA. What?

RUDY. [*shyly*] Never mind.

PATRICIA. Come on, tell me.

RUDY. Who still has his **G.I. Joes**.

PATRICIA. You're cute! [*pause*] You know, I saw you play baseball before.

[RUDY *perks up.*]

PATRICIA. You were at the playground.

RUDY. Was I any good?

PATRICIA. No, but I liked how you tried really hard.

RUDY. Well, I like baseball. It just feels good, standing in the box when the outfielders are playing in. You got to grip the bat like you mean it, kick at the dirt in the batting box, stare at the pitcher like you hate him, and do this. [*spitting into palms*] And before, at home, you got to iron your jersey, put some black shine under your eyes, polish your mitt . . .

[RUDY'S MOTHER *and her friend* ESTELA *enter the restaurant. The* MOTHER *immediately sees* RUDY, *but he doesn't see her.* ESTELA *points at the young couple—*RUDY *and* PATRICIA—*but the* MOTHER *shushes* ESTELA. ALEX *sees* RUDY'S MOTHER; ALEX *gulps and hides behind a menu.* JUAN *raises a finger to his mouth. The two women take seats quietly and hide behind menus.*] **1**

[WAITER *enters and takes away* RUDY's *and* PATRICIA's *plates and gives them a menu.*]

[RUDY *and* PATRICIA *look at each other.* RUDY *takes the menu and opens it up.*]

1 Script/Sensory Images
The most powerful action in a scene may occur when no one speaks. How does the playwright use stage directions to help tell the story on this page?

In Other Words
G.I. Joes action figure toys

WAITER. [*to his new customers*] I'll be with you in a moment.

RUDY. If you want, you can have dessert.

PATRICIA. No, I'm fine. That was good.

RUDY. [*continuing romantically*] Pat, I like your hair.

PATRICIA. Thanks. I had it blow-dried.

RUDY. [*pulls his notepad from his pocket and reads from it* **surreptitiously**] You **exude cool vibrations** that make me feel like a—[*deep voice*] like a man. [*back to regular voice*] You remind me of a crashing ocean, my mermaid. Or flowers in spring.

MOTHER. *¿Qué?* "My mermaid"?

[RUDY *looks around the restaurant; his* MOTHER *raises a menu to her face.* RUDY *continues reading.*]

RUDY. You're the scent of spring—

MOTHER. Scent of spring!

RUDY. [*looks around again*] Your hands are like doves—

ESTELA. *¡Qué romántico!*

RUDY. [*looks in direction of the women*] Excuse me, Pat.

[RUDY *gets up and looks behind the menu. He is shocked but quickly* **recovers**. *He starts to walk back to his table.*]

OLD MAN. [*loudly whispers*] Hey. [RUDY *stops near the* OLD MAN.]

OLD MAN. Say, you know those women who just came in?

RUDY. Not really.

2 Script
What do you learn about the characters and the plot from these stage directions?

▲ **Critical Viewing: Characters** Actors often change their appearance to look like the characters they are playing. What characters are these girls playing? What did these girls do to look like their characters?

Key Vocabulary
recover *v.*, to return to original or normal conditions

In Other Words
surreptitiously without letting Patricia see
exude cool vibrations give off feelings
¿Qué? What? (in Spanish)
¡Qué romántico! How romantic! (in Spanish)

OLD MAN. [*in loud whisper*] The redhead is kind of cute. Go ask if she's married.

RUDY. I can't do that!

OLD MAN. What, you scared of work? I'll give you two dollars.

RUDY. [*still feeling **short of money**, agrees. He goes up to ESTELA.*]  That gentleman asked about you. [*ESTELA looks over at the OLD MAN and waves flirtatiously. RUDY returns to his table.*]

PATRICIA. Do you know them?

RUDY. [*nervously*] No, I never saw them before.

[*JUAN strums dance music.*]

PATRICIA. Let's dance, Rudy.

RUDY. Dance? No, I'm too full. Those crackers filled me up.

3 Script/Sensory Images
What does Estela look like? Which words in the dialogue tell you?

▲ Critical Viewing: Effect Stage performances use lighting to create an effect. Where is the most light in this scene? Why?

In Other Words

short of money like he doesn't have enough money

PATRICIA. Come on, Novio Boy. No one's around, except your friend.

[PATRICIA *lifts* RUDY *from the chair and pulls him almost roughly.* PATRICIA *tries to dance closely but* RUDY *struggles to dance at arm's length,* **conscious** *of his mother's watching. They dance until the* WAITER *coughs for their attention and approaches.*]

WAITER. Your bill, *monsieur.*

RUDY. Thank you. [*gulps as he reads the bill. He digs into his pocket.*]

PATRICIA. We can split this.

RUDY. No, I got it. What's twenty-four dollars and fifty-four cents to me?

PATRICIA. Next time, it's my turn. Oh, wait! I'll pay the tip!

RUDY. OK.

PATRICIA. I have to be home by two o'clock. I had a lot of fun, Rudy.

RUDY. Me, too. [*pause*] You don't mind if I'm younger?

PATRICIA. Of course not. [*pause*] Listen, I'll teach you how to drive a car.

MOTHER. Drive a car!

PATRICIA. [*looks toward the women*] Are those women talking to us?

RUDY. Nah, they're just chattering.

PATRICIA. So—you want to learn? We can practice going back and forth in the driveway.

RUDY. *¡Simón!* And I got my license, too.

PATRICIA. You do?

RUDY. Well, it's not a real license. It's a license on my bike that says RUDY. It hangs behind my seat.

PATRICIA. [*laughs*] You're a fun date. And a good dancer. 5

[PATRICIA *gives* RUDY *a kiss on his cheek. She leaves.* RUDY *looks at his* MOTHER *and* ESTELA *angrily as they slowly lower the menus from their faces.*]

---

4 Sensory Images
Reread the stage directions. Imagine a production of this part of the play. What would you see and hear?

5 Script
What do you learn about Rudy and Patricia from their dialogue?

Monitor Comprehension

Summarize
Who comes into the restaurant? What happens?

Key Vocabulary
conscious *adj.*, feeling or knowing something, aware

In Other Words
¡Simón! Yes! (in Spanish)

RUDY. How come you're spying on me?

MOTHER. I'm not, **m'ijo**! Me and Estela came here to hear your uncle.

[JUAN *strums guitar*.]

MOTHER. I didn't know this is where you were taking your date.

RUDY. You're snooping! I know you are!

MOTHER. Cross my heart. I didn't know, really.

ESTELA. [*to* RUDY'S MOTHER] She's the girl whose hair you cut yesterday, **qué no**?

RUDY. You did her hair, Mom? She knows you?

MOTHER. [*angry*] What, are you embarrassed? **Ashamed** of your mommy?

RUDY. No, it's just that . . . Mom, I can't get any **privacy**! You're here, Estela is here, and Alex, and Uncle! And even the guy we sold apples to. Everyone!

JUAN. [*to* RUDY] Rudy, it's a cosmic thing that we gathered around you. We're watching out for you. [*to* MOTHER] But we got to give him a little space, **hermana**.

[*Bug-eyed, they all stare at* RUDY.]

RUDY. Well, you're doing too much watching. **6**

MOTHER. She's a nice girl.

ESTELA. Pretty, **también**.

6 Script
What do you learn about Rudy's feelings from his dialogue on this page?

Key Vocabulary
ashamed *adj.*, embarrassed, humiliated
privacy *n.*, the state of being away from others, or of keeping things about yourself secret; concealment

In Other Words
m'ijo my son (in Spanish)
Cross my heart. I promise.
qué no right, isn't that so (in Spanish)
hermana sister (in Spanish)
también too (in Spanish)

RUDY. You like her?

MOTHER. She's a good girl. But I don't want you driving a car with her. [*pinching his cheek*] My little boy is growing up.

[ESTELA *eyes the* OLD MAN, *who has gotten up and joined them.*] **7**

OLD MAN. Say, I like your hair.

ESTELA. Thank you.

OLD MAN. And your smile.

ESTELA. That's sweet.

OLD MAN. And you possess an attitude that—

ESTELA. [*angrily*] Why does everyone think I got an attitude?

OLD MAN. A nice attitude. [*pause*] You married?

ESTELA. [*flirting*] Sometimes.

[OLD MAN *smiles, then* **is at a loss as to** *how to continue.*]

OLD MAN. [*whispering to* RUDY] What should I do next?

RUDY. Maybe you should take them on a walk or something. And don't forget to get her number.

OLD MAN. You gals care to go for a walk? And can I get your telephone number?

[OLD MAN, RUDY'S MOTHER, *and* ESTELA *leave the restaurant.* JUAN, RUDY, *and* ALEX *sit down at their table.*]

ALEX. *Mira*, she left a french fry. Here, Novio Boy. [*feeds it to* RUDY]

RUDY. **She wiped me out** for the rest of ninth grade. But **it beats** doing nothing.

[*At this,* JUAN *begins to play a song about "nothing."*]

RUDY. Thanks for helping out, unc.

JUAN. *No problema.* You're my only nephew. About the money . . . You can pay me back later.

ALEX. But me first.

[JUAN *returns to his stool and starts strumming his guitar softly.*] **8**

RUDY. I'm gonna have a yard sale, so I can earn back what I owe you and Mom and Uncle.

ALEX. What are you gonna sell?

7 **Access Vocabulary**
Here the word eyes is used as a verb. What does it mean in this context?

8 **Sensory Images**
What do you imagine this part of the scene would sound like? Look like?

Key Vocabulary
flirt *v.*, to act as if you are attracted to someone, but in a playful way

In Other Words
is at a loss as to does not know, cannot think of
Mira Look (in Spanish)
She wiped me out I spent all the money I had
it beats it is better than
No problema. No problem. (in Spanish)

RUDY. My G.I. Joes. And my baseball cards. And my basketball and my Ninja Turtle lunch box.

ALEX. Not your Ninja Turtle lunch box!

RUDY. This is a clearance sale! *¡La gran pulga!* Out with it all!

ALEX. I'll help you out. I got some stuff underneath my bed. We'll have *una gran* swap meet right on the front lawn.

RUDY. You'll do that for me?

ALEX. *Simón*, bro. We ninth graders got to stick together.

RUDY. Like tortillas *y frijoles*.

ALEX. Guacamole *y* chips!

RUDY. *¡Huevos con chorizo!* ⑨

ALEX. Soda *y* sunflower seeds!

[*They shake hands elaborately.*]

RUDY. You're the best, homes. ⑩

ALEX. Man, it's tough being a Novio Boy. ❖

⑨ **Script**
How do these similes reflect the boys' cultural heritage?

⑩ **Script**
What does this final dialogue tell you about Rudy and Alex?

Monitor Comprehension

Confirm Predictions
What was your prediction about how Rudy would react to his mother? Was it accurate? If not, why?

In Other Words
¡La gran pulga! The big swap meet! (in Spanish)
una gran a big (in Spanish)
y frijoles and beans (in Spanish)
¡Huevos con chorizo! Eggs with sausage! (in Spanish)

ANALYZE Novio Boy: Scene 7, Part 2

1. **Explain** What does Alex mean by "It's tough being a Novio Boy"? How does the script support this meaning?

2. **Vocabulary** Rudy is **reluctant** to dance with Patricia because his mother is watching. Tell how else Rudy's friends and family affect his date.

3. **Analyze Structure: Script** What new things do you learn about Rudy and Patricia from reading Part 2? Show a partner examples of dialogue and stage directions that reveal something new.

4. **Focus Strategy Identify Sensory Images** Look for words in the play that describe how things look, sound, smell, taste, and feel. Share them with a partner.

   Return to the Text

   Reread and Write Pretend that you are Patricia and that you are writing an e-mail to your friend Alicia. Tell how you tried to make an impression on Rudy during the date. Look again at the play to find details to put in your e-mail.

Key Vocabulary
- **reluctant** *adj.*, unsure, unwilling

BEFORE READING Your World

poem by Georgia Douglas Johnson

Reading Strategies

· Plan and Monitor
· Determine Importance
· Make Inferences
· Ask Questions
· Make Connections
· Synthesize
▶ **Visualize**

Analyze Structure: Rhyme and Rhythm

Rhyme is the repetition of the same end sound in two or more words, such as *date* and *wait*. In poetry, the pattern of rhyme at the end of lines is called a **rhyme scheme**. Letters of the alphabet are used to show a rhyme scheme.

You may also notice the **rhythm** of poetry—a pattern of beats, or stresses—that can give a poem a musical sound.

Look Into the Text

Read the first line aloud to hear its rhythm.

	Rhyme Scheme
Your world is as big as you make it.	a
I know, for I used to abide	b
In the narrowest nest in a corner,	c
My wings pressing close to my side.	b

Focus Strategy ▶ Visualize

Poets choose words that describe how things look, sound, smell, feel, and taste. These images express the feeling and meaning of the poem. As you read, look for **sensory images** that help you experience what the poet describes.

HOW TO USE SENSORY IMAGES

Focus Strategy

1. **Look for Descriptive Words** Place a self-stick note next to words that lead you to form sensory images.

> In the narrowest nest in a corner,
> My wings pressing close to my side.

a bird that can't move because there's not enough room

2. **Write Your Ideas** When you form the images, what do you see, hear, smell, feel, or taste? Write what you experience.

3. **Analyze** How do the images improve your understanding? For example, the image of the bird in the nest helps you realize that the speaker felt restricted.

Connect Across Texts

In Part 2 of Novio Boy, *Rudy* becomes more confident. Read this poem about another person who is **reluctant** at first but then changes.

Your World

by Georgia Douglas Johnson

Your world is as big as you make it.
I know, for I used to abide
In the narrowest nest in a corner,
My wings pressing close to my side.

5   But I sighted the distant horizon
Where the skyline encircled the sea
And I throbbed with a burning desire
To travel this immensity.

I battered the cordons around me
10   And cradled my wings on the breeze
Then soared to the uttermost reaches
With rapture, with power, with ease! **1**

▲ **Critical Viewing: Compare Representations** How does the image in this photograph compare to the images in the poem?

1 **Rhyme and Rhythm/ Sensory Images** Which words at the ends of lines 9–12 rhyme? What do you visualize when you read these lines?

Key Vocabulary
- **reluctant** *adj.*, unsure, unwilling
  horizon *n.*, the line where the sky and land or water seem to meet
  desire *n.*, something that you want strongly; a wish

In Other Words
abide live
encircled went all around
immensity huge place
battered the cordons broke the ties
rapture happiness

ANALYZE Your World

1. **Compare** What does the speaker say she is like at the beginning of the poem? What is she like at the end? Use details from the poem to support your answer.

2. **Vocabulary** What was the speaker's burning **desire**? How did she reach it?

3. **Analyze Structure: Rhyme and Rhythm** As you read the poem aloud with a partner, tap out the rhythm, or beat. Then determine the rhyme scheme.

4. **Focus Strategy Use Sensory Images** Share the sensory images you wrote on self-stick notes with a partner. Discuss how the sensory images helped you understand the meaning of the poem.

Return to the Text

Reread and Write Imagine yourself meeting the speaker of the poem. Write a journal entry describing the impression she makes on you. Use details from the poem to help you create your entry.

About the Writer

Georgia Douglas Johnson (1880–1966) published four books of poetry and other writings during her lifetime. In the 1920s, writers and artists gathered each week at her home in Washington, D.C., to discuss their work and encourage one another.

EQ What Do You Do to Make an Impression?

Reading
Critical Thinking

1. **Analyze** With your group, reread the quotations on page 576. Does either apply to Rudy? Does either apply to the speaker of "Your World"? Explain your answer.

EQ 2. **Compare** What do *Novio Boy* and "Your World" say about making impressions on the world? How is the tone, or the way the author speaks about this subject, different in these two selections?

3. **Judge** Rudy says his family does not respect his **desire** for **privacy**. Is he right to be upset, or is he overreacting? Support your opinion with evidence from the play.

4. **Evaluate** What does the speaker of "Your World" compare herself to? Does this comparison make the feelings in the poem more powerful? Explain your answer.

EQ 5. **Synthesize** Consider what you learned about making an impression from Rudy and from the author of the poem. How can you apply this lesson to your own life?

Writing
Write About Literature

Explanation and Comment The first line of the poem is "Your world is as big as you make it." What do you think this means? Do you agree with the statement? Does the statement seem to contradict itself? Is it a paradox? Write an explanation and a comment. Support your comment with evidence and specific quotations from both texts and your own ideas.

Vocabulary
Key Vocabulary Review

Oral Review Work with a partner. Use these words to complete the paragraph.

ashamed	flirting	recovered
conscious	horizon	reluctant
desired	privacy	

> In *Novio Boy* Rudy was surprised to see his uncle, his mother, and his friend in the restaurant. Even the old man was there __(1)__ with Estela, his mother's friend. Rudy __(2)__ from his surprise, however. He just wanted, or __(3)__ , some time alone—some __(4)__ —on his first date. He was aware, or __(5)__ , that his mother was watching him. He was not embarrassed or __(6)__ of Patricia. He just felt uncertain and __(7)__ about being too close to Patricia in front of his mother. He was glad when his mother and Estela left. He watched them walk off toward the __(8)__ , where the sky meets the ground.

Writing Application Think of how teens **flirt** and try to get each other's attention. Write a paragraph describing the way some teens act. Use at least four Key Vocabulary words. Before you write, create a T Chart and list ways that boys and girls are different in the way they flirt.

Fluency
Read with Ease: Intonation

Assess your reading fluency with the passage in the Reading Handbook, p. 684. Then complete the self-check below.

1. I did/did not vary the tone of my voice as I read.

2. My words correct per minute: _____ .

INTEGRATE THE LANGUAGE ARTS

Use the Present Perfect Tense

The **present perfect tense** of a verb can tell about an action that happened at some time in the past.

I **have picked** a restaurant for us.

The present perfect tense can also describe an action that began in the past and is still happening now.

So far I **have enjoyed** this meal.

To form the present perfect tense, use **have** or **has** plus the **past participle** of the main verb. For most verbs, add **-ed** to form the past participle.

The waiter **has delivered** the menus.

We **have looked** at the choices.

Irregular verbs have special past participle forms.

Present	Past	Present Perfect
choose	chose	have chosen, has chosen
eat	ate	have eaten, has eaten
sit	sat	have sat, has sat
write	wrote	have written, has written

Oral Practice (1–5) Choose from each column to make five sentences. Use words more than once.

Rudy Patricia They	have has	ordered eaten written	before many times some notes

Written Practice (6–10) Rewrite the paragraph. Use present perfect verbs.

Rudy and Patricia sat for a while. Uncle Juan waved at Rudy. Patricia chose a big meal. Rudy looks at the prices. He orders a tiny meal.

Use Appropriate Language

Act It Out Pretend you are at a dinner with a friend. Talk about the food. Then pretend you are at a dinner with your boss. Discuss the same topic.

Rhythm and Meter

Rhythm is the pattern of beats that gives poetry its musical quality. The repetition of sounds is one form of rhythm. Another form is **meter**. Meter is a pattern of stressed and unstressed syllables.

Look at this line from "Your World." Each unstressed syllable has the mark ˘ over it. Each stressed syllable has the mark ´.

˘ ˘ ´ ˘ ˘ ´ ˘ ˘ ´
Where the skyline encircled the sea

Read the line aloud. As you do so, tap softly for each ˘ and loudly for each ´. Listen to the rhythm, or beat.

A **foot** is a unit of stressed and unstressed syllables. For example, the line from "Your World" is written in a poetic foot with two unstressed syllables followed by a stressed syllable.

Read the rest of "Your World" and notice the stressed and unstressed syllables. Write the pattern for one line of the poem.

Oral Report

Literature: Compare Responses What did you think of the poem "Your World"? Use online and print resources and interviews to learn what others thought and to find out more about Georgia Douglas Johnson. Evaluate whether the sources are authoritative and provide support for their opinions. Compare your response to the reviews. Give an oral report to share what you learned.

myNGconnect.com
- Read a review of "Your World."
- Learn about Johnson's life.

Language and Learning Handbook, page 616

Idioms

On page 585, Rudy tells Alex, "She wiped me out." Phrases like this are called **idioms**. Idioms mean something different from the literal, or exact, meanings of their words. To figure out the meaning of an unfamiliar idiom:

1. **Study the context of the phrase.** Text that comes after the phrase tells how Rudy has to pay back money.

2. **Predict the meaning.** The date cost Rudy a lot of money. He doesn't have any left.

3. **Test your prediction.** If your definition doesn't fit, revise it.

4. **Use a resource.** If all else fails, look up the phrase or ask a friend or teacher for help.

If these techniques do not work, continue reading. The meaning may become clearer as you read on.

With a partner, use the techniques to figure out the meanings of these idioms in *Novio Boy*:

- page 584: Cross my heart.
- page 584: it's a cosmic thing …
- page 584: We're watching out for you.
- page 584: … give him a little space
- page 585: … it beats doing nothing
- page 586: We … got to stick together.

Write a Theme Analysis

A test may ask you to analyze the theme of a certain piece of literature.

1 **Unpack the Prompt** Read the prompt and underline the important words.

> **Writing Prompt**
> Writers often reveal a theme through a change in a character. Think about how the speaker in "Your World" changes. Write a paragraph to explain the theme. Analyze how the speaker's change reveals the theme.

2 **Plan Your Response** Use a map to organize your thoughts.

> Title:
> How the character changes:
>
> ↓
>
> Theme:

3 **Draft** Organize your paragraph like this. Use information from your map.

> **Paragraph Organizer**
>
> At the beginning of "Your World," the character is [tell what the character is like]. Then she [tell what the character wants]. She [describe the character's new behavior]. This change reveals the theme of the poem, which is [state what you think the theme is].

4 **Check Your Work** Reread your paragraph. Ask yourself:

- Is the change in the character clear?
- Have I shown how this change expresses the theme?
- Have I used the correct verb forms?

5 **Evaluate Your Work** Use the rubric to self-evaluate your writing.

Writing Handbook, page 698

Poetry SLAM

Have you ever seen a talent contest on television? If you've watched singers or bands compete, you know how exciting it can be. The audience can inspire a singer to a great performance, but the judges can be tough. A poetry slam is a contest like that, with poems instead of songs. Here is how to compete in a poetry slam:

1. Choose a Poem

Choose a poem that you enjoy reading and understand the meaning of. These qualities make a poem good for a poetry slam:

- It has a strong rhythm, like a song.
- It has a strong effect on your emotions. It might make you feel very happy, angry, or excited.
- It is short enough to recite in less than two minutes.
- It has ideas or themes that are appropriate for the audience.

2. Practice Speaking the Poem

Practice until you can say the poem well enough to achieve these goals:

- Speak the poem from memory or from brief notes.
- Emphasize the rhythm of the poem. Find the beat behind the words.
- Show the emotions the poem makes you feel.
- Stress the important words.

3. Perform the Poem

Speak the poem in a way that will make the audience like it as much as you do. Use these techniques:

- Make eye contact with the people in the audience.
- Look around the room as you speak, so that you speak to each person.
- Use facial expressions and gestures to show your emotions.
- Speak clearly, so that the audience can understand you.

myNGconnect.com
↻ **Download the rubric.**

4. Rate the Performers

Use the rubric to rate the performers, including yourself.

Poetry Slam Rubric

Scale	Content of the Poem	Speaker's Preparation	Speaker's Delivery
3 Great	• It grabbed my attention. • It had a strong effect on my emotions.	• Memorized the poem • Understood the poem fully	• Spoke in the rhythm of the poem • Spoke clearly and emphasized important words
2 Good	• It was interesting. • It had an effect on my emotions.	• Used brief notes • Understood most of the poem	• Tried to speak in the rhythm of the poem • Spoke all words clearly
1 Needs Work	• It was not interesting. • It did not affect me.	• Had to read the poem • Did not understand the poem	• Hesitated and stumbled • Was not clear

DO IT ▶ Now that you know how to perform poetry, perform your own poetry in a poetry slam!

◗ Language and Learning Handbook, page 616

What techniques is this student using to perform his poem?

EQ

What Do You Do to Make an Impression?
Meet people who are or who want to be unforgettable.

Make a Connection

Quickwrite When people do something important or valuable, we say that they have "made their mark" on the world. How would you like to make your mark? Take five minutes to answer these questions. What kind of success would you like to have in the future? What would you like people to remember about you?

Learn Key Vocabulary

Study the Words Pronounce each word and learn its meaning. You may also want to look up the definitions in the Glossary.

● Academic Vocabulary

Key Words	Examples
anonymous (u-**no**-nu-mus) *adjective* ▶ page 607	An **anonymous** person is someone who is not known or identified. For example, if no one knows who sent a gift, the gift giver is **anonymous**. *Synonyms:* unknown, unnamed; *Antonyms:* recognized, identified
conquer (**kon**-kur) *verb* ▶ page 600	To **conquer** something is to beat or defeat it. *Synonym:* overpower
● **contribute** (kun-**tri**-byūt) *verb* ▶ page 603	When you **contribute** to a project, you help and add your ideas. *Synonyms:* give, donate; *Antonym:* take away
encouragement (in-**kur**-ij-munt) *noun* ▶ page 601	When people give you hope or support, they give you **encouragement**. When a teacher says that I do a good job, it gives me **encouragement**. *Synonyms:* praise, approval
imperfection (im-pur-**fek**-shun) *noun* ▶ page 605	If a new shirt has an **imperfection**, it has something wrong with it, like a rip or a hole. *Synonyms:* defect, problem
inspire (in-**spīr**) *verb* ▶ pages 600, 608, 611	To **inspire** people is to fill them with a feeling or a desire to do something. Who **inspires** you to do well? *Synonym:* encourage; *Antonym:* discourage
overcome (ō-vur-**kum**) *verb* ▶ pages 600, 609	To **overcome** a problem is to solve it. I have **overcome** my fear of speaking in front of the class because I practiced my speech with my friends first.
unforgettable (un-fur-**ge**-tu-bul) *adjective* ▶ pages 600, 603, 609	When something is **unforgettable**, it will not leave your mind. My first visit to the Grand Canyon was **unforgettable**. I will always remember it. *Synonym:* memorable

Practice the Words Work with a partner to make a **Category Chart**. Put the Key Vocabulary words in groups according to part of speech: adjective, noun, or verb. Then write four sentences using Key Vocabulary words from two or more groups. For example: *An unforgettable* person *inspired* me and gave me strength.

Category Chart

Adjective	Noun	Verb
anonymous		conquer

BEFORE READING **To Helen Keller**

letter by Ernst Papanek
poem by Langston Hughes

Reading Strategies

· Plan and Monitor
· Determine Importance
· Make Inferences
· Ask Questions
· Make Connections
· Synthesize
▶ Visualize

Analyze Style

Writers can use different **styles** to deliver the same message. Style is a particular way of writing. It includes a writer's choice of words and type of sentences. Some writers use simple words and short sentences. Others use fancy words and long, complex sentences.

Look Into the Text

Hughes uses simple, everyday words in this poem.

She,
In the dark,
Found light
Brighter than many ever see.

Which kind of sentence does Hughes use here—simple or complex?

Focus Strategy ▶ Visualize

When you read, you see pictures in your mind. These pictures create feelings, or **emotional responses**, in you. Your own experiences, as well as your imagination, help form your emotional responses.

HOW TO IDENTIFY EMOTIONAL RESPONSES

Focus Strategy

1. **Make a Double-Entry Journal** As you read, write words and phrases that make a picture in your mind.

2. **Visualize** Focus on each mental image. How does it make you feel?

3. **Respond** Describe your emotional response in your journal.

Double-Entry Journal

Words and Phrases	My Response
In the dark, Found light	This reminds me of feeling for a light switch in a dark room. I felt nervous at first, then relieved when the lights came on.

Helen Keller
(1880–1968)

*The most important day
I remember in all my life
is the one on which my
teacher came to me.*

Helen **Keller** taught the world to respect people who are blind and deaf. Her inspiration came from her own life. When she was a baby, she lost her vision and hearing. The tragedy "closed my eyes and ears and plunged me into the unconsciousness of a newborn baby," Helen Keller said.

Keller's parents tried many ways to help her. Then, when she was seven, her parents hired a tutor named Anne Sullivan.

Sullivan was partially blind and had gone to a school for the blind. She had learned a form of sign language, which she taught to her new pupil. Soon Keller was using her fingers to spell words, but she didn't understand what the letters meant. All that changed one morning at the water pump. As Keller held one hand under the cold, running water, Sullivan spelled "W-A-T-E-R" into Keller's other hand. Keller suddenly understood! The feeling of running water had turned into a word. On that day, Keller learned thirty words.

From then on, her mind raced ahead. She learned to speak when she was ten. When she was twenty, she entered college. Later, Helen Keller gave speeches around the world and helped raise money for the American Foundation for the Blind. She received dozens of awards, including the Presidential Medal of Freedom.

myNGconnect.com

🔵 **Read more about Helen Keller.**
🔵 **Read about her work for the American Foundation for the Blind.**

To Helen Keller

Helen Keller spoke to
the world through her
courage and kindness,
but what has the world
said to Helen Keller?
Here are the thoughts
of a professor and a poet.

 Comprehension Coach

Letter to Helen Keller

Professor Ernst Papanek wrote this letter to Helen Keller.
He thanks Helen for an inspiring visit she made to children
in Italy who had been injured during World War II.

June 28, 1965

Dear Helen,

In my mind I can still see you clearly, standing for hours talking to the students and answering their questions. The questions were not always the most intelligent ones. For instance: "How can you ride horseback when you can't see where the horse is going?" But you gave a wonderful answer. "I just hold onto the horse and let him run wherever he wishes!" And you and the children had a good laugh over this description. **1** Or when you said that after you had learned to speak, you became **a real blabbermouth**!

It was **unforgettable** and moving to see you touch the face of a blind child or kiss the face of a crippled one. How your face expressed your feelings. And how your love **inspired** the children to carry on in spite of the huge problems they had to **overcome**. You pushed them in the direction of a happier life. You were able to lead them because you had **conquered** your own handicaps and you were concerned with theirs. **2**

1 Style/Emotional Responses
In addition to descriptive sentences, what does Papanek use to tell about this event? How does his style help you see and feel what happened that day?

2 Visualize/ Emotional Responses
Write descriptive phrases from this paragraph in your journal. Picture the scenes. Describe your emotional responses.

Key Vocabulary
unforgettable *adj.*, not able to leave your mind; memorable
inspire *v.*, to encourage or influence
overcome *v.*, to solve a problem
conquer *v.*, to beat, to defeat

In Other Words
a real blabbermouth very talkative

It doesn't sound good enough when I say this. But thank you for what you did for those children, and for all mankind, after that terrible war. Many people have found strength, **encouragement**, and help in your kindness and goodness.

Gratefully yours,
Ernst Papanek

3 Style
How would you describe Papanek's style? Is the letter friendly or formal? Does the writer mostly use long, flowing sentences or short, choppy ones?

In 1946, Helen Keller began a world tour to raise funds to help blind people. In eleven years she traveled to thirty-five countries. Everywhere she went, people crowded around to see her. Here she is shown in Melbourne, Australia.

The radio was a new invention in the early 1900s. Helen Keller realized how important it could be for blind people. In a speech at the Lions Club, she asked business people to help pay for radios for poor blind children in New York City.

Key Vocabulary
encouragement *n.*, hope, support, praise

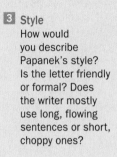
Monitor Comprehension

Describe
What event does Papanek tell about in his letter? Describe the scene.

Helen Keller

by Langston Hughes

She,
In the dark,
Found light
Brighter than many ever see.
5 She,
Within herself,
Found loveliness,
Through the soul's own mastery.
And now the world receives
10 From her dower:
The message of the strength
Of inner power. **4** ❖

4 Style
How would you describe the poet's style in lines 9–12? Is it simple or complicated? Is the speaker's tone playful or serious?

In Other Words
her dower gifts she left behind

Cultural and Historical Background
Historically, a *dower*, or *dowry*, was property a woman brought to her husband when they married, or the property a man gave to or for a bride. Many cultures have practiced such customs. In recent times, a dower is property left to surviving family. Helen Keller never married.

Helen Keller graduated from Radcliffe College in 1904, earning a bachelor of arts degree. As the first blind and deaf person to attend college, she helped pave the way for others with disabilities.

ANALYZE To Helen Keller

1. **Explain** According to Hughes, what gift did Helen Keller **contribute** to the world? Include specific words and phrases from the poem in your answer.

2. **Vocabulary** Who do you think was **unforgettable** to Helen Keller? Explain.

3. **Analyze Style** With a partner, compare the two writers' styles in this selection. Find examples in the text to support your ideas.

4. **Focus Strategy Identify Emotional Responses** Review your **Double-Entry Journal**. Share your most memorable emotional response.

⮌ Return to the Text

Reread and Write Imagine that you were one of the children that Helen Keller visited after World War II. Write a letter to Keller. Tell about the impression she made on you. Look again at the texts to get ideas.

Key Vocabulary
● **contribute** *v.*, to give, to donate

BEFORE READING Marked and Dusting

poems by Carmen Tafolla and Julia Alvarez

Reading Strategies

· Plan and Monitor
· Determine Importance
· Make Inferences
· Ask Questions
· Make Connections
· Synthesize
▶ **Visualize**

Analyze Word Choice: Figurative Language

Figurative language expresses an idea that is different from the literal meaning. Poets use figurative language to spark the reader's imagination by expressing ideas in vivid and original ways. Here are four kinds of figurative language:

- **simile**: compares two unlike things using the words *like* or *as* (The sun is like a glowing flame.)
- **metaphor**: compares two unlike things, usually by saying that one thing is the other (The sun is a gold coin.)
- **allegory**: a type of extended metaphor in which each object or person corresponds to an object or person outside the poem
- **personification**: gives human traits to animals, things, or ideas (The sun raises its head.)
- **symbol**: makes one thing stand for another thing (She is the sun and moon to me.)

Look Into the Text

Each morning I wrote my name
on the dusty cabinet, then crossed
the dining table in script, scrawled
in capitals on the backs of chairs,
practicing signatures like scales
while Mother followed, squirting
linseed from a burping can
into a crumpled-up flannel.

This **simile** compares writing a signature to practicing musical scales.

Why is this an example of **personification**?

Focus Strategy ▶ Visualize

Poets want to create certain **emotional responses**, or feelings, in their readers. They use specific language to try to do this. As you read "Marked" and "Dusting," think about the feelings the poets are trying to create. Decide whether they are successful.

HOW TO ASSESS EMOTIONAL RESPONSES

Focus Strategy

Read the excerpt above. Think about these questions:

1. What words lead you to form images? For example, do the words *dusty cabinet* create an image in your mind?

2. Does the image create an emotional response in you? If so, how do you feel?

3. How well do the poet's words lead you to an emotional response?

> I see my finger writing in the dust. I feel powerful and a little magical. The poet easily led me to these feelings.

Connect Across Texts

Helen Keller made a strong impression on those around her.
Read how these two poets feel about making a mark in the world.

Marked

by Carmen Tafolla

Never write with pencil,
m'ija.
It is for those
who would
5   erase. **1**
Make your mark proud
        and open,
Brave,
            beauty folded into
10   its imperfection,
Like a piece of turquoise
        marked.

Never write
with pencil,
15   m'ija.
Write with ink
        or mud,
or berries grown in
gardens never owned,
20   or, sometimes,
        if necessary,
        blood.

Clearing the bark from sticks and arranging it in swirling patterns, 2003, Strijdom van der Merwe. Land art/photo documentation, Kamiyama, Tokushima, Japan.

1 Figurative Language
In lines 1–5, what object does the poet use to symbolize making a temporary mark on the world?

◀ Critical Viewing: Symbol
Are these sticks like the marks made with a pencil in the poem? Why or why not?

Key Vocabulary
imperfection n., defect, problem

About the Writer

Carmen Tafolla (1951–) grew up in San Antonio, Texas, and started writing poetry when she was a teen. She still lives in San Antonio, in a century-old house with her husband and mother. Tafolla writes fiction as well as poetry. She is also a professor and a public speaker.

Dusting

by Julia Alvarez

Each morning I wrote my name
on the dusty cabinet, then crossed
the dining table in script, scrawled
in capitals on the backs of chairs,

5   practicing signatures like scales
while Mother followed, squirting
linseed from a burping can
into a crumpled-up flannel. **2**

2 Emotional Responses
What is your emotional response to the image of the mother dusting? How well do the author's words lead you to this feeling?

In Other Words
scrawled wrote
scales music notes played for practice
linseed furniture polish
flannel cloth

She erased my fingerprints

10 from the bookshelf and rocker,

polished mirrors on the desk

scribbled with my alphabets.

My name was swallowed in the towel

with which she jeweled the table tops. 3

15 The grain surfaced in the oak

and the pine grew luminous.

But I refused with every mark

to be like her, anonymous. ❖

3 Figurative
Language
What kind of
figurative language
is the poet using in
lines 13–14?

Key Vocabulary
anonymous *adj.*, unknown,
unnamed

About the Writer

Julia Alvarez (1950–) is the author of many
novels and books of poetry. Her family moved
from the Dominican Republic to New York when
she was ten. Alvarez believes that learning
English helped her become a writer. "I had to
pay close attention to each word," she says.

ANALYZE Marked and Dusting

1. **Explain** How does the speaker of "Dusting" feel about her mother? Explain your answer with words and phrases from the poem.

2. **Vocabulary** What do both speakers **inspire** readers to do?

3. **Analyze Word Choice: Figurative Language** What does *blood* symbolize in "Marked"? What does *dusting* symbolize in "Dusting"?

4. **Focus Strategy** **Assess Emotional Responses** Which poet was more successful in creating emotional responses in you? Explain how the poet led you to your responses.

Return to the Text

Reread and Write What do you think each speaker would say about the other's idea of making an impression? Reread both poems. Then write a quotation for each speaker, telling what she would say about the other's poem.

Key Vocabulary
inspire *v.*, to encourage or influence

EQ What Do You Do to Make an Impression?

Critical Thinking

EQ 1. Analyze Go back to your **Quickwrite** on page 596. Have your ideas about success changed after reading these selections? Explain your answer.

2. Compare Which selection about Helen Keller—the letter or the poem—is more helpful in understanding why she is **unforgettable**? Give reasons to support your answer.

3. Analyze In the letter to Helen Keller, what does the writer say that makes the reader have an emotional response? Give specific examples.

4. Evaluate The poems "Helen Keller" and "Marked" contain several short lines. The poem "Dusting" is written in long, regular lines. Explain how the length of the lines affected your responses to the poems.

EQ 5. Judge Of the four writers you have read in this section, whose style made the biggest impression on you? Which writer created the most powerful mental images and most effectively appealed to your emotions? Give examples as you discuss your answer with a partner.

Write About Literature

Poem How do you think people can "make a mark"? Write a short poem to express your feelings and thoughts. Look back at the selections to gather details or ideas for your poem.

Key Vocabulary Review

Oral Review Work with a partner. Use these words to complete the paragraph.

anonymous	encouragement	overcome
conquered	imperfections	unforgettable
contributes	inspire	

I'll never forget Sheila. Because of her, I __(1)__ my fears and learned to walk again after my accident. She is truly __(2)__! She is a volunteer and __(3)__ her time at the hospital to help people like me. She was able to __(4)__ me with her kind words of __(5)__. I did not think I could __(6)__ my problems, but Sheila helped me look past my __(7)__ and get better! I wrote a letter to the hospital to tell them how great Sheila is. I didn't want Sheila to remain just an unknown, or __(8)__, volunteer.

Writing Application Think of someone you know or have heard about who has **overcome** a disability. Write a paragraph about the person. Use at least four Key Vocabulary words.

Read with Ease: Phrasing

Assess your reading fluency with the passage in the Reading Handbook, p. 685. Then complete the self-check below.

1. I did/did not group words properly as I read.

2. My words correct per minute: _____.

INTEGRATE THE LANGUAGE ARTS

Use Compound and Complex Sentences

A **compound sentence** has two independent clauses (complete sentences) joined by *and*, *but*, or *or*. A comma is placed before the conjunction: Helen became sick, **and** she lost her sight.

You can break a run-on sentence into one simple sentence and one compound sentence.

Run-on Sentence: Helen learned to speak and she went to college and she gave many speeches.

Compound and Simple Sentences: Helen learned to speak, and she went to college. Then she gave many speeches.

A complex sentence has one <u>independent</u> clause and at least one <u>dependent</u> clause.

<u>When Helen was seven,</u> <u>her parents hired a tutor.</u>

You can turn a fragment into a complex sentence.

Fragment: Although Helen spelled words.

Complex Sentence: Although Helen spelled words, she did not understand their meanings.

Oral Practice (1–5) With a partner, take turns saying each fragment. Then turn the fragment into a complex sentence.

1. When Helen was a baby.
2. Before Anne Sullivan became her tutor.
3. Because of Anne's help.
4. After Helen learned the meanings of words.
5. Although Helen was deaf and blind.

Written Practice (6–10) Break the run-on sentences apart. Add one more sentence about Helen.

Helen visited injured children and she helped them and she told them how to overcome disabilities. Helen traveled a lot and she was very well known and people loved her.

Analyze Alliteration and Consonance

You have learned how poets "make music" with rhyme. They repeat the ending sounds of words, such as in *abide* and *side*. Poets also use other kinds of repetition.

Sometimes poets use **alliteration**. They repeat the consonant sounds at the beginnings of words, like this: **S**ing **s**ad **s**ongs quietly.

Poets also use **consonance**. They repeat the same consonant sounds within a line or verse of a poem, such as: *Soo**n** the rai**n** stopped and the su**n** sho**ne**.*

- With a partner, discuss the repeated sounds in these lines from "Dusting." Find examples of alliteration.

> Each morning I wrote my name
> on the dusty cabinet, then crossed
> the dining table in script, scrawled
> in capitals on the backs of chairs,
> practicing signatures like scales
> while Mother followed, squirting
> linseed from a burping can
> into a crumpled-up flannel.

- Work with a partner to write a short poem that uses alliteration or consonance or both. Include the other elements and structures of poetry such as rhyme, stanza, metaphor, and simile in your poem. Read your poem aloud to the class.

Elaborate During a Discussion

Group Talk Share your ideas about the poem "Helen Keller" by Langston Hughes. Tell more about how the words sound and what you think the poem means.

Connotation and Denotation

Denotation is the literal, or precise, meaning of a word. For example, *inspire* and *affect* have similar meanings, or denotations. A word's **connotation** is the feeling or idea that the word suggests. *Inspire*, for example, has a more positive connotation than *affect*.

Look up the literal meanings of each pair of words below in a dictionary. Then think about what the words suggest or connote. Use each word in a sentence.

1. talk/blabber
2. delighted/happy
3. write/compose
4. essential/important

Recite Song Lyrics

Choose song lyrics to recite.

1. **Recognize** Take notes as you read the lyrics. Look for metaphors, similes, personification, and symbols. Also note what kinds of words the writer uses and what the sentence structure is like.

2. **Respond** In your notes, write your response to the figurative language and the writer's style. What images do you see in your mind? How do the song lyrics make you feel?

3. **Recite** Choose the most important thoughts from your notes. Write them on note cards. Recite the song lyrics to the class. Share your thoughts about them.

❧ **Language and Learning Handbook**, page 616

Trait: Voice and Style

When you read Ernst Papanek's letter, you get an idea of what he was like. The **voice** in his writing allows his personality to come through. A writer always has the same voice but can vary his or her **style** from one piece of writing to another. Writers choose a style, depending on the topic, the audience, and the genre. Compare these examples from a research report.

Just OK

> Helen Keller was born in 1880. She became deaf and blind when she was really little. Then a teacher named Anne Sullivan helped her. Helen kept learning. As an adult, she helped other people.

Much Better

> Helen Keller was an amazing person. When she was a baby, she became deaf and blind. A teacher named Anne Sullivan rescued her from her lonely world. Helen went on to learn many things and to help many people.

Now it's your turn to use your voice. Revise the following paragraph so it shows your voice and so the style is appropriate for a review.

> Carmen Tafolla and Julia Alvarez wrote poems about making a mark. In "Marked," Carmen talks about making a really permanent mark, like with ink or blood or something. In "Dusting," Julia tells how she's writing in the dust in her house. See, she's trying to make her mark, but her mom keeps dusting it away. Julia wants people to notice her! She doesn't want to be some unknown person.

After you rewrite the review, check your work.

- Does my voice come through?
- Is the style appropriate for a review?
- Did I keep the same ideas that were in the original review?

Make more revisions if necessary.

❧ **Writing Handbook**, page 698

I Believe in All That Has Never Yet Been Spoken

by Rainer Maria Rilke

translated by Anita Barrows
and Joanna Macy

I believe in all that has never yet been spoken.
I want to free what waits within me
so that what no one has dared to wish for

may for once spring clear
5   without my contriving.

If this is arrogant, God, forgive me,
but this is what I need to say.
May what I do flow from me like a river,
no forcing and no holding back,
10   the way it is with children.

Then in these swelling and ebbing currents,
these deepening tides moving out, returning,
I will sing you as no one ever has,

streaming through widening channels
15   into the open sea.

In Other Words
contriving planning
arrogant too proud and self-important
swelling and ebbing growing and retreating

A woman lying on her back playing the ukulele by the sea, Carla Golembe.

Make Music with Your Life

by Bob O'Meally

Make music with your life
a
    jagged
silver tune
5 cuts every deepday madness
Into jewels   that you wear

Carry 16 bars of old blues
wit/you
everywhere you go
10 walk thru azure sadness
howlin
Like a guitar player

In Other Words

jagged rough and uneven
wit/you with you
azure blue

Cultural Background

Blues music was created by African Americans in the early 1900s. It follows a specific progression of sounds divided into groups called bars. Blues has had a powerful influence on other musical styles, including ragtime, jazz, rock and roll, hip-hop, country, and pop.

MAKING IMPRESSIONS

EQ **ESSENTIAL QUESTION:**

What Do You Do to Make an Impression?

myNGconnect.com

Download the rubric.

Present Your Project: Skit

It is time to complete your skit about the Essential Question for this unit: What Do You Do to Make an Impression?

1 Review and Complete Your Plan

Consider these points as you complete your skit:

- How do your characters and plot address the Essential Question?
- Which group members will play which roles?
- What costumes and props will you need?

Practice your skit at least once before performing it for the class. Don't make the skit like a speech. Make the dialogue casual. Talk as you would with your friends.

2 Present Your Skit

Perform your skit for an audience. Afterward, invite audience members to tell you what they think about your skit.

3 Evaluate the Skits

Use the online rubric to evaluate each of the skits, including your own.

Reflect on Your Reading

Think back on your reading of the unit selections, including your choice of Edge Library books. Discuss the following with a partner or in a group.

Genre Focus How is the setting revealed in a play? How is it revealed in a poem? Find examples from the selections in this unit.

Focus Strategy You visualized many images in this unit. Which image do you remember the most? Read aloud the text that inspired the image, and tell why that image was the most memorable for you.

EQ Respond to the Essential Question

Throughout this unit, you have been thinking about what people do to make an impression. Discuss the Essential Question with a group. What have you decided? Support your response with evidence from your reading, discussions, research, and writing.

RESOURCES

Language and Learning Handbook
Language, Learning, Communication

Reading Handbook
Reading, Fluency, Vocabulary

Writing Handbook
Writing Process, Traits, Conventions

Strategies for Learning and Developing Language

Listening & Speaking

Viewing & Representing

Technology and Media

Research

Test-Taking Strategies

Strategies for
Learning and Developing Language

How Do I *Learn* Language?

 1 Listen actively and try out language.

What to Do	Examples
Listen to others and use their language.	**You hear:** "When did our teacher say that the assignment is due?" **You say:** "Our teacher said that the assignment is due May 1."
Listen to yourself to perfect pronunciation of new words.	**You say:** "I see the word *privacy*. *Privacy* has a long *i* sound. Let me practice the long *i* sound to make sure I'm saying the word correctly."
Incorporate language chunks into your speech.	**You hear:** "Send me an e-mail or a text message on my cell." **You think:** "I know what an e-mail is. So a text message must be an e-mail that you send on a phone." **You say:** "I'll e-mail you. I don't think I can send text messages on my cell."
Make connections across content areas. Use the language you learn in one subject area in other subject areas and outside of school.	**You read this in science class:** Studies show that each person in the U.S. produces more than 4 pounds of garbage each day. We don't have enough landfill space. Recycling is essential. **You write this in your reading journal:** Maybe I'll do my persuasive paper for English class on recycling. I have strong feelings about why it is good to recycle. **At home, you might say:** Mom, did you recycle the empty cans and bottles?
Take risks. Use words or phrases you know and use them in another way.	**All of these statements mean the same thing:** My teacher helps me push my thinking. My teacher helps me stretch my mind to see different viewpoints. Before I make a decision, my teacher suggests I role-play different choices in my imagination.
Memorize new words. They will help you build the background knowledge you need to understand more difficult language.	**Make flash cards:** Flash cards are a great way to memorize new words, phrases, or expressions. Write the English meaning on one side of a note card and the meaning in your language on the other side. Look at the words or phrases in your language and try to say the English meaning. Flip the card over to check your answer.

2 Ask for help, feedback, and clarification.

What to Do	Examples
Ask questions about how to use language.	*Did I say that right?*
	Did I use that word the right way?
	Which is right: "brang" or "brought"?
Use your native language or English to ask for clarification. Use what you learned to correct your mistakes.	**You say:** "Wait! Could you go over that point again, a little more slowly, please?"
	Other examples: "Does 'have a heart' mean 'to be kind'?" "Is 'paper' another word for 'essay'?"
Use context clues to confirm your understanding of difficult words.	**You hear:** "The team united, or came together, after they lost the game."
	You think: "I hear the word *or* after the word *united*, so *united* must mean 'came together.'"

3 Use nonverbal clues.

What to Do	Examples
Use gestures and mime to show an idea.	*I will hold up five fingers to show that I need five minutes.*
Look for nonverbal clues.	 *María invited me to a concert where her favorite band will be playing. They are electrifying!* *Electrifying must mean "good." She looks good.*
Identify and respond appropriately to nonverbal and verbal clues.	 *Let's give him a hand.* *Everyone is clapping. "Give him a hand" must mean to clap for him. I should clap for him, too.*

4 **Verify how language works.**

What to Do	Examples
Test hypotheses about how language works.	**You can try out what you learned:** I can add -ation to the verb observe to get the noun observation. So maybe I can make a noun by adding -ation to some verbs that end in -e. Let's see. Prepare and preparation. Yes, that is right! Compare and comparation. That doesn't sound correct. I will see what the dictionary says … Now I understand—it's comparison.
Use spell-checkers, dictionaries, and other available reference aids, such as the Internet.	**You just finished your draft of an essay, so you think:** Now I'll use spell-check to see what words I need to fix.
Use prior knowledge.	You can figure out unfamiliar words by looking for or remembering words you do know or experiences you've learned about previously. Use this prior knowledge to figure out new words. **Example:** We felt embarrassed for Tom when he behaved like a clown. I know the word "clown." Maybe "embarrassed" means the way I feel when one of my friends starts acting like a clown.
Use contrastive analysis to compare how your language works to how English works.	**You hear:** "She is a doctor." **You think:** In English, an article, such as a or an, is used before the title of a job. In my native language, no article is used: "She is doctor."
Use semantic mapping to determine the relationship between the meanings of words.	jogging — tennis — football exercising — weightlifting — swimming — water — goggles — pool **You think:** Where should I place the word ball? It can attach to football or tennis because both activities use a kind of ball.
Use imagery.	Use descriptive language to form a picture in your imagination in order to figure out a word you don't know. You can draw pictures of what you imagined to remind you of the meaning of the word. Say the words while looking at the pictures to make connections.

5 **Monitor and evaluate your learning.**

What to Do	Examples
Self-monitor and self-assess language use.	*Did I use the correct verb form to tell what my plans are for the future?* *Was it all right to use informal language only? Did I use transitions to show how my ideas were connected?*
Take notes about language.	Active Voice Compared to Passive Voice • I should write most sentences in active voice. This is the most common way to construct sentences. The "doer," or actor, of the verb in the sentence should be the subject. **Incorrect**: The race was won by Jon. **Correct**: Jon won the race.
Use visuals to construct or clarify meaning.	*This paragraph is confusing. Maybe I can use a graphic organizer to organize the main ideas.*
Review.	*Do I understand everything that was taught? I should review my notes and graphic organizers.*

How Do I *Use* Language?

Sometimes you use language to clarify ideas or to find out about something. Other times you will want to share information.

How to Ask Questions

Ask about **a person**: *Who* is the girl in the photograph?

Ask about **a place**: *Where* are the people standing?

Ask about **a thing**: *What* is she holding?

Ask about **a time**: *When* do you think Anna plays tennis?

Ask about **reasons**: *Why* is the woman interviewing Anna?

How to Express Feelings

Name **an event**: I won the game.

Name **a feeling**: I was so happy when I won the game.

Tell **more**: I held the trophy over my head with pride!

Use the **subjunctive mood**: If you weren't here, I would be concerned.

How to Express Likes and Dislikes

Tell **what you think**: I like this painting. I think this painting is creative. In my opinion, this is a great painting.

How to Express Ideas, Needs, Intentions, and Opinions

Use words that **express your needs**: I need (require, must have) something to eat.

Be specific about **what you need**: I need a fire extinguisher now!

Elaborate on **why you need** something: I need some tape because I need to attach these two pieces of paper.

Use words that **signal your intentions**: I plan (intend, expect) to arrive at 6:00 p.m.

Use words that **tell your opinions**: I believe (think) the movie is great.

How to Give Oral Directions

Tell the **first thing to do**: Go to the board.

Tell the **next step**. Use a **time order word**: Now pick up the chalk.

Tell **another step**. Use **another time order word**: Next, write your name.

Tell the **last thing to do**: Go back to your seat.

Receive **feedback on directions**: Ask listeners if they were able to follow the directions. Repeat directions as needed.

How to Give Directions

Give **information**: The meeting begins at 3:15 p.m. at the library on Main Street.

Give **one step directions**: Go south on Ridge Road, then turn left on Main Street.

Provide **directions to peers**: The meeting is at the library on Main Street. It is on the same block as the school where last week's football game was held.

How to Give and Respond to Requests and Commands

Make **polite requests**: Could you please give me a pen? May I read aloud?

Respond to a **request**: Of course. You're welcome.

Make a **polite command**: Please listen carefully.

Make a **strong command**: Do not follow me!

Respond to a **command**: Of course. Certainly.

How to Engage in Conversation and Small Talk

Engage in small talk: How are you today? Nice weather we're having, isn't it?

Use social courtesies: May I borrow your pen, please? Thank you.

Ask and answer questions: Do you play baseball? Yes, I do.

Use verbal cues to show that you are listening: Uh-huh. Yes, I see. OK.

Use nonverbal language skills: For example, nod your head, smile at something funny, or make eye contact.

How to Tell an Original Story

Give the main idea of the story first: I want to tell you about my trip to Chicago.

Tell the important events of the story: I visited my cousin at her office. She showed me what her job is like.

Use transition words: First, I got off the bus. Then, I walked down into a tall, modern building.

Give details to make the story interesting: It was very cold that day. I remember I was wearing a big, warm jacket.

Retell a story: Maria said she was on her way to the library when she noticed something strange. Someone was following her.

How to Describe

Be specific by using descriptive words or phrases: I like the actor with the bright red hair.

Use descriptive imagery when possible: The room was as dark as a mountain cave. The butterfly floated gracefully through the air.

Describe a **favorite activity**: Playing volleyball is exciting and competitive.

Describe **people**: Marta has long, brown hair. She is wearing a blue t-shirt.

Describe **places**: The building on the corner had its windows covered with wood, and its yard was filled with trash.

Describe **things**: My house is large and brown. It looks like a barn.

Describe **events**: The jazz band is playing in the auditorium tonight.

Describe **ideas**: We plan to have a car wash next Saturday.

Describe **feelings**: I was bored, but happy.

Describe **experiences**: Playing guitar is relaxing for me.

Describe **immediate surroundings**: There are 28 desks in my English classroom.

Describe **wishes using the subjunctive mood**: I wish that my brother were nicer to me.

How to Elaborate an Idea

Give examples to support your ideas: All students should participate in an activity to fully experience their high school years. For example, people could join the chess club, a sports team, or the school band.

Give details about your ideas: I want to organize a group trip to the museum. We can take the city bus there. We will bring our own lunches to save money. There are many new, exciting exhibits to see at the museum.

Be as specific as possible: It takes several years of school to become a lawyer. First, you have to get a college degree. Then, you need to go to law school. Getting a law degree usually takes about three years.

How to Ask for and Give Information

Use polite requests to ask for information: Can you please tell me your name again?

Give the exact information someone is asking for: To get to the bus stop, walk down this street, then turn left at Carter Avenue.

How to Recognize, Express, and Respond Appropriately to Humor

Listen and watch for clues: For example, a change in a person's voice or facial expression might mean that the person is joking or using humor. Also, watch for more obvious clues such as smiling and laughing.

Use verbal or nonverbal responses to recognize humor: A smile or a nod of the head is a good nonverbal response to humor. You might also respond by saying, "I get it!" or "That's funny!"

Watch others to see how they react: If other people are responding to a humorous situation, then it is usually appropriate to respond to the humor, too.

How to Make Comparisons

Use compare and contrast words: The eagle is a majestic animal. Similarly, many people love dolphins. On the contrary, rats are pests and have few admirers.

Explain with details: The first math problem was difficult. But the second math problem was much more difficult. It required students to read a graph with data.

How to Define and Explain

Give a clear definition: A peacock is a large bird that is known for its colorful feathers.

Give details or examples to clarify: The large tail feathers of the male peacock are often bright green, gold, and blue.

Use a logical order for explanations: The house needs to be cleaned. First, pick up all of the toys and clothes and put them away. Then, vacuum and mop the floors.

Use graphic organizers to help explain: See the Index of Graphic Organizers on p. 772 for graphic organizers you can use to explain and define words and ideas.

How to Clarify Information

Restate your words with new words: The job is a volunteer position. In other words, you do not receive payment for doing the work.

Define some confusing words: Math class is intriguing, meaning it is very interesting.

Use synonyms and antonyms: The information in the memo is confidential, or secret. It is not public information, or common knowledge.

How to Verify and Confirm Information

Ask for repetition: Could you repeat that, please? Would you rephrase that for me?

Restate what you just heard: So, you're saying that it is OK to wear jeans to school?

How to Express Doubts, Wishes, and Possibilities

Understand the subjective mood: Verbs in the subjunctive mood describe doubts, wishes, and possibilities.

Use the subjunctive mood correctly:

- In the present tense, third-person singular verbs in the subjunctive mood do not have the usual -s or -es ending: She demands that he *play* outside.

- In present tense, the subjunctive mood of *be* is *be* (instead of *is* or *are*): She insists that the boys *be* quiet.

- In past tense, the subjunctive mood of *be* is *were*, regardless of the subject: If she *were* kinder, the boys might listen to her.

How to Understand Basic Expressions

Consider the social context:
This video game is so cool!
It's rather cool out today. It's 55 degrees.

Consider the language context: Turn right on Maple Street. The gas station will be just ahead on the left.

How to Justify with Reasons

State your claim clearly: I should be the class president.

Support your claim with evidence: This year I created a scholarship drive, organized career night, and spoke up for students at a school board meeting.

Give clear reasons that connect the evidence and your claim: My actions show that I can be a strong class president.

Combine your sentences to make the logic clear: I should be voted president of our class because I have worked hard to give students new opportunities this year.

How to Persuade or Convince

Use persuasive words: You can be a positive force in your community.

Give suggestions to others: You should listen to what the people in your community believe. You ought to consider all options available.

Give strong support for your persuasive idea: Everyone should ride his or her bicycle to work or school. It will lessen pollution and give people daily exercise.

How to Negotiate

Show that you know both sides of an issue: I see your point about the need for a new parking lot, but a park and soccer field would be more useful.

Use persuasive language: I believe you will agree with me if you consider these facts.

Clearly state your goals: We want to raise $2,000 by April and donate the money to the park fund.

How to Adjust Communication for Your Audience, Purpose, Occasion, and Task

Make sure your language is appropriate for your audience and the situation: You should choose a formal or informal manner of speaking depending on whom you are speaking to and the situation.

If you are addressing your teacher, an employer, or another adult, you might speak in this manner:

> Excuse me, Mr. Johnson. May we please talk about my research paper?

If you are speaking to a friend, you can be less formal:

> Hey Bob, can we talk about my research paper?

If you do not know whether a situation will call for formal or informal language, ask your teacher to help you.

Focus on your purpose: I want to make it very clear to you why that behavior could be hazardous to your health.

How to Engage in an Academic Discussion

Use formal speech: Please review the information at your convenience.

Refer to evidence: In the article we read, the author says that only 40 percent of newspapers have minorities as editors.

Ask questions: Why do you think that? What other options are there? What might have caused that?

Involve others: What do you think?

Express respect for what others say: I understand your opinion. Thank you for sharing that information.

Clarify and verify what others say: Can you explain that in another way? What evidence supports that opinion?

How to Express Social Courtesies

Listen politely and show interest: Yes, I see. Oh, what a good idea!

Wait your turn to speak: May I ask a question? I would just like to say that I disagree.

Use polite terms: Please. Thank you. That was nice of you. You are so welcome.

Use informal language when interacting with friends and family: Hi! How's it going? Thanks! No problem. Bye!

How to Conduct a Transaction or Business Deal

Clearly state numbers, dollar amounts, and other important details: Yes, I would like three textbooks. I cannot spend more than $50.

Be polite and professional: Thank you for your time. I appreciate your help.

Consider the context of the situation: Consider where you are and what is going on. For example, you can infer that when you are asked for your identification at a bank, the teller means your driver's license rather than a school ID.

How to Demonstrate and Interpret Nonverbal Communication

Watch for and use gestures, eye contact, or other visual or nonverbal communication.
Some examples include the following:

* waving to say "hello" or "good-bye"
* direct eye contact to show attention
* nodding to show understanding or approval
* using hands to show a number or a sign, like "stop"
* winking or smiling to show you are joking

Look for clues by combining verbal and nonverbal communication. You can often guess what someone means by watching how they communicate nonverbally while they speak. For example, you will have an easier time understanding someone's directions by watching where he or she points.

Listening and Speaking

Listening

Good listeners are able to learn new information and avoid confusion.

How to Listen Actively and Respectfully

- Set a purpose and prepare for listening.
- Pay close attention to the speaker. Demonstrate appropriate body language by sitting up straight and looking at the speaker as you listen.
- Connect texts or ideas that you are hearing to personal knowledge and experience—this will help you understand.
- Don't interrupt, unless you need to ask the speaker to speak more loudly.
- When the speaker is finished, ask him or her to explain things you did not understand. If the speaker did not talk enough about a topic, ask him or her to tell you more about it.

How to Overcome Barriers to Listening

- Pay close attention to the speaker.
- Try to ignore other noises or distractions around you.
- Politely ask any other people who are talking to be quiet.
- Close the classroom door or any windows if outdoor noises are distracting.
- Raise your hand, and ask the speaker to speak louder if necessary.
- Take notes on the topic being discussed. This will help you stay focused and self-monitor what you hear and track your understanding.
- In your notes, summarize the speaker's main idea and details. Were they effective enough to keep you interested? Was the speech's main idea easy to understand? Did the supporting ideas confirm the speech's main idea?

How to Use Choral Reading and Readers Theater

Choral Reading is a group activity that involves people reading a selection aloud, together. Readers Theater takes a story and treats it like a play. Students are assigned to read different parts, such as the narrator or a character.

During Choral Reading

- Listen carefully to how other readers pronounce words and phrases.
- Listen to how the intonation of the words changes.
- Listen to hear if your pitch and pronunciation sound like everyone else's.

During Readers Theater

- Listen to how different characters have different voices and expressions.
- Watch the speakers for gestures or acting.
- If you are the one who narrates or reads the stage directions, focus on describing where the action takes place.

Speaking

Speaking is saying aloud what you are thinking. Good speakers choose their words and use language effectively. They also choose an appropriate organizational strategy for their ideas. You may be required to speak in class during a discussion or when giving a presentation. Always speak responsibly and ethically. When you speak ethically, you are careful not to offend or upset anyone who is listening to you.

How to Manage Discussions and Presentations

To be a good speaker, you need to effectively share your ideas in class, in a group, or with a partner. There will be times when it is necessary to have a conference with your teacher or another student. In any discussion, whether it is formal or informal, there are things you can do to make it a productive meeting. Discussions are good ways to find information, check your understanding, and share ideas.

- In discussions, make positive comments about the ideas of others. Connect your ideas to what others say.

  > Interesting point! That is a good idea. Thank you for sharing your opinion.

  > I agree that people should recycle and I also think we should focus on saving water.

- Think about the topic that is being discussed. Give ideas about that topic, and exclude nonessential information.

  > He is talking about how climate and weather are different in other parts of the world.

  > There are many tropical climates near the equator.

- Ask questions if you need more information.
- Ask questions to verify or challenge ideas.

  > Can you please repeat that? I do not understand. Can you explain that again?

  > Can you give me evidence to support that idea? I respect your opinion but I think the character was shy, not scared.

- Anticipate, recognize, and adjust to listeners' needs and concerns.

  > He looks confused. I should stop and explain that concept again.

How to Give Presentations

Choose an interesting topic that will engage listeners' attention. You may make a speech, share a poem, or give a performance or report to share your ideas. Be sure to justify your choice of performance technique. That is, does it fit your purpose and audience?

Use an engaging and effective introduction and conclusion. Keep your audience interested by changing your tone and volume and by using varied sentence structure to emphasize meaning. Speak using standard English grammar and syntax. It is fine to make your audience laugh, but be careful to use effective and appropriate humor that does not upset or offend your listeners. Use audience feedback to improve future presentations.

- Change your rate and volume for your audience or purpose. Be sure to speak with appropriate pitch, stress, intonation, and enunciation.

  I will be speaking about how dangerous chemicals are in the chemistry lab. I should use a serious tone during the presentation.

- Use body language such as gestures, facial expressions, and posture while you are speaking to show what you mean.

  I want to show how tall and wide a hockey goal is. I'll use my hands.

- Occasionally make eye contact with specific audience members.

  I do not want to appear nervous or unprepared. If I make eye contact with my audience, my presentation will be natural and relaxed.

How to Overcome Anxiety

Some people get a bit nervous or anxious about speaking in front of others. There are simple ways you can avoid this.

- **Be prepared**. If you plan your presentation well, you can be confident that you will speak well. Practice presenting in front of a mirror or a family member.

- **Use notes**. Use notes, graphic aids, and props as memory aids and to support the message. Notes can guide your speech or presentation. You can refer to the notes if you get confused or forget a topic you want to discuss. See the example on the right for the type of information you can keep track of in notes.

  Civil Wars Around the World
  — Mexico, 1857–1861
  — U.S., 1861–1865
  — Greece, 1946–1949
  — Yugoslavia, 1991–2001

How to Self-Monitor

Monitoring is watching or noticing what is happening as you speak. It is important to monitor your audience's reactions, so you can adjust your presentation if necessary. If possible, tape your speech so you can listen to it before you give it. Analyze the tape to discover anything that might be confusing or inappropriate for the listeners. Use a rubric to prepare, critique, and improve your speech. Create a scoring guide that you can use to self-monitor. For sample rubrics and scoring guides, see page 662–664 and 706–714.

How to Use Rhetorical Devices

Rhetorical devices are ways to use language to make your presentation more interesting, engaging, or effective. Look at the examples below. Then produce one or two examples of your own.

Rhetorical Device	Example
Alliteration: The repetition of the same consonant sounds at the beginning of words.	Pablo prefers pecan pie.
Allusion: A form of literary language in which one text makes the reader think about another text that was written before it.	When Hannah wrote in her essay that vanity was the main character's weak point, or "Achilles' heel," her teacher understood that Hannah was referring to a character in a Greek myth.
Analogy: A way of illustrating or explaining a thing or an idea by comparing it with a more familiar thing or idea.	*Blogs* are to the *Internet* as *journals* are to *paper*.
Irony: When you say one thing, but want the listeners to understand something different. You may say the opposite of what is really true.	Your friend says to you after you trip and fall, "Today must be your lucky day!"
Mood: The attitude or feeling of your presentation. You create this for your listeners with the words you choose.	Slowly the car approached. It rolled to a stop, and a strange looking character stepped out of the back seat.
Quotation: Repeating the exact words of someone using quotation marks.	As Franklin D. Roosevelt said, "The only thing we have to fear is fear itself."
Pun: A humorous use of words that have more than one meaning.	To write with a broken pencil is *point*-less.
Parallelism: Similarity of structure in a pair or series of related words, phrases, or sentences.	We can change our school. We can make a difference. We can do this together.
Repetition: Repeating words, phrases, or ideas. Using this device shows your listeners that you believe the idea is very important.	All people are entitled to freedom. Freedom is something everyone deserves. Freedom will make the world a better place.
Tone: A speaker's attitude toward the topic, audience, or self.	I am definitely not in favor of a shorter lunch period.

Monitoring Your Understanding of Visuals

You encounter visual elements constantly—in print, on TV, on the Internet, and in movies. How can you make sure you accurately understand and interpret what you see? Does the visual enhance your understanding of the oral presentation? Use the following strategies to self-monitor, or check that you understand, what you are viewing.

How to View and Look for Details

Study the image below. Ask these kinds of questions:

- Who or what does the image show? Are there other details that answer *when*, *where*, *why*, or *how* questions about the image?
- How does the image make me feel? Do I enjoy looking at it? Does it worry me, make me laugh, or give me a good or bad feeling?
- What do the details and elements (such as shape, color, and size of the image) add to the meaning?

How to Respond to and Interpret Visuals and Informational Graphics

When you view visuals and informational graphics, think about why they are included and what information they provide. Informational graphics often present facts or statistics. For example, you will sometimes see illustrations or informational graphics used in an oral presentation. Ask yourself:

- What message or information is the visual showing?
- Why did the artist, designer, or illustrator create and include the visual?
- Does the visual represent information accurately and fairly? What information did the creator choose to include or leave out? Why?

How to Self-Correct Your Thoughts as You View

Examine your understanding of visuals to correct any faulty thinking. Always question the validity and accuracy of visuals.

- Be aware of racial, cultural, and gender stereotyping. A **stereotype** is a general opinion that is not always true. A stereotype does not look at the differences between individual people or things. For example, "All cats are lazy." This is a stereotype because although some cats are lazy, some are very active.
- Look again at the image or graphic for more information and details that may change your understanding and for things you did not notice at first.
- Watch for **bias**. Is the writer or creator presenting information that is slanted or manipulated to show a particular point of view?

How to Understand Different Kinds of Visuals

It is important to be familiar with the different kinds of visuals that illustrate ideas for a text or spoken presentation. You will be expected to respond to and interpret these different visuals. Some examples are maps, charts, graphs, photographs, illustrations, and other artwork. As you look at a visual, decide what it is telling you. Visuals should help you better understand the information, especially if the language is elaborate or complex.

Map

A map is a visual layout of a specific location. Maps are an excellent way to gain more information about an idea presented in text.

Graphic Displays

A chart or a graph can show comparisons or provide information more clearly than if the same statistics were only presented in a text. Be sure to evaluate the credibility of the source of the data.

Chart

Number of Endangered Species in the United States	
Classification	Number of Species
Mammals	70
Birds	76
Reptiles	13
Fish	74
Insects	47

Graph

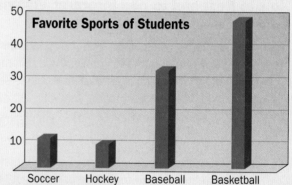

Photographs, Illustrations, Video, Sound, and Artwork

Photographs, illustrations, and other artwork can have a variety of purposes:

- to share an opinion
- to elicit, or draw out, emotions
- to make people think
- to entertain

Multimedia resources include sound, motion, special effects, audio, and visuals. Use what you see and hear. Think about how the creator of a video or media presentation uses music or effects to make a point. Animations and other interactive media change based on what you click or touch.

Using Visuals and Multimedia in Writing and Presenting

Here are some key points to keep in mind when you choose to represent your ideas by using a visual or other media.

Representing Your Ideas Through Visuals

Using visuals in your writing and oral presentations can help you make your point more clearly. Choose visuals that match your purpose and your topic. Strong visuals will make a strong impression. Music and sound effects in multimedia presentations also impact tone and can be used to emphasize ideas or information. For example, if you choose to illustrate a poem about nature, include a picture that will help readers picture the place or feel the mood of the poem.

How Key Elements of Design Create Meaning and Influence the Message

Different visuals share information in different ways.

- If your goal is to entertain, choose a humorous picture.

"Is this seat taken?"

- If your goal is to inform, use a visual that gives additional information about your topic or clarifies the information in some way. See the Index of Graphic Organizers on page 800 for ideas of ways to share information in graphic form.

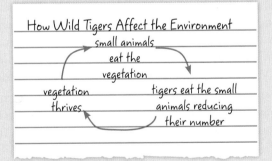

How Wild Tigers Affect the Environment

small animals eat the vegetation → tigers eat the small animals reducing their number → vegetation thrives →

- If your goal is to persuade, or to make people feel or think a certain way, you may want to choose a visual that will appeal to emotions.

- If you use a visual from another source, be sure to identify the source.

The Effects of Visual Arts on Mood

When you choose a visual to represent information in an essay or an oral presentation, make sure it is a visual that your particular audience will understand. A complex graph may not work well if your viewers do not know a lot about your topic. Creating a simple visual is especially important if you have an elaborate presentation. Your audience should be able to use the visual to make sense of the presentation. Make sure it is a visual you would want to view yourself.

In addition, consider the mood that you want the visual to create. The mood should be appropriate to your purpose and audience, such as a classroom of students listening to your oral presentation. If the mood of a presentation or essay is serious, do not use humorous or distracting visuals. For example, if you are giving a presentation on the United States government, you might display a graphic showing the legislative, executive, and judicial branches of government.

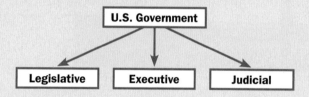

Interpreting and Analyzing Media

Media is the term used to describe the many forms of technology used today to provide communication to a large number of people. As you view media around you, such as the Internet, television, movies, magazines, and newspapers, make sure you remember the key points that are presented. What information is being presented in the visuals that are used? How is it presented? Make decisions about the information you are presented with by the media.

The information and visuals presented may be trustworthy, or they may be suspicious. In today's world, we are surrounded by images and information that we need to analyze and make decisions about. Keep in mind that visual media can easily influence our cultural and social expectations because it is much more visual than traditional texts. Be aware that you can make judgments and decisions while viewing the images and form your own opinions about the information they present.

Sometimes, the same event can be interpreted differently, based on the way the event is covered and the medium in which it is shown. Find a news event discussed in a newspaper and the same event on the Internet or TV. Then compare what is similar and what is different.

- What is the message?
- How do I know it is believable or valid?
- What information is included and what is left out?
- Is the information objective, or is it biased?

Technology and Media

How to Use Technology to Communicate

This section provides examples of the technology used today to communicate in school, in the workplace, and with friends and family.

Cell Phone

A **cell phone** does not need a wire connection to a phone network. It can be used anywhere there is a wireless phone network signal. It is completely portable. Cell phones can allow you to send text messages, connect to the Internet, play music, take photos, and make phone calls.

Personal Computer

A **personal computer** is an electronic tool that helps you create, save, and use information. You can also use a computer to communicate with e-mail, browse the Internet, work with digital photos or movies, or listen to music.

A **desktop computer** is not portable. It has several parts, including a monitor, a mouse, a keyboard, and a CD drive.

A **laptop computer** is smaller than a desktop computer. It is designed to be portable. A laptop computer usually fits in a travel case.

stylus

A **tablet computer** is typically even smaller than a laptop computer. You can use your fingers or a stylus pen to make most tablet computers work.

How to Select and Use Media to Research Information

Modern technology allows us to access a wide range of information. The Internet is a popular source for research and finding information for academic, professional, and personal reasons. Another source for research is your local library. It contains databases where you can gain access to many forms of print and nonprint resources, including audio and video recordings and many other sources of information.

The Internet

The **Internet** is an international network, or connection, of computers that share information with each other. The **World Wide Web** is a part of the Internet that allows you to find, read, and organize information. Using the Web is a fast way to get the most current information about many topics.

Any series of words or phrases can be typed into the "search" section of a search engine, and multiple Web sites with those words will be listed for you to investigate. Once you are at a Web site, you can perform a word or phrase search of the page you are on. This will help direct you to the information you are researching.

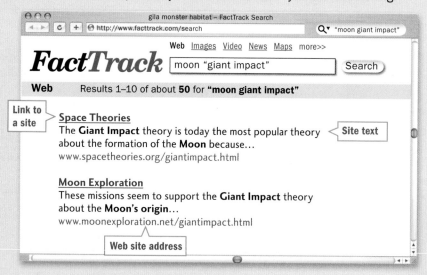

Other Sources of Information

There are many other reliable print and nonprint sources of information to use in your research. For example:

- magazines
- newspapers
- professional or scholarly journal articles
- experts
- political speeches
- press conferences

Most of the information from these sources is also available on the Internet. You should be careful to evaluate and choose the best sources for this information. It is important to double-check the source. Does the source show a bias? Is the source from a professor or from an anonymous blog post?

How to Evaluate the Quality of Information

There is so much information available on the Internet it can be hard to comprehend. It is important to be sure that the information you use as support or evidence is reliable and can be trusted. Use the following checklist as a guideline to decide if a Web page you are reading is reliable and a credible source.

Checklist to Determine Reliable Web Sites

☑ The information is from a well-known and trusted source. For example, Web sites that end in ".edu" are part of an educational institution and usually can be trusted. Other cues for reliable Web sites are sites that end in ".org" for "organization" or ".gov" for "government."

☑ The people who write or are quoted on the Web site are experts, not just everyday people expressing ideas or opinions.

☑ The Web site gives evidence, not just opinions.

☑ The Web site is free of grammatical and spelling errors. This is often a hint that the site was carefully constructed and will not have factual errors.

☑ The Web site is not trying to sell a product or persuade people. It is trying to provide accurate information.

If you are uncertain about the quality of a Web site, contact your teacher for advice.

How to Organize and Discuss Information From Various Media

Devise a system to organize the information you find from various forms of media, such as newspapers, books, and the Internet. You can make photocopies of important newspaper and magazine articles or pages from books and keep them in labeled folders. Web pages can be printed out or bookmarked on your computer for reference. You can discuss the information you find from various media with your classmates or teachers to evaluate its reliability. In fact, explaining aloud what you've gathered from a variety of media is one way to better understand the information. It will also help you to learn how to use specific language and vocabulary related to certain types of media.

How to Analyze and Interpret Information from Various Media

You should always try to analyze and interpret the information you find from various media sources. Many times the same event can be interpreted differently depending on the medium in which it is presented. Ask yourself if the source is reliable or if the information you find shows any bias or opinion. Some writers may only mention facts that support their ideas or opinions and not mention details that are not supportive of their arguments. Find an event that is covered both in your local newspaper and on television. Compare the differences between the coverage in the two media. Do you notice a difference in bias or opinion? Comparing two sources of information about the same topic may help you see that one is more biased than the other. It can help you see ways that different people present similar information.

How to Use Technology to Create Final Products

Technology allows people to create interesting final products to share information. Once you become comfortable with the appropriate equipment and software, there are many ways to create, change, and individualize your work using technology. Here are two examples of products that can be made with technology today.

Electronic Media

Electronic media, or a **word-processing document**, allows you to create and save written work. You can use it to:

- store ideas, plans, and essays
- write drafts of your work
- revise, edit, and proofread your writing
- format, publish, and share your work

There are many different kinds of word-processing programs. If you are not familiar with word-processing programs, talk to your teacher about learning one that will work well for you in class. Review or learn the following basic steps:

1 **Start a File or Document** Open a new document, and choose a place to save it.

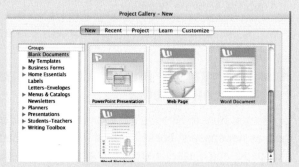

2 **Type and Format Your Work** Review how to do basic tasks, such as change a font, highlight words in color, and make type bold or underlined.

3 **Save and Share Your Work** Continually click the Save icon on the toolbar to ensure your work is not lost by computer error. Once you have a finished document, talk to your teacher about printing or using e-mail options.

Multimedia Presentation

A **multimedia presentation** allows your audience to read, see, and hear your work. You may choose to include visuals, videos, photographs, or audio recordings in your presentation to make the information more interesting for your audience. Be sure to carefully plan and practice your presentation. This will help you avoid errors during your presentation.

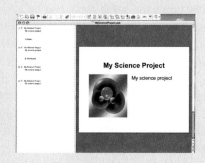

Research

What Is Research?

Research is collecting information about a specific subject. When you research, you are trying to find the answer to a question.

How to Use the Research Process

When you research, you search for information about a specific topic. You can use the information you find to write a story, an article, or a research report.

Choose and Narrow Your Topic

The best way to choose your research topic is to think of something you want to learn more about and that interests you. Make sure your teacher approves your topic. Pick a topic that is not too general. A specific topic is easier to research and write about. It also is more interesting to read about in a report.

Discover What Is Known and What Needs to Be Learned

Get to know your topic. Are there recent articles or reports in the news that relate to your topic? What are researchers and scientists currently working on that relates to the topic?

Formulate Research Questions

What do you know about your topic? What do you want to learn? Write down some questions about your topic that you want to find the answers to. Look at the most important words in your questions, or the key words. These are the words that will be the focus of your research.

> Is there life on Mars?
> Is water or oxygen found on Mars?
> Can life forms live on the surface of Mars?
> What have space missions to Mars discovered about possible life there?

Narrowing the Topic

> Outer Space: This is a very large topic. There are too many things to research in outer space, such as planets, stars, and meteors. There is too much information to cover in one report.

> Planets: This topic is better, but it is still too large. There are many planets in our solar system. It is best to pick a specific planet, and decide on one thing you want to learn about that planet.

> Life on Mars: This topic is more specific than researching the entire planet of Mars. The research can focus just on whether or not plants and animals exist on Mars, or if they ever existed there in the past.

Choose Appropriate Resources to Support Your Topic

Resources can be people you interview, such as experts or teachers. Textbooks, magazines, newspapers, videos, photographs, and the Internet are also resources. The four main types of resources are:

- print
- electronic
- audio visual
- graphic aids

Create a rubric to rate the reliability of your sources. Rate each source on a scale of 1 to 4; 4 is the most reliable, 1 is the least reliable. If you are unsure of the reliability of your sources, ask your teacher, your parents, or a partner.

Gather Information

You may need to survey, skim, or scan a variety of sources to pick the best ones. Use the research questions you formulated to guide your reading.

To Skim Read the title to see if the article is useful for your topic. Read the beginning sentences of the main paragraphs, or any subheads. See if the article may give details about your topic. Read the last paragraph. At the end, there is usually a conclusion that will summarize the main points of the article.

To Scan Look for key words or details. They may be underlined or in bold type. This will tell you if the article will discuss your topic.

Take Notes

As you read, take notes. You will gather the specific information you need from each source. For each resource:

1. Include the key words or important phrases about your topic.

2. Write down the source to record where you found the facts.
   - For a book, list the title, author, page number, publisher, and year of publication.
   - For a magazine or newspaper article, list the name, date, volume, and issue number of the source. Also list the title of the article and the author.
   - For an Internet site, list the Web address, the name of the site, the author (if there is one listed), and the date of the latest site update.

3. List the details and facts that are important to your topic. Be certain to summarize or paraphrase the information in your own words. If you use exact words from a source, you must put the words in quotation marks and note the page you copied it from. If you exactly copy someone else's words, you will be plagiarizing. **Plagiarism** is illegal and can be punished by law.

Notecard for a book

Is there life on Mars?
Mars by Seymour Simon, page 27
-Viking spacecraft supposed to find out if there's life
-Some think experiments showed there isn't

Organize Information from Multiple Sources

After you have taken notes from several sources, **organize** them to see what information is the most important. See how the information from different sources is related.

One of the best ways to organize your information is to use a graphic organizer called an outline. You can also organize your information by using technology. For example, you could type up your notes and save them in a word processing document. It also allows you to choose which data (like dates or times), facts, or ideas are the most relevant.

Analyze, Evaluate, and Use Information

Review your rubric that showed which sources were the most reliable. After you check the reliability, usefulness, relevance, and accuracy of the information, **analyze** and **evaluate** the information. All resources are either primary or secondary sources. A **primary source** is an account of an event by someone who was actually there. A primary source might be a journal, letter, or photograph. A **secondary source** is an account of an event by someone who was not present at the event but that describes the event for other people. A secondary source could be a textbook or an article.

Primary Sources	Secondary Sources
• a soldier's journal	• a book about World War I
• a photograph of a volcano erupting	• a documentary that tells the story of the day a volcano erupted

Synthesize Information from Multiple Sources

Convert your data into graphic aids. Make an outline to **synthesize**, or organize and summarize, your research findings and draw conclusions. Doing this will allow you to identify complexities and discrepancies. You can also use your outline and notes to organize your Works Cited page at the end of your paper. Include the author, title, and page number or Web address.

How to Make an Outline:

1. Put all your notes that have the same keywords or phrases together.

2. Make the first question from your notes into a main idea statement. This will be Roman numeral I.

3. Each of your key research questions will be a Roman numeral heading.

4. Find details that explain each main idea statement. Each important detail about that idea should go below it, and be listed with capital letters.

5. More specific details can be listed with numbers under each capital letter detail.

6. Give your outline a title. This title should state the overall or main idea. It may be a good title to use for your report.

Sample Outline

> The Mystery of Life on Mars
> I. Life on Mars
>   A. How Mars is like Earth
>   1. Volcanoes
>   2. Giant canyons
>   B. Fact-finding missions
>   1. Viking
>   2. Pathfinder
> II. Signs of life on Mars
>   A. Studied by David McKay's team
>   B. Meteorite
>   1. Might contain bacteria fossils
>   2. Found in Antarctica
>   3. Probably from Mars
> III. Continued search for life on Mars
>   A. Look underground
>   B. More study
>   1. Mission planned for future
>   2. Gases in atmosphere
>   3. What rocks are made of.

Design and Write a Research Report

Before you write, ask your teacher to show you which style guide to use. Follow the style guide to learn the proper formatting of the paper. It will also show you how to format your sources into a works cited page. Use the following techniques to complete your research paper.

Write the Title and Introduction

Copy the **title** from your outline. You can make it more interesting if you want. Make sure it gives the main idea of your topic. Next you should write an interesting **introduction** that will explain what the rest of your report will be about. Write an introduction that will get your readers' attention.

Outline

The Mystery of Life on Mars

Title and Introduction

The Mystery of Life on Mars
Perhaps you have heard stories about life on other planets. Or perhaps, you may have only thought about life here on Earth. I am going to explore the research on the planet Mars and discuss with you the studies that have been done to see if there is life on "the red planet."

Write the Body

The body is the main portion of your report. Use your main ideas to write topic sentences for each paragraph. Then use your research details to write sentences about each topic.

Outline

I. Life on Mars
  A. How Mars is like Earth
    1. Volcanoes
    2. Giant canyons

Topic Sentence and Detail

People have always wondered if there is life on other planets, especially Mars. Because Mars is similar to Earth with features like volcanoes and giant canyons, it seems possible that there is life on Mars.

Write the Conclusion

Write about the main ideas of your report in the **conclusion**. This will summarize your report. You can also include an interesting fact or opinion to end your report. This will keep your audience thinking after they have finished reading. For example, "I believe that with all the research still being done on Mars, perhaps in the near future, we will learn more about life on that mysterious planet."

Design Your Report: Graphic and Multimedia Aids

After you write your report, you should consider its **design**, or how it will look on a printed page. This includes choosing the font of the text and deciding whether you will use **graphic aids** to make the information in your report easier to understand or more interesting. Do you want to include illustrations or photographs? Does your audience need a time line or diagram to understand the text better? Is there a video or audio file that might support your ideas? Choose visuals or media that will make your presentation more effective.

Integrate Quotations and Citations

Adding **quotations** and including **citations** are important ways of sharing the information you find during your research. Any words that are not your own must be in quotation marks and the source must be given in the running text in order to avoid plagiarism. If you use an idea that is not your own, even if you paraphrase it in your own words, you must **cite** the source for that information.

To cite a source means to list the information of your source. This helps you to properly note where you found your information. Citing allows other readers to look at the source, too. Use the citation style your teacher tells you to use. Two commonly used citation styles were developed by the Modern Language Association (MLA) and the American Psychological Association (APA). Both of these associations publish style manuals that can help you write research papers. They are available at **www.mla.org** and **www.apastyle.org**.

A common way to cite is to use the MLA style for author and page citation. List the author and the page number of your source right after you use the words or idea of that author. The author's name should be either in the sentence itself or in parentheses following the quotation or paraphrase. The page number(s) should always appear in parentheses, not in the text of your sentence. For example:

> The writer T. S. Eliot has said that poetry expresses an "overflow of powerful feelings" (263).

> Poetry expresses an "overflow of powerful feelings" (Eliot 263).

At the end of your report create a separate **"Works Cited"** page.

> Works Cited
>
> Ackroyd, Peter. *T. S. Eliot: A Life.* London: Simon and Schuster, 1985.
>
> Vendler, Helen. "T. S. Eliot." *Time* 8 June 1998. 70–72.
>
> "T. S. Eliot." *Microsoft Encarta Online Encyclopedia.* 2006.
>
>   <http://encarta.msn.com>

Evaluate Your Research Report and Draw Conclusions

After you complete your research report, you should **evaluate** it, or check its quality. Ask questions about how well you did each step of the report. Look at the paper overall. Does it accomplish what you want it to do? Do you have to do more research or adjust your main idea to achieve the goal of your paper? This will help you to decide if the end product is presented correctly.

Checklist to Evaluate

☑ The title tells what the report is about.

☑ The introduction is interesting, gets the attention of the reader, and gives the main idea of the report.

☑ The body gives the facts you found.

☑ Each paragraph covers a specific topic from your outline.

☑ Each topic in the body paragraphs is connected to the main idea.

☑ Other sentences give specific details about the topic.

☑ The conclusion is a summary of the most important information on your topic.

☑ The conclusion is interesting for the reader.

☑ The paper is formatted according to the style guide used.

☑ All sources are properly formatted per the style guide used.

Share Your Report

Publish your report. You can choose different media for publishing. You can print the final report in paper, put it online, create a poster or display of your final paper, or attach it to an email and send it to trusted friends or adults. Be sure to check your school's Acceptable Use Policy before posting your work.

Questions for Further Study

Now that you have finished the report, you may have questions based on the conclusions you drew. You can consider these questions as other research ideas for the future.

During Your Research

> I see that there were space missions to Mars such as the Viking. How are those machines created? Who designs them? I would like to know more about space technology.

Now

> Maybe my next research report will be about space technology. I could study who designs the machines that go into space and how they work.

Test-Taking Strategies

What Are Test-Taking Strategies?

Test-taking strategies are skills to help you effectively complete a test. These strategies will help you to show what you know on a test without making mistakes.

What to Do Before a Test

Use the following strategies to help you prepare for a test.

- Find out if the test will be multiple-choice, short answers, or essay. Noting the format will allow you to select an appropriate strategy.
- Ask your teacher for practice tests or examples to try before the test day.
- Carefully study the material that will be on the test.
- Make sure you get a good night of rest before a test. This will help you focus.
- Eat a nutritious meal before the test. This will give you energy to get through the test.

What to Do During a Test

Use the following strategies as you complete the test.

Relax: Relax and think carefully during the test. If you feel stressed, take a few deep breaths. Remind yourself that you are prepared.

Plan Your Time: Survey the test to estimate difficulty and plan time. See what questions you can answer easily. Do not work on one question for too long because you might not have enough time to finish the test if you only focus on one question.

Read: Read the directions for each section of the test. Then, read each question carefully. Underline key words in the directions and questions to focus on the most important information. Be certain that you are doing what the question asks. For example, if a question says to "describe," give more than a definition. You may need to give specific details.

You think:

> This question is difficult. I cannot answer this right now.

Then you decide:

> I will return to this question later. I will answer the questions I do know first.

Clarify: Tests ask logical questions. If something seems strange, reread the directions, question, or passage to clarify information. Think about words carefully to be certain you understand their meaning. Use typographic and visual clues to find meaning.

Mark Answers: Carefully mark your answers on the test and check for legibility. This can affect your test grade! Be sure to use the correct writing utensil. For example, some multiple choice tests require the use of a #2 pencil.

Check Completeness: Check to make sure all questions are answered (if there is no penalty for guessing). Always reread your answers or answer choices, if you have time. Finish any questions you may not have finished before.

Tips for Objective Tests

Use the following strategies to help you complete objective tests.

Easy First: Answer the easy questions first. Leave the most difficult ones for last.

Narrow the Choices: If you are uncertain of an answer, determine which choices are definitely not correct. Choose the two that are closest to correct. This will narrow your number of answers to choose from to only two.

Rephrase Questions and Answer Them Mentally: Try to put the question in your own words and think about how you will answer. Then, look at the answer choices to see which one matches your own answer the best.

Make Changes If Needed: Ask yourself if you answered each question correctly. Check your work by reading through the test a second time. Change your answer only if the question was initially misunderstood.

Shuttle Among the Passage, the Question, the Choices: Read the passage, the questions, and the choices until you fully understand what is being asked.

Tips for Essay Tests

Use the following strategies to help you complete essay tests.

Outline: Make an outline of your answer before you write. This way, you can make sure you discuss all the important points of your essay.

Plan: Plan the time for your essay. Know how long you have to write your essay. Mark on your outline how long you plan to spend writing each section of your essay.

Write: Only include information in your essay that you know is accurate and is about your topic. If you are uncertain if it is factual or important, do not include it. Use a topic sentence and supporting details for each paragraph.

Proofread: Carefully proofread your writing. Check for grammar, punctuation, and capitalization. Most importantly, make sure all parts of your essay can be read clearly.

Tips for Online Tests

Use the following strategies to help you complete tests on a computer.

- Find out how the test is designed—Can you go back to questions you have already answered? Can you change your answers? Is there a time limit? Is there a glossary? Audio? Some tests will show you this information on the introduction screen. You can also ask your teacher.

- Find out if this is an adaptive test. When you take adaptive tests, the questions get harder or easier based on whether you are getting answers correct or incorrect. So when you take an adaptive test, take your time and be careful as you answer the first several questions.

- Have a pencil and paper in addition to your computer test. Use your paper to jot down an idea or organize your thoughts with a graphic organizer.

READING HANDBOOK

Reading Strategies

Reading Fluency

Study Skills and Strategies

Vocabulary

Reading Strategies

What Are Reading Strategies?

Reading strategies are hints or techniques you can use to help you become a better reader. They help you interact with the text and take control of your own reading comprehension. Reading strategies can be used before, during, and after you read.

Plan and Monitor

Before you read, plan how to approach the selection by using prereading strategies. **Preview** the selection to see what it is about and try to make a prediction about its content. Keep in mind that English is read from left to right, and that text moves from the top of the page to the bottom. **Set a purpose** for reading, or decide why you will read the selection. You might want or need to adjust your purpose for reading as you read. Monitor your reading to check how well you understand and remember what you read.

How to Select and Use Prereading Strategies	
Title:	Surfing the Pipeline
Author:	Christina Rodriguez
Preview the Text	• Look at the title: Surfing the Pipeline. • Look at the organization of the text, including any chapter titles, heads, and subheads. • Look at any photos and captions. • Think about what the selection is about.
Activate Prior Knowledge	• I know many people surf in the ocean on surfboards. • I've seen a film about people trying to surf on huge waves in California.
Ask Questions	• What is the pipeline? • Where is the pipeline? • Who surfs the pipeline? • Why do people try to surf the pipeline?
Set a Purpose for Reading	• I want to read to find out how people surf the pipeline.

How to Make and Confirm Predictions

Making **predictions** about a selection will help you understand and remember what you read. As you preview a selection, **ask questions** and think about any **prior knowledge** you have about the subject. If you do not learn enough additional information from these steps, read the first few paragraphs of the selection.

Think about the events taking place, and then predict what will happen next. If you are reading fiction or drama, you can use what you know about common plot patterns to help you predict what may happen in the story. After you read each section, confirm your predictions, or see if they were correct. Sometimes you will need to revise your predictions for the next section based on what you read.

Preview to Anticipate Read the title. Think about what the selection will be about as you read the first few paragraphs. Look for clues about the selection's content.

Make and Confirm Predictions As you read, predict what will happen next in the selection based on text evidence or personal experience. Take notes while you are reading, and use a **Prediction Chart** to record your ideas. As you continue to read the selection, confirm your predictions. If a prediction is incorrect, revise it.

Surfing the Pipeline

There Uli was, standing on the white, sandy shores of Oahu, Hawaii. Right in front of her was the famous Banzai Pipeline—one of the most difficult and dangerous places to surf in the world. Uli looked out and saw twelve-foot waves crashing toward her.

Uli had been waiting for this day for a long time. She was ready.

Uli grabbed her surfboard and entered the water. The waves were fierce and strong that morning. It took all of Uli's energy to swim out to the surfing location. Uli could see rocks sticking up through the water. She finally found the perfect starting point and waited anxiously to begin surfing.

Prediction Chart

Prediction	Did It Happen?	Evidence
Uli is going to surf at the Banzai Pipeline.	Not yet, but she will soon.	She is at the starting point to begin surfing. (text evidence)
Surfing the Banzai Pipeline will be hard for Uli.	Not yet, but it will soon.	New activities are always hard when I try them for the first time. (personal experience)

How to Monitor Your Reading

When you **monitor your reading**, you are checking to make sure you understand the information you read. You can check your understanding by keeping track of your thinking while reading. Pause while reading to think about images you may be creating in your mind, connections you are making between words or topics within the text, or problems you are having with understanding the text. When you read something that doesn't make sense to you, use these monitoring strategies to help you.

Strategy	How to Use It	Example Text
Reread to Clarify Ideas	Reread silently the passage you do not understand. Then reread the passage aloud. Continue rereading until you feel more confident about your understanding of the passage.	I will silently reread the first paragraph. Then I will read it aloud. The paragraph is more understandable now.
Use Resources to Clarify Vocabulary	Look up confusing words in a dictionary or thesaurus, or ask a classmate for help.	"... dangerous places to surf ..." I'm not sure what "surf" means. I'll look it up.
Read On and Use Context Clues to Clarify Ideas and Vocabulary	Read past the part of the text where you are confused. What does the rest of the information tell you? Are there nearby words or phrases, context clues or visuals that help you understand?	"... looked out and saw twelve-foot waves ..." Maybe "surf" means riding ocean waves.
Adjust Your Reading Rate	Read slowly when something is confusing or difficult. Keep in mind that English is read from left to right and that text runs down the page from the top. If you are having a difficult time understanding what you're reading, first make sure that you're reading it in the right order.	"Right in front of her was the famous Banzai Pipeline ..." I've never heard of the Banzai Pipeline. I'll read slower to find out what it is.
Adjust Your Purpose for Reading	Think of the purpose you set for reading before you started to read. Have you found a new purpose, or reason to read? If so, adjust your purpose and read on.	I originally wanted to read to find out how people surf the pipeline. Now I want to read to see if Uli actually does it.

How to Use Graphic Organizers

Before you read, you can use graphic organizers to prepare for better comprehension. For example, use a **KWL Chart** to record your prior knowledge about the topic.

KWL Chart

WHAT I <u>K</u>NOW	WHAT I <u>WANT</u> TO KNOW	WHAT I <u>L</u>EARNED

As you read, use a variety of graphic organizers such as diagrams and charts to help keep track of your thinking. Take notes about any ideas or vocabulary that confuse you. Writing down ideas keeps you actively involved in your reading. It also can help clear up any confusion you may have about information in a selection.

Use graphic organizers to capture your thoughts and to help you remember information based on how it was described in the text or based on the text structure. Here are some more examples of graphic organizers:

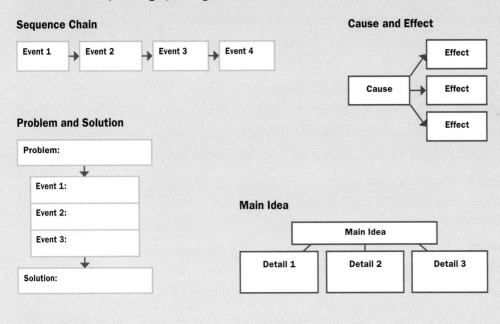

Sequence Chain

Event 1 → Event 2 → Event 3 → Event 4

Cause and Effect

Cause → Effect, Effect, Effect

Problem and Solution

Problem: → Event 1: → Event 2: → Event 3: → Solution:

Main Idea

Main Idea → Detail 1, Detail 2, Detail 3

Definition Map

Definition — Word — Example — Example

Time Line

For more graphic organizers, see the Index of Graphic Organizers on page 800.

Determine Importance

Determining importance is a reading strategy you can use to find the most important details or ideas in a selection. A good way to think about what is important in the selections you read is to **summarize**. When you summarize, you state the main idea and only the most important details in a selection, usually in a sentence or two. To summarize, identify the topic of a paragraph or selection, find the main idea and the most important details, and put them in your own words.

Stated Main Ideas

The main idea of a selection is the most important point a writer wants to relate to readers. Writers often state the main idea in a topic sentence near the beginning of a selection.

What's in a Name?

All college sports teams have special names. Many of these names are common, such as the Bears or the Tigers. However, more teams should have names that are unique and express the school's individuality. The University of Arkansas team names are Razorbacks and Lady Razorbacks. Virginia Tech athletes are called Hokies. Purdue has the Boilermakers. My favorite is the University of California at Santa Cruz's Banana Slugs and Lady Slugs. Slugs are unusual creatures. They have soft, slimy bodies and enjoy moist environments. These unique names make the college sports world a more interesting and fun place.

How to Identify Stated Main Ideas	
What is the paragraph about?	• names of college teams
Look for supporting details.	• Some teams have unique names like Razorbacks, Hokies, Boilermakers, and Lady Slugs. • The author feels these names make the college sports world more fun.
Eliminate unnecessary information or details.	• Slugs are slimy and enjoy moist environments.
Summarize the main idea.	• Unique sports team names are better and more fun than common names.

Implied Main Ideas

Sometimes a main idea is implied, or not directly stated. Readers have to figure out the main idea by studying all of the details in a selection.

The Future of Humankind

Many people agree that space exploration is important. However, when government spending is discussed, many people insist there are problems on Earth that need attention and money first. Don't they realize that the future of the human race depends on space exploration? Someday, the Earth's resources may run out. Paying for more exploration will allow us to learn more about space and how we can better care for our planet.

How to Identify Implied Main Ideas	
What is the paragraph about?	• space exploration
Find and list details.	• Many people feel other issues are more important than space exploration. • Our future depends on exploration.
What message is the author trying to convey?	• If we explore space now, we can better take care of ourselves and Earth.
Summarize the implied main idea.	• Space exploration should be paid for because it is just as important as any other issue. We could die without it.

Personal Relevance

An additional way to determine importance while reading a selection is to look for details that have personal relevance to you. These details may be important to you because they remind you of someone or something in your own life. For example, you might relate to "What's in a Name?" because you have a favorite sports team name. You might understand the main point that the writer is trying to make because you might agree that sports team names should be unique.

Make Connections

Making connections is a reading strategy you can use to better understand or enjoy the information presented in a selection.

As you read, think about what the information reminds you of. Have you seen or heard something like this before? Have you read or experienced something like this? Thinking about what you already know helps you make a connection to the new information.

Type of Connection	Description	Example
Text to Self	A connection between the text you are reading and something that has happened in your own life. A text-to-self connection can also be a feeling, such as happiness or excitement, that you feel as you are reading.	This part of the story reminds me of the first time I drove a car. My dad showed me how to turn and stop. I remember how scared I was. Thinking about this memory helps me better understand how the character is feeling as he learns how to drive.
Text to Text	A connection between the text you are reading and another selection you have read, a film you have seen, or a song you have heard. Sometimes the text you are reading might have a similar theme, or message, to something you've read, seen, or heard before. A text may also belong to a genre, such as mystery or biography, that you are familiar with.	This part of the news article reminds me of a movie I saw about space. Astronauts were taking a trip to the moon, but their spaceship lost all power. I can think about the movie as I read about the most recent space shuttle mission.
Text to World	A connection between something you read in the text and something that is happening or has happened in the world. You might also make a connection with the time period or era that a selection takes place in, such as the Great Depression or the 1980s. The setting may also be familiar.	This part of the text reminds me of presidential elections. I remember candidates giving speeches to tell why they should be president. Thinking about this helps me understand why the characters in the selection give speeches.

Use a chart like the one below to help make and record text-to-self, text-to-text, or text-to-world connections as you read.

Make Connections Chart

The text says ...	This reminds me of ...	This helps me because ...

Make Inferences

Making inferences is a reading strategy in which you make educated guesses about the text's content based on experiences that you've had in everyday life or on facts or details that you read.

Sometimes people call making inferences "reading between the lines." This means looking at *how* the text was written along with what is being discussed. When you "read between the lines," you pay attention to the writer's tone, voice, use of punctuation, or emphasis on certain words. Writers can also use irony, dialogue, or descriptions to infer messages.

When you add your prior knowledge or personal experiences to what you are reading, you can make inferences by reading all the clues and making your best guesses.

How to Make Inferences Using Your Own Experience

Read the following paragraph and chart to learn how to make an inference using your own experiences.

The Waiting

Rain pounded against the windows as Sarah stomped up and down the stairs. She only stopped going up and down to check the time on the clock downstairs every five minutes. She had been dressed and ready to go for more than an hour! Sarah had spent weeks picking out her dress and shoes, and she had even paid $50 to have her hair styled. She threw the flower she had so excitedly bought yesterday in the corner beside the camera. Sarah wondered, "Where is he? Will I have to go alone tonight?"

Inferences Based on Your Own Experience	
You read	Sarah had been dressed and ready to go somewhere for more than an hour. She spent a lot of time selecting her dress and shoes. She threw her flower in the corner by the camera.
You know	I know that people spend a lot of time choosing special outfits for events like dances, weddings, or parties. I know that my parents took a photo of me and my date for the prom last year. My date and I both had flowers for our outfits that night.
You infer	Sarah had a date to a special event that night. She was upset because she cared a lot about the event she was going to and didn't want to be late or go alone.

How to Make Inferences Using Text Evidence

Read the following paragraph and chart to learn how to make an inference by using clues that appear in the text.

The Waiting

Rain pounded against the windows as Sarah stomped up and down the stairs. She only stopped going up and down to check the time on the clock downstairs every five minutes. She had been dressed and ready to go for more than an hour! Sarah had spent weeks picking out her dress and shoes, and she had even paid $50 to have her hair styled. She threw the flower she had so excitedly bought yesterday in the corner beside the camera. Sarah wondered, "Where is he? Will I have to go alone tonight?"

Inferences Based on Text Evidence	
You read	Sarah had been dressed and ready to go somewhere for more than an hour. She spent a lot of time selecting her dress and shoes. She threw her flower in the corner by the camera.
You infer	Sarah had plans to go somewhere special that evening and was waiting for her date. She cared a lot about the event she was going to. Someone is late, and she is angry at him.

Ask Questions

You can **ask questions** to learn new information, to clarify, and to understand or figure out what is important in a selection. Asking questions of yourself and the author while reading can help you locate information you might otherwise miss.

How to Self-Question

Ask yourself questions to understand something that is confusing, keep track of what is happening, or think about what you know.

Ask and Write Questions Use a question word such as *Who, What, When, Where, Why,* or *How* to write your questions.

Examples: How can I figure out what this word means? What are the characters doing? Why is this important? Do I agree with this?

Answer the Questions and Follow Up Use the text, photographs, or other visuals to answer your questions. Write your answer next to the question. Include the page number where you found the answer.

How to Question the Author

Sometimes, you may have questions about what the author is trying to tell you in a selection. Write these types of questions, and then try to answer them by reading the text. The answers to these questions are known as "author and you" answers.

Questions to Ask the Author

- What is the author trying to say here?
- Does the author explain his or her ideas clearly?
- What is the author talking about?
- Does the author support his or her ideas or opinions with facts?

How to Find Question-Answer Relationships

Where you find the answers to your questions is very important. Sometimes the answers are located right in the text. Other times, your questions require you to use ideas and information that are not in the text. Some questions can be answered by using your background knowledge on a topic. Read the chart to learn about question-answer relationships.

Type of Answer	How to Find the Answers
"Right There"	Sometimes you can simply point to the text and say that an answer to one of your questions is "right there."
"Think and Search"	Look back at the selection. Find the information the question is asking about. Think about how the information fits together to answer the question.
"Author and You"	Use ideas and information that are not stated directly in the text. Think about what you have read, and create your own ideas or opinions based on what you know about the author.
"On Your Own"	Use your feelings, what you already know, and your own experiences to find these answers.

Synthesize

When you **synthesize**, you gather your thoughts about what you have read to draw conclusions, make generalizations, and compare the information to information you've read in other texts. You form new overall understandings by putting together ideas and events.

How to Draw Conclusions

Reading is like putting a puzzle together. There are many different parts that come together to make up the whole selection. Synthesizing is the process of putting the pieces together while we read. We combine new information with what we already know to create an original idea or to form new understandings.

Read this passage and the text that follows to help you understand how to synthesize what you read.

Distracted Drivers

Cell phone use in cars has steadily risen in the past decade. Studies from the Departments of Highway Safety show that the more distracted drivers are, the more likely they are to be in an accident. Lawmakers in some states have successfully passed laws requiring drivers to use hands-free accessories while a vehicle is moving. This means they may use an earpiece or a speaker-phone device but not hold the phone in their hands. Many people feel that talking on cell phones is not the only distracting activity that should be illegal for drivers.

Use text evidence from the selection and your own experience to draw conclusions as you read.

Drawing Conclusions	
Look for Details	The more distracted a driver is, the more likely he or she is to be involved in an accident. Cell phones are distracting.
Think About What You Know	I know people who have been in car accidents while talking on their cell phones.
Decide What You Believe	Lawmakers should continue to work on laws to stop drivers from being distracted.

How to Make Generalizations

Generalizations are broad statements that apply to a group of people, a set of ideas, or the way things happen. You can make generalizations as you read, using experience and text evidence from a selection to help you.

- **Take notes about the facts or opinions** Look for the overall theme or message of the selection.
- **Add examples** Think about what you know about the topic from your own knowledge and experience.
- **Construct a generalization** Write a statement that combines the author's statements and your own.

  Example: *Using a cell phone while driving can make you have an accident.*

How to Compare Across Texts

Comparing two or more texts helps you combine ideas, develop judgments, and draw conclusions. Read the following paragraph, and think about how it connects to the paragraph on page 630.

Graduated Driver's License Programs

More and more states are creating graduated driver's license (GDL) laws. Studies show that these programs help teen driver accidents and deaths to decline. The programs differ from state to state, but most GDL programs require an adult with a valid driver's license to be present when a teen is driving, and a teen driver must enroll in a certified driver's education and training course. Each state has various restrictions for teen drivers and punishments for when those restrictions are ignored.

Think About Something You Have Already Read In "Distracted Drivers," you read that cell phones are distracting to drivers and that many people feel it should be illegal to use one while driving.

Think About What You Are Reading Right Now Many states have graduated driver's license programs. Accidents involving teen drivers have declined.

Compare Across Texts and Draw Conclusions Both articles are about laws related to driving. Lawmakers hope that all of the laws they pass related to driving will create safer driving conditions for everyone.

Comparing across texts can help you foster an argument or advance an opinion. Having multiple opinions and facts from different sources makes your argument or opinion more credible.

Visualize

When you **visualize**, you use your imagination to better understand what the author is describing. While reading, create an image or picture in your mind that represents what you are reading about. Look for words that tell how things look, sound, smell, taste, and feel.

My Favorite Car Is a Truck

My name is Stephen, and today was a magical day. I've been working hard and saving money all summer. I finally have enough money for a down payment on a new car. Today my father took me to a car dealership to pick out my car. I immediately found my favorite vehicle. It was a red, shiny pickup truck with gleaming wheels. I climbed inside and looked around. The brown seats were sparkling clean, and the truck still had that new car smell inside the cab. I put the key in the ignition and turned it on. The quiet hum of the engine made me so happy. After a long test-drive, my father and I agreed this was the truck for me.

How to Visualize Using Sketches

- **Read the Text** Look for words that help create pictures in your mind about the characters, setting, and events.
- **Picture the Information in Your Mind** Stop and focus on the descriptive words. Create pictures in your mind using these words.
- **Draw the Events** Sketch pictures to show what is happening. You could draw Stephen climbing inside the pickup truck.

How to Visualize Using Senses

- **Look for Words** Find adjectives and sensory words: smell, look, sound, taste, and feel. Stephen uses the words *red, shiny, with gleaming wheels*; *brown seats, sparkling clean*; *new car smell*; and *quiet hum of the engine* to talk about the truck.
- **Create a Picture in Your Mind of the Scene** What do you hear, feel, see, smell, and taste? Examine how these details improve your understanding.

  I smell: new car smell   **I hear**: engine humming

  I see: red, shiny truck   **I feel**: texture of the seats, the key

How to Recognize Emotional Responses

Do any of the words in the selection make you feel certain emotions? Asking yourself how you feel when you read can help you remember the information.

Example: I feel excited for the main character because I know what it's like to pick out something new.

Reading Fluency

What Is Reading Fluency?

Reading fluency is the ability to read smoothly and expressively with clear understanding. Fluent readers are able to better understand and enjoy what they read. Use the strategies that follow to build your fluency in these four key areas:

- accuracy and rate
- phrasing
- intonation
- expression

How to Improve Accuracy and Rate

Accuracy is the correctness of your reading. Rate is the speed of your reading.

How to read accurately:

- Use correct pronunciation.
- Emphasize correct syllables.

How to read with proper rate:

- Match your reading speed to what you are reading. For example, if you are reading an exciting story, read slightly faster. If you are reading a sad story, read slightly slower.
- Recognize and use punctuation.

Test your accuracy and rate:

- Choose a text you are familiar with, and practice reading it aloud or silently multiple times.
- Ask a friend to use a watch or clock to time you while you read a passage aloud.
- Ask a friend or family member to read a passage for you, so you know what it should sound like.

Use the formula below to measure a reader's accuracy and rate while reading aloud. For passages to practice with, see **Reading Fluency Practice**, pp. 665–685.

Accuracy and Rate Formula

$$\underline{\hspace{3cm}} - \underline{\hspace{3cm}} = \underline{\hspace{3cm}}$$

| words read in one minute | number of errors | words correct per minute (wcpm) |

How to Improve Intonation

Intonation is the rise and fall in the tone of your voice as you read aloud. It means the highness or lowness of the sound.

How to read with proper intonation:

- Change the sound of your voice to match what you are reading.
- Make your voice flow, or sound smooth, while you read.
- Make sure you are pronouncing words correctly.
- Raise the sound of your voice for words that should be stressed, or emphasized.
- Use visual clues. (see box below)

Visual Clue and Meaning	Example	How to Read It
Italics: draw attention to a word to show special importance	She is *smart*.	Emphasize "smart."
Dash: shows a quick break in a sentence	She is—smart.	Pause before saying "smart."
Exclamation: can represent energy, excitement, or anger	She is smart!	Make your voice louder at the end of the sentence.
All capital letters: can represent strong emphasis, or yelling	SHE IS SMART.	Emphasize the whole sentence.
Bold facing: draws attention to a word to show importance	She is **smart**.	Emphasize "smart."
Question mark: shows curiosity or confusion	She is smart?	Raise the pitch of your voice slightly at the end of the sentence.

Use the rubric below to measure how well a reader uses intonation while reading aloud. For intonation passages, see **Reading Fluency Practice**, pp. 665–685.

Intonation Rubric

1	2	3
The reader's tone does not change. The reading all sounds the same.	The reader's tone changes sometimes to match what is being read.	The reader's tone always changes to match what is being read.

How to Improve Phrasing

Phrasing is how you use your voice to group words together.

How to read with proper phrasing:

- Don't read too quickly or too slowly.
- Pause for key words within the text.
- Make sure your sentences sound smooth, not choppy.
- Make sure you sound like you are reading a sentence instead of a list.
- Use punctuation to tell you when to stop, pause, or emphasize. (see box below)

Punctuation	How to Use It
. period	stop at the end of the sentence
, comma	pause within the sentence
! exclamation point	emphasize the sentence and pause at the end
? question mark	emphasize the end of the sentence and pause at the end
; semicolon	pause within the sentence between two related thoughts
: colon	pause within the sentence before giving an example or explanation

One way to practice phrasing is to copy a passage, then place a slash (/), or pause mark, within a sentence where there should be a pause. One slash (/) means a short pause. Two slashes (//) mean a longer pause, such as a pause at the end of a sentence.

Read aloud the passage below, pausing at each pause mark. Then try reading the passage again without any pauses. Compare how you sound each time.

There are many ways to get involved / in your school and community. // Joining a club / or trying out for a sports team / are a few of the options. // Volunteer work can also be very rewarding. // You can volunteer at community centers, / nursing homes, / or animal shelters. //

Use the rubric below to measure how well a reader uses phrasing while reading aloud. For phrasing passages, see **Reading Fluency Practice**, pp. 665–685.

Phrasing Rubric

1	2	3
Reading is choppy. There are few pauses for punctuation.	Reading is mostly smooth. There are some pauses for punctuation.	Reading is very smooth. Punctuation is being used properly.

How to Improve Expression

Expression in reading is how you use your voice to express feeling.

How to read with proper expression:

- Match the sound of your voice to what you are reading. For example, read louder and faster to show strong feeling. Read slower and quieter to show sadness or seriousness.
- Match the sound of your voice to the genre. For example, read a fun, fictional story using a fun, friendly voice. Read an informative, nonfiction article using an even tone and a more serious voice.
- Avoid speaking in monotone, or using only one tone in your voice.
- Pause for emphasis and exaggerate letter sounds to match the mood or theme of what you are reading.

Practice incorrect expression by reading this sentence without changing the tone of your voice: *I am so excited!* Now read the sentence again with proper expression: *I am so excited!* The way you use your voice while reading can help you to better understand what is happening in the text.

For additional practice, read the sentences below aloud with and without changing your expression. Compare how you sound each time.

- I am very sad.
- That was the most *boring* movie I have ever seen.
- We won the game!

Use the rubric below to measure how well a reader uses expression while reading aloud. For expression passages, see **Reading Fluency Practice**, pp. 665–685.

Expression Rubric

1	2	3
The reader sounds monotone. The reader's voice does not match the subject of what is being read.	The reader is making some tone changes. Sometimes, the reader's voice matches what is being read.	The reader is using proper tones and pauses. The reader's voice matches what is being read.

Reading Fluency Practice

Practice Expression: "The Experiment"

Expression in reading is how you use your voice to express feeling. Use this passage to practice reading with proper expression. Print a copy of this passage from myNGconnect.com to help you monitor your progress. To use an Expression Rubric, see page 664.

Finally he turned away from the door and looked around. He tried pushing against the cement blocks to see if any of them were loose. He searched the floor for a trap door. Then he glanced up at the ceiling. The shield! The shield around the light bulb! His mind raced. The metal shield could be used as a tool—the tool he needed! He had found the way to escape!

He moved under the shield and looked closely at it. One good strong pull would free it, he decided. He reached up, grabbed hold of it, and pulled. But the shield stayed attached to the ceiling. He grabbed the shield again, twisting it as he pulled. He felt it rip free, and he fell to the floor clutching his treasure.

The shield was shaped like a cone and had been fastened to the ceiling by three long metal prongs. These prongs were sharp. But they were not strong enough to cut through steel or cement.

From "The Experiment," page 13

Practice Phrasing: "Building Bridges"

Phrasing is how you use your voice to group words together. Use this passage to practice reading with proper phrasing. Print a copy of this passage from myNGconnect.com to help you monitor your progress. To use a Phrasing Rubric, see page 663.

Mama Lil opened her eyes. They looked weary, and her expression looked pained. She sighed. "Bebe, I'm an old woman. I don't have many of my own dreams to go after." Her voice trailed off to silence. Then her face softened. For the first time ever, I saw Mama Lil's eyes fill with regret. "What little bit of dreaming I got left in me," she said, "I'm putting to you."

Mama Lil let out a heavy breath. Then she admitted what we'd both known all along. "Your dreams are the kind that'll take you away from here, Bebe. They'll take you away from your Mama Lil."

I shrugged.

Mama Lil said, "That's an upsetting truth, Bebe. It makes my heart hurt every time I think on it."

"Mama Lil, I got to find my way," I said slowly. "If that bridge renovation wasn't tapping on my soul, I'd go ahead and sweep hair down at Rimley's."

For once, Mama Lil was looking into my face, hearing my words.

"Let me go, Mama Lil. Let me dream," I pleaded softly.

Mama Lil sat as still as a statue. I reached into my pocket to find the bridge project consent form. I unfolded it and set it on the coffee table, next to the application from Rimley's. "Mama Lil," I said carefully, "if you don't sign this—if you *won't* sign it—I'll sign it myself. I been helping you sign checks and letters for years now. I can sign your name on this consent form. Nobody will know the difference."

From "Building Bridges," page 33

Practice Intonation: "One in a Million"

Intonation is the rise and fall in the pitch or tone of your voice as you read aloud. Use this passage to practice reading with proper intonation. Print a copy of this passage from myNGconnect.com to help you monitor your progress. To use an Intonation Rubric, see page 662.

Curious to see what treasure they were after, Hodja pushed through to the center of the group. He was startled to see his donkey! The beast's new owner was shouting, "Look at this fine animal! Have you ever seen a better donkey? See how clean and strong it is! You will never find a better worker. Who will bid for this exceptional creature?"

The buyers pressed forward eagerly. "What a prize! What a find!" they murmured excitedly. One shopper offered forty dinars for the donkey.

Another man offered fifty. A third offered fifty-five!

Puzzlement furrowed Hodja's brow. "I thought that donkey was just an ordinary animal," he said to himself, scratching his scraggly beard. "Was I a fool? It is obviously very special. It's one in a million …"

The new owner swept his arm toward the donkey and cried, "How can you pass up the chance to own such a magnificent beast? See how the muscles ripple under the smooth, silky coat. Look at those bright, intelligent eyes …"

Hodja squeezed his way to the front of the crowd. The man's flowery words floated through the warm air, filling Hodja's ears. "Seventy-five dinars once," the man yelled. "Seventy-five dinars twice …"

Hodja's skin tingled. He raised his hand excitedly and shouted, "I bid eighty dinars!"

From "One in a Million," page 65

Practice Phrasing: "Genes: All in the Family"

Phrasing is how you use your voice to group words together. Use this passage to practice reading with proper phrasing. Print a copy of this passage from myNGconnect.com to help you monitor your progress. To use a Phrasing Rubric, see page 663.

Your genes come from your parents, theirs come from their parents, and so on—all the way back to the first living thing that ever existed. Genes are passed down through families, and that's why you probably look a bit like your parents. Physical characteristics, like long eyelashes, red hair, freckles, or blue eyes, run in families because they are controlled by genes.

Half your genes come from your mother and half come from your father. They were passed on to you in chromosomes carried by sperm and egg cells. Sperm and egg cells have only 23 chromosomes each—half the usual amount. When they meet and form an embryo, they create a new person with a full set of 46 chromosomes.

You actually have two sets of genes: one set from your mother and another from your father. These two genomes give you a mixture of your mother's and father's features—perhaps you have your mother's hair and your father's eyes, for instance.

Every child in a family is different because the parents' genes are shuffled and then divided in two before making each sperm and egg cell. So each child gets a unique set of genes (except for identical twins).

From "Genes: All in the Family," page 101

Practice Intonation: "Fish Cheeks"

Intonation is the rise and fall in the pitch or tone of your voice as you read aloud. Use this passage to practice reading with proper intonation. Print a copy of this passage from myNGconnect.com to help you monitor your progress. To use an Intonation Rubric, see page 662.

When I found out that my parents had invited the minister's family over for Christmas Eve dinner, I cried. What would Robert think of our shabby Chinese Christmas? What would he think of our noisy Chinese relatives who lacked proper American manners? What terrible disappointment would he feel upon seeing not a roasted turkey and sweet potatoes but Chinese food?

On Christmas Eve, I saw that my mother had outdone herself in creating a strange menu. She was pulling black veins out of the backs of fleshy prawns. The kitchen was littered with appalling mounds of raw food: A slimy rock cod with bulging fish eyes that pleaded not to be thrown into a pan of hot oil. Tofu, which looked like stacked wedges of rubbery white sponges. A bowl soaking dried fungus back to life. A plate of squid, crisscrossed with knife markings so they resembled bicycle tires.

And then they arrived—the minister's family and all my relatives in a clamor of doorbells and rumpled Christmas packages. Robert grunted hello, and I pretended he was not worthy of existence.

Dinner threw me deeper into despair. My relatives licked the ends of their chopsticks and reached across the table, dipping into the dozen or so plates of food.

From "Fish Cheeks," page 131

Practice Expression: "Only Daughter"

Expression in reading is how you use your voice to express feeling. Use this passage to practice reading with proper expression. Take turns reading the passage with a classmate or an adult who can check your reading for proper expression. Print a copy of this passage from myNGconnect.com to help you monitor your progress. To use an Expression Rubric, see page 664.

When we were growing up in Chicago, we moved a lot because of my father. He suffered periodic bouts of nostalgia. Then we'd have to let go our flat, store the furniture with mother's relatives, load the station wagon with baggage and bologna sandwiches, and head south. To Mexico City.

We came back, of course. To yet another Chicago flat, another Chicago neighborhood, another Catholic school. Each time, my father would seek out the parish priest in order to get a tuition break, and complain or boast: "I have seven sons."

He meant *siete hijos*, seven children, but he translated it as "sons." "I have seven sons." To anyone who would listen. The Sears Roebuck employee who sold us the washing machine. The short-order cook where my father ate his ham-and-eggs breakfasts. "I have seven sons." As if he deserved a medal from the state.

My papa. He didn't mean anything by that mistranslation, I'm sure. But somehow I could feel myself being erased. I'd tug my father's sleeve and whisper: "Not seven sons. Six! And *one daughter*."

From "Only Daughter," page 143

Practice Intonation: "Heartbeat"

Intonation is the rise and fall in the pitch or tone of your voice as you read aloud. Use this passage to practice reading with proper intonation. Print a copy of this passage from myNGconnect.com to help you monitor your progress. To use an Intonation Rubric, see page 662.

I returned to school in January depressed, because I was still Heartbeat in everyone's eyes. I constantly weighed myself. At least once an hour, no matter where I was, I'd find a bathroom so I could take off my shirt and flex in the mirror for a couple of minutes. I was so frustrated that nothing was working—but the frustration didn't last. I was sitting in study hall two weeks ago when Sarah said the magic words: "Have you been working out, Dave? You look bigger." I couldn't tell if she was being sarcastic. I went home and inspected myself in the mirror. I did look bigger! But then I realized the reason: I'd accidentally worn *two* T-shirts under my rugby shirt that day. It was just an illusion. I was futilely stuffing my face and religiously pumping iron and failing to alter my appearance, and now I'd stumbled on the simplest solution to looking bigger. I felt like I was reborn.

I went to school the next day wearing two T-shirts under my turtleneck. I felt solid. By the end of last week, I was wearing three T-shirts under my rugby shirt. This Monday I tucked four T-shirts under my plaid button-down.

From "Heartbeat," page 191

Practice Phrasing: "I Go Along"

Phrasing is how you use your voice to group words together. Use this passage
to practice reading with proper phrasing. Print a copy of this passage from
myNGconnect.com to help you monitor your progress. To use a Phrasing Rubric,
see page 663.

They're still milling around in the aisle, but there are plenty of
seats. I find an empty double and settle by the window, pulling my
ball cap down in front. It doesn't take us long to get out of town, not
this town. When we go past 7-Eleven, I'm way down in the seat with
my hand shielding my face on the window side. Right about then,
somebody sits down next to me. I flinch.

"Okay?" she says, and I look up, and it's Sharon Willis.

I've got my knee jammed up on the back of the seat ahead of me.
I'm bent double, and my hand's over half my face. I'm cool, and it's
Sharon Willis.

"Whatever," I say.

"How are you doing, Gene?"

I'm trying to be invisible, and she's calling me by name.

"How do you know me?" I ask her.

She shifts around. "I'm a junior, you're a junior. There are about
fifty-three people in our whole year. How could I not?"

Easy, I think, but don't say it. She's got a notebook on her lap.
Everybody seems to, except me.

From "I Go Along," page 213

Practice Expression: "Pale Mare"

Expression in reading is how you use your voice to express feeling. Use this passage to practice reading with proper expression. Print a copy of this passage from myNGconnect.com to help you monitor your progress. To use an Expression Rubric, see page 664.

Papa is disgusted with my long walks. For once Mama tells him to let me be. She knows that I will explode like a star going nova if I am to stay home always.

Each of my strides jars a different, recent memory. Earlier this week at school, my teacher exclaiming over my work in physics, "Excellent work, Consuela. I'll write a letter of recommendation for you. You should really apply to Cal Tech and MIT. You're coming to the weekend astronomy camp, right?" My heart sang. The stars. For the last two years, they are all I've wanted to do: Study them, chart their fierce light, listen to them, learn what they are saying. Stars do talk—really—with radio waves for words. But when I got home from school, an eclipse was on.

Parents, on the dark side: "You will not go to any camp. Isn't school during the week enough? You have to help us with the business."

Me, trying to remain calm in the light: "What about Manuel?" My brother, older by a year.

Parents, astonishment: "He has football practice."

"So what! I'm getting top honors in science! He's playing junior varsity football!"

More genuine astonishment: "But he's the son." Meaning, of course, I'm only the daughter, only a girl.

From "Pale Mare," page 237

Practice Phrasing: "Enabling or Disabling?"

Phrasing is how you use your voice to group words together. Use this passage to practice reading with proper phrasing. Print a copy of this passage from myNGconnect.com to help you monitor your progress. To use a Phrasing Rubric, see page 663.

The relationship can work like this: Janey enabled her boyfriend Frank to take unfair advantage of his asthma. Whenever he was upset, he'd start wheezing, so Janey felt she could never disagree with him. If he wanted to go to the movies, that's where they went, even if Janey had seen the film already. If Frank wanted pizza, then pizza it was, no matter how Janey's mouth watered for a burger.

Janey also tried to keep others from upsetting Frank. When they were with friends, she worried that someone would say something that could send Frank into an asthma attack. She felt she had to control the conversation and the entertainment so he'd stay happy and healthy. She felt personally responsible for his well-being, and took pride in every day that passed without a wheeze.

Her self-esteem was dependent on how Frank felt. If he felt good, so did she. If he was unhappy, so was she. He depended on her to enable him to control others with his asthma.

From "Enabling or Disabling?" page 289

Practice Expression: "Brother Ray"

Expression in reading is how you use your voice to express feeling. Use this passage to practice reading with proper expression. Print a copy of this passage from myNGconnect.com to help you monitor your progress. To use an Expression Rubric, see page 664.

Mama was a country woman with a whole lot of common sense. She understood what most of our neighbors didn't—that I shouldn't grow dependent on anyone except myself. "One of these days I ain't gonna be here," she kept hammering inside my head. Meanwhile, she had me scrub floors, chop wood, wash clothes, and play outside like all the other kids. She made sure I could wash and dress myself. And her discipline didn't stop just 'cause I was blind. She wasn't about to let me get away with any foolishness.

Some of the neighbors gave Mama a hard time. They got on her case when they saw me working out back or helping her in the house.

"He's blind," Mama told them, "but he ain't stupid. He's lost his sight, but he ain't lost his mind."

So you can imagine how strong Mama had to be—and how intelligent—to fight against this outlook and allow me to go out on my own. And she did all this even with the other folks looking down on her.

Not only did she make me help around the house, she made certain that I did the job right.

From "Brother Ray," page 309

Practice Intonation: "He Was No Bum"

Intonation is the rise and fall in the pitch or tone of your voice as you read aloud. Use this passage to practice reading with proper intonation. Take turns reading the passage with a classmate or an adult who can check your reading for proper intonation. Print a copy of this passage from myNGconnect.com to help you monitor your progress. To use an Intonation Rubric, see page 662.

But an older man, who had been in the service himself and was familiar with shell shock, helped Kelly up and said, "That's all right, fellow. You'll be all right." After that, Kelly stayed close to the firehouse.

His mind and his nerves were not good. The firemen had to remind him to bathe, and to change clothes, and to eat properly. They did it, for twenty years and more, without anyone asking. "He's an easygoing fellow," one of them said. "He doesn't harm anybody. It's not so hard for us to take care of him."

Then the firehouse closed down. The firemen were transferred to another station house, at Laflin and Madison. Arthur Joseph Kelly went with them, but it wasn't the same. It wasn't the firehouse he had loved as a child. He didn't want to live there.

So the last fireman to take care of him—George Grant, a fifty-one-year-old father of eight—found Arthur Joseph Kelly a place to live. It wasn't much—it was the room on Madison Street—but every month Grant would take care of the financial arrangements with the bank, and would go to Madison Street to give money to a lady who ran a tavern near Kelly's room. The understanding was that she would give Kelly his meals at the tavern. No liquor. The firemen didn't want Kelly to end up as a Madison Street wino.

From "He Was No Bum," page 331

Practice Phrasing: "Jump Away"

Phrasing is how you use your voice to group words together. Use this passage to practice reading with proper phrasing. Print a copy of this passage from myNGconnect.com to help you monitor your progress. To use a Phrasing Rubric, see page 663.

Fenny wasn't afraid, but even so he really didn't want to jump. No, really he did. But on his own terms. Not forced like what Mike was doing to them here. He wanted to go when he wanted. Better yet, he would've liked to have been fishing instead, like the two people upriver. He looked at them again. He saw one of them standing up, looking in their direction. It was a girl with her hand cupped over her eyes. She was wearing a sleeveless shirt and her arms looked pinkish to Fenny. The day was good for fishing. It was warm enough, almost no current to speak of.

Fenny pulled a stick of gum from his shorts pocket. What am I doing here? he thought. What do I care what Mike thinks about me? Fenny remembered a story he'd read recently in class. It was about a boy who's been challenged to dive fifty feet from a ledge into a pool of water at the base of a waterfall. The boy in the story doesn't dive. Instead he treks back down to the base where the others, a girl included, figure him for a wimp. Easy for a kid to do in a story, Fenny thought.

From "Jump Away," page 375

Practice Intonation: "Fear"

Intonation is the rise and fall in the pitch or tone of your voice as you read aloud. Use this passage to practice reading with proper intonation. Print a copy of this passage from myNGconnect.com to help you monitor your progress. To use an Intonation Rubric, see page 662.

"I said open this door, Alpo! We know you, and you're not gonna stop us. Open up now, and we won't hurt you. You make us get mean and we'll get you, maybe tonight, maybe tomorrow, but trust me, Alpo, we'll get you."

Zo whispers to himself again, "I'd rather be dead than this afraid." He takes another deep breath and pulls his hand back from the lock. "I'd rather be dead than this afraid." Something happens inside his chest—somehow he is able to breathe again, able to think. And now he feels angry. "I'd rather be dead," he whispers.

"We'll get you, Alpo!" the voice says again, full of hate and menace.

"You might," Zo answers back, surprised by the strength of his voice.

"No 'might,' we will!" The voice is cold and murderous.

"You think I don't know you?" Zo says. "You think I can't find out who you are?"

"So what?" one of the voices answers. "You can't do anything!" They both laugh.

"Can't, huh?" Zo snaps back.

The first voice speaks again, another mean laugh in his words. "Oh right, you're all tough and bad, huh?" They laugh again.

From "Fear," page 399

Practice Expression: "Abuela Invents the Zero"

Expression in reading is how you use your voice to express feeling. Use this passage to practice reading with proper expression. Print a copy of this passage from myNGconnect.com to help you monitor your progress. To use an Expression Rubric, see page 664.

The rest of the mass is a blur. All I know is that my grandmother kneels the whole time with her hands over *her* face. She doesn't speak to me on the way home, and she doesn't let me help her walk, even though she almost falls a couple of times.

When we get to the apartment, my parents are at the kitchen table, where my mother is trying to eat some soup. They can see right away that something is wrong. Then Abuela points her finger at me like a judge passing a sentence on a criminal. She says in Spanish, "You made me feel like a zero, like a nothing." Then she goes to her room.

I try to explain what happened. "I don't understand why she's so upset. She just got lost and wandered around for a while," I tell them. But it sounds lame, even to my own ears. My mother gives me a look that makes me cringe and goes into Abuela's room to get her version of the story. She comes out with tears in her eyes.

"Your grandmother says to tell you that of all the hurtful things you can do to a person, the worst is to make them feel as if they are worth nothing."

From "Abuela Invents the Zero," page 423

Practice Intonation: "16: The Right Voting Age"

Intonation is the rise and fall in the pitch or tone of your voice as you read aloud. Use this passage to practice reading with proper intonation. Print a copy of this passage from myNGconnect.com to help you monitor your progress. To use an Intonation Rubric, see page 662.

Youths become physically mature at an earlier age. *Newsday* reports that the average age of puberty has declined. In the mid-1800s, it was 16½. In 1900, it was 15. Today, the average age of puberty is about 12.

Today's youths are smarter than previous generations. Experts cited in *The New York Times* assert that the explosion of television, video games, computer communication, and particularly the Internet, sharpen youths' abilities to think, analyze, and solve problems. Studies begun by Professor James Flynn show that IQ scores grew by 17 points from 1947 to 2001.

Teens are already treated like adults. For example, 16-year-olds can drive legally in many states. Also, young people can be tried for serious crimes as adults. In some states, this can happen at age 16. Sometimes the age is even younger. As a result, the *Jones Law Review* reports that the number of juveniles in adult prisons grew 47% in just five years. If young people can be punished like adults, they should also have the rights of adults.

From "16: The Right Voting Age," page 471

Practice Expression: "Should Communities Set Teen Curfews?"

Expression in reading is how you use your voice to express feeling. Use this passage to practice reading with proper expression. Print a copy of this passage from myNGconnect.com to help you monitor your progress. To use an Expression Rubric, see page 664.

Sure, I wish we didn't have to impose curfews. It's certainly a sad state of affairs. It would be a better solution by far if parents asserted control of their children. But today's parents don't seem to understand the difference between a parent and a buddy. Too many parents want their children to like them.

Used to be, parents could say no and, if their children didn't happen to like them at that moment or that week, the parents held their ground. They survived.

Used to be, when young people were out of the house at 2 o'clock in the morning, they were with their parents or another responsible adult. Once upon a time, chaperoned group activities ended at 11:00 p.m. and those out on dates had to be home by midnight.

Today, there are too many parents who are simply not equipped to be parents. It's sad but true that their offspring are getting into lots of trouble. They are prey to the deviants out on the streets who give them drugs and alcohol, even force them into prostitution.

If a legally imposed curfew can save these kids from that kind of fate, I welcome it.

Used to be, we didn't have to worry so much about our kids. Used to be, but not anymore.

From "Should Communities Set Teen Curfews?," page 489

Practice Phrasing: "What Does Responsibility Look Like?"

Phrasing is how you use your voice to group words together. Use this passage to practice reading with proper phrasing. Print a copy of this passage from myNGconnect.com to help you monitor your progress. To use a Phrasing Rubric, see page 663.

Another option you've mentioned is living in your car while you earned enough money to afford a real place. Where will you park? Police patrol public areas. Storekeepers don't want you in their spaces, and homeowners will not tolerate strangers in front of their houses overnight. The long, leisurely showers you enjoy will be impossible in an automobile, as will clean clothing, home-cooked meals, and nestling down in a warm, comfortable bed.

You've mentioned an even more reckless alternative: joining the homeless. My friend Alan has worked with them for many years. To him, their lives seem like utter misery. They sleep under bridges or in building entrances until the police evict them. Plastic bags and cardboard boxes are their only protection from rain and cold. All of their possessions are in grocery carts. They live in fear of being robbed of what little they have by other vagrants.

Often, the homeless are beaten, stabbed, or shot. Getting enough to eat is difficult. Bathing and clean clothes are luxuries. For any kind of income, teenagers sometimes resort to selling drugs or to prostitution. Hardly happy choices.

Believe me, teenager, you are lucky. There are many worse things than school, curfews, counseling, and parents.

From "What Does Responsibility Look Like?," page 507

Practice Expression: "Novio Boy, Part 1"

Expression in reading is how you use your voice to express feeling. Use this passage to practice reading with proper expression. Print a copy of this passage from myNGconnect.com to help you monitor your progress. To use an Expression Rubric, see page 664.

Patricia. Guess what?

Rudy. You got your driver's permit?

Patricia. How did you know? My dad's going to let me start driving next month. Right now he lets me start up the car in the morning.

Rudy. I'm fourteen, and my mom lets me start up the dryer. [*pause*] What's your mom like? She nice?

Patricia. Tall. Taller than my dad, just about an inch or so. She's pretty nice. But, you know, she's kind of overprotective. She thinks I'm at the library right now.

Rudy. She does?

Patricia. She doesn't like me seeing boys.

Rudy. Maybe if you told her I'm a freshman it would be all right. If she comes, I can jump in a high chair.

Patricia. Maybe, but probably not. She thinks boys are trouble.

Rudy. Am I trouble?

Patricia. [*smiling*] 'Course not. As sweet as you are, how could you be trouble? I mean, you're nicer than most boys, and not stupid, either. [*scoots her chair closer to* RUDY] I can see that there is something behind your eyes.

Rudy. You can?

Patricia. Sure. Your eyes ... they tell me that you're ... daring.

Rudy. Daring?

Patricia. Intelligent.

Rudy. Intelligent?

From "Novio Boy, Part 1," page 555

Practice Intonation: "Novio Boy, Part 2"

Intonation is the rise and fall in the pitch or tone of your voice as you read aloud. Use this passage to practice reading with proper intonation. Print a copy of this passage from myNGconnect.com to help you monitor your progress. To use an Intonation Rubric, see page 662.

Waiter. Your bill, *monsieur.*

Rudy. Thank you. [*gulps as he reads the bill. He digs into his pocket.*]

Patricia. We can split this.

Rudy. No, I got it. What's twenty-four dollars and fifty-four cents to me?

Patricia. Next time, it's my turn. Oh, wait! I'll pay the tip!

Rudy. OK.

Patricia. I have to be home by two o'clock. I had a lot of fun, Rudy.

Rudy. Me, too. [*pause*] You don't mind if I'm younger?

Patricia. Of course not. [*pause*] Listen, I'll teach you how to drive a car.

Mother. Drive a car!

Patricia. [*looks toward the women*] Are those women talking to us?

Rudy. Nah, they're just chattering.

Patricia. So—you want to learn? We can practice going back and forth in the driveway.

Rudy. *¡Simón!* And I got my license, too.

Patricia. You do?

Rudy. Well, it's not a real license. It's a license on my bike that says RUDY. It hangs behind my seat.

Patricia. [*laughs*] You're a fun date. And a good dancer.

From "Novio Boy, Part 2," page 579

Practice Phrasing: "To Helen Keller"

Phrasing is how you use your voice to group words together. Use this passage to practice reading with proper phrasing. Take turns reading the passage with a classmate or an adult who can check your reading for proper phrasing. Print a copy of this passage from myNGconnect.com to help you monitor your progress. To use a Phrasing Rubric, see page 663.

June 28, 1965

Dear Helen,

In my mind I can still see you clearly, standing for hours talking to the students and answering their questions. The questions were not always the most intelligent ones. For instance: "How can you ride horseback when you can't see where the horse is going?" But you gave a wonderful answer. "I just hold onto the horse and let him run wherever he wishes!" And you and the children had a good laugh over this description. Or when you said that after you had learned to speak, you became a real blabbermouth!

It was unforgettable and moving to see you touch the face of a blind child or kiss the face of a crippled one. How your face expressed your feelings. And how your love inspired the children to carry on in spite of the huge problems they had to overcome. You pushed them in the direction of a happier life. You were able to lead them because you had conquered your own handicaps and you were concerned with theirs.

It doesn't sound good enough when I say this. But thank you for what you did for those children, and for all mankind, after that terrible war. Many people have found strength, encouragement, and help in your kindness and goodness.

Gratefully yours,
Ernst Papanek

From "To Helen Keller," page 599

Study Skills and Strategies

Before You Study

Studying can be difficult, especially when you are distracted or have many subjects you need to study all at the same time. There are several ways to prepare to study, including creating a routine and establishing a productive study environment. You can also make studying easier by studying subjects in a specific order and creating a schedule.

How to Create and Maintain a Study Routine

Before you begin studying, create a routine.

- Study at the same time and place for each session.
- Mark the study time in your calendar as an appointment, like going to the doctor. For example, *Tuesday: 3:30–4:30: Study English*.
- Set small, specific goals for each study session.
- Pay attention to what works best for you and repeat that method.
- Give yourself a small reward when you are finished. For example, call a friend or listen to your favorite music.

How to Create a Productive Study Environment

Setting up a study area will help you follow your routine. Find an area where you are comfortable that you can claim as your own.

Set Up Your Workplace
• Make sure your area is quiet or has background noise, depending on which you prefer.
• Make sure you have enough light—get an extra lamp if your area is too dark.
• Have everything you need for studying available beforehand.
• Designate certain places for each necessary item. Don't waste valuable time looking for books, notes, writing materials, self-stick notes, or information.
• After you have assembled the items you need, put them where you can easily access them.
• Keep a calendar and a watch or clock in your study area to help you stay focused on your available time and on your priorities.
• Keep your study area clean.

How to Create an Efficient Study Order

Creating priorities for study time will help you complete your tasks in an efficient order. Making a list of the things you need to do can help you organize your priorities. Look at the chart to understand how to create an efficient order for your study time.

Study Order Tips	
Label Your Assignments by Priority	• **Urgent** Must be done immediately • **Important** Must be done soon • **Upcoming** Must be done in the near future
Make a List	• List the things you have to do in order of importance. • Once you complete a task, cross it off your list.
Stay Organized	• Keep your list nearby to record new tasks or updates.

How to Complete Tasks on Schedule

A good schedule can help you stay focused and complete assignments on time. Create a schedule or purchase a day planner and record homework due dates, quizzes, and tests.

Think about events that might affect your schedule, such as appointments or extracurricular activities. You may need to postpone or cancel other plans to help you stay on schedule. If you are concerned about missing a date, circle the task.

			Weekly Schedule		
Subject	**Monday**	**Tuesday**	**Wednesday**	**Thursday**	**Friday**
Math	Chapter 6: Problems 1-10	None	Chapter 6: Problems 11-20	None	Chapter 7: Problems 1-15
Science	Study for Test	Review for Test	Test	Read Chapter 8	None
History	None	Read Chapter 11	Read Chapter 12	Study for Quiz	Quiz: Chapters 11 and 12
English	Read Chapter 3	Read Chapter 4 Study for Quiz	Quiz: Chapters 3 and 4	Read Chapter 5	None

While You Study

There are many different ways to study. Talk with classmates and your teachers to learn new study techniques and strategies that might work for you, too. No matter which study strategies you use, you should use a variety, such as writing and using graphic organizers, until you figure out which strategies work best for you.

How to Use Writing as a Study Tool

Use writing as a tool to assist you:

- Write your own questions about the topic, and practice answering them.
- Condense your classroom notes onto note cards or into charts for easier reviewing.
- Create an outline from your notes, and then write a summary of the information.
- Write notes on self-stick notes as you read. Later, attach the self-stick notes in an organized manner to a sheet of notebook paper for at-a-glance study.

How to Use Graphic Organizers as a Study Tool

Graphic organizers are effective study tools. For example, a time line can be used to organize the events covered in a nonfiction selection. A word web can be used to learn new vocabulary words. See the Index of Graphic Organizers on page 816 for more examples of graphic organizers you can use as study tools.

How to Review

It is very important to review material. The best time to review is right after you have finished reading something for the first time. Reviewing gives you an opportunity to figure out anything you do not understand and to better remember information in the future.

Review Effectively

- When you read something new, review the information on the same day.
- Reread information to measure what you have learned.
- Go over notes in detail to clarify information you may have missed or don't understand. Combine your notes with any outlines or study guides that you have about the topic.
- Write down any new questions you may have.
- Plan a time to review each day. This will help you learn to review information regularly as part of your daily study schedule.

How to Use a Learning Log and Set Goals

You can use learning logs to record what you have learned, what you found interesting, and questions you have about the text. The purpose of a learning log is to think about your understanding of the material and to clarify your knowledge for further study. Use the **What parts am I struggling with?** and **What will I do next?** columns in the learning log to set future learning goals.

Learning Log			
Title of Selection:			
Dates and page numbers	What have I learned?	What parts am I struggling with?	What will I do next?

How to Seek Help

There will be times when you don't understand certain information, even after studying and careful note taking. You will need to seek help to understand the information. Make a list of the topics or problems that you don't understand. Include the page numbers where they are located in your textbooks. Make a chart that lists people and places you can seek help from. Then use these resources to help clarify confusing information.

Resources for Help

People: teachers, parents, siblings, classmates, librarians, tutors

Places: libraries, museums, study centers, school

Reference Sources: dictionaries, thesauruses, encyclopedias, atlases, newspapers, magazines, Web sites, television programs

Vocabulary

How to Make Words Your Own Routine

When you cook, you follow the steps of a recipe. This helps you make the food correctly. When you read, there are also steps you can follow to learn new words. The following steps will help you practice the words in different ways and make the words your own.

Learning a Word

Follow these steps to add new words to your vocabulary.

1. **Pronounce the Word** Write and say the word one syllable at a time.
   - **realize**: re-a-lize
   - Think about what looks familiar in the word. For example, **real** is part of **realize**.

2. **Study Examples** When you are given examples, read them carefully and think about how and why the word is being used.
   - **Example**: *Marietta did not* **realize** *that Lupe was so busy.* What does this sentence tell you about Marietta and Lupe?
   - Look for more examples to study in books or magazines.

3. **Elaborate** Create new sentences to check your understanding of the word.
   - Finish these sentence frames for practice:
   - I **realized** I was happy when _____.
   - Steve's mom **realized** he was growing up when _____.
   - How did your teacher **realize** that you _____?

4. **Practice the Words** Use the new word to write sentences.
   - Use the word in many different ways. This will help you remember the word and understand its meaning.

How to Relate Words

A good way to build your vocabulary is to **relate new words** to words or concepts you already know. Think about how the new word is similar to or different from words you are already familiar with. You can also create a **semantic map** to help you study the new word.

Semantic Map

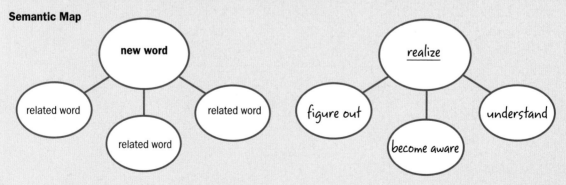

How to Use Context to Understand Words

Context is the surrounding text near a word or phrase that helps explain the meaning of the word or phrase.

Unfamiliar Words

Context clues are hints in a sentence or paragraph that can help define unknown or unfamiliar words. Context clues can include synonyms, antonyms, explanations, definitions, examples, sensory images, or punctuation, such as commas and dashes.

- **Example**: *My fascination with* <u>*celestial bodies*</u>—*such as* **stars, planets,** *and* **moons**—*made me want to buy a* **telescope**. The words *stars*, *planets*, and *moons* are clues that tell me *celestial bodies* are objects in the universe. The word *telescope* tells me I can see these objects from Earth, probably at night.

Multiple-Meaning Words

Some words have different meanings depending on how they are used in a sentence. Check what context the words are used in to help determine which meaning is correct in the material you are reading. Substitute each meaning you know in the context of the sentence until you find the use that makes the best sense.

- **Example**: *Please sign your name before entering the museum.* The word *sign* has more than one meaning. Which meaning is correct in this sentence? *Sign* can mean "to write" or it can mean "something that hangs on a wall to provide information." The first meaning is correct.

Figurative Language

Figurative language is a tool that writers use to help you visualize or relate to what is happening in a selection. This type of language is nonliteral because it does not mean exactly what it looks like it says, or it is using a special meaning. Idioms, similes, and metaphors are common types of nonliteral, or figurative language. It is helpful to use mental images or context clues to better understand what you are reading.

Idioms

An **idiom** is a phrase or an expression that can only be understood as a complete sentence or phrase. The individual words have separate meanings and they will not make sense if they are thought of literally. Read the words before or after the idiom to figure out the meaning. Remember to think about an idiom as a group of words, not as individual words.

- **Example**: Don't *bite off more than you can chew* or you will never finish the job. This is an idiom used to advise people against agreeing to do more work than they are capable of doing. It is not a phrase about biting or chewing.

Similes and Metaphors

Similes use *like* or *as* to compare two things.

- **Example**: *The willow tree's branches are like silken thread.* This simile is comparing a tree's branches to silk thread. Think about the things that are being compared and what they each mean. Silk is very soft and smooth. The simile means the willow's branches are also very soft and smooth.

Metaphors compare two things without using *like* or *as*.

- **Example**: *The night sky is a black curtain.* This metaphor compares the night sky to a black curtain. A black curtain would block out light from coming in a window. This metaphor means the night sky is very dark.

- **Example**: *The company planned an advertising blitz to promote its new product.* The word *blitz* comes from the German word *blitzkrieg*, which refers to the bombing of London, England, by Germany during World War II. The term *advertising blitz*, therefore, is a metaphor that expresses the way advertisements will overwhelm the public.

You can also use sensory images to learn new words by asking yourself or others: What does it look like? Feel like? Sound like?

Technical and Specialized Language

Technical, or specialized, language provides important information about a topic. Many words in English have an everyday meaning and a special meaning in a career field. For example, the word *shift* can mean "to move something from one place to another." In the workplace, however, *shift* can mean "a time period for work."

Example: *Be sure to clean your mouse regularly to make the cursor move smoothly on the computer monitor.*

- Read the sentence to determine the specialized subject.
- Identify technical vocabulary: *mouse, cursor, computer monitor.*
- Use context clues to help you figure out the meaning of the technical language, or jargon.

Denotation and Connotation

Denotation is the actual meaning of a word that you would find in a dictionary. For example, if you looked up the word *snake* in the dictionary, you could find that one of its meanings is "a limbless scaled reptile with a long tapering body."

Connotation is the suggested meaning of the word in addition to its literal meaning. Connotations can be positive or negative. For example, the word *snake* can be used in a positive or negative way.

- **Example**: *Jenny was caught sneaking around Maria's locker. She wanted to steal Maria's homework and copy Maria's answers. Nobody could believe that Jenny would be such a snake.*

By using the context of the paragraph (*sneaking around, steal*), you can understand that the connotation of *snake* in this usage is negative.

Analogies

An **analogy** is a comparison. Think of analogies as word problems. To solve the analogy, figure out what the connection is. Use context to see how the word pairs are related.

- **Example**: *Hard* is to *rocks* as *soft* is to _____. *Hard* describes the feeling of *rocks*. Rocks are hard. What does *soft* describe the feeling of? *Hard* is to *rocks* as *soft* is to *blankets*.

Use the relationships between words in an analogy to infer the meaning of an unfamiliar word. For example, in the analogy "*sparse* is to *meager* as *quarrel* is to *argue*," you can infer that *sparse* and *meager* mean the same thing.

Allusions

An **allusion** is a reference to another text. If you know or can find out about the source that the writer is alluding to, you can better understand the word or phrase.

- **Example**: "It took a herculean effort, but she finally made it to graduation." *Herculean* refers to a character from Greek mythology named Hercules. He fought monsters and faced many dangers. So the character must have faced challenges too.

How to Analyze Word Parts

Each piece in a puzzle fits together to make a picture. Words have pieces that come together, too. Analyzing the parts, or structures, of words will help you learn the meaning of entire words. Use a print or electronic dictionary to confirm your word analysis.

Compound Words

Compound words are made when two separate words are combined to make a new word. To learn the meaning of a compound word, study its parts individually. For example, *doghouse* is one word made from two smaller words, *dog* and *house*. Since you know that *dog* is an animal and *house* is a structure where people live, you can figure out that *doghouse* means a house for a dog.

Greek and Latin Roots

Many words in the English language derived from, or came from, other languages, especially Greek and Latin. It is helpful to know the **origins**, or **roots**, of English words. You may be able to figure out the meaning of an unknown word if you know the meaning of its root. Roots can form many different words and can't be broken into smaller parts. The chart below has examples of roots.

Root Chart		
Root	**Meaning**	**English Example**
crit (Greek)	to judge	*Criticize* means "to find fault." *Critique* means "an act of judgment."
mal (Latin)	bad	*Malady* means "an illness." *Malice* means "desire to harm another."

Prefixes and Suffixes

If you know common roots, **prefixes**, and **suffixes**, you can figure out the meanings of many words. The chart below shows how to analyze the word *constellation*.

Word Part	Definition	Example
Root	The main part of a word	*stella* means "star"
Prefix	A word part placed in front of the root to create a new meaning	*con-* means "together"
Suffix	A word part placed after the root to create a new meaning	*-tion* means "the act of"
Example: A *constellation* is a group of stars.		

Inflected Forms

An **inflection** is a change in the form of a word to show its usage. You can learn new words by analyzing what type of inflection is being used.

Inflection	Meaning	Examples
-er	more	cold**er**, fast**er**
-ed	in the past	call**ed**, talk**ed**
-s	plural	pen**s**, dog**s**

Word Families

A word family is a group of words that all share the same root but have different forms. For example, look at the word family for *success*: *success**ful***, *success**fully***, ***un**success**ful***, ***un**success**fully***. If you know the meaning of the root word *success*, you can use what you know to help you understand the rest of the meanings in the word family.

Cognates and False Cognates

Cognates are words that come from two different languages but that are very similar because they share root origins. Cognates have similar spellings and meanings. For example, the English word *artist* and the Spanish word *artista* both mean "a person who creates art."

False cognates seem like they share a meaning but they do not. For example, the English word *rope* means "a cord to tie things with," but the Spanish word *ropa* means "clothing."

How to Use Cognates to Determine Word Meaning

- Think about what the word means in the language you are most familiar with.
- Substitute the meaning of the word with your language's definition.
- If your language's definition does not make sense, you may be using a false cognate. Try to learn the word using a different resource.

Foreign Words in English

Some foreign words come directly into English, without changes in spelling. For example, the French phrase *avant-garde*, referring to a cutting-edge movement in art or music, is often used in English. Use a print or online dictionary to identify other foreign words in English.

How to Use a Reference

Dictionary

A dictionary lists words with correct spellings, pronunciations, meanings, and uses. It can be used to find the denotation, or exact meaning, of a word. Sometimes a dictionary definition may be helpful in determining the connotation, or feelings associated with a word.

- Read all the definitions of the new word to find the use and meaning you need. Use the dictionary's key to understand any abbreviations or symbols.
- Go back to the selection and reread the paragraph. Substitute the meaning you found for the original word. Check to make sure it is the correct use of the word.

fraud·u·lent
(frȯ' jə lənt), *adj.*: based on or done by fraud or trickery; deceitful. [ME *fraude* fr. L *fraud-*] –fraud'u·lent·ness, *n.* –fraud'u·lent·ly, *adv.*

Key	
ME	Middle English (an old version of English)
L	Latin
fr.	from
ȯ	pronounced like the *a* in *saw*
ə	pronounced like *uh*
'	accented syllable

Thesaurus

A thesaurus lists words with their synonyms and antonyms. Use a thesaurus to confirm word meanings.

- Try to identify a familiar word from the synonyms listed for the new word.
- Go back to the selection and reread the paragraph. Substitute the synonym you chose for the original word. Keep trying synonyms until the words make sense.

Glossary

A glossary is like a dictionary but only defines words found in a specific book.

- Check to see whether there is a glossary at the end of the book you are reading.
- Read the definition of the new word in the glossary.
- Reread the sentence and substitute the definition for the word.

Technology

The Internet links computers and information sites electronically.

Web Sites to Use for Vocabulary Support

- myNGConnect.com This Web site has links to reference sources.
- m-w.com The Merriam-Webster Dictionary Web site includes a dictionary, a thesaurus, Spanish-English translation, and word activities.

Practice Your Vocabulary

When you are trying to learn something new, like a musical instrument, you practice. The more you practice, the better you become. Practicing vocabulary words is an important step in learning new words.

Memorize New Words

- Read the word and its definition silently and aloud.
- Cover the definition and try to restate the word's meaning.
- Write words on one side of index cards and their meanings on the opposite sides to make flashcards. Have someone show you the words, and try to recite their definitions from memory.
- Ask yourself questions using the definition and the word.
- Think of clues or mental images to associate with the new word to help you better remember its definition. You can also use real images to help you remember. For example, look around the classroom. Point to an object and say what it is. Use this to describe the entire classroom.

Review New Words

- Reread the definition of each word.
- Create sentences expressing the correct meaning of each word.
- Make lists of new words with their definitions in a notebook to periodically review.
- Study each word until you are confident you understand its meaning and how to use the word properly.

Word Awareness

It is important to choose the right words in order to clearly say what you mean. You need to be aware of different kinds of words and how they work. For example, remember that some words have multiple meanings. If you are not aware of this as you read, you might use the wrong meaning or misunderstand a sentence.

Synonyms and Antonyms

Synonyms are words that have the same or similar meanings.

- Think of a different word that has the same meaning of the word you want to use. For example, synonyms for the word *loud* include *noisy* and *roaring*.
- Use a thesaurus when trying to identify synonyms.

Antonyms are words that have opposite meanings.

- Think of words that are the exact opposite of the word you want to use. For example, antonyms for the word *break* include *fix* and *repair*.
- Remember that antonyms are usually listed at the end of an entry for a word in a thesaurus.

Homonyms and Homophones

Homonyms are words that are spelled the same but have different meanings.

- **Example**: *I* rose *out of my chair to pick the* rose *from the top of the bush.* In this sentence, *rose* has two meanings. One *rose* is a verb (past tense of *rise*), and the other *rose* is a noun (a type of flower). Using context clues, you can see that *out of my chair* signals that "the past tense of rise" comes at the beginning of the sentence. You can then conclude that "the flower" is the second *rose.*

Homophones are words that sound the same but have different meanings and spellings.

- **Example**: *The wind* blew *the clouds across the* blue *sky. Blew* and *blue* sound alike, but they are spelled differently. *Blew* is a verb (the past tense of *blow*), and *blue* is an adjective (a color). Using context clues, you can see that *the clouds* signals that "the past tense of blow" comes at the beginning of the sentence. You can then conclude that "a color" is the second *blue.*

When you hear a homonym or a homophone read aloud, it is easy to become confused. Visualizing the word can help you figure out its correct meaning and spelling.

Phrasal Verbs, or Two-Word Verbs

Phrasal verbs combine a particle such as *out, up,* or *on* with a verb. These phrases are often idiomatic because the two words on their own mean something different than the phrase.

- **Example**: *I* brought up *my fight with Leon during dinner. Brought* is the past tense of *bring,* and *up* is a direction. But when the words are combined in the context shown in the sample sentence, they mean "mentioned." *I mentioned my fight with Leon during dinner.*

You may be able to find some phrasal verbs in a dictionary. If you do not understand a certain phrase, ask for help or look for English usage resources in the library.

Slang

Slang is language that is informal and specific to certain groups.

- Slang words are created and used in place of standard terms. Popular culture and the media heavily impact slang words and usage.

- Learning when to use slang is important. Slang is OK for casual situations, but not for more formal ones, like school discussions, writing, or presentations.

- If you become familiar with common slang words and phrases, it may help you to better understand everyday conversations. Special dictionaries for slang can help you learn more terms.

Dialect and Regionalism

A **dialect** is a way people in a specific region or area use a language.

- People in different locations often have different ways to express or pronounce words from the same language.

- If you are unfamiliar with a dialect, try to find out more about the way local people use their language. You can use the Internet or library resources to study dialects.

WRITING HANDBOOK

The Writing Process

What Is the Writing Process?

Writing is like anything else—if you want to do it well, you have to work at it. This work doesn't happen all at once, though. Good writers often follow a series of steps called the Writing Process. This process helps the writer break the writing into manageable tasks.

Prewrite

Prewriting is what you do before you write. In this step, you gather ideas, choose your topic, make a plan, and gather details.

❶ Gather Ideas

Great writing ideas are all around you. What interests do you have that other people might want to read about? Think about recent events or things you've read or seen. Brainstorm ideas with your classmates, teachers, and family. Then record your ideas in an "idea bank," such as a notebook, journal, or **word processing** file. Add to your idea bank regularly and draw from it whenever you are given a writing assignment.

❷ Choose Your Topic

Your teacher may give you a topic to write about, or you may have to choose one for yourself. Find several suitable topics in your idea bank; then ask these questions:

- What do I know about this topic?
- Who might want to read about this topic and why?
- Which topic do I feel most strongly about?
- Which topic best fits the assignment?
- What important question can I ask about the topic?

> Writing Ideas
> visiting my family in Mexico
> ✓ my first job
> teens and peer pressure

❸ Make a Plan

Create a Writing Plan to focus and organize your ideas.

Writing Plan
Topic: What will I write about?   my first job
Purpose: Why am I writing?   to share a lesson with others
Audience: Who will read this?   my teacher and classmates
Form: What form works best for my topic, audience, and purpose?   autobiographical narrative
Controlling Idea: What is this mainly about?   learning to do things for myself
Voice/Tone: What attitude and feeling do I want my writing to express?   serious, with a little humor

❹ Gather Details

A 5Ws and H chart will help you gather details for many kinds of writing assignments.

5Ws and H Chart	
Who?	my dad, my boss, and I
What?	first job
Where?	Garcia's Restaurant
When?	last summer to now
Why?	spending money, save for college
How?	fill out application, use bus to get to and from my job

⑤ Research

Some writing forms and topics require research. Use these resources to find out more about your topic:

- **Internet** Develop a list of terms to enter into a search engine. Use sites that end in .edu or .gov for the most reliable information. For more on Internet research, see p. 608.

- **Library** Search the library's catalog and databases for books and articles about your topic. Ask a librarian for help.

- **Interview** You may want to interview a person who has knowledge about your topic. Prepare questions ahead of time and take notes on the responses.

⑥ Get Organized

Review your details and choose a way to organize your writing. Use an appropriate graphic organizer such as a topic outline to show the main idea and details of your paragraphs in order. List your main ideas next to the roman numerals. List any supporting details underneath the main ideas, next to the capital letters.

Topic Outline

My First Job

    I. Introduction: I joined the workforce.
        A. Many teens work.
        B. Work taught me responsibility.
    II. Body: I looked for and got a job.
        A. I searched want ads.
        B. I applied for jobs.
        C. I interviewed.
    III. Body: I learned the job.
        A. My first day was hard.
        B. I improved over time.
    IV. Conclusion: I learned a lesson.
        A. I earned money for college.
        B. I learned responsibility.

For another sample outline, see **Language and Learning Handbook**, page 641.

Draft

The drafting stage is when you put your Writing Plan into action. Don't worry about making things perfect at this point. Drafts are meant to be changed. Instead, concentrate on writing out your ideas in complete sentences and paragraphs. The following ideas will help you organize your main idea and supporting details into a draft.

❶ Remember Purpose, Form, and Audience

Remember, you already made many important decisions about your work during the prewriting stage. Return to your Writing Plan often. Remind yourself of your purpose, form, and controlling idea as you organize your paragraphs. Think carefully about your audience, voice, and tone as you choose words and craft sentences.

❷ Introduce the Controlling Idea and Use Literary Devices

Your first paragraph should introduce your controlling idea and draw readers into your work. You can use any of the following literary devices to begin your paper in a clear and interesting way. Each device is an example of a **topic sentence**, which lets readers know what the text will be about.

- **Position Statement**: *Few things teach responsibility better than a part-time job.*

- **Question**: *Do you remember your first paycheck?*

- **Quotation**: *My dad always says, "If you really want something, you'll work for it."*

- **Statistic**: *In July 2006, almost 22 million teens in the United States held a job. I was one of them. It was my first job.*

The controlling idea is the main thing you are writing about, or the idea you want to express. It is more specific than the topic. The topic is the general area or subject of your writing. For example, if the topic of an article is baseball, the controlling idea could be learning how to hit home runs.

❸ Work Collaboratively

Involve other people in the writing of your draft early and often. Teachers, classmates, and family members can help you improve what you have written and determine what needs to be done. Listen carefully to what they have to say, and take notes on their suggestions.

❹ Use Technology to Draft

Continue writing until you have a complete draft. You can write your draft with a pen and paper or with a **word processor**. In either case, be sure to save a copy of your work.

Draft

My First Job

In July 2006, almost 22 million teens in the United States held a job (Bureau of Labor Statistics). I was one of them. It was my first job. That summer I learned lessons about responsibility that will last me the rest of my life.

The first thing I learned is that knowing how to find, apply for, and interview for a job is as important as knowing how to do the job itself. I searched the want ads in our local newspaper and on the Internet. In fact, I even filled out and submitted applications for several places online. I was sure to fill out each application as completely and honestly as possible. This work proved useful when two restaurants asked me to interview for busboy, or assistant server, positions. I dressed neatly and gave myself plenty of time to make it to the interviews on schedule. When I met the managers, I shook their hands, then listened closely to their questions before responding.

Revise

After you have written a draft, you need to revise it, or make changes. Revision is what takes your writing from good to great.

❶ Revise for Traits of Good Writing

Focus and Unity
- ☑ Do you have a clearly stated controlling idea or opinion?
- ☑ Is your controlling idea supported?
- ☑ Do your ideas and details flow logically?

Organization
- ☑ Do you have a title and an introductory paragraph?
- ☑ Do you transition between ideas?
- ☑ Are your ideas in a sensible order?
- ☑ Do you have a conclusion or ending?
- ☑ Does the organization match your purpose and audience?

Development of Ideas
- ☑ Are your ideas meaningful?
- ☑ Are your details vivid?
- ☑ Do your details answer questions that readers may have about the topic?
- ☑ Have you addressed purpose, audience, and genre to improve subtlety of meaning?

Voice and Style
- ☑ Is your writing unique and engaging?
- ☑ Are most of your sentences in active voice?
- ☑ Do the style and language used match your purpose and audience?
- ☑ Do you use figurative language to address purpose, audience, and genre?

Written Conventions
- ☑ Are your spelling, punctuation, capitalization, grammar, and usage correct?

See pages 706–715 for more information.

❷ Use Technology

The word processing software found on most computers will help you develop and make changes to your work quickly and easily. Here are some hints to help you get the most out of your computer:

- Save your work often. This will prevent the loss of your work in case of a computer malfunction.

- Create a "scrap file" of sentences and paragraphs you deleted as you revised. This deleted material may contain other ideas and details you can use in later writing.

- Think about how you will move your document from computer to computer. For example, if you e-mail yourself a copy, make sure the next computer you plan to use has Internet access.

❸ Hold a Peer Conference

Work with your classmates to improve each other's work.

Peer Review Guidelines

As Writer ...

- Read your draft aloud or supply copies for each member of your group.

- Ask for help on specific points related to the traits of good writing.

- Listen carefully and take notes on your reviewers' comments.

As Reviewer ...

- Read or listen to the complete writing. Take notes as you read or listen.

- Compliment the strong parts of the draft before you criticize weak points.

- Offer specific suggestions.

Edit and Proofread

After you have revised your draft for content, organization, and wording, it is time to check it for mistakes.

❶ Take Your Time

Successful editing and proofreading require attention to detail. The following hints will help you do your best work:

- Use a printed copy of your work. Text looks different on paper than on a computer screen. Many people catch more mistakes when they edit a printed version of their work.

- Set your work aside for a while. Your review may be more effective if you are rested.

- Read line by line. Use a ruler or piece of paper to cover the lines below the one you are reading. This will help you concentrate on the text in front of you.

❷ Check Your Sentences

Make sure your sentences are clear, complete, and correct. Ask yourself:

- Did I include a subject and a predicate in each sentence?

- Did I break up run-on sentences?

- Did I use a variety of sentence structures to keep my writing interesting?

- Did I combine short sentences, when possible, to create longer sentences?

- Did I use the active voice in most of my sentences?

❸ Check for Mistakes

Proofread to find errors in capitalization, punctuation, grammar, and spelling. Look especially for:

- capital letters, end marks, apostrophes, and quotation marks

- subject-verb agreement

- misspelled words

④ Use Reference Tools

Reference tools are an important part of every writer's tool kit. Dictionaries, thesauruses, and electronic sources such as Web sites and the spell-checking features of most word processing programs are all reference tools available to the good writer. When in doubt, check different versions of several sources.

Use a **dictionary** to check the meaning and spelling of your words.

> I worked **diligently** that summer.
> *Is that spelled correctly?*

Use a **thesaurus** to find words that are livelier or more appropriate for your audience.

> I worked ~~diligently~~ **hard** that summer.
> *Maybe this word is clearer to my audience.*

Use a **grammar handbook** to fix sentences and punctuation errors.

> We ~~was~~ **were** cleaning the grill.
> *That's the correct verb.*

Use a **style guide** or **style manual**, which is a publication containing rules and suggestions about grammar, writing, and publishing, for help in **citing** your sources. When you use information and ideas from other authors, you need to give them credit for their work. **Plagiarism** is using someone's words or ideas without giving the person credit. When you reword another author's ideas, you still have to give the author credit for his or her ideas.

> In July 2006, almost 22 million teens in the United States held a job. (Bureau of Labor Statistics)
> *Now the statistic is properly cited, according to the method I found in the style guide.*

⑤ Mark Your Changes

Use proofreader's marks to show changes on a printout of your draft. Then make changes to your word processed document.

> ¶ The first thing I learned is that knowing ~~how~~ how to find, apply for, and interview for a job is as important as knowing how to do the job itself. I *searched* the want ads in our local newspaper and on the Internet. In fact, I even filled out and submitted applications for several places online. I was sure to fill out each application as completely and honestly as possible. I dressed neatly and gave myself plenty of time to make it to the interviews on schedule. This work proved useful when two restaurants asked me to interview for busboy, or assistant server, positions. when I met the Managers, I shook their hands, then listened closely to their questions before responding.

Proofreader's Marks

Mark	Meaning
✏	Delete
∧	Add text
↪	Move to here
⊙	Add period
⌄	Add comma
≡	Capitalize
/	Make lowercase
¶	Start new paragraph

Publish and Evaluate

You've made it! You're now ready for the last step in the Writing Process. First, prepare your final document for your readers. Then, reflect back on what you've done well and what you could do better next time.

❶ Print Your Work

The final version of your work should be neat and easy to read. It should be visually appealing. You can increase the visual impact of the final version of your work by using different font types and sizes, headings, bullet points, or even diagrams and charts as a way to present data. Use the information below to format your document for final publication. Then print out and make copies of your work to share with others. Be sure to keep a copy for yourself.

1 inch top margin

Header with author, class, date

Sam Rodriguez

English 103

October 13, 2007

Centered/ boldfaced title; set in a different font from main text

My First Job

In July 2006, almost 22 million teens in the United States held a job (Bureau of Labor Statistics). I was one of them. It was my first job. That summer I learned lessons about responsibility that will last me the rest of my life.

The first thing I learned is that knowing how to find, apply for, and interview for a job is as important as knowing how to do the job itself. I searched the want ads in our local newspaper and on the Internet. In fact, I even filled out and submitted applications for several places online. I carefully filled out each application as completely and honestly as possible.

This work proved useful when two restaurants asked me to interview for busboy, or assistant server, positions. I dressed neatly and gave myself plenty of time to make it to the interviews on schedule. When I met the managers, I shook their hands, then listened closely to their questions before responding.

1

1 inch bottom margin

1.25 inch left margin

Page number centered, 0.5 inch from bottom

1.25 inch right margin

❷ Publish Your Work

Take your work beyond the classroom and share it in new ways.

- Save examples of your writing in a portfolio. This will allow you to see the improvement in your writing over time. Organize your portfolio by date or form. Each time you add pieces to your portfolio, take some time to self-reflect and compare the new piece to your older work.

Portfolio Review

- ☑ How does this writing compare to other work I've done?
- ☑ What traits am I getting better at?
- ☑ What traits do I need to work on?
- ☑ What is my style? What kinds of sentences and words do I often use?
- ☑ What makes me a super writer?

- Expand your work by making it into a poster or other visual display, such as a video or a Web site. What images best express your ideas? How will the text appear?

- Many newspapers and Web sites publish teen writing. Ask a teacher or librarian for examples, or research them yourself. For writers, there are few things more satisfying than sharing their ideas with as wide an audience as possible.

❸ Evaluate Your Work

Now that you have completed your work, look to see what you can improve.

- Use rubrics to evaluate the quality and effectiveness of your writing. Rubrics contain criteria for evaluating your work. Review the rubrics on pages 706–715.

- Discuss your work with your teacher and classmates, then ask yourself:

What did I do well?

I added some description. My details were sequential and organized.

What are some weaknesses that I could improve on easily?

It lacks uniqueness. I need to vary my sentence structures.

How will I make sure I improve on those weaker areas?

I could pick topics that I feel strongly about. During revision I can check my sentence structure.

What are some weaknesses that may take time to improve?

Expanding my ideas, making my voice more mature.

- Set goals based on your evaluation. Make a list of goals; cross them out as you accomplish them. Then set new goals.

Goals to Improve My Writing
1. I am going to use more descriptive sentences in my next narrative piece.
2. I am going to check all my sentence beginnings and make sure they are different.
3. I am going to add more "important" facts to my expository nonfiction pieces.

What Are Writing Traits?

Writing traits are the characteristics of good writing. Use the traits and writing examples on the following pages to plan, evaluate, and improve your writing.

Focus and Unity

All the ideas in a piece of writing should be related, or go together well. **Focus** your writing by selecting a single central or **controlling idea**. Then give your work **unity** by relating each main idea and detail to that controlling idea. Use the rubric below to help maintain focus and unity in your writing.

Focus and Unity

	How clearly does the writing present a central idea or claim?	How well does everything go together?
4 Wow!	The writing expresses a <u>clear</u> central idea or claim about the topic.	<u>Everything</u> in the writing goes together. • The main idea of each paragraph goes with the central idea or claim of the paper. • The main idea and details within each paragraph are related. • The conclusion is about the central idea or claim.
3 Ahh.	The writing expresses a <u>generally</u> clear central idea or claim about the topic.	<u>Most</u> parts of the writing go together. • The main idea of most paragraphs goes with the central idea or claim of the paper. • In most paragraphs, the main idea and details are related. • Most of the conclusion is about the central idea or claim.
2 Hmm.	The writing includes a topic, but the central idea or claim is <u>not</u> clear.	<u>Some</u> parts of the writing go together. • The main idea of some paragraphs goes with the central idea or claim of the paper. • In some paragraphs, the main idea and details are related. • Some of the conclusion is about the central idea or claim.
1 Huh?	The writing includes many topics and <u>does not</u> express one central idea or claim.	The parts of the writing <u>do not</u> go together. • Few paragraphs have a main idea, or the main idea does not go with the central idea or claim of the paper. • Few paragraphs contain a main idea and related details • None of the conclusion is about the central idea or claim.

Focus and Unity: Strong Example, score of 3 or 4

"Mother to Son"—An Amazing Poem

Nobody writes poetry like Langston Hughes. In the poem "Mother to Son," he shows why he is such an amazing poet. He is a master of theme, rhythm, and figurative language.

The theme of "Mother to Son" is about life's difficulties and the need to keep going. The voice in the poem is that of a mother. She talks about how her life has been such a struggle. The mother shares with her son that he is going to go through some tough times, too, but he has to stay strong and focused when life is hard.

Langston Hughes is also great at creating rhythm with words. His poems read like songs in your head, and "Mother to Son" is no different. He uses quick, short lines with repetitive beginnings to make the poem very rhythmic. Hughes also creates rhythm by adding just a couple of lines that rhyme.

This poem is all about figurative language. The poem really is one big metaphor. The mother compares her life to a rough, worn-out staircase. The metaphor helps me to picture what the mother means about life being difficult sometimes. It also symbolizes that in order to get somewhere, you have to keep trying and working until you get to where you want to be.

Langston Hughes is an amazing poet. He is able to write poems that affect me by making them about something I can relate to and by making them rhythmic and creative.

The beginning states the controlling idea.

The main idea of each paragraph is about the controlling idea.

Details support the main idea.

The end connects to the beginning.

Focus and Unity: Weak Example, score of 1 or 2

An Amazing Poem

The narrator of the poem is that of a mother. She talks about how her life has been such a struggle. The mother shares with her son that he is going to go through some tough times, too, but he has to stay strong and focused when life is hard.

Langston Hughes is a great poet. His poems have theme, figurative language, and rhythm. This poem is all about figurative language. The poem really is one big metaphor. The mother compares her life to a rough, worn-out staircase. The metaphor helps me to picture what the mother means about life being difficult sometimes. It also symbolizes that in order to get somewhere you have to keep trying and working until you get to where you want to be.

He uses quick, short lines with repetitive beginnings to make the poem very rhythmic. Hughes also creates rhythm by adding just a couple of lines that rhyme.

Langston Hughes is an amazing poet.

The controlling idea is unclear.

The paragraphs have no clear main idea.

The conclusion is vague and abrupt.

Organization

Having a clear central idea and supporting details is important, but in order for your audience to understand your ideas, make sure your writing is organized. Good **organization** helps readers move through your writing easily. In a well-organized work, all paragraphs work together to fulfill the author's purpose clearly and smoothly.

Organization

Scale	Does the writing have a clear and appropriate structure?	How smoothly do the ideas flow together?
4 Wow!	The writing has a structure that is <u>clear</u> and appropriate for the writer's audience, purpose, and type of writing.	The ideas progress in a smooth and orderly way. • The introduction is strong. • The ideas flow well from paragraph to paragraph. • The ideas in each paragraph flow well from one sentence to the next. • Effective transitions connect ideas. • The conclusion is strong.
3 Ahh.	The writing has a structure that is <u>generally</u> clear and appropriate for the writer's audience, purpose, and type of writing.	<u>Most</u> of the ideas progress in a smooth and orderly way. • The introduction is adequate. • Most of the ideas flow well from paragraph to paragraph. • Most ideas in each paragraph flow from one sentence to the next. • Effective transitions connect most of the ideas. • The conclusion is adequate.
2 Hmm.	The structure of the writing is <u>not</u> clear or <u>not</u> appropriate for the writer's audience, purpose, and type of writing.	<u>Some</u> of the ideas progress in a smooth and orderly way. • The introduction is weak. • Some of the ideas flow well from paragraph to paragraph. • Some ideas in each paragraph flow from one sentence to the next. • Transitions connect some ideas. • The conclusion is weak.
1 Huh?	The writing is not clear or organized.	<u>Few or none</u> of the ideas progress in a smooth and orderly way.

Common patterns of organization include:

* **chronological order**, in which details are told in time order
* **compare and contrast**, in which similarities and differences between two or more things are discussed
* **problem-solution**, in which a problem is discussed first and then one or more solutions are presented
* **order of importance**, in which the writer presents the strongest arguments first and last, and presents weaker arguments in the middle.

Organization: Strong Example, score of 3 or 4

Say No to Raising the Legal Driving Age

For teens in the United States, receiving a driver's license at age sixteen is an important part of growing up. However, some states are considering raising the legal driving age to eighteen years old. I believe that this idea would negatively affect teens and parents.

One reason teens need to be able to drive at the age of sixteen is so they can get a job. Many teens need to get jobs to have money for food, clothes, and entertainment. Often, a teen who has a job must have a car and be able to drive it to work.

Teens also want to be able to date and do other social activities on their own. Teens need the opportunity to be responsible and feel trusted. Being able to drive at sixteen helps teens earn this trust.

Perhaps most importantly, teen students have to be able to drive to and from school. A lot of parents and guardians go to work before school starts and have to work until after school is out. The only way for some students to get to school or get to school events and practices is to drive. Without driver's licenses, students may end up missing a lot of school and school activities.

While there may be some good reasons why the legal driving age should be raised, it is important to teens and parents that it stays the same. Sixteen-year-olds need to be able to drive to work, to social events, and to school functions.

The beginning makes the purpose clear: to persuade.

There are effective transitions between paragraphs.

Details support the main idea.

Each paragraph gives reasons that support the author's opinion.

Organization: Weak Example, score of 1 or 2

Teens and Driving

Can you imagine having your mom drive you to your high school graduation or to prom? How would you feel if you couldn't get a job? Many states want to make eighteen the legal driving age.

Many teens do not reach age eighteen until after they have been graduated from high school. It wouldn't be fun waiting until eighteen before you could drive. My friends and I drove once when we were fifteen. Many kids need to work to earn money. It would be difficult to get a job if the legal driving age was eighteen.

Students need to be able to drive to school. If the driving age is eighteen, lots of kids will have to take the bus. My friends and I rode the bus for many years. There are thousands of students who have to ride the bus each year.

Can you imagine going on a date with your parents in the front seat? My mom drove me to a dance once, and I was so embarrassed. Students need to be able to go on dates.

The legal driving age needs to stay the same so teens can drive to school, work, and on dates.

The purpose is not clear.

Paragraphs lack transitions.

The details here do not support the author's opinion.

Development of Ideas

Good ideas are important, but so are the details that describe the ideas. Details develop your ideas, or help your reader to understand them. They also make your writing much more interesting to read. When you are writing, there may be many ideas to choose from, so consider which ideas are most important to your audience and support your purpose for writing.

Development of Ideas

Scale	How thoughtful and interesting is the writing?	How well are the ideas or claims explained and supported?
4 Wow!	The writing engages the reader with meaningful ideas or claims and presents them in a way that is interesting and appropriate to the audience, purpose, and type of writing.	**The ideas or claims are fully explained and supported.** • The ideas or claims are well developed with important details, evidence, and/or description. • The writing feels complete, and the reader is satisfied.
3 Ahh.	<u>Most</u> of the writing engages the reader with meaningful ideas or claims and presents them in a way that is interesting and appropriate to the audience, purpose, and type of writing.	<u>Most</u> **of the ideas or claims are explained and supported.** • Most of the ideas or claims are developed with important details, evidence, and/or description. • The writing feels mostly complete, but the reader still has some questions.
2 Hmm.	<u>Some</u> of the writing engages the reader with meaningful ideas or claims and presents them in a way that is interesting and appropriate to the audience, purpose, and type of writing.	<u>Some</u> **of the ideas or claims are explained and supported.** • Only some of the ideas or claims are developed. Details, evidence, and/or description are limited or not relevant. • The writing leaves the reader with many questions.
1 Huh?	The writing does <u>not</u> engage the reader. It is not appropriate to the audience, purpose, and type of writing.	**The ideas or claims are <u>not</u> explained or supported.** The ideas or claims lack details, evidence, and/or description, and the writing leaves the reader unsatisfied.

Development of Ideas: Strong Example, score of 3 or 4

Parent-for-a-Day

Have you ever wondered what it would be like if we could change places with our parents just for the day? I have, and there are a few things I would like to do.

No school! Making my parents go to school for me would be the first thing I would do as parent for the day. Oh, what fun to be the one to tell my parents to "wake up, eat your breakfast, get to school!" Off they would go to sit in classrooms while I headed to the park for a long game of soccer.

No chores! When my parents got home from school, they would take out the trash, they would do the dishes, and they would clean the house. Meanwhile, I would sit in front of the television and watch my favorite shows.

No bedtime! The last and best part of being a parent for the day is that there would be no bedtime. I would stay up until the wee hours of the morning watching television and finishing my favorite mystery novel.

I have my "parent-for-a-day" all planned out, but the hardest part remains. I still need to convince my parents it is a good idea.

The writer asks a question to engage the audience.

Each paragraph explains and supports the main idea.

The end returns to the topic in a new way.

Development of Ideas: Weak Example, score of 1 or 2

Parent-for-a-Day

Have you ever wondered what it would be like if we could change places with our parents just for the day?

No school! Making my parents go to school for me would be the first thing I would do as parent for the day.

No chores! When my parents got home from school, I would make them do all the chores.

No bedtime! The last and best part of being a parent for the day is that there would be no bedtime.

Now I just need to talk my parents into the idea.

Paragraphs offer little explanation or support.

The ending is abrupt.

Voice and Style

Voice and **style** in writing contribute to communicating the meaning of writing. These qualities make each writer and piece of writing unique.

- **Voice** in writing is the quality that makes the words sound as if they are being spoken by someone. Voice communicates the author's or speaker's attitude.

- **Style** is the characteristic way a writer expresses his or her ideas. Part of that style is the author's **tone**, or attitude toward his or her subject as reflected in word choice. Tone, word choice, and sentence structure are all parts of a writer's style.

Matching Voice and Style to Audience

Because writing is intended to communicate, it is important to match voice and style to the audience. A serious subject may require a serious tone. The intended audience may also dictate whether you can use informal English. If the audience is your classmates, you might be able to use informal or casual English as you would in everyday conversation. If your audience is your teacher or other adults, use formal English in your writing. Whoever the audience, choose vivid words, and vary your sentence patterns.

Voice and Style

Scale	Does the writing have a clear voice and is it the best style for the type of writing?	Is the language interesting and are the words and sentences appropriate for the purpose, audience, and type of writing?
4 Wow!	The writing <u>fully</u> engages the reader with its individual voice. The writing style is best for the type of writing.	The words and sentences are interesting and appropriate to the purpose and audience. • The words are precise and engaging. • The sentences are varied and flow together smoothly.
3 Ahh.	<u>Most</u> of the writing engages the reader with an individual voice. The writing style is mostly best for the type of writing	<u>Most</u> of the words and sentences are interesting and appropriate to the purpose and audience. • Most words are precise and engaging. • Most sentences are varied and flow together.
2 Hmm.	<u>Some</u> of the writing engages the reader, but it has no individual voice and the style is not best for the writing type.	<u>Some</u> of the words and sentences are interesting and appropriate to the purpose and audience. • Some words are precise and engaging. • Some sentences are varied, but the flow could be smoother.
1 Huh?	The writing does <u>not</u> engage the reader.	<u>Few or none</u> of the words and sentences are appropriate to the purpose and audience. • The words are often vague and dull. • The sentences lack variety and do not flow together.

Voice and Style: Strong Example, score of 3 or 4

Dried Up

Some people are meant to make speeches, and others are meant to listen. I learned the hard way that I am definitely a listener.

I have always been comfortable speaking out in class, so when my friend Heather joined the speech team, I decided to give it a try. This kind of activity looks great on college applications, I figured. Moreover, how hard could it be?

I learned just how hard on the afternoon of the regional speech competition. Preparation certainly wasn't a problem. I had spent hours crafting my words. Each of us had rehearsed time and time again in front of our coach and each other. The rhythm and accents of my speech had been drilled into my mind and body.

When I stepped on stage, however, all that preparation dried up under the hot lights. My mouth felt as if it were filled with cotton, and I thought even the packed auditorium could hear my dry bones tremble. As I began to speak, my voice creaked like a rusty door.

I would like to say that I overcame that rough start, but I barely recall giving the rest of my speech. I slouched off stage and took my seat to the sound of weak applause, eager to take my place as the quietest, most intent listener in the room.

The voice is light-hearted and clear.

The sentence lengths are varied.

Vivid verbs and modifiers make the scene seem real and exciting.

Voice and Style: Weak Example, score of 1 or 2

A Bad Day

It was one of the worst days of my life. I tried to give a speech in front of a lot of people and ended up a failure.

This is what happened. My friend was part of the speech team. She talked me into trying out. I thought that it would be easy and it was, at least in front of my classmates.

At our first competition, I sat waiting until the judge called my name. I went on stage, and I could see a lot of people in the audience. I couldn't move, and then I almost passed out. The speech didn't go well at all.

It was an embarrassing moment, but I am glad I at least tried.

The voice is flat and lifeless.

Sentences have little variety.

Words are general and uninteresting.

Written Conventions

You want readers to focus on your ideas, but errors can make it hard to understand what you mean. Good writers pay attention to **written conventions**, that is, the accepted methods and rules for grammar, punctuation, spelling, and capitalization that are commonly used to write English.

Written Conventions Rubric

Scale	Grammar: Are the sentences grammatically correct?	Mechanics and Spelling: Are there errors in spelling, punctuation, or capitalization that affect understanding?
4 Wow!	The writing contains grammatically correct sentences throughout.	There are few or no mistakes in spelling, punctuation, or capitalization.
3 Looks Good.	Most of the sentences contain proper grammar.	There are mistakes in spelling, punctuation, or capitalization, but they do not affect understanding.
2 Hmm.	Some of the sentences contain grammar errors.	There are some mistakes in spelling, punctuation, and capitalization that affect understanding.
1 Huh?	Many sentences contain grammar errors.	There are many mistakes in spelling, punctuation, and capitalization that make the writing difficult to understand.

Written conventions also include using **complete sentences**, **organization**, and **text features** that people understand. Complete sentences have a subject and a predicate and express a complete thought. For more help with written conventions, see Grammar, Usage, Mechanics, and Spelling on page 738.

Written Conventions: Strong Example, score of 3 or 4

A True Hispanic Hero

There are many Hispanic heroes, but my favorite is Miriam Colon Valle. With hard work and a strong belief in herself and her profession, she has become a role model for all.

Early Years

Miriam Colon Valle grew up in Puerto Rico in the 1940s. She participated in drama in high school, and her teacher saw that she had a lot of talent. Valle was then asked to take part in the drama program at the University of Puerto Rico. Her work at the university earned her scholarships that allowed her to attend the Lee Strasberg Acting Studio in the United States.

Rise to Stardom

In the United States, Valle worked hard. She played roles in more than thirty movies; one of her most famous was as the mother of Al Pacino in the movie *Scarface*. Valle was also on television shows, such as the soap opera *The Guiding Light*.

Valle also loved the theater. In the 1950s she started her own theater group. She also acted in numerous Broadway productions. Her drive to help other Hispanic actors and to share theater with poor people inspired her to start the Puerto Rican Traveling Theater.

Because of her love for acting and her love for Hispanic culture and theater, she was awarded a Lifetime Achievement Award in Theater. Miriam Colon Valle is an inspiration to Hispanics and people of all races.

Grammar is correct throughout.

Heads separate sections and give information.

Readers can easily understand the sequence of events.

Names and titles are properly formatted.

Punctuation occurs in the proper places throughout.

Written Conventions: Weak Example, score of 1 or 2

A true Hispanic Hero

There are many hispanic heroes. My favorite is Miriam Colon Valle. She is a role model for evrybody.

Miriam Colon Valle grew up in puerto rico in the 1940s she participated in drama in high school. Valle then taken part in the drama program at the "university of puerto rico." Her work at the university lead her to The United States eventually.

Valle also loved the theater. In the 1950s she started her own theater group. She also acted in a bunch of Broadway productions. She also started the Puerto Rican Traveling Theater. She was awarded a "Lifetime Achievement Award in Theater." Because of her love for acting and her love for hispanic culture and theater. Miriam Colon Valle is an inspiration to hispanics and people of all races.

In The United States, Valle worked hard. She played roles in more than thirty movies. Valle was also on television shows. Including the soap opera The Guiding Light.

There are many misspellings.

Names and titles are not properly capitalized or formatted.

Poor organization and lack of heads make it difficult to follow information.

Sentences are incorrectly punctuated or too long.

Writing Purposes, Modes, and Forms

There are many **forms** of writing, which appear in a number of **modes**, or types, based on the author's purpose and audience. Some writing is meant strictly to inform; other writing is meant to entertain. Other writing forms are intended to persuade or convince readers or listeners to act in certain ways or change their opinions or beliefs. Writing forms can often be categorized into more than one mode.

Writing Modes

A writing mode, or type, is defined by its purpose. Most of your writing tasks will occur in one of the modes described below.

Write to Inform or Explain

The purpose of **expository writing** is to present information or explanations about a topic. Many academic writing forms, such as research papers and literary response papers, are expository. Expository texts usually include a strong controlling idea or thesis in the first paragraph. Each of the body paragraphs presents a main idea and details related to the controlling idea. The final paragraph, or conclusion, restates, or sums up, the controlling idea.

Write Narratives

The purpose of **narrative writing** is to tell readers something they can follow in story form. Narratives can be fiction or nonfiction. They are often used for entertainment or to explain something that really happened. They offer a way of making sense of the world by ordering events into a clear beginning, middle, and end. Strong characters and interesting settings are usually key parts of narrative fiction. Most short stories are narratives, as are autobiographical and biographical essays.

Write Arguments

You can argue to defend your own ideas or opinions or you can try to influence the thinking or actions of other people. When you try to convince others, it's called **persuasive writing**. All arguments include a claim. A claim clearly states the writer's idea or opinion. Good arguments include evidence like facts, statistics, expert opinions, or personal experiences. Clear explanations, or reasons, connect evidence to claims. The reasons may appeal to the reader's emotions, ethics (sense of right and wrong), or to logic and understanding of facts. Persuasive texts should have an appropriate voice and tone for the intended audience, clear organization of ideas, and strong supporting details.

Common Academic Writing Forms

The following pages explain the most common writing forms you will use in school. You may be asked to write, read, evaluate, and respond to any of these forms while you are a student.

Cause-and-Effect Essay

A **cause-and-effect essay** traces the relationship between events. A cause is the reason something happens. An effect is the result of that cause.

Use a graphic organizer like the one below to develop your cause-and-effect essays.

Single Cause/Multiple Effects

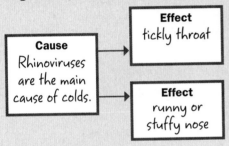

Multiple Causes/Single Effect

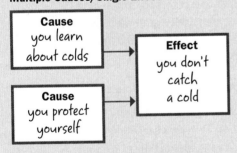

Check your essay for the following:

- A clear statement of the relationship that is being analyzed and discussed.

Causes and Effects of Colds

Cold season is almost here. It's a good time to review the causes and symptoms, or effects, of colds. The more you know, the better prepared you will be to protect yourself from catching a cold.

- A clear main idea for each paragraph.
- Appropriate supporting details.
- Signal words like *if/then* and *because*.

Most colds are caused by rhinoviruses. There are more than one hundred kinds of these tiny, disease-causing organisms. If a rhinovirus infects the lining of your nose or throat, then you have a cold.

The first effects of a cold are a tickling feeling in the throat and a runny or stuffy nose. Other symptoms include sneezing, headaches, and achiness.

A severe cold may cause further effects. For example, the cold sufferer may develop a low-grade temperature, or fever. If his or her chest becomes congested, then the person may also develop a cough.

College Entry Essay

If you apply to a college or university, you may be asked to submit an **entrance essay** as part of the application. A college entrance essay is a kind of **reflective essay**, in which a person tells stories about their experiences. Your essay should do more than introduce who you are to the college board. It should detail specific events in your life and how these events impacted you. Choose words that show your personality, point out your skills and talents, and outline your future plans. A good college entrance essay should explain how your unique talents and personality will make you a successful student.

A college may provide you with a topic to write about, or it may ask you to select your own topic.

Writing Purposes, Modes, and Forms

Common Academic Writing Forms, continued

Use the graphic organizer below to develop your college entry essay.

College Entry Essay Overview

> **Beginning**
>
> Introduce yourself by writing in your own conversational tone. Get the reader interested with a good story or description. You might also present your controlling idea here.

> **Middle**
>
> Develop your main ideas with clearly organized supporting details. These details should help readers understand how your experiences have helped you grow as a person. Focus on how one or a few experiences helped you grow in one very important way.

> **End**
>
> Lead the reader back to the controlling idea. Leave a lasting, positive impression with a strong ending that tells who you are and why you should be accepted at the college.

Check your college entry essay for the following elements:

- clear focus on your own experience
- a personal voice and tone
- interesting details
- correct grammar, spelling, and punctuation

> "Travel broadens the mind," my dad always says just before our summer road trip. Every June, he piles Mom, me, my sisters, and our dog into the car, and away we go. Though I used to dread our trips, I now realize how much I have gained from them. Our road trips have broadened my mind in many ways.

Comparison-Contrast Essay

A **comparison-contrast essay** tells how things are similar and different. Comparisons show how two or more things are alike. Contrasts show how they differ.

Use a Venn diagram to collect information for your comparison-contrast essay. List characteristics of each thing being described. Then, in the center, list the characteristics they share.

Venn Diagram

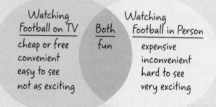

Watching Football on TV
cheap or free
convenient
easy to see
not as exciting

Both
fun

Watching Football in Person
expensive
inconvenient
hard to see
very exciting

Check your essay for the following:

- A clear statement of what is being compared and contrasted
- A clear main idea for each paragraph
- Appropriate supporting details
- Signal words like *both/and*, *similar*, and *like* for comparisons; signal words like *but*, *however*, and *on the other hand* for contrasts

> **At Home or at the Stadium?**
>
> If you really like football, you probably watch it on TV every chance you get. You may even go to the stadium to see your home team play. Though both ways of watching football are fun, there are some important differences between the two.
>
> The first big difference is cost. Watching a football game on TV costs little or nothing. If the game is on network TV, it's free. If the game is on cable, it may be included in the cable package. But a ticket to a professional football game is expensive. The average price for a ticket to an NFL game is $50.

Descriptive Essay

A **descriptive essay** provides the reader with a strong impression of a setting, event, person, animal, or object. The essay may contain many different sensory details, but all the details should work together to support the author's controlling idea.

Use a details web to gather and organize sensory details for your descriptive essay.

Details Web

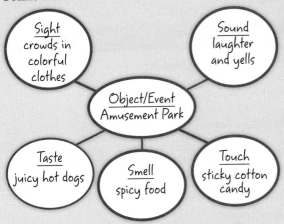

Check your descriptive essay for the following elements:

- a controlling idea that presents a single, strong impression that appeals to the five senses
- Information about how the subject affects more than one of the senses
- Vivid verbs, adjectives, and adverbs
- Clear organization of information, using a pattern such as spatial order (describing items from left to right, top to bottom, etc.)
- A unique style and appropriate tone for the audience

An Amusing Mixture

When summer vacation starts, I want to go to Alman's Amusement Park. Of course, I enjoy the thrilling rides there. But I enjoy the mixture of sights, sounds, smells, tastes, and feelings even more.

As I stroll past the Tilt-A-Whirl, I always see a blur of colors. People in bright summer clothes madly twirl, staining the sky with swirls of red, blue, green, and yellow. I hear the kids laughing and giggling, and I want to stop and watch. But I can't. The tempting scent of spicy food is in the air. I follow my nose to the Food Court for a juicy hot dog.

How-To Essay

A **how-to essay** explains a process. This kind of essay is also known as a process description or a technical document. A how-to essay describes the equipment, materials, and steps needed to complete a task. It answers any possible questions readers might have in order to make the process clear. The essay also often explains why the process is worth doing.

Use the chart below to collect information for your how-to essay.

How-To Planner

Task: Making a grilled cheese sandwich

Materials:	Steps:
2 slices rye bread	First, butter one side of each piece of bread.
1 tablespoon butter	Next, place the cheese between the bread.
1, one ounce slice sharp cheddar cheese	Next, fry the sandwich until brown.
1 slice tomato	Then, add the tomato to the sandwich.
1 nonstick frying pan	Finally, serve the sandwich with chips.

Check your **how-to essay** for the following elements:

- a clear statement of the process
- a complete list of materials and equipment needed to complete the process
- chronological organization of steps
- signal words such as *first*, *next*, and *then*
- complete description of the actions to take during each step
- benefits of performing the process

Deluxe Grilled Cheese Sandwich

A grilled cheese sandwich is delicious and easy to make. Try this simple but yummy recipe. All you need are two pieces of rye bread, a tablespoon of butter, a one-ounce slice of sharp cheddar cheese, a slice of tomato, and a nonstick frying pan.

First, spread half a tablespoon of butter on one side of each slice of bread. Be sure to spread the butter evenly, from corner to corner, so that the sandwich browns evenly when you fry it.

Next, place the unbuttered sides of the bread slices together. Put the piece of cheese inside the slices to form a sandwich. Make sure that the cheese slice is not larger than the bread. If it is, trim the cheese so that it fits inside the bread. Otherwise, when the cheese melts it will drip over the sides of the bread.

Literary Response Essay

In a **literary response essay**, you present your reactions to and analysis of a text. In an analysis, you look at elements that make up the text. For an analysis of fiction, for example, you might look at characters and conflict. For an analysis of nonfiction, you might look at word choice and meaning.

Use a graphic organizer like the one below to collect information and organize your literary response essay.

Literary Response Essay
Text Title: "Gettysburg Address"
Author: Abraham Lincoln
Date Written: November, 1863
Publishing Information: first published in newspapers
My Overall Impression of the Text: powerful speech!
Main Idea 1 about Text: nation founded on equality
Supporting Detail: "soldiers gave their lives" for this
Main Idea 2 about Text: other founding principles
Supporting Detail: "of the people, by the people, for the people"
My Responses to Main Idea 1: Soldiers' sacrifices keep us free.
My Responses to Main Idea 2: I, too, have responsibilities to my country.

The text a writer responds to is called *a source text*. Read the source text below. Then note how the reader responded to it.

The Gettysburg Address
By Abraham Lincoln

Four score and seven years ago our fathers brought forth on this continent a new nation, conceived in liberty, and dedicated to the proposition that all men are created equal.

Now we are engaged in a great civil war, testing whether that nation, or any nation so conceived and so dedicated, can long endure. We are met on a great battle-field of that war. We have come to dedicate a portion of that field as a final resting place for those who here gave their lives that this nation might live. It is altogether fitting and proper that we should do this.

But, in a larger sense, we can not dedicate—we can not consecrate—we can not hallow—this ground. The brave men, living and dead, who struggled here, have consecrated it, far above our poor power to add or detract.... It is rather for us to be here dedicated to the great task remaining before us—that from these honored dead we take increased devotion to that cause for which they gave the last full measure of devotion— that we here highly resolve that these dead shall not have died in vain—that this nation, under God, shall have a new birth of freedom—and that government of the people, by the people, for the people, shall not perish from the earth.

The Message of Gettysburg

In 1863, President Abraham Lincoln traveled to Pennsylvania. The occasion was the dedication of a cemetery for the soldiers who had died at the Battle of Gettysburg. Lincoln's brief comments are today known as "The Gettysburg Address," and they present a new vision of the founding principles of the United States.

Lincoln begins his speech by noting that our nation was founded on the idea of equality just eighty-seven years prior to his speech. He then notes that the men buried at Gettysburg "gave their lives that this nation might live." This point makes me think of all the wars since then and the ways that soldiers' sacrifices allow me to enjoy the benefits of a democratic society.

Most powerfully, Lincoln ends his speech by restating the founding principles of the Declaration of Independence and the U.S. Constitution. Ours is a government "of the people, by the people, for the people." It was the brave sacrifice of those people and the ones who died at Gettysburg that Lincoln so beautifully honors in his speech. It reminds me that I have responsibilities to be a part of the government that so many have fought to keep alive.

In the introductory paragraph, identify the author and date.

State controlling idea of the text.

Include quotations from the text.

Describe reaction to a main idea.

Describe reaction to a main idea.

Narratives

Narratives can be either fiction or nonfiction. Fiction narratives tell stories featuring characters, settings, and plots. The forms of nonfiction narrative include:

- autobiographical essays/personal essays
- biographical essays
- diary or journal entries

Personal Essay or Autobiographical Narrative

In a personal essay, a writer describes events that he or she actually experienced. The purpose is often to entertain readers or to teach them.

Personal/Autobiographical Narrative Overview

Beginning
Introduce the people, setting, and situation. State why the event or experience was important.

Middle
Give details about what happened in the order that it happened. Share your thoughts and feelings. Use lively details and dialogue.

End
Explain how the action came to an end or the problem was solved. Summarize why the event or experience was important.

Personal Narrative Model

A Hard Lesson Learned

When Marie invited me to her birthday party, I was thrilled. She was the most popular girl in school. My best friend said, "Why do you want to go? Marie is not nice. She doesn't know how to be a friend." I wish I had listened, because my friend was right. The best I can say about my time with Marie is that it taught me a hard but valuable lesson about friendship.

Journal or Diary Entry

Journal entries are the least formal kind of nonfiction narrative. They are often used to record events from a person's life, but they can also be used as learning tools, such as when a person documents a research process or traces thoughts about something over time.

Journal Entry Model

January 4, 2007
I went to the library today to research my paper about hip-hop music. I was worried that I wouldn't find anything, but then I remembered a tip my teacher gave me: ask a librarian! So I did, and he was very helpful. We found three books, six magazine articles, and even a documentary film. I'm glad I thought to ask. It definitely made doing the assignment easier for me.

Short Story or Novel

Short stories and **novels** are common forms of narrative fiction. Novels are typically longer than short stories, with more developed characters and plots. Both of these forms usually include descriptive elements, such as figurative language and vivid word choice.

Plot Diagram for Fiction

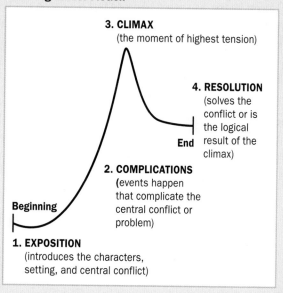

3. CLIMAX
(the moment of highest tension)

4. RESOLUTION
(solves the conflict or is the logical result of the climax)

End

2. COMPLICATIONS
(events happen that complicate the central conflict or problem)

Beginning

1. EXPOSITION
(introduces the characters, setting, and central conflict)

Using Persuasive Strategies

Good persuasive essays demonstrate effective use of persuasive strategies. Use persuasive strategies, such as appeals, to support your opinions. Note in the following examples how the writer's opinion statement changes depending on the appeal chosen.

Persuasive Essay

In a **persuasive essay**, you try to convince readers to agree with you or take a particular action. TV commercials, magazine ads, newspaper editorials, and campaign speeches are all kinds of persuasive media that begin as persuasive writing.

Persuasive Essay Planner

OPINION STATEMENT	I BELIEVE THAT WE SHOULD ... KEEP OUR CATS INDOORS
Reason 1:	It's safe for the cat.
Evidence:	Many cats catch diseases outdoors.
Reason 2:	It's safer for wildlife.
Evidence:	Many animals are killed by outdoor cats each year.
Reason 3:	Cats lead happy lives indoors.
Evidence:	Experts say house cats are content.
Counter-argument	Cats like to be outside. However, they don't need to be.

Start a persuasive essay by stating an issue in a way that will make the audience care about it. Then state your opinion about the issue.

Keep Cats Indoors!

According to the American Bird Conservancy, pet cats kill thousands of birds each year. Now, I love cats. In fact, I own one. But I never let him go outdoors unless he is in his cat carrier. If you are a true animal lover, you will keep your cat indoors, too.

Support your opinion with reasons, evidence, and other appeals.

- An ethical appeal is directed at the reader's sense of right and wrong.

It's just plain wrong to let your cat hunt and hurt other animals. Birds, rabbits, and other wildlife animals have the right to live just as your cat does.

- A logical appeal is directed at the reader's common sense.

The fact is that it is dangerous for your cat to be outdoors. Your pet may be hit by a car. It may catch a serious disease from an infected animal. It may be chased by a dog or other larger animal.

- An emotional appeal is directed at the reader's feelings.

Do you really want your cat to be lost? Picture how cold, lonely, scared, and hungry your pet might become while it is looking for your home.

Now picture what it is like for a bird or a rabbit to be chased by a cat. Can you feel the terror of these little animals?

Additional things to remember:

- A personal anecdote, case study, or analogy validates your opinion.
- Think of questions or concerns your reader might have and address them.

Position Paper

In a **position paper**, you state your opinion, or position, on an issue that has at least two sides to it. You also give reasons and evidence to support your position. The purpose of position papers is to persuade, or convince, your readers to agree with you.

Unlike a persuasive essay, a position paper does not necessarily include a call to action. A position paper also does not necessarily contain counter-arguments. The main purpose of a position paper is to state and support an opinion.

Position Paper Overview

> **Beginning**
> Introduce the issue. Show readers why they should care about it; then state your position, the controlling idea of the paper.

> **Middle**
> Support your position with reasons that will convince your audience. Organize the reasons strategically. Use transitions to help readers move smoothly from one reason to another.

> **End**
> Restate your position in a memorable way.

Check your position paper for the following elements:

- an attention-grabbing introduction with a clear statement of opinion
- supporting reasons with evidence for each reason
- clear organization and transition words, such as *first*, *next*, and *most important*

Play Your Way to Good Health

Recently, I joined the swim team. I had never been particularly interested in sports before. However, I have always been interested in having good health and making new friends. I received these benefits and many more from being on the swim team. Therefore, I think that all students should become involved in sports.

The first big benefit of becoming involved in a sport is that it will improve your health.

Persuasive Speech

A **persuasive speech** tries to convince the audience to take an action or believe something.

Persuasive Speech Overview

> **Beginning**
> Introduce the topic. Get listeners' attention. You might tell a story from your own experience or describe a case study of someone else's experience. Give necessary background information. End by stating your opinion. It is your controlling idea.

> **Middle**
> Support your position. Give reasons readers or listeners should agree with you. Also use ethical or emotional appeals when appropriate. Then state at least one possible objection, or counterargument, to your opinion and respond to it respectfully.

> **End**
> Sum up your reasons and give a call to action. Tell readers what action you want them to take or what belief you want them to have.

Check your persuasive speech for the following elements:

- An attention-grabbing introduction with a clear statement of opinion.
- Paragraphs organized by reason.
- Strong appeals appropriate to the topic and audience.
- A counterargument with reasons and evidence against that argument.
- A summary of your opinion and a call to action.
- Respectful tone throughout.

Watch Educational Television

Can watching TV actually be good for you? Surprisingly, a recent university study suggests that it can. However, there's a catch. You have to watch educational TV, like nature shows and history programs. According to the study, watching shows like these can help improve your scores on standardized tests. Based on this study, I urge you to examine your TV habits and, if necessary, form a new habit: watching educational TV.

Though you may not at first believe it, watching educational TV shows can be fun. They can make a dry subject come alive for you. And when that happens, you learn and remember more. Let me give you an example. I had a hard time remembering anything I read about World War II. For me, the war happened so long ago that it did not seem real or interesting. When I watched a Public Broadcasting System series about the war, however, I began to feel differently. The subject became interesting to me when I watched and listened to interviews with people who lived through World War II. After watching the series, I reread my history book, and it made a lot more sense to me.

Problem-Solution Essay

A **problem-solution essay** informs readers about a problem and suggests one or more ways to solve it. A problem-solution essay has five main parts:

Problem-Solution Essay Planner

1. PROBLEM	Clearly state the problem. Where does it take place? When does it happen? Why does it matter?
2. CAUSES	Why does the problem happen? Who or what is to blame?
3. EFFECTS	Who is affected? How?
4. SOLUTIONS	Think about possible solutions. What has already been done? Has it helped? Think of new solutions. What are the benefits and risks of each idea?
5. CONCLUSION	Which solution is best? What makes it best? How could it be carried out? What do you want your reader or listener to understand? What do you want your reader or listener to do?

Reduce, Reuse, and Recycle

The United States is running out of land—land for landfills, that is. Landfills are where trash is taken and buried after workers collect it from homes or businesses and haul it away. Our landfill system is a good one. Or it would be, if we did not generate so much trash. Unfortunately, the average American throws away more than four pounds of paper, packaging, meal scraps, and other kinds of garbage each day. Multiply four pounds by the number of Americans, and you can see why we have a problem. Fortunately, there are simple solutions that anyone can put into effect. They are the "Three *Rs*": Reduce, Reuse, and Recycle.

Summary or Abstract

A **summary** is a brief restatement of the main points of a text or visual medium, such as plays or books. An **abstract** is a summary of a research report that appears before the report. It tells the reader what your report is about. Begin a summary by giving information about the original work. Then present the main ideas and the most important supporting details. Use quotations and proper citation when necessary. (For sample citations, see the model research report on pp. 727–728.)

Summary Model

> William Shakespeare wrote the tragic play *Hamlet* in about 1600. Since then, it has become one of the most famous plays in the English language.
>
> As the play opens, Hamlet, the Prince of Denmark, is visited by the ghost of his father, the king. The king's ghost tells Hamlet that the king was murdered, and Hamlet decides to find out by whom. He suspects that his uncle Claudius, who has married his mother and taken over the role of king, is the murderer.
>
> Hamlet's behavior grows stranger over the course of the play, as he is tormented by the idea of his father's murder and his mother's betrayal. He decides to create a play that he believes will show that Claudius is guilty. When Claudius does indeed show himself to be guilty, Hamlet's words and actions grow increasingly violent.
>
> In the end, Hamlet, his mother, and Claudius are all killed during a duel. An invading army stumbles upon the bloody scene, and Hamlet is carried away to be buried.

Research Reports

A **research report** is a presentation of information about a topic. In a research report, you combine and organize facts from different sources of information. You put the information in your own words and let your readers know where you found the information you cite, or use, in your report.

Research reports are typically researched, written, and cited using either the Modern Language Association (MLA) style or the American Psychological Association (APA) style. The style is often determined by the subject matter.

To learn more about research, see the **Language and Learning Handbook**, pp. 639–644.

Analysis of an Issue

To write an **analysis of an issue**, research a controversial situation—one that has at least two sides to it. Then use the information to write a report that answers the question *How?* or *Why?* In an analysis, the writer's personal opinion does not need to be included. The purpose of the analysis is to inform and explain, not to persuade.

Use the following graphic organizer to organize your report.

Issue Analysis Overview

Beginning
Start with an interesting fact or idea about the issue. Make readers care about it. Give background if necessary. Then state your controlling idea.

Middle
Analyze the issue. Take it apart, and examine each part. Answer the question *How?* or *Why?*

End
Sum up the results of your analysis. You might state the importance, or significance, of what you discovered. Or you might restate your controlling idea in an interesting way.

Works Cited
List the sources of information you used.

The following pages show a Research Report with citations done in MLA style.

J. Smith
Mrs. Walker
English 100
January 10, 2013

An Analysis of the Global Warming Debate

The issue of global warming has divided the scientific community. Some scientists believe that carbon dioxide and other greenhouse gases are warming Earth, causing dangerous changes in the climate. Other scientists disagree. They believe that there is no proof of global warming or its effects on the climate. Is global warming real? And if it is, should we be worried about it?

The theory of global warming is not new. It was first proposed in 1896 by Svante Arrhenius, a Swedish scientist. He said that people were unknowingly causing Earth's temperature to rise. The rise, he believed, was caused by people releasing carbon dioxide into the atmosphere when they burned coal and other carbon-based fuels. The carbon dioxide, he believed, raised Earth's temperature (Maslin 24).

Over the years, other scientists further developed Arrhenius's theory, which has evolved into a scientific model called the "greenhouse effect." According to the effect, Earth's atmosphere is like the glass in a greenhouse. Glass lets sunlight in and re-reflects it, bouncing heat from sunrays back into the house and trapping it there. Similarly, carbon dioxide and other greenhouse gases re-reflect rays from the sun, trapping heat in the atmosphere around Earth.

The greenhouse effect is a natural process that protects us and our planet. Without the greenhouse effect, it would not be warm enough on Earth for plants and animals to live (Fridell 25). However, many scientists believe that problems occur when the level of greenhouse gases rises, causing the amount of heat energy trapped around Earth also to rise. This process, it is believed, may cause Earth to become warmer than it has ever been.

Most scientists believe that this temperature change has already happened. For example, scientists at the U.S. Environmental Protection Agency (EPA) say that over the past century Earth's surface temperature has increased about 1.4 degrees F ("Basic Information"). The EPA believes that the rise has been caused by carbon dioxide produced by the burning of gasoline, oil, and coal.

Does such a small rise in temperature really matter? Many scientists believe it does. They think that the higher surface temperature of Earth is causing dangerous changes to our planet. Temperature changes will result in changes in rainfall patterns like drought and flooding. As ice in the north and south poles melts, global sea levels will rise. People living near

The introductory paragraph is clear and effective and states the controlling idea.

The analysis focuses on these controlling ideas.

Parenthetical citations like this one tell readers where the student found information.

Background helps readers understand the issue.

The student uses a variety of sentence structures.

The student develops the analysis by explaining a main viewpoint on global warming.

Smith 2

the ocean may lose land or experience more severe storms. People and animals will be impacted. ("Global Warming"). These changes will impact citizens across the globe, including people in the United States (Karl, J.M. et al).

Kerry Emanuel, a scientist at the Massachusetts Institute of Technology (MIT) is a strong believer in global warming. He thinks that global warming has caused hurricanes to be more powerful and destructive. After studying about 5,000 hurricanes, he found that storms increased in intensity during the same period that Earth's temperature began to rise. The number of big storms has increased since 1923 (Tollefson 2012). Emanuel believes that warmer ocean temperatures are to blame for the increase in storms' destructive power (Kluger 92).

Not all scientists agree that global warming is causing climate changes. Physicist S. Fred Singer is representative of this group. In an interview for the Public Broadcasting System (PBS), Singer said that "whether or not human beings can produce a global climate change is an important question [that] is not at all settled. It can only be settled by actual measurements, data. And the data are ambiguous.... Since 1979, our best measurements show that the climate has been cooling just slightly. Certainly, it has not been warming" ("What's up?"). Singer bases his conclusion on measurements from weather satellites, which he believes to be more accurate than measurements from ground-based thermometers.

Dr. Richard Lindzen, a scientist at MIT, shares Singer's doubts about global warming and climate change. According to Dr. Lindzen, rises in Earth's temperature and carbon dioxide levels "neither constitute support for alarm nor establish man's responsibility for the small amount of global warming that has occurred" (Lindzen). He believes that the computer models on which global warming forecasts have been made are flawed and incorrect.

The student develops the analysis by explaining a different main viewpoint on global warming.

Why, then, do so many scientists believe in global warming? Lindzen believes the answer has more to do with money than with science. He believes that government money is more often given to scientists whose work appears to predict and prevent disasters than to scientists whose work does not predict gloom and doom. Lindzen feels that because these kinds of projects tend to attract funding, some scientists have exaggerated the effects of global warming to get government grants (Lindzen).

The student answers the question Why?

And so the debate continues. Perhaps this is for the best. As James Hansen of the National Aeronautics and Space Administration (NASA) put it, "Science thrives on repeated challenges . . . and there is even special pleasure in trying to find something wrong with well-accepted theory. Such challenges eventually strengthen our understanding of the subject" (Hansen).

In the conclusion, the student effectively sums up the report.

Works Cited

"Basic Information." *Climate Change*. 14 Dec. 2006. U.S. Environmental
Protection Agency. 5 Jan. 2007
<http://www.epa.gov/climatechange/basicinfo.html>.

Fridell, Ron. *Global Warming*. New York: Franklin Watts, 2002.

"Global Warming: A Way Forwrad: Facing Climate Change." National
Geographic. Video and Audio. 30 Nov. 2012.
<http://video.nationalgeographic.com/video/environment/
global-warming-environment/way-forward-climate/>.

Hansen, James. "The Global Warming Debate." Education. Jan. 1999. NASA
Goddard Institute for Space Studies. 7 Jan. 2007
<http://www.giss.nasa.gov/edu/gwdebate>.

Karl, T.R, Melillo, J.M, and Peterson T.C. *U.S. Global Change Research Program.
2009. Global climate change impacts in the United States.* Cambridge:
Cambridge University Press, 2009.

Kluger, Jeffrey. "The Man Who Saw Katrina Coming." *Time* 8 May 2006: 92.

Lindzen, Richard. "Climate of Fear." Opinion Journal from the Wall Street
Journal Editorial Page. 12 April 2006. WSJ.com. 2 Jan. 2007
<http://www.opinionjournal.com/extra/?id=110008220&mod=RSS_O>.

Maslin, Mark. *Global Warming: A Very Short Introduction*. Oxford: Oxford
University Press, 2004.

Tollefson, J. "Hurricane Sandy Spins Up Climate Change Discussion."
Nature. October 2012.
<http://www.nature.com/news/hurricane-sandy-spins-up-climate-
discussion-1.11706>. Accessed November 23, 2012.

"What's up with the Weather?" NOVA Frontline. 2000. WGBH/NOVA/
FRONTLINE. 4 Jan. 2007
<http://www.pbs.org/wgbh/warming>.

The student lists
all the sources of
information cited in
the research report.

Career and Workplace Communication

In the world of work, there are expectations about the form and style of written communications. The following writing forms will help you at your workplace.

Business Letter

Business letters serve many purposes. You might write a business letter to make a request or to register a complaint with a business or other organization. The example below is a cover letter, a type of business letter in which the sender introduces himself or herself to an employer and states his or her qualifications for a job. Business letters should be typed on a computer or other word processor and should sound and look professional. Follow the business letter format below, and always check your letters carefully for grammatical or spelling errors.

Adam Russell
1297 Newport Ave.
Chicago, IL 79910
(555) 212-9402
May 18, 2013

Ms. Carlita Ortiz
Ortiz Corner Grocery
2480 North Lincoln Ave.
Chicago, IL 79919

Dear Ms. Ortiz:

I recently read in the *Chicago Tribune* that you are taking applications for the position of full-time checkout clerk. I am very interested in interviewing for this position.

I worked for supermarkets for the previous two summers in similar positions, first at Green Grocers and then at The Grainery Foods. My managers always gave me good performance reviews, and I truly enjoy the work.

I currently attend Julius Jones High School, but I am available for work in the evenings and will be available in the summer after June 10, 2013. I can be reached after 4 p.m. on weekdays. I look forward to hearing from you about this opportunity and thank you for your consideration.

Sincerely,

Adam Russell

Adam Russell

Insert contact information for yourself followed by the person you are writing to.

Insert a space between the date and the contact information.

Use a formal greeting, addressing a specific person. Use formal titles and last names to show respect in business letters.

Do not indent paragraphs.

Use single-spaced paragraphs. Separate paragraphs with an extra space.

Always thank recipients for their attention.

Include a traditional closing with a handwritten and typed signature.

Résumé

A résumé is a document that describes your qualifications for a job. A well-written résumé includes the kind of information a potential employer would like to know about you. Examples include previous work experience, skills, and achievements. It is very important that résumés be free of errors, so that the employer can see that you would take a job seriously and pay attention to detail. Use the format below to set apart your résumé from all the résumés of other applicants.

Adam Russell

1297 Newport Ave.

Chicago, IL 79910

(555) 212-9402

Objective

To obtain full-time, seasonal work in the food service industry.

Work History

2012, Grainery Foods

Full-time checkout and stock clerk at a busy supermarket

- Used a standard register and invoice-tracking equipment

- Trained new employees

- Met and exceeded cash handling accuracy reviews

2011, Green Grocers

Full-time retail assistant at a local outdoor market

- Set up and closed market stalls

- Supervised volunteer staff

- Assisted customers with pricing and selection

Education

Currently enrolled at Julius Jones High School.

Awards

Student of the Month, April 2013.

References

Available upon request.

Include your contact information clearly at the top of the page.

Use boldface type, italics, or underlining to make important information or headings stand out.

List your experience, starting with your most recent job.

Use bullet points to draw attention to specific skills or responsibilities.

Include information about your education and any information that would show what you have done well in the past.

Keep a list of 3 to 5 references available. Check with your references before you give their names out.

Job Application

Many jobs require you to fill out an **application**. Follow the instructions closely and write as neatly as possible or type the information. You will often need to provide reference information for your work ability or character. It is important to have personal identification with you when completing job applications. Ask a manager if you have any questions.

Please type or print neatly.

Today's Date: 5 / 1 / 13

First Name: Adam   Last Name: Russell

Address: 1297 Newport Ave.

City: Chicago   State: IL   Zip: 79910

Phone: (555) 212-9402   Birth date: 7 / 20 / 99

Sex: M ☑ F ☐

Education

High School Name: Currently attending Julius Jones High School.

Employment History (List each job, starting with most recent.)

1. Employer: The Grainery Foods   Phone: (555) 436-0090

   Dates: 5/2013 – 9/2013   Position: Full-time checkout and stock clerk

   Duties: Check out orders and stock inventory.

References

1. Name: Consuela Ybarra   Relationship: supervisor

   Company: The Grainery Foods

   Address: 123 Main Street, Chicago   Phone: (555) 436-0092

2. Name: Roman Hrbanski   Relationship: teacher/coach

   Company: Julius Jones High School

   Address: 321 N. Elm Street, Chicago   Phone: (555) 233-0765

Follow instructions.

Provide complete and accurate information.

Provide contact information for people who can tell the employer that you are a good and dependable worker.

Business Memo

A memo, or memorandum, provides employees with information concerning the business or organization.

Date: June 28, 2013
From: Carlita Ortiz, General Manager
To: All Full-Time and Part-Time Staff
Re: Independence Day Sale Hours

Please remember that all employees scheduled to work the morning of Sunday, July 1, should report at 7:00 A.M., one hour earlier than usual, as we will need special help setting up the Independence Day Sale.

Thank you for your attention.

Give information regarding date, sender, recipients, and the topic.

State the purpose of the memo and any supporting information.

Be short and specific.

Creative Writing

Your imagination is the most important tool in building the forms of creative writing. Some of these forms, such as plays and some kinds of poetry, have set structures. Others, such as parody, are defined by their purpose rather than their structure. Creative writing allows you to describe people, things, and events in new and interesting ways.

To learn more about these forms, see the **Literary Terms**.

Poetry

Poetry is a literary form in which special emphasis is given to ideas through the use of style and rhythm. In poetry, lines of text are called verses, and groups of verses are called stanzas. Rhyme and other sound effects within and among lines and words are popular elements of poetic style.

Some poems are written in conventional poetic forms. The number of lines, rhythm, and rhyme patterns are defined by the form. Other poems have a style all their own. These are called free verse:

> **Friendship**
>
> To never judge
> To accept your true self
> Through all your faults
> Still loyal and caring.
> That is the making,
> An act of giving and taking,
> of what we call a true friend.

Song Lyrics

A **song lyric** is text set to music and meant to be sung. Like lyric poetry, song lyrics often express personal feelings using rhythm and sound effects. These effects provide musical qualities similar to those often found in lyric poetry. In fact, the word *lyric* comes from the ancient Greek word for *lyre*, a musical instrument with strings.

Parody

A **parody** makes fun of, imitates, or exaggerates another creation or work. The parody can be sarcastic, and it is often used to make a point in a funny way. A parody can be in any form, from plays to essays to poems.

> **Twinkle, Twinkle?**
>
> Twinkle, twinkle unseen star,
> Covered in our smog you are.
> Up above our town once bright,
> Now we cannot see your light.

Play/Skit

A **play** is a narrative that is meant to be performed before an audience. The text of a play consists of dialogue spoken by the characters and brief descriptions of sets, lighting, stage movements, and vocal tone. A **skit** is a very short play:

> **James.** You mean I won? [*grabbing Paula's hands*]
>
> **Paula.** Yes, you did. You won the Battle of the Singers competition!
>
> **James.** [*shocked, then jumps, screaming and hooting*] I can't believe it!

Poster

A **poster** is used to get people's attention and give information in a visually appealing way. Posters should have the following:

- a purpose: What do you want people to know or think?
- attention-grabbing colors or pictures
- a large heading that tells people what the poster is about
- large print so people can read the poster from a distance
- just enough details to convey your message

Electronic Communication

More and more, people are writing to each other using electronic forms of communication. Computers and portable devices, such as cell phones, offer a number of ways to research school assignments, conduct business, and keep in contact with friends and family. You need to protect your identity and stay safe online. Check your school's Acceptable Use Policy for guidance on how to protect your hardware and, more importantly, yourself.

E-mail

Electronic mail, or **e-mail**, allows users to exchange written messages and digital files over the Internet. Like traditional mail, e-mail requires an address to enable users to send and receive messages. This address is attached to an account that a user accesses through the Internet or through an e-mail software program. Keep the following rules in mind when writing e-mail:

- Carefully check the address of your recipient.
- Include the subject of the e-mail.
- Include a greeting.
- Be sure to supply enough background information to help the reader understand the topic and purpose of your e-mail.
- Unless you are writing to a peer, such as a friend or classmate, use a formal tone, proper punctuation, and grammar.
- Include a closing, and give your name.

From: student@studentweb.edu
To: n.patterson@njc.library.org
Subject: Library Books

Dear Ms. Patterson:

I have returned the books that you asked me about. I put the books in the return box. Please let me know if you don't receive them.

Thank you,
Jamie

Instant Messaging and Text Messaging

Instant messaging, or **IM**, allows two users to exchange messages instantly over the Internet. **Text messages** are sent over cell phone lines. Like e-mail, these messages require each user to have an account. Messaging is used most frequently by peers, so the writing style may be very casual. Abbreviations are often used to shorten the amount of time and space needed for the message.

Blogs

Web logs, or **blogs**, are Internet newsletters. Many individuals and organizations use blogs to communicate their ideas to a wide audience. Some blogs offer articles on a particular topic, much like a newspaper or magazine. Others are more like journals, with individuals documenting their interests or events from their lives. Most blogs are updated regularly.

Listserves

A **listserve** is an electronic forum in which users discuss and share information about a particular topic. Users sign up for the listserve, then post and respond to questions using their e-mail account. Many experts use listserves to exchange information with others in their field.

Message Boards

A **message board**, or **forum**, allows users to post thoughts and questions about a topic to a Web site and then see what others have to say about it. The site is usually organized by individual topics, called threads.

Social Media

There are many different kinds of tools and web sites that connect individuals to friends or groups. Individuals choose whether to subscribe, follow, or "like" an individual or group. This gives you access to that group. After you have access to a group, messages can be created or shared. You can join study groups, or connect with other readers or authors.

Media and Feature Writing

Many forms of **media and feature writing** are used in newspapers, magazines, radio, and television programs. Some of these forms are like narration because they tell a story. Other forms are types of persuasive writing. The most common forms are described below.

Advertisement

Advertisements, or **ads**, are meant to persuade readers to buy a product or service. Ad text should make an immediate impact on the reader and be easily remembered. Usually, advertisements appeal to people's emotions rather than to logic. Advertising messages are usually presented in visually interesting ways. Ads on TV may use visual techniques and background music to increase their effectiveness.

News Article and Feature Article

The purpose of a **news article** is to provide information. It should provide well-researched facts about a current event. It answers the questions: *Who? What? Where? When? Why?* and *How?* The first paragraph of a news article introduces the main facts, and the following paragraphs provide supporting details.

The purpose of a **feature article** is to provide information and points of view about something fun, entertaining, or important in people's daily lives. Feature articles are lively, fact-based discussions. Magazines contain many examples of feature writing, such as "Great Prom Ideas" or "The Year's Best Music." One characteristic of feature articles is a strong lead, or first paragraph, that draws readers into the piece.

Because they are based in fact, both news articles and feature articles can be considered narrative nonfiction.

Editorial/Letter to the Editor

Editorials are common features of most newspapers. These articles give newspaper staff writers the chance to voice their opinions on important issues. Many periodicals also publish letters to the editor, in which the public can voice opinions on a periodical's content or other topics of interest to its readers. When writing a letter to the editor, be sure to support your opinion with facts and evidence. Editorials and letters to the editor are usually persuasive in tone.

Critique or Review

A **critique**, or **review**, presents the author's opinion of a book, movie, or other work. The review usually includes a brief plot summary or description of the work of art. A critique does more than just summarize the main ideas of a work, however. Details about performances or the author's opinion of the quality of the work supports the author's opinion. In an effective review, the author's opinions about the work are always supported by specific details. The purpose of critiques and reviews is to help readers decide whether to experience the work for themselves.

Worth Seeing?

The Fellowship of the Ring is a movie version of the epic J. R. R. Tolkien novel about a mythical world threatened by the power of an evil ring. Director Peter Jackson uses beautiful computer graphics to show the struggle of a small group of adventurers who set out to destroy the ring. The rich characters, exciting action scenes, and incredible music make *The Fellowship of the Ring* a must-see for all fans of fantasy and adventure films.

Speech

A **speech** is a type of spoken message, often planned in advance and later delivered to a group of people. A speech can have many purposes:

- **to inform or explain,** as when a community leader speaks to a group of news reporters about a new neighborhood program

- **to argue,** as when a political candidate makes a speech on TV to convince people to vote for him or her

- **to tell a story** and build relationships, as when a business leader makes a humorous after-dinner speech at a business convention, or tells their life story to inspire others to reach success.

Before planning a speech, identify the occasion for speaking, the audience, and your purpose. These three elements will help you select an appropriate tone, words, and details. For example, if you are planning a speech about computers for the members of a computer club, you will not need to define computer terms for your audience. If you were to give the same speech to a general audience, however, you might need to define the terms because some members of the audience may not know what the words mean.

> ### Computer Speech for Computer Club
>
> I am here to give you tips on creating Web pages. I will speak to you about the asynchronous qualities of Ajax and the advantages and disadvantages of pulling content with it.

> ### Computer Speech for General Audience
>
> I am here to give you tips on creating Web pages. I will speak to you about Ajax, which stands for "Asynchronous JavaScript and XML." Simply put, Ajax is a way to put content on a Web page by using codes that pull information from a server for you.

Script or Transcript

A **nonfiction script** is the prewritten text for a presentation or broadcast program. Like a news story, a nonfiction script contains the five Ws, but no unnecessary details. A **transcript** is a written record of a live discussion or broadcast.

Scripts and transcripts usually follow the written conventions of plays. The names of the speakers are followed by their dialogue and brief descriptions of movement, visual material, and other information necessary to describe how the presentation should look when it happens or how it looked when it happened.

> ### Transcript of WXQV TV Interview
>
> **MARCY RAY, INTERVIEWER:** Coach, you must be very excited about the big win today. Can you describe your feelings for me and our viewers?
>
> **COACH:** It's hard to put my feelings into words right now, Marcy. I guess what I'm feeling most is pride. The team worked so hard this year. Every one of those kids earned this win, and I'm very, very proud of the entire team.
>
> [*Background cheers from team members*]
>
> **RAY:** How will you and the team celebrate, Coach?
>
> **COACH:** We won't be celebrating alone. This win belongs to the whole school. So there will be a celebration and ceremony in the school gym Monday morning at 9 a.m. Students, parents, faculty, staff— everyone in the school community— are invited.

Social Communication

The forms of **social communication** help people establish and maintain relationships with friends and family. When you communicate socially, always think about the occasion for writing and how well you know the recipients. For example, if the occasion is informal and you know the recipients well, your tone and word choice can be informal. However, if the occasion is formal and you are not well acquainted with the recipients, a formal tone and formal language are more appropriate.

Friendly Letter

Before the development of electronic forms of communication, **friendly letters** were the most common way of exchanging ideas with friends and family. Today, the conventions of friendly letters are still used to write e-mail messages. The extra time and effort it takes to write and mail a letter show the recipient how much you care. Use the following rules to develop your friendly letters.

- Friendly letters can be handwritten or typed.
- Include the date.
- Include a salutation, or greeting, such as "Dear Joe."
- Indent the paragraphs.
- End the letter with a complimentary closing like "Sincerely," and your signature.
- Be sure to include the proper address and postage on the envelope.

> November 3, 2007
> Dear Grandfather,
>
> I want you to know how much we are all looking forward to your visit. It's been so long since we've seen you! Dad has already planned some special events for us, but I hope that we can go fishing.
>
> Yours truly,
> Carlos

Thank-You Letter

A **thank-you letter** is a brief, friendly letter in which the sender expresses appreciation for a gift or an act of kindness.

> September 4, 2007
> Dear Janita,
>
> Thank you so much for your help on the school newsletter. Your attention to detail and hard work were a big part of our success.
>
> Thanks again,
> Mr. Hahn

Invitation

An **invitation** gives the date, time, place, and purpose of a social event. An invitation often includes an RSVP. This is an abbreviation of *répondez, s'il vous plaît,* a French phrase for "please respond." Including an RSVP can help you plan for the number of people attending your event.

> ### Come One, Come All!
>
> Come celebrate Crystal's sixteenth birthday!
>
> Where: Elm Park
> 1900 Elm Street
>
> When: Friday, May 25
> 6:00–8:30 p.m.
>
> RSVP: Please let Crystal know by Wednesday, May 23, whether you can attend.

Grammar, Usage, Mechanics, and Spelling

Parts of Speech Overview

All the words in the English language can be put into one of eight groups. These groups are the eight **parts of speech**. You can tell a word's part of speech by looking at how it functions, or the way it is used, in a sentence. Knowing about the functions of words can help you become a better writer.

The Eight Parts of Speech	Examples
A **noun** names a person, place, thing, or idea.	**Erik Weihenmayer** climbed the highest **mountain** in the **world**. The **journey** up **Mount Everest** took **courage**.
A **pronoun** takes the place of a noun.	**He** made the journey even though **it** was dangerous.
An **adjective** describes a noun or a pronoun.	Erik is a **confident** climber. He is **strong**, too.
A **verb** can tell what the subject of a sentence does or has. A **verb** can also link a noun or an adjective in the predicate to the subject.	Erik also **skis** and **rides** a bike. He **has** many hobbies. Erik **is** an athlete. He **is** also blind.
An **adverb** describes a verb, an adjective, or another adverb.	Illness **slowly** took his eyesight, but it **never** affected his spirit. His accomplishments have made him **very** famous. He has been interviewed **so** often.
A **preposition** shows how two things or ideas are related. It introduces a prepositional phrase.	Erik speaks **to** people **around** the world. **In** his speeches, he talks **about** his life.
A **conjunction** connects words or groups of words.	Courage **and** skill have carried him far. He has one disability, **but** he has many abilities.
An **interjection** expresses strong feeling.	**Wow**! What an amazing person he is. **Hurray**! He reached the mountain top.

Grammar and Usage

Grammar and **usage** rules tell us how to correctly identify and use the parts of speech and types of sentences.

Nouns

A **noun** names a person, place, thing, or idea. There are different kinds of nouns.

Common and Proper Nouns	Examples
A **common noun** names a general person, thing, or idea.	A **teenager** sat by the **ocean** and read a **magazine**.
Capitalize a common noun only when it begins a sentence.	**Magazines** are the perfect thing to read at the beach.
A **proper noun** names a specific person, place, thing, or idea. Always capitalize a proper noun.	**Jessica** sat by the **Pacific Ocean** and read *Teen Talk Magazine*.

Count and Noncount Nouns	Examples
Count nouns name things that you can count. The singular form of a count noun names one thing. The plural form names more than one thing.	<table><tr><td>Singular</td><td>Plural</td></tr><tr><td>one desk</td><td>two desks</td></tr><tr><td>one book</td><td>many books</td></tr><tr><td>one teacher</td><td>several teachers</td></tr></table>
You can count some food items by using a measurement word like **cup**, **slice**, or **glass** followed by the word **of**. To show the plural form, make the measurement word plural.	Jessica drank **a glass of water** after school. Jessica drank **two glasses of water** while she was reading her book.
Noncount nouns name things that you cannot count. They can be divided into different categories.	

Activities and Sports:	baseball, camping, dancing, golf, singing, soccer
Category Nouns:	clothing, equipment, furniture, machinery, mail
Food:	bread, cereal, cheese, lettuce, meat, milk, soup, tea
Ideas and Feelings:	democracy, enthusiasm, freedom, honesty, health
Materials:	air, fuel, gasoline, metal, paper, water, dust, soil
Weather:	fog, hail, heat, rain, smog, snow, humidity, sunshine

Some nouns can be either count or noncount nouns. It depends on how the nouns are used.	Jessica has read the book two **times**. She is fascinated by the idea of traveling through **time**.

Plural Nouns	Examples
Plural nouns name more than one person, place, thing, or idea. Add **-s** to most count nouns to make them plural. Other count nouns follow simple rules to form the plural.	My favorite **guitar** was made in Spain, but I also like my two American **guitars**.

Forming Noun Plurals

When a Noun Ends in:	Form the Plural by:	Examples
ch, **sh**, **s**, **x**, or **z**	adding **-es**	box—box**es** brush—brush**es**
a consonant + **y**	changing the **y** to **i** and adding **-es**	story—stor**ies**
a vowel + **y**	just adding **-s**	boy—boy**s**
f or **fe**	changing the **f** to **v** and adding **-es**, in most cases for some nouns that end in **f** or **fe**, just add **-s**	leaf—lea**ves** knife—kni**ves** cliff—cliff**s** safe—safe**s**
a vowel + **o**	adding **-s**	radio—radio**s** kangaroo—kangaroo**s**
a consonant + **o**	adding **-s**, in most cases; other times adding **-es** some nouns take either **-s** or **-es**	photo—photo**s** potato—potato**es** zero—zero**s**/zero**es**

A few count nouns are **irregular**. These nouns do not follow the rules to form the plural.

Forming Plurals of Irregular Count Nouns

For some irregular count nouns, change the spelling to form the plural.	one child many **children** one foot many **feet**	one man several **men** one ox ten **oxen**	a few **people** one person one woman most **women**
For other irregular count nouns, keep the same form for the singular and the plural.	one deer two **deer**	one fish many **fish**	one sheep twelve **sheep**

Possessive Nouns	Examples
Possessive nouns show ownership or relationship of persons, places, or things.	**Ted's** daughter made the guitar. The **guitar's** tone is beautiful.
Follow these rules to make a noun possessive: • Add **'s** to a singular noun or a plural noun that does not end in **s**.	 When she plays the piano, it attracts **people's** attention.
• If the owner's name ends in **s**, form the possessive by adding **'s** or just an apostrophe. Either is correct.	**Louis's** music is playful and funny. **Louis'** music is playful and funny.
• Add an apostrophe after the final **s** in a plural noun that ends in **s**.	Three **musicians'** instruments were left on the bus.

Noun Phrases and Clauses	Examples
A **noun phrase** is made up of a noun and its modifiers. Modifiers are words that describe, such as adjectives.	**The flying frog** does not actually fly. It glides on **special skin flaps**. Thailand is **a frog-friendly habitat**.
A **noun clause** is a group of words that functions as a noun and has a subject and a verb. It may begin with *that*, *how*, or a *wh-* word such as *why*, *what*, or *when*.	**How any animal flies** is hard to understand. He explained **that it is called a flying frog**. Its name makes sense to **whoever sees it**.

Articles

An **article** is a word that helps identify a noun.

Articles	Examples
A, **an**, and **the** are **articles**. An article often comes before a count noun. Do not use the articles **a** or **an** before a noncount noun.	It is **an** amazing event when **a** flying frog glides in **the** forest.
A and **an** are **indefinite articles**. Use **a** or **an** before a noun that names a nonspecific thing.	**A flying frog** stretched its webbed feet. **An owl** watched from a nearby tree.
• Use **a** before a word that starts with a consonant sound.	a **f**oot a **r**ainforest a **p**ool a **u**nion (*u* is pronounced like *y*, a **n**est a consonant)
• Use **an** before a word that starts with a vowel sound.	an **e**gg an **a**nimal an **a**dult an **a**mount an **o**cean an **h**our (The *h* is silent.)
The is a **definite article**. Use **the** before a noun that names a specific thing.	Leiopelmids are **the** oldest kind of frog in **the** world. They are survivors of **the** Jurassic period.

Pronouns

A **pronoun** is a word that takes the place of a noun. **Case** refers to the form that a pronoun takes to show how it is used in a sentence.

Subjective Case Pronouns	Examples
Use a **subject pronoun** as the subject of a sentence.	**Antonio** is looking forward to the homecoming dance. **He** is trying to decide what to wear.

Subject Pronouns	
Singular	**Plural**
I	we
you	you
he, she, it	they

The pronoun **it** can be used as a **subject** to refer to a noun.	The **dance** starts at 7:00. **It** ends at 10:00.
But: The pronoun **it** can be the subject without referring to a specific noun.	**It** is important to arrive on time. **It** is fun to see your friends in formal clothes.

Objective Case Pronouns	Examples
Use an **object pronoun** after an **action verb**.	Tickets are on sale, so buy **them** now.

Object Pronouns	
Singular	**Plural**
me	us
you	you
him, her, it	them

Use an **object pronoun** after a **preposition**.	Antonio invited Caryn. He ordered flowers for **her**.
Use **reciprocal pronouns** to show a two-way action between two or more people.	Mary and Juan tossed the ball to **each other**. Mary, Juan, and Lorenzo tested **one another** on the new math skills.

Possessive Words	Examples
A **possessive pronoun** tells who or what owns something.	**His** photograph of a tree won an award.
Possessive pronouns take the place of a **possessive noun and the person**, **place**, **or thing it owns**. Possessive pronouns always stand alone.	Which camera is Aleina's? The expensive camera is **hers**. **Mine** is a single-use, disposable camera.

Possessive Pronouns	
Singular	**Plural**
mine	ours
yours	yours
his, hers	theirs

Possessive Words (cont.)	Examples
Some possessive words act as **adjectives**, so they are called **possessive adjectives**. Possessive adjectives always come before a noun.	Aleina's photographs are beautiful because of **her** eye for detail.

Possessive Adjectives	
Singular	**Plural**
my	our
your	your
his, her, its	their

Demonstrative Words	Examples
A **demonstrative pronoun** points out a specific person, place, or thing. It can point to something near or far away.	**That** is a good photo of my grandparents. **These** are good photos, too.

Demonstrative Words		
	Singular	**Plural**
Near	this	these
Far	that	those

Demonstrative Words (cont.)	Examples
A demonstrative word can **act as an adjective**, answering the question *Which one?* or *Which ones?*	**This** photo album has pictures of my family. **These** photographs are of my grandparents.

Indefinite Pronouns	Examples
Use an **indefinite pronoun** when you are not talking about a specific person, place, or thing.	**Someone** has to lose the game. **Nobody** knows who the winner will be.

Some Indefinite Pronouns

These **indefinite pronouns** are always singular and need a **singular verb**.	
another either nobody someone anybody everybody no one something anyone everyone nothing anything everything one each neither somebody	**Something is** happening on the playing field. We hope that **everything goes** well for our team.
These **indefinite pronouns** are always plural and need a **plural verb**. both few many several	**Many** of us **are** hopeful.
These **indefinite pronouns** can be either singular or plural. all any most none some Look at the phrase that follows the indefinite pronoun. If the noun or pronoun in the phrase is plural, use a **plural verb**. If the noun or pronoun is singular, use a **singular verb**.	**Most** of the players **are** tired. **Most** of the game **is** over.

Relative Pronouns	Examples
A **relative pronoun** introduces **a relative clause**. It connects, or relates, the clause to a word in the sentence. Relative pronouns are used in restrictive and nonrestrictive clauses.	**Relative Pronouns** who whoever whosoever whom whomever whomsoever whose which whichever what whatever whatsoever

Grammar Tip
In informal speech, it is acceptable to say "**Who** did you ask?" In formal writing, use the correct form, "**Whom** did you ask?"

Use **who**, **whom**, or **whose** for people. The pronouns **whoever**, **whomever**, **whosoever**, and **whomsoever** also refer to people.	The student **who** was injured is Joe. We play **whomever** we are scheduled to play.
Use **which**, **whichever**, **what**, **whatever**, and **whatsoever** for things.	Joe's wrist, **which** is sprained, will heal.
Use **that** for people or things.	The trainer **that** examined Joe's wrist is sure. The injury **that** Joe received is minor.

Reflexive and Intensive Pronouns	Examples
Reflexive and **intensive pronouns** refer to nouns or other pronouns in a sentence. These pronouns end with -**self** or -**selves**.	**I** will go to the store by **myself**.
Use a **reflexive pronoun** when the object **refers back to the subject**.	To surprise her technology teacher, **Kim** taught **herself** how to create a Web site on the computer.

Reflexive and Intensive Pronouns

Singular	Plural
myself	ourselves
yourself	yourselves
himself, herself, itself	themselves

Use an **intensive pronoun** when you want **to emphasize a noun or a pronoun** in a sentence.	The technology **teacher himself** learned some interesting techniques from Kim.

Agreement and Reference	Examples
When nouns and pronouns **agree**, they both refer to the same person, place, or thing. The **noun** is the **antecedent**, and the **pronoun** refers to it.	**Rafael and Felicia** visited a local college. **They** toured the campus. *antecedent* *pronoun*
A pronoun must agree (match) in **number** with the noun it refers to. • **Singular pronouns** refer to one person. • **Plural pronouns** refer to more than one person.	**Rafael** plays violin. **He** enjoyed the music school. **The teenagers** were impressed. **They** liked this college.
Pronouns and adjectives must agree in **gender** with the nouns they refer to. Use **she**, **her**, and **hers** to refer to females. Use **he**, **him**, and **his** to refer to males.	Felicia told **her** uncle about the college visit. **Her** uncle told **her** that **he** received **his** graduate degree from that school.

Editing Tip

Find each pronoun in your paper. Find the noun it is replacing. Do they match?

Adjectives

An **adjective** describes, or modifies, a noun or a pronoun. It can tell what kind, which one, how many, or how much.

Adjectives	Examples
Adjectives provide more detailed information about a noun. Usually, an adjective comes before the noun it describes. But an adjective can also come after the noun.	Deserts have a **dry** climate. The climate is also **hot**.

Adjectives That Compare	Examples
Comparative adjectives help show the similarities or differences between two nouns.	Deserts are **more fun** to study than forests are.
To form the comparative of one-syllable adjectives and two-syllable adjectives that end in a consonant + **y**, add -**er**, and use **than**. Use **more** ... **than** if the adjective has three or more syllables.	The Sechura Desert in South America is small**er than** the Kalahari Desert in Africa. Is that desert **more interesting than** this one?
Superlative adjectives help show how three or more nouns are alike or different.	Of the Sechura, Kalahari, and Sahara, which is the **largest**?
To form the superlative of one-syllable adjectives and two-syllable adjectives that end in a consonant + **y**, add -**est**. Use **most** if the adjective has three or more syllables.	Which of the three deserts is the **smallest**? I think the Sahara is the **most beautiful**.
Irregular adjectives form the comparative and superlative differently. good better best some more most bad worse worst little less least	I had the **best** time ever visiting the desert. But the desert heat is **worse** than city heat.
Some two-syllable adjectives form the comparative with either -**er** or **more** and superlative with either -**est** or **most**. **Do not form a double comparison by using both.**	Most desert animals are **more lively** at night than during the day. Most desert animals are **livelier** at night than during the day.

Adjective Phrases and Clauses	Examples
An **adjective phrase** is a group of words that work together to modify a noun or a pronoun. A phrase has no verb.	Plants **in the desert** have developed adaptations.
An **adjective clause** is also a group of words that work together to modify a noun or a pronoun. Unlike a phrase, however, a clause has both a subject and a verb.	Desert plants **that have long roots** tap into water deep in the earth.

Verbs

Every sentence has two parts: a subject and a predicate. The subject tells who or what the sentence is about. The predicate tells something about the subject. For example:
The dancers / **performed** on stage.

The **verb** is the key word in the predicate because it tells what the subject does or has. Verbs can also link words.

Action Verbs	Examples
An **action verb** tells what the subject of a sentence does. Most verbs are action verbs.	Dancers **practice** for many hours. They **stretch** their muscles and **lift** weights.
Some **action verbs** tell about an action that you cannot see.	The dancers **recognize** the rewards that come from their hard work.

Linking Verbs	Examples
A **linking verb** connects, or links, the subject of a sentence to a word in the predicate.	**Linking Verbs** **Forms of the Verb *Be*** am / is / are — was / were **Other Linking Verbs** appear / feel / look — seem / smell — become / taste
The word in the predicate can describe the subject.	Their feet **are** calloused.
Or the word in the predicate can rename the subject.	These dancers **are** athletes.

Conditional Verbs	Examples
Conditional verbs show, in the present, how one event depends on another event in the future.	Dancers **should** stretch to prevent injuries. An injury **might** prevent a dancer from performing.
Some Conditional Verbs can / could / might / must shall / should / will / would	
Sentences with conditional verbs often use **if** and **then** to show how two events are connected. Conditional verbs are sometimes called **modal verbs**.	**If** a principal dancer is unable to perform, **then** the understudy will perform the role.

Helping Verbs	Examples
Verb phrases have more than one verb: helping verbs and a main verb.	Ballet **is considered** a dramatic art form. *helping verb* *main verb*
The action word is called the **main verb**. It shows what the subject does, has, or is.	This dance form **has been evolving** over the years. *helping verbs* *main verb*
Any verbs that come before the main verb are the **helping verbs**.	Ballet **must have been** very different in the 1500s. *helping verbs* *main verb*
Helping verbs agree with the subject.	Baryshnikov **has performed** around the world. Many people **have praised** this famous dancer.
Adverbs can be in several places in a sentence. The adverb **not** always comes between the **helping verb** and the **main verb**.	If you **have** not **heard** of him, you can watch the film *Dancers* to see him perform. He sometimes **has danced** in films. Usually, he dances on stage.
In questions, the subject comes between the **helping verb** and the **main verb**.	**Have** you **heard** of Mikhail Baryshnikov?

Helping Verbs

Forms of the Verb *Be*	Forms of the Verb *Do*	Forms of the Verb *Have*
am was is were are	do did does	have had has

Other Helping Verbs

To express ability: **can**, **could**	I **can** dance.
To express possibility: **may**, **might**, **could**	I **might** dance tonight.
To express necessity or desire: **must**, **would like**	I **must** dance more often. I **would like** to dance more often.
To express certainty: **will**, **shall**	I **will** dance more often.
To express obligation: **should**, **ought to**	I **should** practice more often. I **ought to** practice more often.

Verb Tense

The **tense** of a verb shows when an action happens.

Present Tense Verbs	Examples
The **present tense** of a verb tells about an action that happens now.	Greg **checks** his watch to see if it is time to leave. He **starts** work at 5:00 today.

Habitual Present Tense Verbs	Examples
The **habitual present tense** of a verb tells about an action that happens regularly or all the time.	Greg **works** at a pizza shop on Saturdays and Sundays. He **makes** pizzas and **washes** dishes.

Past Tense Verbs (Regular and Irregular)	Examples
The **past tense** of a verb tells about an action that happened earlier, or in the past.	Yesterday, Greg **worked** until the shop closed. He **made** 50 pizzas.
• The past tense form of **regular verbs** ends with -**ed**.	He **learned** how to make a stuffed-crust pizza. Then Greg **chopped** onions and peppers.
• **Irregular verbs** have **special forms** to show the past tense. For more irregular verbs, see the **Troubleshooting Guide**, page 773.	Greg **cut** the pizza. It **was** delicious. We **ate** all of it!

Some Irregular Verbs

Present Tense	Past Tense
cut	cut
is	was
eat	ate

Future Tense Verbs	Examples
The **future tense** of a verb tells about an action that will happen later, or in the future. To talk about the future, use:	Greg **will ride** the bus home after work tonight.
• the helping verb **will** plus a main verb.	Greg's mother **will drive** him to work tomorrow. On Friday, he **will get** his first paycheck.
• the phrase **am going to**, **is going to**, or **are going to** plus a **main verb**.	He **is going to take** a pizza home to his family. They **are going to eat** the pizza for dinner.

Perfect Tense Verbs

All verbs in the **perfect tenses**—**present**, **past**, and **future**—have a helping verb and a form of the main verb that is called the **past participle**.

Present Perfect Tense Verbs	Examples
For **regular verbs**, the past tense and the past participle end in -**ed**. To form the present perfect, use **has** or **have** with the past participle. **Present Tense** like **Past Tense** liked **Present Perfect** has/have liked **Irregular verbs** have **special forms** for the past tense and past participle. Always use **has** or **have** with the past participle. See page 773. **Present Tense** know **Past Tense** knew **Present Perfect** has/have known	 I **like** the Internet. I **liked** the Internet. I **have** always **liked** the Internet. I **know** a lot about the Internet. I **knew** very little about the Internet last year. I **have known** about the Internet for a long time.
The **present perfect tense** of a verb can tell about an action that began in the past and is still going on.	The public **has used** the Internet since the 1980s. **Have** you **done** research on the Internet?

Past Perfect Tense Verbs	Examples
The **past perfect tense** of a verb tells about an action that was completed before some other action in the past. It uses the helping verb **had** and the past participle of the main verb.	Before the Internet became popular, people **had done** their research in the library.

Future Perfect Tense Verbs	Examples
The **future perfect tense** of a verb tells about an action that will be completed at a specific time in the future. It uses the helping verbs **will have** and the past participle of the main verb.	By the end of next year, 100,000 people **will have visited** our Web site.

Contractions

A **contraction** is a shortened form of a verb or verb and pronoun combination.

Contractions	Examples
Use an **apostrophe** to show which letters have been left out of the contraction.	I would = I'd is not = isn't they are = they're can not = can't
In contractions made up of a verb and the word **not**, the word **not** is usually shortened to **n't**.	I **can't** stop eating these cookies!

Verb Forms

The **form** a verb takes changes depending on how it is used in a sentence, phrase, or clause.

Progressive Verbs	Examples
The **progressive verb** form tells about an action that occurs over a period of time.	
The **present progressive tense** of a verb tells about an action as it is happening.	They **are expecting** a big crowd for the fireworks show this evening.
• It uses the helping verb **am**, **is**, or **are**. The main verb ends in -**ing**.	**Are** you **expecting** the rain to end before the show starts?
The **past progressive tense** of a verb tells about an action that was happening over a period of time in the past.	They **were thinking** of canceling the fireworks.
• It uses the helping verb **was** or **were** and a main verb. The main verb ends in -**ing**.	A tornado **was heading** in this direction.
The **future progressive tense** of a verb tells about an action that will be happening over a period of time in the future.	The weather forecasters **will be watching** for the path of the tornado.
• It uses the helping verbs **will be** plus a main verb. The main verb ends in -**ing**.	I hope that they **will** not **be canceling** the show.

Transitive and Intransitive Verbs	Examples
Action verbs can be transitive or intransitive. A **transitive verb** needs an **object** to complete its meaning and to receive the action of the verb.	**Not complete:** **Complete:** Many cities **use** Many cities **use** fireworks.
The object can be a **direct object**. A direct object answers the question *Whom?* or *What?*	**Whom:** The noise **surprises** the audience. **What:** The people in the audience **cover** their ears.
An **intransitive verb** does not need an object to complete its meaning.	**Complete:** The people in our neighborhood **clap**. They **shout**. They **laugh**.
An **intransitive verb** may end the sentence, or it may be followed by other words that tell how, where, or when. These words are not objects since they do not receive the action of the verb.	The fireworks **glow** brightly. Then, slowly, they **disappear** in the sky. The show **ends** by midnight.

Active and Passive Voice	Examples
A verb is in **active voice** if the **subject** is doing the action.	Many cities **hold** fireworks displays for the Fourth of July.
A verb is in **passive voice** if the **subject** is not doing the action. A verb in passive voice always includes a form of the verb **be**, plus the past participle of the main verb. Use active voice to emphasize the subject. Use passive voice to put less emphasis on the subject, such as when:	Fireworks displays **are held** by many cities for the Fourth of July.
• the object, or receiver of the action, is more important than the doer	Our celebration **was held** after the winds died down.
• you don't know who the doer is	The fireworks **were made** in the U.S.
• you don't want to name the doer or place blame	The start time **is listed** incorrectly in the newspaper.

Two-Word Verbs

A **two-word verb** is a verb followed by a preposition. The meaning of the two-word verb is different from the meaning of the verb by itself.

Some Two-Word Verbs

Verb	Meaning	Example
break	to split into pieces	I didn't **break** the window with the ball.
break down	to stop working	Did the car **break down** again?
break up	to end	The party will **break up** before midnight.
	to come apart	The ice on the lake will **break up** in the spring.
bring	to carry something with you	**Bring** your book to class.
bring up	to suggest	She **brings up** good ideas at every meeting.
	to raise children	**Bring up** your children to be good citizens.
check	to make sure you are right	We can **check** our answers at the back of the book.
check in	to stay in touch with someone	I **check in** with my mom at work.
check up	to see if everything is okay	The nurse **checks up** on the patient every hour.
check off	to mark off a list	Look at your list and **check off** the girls' names.
check out	to look at something carefully	Hey, Marisa, **check out** my new bike!

Verb	Meaning	Example
fill	to place as much as can be held	**Fill** the pail with water.
fill in	to color or shade in a space	Please **fill in** the circle.
fill out	to complete	Marcos **fills out** a form to order a book.
get	to go after something	I'll **get** some milk at the store.
	to receive	I often **get** letters from my pen pal.
get ahead	to go beyond what is expected	She worked hard to **get ahead** in math class.
get along	to be on good terms with	Do you **get along** with your sister?
get out	to leave	Let's **get out** of the kitchen.
get over	to feel better	I hope you'll **get over** the flu soon.
get through	to finish	I can **get through** this book tonight.
give	to hand something to someone	We **give** presents to the children.
give out	to stop working	If she runs ten miles, her energy will **give out**.
give up	to quit	I'm going to **give up** eating candy.
go	to move from place to place	Did you **go** to the mall on Saturday?
go on	to continue	Why do the boys **go on** playing after the bell rings?
go out	to go someplace special	Let's **go out** to lunch on Saturday.
look	to see or watch	Don't **look** directly at the sun.
look over	to review	She **looks over** her test before finishing.
look up	to hunt for and find	We **look up** information on the Internet.
pick	to choose	I'd **pick** Lin for class president.
pick on	to bother or tease	My older brothers always **pick on** me.
pick up	to go faster	Business **picks up** in the summer.
	to gather or collect	**Pick up** your clothes!
run	to move quickly	Juan will **run** in a marathon.
run into	to see someone unexpectedly	Did you **run into** Chris at the store?
run out	to suddenly have nothing left	The cafeteria always **runs out** of nachos.
stand	to be on one's feet	I have to **stand** in line to buy tickets.
stand for	to represent	A heart **stands for** love.
stand out	to be easier to see	You'll **stand out** with that orange cap.
turn	to change direction	We **turn** right at the next corner.
turn up	to raise the volume	Please **turn up** the radio.
turn in	to give back	You didn't **turn in** the homework yesterday.
turn off	to make something stop	Please **turn off** the radio.

Forms of Irregular Verbs

Irregular verbs form the past tense and the past participle in a different way than regular verbs. These verb forms have to be memorized.

Some Irregular Verbs

Irregular Verb	Past Tense	Past Participle	Irregular Verb	Past Tense	Past Participle
be: am, is be: are	was were	been been	eat	ate	eaten
beat	beat	beaten	fall (*intr.*)	fell	fallen
become	became	become	feed	fed	fed
begin	began	begun	feel	felt	felt
bend	bent	bent	fight	fought	fought
bind	bound	bound	find	found	found
bite	bit	bitten	fly	flew	flown
blow	blew	blown	forget	forgot	forgotten
break	broke	broken	forgive	forgave	forgiven
bring	brought	brought	freeze	froze	frozen
build	built	built	get	got	got, gotten
burst	burst	burst	give	gave	given
buy	bought	bought	go	went	gone
catch	caught	caught	grow	grew	grown
choose	chose	chosen	have	had	had
come	came	come	hear	heard	heard
cost	cost	cost	hide	hid	hidden
creep	crept	crept	hit	hit	hit
cut	cut	cut	hold	held	held
dig	dug	dug	hurt	hurt	hurt
do	did	done	keep	kept	kept
draw	drew	drawn	know	knew	known
dream	dreamed, dreamt	dreamed, dreamt	lay (*tr.*)	laid	laid
drink	drank	drunk	lead	led	led
drive	drove	driven	leave	left	left

Irregular Verb	Past Tense	Past Participle	Irregular Verb	Past Tense	Past Participle
lend	lent	lent	sing	sang	sung
lie (*intr.*)	lay	lain	sink	sank	sunk
let	let	let	sit	sat	sat
light	lit	lit	sleep (*intr.*)	slept	slept
lose	lost	lost	slide	slid	slid
make	made	made	speak	spoke	spoken
mean	meant	meant	spend	spent	spent
meet	met	met	stand	stood	stood
pay	paid	paid	steal	stole	stolen
prove	proved	proved, proven	stick	stuck	stuck
put	put	put	sting	stung	stung
quit	quit	quit	strike	struck	struck
read	read	read	swear	swore	sworn
ride	rode	ridden	swim	swam	swum
ring	rang	rung	swing	swung	swung
rise (*intr.*)	rose	risen	take	took	taken
run	ran	run	teach	taught	taught
say	said	said	tear	tore	torn
see	saw	seen	tell	told	told
seek	sought	sought	think	thought	thought
sell	sold	sold	throw	threw	thrown
send	sent	sent	understand	understood	understood
set	set	set	wake	woke, waked	woken, waked
shake	shook	shaken	wear	wore	worn
show	showed	shown	weep	wept	wept
shrink	shrank	shrunk	win	won	won
shut	shut	shut	write	wrote	written

Verbals

A **verbal** is a word made from a verb but used as another part of speech.

Gerunds	Examples
A **gerund** is a verb form that ends in -**ing** and that is used as a noun. Like all nouns, a gerund can be the subject of a sentence or an object.	**Cooking** is Mr. Jimenez's favorite hobby. *subject* Mr. Jimenez truly enjoys **cooking**. *direct object* Mr. Jimenez is very talented at **cooking**. *object of preposition*

Infinitives	Examples
An **infinitive** is a verb form that begins with **to**. It can be used as a noun, an adjective, or an adverb.	Mr. Jimenez likes **to cook**. *noun* Mr. Jimenez's beef tamales are a sight **to see**. *adjective* Mr. Jimenez cooks **to relax**. *adverb*

Participial Phrases	Examples
A **participle** is a verb form that is used as an adjective. For regular verbs, it ends in -**ing** or -**ed**. Irregular verbs take the past participle form.	His **sizzling** fajitas taste delicious. Mr. Jimenez also makes tasty **frozen** desserts.
A **participial phrase** begins with a participle. Place the phrase next to the noun it describes.	**Standing by the grill**, he cooked meat. **Not**: He cooked meat, standing by the grill.

Absolutes

An **absolute** is a sentence-like phrase. It is usually formed with a subject and a participle.

Absolutes	Examples
An **absolute** modifies all the remaining parts of the sentence.	**More guests having arrived,** Mr. Jimenez added burgers to the grill.
Use a comma to set off the **absolute** from the rest of the sentence.	Mr. Jimenez, **his plans for a good party accomplished**, smiled broadly.

A phrase that utilizes a gerund, an infinitive, a participle, or an absolute is known as a **verbal phrase**.

Adverbs

An **adverb** describes a verb, an adjective, or another adverb.

Adverbs	Examples
Adverbs answer one of the following questions: • How? • Where? • When? • How often?	**Carefully** aim the ball. Kick the ball **here**. Try again **later** to make a goal. Cathy **usually** scores.
Adverbs that tell how often usually come before the main verb or after a form of **be**. Other adverbs often come after the verb.	Our team **always wins**. The whole team **plays well**.
An adverb can strengthen the meaning of an **adjective** or another **adverb**.	Gina is **really good** at soccer. She plays **very well**.

Grammar Tip

Use an adjective, rather than an adverb, after a linking verb.

My teacher is fairly.

Adverbs That Compare	Examples
Some **adverbs** compare actions. Add -**er** to compare the actions of two people. Add -**est** to compare the actions of three or more people.	Gina runs **fast**. Gina runs **faster** than Maria. Gina runs **the fastest** of all the players.
If the adverb ends in -**ly**, use **more** or **less** to compare two actions.	Gina aims **more carefully** than Jen. Jen aims **less carefully** than Gina.
Use **the most** or **the least** to compare three or more actions.	Gina aims **the most carefully** of all the players. Jen aims **the least carefully** of all the players.

Adverbial Phrases and Clauses	Examples
An **adverb phrase** is a prepositional phrase that modifies a verb, an adjective, or another adverb.	When Gina kicked the ball, it **went into the net**. The coach was **happy about the score**. Gina plays **best under pressure**.
An **adverb clause** has a subject and a verb. It modifies an independent main clause and cannot stand alone. Adverb clauses can tell when, why, or where.	**After the team won**, the coach praised the players. Everyone was muddy **because it had rained**. Soccer is popular **wherever there are fields available**.

Prepositions

A **preposition** comes at the beginning of a prepositional phrase. **Prepositional phrases** add details to sentences.

Uses of Prepositions	Examples
Some prepositions show **location**.	The Chávez Community Center is **by my house**. The pool is **behind the building**.
Some prepositions show **time**.	The Teen Club's party will start **after lunch**.
Some prepositions show **direction**.	Go **through the building** and **around the fountain** to get **to the pool**. The snack bar is **down the hall**.
Some prepositions have **multiple uses**.	We might see Joshua **at the party**. Meet me **at my house**. Come **at noon**.

Prepositional Phrases	Examples
A **prepositional phrase** starts with a preposition and ends with a noun or a pronoun. It includes all the words in between. The noun or pronoun is the **object of the preposition**.	I live **near the Chávez Community Center**. *object of preposition* Tom wants to walk there **with you and me**. *objects of preposition*
Prepositional phrases are often consecutive.	The Community Center is **up the street** and **on the right**.

Some Prepositions

Location		Time	Direction	Other Prepositions	
above	near	after	across	about	for
behind	next to	before	around	against	from
below	off	during	down	along	of
beside	on	till	into	among	to
between	out	until	out of	as	with
by	outside		through	at	without
in	over		toward	except	
inside	under		up		

Conjunctions and Interjections

A **conjunction** connects words or groups of words. An **interjection** expresses strong feeling or emotion.

Conjunctions	Examples
A **coordinating conjunction** connects words, phrases, or clauses.	
To show similarity: **and**	Irena **and** Irving are twins.
To show difference: **but**, **yet**	I know Irena, **but** I do not know Irving.
To show choice: **or**	They will celebrate their birthday Friday **or** Saturday night.
To show cause/effect: **so**, **for**	I have a cold, **so** I cannot go to the party.
To put negative ideas together: **nor**	My mother will not let me go, **nor** will my father.
Correlative conjunctions are used in pairs. The pair connects phrases or words.	**Some Correlative Conjunctions** both … and not only … but also either … or whether … or neither … nor
A **subordinating conjunction** introduces a **dependent clause** in a complex sentence. It connects the **dependent clause** to the main clause.	**Some Subordinating Conjunctions** after before till although if until as in order that when as if since where as long as so that while because though
A **conjunctive adverb** joins two independent clauses. Use a semicolon before the conjunction and a comma after it.	**Some Conjunctive Adverbs** besides meanwhile then consequently moreover therefore however nevertheless thus

Grammar Tip

When you use paired words, make sure you use both words in the sentence. Don't leave one out!

Interjections	Examples
An **interjection** shows emotion. If an interjection stands alone, follow it with an exclamation point.	**Help!** **Oops!** **Oh boy!**
An interjection used in a sentence can be followed by a comma or an exclamation mark. Use a comma after a weak interjection. Use an exclamation mark after a strong interjection.	**Oh**, it's a baby panda! **Hooray**! The baby panda has survived!

Sentences

A **sentence** is a group of words that expresses a complete thought. Every sentence has a subject (a main idea) and a predicate that describes what the main idea is, has, or does. Sentences can be classified according to their function and structure.

Sentence Types	Examples
A **declarative sentence** makes a statement. It ends with a period.	The football game was on Friday. The coach made an important announcement.
An **interrogative sentence** asks a question. It ends with a question mark.	Who heard the announcement? What did the coach say?
An **exclamatory sentence** shows surprise or strong emotion. It ends with an exclamation point.	That's fantastic news! I can't believe it!
An **imperative sentence** gives a command.	Give the team my congratulations.
• An imperative sentence usually begins with a verb and ends with a period.	**Be** on time.
• If an imperative sentence shows strong emotion, it ends with an exclamation point.	Beat the opponent!

> **Grammar Tip**
>
> Use **please** to make a command more polite:
>
> *Please* call me if you have any questions.

Negative Sentences	Examples
A **negative sentence** uses a **negative word** to say "no."	The game in Hawaii was **not** boring! **Nobody** in our town missed it on TV. Our team **never** played better.

Negative Words

no	none	no one	not
nowhere	never	nobody	nothing

Use only one negative word in a sentence. Using two negatives in one sentence is called a **double negative**. Two negatives cancel each other out. **I did not see no one**, means **I saw someone**.	The other team could not do ~~nothing~~ right. (anything) Their team never scored ~~no~~ points. (any)

Conditional Sentences	Examples
Conditional sentences tell how one action depends on another. These sentences often use conditional or modal verbs, such as **can**, **will**, **could**, **would**, or **might**.	**If** our team returns today, **then** we **will** have a party. **Unless** it rains, we **can** have the party outside.
Sometimes a conditional sentence tells about an imaginary condition and its imaginary result.	If my dog **could talk**, he **would tell** me his thoughts.

Sentence Structure

Phrases	Examples
A **phrase** is a group of related words that does not have both a subject and a verb. English can have noun phrases, verb phrases, adjective phrases, adverb phrases, prepositional phrases, and more.	The football team has won many games in overtime. *noun phrase*　*verb phrase*　*noun phrase*　*prepositional phrase*

Clauses	Examples
A **clause** is a group of words that has both a **subject** and a **predicate**. A clause can be a complete sentence.	California's population / grew during the 1840s. *subject*　*predicate*
An **independent clause** can stand alone as a complete sentence.	California's population / increased. *subject*　*predicate*
A **dependent clause** cannot stand alone as a complete sentence.	**because** gold / was found there during that time
An **adjective clause** gives more details about the noun or pronoun that it describes.	The news **that gold had been found** spread fast.
An **adverb clause** can tell when, where, or why.	**When someone found gold**, people celebrated.
A **noun clause** can function as a subject, a direct object, or an object of a preposition.	The reporter knew **why the miners were celebrating.**
A **nonrestrictive clause** is a clause that adds non-essential detail to your sentence. Set it off with commas.	The miners, **who were happy to hear the news,** leaped for joy.

Simple Sentences	Examples
A **simple sentence** is one independent clause with a subject and a predicate. It has no dependent clauses.	Supplies / were scarce. The miners / needed goods and services.

Compound Sentences	Examples
When you join two independent clauses, you make a **compound sentence**.	
Use either a comma and a **coordinating conjunction**, or a **semicolon**, to join independent clauses.	People opened stores, **but** supplies were scarce.
Or use a **conjunctive adverb** with a semicolon before it and a comma after it.	People opened stores; supplies slowly arrived. Miners made money; **however**, merchants made more money.

Complex Sentences	Examples
To make a **complex sentence**, join an independent clause with one or more dependent clauses.	Many writers visited camps **where miners worked**.
	independent *dependent*
If the dependent clause comes first, put a **comma** after it.	**While the writers were there**, they wrote stories about the miners.
Use a comma or commas to separate the nonrestrictive clause from the rest of the sentence.	The writers, **who were from California,** lived in the same tents as the miners.

Compound-Complex Sentences	Examples
You can make a **compound-complex sentence** by joining two or more independent clauses and one or more dependent clauses.	Many miners never found gold, **but** they stayed in California **because they found other jobs there**.
	dependent

Properly Placed Modifiers and Clauses	Examples
Place **modifiers** as closely as possible to the word or words that they describe. The meaning of a clause may be unclear if a modifier is not placed properly.	Unclear: Some miners **only** found fool's gold. (Does *only* describe *found* or *fool's gold*?) Clear: Some miners found **only** fool's gold.
A **misplaced clause** may make a sentence unclear and accidentally funny. When the clause is placed properly, it makes the meaning of the sentence clear.	Unclear: I read that miners traveled by mule **when I studied American history.** (Did the miners travel while you studied?) Clear: **When I studied American history**, I read that miners traveled by mule.
A **misplaced modifier** is a phrase placed too far away from the word or words it describes. Correct a misplaced modifier by placing it closer to the word or words it describes.	Unclear: The stream rushed past the miners, **splashing wildly.** (Did the miners or the stream splash wildly?) Clear: **Splashing wildly**, the stream rushed past the miners.
A **dangling modifier** occurs when you accidentally forget to include the word being described. Correct a dangling modifier by adding the missing word being described, adding words to the modifier, or rewording the sentence.	**Standing in rushing streams**, the search for gold was dangerous. (Who stood in the streams?) The search for gold was dangerous for **miners** standing in rushing streams.

Parenthetical Phrases and Appositives	Examples
A **parenthetical phrase** adds nonessential information to a sentence. You can leave out a nonessential phrase without changing the meaning of the sentence. Use commas to set off a nonessential phrase.	Most miners did not, **in fact**, find gold. Gold, **every miner's dream**, lay deeply buried.
An **appositive phrase** renames the noun next to it. An appositive phrase usually comes after the noun or pronoun it refers to. Use commas to set off an appositive.	James Marshall, **a mill worker**, started the Gold Rush when he found gold nuggets in 1848.

Clauses with Missing Words	Examples
In an **elliptical clause**, a word or words are left out to shorten a sentence and avoid repetition. You can tell what word is missing by reading the rest of the sentence.	Henry found six nuggets; **James**, **eight**. (You can tell that the missing word is "found.")
You may also combine two or more sentences that are similar and include related information. Some words, usually any pronouns that refer back to the subject, can be left out of the combined sentence. This is called **structural omission**. In this example, the three sentences are combined, using commas and the conjunction **and**. The pronoun *he* is omitted from the final two sentences.	James counted his gold nuggets. He put them away. He counted them again later. James counted his gold nuggets, put them away, **and** counted them again later.

Restrictive Relative Clauses	Examples
A **restrictive relative clause** is a clause that begins with a relative pronoun, such as **who**, **whom**, **which**, or **that**. You cannot remove the clause without changing its meaning. Do not use commas.	Only people **who have a ticket** can come in. The man **who found the dog** received a reward.

Coordination and Subordination	Examples
Use **coordination** to join clauses of equal weight, or importance.	Gold was often found next to streams, **and** it was also found deep beneath the earth.
Use **subordination** to join clauses of unequal weight, or importance.	The miners were called '49ers. *main idea*
Put the main idea in the main clause and the less important detail in the dependent clause.	Many miners arrived in 1849. *less important detail* The miners were called '49ers because many miners arrived in 1849.

Subjects and Predicates

A **subject** tells who or what the sentence is about. A **predicate** tells something about the subject.

Complete and Simple Subjects	Examples
The **complete subject** includes all the words in the subject.	**Many people** visit our national parks. **My favorite parks** are in the West.
The **simple subject** is the most important word in the complete subject.	Many <u>people</u> visit our national parks. My favorite <u>parks</u> are in the West.

Understood Subject	Examples
When you give a command, you do not state the subject. The subject **you** is understood in an imperative sentence.	Watch the geysers erupt. Soak in the hot springs. See a petrified tree.

It as the Subject	Examples
As the subject of a sentence, the pronoun *it* may refer to a specific noun. Or *it* can be the subject without referring to a specific noun.	See that **stone structure**? **It** is a natural bridge. **It** is amazing to see the natural wonders in these parks.

Complete and Simple Predicate	Examples
The predicate of a sentence tells what the subject is, has, or does. The **complete predicate** includes all the words in the predicate.	People **explore caves in Yellowstone Park**. Many flowers **grow wild throughout the park**. Some people **climb the unusual rock formations**.
The **simple predicate** is the **verb**. It is the most important word in the predicate.	People <u>explore</u> caves in Yellowstone Park. Many flowers <u>grow</u> wild throughout the park. Some people <u>climb</u> the unusual rock formations.

Compound Subject	Examples
A **compound subject** is two or more simple subjects joined by **and** or **or**.	<u>Yosemite</u> and <u>Yellowstone</u> are both in the West. Either <u>spring</u> or <u>fall</u> is a good time to visit.

Compound Predicate	Examples
A **compound predicate** has two or more verbs joined by **and** or **or**.	At Yosemite, some people **fish and swim**. My family **hikes** to the river **or stays** in the cabin. I **have seen** the falls **and have ridden** the trails.

Complete Sentences and Fragments

A **complete sentence** has both a **subject** and a **predicate** and expresses a complete thought. A **fragment** is written like a sentence but is not a complete thought.

Sentences and Fragments	Examples
Begin a complete sentence with a capital letter, and end it with a period or other end mark.	These parks / have many tourist attractions. _subject_ _predicate_
A **fragment** is a sentence part that is incorrectly used as a complete sentence. For example, the fragment may be missing a subject. Add a subject to correct the problem.	**Incorrect:** Fun to visit because they have many attractions. **Correct:** Parks are fun to visit because they have many attractions.
Writers sometimes use fragments on purpose to emphasize an idea or for another effect.	I did not camp in bear country. **No way. Too dangerous.**

Subject-Verb Agreement

The number of a subject and the number of a verb must agree.

Subject-Verb Agreement	Examples
Use a **singular subject** with a **singular verb**. Use a **plural subject** with a **plural verb**.	Another popular **park is** the Grand Canyon. We **were amazed** by the colors of its cliffs.
If the simple subjects in a **compound subject** are connected by **and**, use a plural verb. If the compound subject is connected by **or**, look at the last simple subject. If it is singular, use a **singular verb**. If it is plural, use a **plural verb**.	A **mule** and a **guide are** available for a trip down the canyon. These **rafts or** this **boat is** the best way to go. This **boat or** these **rafts are** the best way to go.
The **subject** and **verb** must agree, even when other words come between them.	The **bikers** in the park **are looking** for animals.
The **subject** and **verb** must agree even if the subject comes after the verb.	There **are** other amazing **parks** in Arizona. Here **is** a **list** of them.

Editing Tip

Read your writing aloud to find mistakes in subject-verb agreement.

Grammar Tip

Subjects and verbs are not in prepositional phrases. Drop these phrases to find the subject and verb more easily.

Parallel Structure

A sentence is **parallel** when all of its parts have the same form.

Parallel Structure	Examples
The parts of a sentence must be **parallel**. Words, phrases, or clauses in a sentence that do the same job should have the same form.	They went hik**ing**, raft**ing**, and horseback rid**ing**. I know **that we must be** in shape to hike the Canyon, **that we have to carry** plenty of water, and **that we need to take and eat** salty snacks.

Mechanics

Proper use of capital letters and correct punctuation is important to effective writing.

Capitalization

Knowing when to use capital letters is an important part of clear writing.

First Word in a Sentence	Examples
Capitalize the first word in a sentence.	**W**e are studying the Lewis and Clark Expedition.

In Direct Quotations	Examples
Capitalize the first word in a **direct quotation**.	Clark said, "**There is great joy in camp.**" "**We are in view of the ocean**," he said. "**It's the Pacific Ocean**," he added.

In Letters	Examples
Capitalize the first word used in the **greeting** or in the **closing** of a letter.	**D**ear Kim, **Y**our friend,

In Titles of Works	Examples
All important words in a **title** begin with a capital letter. Articles (**a, an, the**), short conjunctions (**and, but, or, so**), and short prepositions (**at, for, from, in, of, with,** etc.) are not capitalized unless they are the first or last word in the title.	**book:** *The Longest Journey* **poem:** "Leaves of Grass" **magazine:** *Flora and Fauna of Arizona* **newspaper:** *The Denver Post* **song:** "Star-Spangled Banner" **game:** Exploration! **TV series:** "The Gilmore Girls" **movie:** *The Lion King*

Pronoun *I*	Examples
Capitalize the pronoun *I* no matter where it is located in a sentence.	**I** was amazed when **I** learned that Lewis and Clark's expedition was over 8,000 miles.

Proper Nouns and Adjectives	Examples
Common nouns name a general person, place, thing, or idea. Proper nouns name a particular person, place, thing, or idea. All the important words in a **proper noun** start with a capital letter.	**Common Noun:** **t**eam **Proper Noun:** **C**orps of **D**estiny

Proper Nouns and Adjectives, continued	Examples
Proper nouns include the following: • names of people and their titles	**S**tephanie **E**ddins **C**aptain **M**eriwether **L**ewis
Do not capitalize a title if it is used without a name.	The **captain's** co-leader on the expedition was William Clark.
• family titles like **Mom** and **Dad** when they are used as names.	"William Clark is one of our ancestors," **Mom** said. I asked my **mom** whose side of the family he was on, hers or my **dad's**.
• names of organizations	United Nations History Club Wildlife Society
• names of languages and religions	Spanish Christianity
• months, days, special days, and holidays	April Sunday Thanksgiving
Names of geographic places are proper nouns. Capitalize street, city, and state names in mailing addresses.	**Cities and States**: Dallas, Texas **Streets and Roads**: Main Avenue **Bodies of Water**: Pacific Ocean **Countries**: Ecuador **Landforms**: Sahara Desert **Continents**: North America **Public Spaces**: Muir Camp **Buildings, Ships, and Monuments**: *Titanic* **Planets and Heavenly Bodies**: Neptune
A **proper adjective** is formed from a **proper noun**. Capitalize proper adjectives.	Napoleon Bonaparte was from **Europe**. He was a **European** leader in the 1800s.

Grammar Tip

If the family title is preceded by a possessive pronoun, always use lower case.

Abbreviations of Proper Nouns

Abbreviations of geographic places are also capitalized.

Geographic Abbreviations

Words Used in Addresses				Some State Names Used in Mailing Addresses			
Avenue	Ave.	Highway	Hwy.	California	CA	Michigan	MI
Boulevard	Blvd.	Lane	Ln.	Florida	FL	Ohio	OH
Court	Ct.	Place	Pl.	Georgia	GA	Texas	TX
Drive	Dr.	Street	St.	Illinois	IL	Virginia	VA

Abbreviations of Personal Titles

Capitalize abbreviations for a personal title. Follow the same rules for capitalizing a personal title.

Mr. . . . . Mister	**Mrs.** . . . . . . Mistress	**Dr.** . . . . Doctor
Jr. . . . . Junior	**Capt.** . . . . . Captain	**Sen.** . . . . . . Senator

Punctuation

Punctuation marks are used to emphasize or clarify meanings.

Apostrophe	Examples
Use an **apostrophe** to punctuate a **possessive noun**.	
If there is one owner, add **'s** to the owner's name. If the owner's name ends in s, it is correct to add **'s** *or* just the apostrophe. If there is more than one owner, add **'** if the plural noun ends in **s**. Add **'s** if it does not end in **s**.	Mrs. Ramos's sons live in New Mexico. Mrs. Ramos' sons live in New Mexico. Her sons' birthdays are both in January. She sends cards for her children's birthdays.
Use an **apostrophe** to replace the letters left out of a contraction.	could n̶o̶t̶ = couldn't he w̶o̶u̶l̶d̶ = he'd

> **Grammar Tip**
>
> Never use an apostrophe to form a plural—only to show possession or contraction.

End Marks	Examples
Use a **period** at the end of a statement or a polite command. Use a period after an indirect question. An indirect question tells about a question you asked.	Georgia read the paper to her mom. Tell me if there are any interesting articles. She asked if there were any articles about the new restaurant on Stone Street near their house.
Use a **question mark** at the end of a question. Use a question mark after a tag question that comes at the end of a statement.	What kind of food do they serve? The food is good, isn't it?
Use an **exclamation point** after an interjection. Use an exclamation point at the end of a sentence to show you feel strongly about something.	Wow! The chicken parmesan is delicious!

Comma	Examples
Use a **comma**:	
• before the **coordinating conjunction** in a compound sentence	Soccer is a relatively new sport in the United States, **but** it has been popular in England for a long time.
• to set off words that interrupt a sentence, such as an **appositive phrase** or a **nonrestrictive clause** that is not needed to identify the word it describes	Mr. Okada, **the soccer coach,** had the team practice skills like passing, **for example,** for the first hour. Passing, **which is my favorite skill,** was fun.
• to separate three or more items in a **series**	Shooting, passing, and dribbling are important skills.
• between two or more adjectives that tell equally about the same noun	The midfielder's quick, unpredictable passes made him the team's star player.
• after an **introductory phrase or clause**	**In the last game,** he made several goals.
• to separate a **nonrestrictive phrase** or **clause**, or a **nonrestrictive relative clause.**	The cook, **who used to be a teacher,** made enough soup to feed all of us.
• before someone's exact words and after them if the sentence continues	Mr. Okada said, "Meet the ball after it bounces," as we practiced our half-volleys.
• before and after a **nonrestrictive clause**	At the end of practice, **before anyone left,** Mr. Okada handed out revised game schedules.
• to set off a short phrase at the beginning of a sentence	**At last**, we could go home.
• to separate contrasting phrases	I like to watch movies, **not plays**.
Use a comma in these places in a letter:	
• between the city and the state • between the date and the year • after the greeting of a personal letter • after the closing of a letter	Milpas, AK July 3, 2008 Dear Mr. Okada, Sincerely,

Dash	Examples
Use a **dash** to show a break in an idea or the tone in a sentence.	Water—a valuable resource—is often taken for granted.
Or use a dash to emphasize a word, a series of words, a phrase, or a clause.	It is easy to conserve water—wash full loads of laundry, use water-saving devices, fix leaky faucets.

Ellipsis	Examples
Use an **ellipsis** to show that you have left out words.	A recent survey documented ... water usage.
Or use an ellipsis to show an idea that trails off.	The survey reported the amount of water wasted ...

Hyphen	Examples
Use a **hyphen** to:	
• connect words in a number and in a fraction	**One-third** of the people wasted water every day.
• join some words to make a compound word	A **15-year-old boy** and his **great-grandmother** have started an awareness campaign.
• connect a letter to a word	They designed a **T-shirt** for their campaign.
• divide words at the end of a line. Always divide the word between two syllables.	Please join us in our awareness campaign.

Italics and Underlining	Examples
When you are using a computer, use **italics** for the names of:	
• magazines and newspapers	I like to read **Time Magazine** and the **Daily News**.
• books	They help me understand our history book, **The U.S. Story**.
• plays	Did you see the play **Abraham Lincoln in Illinois**?
• movies	It was made into the movie **Young Abe**.
• musicals	The musical **Oklahoma!** is about Southwest pioneers.
• music albums	**Greatest Hits from Musicals** is my favorite album.
• TV series	Do you like the singers on the TV show **American Idol**?
If you are using handwriting, underline.	

Parentheses	Examples
Use **parentheses** around extra information in a sentence.	The new story (in the evening paper) is very interesting.

Quotation Marks	Examples
Use **quotation marks** to show:	
• a speaker's exact words	"Listen to this!" Jim said.
• the exact words quoted from a book or other printed material	The announcement in the paper was: "The writer Josie Ramón will be at Milpas Library on Friday."
• the title of a song, poem, short story, magazine article, or newspaper article	Her famous poem "Speaking" appeared in the magazine article "How to Talk to Your Teen."
• the title of a chapter from a book	She'll be reading "Getting Along," a chapter from her new book.
• words used in a special way	We will be "all ears" at the reading.

Grammar Tip

Always put **periods** and **commas** inside quotation marks.

Semicolon	Examples
Use a **semicolon**:	
• to separate two simple sentences used together without a conjunction	A group of Jim's classmates plan to attend the reading; he hopes to join them.
• before a **conjunctive adverb** that joins two simple sentences. Use a comma after the adverb.	Jim wanted to finish reading Josie Ramón's book this evening; **however,** he forgot it at school.
• to separate a group of words in a series if the words in the series already have commas	After school, Jim has to study French, health, and math; walk, feed, and brush the dog; and eat dinner.

Colon	Examples
Use a **colon**:	
• after the greeting in a business letter	Dear Sir or Madam**:**
• to separate hours and minutes	The restaurant is open until 11:30 p.m.
• to start a list	If you decide to hold your banquet here, we can: 1. Provide a private room 2. Offer a special menu 3. Supply free coffee and lemonade.
• to set off a quotation	According to the review in *The Gazette:* El Gato Azul is *the* best place for tapas.
• to set off a list in running text	Among their best tapas are: fried goat cheese, caprece, and crab quesadilla.
• after a signal word like "the following" or "these"	Be sure to try these: black bean cakes, wontons con queso, and calamari frita.

Spelling

Correct spelling is important for clarity.

How to Be a Better Speller
To learn a new word: • Study the word and look up its meaning. • Say the word aloud. Listen as you repeat it. • Picture how the word looks. • Spell the word aloud several times. • Write the word several times for practice. • Use the word often in writing until you are sure of its spelling. • Keep a notebook of words that are hard for you to spell. • Use a dictionary to check your spelling.
Knowing spelling rules can help you when you get confused. Use the rules shown in the boxes to help improve your spelling.

Memorize Reliable Generalizations	Examples
Always put a **u** after a **q**.	The **qu**ick but **qu**iet **qu**arterback asked **qu**antities of **qu**estions. *Exceptions*: Iraq Iraqi
Use **i** before **e** except after **c**.	The f**ie**rce rec**ei**ver was ready to catch the ball. *Exceptions*: • **ei**ther, h**ei**ght, th**ei**r, w**ei**rd, s**ei**ze • w**ei**gh, n**ei**ghbor (and other words where **ei** has the long **a** sound)

Spell Correctly	Examples
If a word ends in a consonant plus **y**, change the **y** to **i** before you add -**es**, -**ed**, -**er**, or -**est**.	The coach was the happ**iest** when his players tried their best.
For words that end in a vowel plus **y**, just add -**s** or -**ed**.	For five days before the game, the team sta**yed** at practice an extra 30 minutes.
If you add -**ing** to a verb that ends in -**y**, do not change the **y** to **i**.	The players learned a lot from stud**ying** the videos of their games.

Troubleshooting Guide

In this section you will find helpful solutions to common problems with grammer, usage, and sentences. There is also an alphabetical list of words that are often misused in English. Use these to help improve your writing skills.

Grammar and Usage: Problems and Solutions

Use these solutions to fix grammar and usage problems.

Problems with Nouns

Problem: The sentence has the wrong plural form of an irregular noun.	**Incorrect:** Many deers live there.
Solution: Rewrite the sentence using the correct plural form. (Check a dictionary.)	**Correct:** Many deer live there.
Problem: The noun should be possessive, but it is not.	**Incorrect:** The beginning should capture the readers interest.
Solution: Add an apostrophe to make the noun possessive.	**Correct:** The beginning should capture the readers' interest.

Problems with Pronouns

Problem: The pronoun does not agree in number or gender with the noun it refers to.	**Incorrect:** Mary called Robert, but they did not answer him.
Solution: Match a pronoun's number and gender to the number and gender of the noun it is replacing.	**Correct:** Mary called Robert, but he did not answer her.
Problem: A pronoun does not agree in number with the indefinite pronoun it refers to.	**Incorrect:** Everyone brought their book to class.
Solution: Make the pronoun and the word it refers to agree in number, so that both are singular or plural.	**Correct:** Everyone brought his or her book to class. All the students brought their books to class.
Problem: A reciprocal pronoun does not agree with the number of nouns it refers to.	**Incorrect:** The three boys gave presents to each other.
Solution: Use *each other* when referring to two people, and use *one another* when referring to more than two people.	**Correct:** The three boys gave presents to one another.

Problems with Pronouns, continued

Problem: It is hard to tell which noun in a compound subject is referred to or replaced. **Solution:** Replace the unclear pronoun with the noun it refers to.	**Incorrect:** Ana and Dawn own a car, but only she drives it. **Correct:** Ana and Dawn own a car, but only Dawn drives it.
Problem: It is unclear which antecedent a pronoun refers to. **Solution:** Rewrite the sentence to make it clearer.	**Incorrect:** The kitten's mother scratched its ear. **Correct:** The mother cat scratched her kitten's ear.
Problem: The object pronoun *them* is used as a demonstrative adjective. **Solution:** Replace *them* with the correct demonstrative adjectives.	**Incorrect:** Were any of them packages delivered? **Correct:** Were any of those packages delivered?
Problem: An object pronoun is used in a compound subject. *Remember that subjects do actions and objects receive actions.* **Solution:** Replace the object pronoun with a subject pronoun.	**Incorrect:** My brother and me rebuild car engines. **Correct:** My brother and I rebuild car engines.
Problem: A subject pronoun is used in a compound object. **Solution:** Replace the subject pronoun with an object pronoun.	**Incorrect:** Leticia asked my brother and I to fix her car. **Correct:** Leticia asked my brother and me to fix her car.
Problem: A subject pronoun is used as the object of a preposition. **Solution:** Replace the subject pronoun with an object pronoun.	**Incorrect:** Give your timesheet to Colin or I. **Correct:** Give your timesheet to Colin or me.
Problem: The subject pronoun *who* is used as an object. **Solution:** Replace *who* with the object pronoun *whom*.	**Incorrect:** Who am I speaking to? **Correct:** Whom am I speaking to?
Problem: The object pronoun *whom* is used as a subject. **Solution:** Replace *whom* with the subject pronoun *who*.	**Incorrect:** Whom shall I say is calling? **Correct:** Who shall I say is calling?

Problems with Verbs

Problem:	Incorrect:
In a sentence with two verbs, the tense of the second verb doesn't match the first.	Yesterday, Alberto called me and says he has tickets for the game.
Solution:	**Correct:**
Keep the verb tense the same unless there is a change in time, such as from past to present.	Yesterday, Alberto called me and said he had tickets for the game.
Problem:	**Incorrect:**
The -*ed* ending is missing from a regular past-tense verb.	This morning, I ask my brother to go with us.
Solution:	**Correct:**
Add the -*ed* ending.	This morning, I asked my brother to go with us.
Problem:	**Incorrect:**
The wrong form of an irregular verb is used.	We brang our portable TV to the game.
Solution:	**Correct:**
Replace the wrong form with the correct one. (Check a dictionary.)	We brought our portable TV to the game.
Problem:	**Incorrect:**
The participle form is used when the past-tense form is required.	After the game, we run over to Marcia's house.
Solution:	**Correct:**
Replace the wrong form with the correct one. (Check a dictionary.)	After the game, we ran over to Marcia's house.
Problem:	**Poor:**
The passive voice is overused.	A new activity schedule will be created by the camp counselors. Several fun activities are being considered by the counselors.
Solution:	**Better:**
Put the sentence in the active voice so that the subject does the action instead of receiving it.	The camp counselors are creating a new activity schedule. The counselors are considering several fun activities.
Problem:	**Poor:**
The sentence has a split infinitive.	The boy wanted to slowly walk to school.
Solution:	**Better:**
Rewrite the sentence to keep the infinitive as a single unit.	The boy wanted to walk to school slowly.

Problems with Adjectives

Problem: The sentence contains a double comparison, using both an *-er* ending and the word *more*, for example.	**Incorrect:** Joseph is more older than he looks.
Solution: Delete the incorrect comparative form.	**Correct:** Joseph is older than he looks.
Problem: The wrong form of an irregular adjective appears in a sentence that makes a comparison.	**Incorrect:** Cal feels worser since he ran out of medicine.
Solution: Replace the wrong form with the correct one. (Check a dictionary.)	**Correct:** Cal feels worse since he ran out of medicine.
Problem: The wrong demonstrative adjective is used.	**Incorrect:** That car here is really fast. This car there is not as fast.
Solution: Use *this* or the plural *these* for things that are near or "here." Use *that* or the plural *those* for things that are farther away or "there."	**Correct:** This car here is really fast. That car there is not as fast.
Problem: The adjective *good* is used to modify a verb.	**Incorrect:** Julia did good on her test.
Solution: Rewrite the sentence using the adverb *well*, or add a noun for the adjective to describe.	**Correct:** Julia did well on her test. Julia did a good job on her test.

Problems with Adverbs

Problem: An adverb is used to modify a noun or pronoun after the linking verb *feel*.	**Incorrect:** I feel badly about the mistake.
Solution: Rewrite the sentence using an adjective.	**Correct:** I feel bad about the mistake.
Problem: An adverb is used but does not modify anything in the sentence.	**Incorrect:** Hopefully, I didn't make too many mistakes on the test.
Solution: Rewrite the sentence changing the adverb to a verb.	**Correct:** I hope I didn't make too many mistakes on the test.
Problem: Two negative words are used to express one idea.	**Incorrect:** We don't have no aspirin.
Solution: Change one negative word to a positive word.	**Correct:** We don't have any aspirin.

Sentences: Problems and Solutions

Some problems with sentences in English are the result of missing parts of speech or incorrect punctuation. Two common problems are sentence fragments and run on sentences.

Problems with Sentence Fragments

Problem: An infinitive phrase is punctuated as a complete sentence. **Solution:** Add a complete sentence to the phrase.	**Incorrect:** To show students alternative ways to learn. **Correct:** To show students alternative ways to learn, Mr. Harris organized the trip.
Problem: A clause starting with a relative pronoun is punctuated as a complete sentence. **Solution:** Add a subject and predicate to the sentence.	**Incorrect:** Who might be interested in going on the trip. **Correct:** Anyone who might be interested in going on the trip should see Mr. Harris.
Problem: A participial phrase is punctuated as a complete sentence. **Solution:** Add a sentence to the participial phrase.	**Incorrect:** When traveling overseas. **Correct:** When traveling overseas, always try to speak to people in their native language.

Problems with Run On Sentences

Problem: Two main clauses are separated by a comma. This is known as a comma splice. **Solution:** Add a semicolon between the clauses.	**Incorrect:** Many music students fail to practice regularly, this is frustrating for teachers. **Correct:** Many music students fail to practice regularly; this is frustrating for teachers.
Problem: Two or more main clauses are run together with no punctuation. This is known as a fused sentence. **Solution:** Change one of the clauses into a subordinate clause. Rewrite the sentence as two sentences.	**Incorrect:** I started playing guitar when I was twelve I thought I was great I knew very little. **Correct:** I thought I was great when I started playing guitar at age twelve. I knew very little!
Problem: Two or more main clauses are joined with a conjunction, but without a comma. **Solution:** Use a comma after the first main clause and before the conjunction.	**Incorrect:** I continued to take lessons and I realized that I had much to learn to become a good guitarist. **Correct:** I continued to take lessons, and I realized that I had much to learn to become a good guitarist.

Words Often Confused

This section will help you to choose between words that are often confused.

a lot, allot

A lot means "many" and is always written as two words, never as one word. *Allot* means "to assign."

I have **a lot** of friends who like to run.

We are **allotted** 30 minutes for lunch.

a while, awhile

The two-word form *a while* is a noun phrase and is often preceded by the prepositions *after*, *for*, or *in*. The one-word form *awhile* is an adverb and cannot be used with a preposition.

Let's stop here for **a while**.

Let's stop here **awhile**.

accept, except

Accept is a verb that means "to receive." *Except* can be a verb meaning "to leave out" or a preposition meaning "excluding."

I **accept** everything you say, **except** your point about music.

advice, advise

Advice is a noun that means "ideas about how to solve a problem." *Advise* is a verb and means "to give advice."

I will give you **advice** about your problem today, but do not ask me to **advise** you again tomorrow.

affect, effect

Affect is a verb. It means "to cause a change in" or "to influence." *Effect* as a verb means "to bring about." As a noun, *effect* means "a result."

The sunshine will **affect** my plants.

The governor is working to **effect** change.

The rain had no **effect** on our spirits.

aren't

Ain't is not used in formal English. Use the correct form of the verb *be* with the word *not*: *is not*, *isn't*; *are not*, or *aren't*.

We **are not going to sing** in front of you.

I **am not going to practice** today.

all ready, already

Use the two-word form, *all ready*, to mean "completely finished." Use the one-word form, *already*, to mean "before."

We waited an hour for dinner to be **all ready**.

It is a good thing I have **already** eaten today.

all right

The expression *all right* means "OK" and should be written as two words. The one-word form, *alright*, is not used in formal writing.

I hope it is **all right** that I am early.

all together, altogether

The two-word form, *all together*, means "in a group." The one-word form, *altogether*, means "completely."

It is **altogether** wrong that we will not be **all together** this holiday.

among, between

Use *among* when comparing more than two people or things. Use *between* when comparing a person or thing with one other person, thing, or group.

You are **among** friends.

We will split the money **between** Sal and Jess.

amount of, number of

Amount of is used with nouns that cannot be counted. *Number of* is used with nouns that can be counted.

The **amount of** pollution in the air is increasing.

A record **number of** people attended the game.

assure, ensure, insure

Assure means "to make feel better." *Ensure* means "to guarantee." *Insure* means "to cover financially."

I **assure** you that he is OK.

I will personally **ensure** his safety.

If the car is **insured,** the insurance company will pay to fix the damage.

being as, being that

Neither of these is used in formal English. Use *because* or *since* instead.

> I went home early **because** I was sick.

beside, besides

Beside means "next to." *Besides* means "plus" or "in addition to."

> Located **beside** the cafeteria is a vending machine.

> **Besides** being the fastest runner, she is also the nicest team member.

bring, take

Bring means "to carry closer." *Take* means "to grasp." *Take* is often used with the preposition *away* to mean "carry away from."

> Please **bring** the dictionary to me and **take** the thesaurus from my desk.

bust, busted

Neither of these is used in formal English. Use *broke* or *broken* instead.

> I **broke** the vase by accident.

> The **broken** vase cannot be fixed.

can't; hardly; scarcely

Do not use *can't* with *hardly* or *scarcely*. That would be a double negative. Use only *can't*, or use *can* plus a negative word.

> I **can't** get my work done in time.

> I **can scarcely** get my work done in time.

capital, capitol

A *capital* is a place where a government is located. A *capitol* is an actual government building.

> The **capital** of the U.S. is Washington, D.C.

> The senate met at the **capitol** to vote.

cite, site, sight

To *cite* means "to quote a source." A *site* is "a place." *Sight* can mean "the ability to see" or it can mean "something that can be seen."

> Be sure to **cite** all your sources.

> My brother works on a construction **site**.

> Dan went to the eye doctor to have his **sight** checked.

> The sunset last night was a beautiful **sight**.

complement, compliment

Complement means "something that completes" or "to complete." *Compliment* means "something nice someone says about another person" or "to praise."

> The colors you picked really **complement** each other.

> I would like to **compliment** you on your new shoes.

could have, should have, would have, might have

Be sure to use "have," not "of," with words like *could*, *should*, *would*, and *might*.

> I **would have** gone, but I didn't feel well.

council, counsel

A *council* is a group that gives advice. To *counsel* is to give advice to someone.

> The city **council** met to discuss traffic issues.

> Mom, please **counsel** me on how to handle this situation.

coup d'état, coup de grâce

A *coup d'état* ("stroke of state") usually refers to the overthrow of a government. A coup de *grâce* ("stroke, or blow, or mercy") refers to a final action that brings victory.

different from, different than

Different from is preferred in formal English and is used when the comparison is between two persons or things. *Different than*, when used, is used with full clauses.

> My interest in music is **different from** my friend's.

> Movies today are **different than** they used to be in the 1950s.

each other, one another

Each other refers to two people. *One another* refers to more than two people.

> Mika and I gave **each other** presents for Christmas.

The five of us looked out for **one another** on the field trip.

farther, further

Farther refers to a physical distance. *Further* refers to time or amount.

If you go down the road a little **farther**, you will see the sign.

We will discuss this **further** at lunch.

fewer, less

Fewer refers to things that can be counted individually. *Less* refers to things that cannot be counted individually.

The farm had **fewer** animals than the zoo, so it was **less** fun to visit.

good, well

The adjective *good* means "kind." The adjective *well* means "healthy." The adverb *well* means "ably."

She is a **good** person.

I am glad to see that you are **well** again after that illness.

You have performed **well**.

immigrate to, emigrate from

Immigrate to means "to move to a country." *Emigrate from* means "to leave a country."

I **immigrated to** America in 2001 from Panama.

I **emigrated from** El Salvador because of the war.

it's, its

It's is a contraction of *it is*. *Its* is a possessive word meaning "belonging to it."

It's going to be a hot day.

The dog drank all of **its** water already.

kind of, sort of

These words mean "a type of." In formal English, do not use them to mean "partly." Use *somewhat* or *rather* instead.

The peanut is actually a **kind of** bean.

I feel **rather** silly in this outfit.

lay, lie

Lay means "to put in a place." It is used to describe what people do with objects. *Lie* means

"to recline." People can *lie* down, but they *lay* down objects. Do not confuse this use of *lie* with the noun that means "an untruth."

I will **lay** the book on this desk for you.

She **lay** the baby in his crib.

I'm tired and am going to **lie** on the couch.

If you **lie** in court, you will be punished.

learn, teach

To *learn* is "to receive information." To *teach* is "to give information."

If we want to **learn**, we have to listen.

She will **teach** us how to drive.

leave (alone), let

Leave alone means "not to disturb someone." *Let* means "to allow or permit."

Leave her **alone**, and she will be fine.

Let them go.

like, as

Like can be used either as a preposition meaning "in the manner of" or as a verb meaning "to care about something." *As* is a conjunction and should be used to introduce a subordinate clause.

She sometimes acts **like** a princess. But I still **like** her.

She acts **as** if she owns the school.

loose, lose

Loose can be used as an adverb or adjective meaning "free" or "not securely attached." The verb *lose* means "to misplace" or "not to win."

I let the dog **loose** and he is missing.

Did you **lose** your homework?

Did they **lose** the game by many points?

passed, past

Passed is a verb that means "moved ahead of" or "succeeded." *Past* is a noun that means "the time before the present."

The car **passed** us quickly.

I **passed** my English test.

Poor grades are in the **past** now.

precede, proceed

Precede means "to come before." *Proceed* means "to go forward."

> Prewriting **precedes** drafting in the writing process.

> Turn left; then **proceed** down the next street.

principal, principle

A *principal* is "a person of authority." Principal can also mean "main." A *principle* is "a general truth or belief."

> The **principal** of our school makes an announcement every morning.

> The **principal** ingredient in baking is flour.

> The essay was based on the **principles** of effective persuasion.

raise, rise

The verb *raise* takes an object and means "to lift" or "to be brought up." The verb *rise* means "to lift oneself up." People can *rise*, but objects are *raised*.

> **Raise** the curtain for the play.

> She **raises** baby rabbits on her farm.

> I **rise** from bed every morning at six.

real, really

Real means "actual." It is an adjective used to describe nouns. *Really* means "actually" or "truly." It is an adverb used to describe verbs, adjectives, or other adverbs.

> The diamond was **real**.

> The diamond was **really** beautiful.

set, sit

The verb *set* usually means "to put something down." The verb *sit* means "to go into a seated position."

> I **set** the box on the ground.

> Please **sit** while we talk.

than, then

Than is used to compare things. *Then* means "next" and is used to tell when something took place.

> She likes fiction more **than** nonfiction.

> First, we will go to town; **then** we will go home.

they're, their, there

They're is the contraction of *they are*. *Their* is the possessive form of the pronoun *they*. *There* is used to indicate location.

> **They're** all on vacation this week.

> I want to use **their** office.

> The library is right over **there**.

> **There** are several books I want to read.

this, these, that, those

This indicates something specific that is near someone. *These* is the plural form. *That* indicates something specific that is farther from someone. *Those* is the plural form of *that*.

> **This** book in my hand belongs to me. **These** pens are also mine.

> **That** book is his. **Those** notes are his, too.

where

Do not use *at* or *to* after *where*. Simply use *where*.

> The restaurant is **where** I am right now.

> **Where** is Ernesto?

who, whom

Who is a subject. *Whom* is an object.

> **Who** is going to finish first?

> My grandmother is a woman to **whom** I owe many thanks.

who's, whose

Who's is a contraction of *who is*. *Whose* is the possessive form of *who*.

> **Who's** coming to our dinner party?

> **Whose** car is parked in the garage?

you're, your

You're is a contraction of *you are*. *Your* is a possessive adjective meaning "belonging to you."

> **You're** going to be late if you don't hurry.

> Is that **your** backpack under the couch?

Grammar Tip

If you can replace *who* or *whom* with *he*, *she*, or *they*, use *who*. If you can replace the word with *him*, *her*, or *them*, use *whom*.

Literary Terms

A

Alliteration The repetition of the same sounds (usually consonants) at the beginning of words that are close together. *Example:* Molly makes magnificent mousse, though Pablo prefers pecan pie.

    See also **Assonance; Consonance; Repetition**

Allusion A key form of literary language, in which one text makes the reader think about another text that was written before it. Allusion can also mean a reference to a person, place, thing, or event that is not specifically named. *Example:* When Hannah wrote in her short story that vanity was the talented main character's "Achilles heel," her teacher understood that Hannah was referring to a character in a Greek myth. So, she suspected that the vanity of the main character in Hannah's short story would prove to be the character's greatest weakness.

    See also **Connotation; Literature; Poetry**

Analogy A way of illustrating a thing or an idea by comparing it with a more familiar thing or idea. *Example: Blogs* are to the *Internet* as *journals* are to *paper.*

    See also **Illustration; Metaphor; Rhetorical device; Simile**

Antagonist A major character who opposes the main character, or protagonist, in a fictional narrative or a play. *Example:* In many fairy tales, a wolf is the antagonist.

    See also **Protagonist**

Argument A type of writing or speaking that supports a position or attempts to convince the reader or listener. Arguments include a claim that is supported by reasons and evidence.

    See also **Claim; Reason; Evidence**

Article A short piece of nonfiction writing on a specific topic. Articles usually appear in newspapers and magazines.

    See also **Nonfiction; Topic**

Assonance The repetition of the same or similar vowel sounds between consonants in words that are close together. *Example:* The expression, "mad as a hatter."

    See also **Alliteration; Consonance; Repetition**

Autobiography The story of a person's life, written by that person. *Example:* Mahatma Gandhi wrote an autobiography titled *Gandhi: An Autobiography: The Story of My Experiments With Truth.*

    See also **Biography; Diary; Journal; Memoir; Narration; Personal narrative**

B

Biography The story of a person's life, written by another person.

    See also **Autobiography; Narration**

Blank verse A form of unrhymed verse in which each line normally has 10 syllables divided into five pairs of one unstressed and one stressed syllable. Of all verse forms, blank verse comes closest to the natural rhythms of English speech. Consequently, it has been used more often, in more ways than any other verse form in English. *Example:* Today she darts from the room with delight./Bizarre she does seem, like a haughty queen./I long to make her hot cinnamon tea/ One day, she will love me as I do her./

    See also **Meter; Rhyme; Stress; Verse**

C

Character A person, an animal, or an imaginary creature in a work of fiction.

    See also **Characterization; Character traits; Fiction**

Characterization The way a writer creates and develops a character. Writers use a variety of ways to bring a character to life: through descriptions of the character's appearance, thoughts, feelings, and actions; through the character's words; and through the words or thoughts of other characters.

    See also **Character; Character traits; Dynamic character; Motive; Point of view; Short story; Static character**

Character traits The special qualities of personality that writers give their characters.

    See also **Character; Characterization**

Claim A statement that clearly identifies an author's ideas or opinion.

    See also **Argument, Reason, Evidence**

Climax The turning point or most important event in a plot.

    See also **Falling action; Plot; Rising action**

Comedy A play or a fictional story written mainly to amuse an audience. Most comedies end happily for the leading characters.

    See also **Drama; Narration; Play**

Complication *See* **Rising action**

Conflict The main problem faced by the protagonist in a story or play. The protagonist may be involved in a struggle against nature, another character (usually the *antagonist*), or society. The struggle may also be between two elements in the protagonist's mind.

    See also **Plot**

Connotation The feelings suggested by a word or phrase, apart from its dictionary meaning. *Example:* The terms "used car" and "previously owned vehicle" have different connotations. To most people, the phrase "previously owned vehicle" sounds better than "used car."

    See also **Denotation; Poetry**

Consonance The repetition of the same or similar consonant sounds that come after different vowel sounds in words that are close together. *Example:* Sid did bid on a squid, he did.

    See also **Alliteration; Assonance; Repetition**

D

Denotation The dictionary meaning of a word or phrase. Denotation is especially important in functional texts and other types of nonfiction used to communicate information precisely.

    See also **Connotation; Functional text; Nonfiction**

Description Writing that creates a "picture" of a person, place, or thing—often using language that appeals to the five senses: sight, hearing, touch, smell, and taste. *Example:* The bright, hot sun beat down on Earth's surface. Where once a vibrant lake cooled the skin of hippos and zebras, only thin, dry cracks remained, reaching across the land like an old man's fingers, as far as the eye could see. The smell of herds was gone, and only silence filled the space.

    See also **Imagery**

Dialect A form of a language commonly spoken in a certain place or by a certain group of people— especially a form that differs from the one most widely accepted. Dialect includes special words or phrases as well as particular pronunciations and grammar. Writers use dialect to help make their characters and settings lively and realistic. *Example:* While someone from the southern United States might say "ya'll" when referring to several friends, someone from the Northeast or Midwest might say "you guys."

    See also **Diction; Jargon**

Dialogue What characters say to each other. Writers use dialogue to develop characters, move the plot forward, and add interest. In most writing, dialogue is set off by quotation marks; in play scripts, however, dialogue appears without quotation marks.

Diary A book written by a person about his or her own life as it is happening. Unlike an autobiography, a diary is not usually meant to be published. It is made up of entries that are written shortly after events occur. The person writing a diary often expresses feelings and opinions about what has happened.

    See also **Autobiography; Journal**

Drama A kind of writing, in verse or prose, in which a plot unfolds in the words and actions of characters performed by actors. Two major genres of drama are comedy and tragedy.

    See also **Comedy; Genre; Play; Plot; Tragedy**

Dramatic conventions The usual ways of making drama seem real. Dramatic conventions include imagining that actors really are the characters they pretend to be and that a stage really is the place it represents.

Dynamic character A character who changes because of actions and experiences.

> See also **Character; Static character**

E

Editorial An article in a newspaper or magazine that gives the opinions of the editors or publishers. *Example:* Rather than just reporting the facts, a newspaper editorial might argue that the city government should not clear preserved woodlands in order to build a shopping mall.

Electronic text Writing that a computer can store or display on a computer screen. Forms of electronic text include *Web sites* (groupings of World Wide Web pages that usually contain hyperlinks), *blogs* (Web logs—sites maintained by an individual or organization that contain various kinds of informal writing, such as diaries, opinion pieces, and stories), and *e-mail*.

Epic A long, fictional, narrative poem, written in a lofty style, that celebrates the great deeds of one or more heroes or heroines. *Example:* Homer's *The Odyssey* is a famous epic poem of over 12,000 lines. The hero, Odysseus, spends ten years overcoming various obstacles in order to return home to his wife and son after the end of the Trojan War.

> See also **Fiction; Hero** or **Heroine; Poetry**

Essay A short piece of nonfiction, normally in prose, that discusses a single topic without claiming to do so thoroughly. Its purpose may be to inform, entertain, or persuade.

> See also **Exposition; Nonfiction; Persuasion; Photo-essay; Review; Topic**

Evidence Information provided to support a claim. Facts, statistics, and quotes from experts are commonly used as evidence.

> See also **Argument; Claim; Reasons**

Exposition The rising action of a story in which characters and the problems they face are introduced.

> See also **Description; Functional text; Narration; Persuasion; Rising action**

F

Fable A brief fictional narrative that teaches a lesson about life. Many fables have animals instead of humans as characters. Fables often end with a short, witty statement of their lesson. *Example:* "The Tortoise and the Hare" is a famous fable in which a boastful, quick-moving hare challenges a slow-moving tortoise to a race. Because the overconfident hare takes a nap during the race, the tortoise wins. The moral of the fable is that slow and steady wins the race.

> See also **Fiction; Folk tale; Narration**

Falling action The actions and events in a plot that happen after the climax. Usually, the major problem is solved in some way, so the remaining events serve to bring the story to an end.

> See also **Climax; Conflict; Plot, Rising action**

Fantasy Fiction in which imaginary worlds differ from the "real" world outside the text. Fairy tales, science fiction, and fables are examples of fantasy.

> See also **Fable; Fiction; Science fiction**

Fiction Narrative writing about imaginary people, places, things, or events.

> See also **Fable; Fantasy; Folk tale; Historical fiction; Myth; Narration; Nonfiction; Novel; Realistic fiction; Science fiction; Short story; Tall tale**

Figurative language The use of a word or phrase to say one thing and mean another. Figurative language is especially important in literature and poetry because it gives writers a more effective way of expressing what they mean than using direct, literal language. *Example:* Upon receiving her monthly bills, Victoria complained that she was "drowning in debt."

> See also **Hyperbole; Idiom; Imagery; Irony; Literature; Metaphor; Personification; Poetry; Simile; Symbol**

Flashback An interruption in the action of a narrative to tell about something that happened earlier. It is often used to give the reader background information about a character or situation.

See also **Character; Narration**

Folk literature The collection of a people's literary works shared mainly orally rather than in writing. Such works include spells, songs, ballads (songs that tell a story), jokes, riddles, proverbs, nursery rhymes, and folk tales.

See also **Folk tale; Folklore; Literature; Song lyrics**

Folk tale A short, fictional narrative shared orally rather than in writing, and thus partly changed through its retellings before being written down. Folk tales include myths, legends, fables, tall tales, ghost stories, and fairy tales.

See also **Fable; Folk literature; Myth; Tall tale**

Folklore The collection of a people's beliefs, customs, rituals, spells, songs, sayings, and stories as shared mainly orally rather than in writing.

See also **Folk literature; Folk tale**

Foreshadowing A hint that a writer gives about an event that will happen later in a story. *Example:* In a story about a teenage girl who starts getting into trouble, an early scene may show her friend stealing earrings from a jewelry store. Later the girl herself begins stealing. Based on the earlier scene, the reader might guess this is what the girl would do.

Free verse Writing that is free of meter, and thus not really verse at all. It is closer to rhythmic prose or speech. But like verse, and unlike prose or speech, it is arranged in lines, which divide the text into units of rhythm. Free verse may be rhymed or unrhymed.

See also **Meter; Prose; Rhyme; Rhythm; Verse**

Functional text Writing in which the main purpose is to communicate the information people need to accomplish tasks in everyday life. *Examples:* résumés, business letters, instruction manuals, and the help systems of word-processing programs.

G

Genre A type or class of literary works grouped according to form, style, and/or topic. Major genres include fictional narrative prose (such as short stories and most novels), nonfiction narrative prose (such as autobiographies, historical accounts, and memoirs), drama (such as comedies and tragedies), verse (such as lyrics and epics), and the essay.

See also **Essay; Fiction; Literature; Narration; Nonfiction; Prose; Style; Topic; Verse**

H

Haiku A form of short, unrhymed poetry that expresses a moment of sudden, intensely felt awareness. The words in haiku focus on what can be seen, smelled, tasted, touched, or heard. The haiku was invented in Japan, and it traditionally consists of 17 syllables in three lines of 5, 7, and 5 syllables. *Example:*

Gold, red leaves rustle
A baby cries somewhere near
Blue sky fades to gray.

See also **Imagery; Lyric; Poetry**

Hero or **Heroine** In myths and legends, a man or woman of great courage and strength who is celebrated for his or her daring feats; also, any protagonist, or main character.

See also **Myth; Protagonist**

Historical account A piece of nonfiction writing about something that happened in the past.

See also **Memoir; Nonfiction**

Historical fiction Fiction based on events that actually happened or on people who actually lived. It may be written from the point of view of a "real" or an imaginary character, and it usually includes invented dialogue.

See also **Fiction**

Humor A type of writing meant to be funny in a good-natured way. It often makes what characters look like, say, or do seem serious to them but ridiculous to the reader.

See also **Parody**

Hyperbole Figurative language that exaggerates, often to the point of being funny, to emphasize something. *Example:* When his mother asked how long he had waited for the school bus that morning, Jeremy grinned and said, "Oh, not long. Only about a million years."

See also **Figurative language; Tall tale**

I

Idiom A phrase or expression that means something different from the word or words' dictionary meanings. Idioms cannot be translated word for word into another language because an idiom's meaning is not the same as that of the individual words that make it up. *Example:* "Mind your p's and q's" in English means to be careful, thoughtful, and behave properly.

Illustration Writing that uses examples to support a main idea. Illustration is often used to help the reader understand general, abstract, or complex ideas.

Imagery Figurative language that communicates sensory experience. Imagery can help the reader imagine how people, places, and things look, sound, taste, smell, and feel. It can also make the reader think about emotions and ideas that commonly go with certain sensations. Because imagery appeals to the senses, it is sometimes called *sensory language*.

See also **Description; Figurative language; Symbol**

Interview A discussion between two or more people in which questions are asked and answered so that the interviewer can get information. The record of such a discussion is also called an interview.

Irony A type of figurative language that takes three forms: (1) *verbal irony* means the opposite of what is said, or it means both what is said and the opposite of what is said, at once; (2) *dramatic irony* (a) contrasts what a speaker or character says with what the writer means or thinks, or (b) in a story, presents a speech or an action that means more to the audience than to the character who speaks or performs it, because the audience knows something the character does not; (3)

situational irony (a) contrasts an actual situation with what would seem appropriate, or (b) contrasts what one expects with what actually happens. *Examples:* 1. Verbal Irony: After having her car towed, getting drenched in a thunderstorm, and losing her wallet, Kate told her friend, "Let me tell you, today has been a real picnic."
2. Dramatic Irony: In the final scene of William Shakespeare's play *Romeo and Juliet*, Romeo finds Juliet drugged. While the audience knows that she is still alive, Romeo presumes that she is dead and decides to kill himself. Juliet shortly thereafter awakes and, upon finding Romeo dead, kills herself.
3. Situational Irony: In O. Henry's short story "The Gift of the Magi," a husband and wife each want to buy a Christmas present for the other. The wife buys her husband a chain for his watch; the husband buys the wife combs for her hair. To get enough money to buy these gifts, the wife cuts and sells her hair, and the husband sells his watch.

See also **Figurative language**

J

Jargon Specialized language used by people to describe things that are specific to their group or subject. *Example: Mouse* in a computer class means "part of a computer system," not "a rodent."

See also **Dialect; Diction**

Journal A personal record, similar to a diary. It may include accounts of actual events, stories, poems, sketches, thoughts, essays, a collection of interesting information, or just about anything the writer wishes to include.

See also **Diary**

L

Literature A body of written works in prose or verse.

See also **Functional text; Poetry; Prose; Verse**

Literary criticism The careful study and discussion of works of literature, mainly to understand them and judge their effectiveness.

See also **Literature**

Lyric One of the main types of poetry. Lyrics tend to be short and songlike, and express the state of mind—or the process of observing, thinking, and feeling—of a single "speaker."

See also **Haiku; Poetry; Song lyrics; Sonnet**

M

Memoir A written account of people the author has known and events he or she has witnessed. *Example:* Elie Wiesel's novel *Night* is a memoir. It documents his personal experiences in a concentration camp during World War II.

See also **Autobiography; Historical account**

Metaphor A type of figurative language that compares two unlike things by saying that one thing is the other thing. *Example:* Dhara says her grandfather can be a real mule when he doesn't get enough sleep.

See also **Figurative language; Simile; Symbol**

Meter The patterning of language into regularly repeating units of rhythm. Language patterned in this way is called *verse.* Most verse in English has been written in one of two main types of meter: (1) *accentual,* which depends on the number of stressed syllables in a line; (2) *accentual-syllabic,* which depends on the number of stressed and unstressed syllables in a line. By varying the rhythm within a meter, the writer can heighten the reader's attention to what is going on in the verse and reinforce meaning.

See also **Poetry; Rhythm; Stress; Verse**

Mood The overall feeling or atmosphere a writer creates in a piece of writing.

See also **Tone**

Motive The reason a character has for his or her thoughts, feelings, actions, or words. *Example:* Maria's motive for bringing cookies to her new neighbors was to learn what they were like.

See also **Characterization**

Myth A fictional narrative, often a folk tale, that tells of supernatural events as a way of explaining natural events and their relation to human life. Myths commonly involve gods, goddesses, monsters, and superhuman heroes or heroines.

See also **Folk tale; Hero** or **Heroine**

N

Narration The telling of events (a story), mostly through explanation and description, rather than through dialogue.

See also **Narrator; Point of view; Story**

Narrative Writing that gives an account of a set of real or imaginary events (the story), which the writer selects and arranges in a particular order (the plot). Narrative writing includes nonfiction works such as news articles, autobiographies, and historical accounts, as well as fictional works such as short stories, novels, and epics.

See also **Autobiography; Fiction; Historical account; Narrator; Nonfiction; Plot; Story**

Narrator Someone who gives an account of events. In fiction, the narrator is the teller of a story (as opposed to the real author, who invented the narrator as well as the story). Narrators differ in how much they participate in a story's events. In a first-person narrative, the narrator is the "I" telling the story. In a third-person narrative, the narrator is not directly involved in the events and refers to characters by name or as *he, she, it,* or *they.* Narrators also differ in how much they know and how much they can be trusted by the reader.

See also **Character; Narration; Point of view; Voice**

Nonfiction Written works about events or things that are not imaginary; writing other than fiction.

See also **Autobiography; Biography; Diary; Encyclopedia; Essay; Fiction; Historical account; Journal; Memoir; Personal narrative; Photo-essay; Report; Textbook**

Novel A long, fictional narrative, usually in prose. Its length enables it to have more characters, a more complicated plot, and a more fully developed setting than shorter works of fiction.

See also **Character; Fiction; Narration; Plot; Prose; Setting; Short story**

O

Onomatopoeia The use of words that imitate the sounds they refer to. *Examples: buzz, slam, hiss*

P

Paradox A statement or an expression that seems to contradict itself but may, when thought about further, begin to make sense and seem true. Paradox can shock the reader into attention, thus underscoring the truth of what is being said. *Example:* The Time Paradox: A man travels back in time and kills his grandfather. The paradox is that if he killed his grandfather, the man himself never would have been born.

Parody A piece of writing meant to amuse by imitating the style or features of another (usually serious) piece. It makes fun of the original by taking the elements it imitates to extreme or ridiculous lengths or by applying them to a lowly or comically inappropriate subject. *Example:* In 1729, Jonathan Swift wrote a pamphlet titled "A Modest Proposal." In it, he outrageously recommends that the poor sell their children as food to the wealthy in order to make money. "A Modest Proposal" is a parody of similar pamphlets distributed by the wealthy business class, whose practices, Swift believed, neglected human costs and made it difficult for the poor to overcome poverty.
> See *also* **Genre; Humor; Style**

Personal narrative An account of a certain event or set of events in a person's life, written by that person.
> See *also* **Autobiography; Narration**

Personification Figurative language that describes animals, things, or ideas as having human traits. *Examples:* in the movie *Babe* and in the book *Charlotte's Web*, the animals are all personified
> See *also* **Figurative language**

Persuasion Writing that attempts to get someone to do or agree to something by appealing to logic or emotion. Persuasive writing is used in advertisements, editorials, sermons, and political speeches.
> See *also* **Description; Editorial; Exposition; Narration; Rhetorical device**

Photo-essay A short nonfiction piece made up of photographs and captions. The photographs are as important as the words in giving information to the reader.
> See *also* **Essay; Nonfiction**

Play A work of drama, especially one written to be performed on a stage. *Example:* Lorraine Hansberry's *A Raisin in the Sun*
> See *also* **Drama**

Plot The pattern of events and situations in a story or play. Plot is usually divided into four main parts: *conflict* (or *problem*), *rising action* (or *exposition* or *complication*), *climax*, and *falling action* (or *resolution*).
> See *also* **Climax; Conflict; Drama; Falling action; Fiction; Narration; Rising action; Story**

Poetry A form of literary expression that uses line breaks for emphasis. Poems often use connotation, imagery, metaphor, symbol, paradox, irony, allusion, repetition, and rhythm. Word patterns in poetry include rhythm or meter, and often rhyme and alliteration. The three main types of poetry are narrative, dramatic, and lyric.
> See *also* **Alliteration; Connotation; Figurative language; Literature; Lyric; Meter; Narration; Repetition; Rhyme; Rhythm; Verse**

Point of view The position from which the events of a story seem to be observed and told. A first-person point of view tells the story through what the narrator knows, experiences, concludes, or can find out by talking to other characters. A third-person point of view may be *omniscient*, giving the narrator unlimited knowledge of things, events, and characters, including characters' hidden thoughts and feelings. Or it may be *limited* to what one or a few characters know and experience. *Example* of First-Person Point of View: I'm really hungry right now, and I can't wait to eat my lunch. *Example* of Third-Person Limited Point of View: Olivia is really hungry right now and she wants to eat her lunch. *Example* of Third-Person Omniscient Point of View: Olivia is really hungry right now and she wants to eat her lunch. The other students are thinking about their weekend plans. The teacher is wondering how she will finish the lesson before the bell rings.
> See *also* **Character; Fiction; Narration; Narrator; Voice**

Prose A form of writing in which the rhythm is less regular than that of verse and more like that of ordinary speech.

See also **Rhythm; Verse**

Protagonist The main character in a fictional narrative or a play. He or she may be competing with an antagonist; sometimes called the hero or heroine. *Example:* Although the Tin Man, the Cowardly Lion, and the Scarecrow are important characters in *The Wizard of Oz*, Dorothy is the protagonist.

See also **Antagonist; Hero** or **Heroine**

Pun An expression, used for emphasis or humor, in which two distinct meanings are suggested by one word or by two similar-sounding words. *Example:* The following joke uses a pun on the way that the word "lettuce" sounds similar to "let us":

Q: Knock, knock.   **A**: Who's there?
Q: Lettuce.   **A**: Lettuce who?
Q: Lettuce in, it's cold out here!

See also **Humor**

R

Realistic fiction Fiction in which detailed handling of imaginary settings, characters, and events produces a lifelike illusion of a "real" world. *Example:* Although Upton Sinclair's *The Jungle* is a work of fiction, the author's graphic, detailed descriptions of the slaughterhouse workers' daily lives led to real changes in the meat packing industry.

See also **Fiction**

Reason A logical explanation that connects a piece of evidence to a writer or speaker's claim.

See also **Argument; Claim; Evidence**

Refrain A line, group of lines, or part of a line repeated (sometimes with slight changes) at various points in poetry or song.

See also **Poetry; Repetition; Song lyrics**

Repetition The repeating of individual vowels and consonants, syllables, words, phrases, lines, or groups of lines. Repetition can be used because it sounds pleasant, to emphasize the words in which it occurs, or to help tie the parts of a text into one structure. It is especially important in creating the musical quality of poetry, where it can take such forms as alliteration, assonance, consonance, rhyme, and refrain.

See also **Alliteration; Assonance; Consonance; Poetry; Refrain; Rhyme**

Report A usually short piece of nonfiction writing on a particular topic. It differs from an essay in that it normally states only facts and does not directly express the writer's opinions.

See also **Essay; Nonfiction; Topic**

Resolution See **Falling action**

Review An essay describing a work or performance and judging its effectiveness.

See also **Description; Essay**

Rhetorical device A use of language that differs from ordinary use in order to emphasize a point. It achieves its effects mainly by arranging words in a special way rather than by changing the meaning of the words themselves. Rhetorical devices include *analogy*, *antithesis* (placing words in contrast with one another), *anaphora* (repeating the same word or phrase in a series of lines, clauses, or sentences), the *rhetorical question* (asking a question not to request information, but to make a point more forcefully than simply stating it would do), and *apostrophe* (directly addressing an absent person, nonhuman, or an idea).

See also **Analogy; Figurative language**

Rhyme The repetition of ending sounds in different words. Rhymes usually come at the end of lines of verse, but they may also occur within a line. If rhymed sounds are exactly the same, they make a *perfect rhyme*. If the endings of rhyming words are spelled the same but sound different, they make an *eye rhyme*. And if the last stressed vowels of rhyming words are only similar but the rhyming consonants are the same (or nearly so), the words make a *partial rhyme* (also called *slant rhyme*, *near rhyme*, or *imperfect rhyme*). *Examples:* The words "look" and "brook" and "shook" are perfect rhymes. The words "slaughter" and "laughter" are an eye rhyme. The words "ought" and "fault" form a partial rhyme.

See also **Poetry; Repetition; Rhyme scheme; Stress; Verse**

Rhyme scheme The pattern of rhymed line endings in a work of verse or a stanza. It can be represented by giving a certain letter of the alphabet to each line ending on the same rhyme. *Example:* Because the end word of every other line rhymes in the following poem, the rhyme scheme is *abab*:

Winter night falls quick (a)
The pink sky gone, blackness overhead (b)
Looks like the snow will stick (a)
Down the street and up the hill I tread (b)
> See also **Rhyme; Stanza; Verse**

Rhythm The natural rise and fall, or "beat," of language. In English it involves a back-and-forth movement between stressed and unstressed syllables. Rhythm is present in all language, including ordinary speech and prose, but it is most obvious in verse.
> See also **Meter; Prose; Stress; Verse**

Rising action The part of a plot that presents actions or events that lead to the climax.
> See also **Climax; Conflict; Exposition; Falling action; Plot**

S

Science fiction A genre of fantasy writing based on real or imaginary scientific discoveries. It often takes place in the future.
> See also **Fantasy; Fiction**

Script The text of a play, radio or television broadcast, or movie.

Setting The time and place in which the events of a story occur.
> See also **Drama; Narration**

Short story A brief, fictional narrative in prose. Like the novel, it organizes the action, thought, and dialogue of its characters into a plot. But it tends to focus on fewer characters and to center on a single event, which reveals as much as possible about the protagonist's life and the traits that set him or her apart.
> See also **Character; Fiction; Narration; Novel; Plot; Prose; Protagonist; Story**

Simile A type of figurative language that compares two unlike things by using a word or phrase such as *like, as, than, similar to, resembles,* or *seems. Examples:* The tall, slim man had arms as willowy as a tree's branches. The woman's temper is like an unpredictable volcano.
> See also **Figurative language; Metaphor**

Song lyrics Words meant to be sung. Lyrics have been created for many types of songs, including love songs, religious songs, work songs, sea chanties, and children's game songs. Lyrics for many songs were shared orally for generations before being written down. Not all song lyrics are lyrical like poems; some are the words to songs that tell a story. Not all poems called songs were written to be sung.
> See also **Folk literature; Lyric; Narration; Poetry; Refrain**

Sonnet A major form of poetry made up of 14 rhyming lines of equal length. Most sonnets in English take one of two basic patterns: (1) The Italian, or Petrarchan, sonnet consists of two parts: a group of eight lines rhyming *abbaabba*, followed by a group of six lines usually rhyming *cdecde*; (2) The English, or Shakespearean, sonnet is divided into three groups of four lines rhyming *abab cdcd efef* and a pair rhyming *gg*.
> See also **Lyric; Meter; Rhyme; Rhyme scheme; Verse**

Speech A message on a specific topic, spoken before an audience; also, spoken (not written) language.

Stanza A group of lines that forms a section of a poem and has the same pattern (including line lengths, meter, and usually rhyme scheme) as other sections of the same poem. In printed poems, stanzas are separated from each other by a space.
> See also **Meter; Rhyme scheme; Verse**

Static character A character who changes little, if at all. Things happen *to,* rather than *within,* him or her. *Example:* In Charles Dickens's novel *Great Expectations,* Joe Gargery is a static character. He is a poor, uneducated blacksmith who endures the cruelty of his wife and Pip, the main character. Throughout the novel, Joe remains humble, loyal, and supportive of those he loves.
> See also **Character; Characterization; Dynamic character**

Story A series of events (actual or imaginary) that can be selected and arranged in a certain order to form a narrative or dramatic plot. It is the raw material from which the finished plot is built. Although there are technical differences, the word *story* is sometimes used in place of *narrative*.

 See also **Drama; Narration; Plot**

Stress The force with which a syllable is spoken compared with neighboring syllables in a line of verse. A stressed syllable is spoken more forcefully than an unstressed one.

 See also **Meter; Rhythm; Verse**

Style The way a writer uses language to express the feelings or thoughts he or she wants to convey. Just as no two people are alike, no two styles are exactly alike. A writer's style results from his or her choices of vocabulary, sentence structure and variety, imagery, figurative language, rhythm, repetition, and other resources.

 See also **Diction; Figurative language; Genre; Imagery; Parody; Repetition; Rhythm; Voice**

Suspense A feeling of curiosity, tension, or excitement a narrative creates in the reader about what will happen next. Mystery novels, like horror movies, are often full of suspense.

 See also **Narration**

Symbol A word or phrase that serves as an image of some person, place, thing, or action but that also calls to mind some other, usually broader, idea or range of ideas. *Example:* An author might describe doves flying high in the sky to symbolize a peaceful setting.

 See also **Figurative language; Imagery**

T

Tall tale A kind of folk tale that wildly exaggerates a character's strength and ability, usually for comic effect. *Example:* Stories about Paul Bunyan, the enormous lumberjack whose footprints created Minnesota's 10,000 lakes, are considered tall tales.

 See also **Hyperbole**

Textbook A book prepared for use in schools for the study of a subject.

Theme The underlying message or main idea of a piece of writing. It expresses a broader meaning than the topic of the piece.

 See also **Topic**

Tone A writer's or speaker's attitude toward his or her topic or audience or toward him- or herself. A writer's tone may be positive, negative, or neutral. The words the writer chooses, the sentence structure, and the overall pattern of words convey the intended tone.

 See also **Connotation; Figurative language; Literature; Mood; Rhythm; Topic**

Topic What or who is being discussed in a piece of writing; the subject of the piece.

 See also **Theme**

Tragedy A play or a fictional narrative about the disastrous downfall of the protagonist, usually because of a flaw in his or her moral character. Though brought to ruin, the protagonist comes to understand the meaning of his or her actions and to accept the consequences. *Example:* William Shakespeare's play *Hamlet* is about the downfall and eventual death of the protagonist, Hamlet, so it is considered a tragedy.

 See also **Drama; Narration; Protagonist**

V

Verse Language that differs from prose and ordinary speech by being arranged in regular units of rhythm called *meter*. The meter, in turn, occurs within a larger unit of rhythm and meaning: the *line*. In written verse, unlike written prose, the writer rather than the printer decides where one line ends and the next begins. Not all poetry is written in verse (poetry can even be written in prose), and not all verse is poetry (even skillfully written verse can be ineffective in communicating experience).

 See also **Blank verse; Free verse; Meter; Poetry; Prose; Rhythm; Sonnet**

Voice The specific group of traits conveyed by the narrator or "speaker" in a literary work.

 See also **Narrator**

Vocabulary Glossary

The definitions in this glossary are for words as they are used in the selections in this book. Use the Pronunciation Key below to help you use each word's pronunciation. Then read about the parts of an entry.

Pronunciation Key

Symbols for Consonant Sounds				Symbols for Short Vowel Sounds		Symbols for R-controlled Sounds		Symbols for Variant Vowel Sounds	
b	box	**p**	pan	**a**	hat	**ar**	barn	**ah**	father
ch	chick	**r**	ring	**e**	bell	**air**	chair	**aw**	ball
d	dog	**s**	bus	**i**	chick	**ear**	ear	**oi**	boy
f	fish	**sh**	fish	**o**	box	**īr**	fire	**ow**	mouse
g	girl	**t**	hat	**u**	bus	**or**	corn	**oo**	book
h	hat	**th**	earth			**ur**	girl	**ü**	fruit
j	jar	**th**	father	**Symbols for Long Vowel Sounds**					
k	cake	**v**	vase	**ā**	cake			**Miscellaneous Symbols**	
ks	box	**w**	window	**ē**	key				
kw	queen	**wh**	whale	**ī**	bike			**shun**	fraction
l	bell	**y**	yarn	**ō**	goat			**chun**	question
m	mouse	**z**	zipper	**yū**	mule			**zhun**	division
n	pan	**zh**	treasure						
ng	ring								

Academic Vocabulary

Certain words in this glossary have a red dot indicating that they are academic vocabulary words. These are the words that are necessary for you to learn in order to understand the concepts being taught in school.

Parts of an Entry

The **entry** shows how the word is spelled and how it is broken into syllables.

The **pronunciation** shows you how to say the word.

part of speech
n. for noun
v. for verb
adj. for adjective
adv. for adverb.

The red dot signals that a word is an **academic vocabulary** word. Not all words have a red dot.

The **definition** gives the meaning of the word.

The **sample sentence** uses the word in a way that shows its meaning.

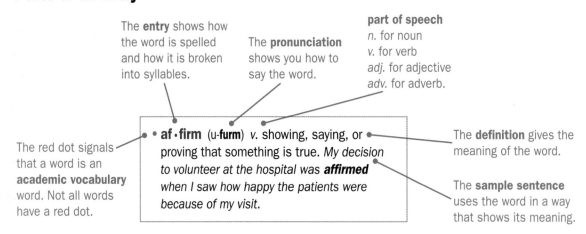

• **af·firm** (u-**furm**) *v.* showing, saying, or proving that something is true. *My decision to volunteer at the hospital was **affirmed** when I saw how happy the patients were because of my visit.*

A

abusive (u-**byū**-siv) *adj.* hurtful, cruel, harsh. *A factory that pollutes the air and water is **abusive** to the environment.*

accountable (u-**kown**-tu-bul) *adj.* responsible. *Who is **accountable** for the grades you get in school?*

advanced (ud-**vanst**) *adj.* more challenging. *The students in the **advanced** art class draw very well.*

advice (ud-**vīs**) *n.* ideas about how to solve a problem, suggestions. *When you ask a friend for **advice**, you want ideas on how to solve a problem.*

afford (u-**ford**) *v.* to have enough money for something. *Gwen had two jobs in order to **afford** her bills.*

agony (**a**-gu-nē) *n.* great suffering and worry. *The athlete was in **agony** when she broke her leg.*

anonymous (u-**no**-nu-mus) *adj.* unknown, unnamed. *If no one knows who sent a gift, the gift giver is **anonymous**.*

appearance (u-**pear**-uns) *n.* the way someone or something looks. *Changing your hairstyle can completely change your **appearance**.*

- **appreciate** (u-**prē**-shē-āt) *v.* to understand that something is good, to act grateful for it, to value it. *I always **appreciate** when people help me wash the dishes after a big dinner.*

approval (u-**prü**-vul) *n.* accepting something as good or correct; a good opinion of something. *"Thumbs up" is a sign of **approval**.*

arrange (u-**rānj**) *v.* to organize. *Do you **arrange** for a ride to school, or does the bus pick you up?*

ashamed (u-**shāmd**) *adj.* embarrassed, humiliated. *I was **ashamed** when I forgot my homework.*

- **assume** (u-**süm**) *v.* to think that something is true. *Do you **assume** that you will take exams at school?*

- **attitude** (**a**-tu-tüd) *n.* 1. a way of feeling about or looking at the world. *Having a positive **attitude** is important.*; 2. unfriendly or negative feelings toward someone or something. *I had a negative **attitude** about math homework when I did not understand how to do it.*

- **authority** (u-**thor**-u-tē) *n.* power over others. *The police have the **authority** to arrest people who break the law.*

avoid (u-**void**) *v.* to stay away from. *Do you try to **avoid**, or stay away from, unhealthy foods?*

B

behavior (bi-**hā**-vyur) *n.* the way a person acts, conduct. *Students with good **behavior** may be named "Student of the Month."*

belief (bu-**lēf**) *n.* something you think is true. *Different people have different **beliefs**.*

- **beneficial** (be-nu-**fi**-shul) *adj.* useful, helpful. *Exercise is **beneficial**.*

- **bond** (**bond**) *n.* attachment, connection, tie. *My grandmother and I share a special **bond**.*

bully (**boo**-lē) *n.; v. n*: a person who is repeatedly mean to others. *The school **bully** was suspended when he started a fight with a smaller, weaker student.*; *v*: to threaten. *Even though I didn't want to, my brother **bullied** me into cleaning his room.*

C

career (ku-**rear**) *n.* life's work, profession. *You need a lot of training to have a **career** as a doctor or a nurse.*

- **category** (**ca**-tu-gor-ē) *n.* a group of items that are similar in some way. *Cauliflower, lettuce, and broccoli are all in the vegetable **category**.*

- **challenge** (**cha**-lunj) *v.* to try to get someone to do something difficult; to dare someone. *Has anyone ever **challenged** you to run ten miles?*

- **circumstances** (**sur**-kum-stans-uz) *n.* how things are or what happens. *What **circumstance** might make you late for school?*

claim (**klām**) *v.* to say you have the right to something. *If you win a contest, you **claim** the prize.*

comedian (ku-**mē**-dē-un) *n.* a person who makes people laugh. *The **comedian** told jokes until everyone was laughing.*

- **communicate** (ku-**myū**-nu-kāt) *v.* to talk. *Some people **communicate** using hand signs to express their ideas.*

compliment (**kom**-plu-munt) *n.* something nice that someone says about another person. *How do you feel when you receive a **compliment**?*

compromise (**kom**-pru-mīz) *n.* an agreement in which each side gets something it wants and gives up something it wants. *You can make a **compromise** to end a fight.*

conceal (kun-**sēl**) *v.* to keep something secret or to hide something. *Lisa decided to **conceal** her feelings about Laurie's new dress so she wouldn't hurt Laurie's feelings.*

condition (kun-**di**-shun) *n.* a problem with a person's health. *The man's medical **condition** prevented him from going on an active vacation.*

confident (**kon**-fu-dunt) *adj.* to feel sure of yourself. *If you study, you might feel **confident** that you will do well on a test.*

confront (kun-**frunt**) *v.* to meet someone face-to-face about a problem or to face a difficult situation. *Your teacher may **confront** a student who is late to class.*

conquer (**kahn**-kur) *v.* to beat, to defeat. *The army **conquered** the invaders.*

conscious (**kon**-shus) *adj.* feeling or knowing something; aware. *We were **conscious** of the cell phone ringing in the quiet movie theater.*

• **consent** (kun-**sent**) *n.* permission. *When you give your **consent**, you give your approval.*

consequence (**kon**-su-kwens) *n.* the result of some action. *If you cheat, you should be prepared to face the **consequence**.*

• **consume** (kun-**süm**) *v.* to use things up, to eat. *When you eat food, you **consume** it.*

• **contribute** (kun-**tri**-byūt) *v.* to give, to donate. *When you **contribute** to a project, you help and add your ideas.*

control (kun-**trōl**) *v.* to have the power to manage or direct something. *Who **controls** a team—a player or the coach?*

• **convince** (kun-**vins**) *v.* to make someone believe something. *The father tried to **convince** his children that the healthy green peas tasted good.*

D

• **data** (**dā**-tu) *n.* information collected and organized for a topic. ***Data** must be gathered in order to write an accurate report.*

defiant (di-**fī**-unt) *adj.* going against or trying to oppose power or authority; not obedient. *Are you **defiant** when someone tries to make you do something you don't want to do?*

dependent (di-**pen**-dunt) *adj.* needing help most of the time. *Children are **dependent** on their parents for food and housing.*

• **depressed** (di-**prest**) *adj.* unhappy, sad. *Some people get **depressed** during the dark, cold days of winter.*

desire (di-**zīr**) *n.* something that you want strongly; a wish. *My **desire** is to travel to Africa one day.*

destiny (**des**-tu-nē) *n.* what is supposed to happen to you in the future; fate. *Is it your **destiny** to become like your parents?*

destruction (di-**struk**-shun) *n.* what is left behind after something is ruined. *The hurricane caused **destruction** all along the coast.*

dignity (**dig**-nu-tē) *n.* self-respect. *The basketball team kept their **dignity** even when they lost the game.*

disabilities (dis-u-**bi**-lu-tēz) *n.* problems that can limit what a person does. *Some people with physical **disabilities** use wheelchairs to move around.*

discipline (**di**-su-plun) *n.* training on how to behave. *Punishment can be one form of **discipline**.*

• **discrimination** (dis-kri-mu-**nā**-shun) *n.* treating people unfairly. *He faced **discrimination** at his job.*

• **distorted** (di-**stor**-ted) *adj.* twisted out of shape, not representing the truth. ***Distorted** facts do not represent the truth well.*

doubt (**dowt**) *v.* to be unsure if you believe something. *I **doubt** the story is true, because it is so unbelievable.*

dropout (**drop**-owt) *n.* a person who quits school before graduating. *Most high school **dropouts** have a hard time getting a good job.*

E

elegance (**e**-li-guns) *n.* high quality, beauty, and style. *The wealthy person's home was decorated with great **elegance**.*

embarrass (im-**bair**-us) *v.* to make someone feel confused, uneasy, or ashamed. *I used to **embarrass** my older brother by teasing him at school.*

• **enable** (i-**nā**-bul) *v.* to help make something possible. *Parents who pay for their children's college **enable** them to succeed.*

encouragement (in-**kur**-ij-munt) *n.* hope, support, praise. *When a teacher says that I do a good job, it gives me **encouragement**.*

engineer (en-ju-**near**) *n.* a person who plans how to build things like bridges and buildings. *The **engineer** designed the new museum.*

escape (is-**kāp**) *v.* to get free. *If you are in danger, you try to **escape**.*

• **establish** (i-**sta**-blish) *v.* to set up, to create. *I went to the bank to **establish** a savings account.*

• **evidence** (**e**-vu-duns) *n.* clues or proof that something is true. *The police use **evidence** to determine who committed a crime.*

existence (ig-**zis**-tuns) *n.* the state of living or being; life. *Your **existence** depends on food and water.*

experience (ik-**spear**-ē-uns) *n.* something you have done, or skills you have learned. *An after-school job can give you work **experience**.*

experiment (ik-**spair**-u-munt) *n.* a test or a trial. *What **experiments** do you do in science class?*

• **extraction** (ik-**strak**-shun) *n.* the act of removing one thing from another thing. *A dentist might perform an **extraction** of a bad tooth.*

F

failure (**fāl**-yur) *n.* a bad result. *After the heavy rainstorm, we had no electricity because of a power **failure**.*

flirt (**flurt**) *v.* to act as if you are attracted to someone, but in a playful way. *Dan likes to **flirt** with all the girls, but he is not serious about any of them.*

foolish (**fū**-lish) *adj.* not wise, silly. ***Foolish** people believe things that are untrue or that don't make sense.*

freedom (**frē**-dum) *n.* the power to do, say, or be whatever you want. *In the United States, people have **freedom** of speech and assembly.*

G

• **generation** (je-nu-**rā**-shun) *n.* a group of people who are born and who live around the same time. *Grandparents, parents, and children form three **generations**.*

• **goal** (**gōl**) *n.* a purpose. *When you set a **goal** for yourself, you know what you want to do.*

guardian (**gar**-dē-un) *n.* a person who is responsible for someone else. *A grandparent may become the **guardian** for a child whose parents die.*

H

hero (**hear**-ō) *n.* someone whom others admire; someone who acts with courage to help others. *A firefighter who saves someone's life is one kind of **hero**.*

horizon (hu-**rī**-zun) *n.* the line where the sky and land or water seem to meet. *At the beach you can clearly see the sun set on the **horizon**.*

I

ideals (ī-**dē**-ulz) *n.* ideas about the right way to live or act. *If you believe in treating people fairly, then fairness is one of your **ideals**.*

ignore (ig-**nor**) *v.* to pay no attention to something. *Usually it is best to **ignore** bullies.*

illusion (i-**lū**-zhun) *n.* image that does not match reality. *When a magician changes flowers into a bird, it is an **illusion**.*

imperfection (im-pur-**fek**-shun) *n.* defect, problem. *Only after I bought the television did I notice the **imperfection**.*

implore (im-**plor**) *v.* to beg. *I **implore** you not to tell this secret.*

- **impose** (im-**pōz**) *v.* to establish, to apply. *When parents **impose** rules, they are setting rules that their children must follow.*

income (**in**-kum) *n.* money that you earn. *Rudy's only **income** was the money he earned washing cars on Saturdays.*

inconvenient (in-kun-**vē**-nyunt) *adj.* happening at a bad time; troublesome. *When you're in a hurry, it is **inconvenient** to help your little sister get ready for school.*

independent (in-du-**pen**-dunt) *adj.* on your own. *When I moved into my own place I was finally **independent**.*

inherit (in-**hair**-ut) *v.* to get things from family members who lived before us. *We might **inherit** money and property from a grandparent.*

inspire (in-**spīr**) *v.* to encourage or influence. *My grandmother, who worked hard all her life to provide for her children, **inspires** me to do well.*

insult (in-**sult**) *v.* to say or do something mean to someone. *I felt hurt when he **insulted** me.*

- **intervene** (in-tur-**vēn**) *v.* to get involved. *When should you **intervene** to help someone in trouble?*

intimidate (in-**ti**-mu-dāt) *v.* to make someone feel unimportant or afraid. *I did not let my older brother **intimidate** me.*

intruder (in-**trüd**-ur) *n.* someone who goes where he or she should not go. *An **intruder** might break into a house to steal something.*

J

judgment (**juj**-munt) *n.* the ability to make good decisions. *A person who has good **judgment** thinks carefully before deciding something.*

M

- **mature** (mu-**choor**) *adj.* like a grown-up. *People become physically **mature** at different ages.*

misfortune (mis-**for**-chun) *n.* something bad that happens that you did not expect. *Has something bad happened to you that you did not expect? If so, you have suffered from **misfortune**.*

mistaken (mi-**stā**-kun) *v.* mixed up, confused. *I have **mistaken** a doorbell for a cell phone ring tone.*

molecule (**mo**-li-kyūl) *n.* a very small particle or piece of a substance. *A **molecule** of water is made up of two hydrogen atoms and one oxygen atom.*

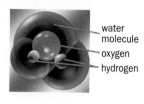

water molecule
oxygen
hydrogen

- **motivate** (**mō**-tu-vāt) *v.* to give reason to; to inspire; to stimulate. *Prizes and money can **motivate** people, or give them a reason, to work hard.*

N

neglect (ni-**glekt**) *n.* a lack of care and attention. *If you don't take care of plants, they can die from **neglect**.*

nerves (**nurvz**) *n.* worried and scared feelings. *Some actors suffer from **nerves** before they go on stage.*

nervous (**nur**-vus) *adj.* restless, anxious, worried. *Do you feel **nervous** when you have to speak in front of the class?*

- **normal** (**nor**-mul) *adj.* usual, ordinary. *On a **normal**, or ordinary, school day, the first class begins at 8:00 in the morning and the last class ends at 3:00 in the afternoon.*

O

obstacle (**ahb**-sti-kul) *n.* something that stands in your way or prevents you from doing something. *Lack of money may be an **obstacle** to buying a new car.*

outlook (**owt**-look) *n.* point of view, opinion. *A difficult job can be fun when you have a positive **outlook** about it.*

overcome (ō-vur-**kum**) *v.* to solve a problem. *I have **overcome** my fear of speaking in front of the class because I practiced my speech with my friends first.*

- **overprotective** (ō-vur-pru-**tek**-tiv) *adj.* too concerned about someone's safety or health. *Some parents can be **overprotective** of their children.*

P

- **participate** (par-**ti**-su-pāt) *v.* to take part in an activity or event. *What sports do you **participate** in at school?*

personality (pur-su-**na**-lu-tē) *n.* a person's characteristics and behavior. *Whom do you know with a friendly **personality**?*

poet (**pō**-ut) *n.* person who writes poems. *The **poet** wrote beautiful poems about life.*

politics (**pah**-lu-tiks) *n.* the government and what people think about it. *At lunch we like to talk about **politics**.*

position (pu-**zi**-shun) *n.* a specific job. *You could be hired to fill the **position** of assistant manager.*

- **positive** (**po**-zu-tiv) *adj.* good, helpful, favorable. *What are **positive**, or good, things in your life?*

- **potential** (pu-**ten**-shul) *n.* possibility; the ability to do something, given the chance. *If you can sing very well, you have the **potential** to be a singer in the future.*

presence (**pre**-zuns) *n.* the fact or feeling that someone is there. *Sometimes you can feel a person's **presence** even if he or she is not really there.*

privacy (**prī**-vu-sē) *n.* the state of being away from others, or of keeping things about yourself secret; concealment. *It is hard to have **privacy** when you share a room with two sisters.*

program (**prō**-gram) *n.* a planned event, performance, show. *What TV **program** is your favorite?*

- **prohibit** (prō-**hi**-but) *v.* to keep people from doing something, to prevent. *My parents **prohibit** me from going out until I finish my homework.*

- **project** (**prah**-jekt) *n.* job, task, assignment. *A school **project**, such as a video presentation, takes time and planning.*

Q

qualified (**kwah**-lu-fīd) *adj.* well-trained and prepared. *We hired a **qualified** plumber to fix the broken water pipe.*

R

- **react** (rē-**akt**) *v.* to act in response to something. *How do you **react** when you hear good news?*

- **reaction** (rē-**ak**-shun) *n.* what you think or do because of something else. *To cry is a natural **reaction** to pain.*

reality (rē-**a**-lu-tē) *n.* the sum of everything real. *What I see with my own eyes is **reality**.*

realize (**rē**-u-līz) *v.* to figure out. *A math problem may be seem hard, but when you solve it, you **realize** it was easy.*

reckless (**re**-klus) *adj.* taking foolish risks. ***Reckless** drivers often cause car accidents.*

recover (ri-**ku**-vur) *v.* to return to original or normal conditions. *After my accident, it took me some time to **recover**.*

reform (ri-**form**) *v.* to change for the better. *When criminals **reform**, they no longer commit crimes.*

relationship (ri-**lā**-shun-ship) *n.* the way that people are connected to each other. *Friendship and marriage are two different kinds of **relationships**.*

- **reluctant** (ri-**luk**-tunt) *adj.* unsure, unwilling, uncertain. *I was **reluctant** to do my chores after being in school all day.*

rescue (**res**-kyū) *v.* to save someone from harm. *If you fall into a lake, you may need someone to **rescue** you.*

- **research** (ri-**surch**) *n.* the gathering of information. *My **research** reveals that my family has lived in this city for seventy-six years.*

- **response** (ri-**spons**) *n.* an answer or reply. *You can give a **response** to many things, such as a question, an invitation, or a short story.*

responsibility (ri-spon-su-**bi**-lu-tē) *n.* job, duty. *The **responsibility** of a student is to go to school, study, and learn.*

- **restriction** (ri-**strik**-shun) *n.* something that limits activity. *A leash is a **restriction** on a dog's freedom.*

reveal (ri-**vēl**) *v.* to show, to make known. *I did not want to **reveal** to the teacher that I was nervous about giving my speech.*

revelation (re-vu-**lā**-shun) *n.* something that is revealed, or made known. *The whole family was surprised by the **revelation** that they were related to royalty.*

revenge (ri-**venj**) *n.* the act of hurting someone who has hurt you. *After he insulted me, I wanted **revenge**.*

ridiculous (ru-**di**-kyu-lus) *adj.* silly, foolish. *Do dogs wearing sunglasses look **ridiculous**?*

role (**rōl**) *n.* a part you play on stage or in real life. *What is your **role** in your family?*

romantic (rō-**man**-tik) *adj.* filled with love. *A bouquet of flowers is a **romantic** gift to give to someone you love.*

roots (**rüts**) *n.* 1. ties to family or the place you come from.; 2. part of a plant that is under the ground. *A carrot is actually a **root**.*

S

sequence (**sē**-kwuns) *n.* order. *The alphabet follows a certain **sequence**.*

serious (**sear**-ē-us) *adj.* not joking. *The teacher was very **serious** when talking about the student's future.*

shock (**shok**) *n.* surprise and fear. *People who receive bad news often suffer a great **shock**.*

solution (su-**lü**-shun) *n.* answer to a problem. *Better public transportation is one **solution** to traffic problems.*

struggle (**stru**-gul) *v.* to work hard for something. *The men **struggle** to lift the heavy boxes.*

stubborn (**stu**-burn) *adj.* not willing to change or quit. *My little sister can be very **stubborn** when she wants to do something her way.*

superstition (sü-pur-**sti**-shun) *n.* an idea based on fear, not logic. *There is a **superstition** that black cats cause bad luck.*

survey (sur-**vā**) *n.* a poll. *When you conduct a **survey**, you ask people questions to find out what they think or do.*

survive (sur-**vīv**) *v.* to live, to last. *If someone **survives** a bad storm, the person is still alive when the storm has ended.*

sympathetic (sim-pu-**the**-tik) *adj.* kind, understanding, caring. *When you are upset, a **sympathetic** friend can make you feel better.*

T

tradition (tru-**di**-shun) *n.* a belief or a way of doing things. *It is an American **tradition** to watch fireworks on the Fourth of July.*

tragedy (**tra**-ju-dē) *n.* a very sad event. *The death of a loved one is a **tragedy**.*

trait (**trāt**) *n.* a certain way something is, a feature of something. *Eye color is one **trait** for a person's appearance.*

transform (trans-**form**) *v.* change into something else. *You can **transform** a dark room by painting the walls white.*

transmit (trans-**mit**) *v.* to pass on or send. *My friend **transmits** text messages on her cell phone.*

U

understand (un-dur-**stand**) *v.* to know the meaning of something well. *Do you **understand** that math problem, or are you still confused?*

unforgettable (un-fur-**ge**-tu-bul) *adj.* not able to leave your mind; memorable. *My first visit to the Grand Canyon was **unforgettable**.*

unique (yū-**nēk**) *adj.* one of a kind. *Each of us has a **unique** set of fingerprints.*

united (yū-**nī**-tid) *adj.* joined, together. *When a team is **united**, the players work well together.*

V

valuable (**val**-yū-bul) *adj.* having worth, important. *What is the most **valuable** thing you own?*

value (**val**-yū) *v.* to believe that something is important or has worth; to care for, to prize. *You might **value** a good friend or your school.*

veteran (**ve**-tu-run) *n.* someone who was in the military. *The **veteran** was given a medal for bravery.*

violate (**vī**-u-lāt) *v.* to go against. *You can receive a fine or go to jail if you **violate** the law.*

violence (**vī**-luns) *n.* physical action that is very rough, harmful, and mean. *Someone may use* ***violence*** *to injure another person.*

vote (**vōt**) *v.* to make choices in elections. *If you could* ***vote****, who would you want for president?*

W

weight (**wāt**) *n.* 1. heavy gym equipment used for exercising. *To build his muscles, the teenage boy lifted* ***weights*** *every other day.* 2. how heavy an object is. *The* ***weight*** *of the refrigerator made it impossible for one man to lift.*

willingly (**wi**-ling-lē) *adv.* without being forced. *He ate the ice cream* ***willingly****.*

worthless (**wurth**-lus) *adj.* useless. *A smashed remote control is* ***worthless*** *because you can't use it or sell it.*

Beginning-Middle-End

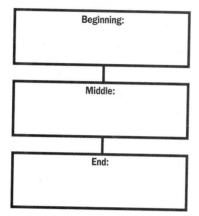

Character-Setting-Plot

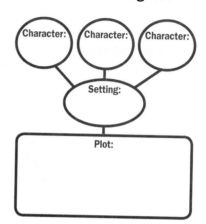

Character Description

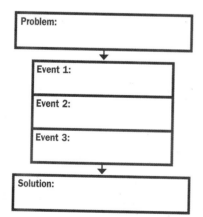

Goal-and-Outcome

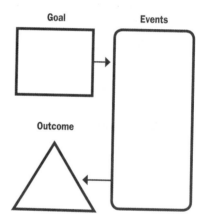

Problem-and-Solution

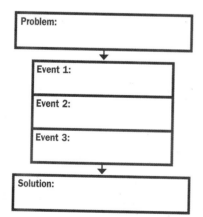

Cause-and-Effect Chart

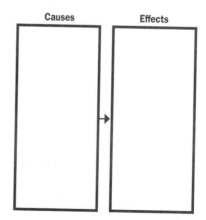

Cycle Diagram

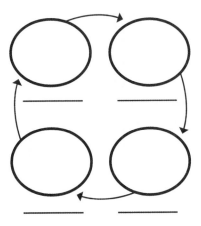

Sequence Chain

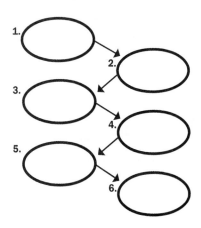

Time Line

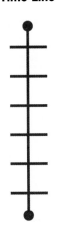

Main-Idea Diagram

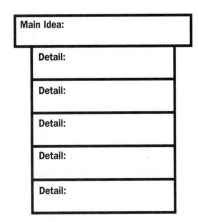

Idea Web

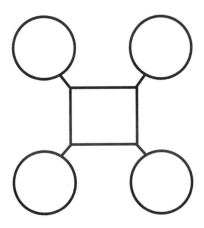

Topic Triangle

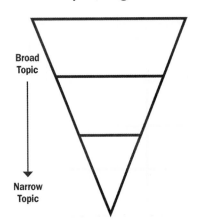

Venn Diagram

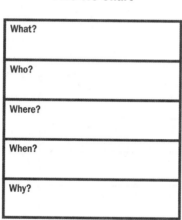

Classification Chart

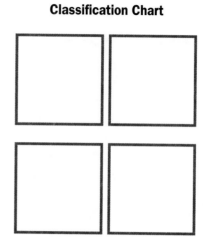

Five-Ws Chart

What?	
Who?	
Where?	
When?	
Why?	

KWL Chart

K What Do I Know?	W What Do I Want to Learn?	L What Did I Learn?

Table

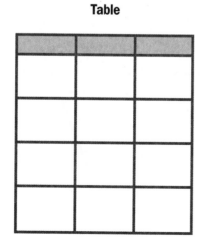

Outline

I. _____

   A. _____

   B. _____

II. _____

   A. _____

   B. _____

III. _____

   A. _____

   B. _____

Graph

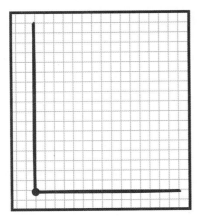

T Chart

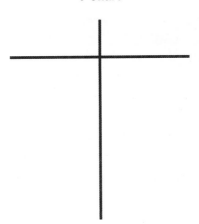

Word Map

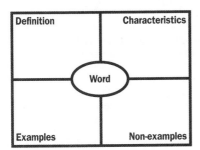

Common Core State Standards

UNIT 1: Think Again

SE Pages	Lesson	Code	Standards Text
0–1	Discuss the Essential Question	SL.9-10.1.b	Work with peers to set rules for collegial discussions and decision-making, clear goals and deadlines, and individual roles as needed.
		SL.9-10.3	Evaluate a speaker's point of view, reasoning, and use of evidence and rhetoric, identifying any fallacious reasoning or exaggerated or distorted evidence.
2	Analyze and Debate	SL.9-10.4	Present information, findings, and supporting evidence clearly, concisely, and logically such that listeners can follow the line of reasoning and the organization, development, substance, and style are appropriate to purpose, audience, and task.
3	Plan a Project	SL.9-10.1.b	Work with peers to set rules for collegial discussions and decision-making, clear goals and deadlines, and individual roles as needed.
3	Choose More to Read	RL.9-10.10	By the end of grade 10, read and comprehend literature, including stories, dramas, and poems, at the high end of the grades 9–10 text complexity band independently and proficiently.
		RI.9-10.10	By the end of grade 10, read and comprehend literary nonfiction at the high end of the grades 9–10 text complexity band independently and proficiently.
4–5	How to Read Using Reading Strategies	L.9-10.6	Acquire and use accurately general academic and domain-specific words and phrases, sufficient for reading, writing, speaking, and listening at the college and career readiness level; demonstrate independence in gathering vocabulary knowledge when considering a word or phrase important to comprehension or expression.
		RI.9-10.10	By the end of grade 10, read and comprehend literary nonfiction at the high end of the grades 9–10 text complexity band independently and proficiently.
6–9	How to Read Short Stories	RL.9-10.1	Cite strong and thorough textual evidence to support analysis of what the text says explicitly as well as inferences drawn from the text.
		RL.9-10.3	Analyze how complex characters develop over the course of a text, interact with other characters, and advance the plot or develop the theme.
		RL.9-10.10	By the end of grade 10, read and comprehend literature, including stories, dramas, and poems, at the high end of the grades 9–10 text complexity band independently and proficiently.

Cluster 1

SE Pages	Lesson	Code	Standards Text
10	Prepare to Read	RL.9-10.4	Determine the meaning of words and phrases as they are used in a text, including figurative, connotative, and technical meanings; analyze the cumulative impact of specific word choices on meaning and tone.
		SL.9-10.3	Evaluate a speaker's point of view, reasoning, and use of evidence and rhetoric, identifying any fallacious reasoning or exaggerated or distorted evidence.
		L.9-10.6	Acquire and use accurately general academic and domain-specific words and phrases, sufficient for reading, writing, speaking, and listening at the college and career readiness level; demonstrate independence in gathering vocabulary knowledge when considering a word or phrase important to comprehension or expression.
11	Before Reading: The Experiment	RL.9-10.3	Analyze how complex characters develop over the course of a text, interact with other characters, and advance the plot or develop the theme.

Cluster 1, continued

SE Pages	Lesson	Code	Standards Text
11	**Before Reading: The Experiment** continued	RL.9-10.10	By the end of grade 10, read and comprehend literature, including stories, dramas, and poems, at the high end of the grades 9–10 text complexity band independently and proficiently.
12–19	**Read The Experiment**	RL.9-10.2	Determine a theme or central idea of a text and analyze in detail its development over the course of the text, including how it emerges and is shaped and refined by specific details; provide an objective summary of the text.
		RL.9-10.3	Analyze how complex characters develop over the course of a text, interact with other characters, and advance the plot or develop the theme.
		RL.9-10.10	By the end of grade 10, read and comprehend literature, including stories, dramas, and poems, at the high end of the grades 9–10 text complexity band independently and proficiently.
		W.9-10.9.a	Apply grades 9–10 Reading standards to literature.
		L.9-10.1.b	Use various types of phrases (noun, verb, adjectival, adverbial, participial, prepositional, absolute) and clauses (independent, dependent; noun, relative, adverbial) to convey specific meanings and add variety and interest to writing or presentations.
		L.9-10.2	Demonstrate command of the conventions of standard English capitalization, punctuation, and spelling when writing.
		L.9-10.4.a	Use context as a clue to the meaning of a word or phrase.
		L.9-10.6	Acquire and use accurately general academic and domain-specific words and phrases, sufficient for reading, writing, speaking, and listening at the college and career readiness level; demonstrate independence in gathering vocabulary knowledge when considering a word or phrase important to comprehension or expression.
20	**Before Reading: Superstitions: The Truth Uncovered**	RI.9-10.7	Analyze various accounts of a subject told in different mediums, determining which details are emphasized in each account.
		RI.9-10.10	By the end of grade 10, read and comprehend literary nonfiction at the high end of the grades 9–10 text complexity band independently and proficiently.
21–24	**Read Superstitions: The Truth Uncovered**	RI.9-10.1	Cite strong and thorough textual evidence to support analysis of what the text says explicitly as well as inferences drawn from the text.
		RI.9-10.7	Analyze various accounts of a subject told in different mediums, determining which details are emphasized in each account.
		RI.9-10.10	By the end of grade 10, read and comprehend literary nonfiction at the high end of the grades 9–10 text complexity band independently and proficiently.
		W.9-10.9.b	Apply grades 9–10 Reading standards to literary nonfiction.
		W.9-10.10	Write routinely over extended time frames (time for research, reflection, and revision) and shorter time frames (a single sitting or a day or two) for a range of tasks, purposes, and audiences.
		L.9-10.1.b	Use various types of phrases (noun, verb, adjectival, adverbial, participial, prepositional, absolute) and clauses (independent, dependent; noun, relative, adverbial) to convey specific meanings and add variety and interest to writing or presentations.

Common Core State Standards, continued

SE Pages	Lesson	Code	Standards Text
21–24	**Read Superstitions: The Truth Uncovered** continued	L.9-10.6	Acquire and use accurately general academic and domain-specific words and phrases, sufficient for reading, writing, speaking, and listening at the college and career readiness level; demonstrate independence in gathering vocabulary knowledge when considering a word or phrase important to comprehension or expression.
25	**Reflect and Assess Critical Thinking**	RL.9-10.1	Cite strong and thorough textual evidence to support analysis of what the text says explicitly as well as inferences drawn from the text.
		RI.9-10.1	Cite strong and thorough textual evidence to support analysis of what the text says explicitly as well as inferences drawn from the text.
	Write About Literature	W.9-10.1	Write arguments to support claims in an analysis of substantive topics or texts, using valid reasoning and relevant and sufficient evidence.
	Key Vocabulary Review	L.9-10.6	Acquire and use accurately general academic and domain-specific words and phrases, sufficient for reading, writing, speaking, and listening at the college and career readiness level; demonstrate independence in gathering vocabulary knowledge when considering a word or phrase important to comprehension or expression.
	Read with Ease: Expression	RL.9-10.10	By the end of grade 10, read and comprehend literary nonfiction at the high end of the grades 9–10 text complexity band independently and proficiently.
26	**Grammar: Write Complete Sentences**	SL.9-10.1.b	Work with peers to set rules for collegial discussions and decision-making, clear goals and deadlines, and individual roles as needed.
		L.9-10.1.b	Use various types of phrases (noun, verb, adjectival, adverbial, participial, prepositional, absolute) and clauses (independent, dependent; noun, relative, adverbial) to convey specific meanings and add variety and interest to writing or presentations.
26	**Language Development: Ask and Answer Questions**	SL.9-10.1.b	Work with peers to set rules for collegial discussions and decision-making, clear goals and deadlines, and individual roles as needed.
26	**Literary Analysis: Analyze Plot: Climax**	RL.9-10.5	Analyze how an author's choices concerning how to structure a text, order events within it, and manipulate time create such effects as mystery, tension, or surprise.
27	**Vocabulary Study: Prefixes**	L.9-10.4.b	Identify and correctly use patterns of word changes that indicate different meanings or parts of speech.
27	**Research.:/Speaking: Oral Report**	W.9-10.7	Conduct short as well as more sustained research projects to answer a question (including a self-generated question) or solve a problem; narrow or broaden the inquiry when appropriate; synthesize multiple sources on the subject, demonstrating understanding of the subject under investigation.
		SL.9-10.4	Present information, findings, and supporting evidence clearly, concisely, and logically such that listeners can follow the line of reasoning and the organization, development, substance, and style are appropriate to purpose, audience, and task.
27	**Writing: Write a Narrative Paragraph**	W.9-10.3	Write narratives to develop real or imagined experiences or events using effective technique, well-chosen details, and well-structured event sequences.
		W.9-10.7	Conduct short as well as more sustained research projects to answer a question (including a self-generated question) or solve a problem; narrow or broaden the inquiry when appropriate; synthesize multiple sources on the subject, demonstrating understanding of the subject under investigation.

Cluster 1, continued

SE Pages	Lesson	Code	Standards Text
28	Workplace Workshop: At a Television Station	W.9-10.4	Produce clear and coherent writing in which the development, organization, and style are appropriate to task, purpose, and audience.
		W.9-10.7	Conduct short as well as more sustained research projects to answer a question (including a self-generated question) or solve a problem; narrow or broaden the inquiry when appropriate; synthesize multiple sources on the subject, demonstrating understanding of the subject under investigation.
		W.9-10.10	Write routinely over extended time frames (time for research, reflection, and revision) and shorter time frames (a single sitting or a day or two) for a range of tasks, purposes, and audiences.
		L.9-10.6	Acquire and use accurately general academic and domain-specific words and phrases, sufficient for reading, writing, speaking, and listening at the college and career readiness level; demonstrate independence in gathering vocabulary knowledge when considering a word or phrase important to comprehension or expression.
29	Vocabulary Workshop: Use Word Parts	L.9-10.4.b	Identify and correctly use patterns of word changes that indicate different meanings or parts of speech.
		L.9-10.4.c	Consult general and specialized reference materials, both print and digital, to find the pronunciation of a word or determine or clarify its precise meaning, its part of speech, or its etymology.
		L.9-10.4.d	Verify the preliminary determination of the meaning of a word or phrase.

Cluster 2

SE Pages	Lesson	Code	Standards Text
30	Prepare to Read	RI.9-10.4	Determine the meaning of words and phrases as they are used in a text, including figurative, connotative, and technical meanings; analyze the cumulative impact of specific word choices on meaning and tone.
		SL.9-10.1	Initiate and participate effectively in a range of collaborative discussions (one-on-one, in groups, and teacher-led) with diverse partners on grades 9–10 topics, texts, and issues, building on others' ideas and expressing their own clearly and persuasively.
		L.9-10.4.c	Consult general and specialized reference materials, both print and digital, to find the pronunciation of a word or determine or clarify its precise meaning, its part of speech, or its etymology.
		L.9-10.6	Acquire and use accurately general academic and domain-specific words and phrases, sufficient for reading, writing, speaking, and listening at the college and career readiness level; demonstrate independence in gathering vocabulary knowledge when considering a word or phrase important to comprehension or expression.
31	Before Reading: Building Bridges	RL.9-10.3	Analyze how complex characters develop over the course of a text, interact with other characters, and advance the plot or develop the theme.
		RL.9-10.4	Determine the meaning of words and phrases as they are used in the text, including figurative and connotative meanings; analyze the cumulative impact of specific word choices on meaning and tone.
32–43	Read Building Bridges	RL.9-10.1	Cite strong and thorough textual evidence to support analysis of what the text says explicitly as well as inferences drawn from the text.

Common Core State Standards, continued

Cluster 2, continued

SE Pages	Lesson	Code	Standards Text
32–43	**Read Building Bridges** continued	RL.9-10.3	Analyze how complex characters develop over the course of a text, interact with other characters, and advance the plot or develop the theme.
		RL.9-10.4	Determine the meaning of words and phrases as they are used in the text, including figurative and connotative meanings; analyze the cumulative impact of specific word choices on meaning and tone.
		RL.9-10.7	Analyze the representation of a subject or a key scene in two different artistic mediums, including what is emphasized or absent in each treatment.
		RL.9-10.10	By the end of grade 10, read and comprehend literature, including stories, dramas, and poems, at the high end of the grades 9–10 text complexity band independently and proficiently.
		W.9-10.9.a	Apply grades 9–10 Reading standards to literature.
		W.9-10.10	Write routinely over extended time frames (time for research, reflection, and revision) and shorter time frames (a single sitting or a day or two) for a range of tasks, purposes, and audiences.
		L.9-10.5.b	Analyze nuances in the meaning of words with similar denotations.
		L.9-10.6	Acquire and use accurately general academic and domain-specific words and phrases, sufficient for reading, writing, speaking, and listening at the college and career readiness level; demonstrate independence in gathering vocabulary knowledge when considering a word or phrase important to comprehension or expression.
44	**Before Reading: The Rights Words at the Right Time**	RI.9-10.1	Cite strong and thorough textual evidence to support analysis of what the text says explicitly as well as inferences drawn from the text.
		RI.9-10.10	By the end of grade 10, read and comprehend literary nonfiction at the high end of the grades 9–10 text complexity band independently and proficiently.
45–48	**Read The Right Words at the Right Time**	RI.9-10.1	Cite strong and thorough textual evidence to support analysis of what the text says explicitly as well as inferences drawn from the text.
		RI.9-10.2	Determine a central idea of a text and analyze its development over the course of the text, including how it emerges and is shaped and refined by specific details; provide an objective summary of the text.
		RI.9-10.4	Determine the meaning of words and phrases as they are used in the text, including figurative and connotative meanings; analyze the cumulative impact of specific word choices on meaning and tone.
		RI.9-10.10	By the end of grade 10, read and comprehend literary nonfiction at the high end of the grades 9–10 text complexity band independently and proficiently.
		W.9-10.9.b	Apply grades 9–10 Reading standards to literary nonfiction.
		W.9-10.10	Write routinely over extended time frames (time for research, reflection, and revision) and shorter time frames (a single sitting or a day or two) for a range of tasks, purposes, and audiences.
		L.9-10.1	Demonstrate command of the conventions of standard English grammar and usage when writing or speaking.

SE Pages	Lesson	Code	Standards Text
45–48	**Read The Right Words at the Right Time** continued	L.9-10.6	Acquire and use accurately general academic and domain-specific words and phrases, sufficient for reading, writing, speaking, and listening at the college and career readiness level; demonstrate independence in gathering vocabulary knowledge when considering a word or phrase important to comprehension or expression.
49	**Reflect and Assess Critical Thinking**	RL.9-10.1	Cite strong and thorough textual evidence to support analysis of what the text says explicitly as well as inferences drawn from the text.
		RI.9-10.1	Cite strong and thorough textual evidence to support analysis of what the text says explicitly as well as inferences drawn from the text.
	Write About Literature	W.9-10.3	Write narratives to develop real or imagined experiences or events using effective technique, well-chosen details, and well-structured event sequences.
	Key Vocabulary Review	L.9-10.6	Acquire and use accurately general academic and domain-specific words and phrases, sufficient for reading, writing, speaking, and listening at the college and career readiness level; demonstrate independence in gathering vocabulary knowledge when considering a word or phrase important to comprehension or expression.
	Read with Ease: Phrasing	RI.9-10.10	By the end of grade 10, read and comprehend literary nonfiction at the high end of the grades 9–10 text complexity band independently and proficiently.
50	**Grammar: Make Subjects and Verbs Agree**	L.9-10.1	Demonstrate command of the conventions of standard English grammar and usage when writing or speaking.
50	**Language Development: Ask and Answer Questions**	L.9-10.1.c	Spell correctly.
50	**Literary Analysis: Dialect**	RI.9-10.4	Determine the meaning of words and phrases as they are used in a text, including figurative, connotative, and technical meanings; analyze the cumulative impact of specific word choices on meaning and tone.
51	**Vocabulary Study: Prefixes**	L.9-10.4.b	Identify and correctly use patterns of word changes that indicate different meanings or parts of speech.
51	**Research/Writing: Career Chart**	W.9-10.7	Conduct short as well as more sustained research projects to answer a question (including a self-generated question) or solve a problem; narrow or broaden the inquiry when appropriate; synthesize multiple sources on the subject, demonstrating understanding of the subject under investigation.
51	**Writing on Demand: Write a Short Comparison**	W.9-10.2.b	Develop the topic with well-chosen, relevant, and sufficient facts, extended definitions, concrete details, quotations, or other information and examples appropriate to the audience's knowledge of the topic.
		W.9-10.4	Produce clear and coherent writing in which the development, organization, and style are appropriate to task, purpose, and audience.
52–53	**Listening and Speaking Workshop: Role-Play**	SL.9-10.1.b	Work with peers to set rules for collegial discussions and decision-making, clear goals and deadlines, and individual roles as needed.
		SL.9-10.6	Adapt speech to a variety of contexts and tasks, demonstrating command of formal English when indicated or appropriate.
		L.9-10.3	Apply knowledge of language to understand how language functions in different contexts, to make effective choices for meaning or style, and to comprehend more fully when reading or listening.

Common Core State Standards, continued

SE Pages	Lesson	Code	Standards Text
54	**Prepare to Read**	RI.9-10.4	Determine the meaning of words and phrases as they are used in a text, including figurative, connotative, and technical meanings; analyze the cumulative impact of specific word choices on meaning and tone.
		SL.9-10.1	Initiate and participate effectively in a range of collaborative discussions (one-on-one, in groups, and teacher-led) with diverse partners on grades 9–10 topics, texts, and issues, building on others' ideas and expressing their own clearly and persuasively.
		L.9-10.6	Acquire and use accurately general academic and domain-specific words and phrases, sufficient for reading, writing, speaking, and listening at the college and career readiness level; demonstrate independence in gathering vocabulary knowledge when considering a word or phrase important to comprehension or expression.
55	**Before Reading: The Open Window**	RL.9-10.3	Analyze how complex characters develop over the course of a text, interact with other characters, and advance the plot or develop the theme.
		RL.9-10.4	Determine the meaning of words and phrases as they are used in the text, including figurative and connotative meanings; analyze the cumulative impact of specific word choices on meaning and tone.
56–63	**Read The Open Window**	RL.9-10.1	Cite strong and thorough textual evidence to support analysis of what the text says explicitly as well as inferences drawn from the text.
		RL.9-10.3	Analyze how complex characters develop over the course of a text, interact with other characters, and advance the plot or develop the theme.
		RL.9-10.4	Determine the meaning of words and phrases as they are used in the text, including figurative and connotative meanings; analyze the cumulative impact of specific word choices on meaning and tone.
		RL.9-10.7	Analyze the representation of a subject or a key scene in two different artistic mediums, including what is emphasized or absent in each treatment.
		RL.9-10.10	By the end of grade 10, read and comprehend literature, including stories, dramas, and poems, at the high end of the grades 9–10 text complexity band independently and proficiently.
		W.9-10.9.a	Apply grades 9–10 Reading standards to literature.
		L.9-10.1	Demonstrate command of the conventions of standard English grammar and usage when writing or speaking.
		L.9-10.6	Acquire and use accurately general academic and domain-specific words and phrases, sufficient for reading, writing, speaking, and listening at the college and career readiness level; demonstrate independence in gathering vocabulary knowledge when considering a word or phrase important to comprehension or expression.
64	**Before Reading: One in a Million**	RL.9-10.4	Determine the meaning of words and phrases as they are used in the text, including figurative and connotative meanings; analyze the cumulative impact of specific word choices on meaning and tone.
		RL.9-10.6	Analyze a particular point of view or cultural experience reflected in a work of literature from outside the United States, drawing on a wide reading of world literature.
65–66	**Read One in a Million**	RL.9-10.1	Cite strong and thorough textual evidence to support analysis of what the text says explicitly as well as inferences drawn from the text.

SE Pages	Lesson	Code	Standards Text
65–66	**Read One in a Million** continued	RL.9-10.3	Analyze how complex characters develop over the course of a text, interact with other characters, and advance the plot or develop the theme.
		RL.9-10.4	Determine the meaning of words and phrases as they are used in the text, including figurative and connotative meanings; analyze the cumulative impact of specific word choices on meaning and tone.
		RL.9-10.6	Analyze a particular point of view or cultural experience reflected in a work of literature from outside the United States, drawing on a wide reading of world literature.
		RL.9-10.10	By the end of grade 10, read and comprehend literature, including stories, dramas, and poems, at the high end of the grades 9–10 text complexity band independently and proficiently.
		W.9-10.9.a	Apply grades 9–10 Reading standards to literature.
		W.9-10.10	Write routinely over extended time frames (time for research, reflection, and revision) and shorter time frames (a single sitting or a day or two) for a range of tasks, purposes, and audiences.
		L.9-10.6	Acquire and use accurately general academic and domain-specific words and phrases, sufficient for reading, writing, speaking, and listening at the college and career readiness level; demonstrate independence in gathering vocabulary knowledge when considering a word or phrase important to comprehension or expression.
67	**Reflect and Assess**	RL.9-10.1	Cite strong and thorough textual evidence to support analysis of what the text says explicitly as well as inferences drawn from the text.
67	**Critical Thinking**	RL.9-10.3	Analyze how complex characters develop over the course of a text, interact with other characters, and advance the plot or develop the theme.
67	**Write About Literature**	W.9-10.1	Write arguments to support claims in an analysis of substantive topics or texts, using valid reasoning and relevant and sufficient evidence.
67	**Key Vocabulary Review**	L.9-10.6	Acquire and use accurately general academic and domain-specific words and phrases, sufficient for reading, writing, speaking, and listening at the college and career readiness level; demonstrate independence in gathering vocabulary knowledge when considering a word or phrase important to comprehension or expression.
67	**Read with Ease: Intonation**	RL.9-10.10	By the end of grade 10, read and comprehend literature, including stories, dramas, and poems, at the high end of the grades 9–10 text complexity band independently and proficiently.
68	**Grammar: Fix Sentence Fragments**	L.9-10.1	Demonstrate command of the conventions of standard English grammar and usage when writing or speaking.
68	**Language Development: Ask and Answer Questions**	SL.9-10.1.a	Come to discussions prepared, having read and researched material under study; explicitly draw on that preparation by referring to evidence from texts and other research on the topic or issue to stimulate a thoughtful, well-reasoned exchange of ideas.
68	**Literary Analysis: Compare Settings**	RL.9-10.3	Analyze how complex characters develop over the course of a text, interact with other characters, and advance the plot or develop the theme.
69	**Vocabulary Study: Suffixes**	L.9-10.4.b	Identify and correctly use patterns of word changes that indicate different meanings or parts of speech.

Common Core State Standards, continued

SE Pages	Lesson	Code	Standards Text
69	Research/Speaking: Folk Tales	W.9-10.7	Conduct short as well as more sustained research projects to answer a question (including a self-generated question) or solve a problem; narrow or broaden the inquiry when appropriate; synthesize multiple sources on the subject, demonstrating understanding of the subject under investigation.
		SL.9-10.1.a	Come to discussions prepared, having read and researched material under study; explicitly draw on that preparation by referring to evidence from texts and other research on the topic or issue to stimulate a thoughtful, well-reasoned exchange of ideas.
69	Writing Trait: Focus and Unity	W.9-10.5	Develop and strengthen writing as needed by planning, revising, editing, rewriting, or trying a new approach, focusing on addressing what is most significant for a specific purpose and audience.

Close Reading

SE Pages	Lesson	Code	Standards Text
70–73	Read Ambush	RL.9-10.10	By the end of grade 10, read and comprehend literature, including stories, dramas, and poems, at the high end of the grades 9–10 text complexity band independently and proficiently.

Unit Wrap-Up

SE Pages	Lesson	Code	Standards Text
74	Unit Wrap-Up Present Your Project	W.9-10.4	Produce clear and coherent writing in which the development, organization, and style are appropriate to task, purpose, and audience.
		SL.9-10.4	Present information, findings, and supporting evidence clearly, concisely, and logically such that listeners can follow the line of reasoning and the organization, development, substance, and style are appropriate to purpose, audience, and task.
74	Reflect on Your Reading	SL.9-10.1.a	Come to discussions prepared, having read and researched material under study; explicitly draw on that preparation by referring to evidence from texts and other research on the topic or issue to stimulate a thoughtful, well-reasoned exchange of ideas.
74	Respond to the Essential Question	SL.9-10.1.a	Come to discussions prepared, having read and researched material under study; explicitly draw on that preparation by referring to evidence from texts and other research on the topic or issue to stimulate a thoughtful, well-reasoned exchange of ideas.

Unit 1 Writing Project: Personal Narrative

SE Pages	Lesson	Code	Standards Text
76–79	Study Personal Narratives and Prewrite	W.9-10.3.c	Use a variety of techniques to sequence events so that they build on one another to create a coherent whole.
		W.9-10.4	Produce clear and coherent writing in which the development, organization, and style are appropriate to task, purpose, and audience.
		W.9-10.5	Develop and strengthen writing as needed by planning, revising, editing, rewriting, or trying a new approach, focusing on addressing what is most significant for a specific purpose and audience.
80–81	Personal Narrative: Draft	W.9-10.3	Write narratives to develop real or imagined experiences or events using effective technique, well-chosen details, and well-structured event sequences.
		W.9-10.3.a	Engage and orient the reader by setting out a problem, situation, or observation, establishing one or multiple point(s) of view, and introducing a narrator and/or characters; create a smooth progression of experiences or events.

Unit 1 Writing Project: Personal Narrative, continued

SE Pages	Lesson	Code	Standards Text
80–81	**Personal Narrative: Draft** continued	W.9-10.4	Produce clear and coherent writing in which the development, organization, and style are appropriate to task, purpose, and audience.
		W.9-10.6	Use technology, including the Internet, to produce, publish, and update individual or shared writing products, taking advantage of technology's capacity to link to other information and to display information flexibly and dynamically.
82–85	**Personal Narrative: Revise** **Trait: Focus and Unity**	W.9-10.3.a	Engage and orient the reader by setting out a problem, situation, or observation, establishing one or multiple point(s) of view, and introducing a narrator and/or characters; create a smooth progression of experiences or events.
		W.9-10.3.b	Use narrative techniques, such as dialogue, pacing, description, reflection, and multiple plot lines, to develop experiences, events, and/or characters.
		W.9-10.3.c	Use a variety of techniques to sequence events so that they build on one another to create a coherent whole.
		W.9-10.3.e	Provide a conclusion that follows from and reflects on what is experienced, observed, or resolved over the course of the narrative.
		W.9-10.5	Develop and strengthen writing as needed by planning, revising, editing, rewriting, or trying a new approach, focusing on addressing what is most significant for a specific purpose and audience.
		SL.9-10.1	Initiate and participate effectively in a range of collaborative discussions (one-on-one, in groups, and teacher-led) with diverse partners on grades 9–10 topics, texts, and issues, building on others' ideas and expressing their own clearly and persuasively.
		SL.9-10.1.d	Respond thoughtfully to diverse perspectives, summarize points of agreement and disagreement, and, when warranted, qualify or justify their own views and understanding and make new connections in light of the evidence and reasoning presented.
86–88	**Personal Narrative: Edit and Proofread** **Capitalization: First Word of a Sentence and the Pronoun I** **End Punctuation** **Spelling** **Complete Sentences**	W.9-10.6	Use technology, including the Internet, to produce, publish, and update individual or shared writing products, taking advantage of technology's capacity to link to other information and to display information flexibly and dynamically.
		L.9-10.1	Demonstrate command of the conventions of standard English grammar and usage when writing or speaking.
		L.9-10.2	Demonstrate command of the conventions of standard English capitalization, punctuation, and spelling when writing.
		L.9-10.2.c	Spell correctly.
		L.9-10.3.a	Write and edit work so that it conforms to the guidelines in a style manual appropriate for the discipline and writing type.
89	**Personal Narrative: Publish and Present**	W.9-10.4	Produce clear and coherent writing in which the development, organization, and style are appropriate to task, purpose, and audience.
		W.9-10.5	Develop and strengthen writing as needed by planning, revising, editing, rewriting, or trying a new approach, focusing on addressing what is most significant for a specific purpose and audience.
		SL.9-10.1	Initiate and participate effectively in a range of collaborative discussions (one-on-one, in groups, and teacher-led) with diverse partners on grades 9–10 topics, texts, and issues, building on others' ideas and expressing their own clearly and persuasively.

Common Core State Standards, continued

UNIT 2: Family Matters

SE Pages	Lesson	Code	Standards Text
90–91	Discuss the Essential Question	SL.9-10.1.b	Work with peers to set rules for collegial discussions and decision-making, clear goals and deadlines, and individual roles as needed.
		SL.9-10.3	Evaluate a speaker's point of view, reasoning, and use of evidence and rhetoric, identifying any fallacious reasoning or exaggerated or distorted evidence.
92	Analyze and Debate	SL.9-10.4	Present information, findings, and supporting evidence clearly, concisely, and logically such that listeners can follow the line of reasoning and the organization, development, substance, and style are appropriate to purpose, audience, and task.
93	Plan a Project	SL.9-10.1.b	Work with peers to set rules for collegial discussions and decision-making, clear goals and deadlines, and individual roles as needed.
93	Choose More to Read	RL.9-10.10	By the end of grade 10, read and comprehend literature, including stories, dramas, and poems, at the high end of the grades 9–10 text complexity band independently and proficiently.
		RI.9-10.10	By the end of grade 10, read and comprehend literary nonfiction at the high end of the grades 9–10 text complexity band independently and proficiently.
94–97	How to Read Nonfiction	RI.9-10.1	Cite strong and thorough textual evidence to support analysis of what the text says explicitly as well as inferences drawn from the text.
		RI.9-10.2	Determine a central idea of a text and analyze its development over the course of the text, including how it emerges and is shaped and refined by specific details; provide an objective summary of the text.
		RI.9-10.6	Determine an author's point of view or purpose in a text and analyze how an author uses rhetoric to advance that point of view or purpose.
		SL.9-10.1	Initiate and participate effectively in a range of collaborative discussions (one-on-one, in groups, and teacher-led) with diverse partners on grades 9–10 topics, texts, and issues, building on others' ideas and expressing their own clearly and persuasively.
		L.9-10.6	Acquire and use accurately general academic and domain-specific words and phrases, sufficient for reading, writing, speaking, and listening at the college and career readiness level; demonstrate independence in gathering vocabulary knowledge when considering a word or phrase important to comprehension or expression.

Cluster 1

SE Pages	Lesson	Code	Standards Text
98	Prepare to Read	RI.9-10.4	Determine the meaning of words and phrases as they are used in a text, including figurative, connotative, and technical meanings; analyze the cumulative impact of specific word choices on meaning and tone.
		SL.9-10.1	Initiate and participate effectively in a range of collaborative discussions (one-on-one, in groups, and teacher-led) with diverse partners on grades 9–10 topics, texts, and issues, building on others' ideas and expressing their own clearly and persuasively.
		L.9-10.6	Acquire and use accurately general academic and domain-specific words and phrases, sufficient for reading, writing, speaking, and listening at the college and career readiness level; demonstrate independence in gathering vocabulary knowledge when considering a word or phrase important to comprehension or expression.

SE Pages	Lesson	Code	Standards Text
99	Before Reading: Genes: All in the Family	RI.9-10.1	Cite strong and thorough textual evidence to support analysis of what the text says explicitly as well as inferences drawn from the text.
		RI.9-10.6	Determine an author's point of view or purpose in a text and analyze how an author uses rhetoric to advance that point of view or purpose.
100–109	Read Genes: All in the Family	RI.9-10.1	Cite strong and thorough textual evidence to support analysis of what the text says explicitly as well as inferences drawn from the text.
		RI.9-10.2	Determine a theme or central idea of a text and analyze in detail its development over the course of the text, including how it emerges and is shaped and refined by specific details; provide an objective summary of the text.
		RI.9-10.4	Determine the meaning of words and phrases as they are used in the text, including figurative and connotative meanings; analyze the cumulative impact of specific word choices on meaning and tone.
		RI.9-10.6	Determine an author's point of view or purpose in a text and analyze how an author uses rhetoric to advance that point of view or purpose.
		RI.9-10.7	Analyze various accounts of a subject told in different mediums, determining which details are emphasized in each account.
		RI.9-10.10	By the end of grade 10, read and comprehend literature, including stories, dramas, and poems, at the high end of the grades 9–10 text complexity band independently and proficiently.
		W.9-10.9.b	Apply grades 9–10 Reading standards to literary nonfiction.
		W.9-10.10	Write routinely over extended time frames (time for research, reflection, and revision) and shorter time frames (a single sitting or a day or two) for a range of tasks, purposes, and audiences.
		L.9-10.1	Demonstrate command of the conventions of standard English grammar and usage when writing or speaking.
		L.9-10.4	Determine or clarify the meaning of unknown and multiple-meaning words and phrases based on grades 9-10 reading and content, choosing flexibly from a range of strategies.
		L.9-10.6	Acquire and use accurately general academic and domain-specific words and phrases, sufficient for reading, writing, speaking, and listening at the college and career readiness level; demonstrate independence in gathering vocabulary knowledge when considering a word or phrase important to comprehension or expression.
110	Before Reading: How to See DNA	RI.9-10.1	Cite strong and thorough textual evidence to support analysis of what the text says explicitly as well as inferences drawn from the text.
		RI.9-10.6	Determine an author's point of view or purpose in a text and analyze how an author uses rhetoric to advance that point of view or purpose.
111–114	Read How to See DNA	RI.9-10.1	Cite strong and thorough textual evidence to support analysis of what the text says explicitly as well as inferences drawn from the text.
		RI.9-10.2	Determine a central idea of a text and analyze its development over the course of the text, including how it emerges and is shaped and refined by specific details; provide an objective summary of the text.

Common Core State Standards, continued

SE Pages	Lesson	Code	Standards Text
111–114	**Read How to See DNA** continued	RI.9-10.6	Determine an author's point of view or purpose in a text and analyze how an author uses rhetoric to advance that point of view or purpose.
		RI.9-10.10	By the end of grade 10, read and comprehend literature, including stories, dramas, and poems, at the high end of the grades 9–10 text complexity band independently and proficiently.
		W.9-10.9.b	Apply grades 9–10 Reading standards to literary nonfiction.
		W.9-10.10	Write routinely over extended time frames (time for research, reflection, and revision) and shorter time frames (a single sitting or a day or two) for a range of tasks, purposes, and audiences.
		L.9-10.1	Demonstrate command of the conventions of standard English grammar and usage when writing or speaking.
		L.9-10.6	Acquire and use accurately general academic and domain-specific words and phrases, sufficient for reading, writing, speaking, and listening at the college and career readiness level; demonstrate independence in gathering vocabulary knowledge when considering a word or phrase important to comprehension or expression.
115	**Reflect and Assess** **Critical Thinking**	RI.9-10.1	Cite strong and thorough textual evidence to support analysis of what the text says explicitly as well as inferences drawn from the text.
	Write About Literature	RI.9-10.1	Cite strong and thorough textual evidence to support analysis of what the text says explicitly as well as inferences drawn from the text.
		W.9-10.1	Write arguments to support claims in an analysis of substantive topics or texts, using valid reasoning and relevant and sufficient evidence.
	Key Vocabulary Review	L.9-10.6	Acquire and use accurately general academic and domain-specific words and phrases, sufficient for reading, writing, speaking, and listening at the college and career readiness level; demonstrate independence in gathering vocabulary knowledge when considering a word or phrase important to comprehension or expression.
	Read with Ease: Phrasing	RI.9-10.10	By the end of grade 10, read and comprehend literary nonfiction at the high end of the grades 9–10 text complexity band independently and proficiently.
116	**Grammar:** **Use Subject Pronouns**	L.9-10.1	Demonstrate command of the conventions of standard English grammar and usage when writing or speaking.
116	**Research/Writing:** **Poster**	W.9-10.7	Conduct short as well as more sustained research projects to answer a question (including a self-generated question) or solve a problem; narrow or broaden the inquiry when appropriate; synthesize multiple sources on the subject, demonstrating understanding of the subject under investigation.
116	**Language Development:** **Express Likes and Dislikes**	SL.9-10.1	Initiate and participate effectively in a range of collaborative discussions (one-on-one, in groups, and teacher-led) with diverse partners on grades 9–10 topics, texts, and issues, building on others' ideas and expressing their own clearly and persuasively.
117	**Vocabulary Study:** **Context Clues**	L.9-10.4.a	Use context as a clue to the meaning of a word or phrase.
117	**Literary Analysis:** **Summarize**	RI.9-10.2	Determine a theme or central idea of a text and analyze in detail its development over the course of the text, including how it emerges and is shaped and refined by specific details; provide an objective summary of the text.

Cluster 1, continued

SE Pages	Lesson	Code	Standards Text
117	**Writing on Demand: Write and Expository Paragraph**	W.9-10.2	Write informative/explanatory texts to examine and convey complex ideas, concepts, and information clearly and accurately through the effective selection, organization, and analysis of content.
117	**Workplace Workshop: Inside a Medical Laboratory**	W.9-10.7	Conduct short as well as more sustained research projects to answer a question (including a self-generated question) or solve a problem; narrow or broaden the inquiry when appropriate; synthesize multiple sources on the subject, demonstrating understanding of the subject under investigation.
		W.9-10.10	Write routinely over extended time frames (time for research, reflection, and revision) and shorter time frames (a single sitting or a day or two) for a range of tasks, purposes, and audiences.
		L.9-10.6	Acquire and use accurately general academic and domain-specific words and phrases, sufficient for reading, writing, speaking, and listening at the college and career readiness level; demonstrate independence in gathering vocabulary knowledge when considering a word or phrase important to comprehension or expression.
119	**Vocabulary Workshop: Use Context Clues**	L.9-10.4.a	Use context as a clue to the meaning of a word or phrase.
		L.9-10.4.c	Consult general and specialized reference materials, both print and digital, to find the pronunciation of a word or determine or clarify its precise meaning, its part of speech, or its etymology.
		L.9-10.4.d	Verify the preliminary determination of the meaning of a word or phrase.

Cluster 2

SE Pages	Lesson	Code	Standards Text
120	**Prepare to Read**	RI.9-10.4	Determine the meaning of words and phrases as they are used in a text, including figurative, connotative, and technical meanings; analyze the cumulative impact of specific word choices on meaning and tone.
		SL.9-10.1	Initiate and participate effectively in a range of collaborative discussions (one-on-one, in groups, and teacher-led) with diverse partners on grades 9–10 topics, texts, and issues, building on others' ideas and expressing their own clearly and persuasively.
		L.9-10.6	Acquire and use accurately general academic and domain-specific words and phrases, sufficient for reading, writing, speaking, and listening at the college and career readiness level; demonstrate independence in gathering vocabulary knowledge when considering a word or phrase important to comprehension or expression.
121	**Before Reading: Do Family Meals Matter?**	RI.9-10.1	Cite strong and thorough textual evidence to support analysis of what the text says explicitly as well as inferences drawn from the text.
		RI.9-10.6	Determine an author's point of view or purpose in a text and analyze how an author uses rhetoric to advance that point of view or purpose.
122–129	**Read Do Family Meals Matter?**	RI.9-10.1	Cite strong and thorough textual evidence to support analysis of what the text says explicitly as well as inferences drawn from the text.
		RI.9-10.2	Determine a central idea of a text and analyze its development over the course of the text, including how it emerges and is shaped and refined by specific details; provide an objective summary of the text.

Common Core State Standards, continued

Cluster 2, continued

SE Pages	Lesson	Code	Standards Text
122–129	**Read Do Family Meals Matter?** continued	RI.9-10.4	Determine the meaning of words and phrases as they are used in a text, including figurative, connotative, and technical meanings; analyze the cumulative impact of specific word choices on meaning and tone.
		RI.9-10.6	Determine an author's point of view or purpose in a text and analyze how an author uses rhetoric to advance that point of view or purpose.
		RI.9-10.7	Analyze various accounts of a subject told in different mediums, determining which details are emphasized in each account.
		RI.9-10.10	By the end of grade 10, read and comprehend literary nonfiction at the high end of the grades 9–10 text complexity band independently and proficiently.
		W.9-10.9.b	Apply grades 9–10 Reading standards to literary nonfiction.
		W.9-10.10	Write routinely over extended time frames (time for research, reflection, and revision) and shorter time frames (a single sitting or a day or two) for a range of tasks, purposes, and audiences.
		L.9-10.1	Demonstrate command of the conventions of standard English grammar and usage when writing or speaking.
		L.9-10.2.c	Spell correctly.
		L.9-10.6	Acquire and use accurately general academic and domain-specific words and phrases, sufficient for reading, writing, speaking, and listening at the college and career readiness level; demonstrate independence in gathering vocabulary knowledge when considering a word or phrase important to comprehension or expression.
130	**Before Reading: Fish Cheeks**	RI.9-10.1	Cite strong and thorough textual evidence to support analysis of what the text says explicitly as well as inferences drawn from the text.
		RI.9-10.6	Determine an author's point of view or purpose in a text and analyze how an author uses rhetoric to advance that point of view or purpose.
131–134	**Read Fish Cheeks**	RI.9-10.1	Cite strong and thorough textual evidence to support analysis of what the text says explicitly as well as inferences drawn from the text.
		RI.9-10.2	Determine a central idea of a text and analyze its development over the course of the text, including how it emerges and is shaped and refined by specific details; provide an objective summary of the text.
		RI.9-10.4	Determine the meaning of words and phrases as they are used in a text, including figurative, connotative, and technical meanings; analyze the cumulative impact of specific word choices on meaning and tone.
		RI.9-10.6	Determine an author's point of view or purpose in a text and analyze how an author uses rhetoric to advance that point of view or purpose.
		RI.9-10.10	By the end of grade 10, read and comprehend literary nonfiction at the high end of the grades 9–10 text complexity band independently and proficiently.
		W.9-10.9.b	Apply grades 9–10 Reading standards to literary nonfiction.
		W.9-10.10	Write routinely over extended time frames (time for research, reflection, and revision) and shorter time frames (a single sitting or a day or two) for a range of tasks, purposes, and audiences.

SE Pages	Lesson	Code	Standards Text
131–134	**Read Fish Cheeks** continued	L.9-10.1.b	Use various types of phrases (noun, verb, adjectival, adverbial, participial, prepositional, absolute) and clauses (independent, dependent; noun, relative, adverbial) to convey specific meanings and add variety and interest to writing or presentations.
		L.9-10.6	Acquire and use accurately general academic and domain-specific words and phrases, sufficient for reading, writing, speaking, and listening at the college and career readiness level; demonstrate independence in gathering vocabulary knowledge when considering a word or phrase important to comprehension or expression.
135	**Reflect and Assess Critical Thinking**	RI.9-10.1	Cite strong and thorough textual evidence to support analysis of what the text says explicitly as well as inferences drawn from the text.
	Write About Literature	W.9-10.1	Write arguments to support claims in an analysis of substantive topics or texts, using valid reasoning and relevant and sufficient evidence.
	Key Vocabulary Review	L.9-10.6	Acquire and use accurately general academic and domain-specific words and phrases, sufficient for reading, writing, speaking, and listening at the college and career readiness level; demonstrate independence in gathering vocabulary knowledge when considering a word or phrase important to comprehension or expression.
	Read with Ease: Intonation	RI.9-10.10	By the end of grade 10, read and comprehend literary nonfiction at the high end of the grades 9–10 text complexity band independently and proficiently.
136	**Grammar: Use Action Verbs in the Present**	L.9-10.1.b	Use various types of phrases (noun, verb, adjectival, adverbial, participial, prepositional, absolute) and clauses (independent, dependent; noun, relative, adverbial) to convey specific meanings and add variety and interest to writing or presentations.
136	**Language Development: Express Ideas and Feelings**	SL.9-10.1	Initiate and participate effectively in a range of collaborative discussions (one-on-one, in groups, and teacher-led) with diverse partners on grades 9–10 topics, texts, and issues, building on others' ideas and expressing their own clearly and persuasively.
137	**Literary Analysis: Analyze Descriptive Language**	RI.9-10.4	Determine the meaning of words and phrases as they are used in a text, including figurative, connotative, and technical meanings; analyze the cumulative impact of specific word choices on meaning and tone.
137	**Vocabulary Study: Context Clues**	L.9-10.4.a	Use context as a clue to the meaning of a word or phrase.
137	**Research/Speaking: Oral Report**	W.9-10.7	Conduct short as well as more sustained research projects to answer a question (including a self-generated question) or solve a problem; narrow or broaden the inquiry when appropriate; synthesize multiple sources on the subject, demonstrating understanding of the subject under investigation.
		SL.9-10.4	Present information, findings, and supporting evidence clearly, concisely, and logically such that listeners can follow the line of reasoning and the organization, development, substance, and style are appropriate to purpose, audience, and task.
137	**Writing: Write a Biographical Sketch**	W.9-10.2	Write informative/explanatory texts to examine and convey complex ideas, concepts, and information clearly and accurately through the effective selection, organization, and analysis of content.
		W.9-10.5	Develop and strengthen writing as needed by planning, revising, editing, rewriting, or trying a new approach, focusing on addressing what is most significant for a specific purpose and audience.

Common Core State Standards, continued

Cluster 2, continued

SE Pages	Lesson	Code	Standards Text
138–139	Listening and Speaking Workshop: Interview	SL.9-10.1.c	Propel conversations by posing and responding to questions that relate the current discussion to broader themes or larger ideas; actively incorporate others into the discussion; and clarify, verify, or challenge ideas and conclusions.
		L.9-10.3	Apply knowledge of language to understand how language functions in different contexts, to make effective choices for meaning or style, and to comprehend more fully when reading or listening.

Cluster 3

SE Pages	Lesson	Code	Standards Text
140	Prepare to Read	RI.9-10.4	Determine the meaning of words and phrases as they are used in a text, including figurative, connotative, and technical meanings; analyze the cumulative impact of specific word choices on meaning and tone.
		SL.9-10.1	Initiate and participate effectively in a range of collaborative discussions (one-on-one, in groups, and teacher-led) with diverse partners on grades 9–10 topics, texts, and issues, building on others' ideas and expressing their own clearly and persuasively.
		L.9-10.4.c	Consult general and specialized reference materials, both print and digital, to find the pronunciation of a word or determine or clarify its precise meaning, its part of speech, or its etymology.
		L.9-10.6	Acquire and use accurately general academic and domain-specific words and phrases, sufficient for reading, writing, speaking, and listening at the college and career readiness level; demonstrate independence in gathering vocabulary knowledge when considering a word or phrase important to comprehension or expression.
141	Before Reading: Only Daughter	RI.9-10.1	Cite strong and thorough textual evidence to support analysis of what the text says explicitly as well as inferences drawn from the text.
		RI.9-10.6	Determine an author's point of view or purpose in a text and analyze how an author uses rhetoric to advance that point of view or purpose.
142–151	Read Only Daughter	RI.9-10.1	Cite strong and thorough textual evidence to support analysis of what the text says explicitly as well as inferences drawn from the text.
		RI.9-10.2	Determine a central idea of a text and analyze its development over the course of the text, including how it emerges and is shaped and refined by specific details; provide an objective summary of the text.
		RI.9-10.6	Determine an author's point of view or purpose in a text and analyze how an author uses rhetoric to advance that point of view or purpose.
		RI.9-10.10	By the end of grade 10, read and comprehend literary nonfiction at the high end of the grades 9–10 text complexity band independently and proficiently.
		W.9-10.9.b	Apply grades 9–10 Reading standards to literary nonfiction.
		W.9-10.10	Write routinely over extended time frames (time for research, reflection, and revision) and shorter time frames (a single sitting or a day or two) for a range of tasks, purposes, and audiences.
		L.9-10.1.b	Use various types of phrases (noun, verb, adjectival, adverbial, participial, prepositional, absolute) and clauses (independent, dependent; noun, relative, adverbial) to convey specific meanings and add variety and interest to writing or presentations.

Cluster 3, continued

SE Pages	Lesson	Code	Standards Text
142–151	**Read Only Daughter** continued	L.9-10.6	Acquire and use accurately general academic and domain-specific words and phrases, sufficient for reading, writing, speaking, and listening at the college and career readiness level; demonstrate independence in gathering vocabulary knowledge when considering a word or phrase important to comprehension or expression.
152	**Before Reading: Calling a Foul**	RI.9-10.1	Cite strong and thorough textual evidence to support analysis of what the text says explicitly as well as inferences drawn from the text.
		RI.9-10.6	Determine an author's point of view or purpose in a text and analyze how an author uses rhetoric to advance that point of view or purpose.
153–155	**Read Calling a Foul**	RI.9-10.1	Cite strong and thorough textual evidence to support analysis of what the text says explicitly as well as inferences drawn from the text.
		RI.9-10.2	Determine a central idea of a text and analyze its development over the course of the text, including how it emerges and is shaped and refined by specific details; provide an objective summary of the text.
		RI.9-10.6	Determine an author's point of view or purpose in a text and analyze how an author uses rhetoric to advance that point of view or purpose.
		RI.9-10.10	By the end of grade 10, read and comprehend literary nonfiction at the high end of the grades 9–10 text complexity band independently and proficiently.
		W.9-10.9.b	Apply grades 9–10 Reading standards to literary nonfiction.
		W.9-10.10	Write routinely over extended time frames (time for research, reflection, and revision) and shorter time frames (a single sitting or a day or two) for a range of tasks, purposes, and audiences.
		L.9-10.1.b	Use various types of phrases (noun, verb, adjectival, adverbial, participial, prepositional, absolute) and clauses (independent, dependent; noun, relative, adverbial) to convey specific meanings and add variety and interest to writing or presentations.
		L.9-10.6	Acquire and use accurately general academic and domain-specific words and phrases, sufficient for reading, writing, speaking, and listening at the college and career readiness level; demonstrate independence in gathering vocabulary knowledge when considering a word or phrase important to comprehension or expression.
156	**Postscript: Calling a Foul**	RI.9-10.1	Cite strong and thorough textual evidence to support analysis of what the text says explicitly as well as inferences drawn from the text.
		RI.9-10.7	Analyze various accounts of a subject told in different mediums, determining which details are emphasized in each account.
		SL.9-10.1	Initiate and participate effectively in a range of collaborative discussions (one-on-one, in groups, and teacher-led) with diverse partners on grades 9–10 topics, texts, and issues, building on others' ideas and expressing their own clearly and persuasively.
157	**Reflect and Assess Critical Thinking**	RI.9-10.1	Cite strong and thorough textual evidence to support analysis of what the text says explicitly as well as inferences drawn from the text.
	Write About Literature	W.9-10.1	Write arguments to support claims in an analysis of substantive topics or texts, using valid reasoning and relevant and sufficient evidence.

Common Core State Standards, continued

Cluster 3, continued

SE Pages	Lesson	Code	Standards Text
157	Reflect and Assess continued Key Vocabulary Review	L.9-10.6	Acquire and use accurately general academic and domain-specific words and phrases, sufficient for reading, writing, speaking, and listening at the college and career readiness level; demonstrate independence in gathering vocabulary knowledge when considering a word or phrase important to comprehension or expression.
	Read with Ease: Expression	RI.9-10.10	By the end of grade 10, read and comprehend literary nonfiction at the high end of the grades 9–10 text complexity band independently and proficiently.
158	Grammar: Use Verbs to Talk About the Present	L.9-10.1.b	Use various types of phrases (noun, verb, adjectival, adverbial, participial, prepositional, absolute) and clauses (independent, dependent; noun, relative, adverbial) to convey specific meanings and add variety and interest to writing or presentations.
158	Language Development: Express Needs and Intentions	SL.9-10.1	Initiate and participate effectively in a range of collaborative discussions (one-on-one, in groups, and teacher-led) with diverse partners on grades 9–10 topics, texts, and issues, building on others' ideas and expressing their own clearly and persuasively.
158	Literary Analysis: Analyze Style	RI.9-10.4	Determine the meaning of words and phrases as they are used in a text, including figurative, connotative, and technical meanings; analyze the cumulative impact of specific word choices on meaning and tone.
159	Vocabulary Study: Context Clues	L.9-10.4.a	Use context as a clue to the meaning of a word or phrase.
159	Research/Writing: Flier	W.9-10.7	Conduct short as well as more sustained research projects to answer a question (including a self-generated question) or solve a problem; narrow or broaden the inquiry when appropriate; synthesize multiple sources on the subject, demonstrating understanding of the subject under investigation.
159	Writing Trait: Trait: Development of Ideas	W.9-10.3	Write narratives to develop real or imagined experiences or events using effective technique, well-chosen details, and well-structured event sequences.
		W.9-10.4	Produce clear and coherent writing in which the development, organization, and style are appropriate to task, purpose, and audience.

Close Reading

SE Pages	Lesson	Code	Standards Text
160–163	Read The Color of Water	RI.9-10.10	By the end of grade 10, read and comprehend literary nonfiction at the high end of the grades 9–10 text complexity band independently and proficiently.

Unit Wrap-Up

SE Pages	Lesson	Code	Standards Text
164	Unit Wrap-Up Present Your Project	SL.9-10.2	Integrate multiple sources of information presented in diverse media or formats evaluating the credibility and accuracy of each source.
		SL.9-10.5	Make strategic use of digital media in presentations to enhance understanding of findings, reasoning, and evidence and to add interest.
	Reflect on Your Reading	SL.9-10.1.a	Come to discussions prepared, having read and researched material under study; explicitly draw on that preparation by referring to evidence from texts and other research on the topic or issue to stimulate a thoughtful, well-reasoned exchange of ideas.
	Respond to the Essential Question	SL.9-10.1.a	Come to discussions prepared, having read and researched material under study; explicitly draw on that preparation by referring to evidence from texts and other research on the topic or issue to stimulate a thoughtful, well-reasoned exchange of ideas.

Unit 2 Writing Project: News Article

SE Pages	Lesson	Code	Standards Text
166–169	Study News Articles and Prewrite	W.9-10.2.a	Introduce a topic; organize complex ideas, concepts, and information to make important connections and distinctions; include formatting, graphics, and multimedia when useful to aiding comprehension.
		W.9-10.2.b	Develop the topic with well-chosen, relevant, and sufficient facts, extended definitions, concrete details, quotations, or other information and examples appropriate to the audience's knowledge of the topic.
		W.9-10.5	Develop and strengthen writing as needed by planning, revising, editing, rewriting, or trying a new approach, focusing on addressing what is most significant for a specific purpose and audience.
170–171	News Article: Draft	W.9-10.2	Write informative/explanatory texts to examine and convey complex ideas, concepts, and information clearly and accurately through the effective selection, organization, and analysis of content.
		W.9-10.2.a	Introduce a topic; organize complex ideas, concepts, and information to make important connections and distinctions; include formatting, graphics, and multimedia when useful to aiding comprehension.
		W.9-10.4	Produce clear and coherent writing in which the development, organization, and style are appropriate to task, purpose, and audience.
172–175	News Article: Revise Trait: Development of Ideas	W.9-10.2	Write informative/explanatory texts to examine and convey complex ideas, concepts, and information clearly and accurately through the effective selection, organization, and analysis of content.
		W.9-10.2.a	Introduce a topic; organize complex ideas, concepts, and information to make important connections and distinctions; include formatting, graphics, and multimedia when useful to aiding comprehension.
		W.9-10.2.b	Develop the topic with well-chosen, relevant, and sufficient facts, extended definitions, concrete details, quotations, or other information and examples appropriate to the audience's knowledge of the topic.
		W.9-10.2.c	Use appropriate and varied transitions to link the major sections of the text, create cohesion, and clarify the relationships among complex ideas and concepts.
		W.9-10.2.d	Use precise language and domain-specific vocabulary to manage the complexity of the topic.
		W.9-10.2.e	Establish and maintain a formal style and objective tone while attending to the norms and conventions of the discipline in which they are writing.
		W.9-10.5	Develop and strengthen writing as needed by planning, revising, editing, rewriting, or trying a new approach, focusing on addressing what is most significant for a specific purpose and audience.
		SL.9-10.1	Initiate and participate effectively in a range of collaborative discussions (one-on-one, in groups, and teacher-led) with diverse partners on grades 9–10 topics, texts, and issues, building on others' ideas and expressing their own clearly and persuasively.
		SL.9-10.1.d	Respond thoughtfully to diverse perspectives, summarize points of agreement and disagreement, and, when warranted, qualify or justify their own views and understanding and make new connections in light of the evidence and reasoning presented.

Common Core State Standards, continued

Unit 2 Writing Project: News Article, continued

SE Pages	Lesson	Code	Standards Text
176–178	News Article: Edit and Proofread	L.9-10.1	Demonstrate command of the conventions of standard English grammar and usage when writing or speaking.
Capitalization: Names of Groups		L.9-10.2	Demonstrate command of the conventions of standard English capitalization, punctuation, and spelling when writing.
Semicolons		L.9-10.2.a	Use a semicolon (and perhaps a conjunctive adverb) to link two or more closely related independent clauses.
Spelling Subject Pronouns		L.9-10.2.c	Spell correctly.
		L.9-10.3.a	Write and edit work so that it conforms to the guidelines in a style manual appropriate for the discipline and writing type.
179	News Article: Publish and Present	W.9-10.2.a	Introduce a topic; organize complex ideas, concepts, and information to make important connections and distinctions; include formatting, graphics, and multimedia when useful to aiding comprehension.
		W.9-10.6	Use technology, including the Internet, to produce, publish, and update individual or shared writing products, taking advantage of technology's capacity to link to other information and to display information flexibly and dynamically.
		W.9-10.8	Gather relevant information from multiple authoritative print and digital sources, using advanced searches effectively; assess the usefulness of each source in answering the research question; integrate information into the text selectively to maintain the flow of ideas, avoiding plagiarism and following a standard format for citation.
		SL.9-10.1	Initiate and participate effectively in a range of collaborative discussions (one-on-one, in groups, and teacher-led) with diverse partners on grades 9–10 topics, texts, and issues, building on others' ideas and expressing their own clearly and persuasively.

UNIT 3: True Self

SE Pages	Lesson	Code	Standards Text
180–181	Discuss the Essential Question	SL.9-10.1.b	Work with peers to set rules for collegial discussions and decision-making, clear goals and deadlines, and individual roles as needed.
		SL.9-10.3	Evaluate a speaker's point of view, reasoning, and use of evidence and rhetoric, identifying any fallacious reasoning or exaggerated or distorted evidence.
182	Analyze and Debate	SL.9-10.4	Present information, findings, and supporting evidence clearly, concisely, and logically such that listeners can follow the line of reasoning and the organization, development, substance, and style are appropriate to purpose, audience, and task.
183	Plan a Project	SL.9-10.1.b	Work with peers to set rules for collegial discussions and decision-making, clear goals and deadlines, and individual roles as needed.
183	Choose More to Read	RL.9-10.10	By the end of grade 10, read and comprehend literature, including stories, dramas, and poems, at the high end of the grades 9–10 text complexity band independently and proficiently.
		RI.9-10.10	By the end of grade 10, read and comprehend literary nonfiction at the high end of the grades 9–10 text complexity band independently and proficiently.
184–187	How to Read Short Stories	RL.9-10.1	Cite strong and thorough textual evidence to support analysis of what the text says explicitly as well as inferences drawn from the text.

UNIT 3: True Self, continued

SE Pages	Lesson	Code	Standards Text
184–187	**How to Read Short Stories** continued	RL.9-10.4	Determine the meaning of words and phrases as they are used in the text, including figurative and connotative meanings; analyze the cumulative impact of specific word choices on meaning and tone.
		SL.9-10.3	Evaluate a speaker's point of view, reasoning, and use of evidence and rhetoric, identifying any fallacious reasoning or exaggerated or distorted evidence.
Cluster 1			
188	**Prepare to Read**	RI.9-10.4	Determine the meaning of words and phrases as they are used in a text, including figurative, connotative, and technical meanings; analyze the cumulative impact of specific word choices on meaning and tone.
		SL.9-10.1	Initiate and participate effectively in a range of collaborative discussions with diverse partners on grades 9–10 topics, texts, and issues, building on others' ideas and expressing their own clearly and persuasively.
		L.9-10.4.c	Consult general and specialized reference materials, both print and digital, to find the pronunciation of a word or determine or clarify its precise meaning, its part of speech, or its etymology.
		L.9-10.6	Acquire and use accurately general academic and domain-specific words and phrases, sufficient for reading, writing, speaking, and listening at the college and career readiness level; demonstrate independence in gathering vocabulary knowledge when considering a word or phrase important to comprehension or expression
189	**Before Reading: Heartbeat**	RL.9-10.1	Cite strong and thorough textual evidence to support analysis of what the text says explicitly as well as inferences drawn from the text.
		CCRA.R.6	Assess how point of view or purpose shapes the content and style of a text.
190–199	**Read Heartbeat**	RL.9-10.1	Cite strong and thorough textual evidence to support analysis of what the text says explicitly as well as inferences drawn from the text.
		RL.9-10.2	Determine a theme or central idea of a text and analyze in detail its development over the course of the text, including how it emerges and is shaped and refined by specific details; provide an objective summary of the text.
		RL.9-10.4	Determine the meaning of words and phrases as they are used in the text, including figurative and connotative meanings; analyze the cumulative impact of specific word choices on meaning and tone.
		RL.9-10.10	By the end of grade 10, read and comprehend literature, including stories, dramas, and poems, at the high end of the grades 9–10 text complexity band independently and proficiently.
		W.9-10.9.a	Apply grades 9–10 Reading standards to literature.
		W.9-10.10	Write routinely over extended time frames (time for research, reflection, and revision) and shorter time frames (a single sitting or a day or two) for a range of tasks, purposes, and audiences.
		L.9-10.1.a	Use parallel structure.
		L.9-10.2.c	Spell correctly.

Common Core State Standards, continued

Cluster 1, continued

SE Pages	Lesson	Code	Standards Text
190–199	**Read Heartbeat** continued	L.9-10.6	Acquire and use accurately general academic and domain-specific words and phrases, sufficient for reading, writing, speaking, and listening at the college and career readiness level; demonstrate independence in gathering vocabulary knowledge when considering a word or phrase important to comprehension or expression.
		CCRA.R.6	Assess how point of view or purpose shapes the content and style of a text.
200	**Before Reading: Behind the Bulk**	RL.9-10.1	Cite strong and thorough textual evidence to support analysis of what the text says explicitly as well as inferences drawn from the text.
		CCRA.R.6	Assess how point of view or purpose shapes the content and style of a text.
201–204	**Read Behind the Bulk**	RI.9-10.1	Cite strong and thorough textual evidence to support analysis of what the text says explicitly as well as inferences drawn from the text.
		RI.9-10.2	Determine a theme or central idea of a text and analyze in detail its development over the course of the text, including how it emerges and is shaped and refined by specific details; provide an objective summary of the text.
		RI.9-10.4	Determine the meaning of words and phrases as they are used in the text, including figurative and connotative meanings; analyze the cumulative impact of specific word choices on meaning and tone.
		RI.9-10.7	Analyze various accounts of a subject told in different mediums, determining which details are emphasized in each account.
		RI.9-10.10	By the end of grade 10, read and comprehend literature, including stories, dramas, and poems, at the high end of the grades 9–10 text complexity band independently and proficiently.
		W.9-10.9.b	Apply grades 9–10 Reading standards to literary nonfiction.
		W.9-10.10	Write routinely over extended time frames (time for research, reflection, and revision) and shorter time frames (a single sitting or a day or two) for a range of tasks, purposes, and audiences.
		L.9-10.1	Demonstrate command of the conventions of standard English grammar and usage when writing or speaking.
		L.9-10.6	Acquire and use accurately general academic and domain-specific words and phrases, sufficient for reading, writing, speaking, and listening at the college and career readiness level; demonstrate independence in gathering vocabulary knowledge when considering a word or phrase important to comprehension or expression.
		CCRA.R.6	Assess how point of view or purpose shapes the content and style of a text.
205	**Reflect and Assess Critical Thinking**	RL.9-10.1	Cite strong and thorough textual evidence to support analysis of what the text says explicitly as well as inferences drawn from the text.
		RI.9-10.1	Cite strong and thorough textual evidence to support analysis of what the text says explicitly as well as inferences drawn from the text.
	Write About Literature	W.9-10.2	Write informative/explanatory texts to examine and convey complex ideas, concepts, and information clearly and accurately through the effective selection, organization, and analysis of content.

Cluster 1, continued

SE Pages	Lesson	Code	Standards Text
205	**Reflect and Assess Critical Thinking** continued **Key Vocabulary Review**	L.9-10.6	Acquire and use accurately general academic and domain-specific words and phrases, sufficient for reading, writing, speaking, and listening at the college and career readiness level; demonstrate independence in gathering vocabulary knowledge when considering a word or phrase important to comprehension or expression.
	Read with Ease: Intonation	RL.9-10.10	By the end of grade 10, read and comprehend literature, including stories, dramas, and poems, at the high end of the grades 9–10 text complexity band independently and proficiently.
206	**Grammar: Use Verb Tenses**	L.9-10.1.a	Use parallel structure.
206	**Literary Analysis: Analyze Point of View**	CCRA.R.6	Assess how point of view or purpose shapes the content and style of a text.
206	**Language Development: Give and Respond to Commands**	SL.9-10.1	Initiate and participate effectively in a range of collaborative discussions (one-on-one, in groups, and teacher-led) with diverse partners on grades 9–10 topics, texts, and issues, building on others' ideas and expressing their own clearly and persuasively.
207	**Vocabulary Study: Word Families**	L.9-10.4.b	Identify and correctly use patterns of word changes that indicate different meanings or parts of speech.
		L.9-10.4.d	Verify the preliminary determination of the meaning of a word or phrase.
207	**Listening/Speaking: Critique**	SL.9-10.1.a	Come to discussions prepared, having read and researched material under study; explicitly draw on that preparation by referring to evidence from texts and other research on the topic or issue to stimulate a thoughtful, well-reasoned exchange of ideas.
207	**Writing Trait: Trait: Organization**	W.9-10.1	Write arguments to support claims in an analysis of substantive topics or texts, using valid reasoning and relevant and sufficient evidence.
208	**Workplace Workshop: Inside a Health Club**	W.9-10.7	Conduct short as well as more sustained research projects to answer a question (including a self-generated question) or solve a problem; narrow or broaden the inquiry when appropriate; synthesize multiple sources on the subject, demonstrating understanding of the subject under investigation.
		W.9-10.10	Write routinely over extended time frames (time for research, reflection, and revision) and shorter time frames (a single sitting or a day or two) for a range of tasks, purposes, and audiences.
		L.9-10.6	Acquire and use accurately general academic and domain-specific words and phrases, sufficient for reading, writing, speaking, and listening at the college and career readiness level; demonstrate independence in gathering vocabulary knowledge when considering a word or phrase important to comprehension or expression.
209	**Vocabulary Workshop: Use What You Know**	L.9-10.4.b	Identify and correctly use patterns of word changes that indicate different meanings or parts of speech.
		L.9-10.4.d	Verify the preliminary determination of the meaning of a word or phrase.

Cluster 2

SE Pages	Lesson	Code	Standards Text
210	**Prepare to Read**	RI.9-10.4	Determine the meaning of words and phrases as they are used in a text, including figurative, connotative, and technical meanings; analyze the cumulative impact of specific word choices on meaning and tone.

Common Core State Standards, continued

SE Pages	Lesson	Code	Standards Text
210	Prepare to Read continued	SL.9-10.1	Initiate and participate effectively in a range of collaborative discussions (one-on-one, in groups, and teacher-led) with diverse partners on grades 9–10 topics, texts, and issues, building on others' ideas and expressing their own clearly and persuasively.
		L.9-10.6	Acquire and use accurately general academic and domain-specific words and phrases, sufficient for reading, writing, speaking, and listening at the college and career readiness level; demonstrate independence in gathering vocabulary knowledge when considering a word or phrase important to comprehension or expression.
211	Before Reading: I Go Along	RL.9-10.1	Cite strong and thorough textual evidence to support analysis of what the text says explicitly as well as inferences drawn from the text.
		CCRA.R.6	Assess how point of view or purpose shapes the content and style of a text.
212–224	Read I Go Along	RL.9-10.1	Cite strong and thorough textual evidence to support analysis of what the text says explicitly as well as inferences drawn from the text.
		RL.9-10.3	Analyze how complex characters develop over the course of a text, interact with other characters, and advance the plot or develop the theme.
		RL.9-10.7	Analyze the representation of a subject or a key scene in two different artistic mediums, including what is emphasized or absent in each treatment.
		RL.9-10.10	By the end of grade 10, read and comprehend literature, including stories, dramas, and poems, at the high end of the grades 9–10 text complexity band independently and proficiently.
		W.9-10.9.a	Apply grades 9–10 Reading standards to literature.
		W.9-10.10	Write routinely over extended time frames (time for research, reflection, and revision) and shorter time frames (a single sitting or a day or two) for a range of tasks, purposes, and audiences.
		L.9-10.1.a	Use parallel structure.
		L.9-10.1.b	Use various types of phrases (noun, verb, adjectival, adverbial, participial, prepositional, absolute) and clauses (independent, dependent; noun, relative, adverbial) to convey specific meanings and add variety and interest to writing or presentations.
		L.9-10.2.c	Spell correctly.
		L.9-10.3	Apply knowledge of language to understand how language functions in different contexts, to make effective choices for meaning or style, and to comprehend more fully when reading or listening.
		L.9-10.6	Acquire and use accurately general academic and domain-specific words and phrases, sufficient for reading, writing, speaking, and listening at the college and career readiness level; demonstrate independence in gathering vocabulary knowledge when considering a word or phrase important to comprehension or expression.
		CCRA.R.6	Assess how point of view or purpose shapes the content and style of a text.
225	Before Reading: Theme for English B	RL.9-10.1	Cite strong and thorough textual evidence to support analysis of what the text says explicitly as well as inferences drawn from the text.
		RL.9-10.5	Analyze how an author's choices concerning how to structure a text, order events within it, and manipulate time create such effects as mystery, tension, or surprise.

Cluster 2, continued

SE Pages	Lesson	Code	Standards Text
226–228	Read Theme for English B	RL.9-10.1	Cite strong and thorough textual evidence to support analysis of what the text says explicitly as well as inferences drawn from the text.
		RL.9-10.2	Determine a theme or central idea of a text and analyze in detail its development over the course of the text, including how it emerges and is shaped and refined by specific details; provide an objective summary of the text.
		RL.9-10.5	Analyze how an author's choices concerning how to structure a text, order events within it, and manipulate time create such effects as mystery, tension, or surprise.
		RL.9-10.10	By the end of grade 10, read and comprehend literature, including stories, dramas, and poems, at the high end of the grades 9-10 text complexity band independently and proficiently.
		W.9-10.9.a	Apply grades 9–10 Reading standards to literature.
		W.9-10.10	Write routinely over extended time frames (time for research, reflection, and revision) and shorter time frames (a single sitting or a day or two) for a range of tasks, purposes, and audiences.
		L.9-10.6	Acquire and use accurately general academic and domain-specific words and phrases, sufficient for reading, writing, speaking, and listening at the college and career readiness level; demonstrate independence in gathering vocabulary knowledge when considering a word or phrase important to comprehension or expression.
229	Reflect and Assess Critical Thinking	RL.9-10.1	Cite strong and thorough textual evidence to support analysis of what the text says explicitly as well as inferences drawn from the text.
	Write About Literature	W.9-10.1	Write arguments to support claims in an analysis of substantive topics or texts, using valid reasoning and relevant and sufficient evidence.
	Key Vocabulary Review	L.9-10.6	Acquire and use accurately general academic and domain-specific words and phrases, sufficient for reading, writing, speaking, and listening at the college and career readiness level; demonstrate independence in gathering vocabulary knowledge when considering a word or phrase important to comprehension or expression.
	Read with Ease: Phrasing	RL.9-10.10	By the end of grade 10, read and comprehend literature, including stories, dramas, and poems, at the high end of the grades 9-10 text complexity band independently and proficiently.
230	Grammar: Use Verb Tenses	L.9-10.1.a	Use parallel structure.
		L.9-10.1.b	Use various types of phrases (noun, verb, adjectival, adverbial, participial, prepositional, absolute) and clauses (independent, dependent; noun, relative, adverbial) to convey specific meanings and add variety and interest to writing or presentations.
230	Language Development: Make and Respond to Requests	SL.9-10.1.a	Come to discussions prepared, having read and researched material under study; explicitly draw on that preparation by referring to evidence from texts and other research on the topic or issue to stimulate a thoughtful, well-reasoned exchange of ideas.
230	Literary Analysis: Analyze Style	RL.9-10.4	Determine the meaning of words and phrases as they are used in the text, including figurative and connotative meanings; analyze the cumulative impact of specific word choices on meaning and tone.

Common Core State Standards, continued

Cluster 2, continued

SE Pages	Lesson	Code	Standards Text
231	Vocabulary Study: Latin and Greek Roots	L.9-10.4.d	Verify the preliminary determination of the meaning of a word or phrase.
231	Writing: Write a Comparison/Contrast Piece	SL.9-10.4	Present information, findings, and supporting evidence clearly, concisely, and logically such that listeners can follow the line of reasoning and the organization, development, substance, and style are appropriate to purpose, audience, and task.
231	Listening/Speaking: Evaluation	W.9-10.2	Write informative/explanatory texts to examine and convey complex ideas, concepts, and information clearly and accurately through the effective selection, organization, and analysis of content.
		W.9-10.5	Develop and strengthen writing as needed by planning, revising, editing, rewriting, or trying a new approach, focusing on addressing what is most significant for a specific purpose and audience.
232–233	Listening and Speaking Workshop: Retell a Story	SL.9-10.6	Adapt speech to a variety of contexts and tasks, demonstrating command of formal English when indicated or appropriate.
		L.9-10.3	Apply knowledge of language to understand how language functions in different contexts, to make effective choices for meaning or style, and to comprehend more fully when reading or listening.

Cluster 3

SE Pages	Lesson	Code	Standards Text
234	Prepare to Read	RI.9-10.4	Determine the meaning of words and phrases as they are used in a text, including figurative, connotative, and technical meanings; analyze the cumulative impact of specific word choices on meaning and tone.
		SL.9-10.1	Initiate and participate effectively in a range of collaborative discussions (one-on-one, in groups, and teacher-led) with diverse partners on grades 9–10 topics, texts, and issues, building on others' ideas and expressing their own clearly and persuasively.
		L.9-10.6	Acquire and use accurately general academic and domain-specific words and phrases, sufficient for reading, writing, speaking, and listening at the college and career readiness level; demonstrate independence in gathering vocabulary knowledge when considering a word or phrase important to comprehension or expression.
235	Before Reading: The Pale Mare	CCRA.R.6	Assess how point of view or purpose shapes the content and style of a text.
		RL.9-10.1	Cite strong and thorough textual evidence to support analysis of what the text says explicitly as well as inferences drawn from the text.
236-250	Read The Pale Mare	CCRA.R.6	Assess how point of view or purpose shapes the content and style of a text.
		RL.9-10.1	Cite strong and thorough textual evidence to support analysis of what the text says explicitly as well as inferences drawn from the text.
		RL.9-10.2	Determine a theme or central idea of a text and analyze in detail its development over the course of the text, including how it emerges and is shaped and refined by specific details; provide an objective summary of the text.
		RL.9-10.3	Analyze how complex characters develop over the course of a text, interact with other characters, and advance the plot or develop the theme.
		RL.9-10.4	Determine the meaning of words and phrases as they are used in a text, including figurative, connotative, and technical meanings; analyze the cumulative impact of specific word choices on meaning and tone.

SE Pages	Lesson	Code	Standards Text
236-250	**Read The Pale Mare** continued	RL.9-10.7	Analyze the representation of a subject or a key scene in two different artistic mediums, including what is emphasized or absent in each treatment.
		RL.9-10.10	By the end of grade 10, read and comprehend literature, including stories, dramas, and poems, at the high end of the grades 9–10 text complexity band independently and proficiently.
		W.9-10.9.a	Apply grades 9–10 Reading standards to literature.
		W.9-10.10	Write routinely over extended time frames (time for research, reflection, and revision) and shorter time frames (a single sitting or a day or two) for a range of tasks, purposes, and audiences.
		L.9-10.1	Demonstrate command of the conventions of standard English grammar and usage when writing or speaking.
		L.9-10.4	Determine or clarify the meaning of unknown and multiple-meaning words and phrases based on grades 9–10 reading and content, choosing flexibly from a range of strategies.
		L.9-10.5	Demonstrate understanding of figurative language, word relationships, and nuances in word meanings.
		L.9-10.6	Acquire and use accurately general academic and domain-specific words and phrases, sufficient for reading, writing, speaking, and listening at the college and career readiness level; demonstrate independence in gathering vocabulary knowledge when considering a word or phrase important to comprehension or expression.
251	**Before Reading: Caged Bird**	RL.9-10.1	Cite strong and thorough textual evidence to support analysis of what the text says explicitly as well as inferences drawn from the text.
		RL.9-10.5	Analyze how an author's choices concerning how to structure a text, order events within it, and manipulate time create such effects as mystery, tension, or surprise.
252-254	**Read Caged Bird**	RL.9-10.1	Cite strong and thorough textual evidence to support analysis of what the text says explicitly as well as inferences drawn from the text.
		RL.9-10.2	Determine a theme or central idea of a text and analyze in detail its development over the course of the text, including how it emerges and is shaped and refined by specific details; provide an objective summary of the text.
		RL.9-10.5	Analyze how an author's choices concerning how to structure a text, order events within it, and manipulate time create such effects as mystery, tension, or surprise.
		RL.9-10.10	By the end of grade 10, read and comprehend literature, including stories, dramas, and poems, at the high end of the grades 9–10 text complexity band independently and proficiently.
		W.9-10.9.a	Apply grades 9–10 Reading standards to literature.
		W.9-10.10	Write routinely over extended time frames (time for research, reflection, and revision) and shorter time frames (a single sitting or a day or two) for a range of tasks, purposes, and audiences.
		L.9-10.6	Acquire and use accurately general academic and domain-specific words and phrases, sufficient for reading, writing, speaking, and listening at the college and career readiness level; demonstrate independence in gathering vocabulary knowledge when considering a word or phrase important to comprehension or expression.

Common Core State Standards, continued

Cluster 3, continued

SE Pages	Lesson	Code	Standards Text
255	Reflect and Assess Critical Thinking	RL.9-10.1	Cite strong and thorough textual evidence to support analysis of what the text says explicitly as well as inferences drawn from the text.
	Write About Literature	W.9-10.1	Write arguments to support claims in an analysis of substantive topics or texts, using valid reasoning and relevant and sufficient evidence.
	Key Vocabulary Review	L.9-10.6	Acquire and use accurately general academic and domain-specific words and phrases, sufficient for reading, writing, speaking, and listening at the college and career readiness level; demonstrate independence in gathering vocabulary knowledge when considering a word or phrase important to comprehension or expression.
	Read with Ease: Expression	RL.9-10.10	By the end of grade 10, read and comprehend literature, including stories, dramas, and poems, at the high end of the grades 9–10 text complexity band independently and proficiently.
256	Grammar: Use Subject and Object Pronouns	L.9-10.1	Demonstrate command of the conventions of standard English grammar and usage when writing or speaking.
256	Language Development: Give Directions	SL.9-10.1	Initiate and participate effectively in a range of collaborative discussions (one-on-one, in groups, and teacher-led) with diverse partners on grades 9–10 topics, texts, and issues, building on others' ideas and expressing their own clearly and persuasively.
256	Literary Analysis: Analyze Point of View	CCRA.R.6	Assess how point of view or purpose shapes the content and style of a text.
257	Vocabulary Study: Word Families	L.9-10.4.b	Identify and correctly use patterns of word changes that indicate different meanings or parts of speech.
		L.9-10.4.c	Consult general and specialized reference materials, both print and digital, to find the pronunciation of a word or determine or clarify its precise meaning, its part of speech, or its etymology.
257	Writing on Demand: Write a Response to Literature	W.9-10.1	Write arguments to support claims in an analysis of substantive topics or texts, using valid reasoning and relevant and sufficient evidence.
257	Listening/Speaking: Dramatic Reading	SL.9-10.6	Adapt speech to a variety of contexts and tasks, demonstrating command of formal English when indicated or appropriate.

Close Reading

SE Pages	Lesson	Code	Standards Text
258–261	Read Outliers	RI.9-10.10	By the end of grade 10, read and comprehend literary nonfiction at the high end of the grades 9–10 text complexity band independently and proficiently.

Unit Wrap-Up

SE Pages	Lesson	Code	Standards Text
262	Unit Wrap-Up Present Your Project	SL.9-10.5	Make strategic use of digital media in presentations to enhance understanding of findings, reasoning, and evidence and to add interest.
	Reflect on Your Reading	SL.9-10.1.a	Come to discussions prepared, having read and researched material under study; explicitly draw on that preparation by referring to evidence from texts and other research on the topic or issue to stimulate a thoughtful, well-reasoned exchange of ideas.
	Respond to the Essential Question	SL.9-10.1.a	Come to discussions prepared, having read and researched material under study; explicitly draw on that preparation by referring to evidence from texts and other research on the topic or issue to stimulate a thoughtful, well-reasoned exchange of ideas.

Unit 3 Writing Project: Short Story

SE Pages	Lesson	Code	Standards Text
264–267	**Study Short Stories and Prewrite**	W.9-10.3.c	Use a variety of techniques to sequence events so that they build on one another to create a coherent whole.
		W.9-10.5	Develop and strengthen writing as needed by planning, revising, editing, rewriting, or trying a new approach, focusing on addressing what is most significant for a specific purpose and audience.
268–269	**Short Story: Draft**	W.9-10.3	Write narratives to develop real or imagined experiences or events using effective technique, well-chosen details, and well-structured event sequences.
		W.9-10.3.b	Use narrative techniques, such as dialogue, pacing, description, reflection, and multiple plot lines, to develop experiences, events, and/or characters.
		W.9-10.3.d	Use precise words and phrases, telling details, and sensory language to convey a vivid picture of the experiences, events, setting, and/or characters.
		W.9-10.4	Produce clear and coherent writing in which the development, organization, and style are appropriate to task, purpose, and audience.
270–273	**Short Story: Revise** **Trait: Organization**	W.9-10.3.a	Engage and orient the reader by setting out a problem, situation, or observation, establishing one or multiple point(s) of view, and introducing a narrator and/or characters; create a smooth progression of experiences or events.
		W.9-10.3.b	Use narrative techniques, such as dialogue, pacing, description, reflection, and multiple plot lines, to develop experiences, events, and/or characters.
		W.9-10.3.c	Use a variety of techniques to sequence events so that they build on one another to create a coherent whole.
		W.9-10.3.d	Use precise words and phrases, telling details, and sensory language to convey a vivid picture of the experiences, events, setting, and/or characters.
		W.9-10.3.e	Provide a conclusion that follows from and reflects on what is experienced, observed, or resolved over the course of the narrative.
		W.9-10.5	Develop and strengthen writing as needed by planning, revising, editing, rewriting, or trying a new approach, focusing on addressing what is most significant for a specific purpose and audience.
		SL.9-10.1.d	Respond thoughtfully to diverse perspectives, summarize points of agreement and disagreement, and, when warranted, qualify or justify their own views and understanding and make new connections in light of the evidence and reasoning presented.
274–276	**Short Story:** **Edit and Proofread**	W.9-10.6	Use technology, including the Internet, to produce, publish, and update individual or shared writing products, taking advantage of technology's capacity to link to other information and to display information flexibly and dynamically.
	Capitalization: Quotations	L.9-10.1	Demonstrate command of the conventions of standard English grammar and usage when writing or speaking.
	Quotation Marks	L.9-10.2	Demonstrate command of the conventions of standard English capitalization, punctuation, and spelling when writing.
	Spelling	L.9-10.2.c	Spell correctly.

Common Core State Standards, continued

Unit 3 Writing Project: Short Story, continued

SE Pages	Lesson	Code	Standards Text
274–276	Short Story: continued	L.9-10.3	Apply knowledge of language to understand how language functions in different contexts, to make effective choices for meaning or style, and to comprehend more fully when reading or listening.
		L.9-10.3.a	Write and edit work so that it conforms to the guidelines in a style manual appropriate for the discipline and writing type.
277	Short Story: Publish and Present	W.9-10.6	Use technology, including the Internet, to produce, publish, and update individual or shared writing products, taking advantage of technology's capacity to link to other information and to display information flexibly and dynamically.
		SL.9-10.1	Initiate and participate effectively in a range of collaborative discussions (one-on-one, in groups, and teacher-led) with diverse partners on grades 9–10 topics, texts, and issues, building on others' ideas and expressing their own clearly and persuasively.
		SL.9-10.5	Make strategic use of digital media in presentations to enhance understanding of findings, reasoning, and evidence and to add interest.

UNIT 4: Give & Take

SE Pages	Lesson	Code	Standards Text
278–279	Discuss the Essential Question	SL.9-10.1.b	Work with peers to set rules for collegial discussions and decision-making, clear goals and deadlines, and individual roles as needed.
		SL.9-10.3	Evaluate a speaker's point of view, reasoning, and use of evidence and rhetoric, identifying any fallacious reasoning or exaggerated or distorted evidence.
280	Analyze and Debate	SL.9-10.4	Present information, findings, and supporting evidence clearly, concisely, and logically such that listeners can follow the line of reasoning and the organization, development, substance, and style are appropriate to purpose, audience, and task.
281	Plan a Project	SL.9-10.1.b	Work with peers to set rules for collegial discussions and decision-making, clear goals and deadlines, and individual roles as needed.
281	Choose More to Read	RL.9-10.10	By the end of grade 10, read and comprehend literature, including stories, dramas, and poems, at the high end of the grades 9–10 text complexity band independently and proficiently.
		RI.9-10.10	By the end of grade 10, read and comprehend literary nonfiction at the high end of the grades 9–10 text complexity band independently and proficiently.
282–285	How to Read Nonfiction	RI.9-10.2	Determine a central idea of a text and analyze its development over the course of the text, including how it emerges and is shaped and refined by specific details; provide an objective summary of the text.
		RI.9-10.3	Analyze how the author unfolds an analysis or series of ideas or events, including the order in which the points are made, how they are introduced and developed, and the connections that are drawn between them.
		RI.9-10.4	Determine the meaning of words and phrases as they are used in the text, including figurative and connotative meanings; analyze the cumulative impact of specific word choices on meaning and tone.
		RI.9-10.5	Analyze in detail how an author's ideas or claims are developed and refined by particular sentences, paragraphs, or larger portions of a text.
		RI.9-10.10	By the end of grade 10, read and comprehend literary nonfiction at the high end of the grades 9–10 text complexity band independently and proficiently.

Cluster 1

SE Pages	Lesson	Code	Standards Text
286	**Prepare to Read**	RI.9-10.4	Determine the meaning of words and phrases as they are used in a text, including figurative, connotative, and technical meanings; analyze the cumulative impact of specific word choices on meaning and tone.
		SL.9-10.1	Initiate and participate effectively in a range of collaborative discussions (one-on-one, in groups, and teacher-led) with diverse partners on grades 9–10 topics, texts, and issues, building on others' ideas and expressing their own clearly and persuasively.
		L.9-10.6	Acquire and use accurately general academic and domain-specific words and phrases, sufficient for reading, writing, speaking, and listening at the college and career readiness level; demonstrate independence in gathering vocabulary knowledge when considering a word or phrase important to comprehension or expression.
287	**Before Reading: Enabling or Disabling?**	RI.9-10.2	Determine a central idea of a text and analyze its development over the course of the text, including how it emerges and is shaped and refined by specific details; provide an objective summary of the text.
		RI.9-10.3	Analyze how the author unfolds an analysis or series of ideas or events, including the order in which the points are made, how they are introduced and developed, and the connections that are drawn between them.
288–295	**Read Enabling or Disabling?**	RI.9-10.1	Cite strong and thorough textual evidence to support analysis of what the text says explicitly as well as inferences drawn from the text.
		RI.9-10.2	Determine a central idea of a text and analyze its development over the course of the text, including how it emerges and is shaped and refined by specific details; provide an objective summary of the text.
		RI.9-10.3	Analyze how the author unfolds an analysis or series of ideas or events, including the order in which the points are made, how they are introduced and developed, and the connections that are drawn between them.
		RI.9-10.4	Determine the meaning of words and phrases as they are used in a text, including figurative, connotative, and technical meanings; analyze the cumulative impact of specific word choices on meaning and tone.
		RI.9-10.7	Analyze various accounts of a subject told in different mediums, determining which details are emphasized in each account.
		RI.9-10.10	By the end of grade 10, read and comprehend literary nonfiction at the high end of the grades 9–10 text complexity band independently and proficiently.
		W.9-10.9.b	Apply grades 9–10 Reading standards to literary nonfiction.
		L.9-10.1.b	Use various types of phrases (noun, verb, adjectival, adverbial, participial, prepositional, absolute) and clauses (independent, dependent; noun, relative, adverbial) to convey specific meanings and add variety and interest to writing or presentations.
		L.9-10.2.c	Spell correctly.
		L.9-10.6	Acquire and use accurately general academic and domain-specific words and phrases, sufficient for reading, writing, speaking, and listening at the college and career readiness level; demonstrate independence in gathering vocabulary knowledge when considering a word or phrase important to comprehension or expression.

Common Core State Standards, continued

Student Handbooks, continued

Cluster 1, continued

SE Pages	Lesson	Code	Standards Text
296	Before Reading: This I Believe	RI.9-10.2	Determine a central idea of a text and analyze its development over the course of the text, including how it emerges and is shaped and refined by specific details; provide an objective summary of the text.
		RI.9-10.3	Analyze how the author unfolds an analysis or series of ideas or events, including the order in which the points are made, how they are introduced and developed, and the connections that are drawn between them.
297–300	Read This I Believe	RI.9-10.1	Cite strong and thorough textual evidence to support analysis of what the text says explicitly as well as inferences drawn from the text.
		RI.9-10.2	Determine a central idea of a text and analyze its development over the course of the text, including how it emerges and is shaped and refined by specific details; provide an objective summary of the text.
		RI.9-10.3	Analyze how the author unfolds an analysis or series of ideas or events, including the order in which the points are made, how they are introduced and developed, and the connections that are drawn between them.
		RI.9-10.10	By the end of grade 10, read and comprehend literary nonfiction at the high end of the grades 9–10 text complexity band independently and proficiently.
		W.9-10.9.b	Apply grades 9–10 Reading standards to literary nonfiction.
		W.9-10.10	Write routinely over extended time frames (time for research, reflection, and revision) and shorter time frames (a single sitting or a day or two) for a range of tasks, purposes, and audiences.
		L.9-10.1	Demonstrate command of the conventions of standard English grammar and usage when writing or speaking.
		L.9-10.6	Acquire and use accurately general academic and domain-specific words and phrases, sufficient for reading, writing, speaking, and listening at the college and career readiness level; demonstrate independence in gathering vocabulary knowledge when considering a word or phrase important to comprehension or expression.
301	Reflect and Assess Critical Thinking	RI.9-10.1	Cite strong and thorough textual evidence to support analysis of what the text says explicitly as well as inferences drawn from the text.
		RI.9-10.2	Determine a central idea of a text and analyze its development over the course of the text, including how it emerges and is shaped and refined by specific details; provide an objective summary of the text.
	Write About Literature	W.9-10.2	Write informative/explanatory texts to examine and convey complex ideas, concepts, and information clearly and accurately through the effective selection, organization, and analysis of content.
	Key Vocabulary Review	L.9-10.6	Acquire and use accurately general academic and domain-specific words and phrases, sufficient for reading, writing, speaking, and listening at the college and career readiness level; demonstrate independence in gathering vocabulary knowledge when considering a word or phrase important to comprehension or expression.
	Read with Ease: Phrasing	RI.9-10.10	By the end of grade 10, read and comprehend literary nonfiction at the high end of the grades 9–10 text complexity band independently and proficiently.

Cluster 1, continued

SE Pages	Lesson	Code	Standards Text
302 Grammar: Show Possession		L.9-10.1.b	Use various types of phrases (noun, verb, adjectival, adverbial, participial, prepositional, absolute) and clauses (independent, dependent; noun, relative, adverbial) to convey specific meanings and add variety and interest to writing or presentations.
302	**Language Development: Describe an Experience**	SL.9-10.1.a	Come to discussions prepared, having read and researched material under study; explicitly draw on that preparation by referring to evidence from texts and other research on the topic or issue to stimulate a thoughtful, well-reasoned exchange of ideas.
302	**Literary Analysis: Analyze Style**	RI.9-10.4	Determine the meaning of words and phrases as they are used in a text, including figurative, connotative, and technical meanings; analyze the cumulative impact of specific word choices on meaning and tone.
303	**Vocabulary Study: Multiple-Meaning Words**	L.9-10.4.a	Use context as a clue to the meaning of a word or phrase.
		L.9-10.4.c	Consult general and specialized reference materials, both print and digital, to find the pronunciation of a word or determine or clarify its precise meaning, its part of speech, or its etymology.
		L.9-10.4.d	Verify the preliminary determination of the meaning of a word or phrase.
303 Writing: Write a Paragraph to Express an Idea		W.9-10.1	Write arguments to support claims in an analysis of substantive topics or texts, using valid reasoning and relevant and sufficient evidence.
		W.9-10.5	Develop and strengthen writing as needed by planning, revising, editing, rewriting, or trying a new approach, focusing on addressing what is most significant for a specific purpose and audience.
303	**Research/Writing: Poster**	W.9-10.7	Conduct short as well as more sustained research projects to answer a question (including a self-generated question) or solve a problem; narrow or broaden the inquiry when appropriate; synthesize multiple sources on the subject, demonstrating understanding of the subject under investigation.
304	**Workplace Workshop: Inside a Mental Health Center**	W.9-10.7	Conduct short as well as more sustained research projects to answer a question (including a self-generated question) or solve a problem; narrow or broaden the inquiry when appropriate; synthesize multiple sources on the subject, demonstrating understanding of the subject under investigation.
		W.9-10.10	Write routinely over extended time frames (time for research, reflection, and revision) and shorter time frames (a single sitting or a day or two) for a range of tasks, purposes, and audiences.
		L.9-10.6	Acquire and use accurately general academic and domain-specific words and phrases, sufficient for reading, writing, speaking, and listening at the college and career readiness level; demonstrate independence in gathering vocabulary knowledge when considering a word or phrase important to comprehension or expression.
305	**Vocabulary Workshop: Access Words During Reading**	L.9-10.4.a	Use context as a clue to the meaning of a word or phrase.
		L.9-10.4.d	Verify the preliminary determination of the meaning of a word or phrase.
Cluster 2			
306	**Prepare to Read**	RI.9-10.4	Determine the meaning of words and phrases as they are used in a text, including figurative, connotative, and technical meanings; analyze the cumulative impact of specific word choices on meaning and tone.

Common Core State Standards, continued

SE Pages	Lesson	Code	Standards Text
306	**Prepare to Read** continued	SL.9-10.1	Initiate and participate effectively in a range of collaborative discussions (one-on-one, in groups, and teacher-led) with diverse partners on grades 9–10 topics, texts, and issues, building on others' ideas and expressing their own clearly and persuasively.
		L.9-10.6	Acquire and use accurately general academic and domain-specific words and phrases, sufficient for reading, writing, speaking, and listening at the college and career readiness level; demonstrate independence in gathering vocabulary knowledge when considering a word or phrase important to comprehension or expression.
307	**Before Reading: Brother Ray**	RI.9-10.2	Determine a central idea of a text and analyze its development over the course of the text, including how it emerges and is shaped and refined by specific details; provide an objective summary of the text.
		RI.9-10.5	Analyze in detail how an author's ideas or claims are developed and refined by particular sentences, paragraphs, or larger portions of a text.
308–315	**Read Brother Ray**	RI.9-10.1	Cite strong and thorough textual evidence to support analysis of what the text says explicitly as well as inferences drawn from the text.
		RI.9-10.2	Determine a central idea of a text and analyze its development over the course of the text, including how it emerges and is shaped and refined by specific details; provide an objective summary of the text.
		RI.9-10.4	Determine the meaning of words and phrases as they are used in a text, including figurative, connotative, and technical meanings; analyze the cumulative impact of specific word choices on meaning and tone.
		RI.9-10.5	Analyze in detail how an author's ideas or claims are developed and refined by particular sentences, paragraphs, or larger portions of a text (e.g., a section or chapter).
		RI.9-10.10	By the end of grade 10, read and comprehend literary nonfiction at the high end of the grades 9–10 text complexity band independently and proficiently.
		W.9-10.9.b	Apply grades 9–10 Reading standards to literary nonfiction.
		W.9-10.10	Write routinely over extended time frames (time for research, reflection, and revision) and shorter time frames (a single sitting or a day or two) for a range of tasks, purposes, and audiences.
		L.9-10.1.b	Use various types of phrases (noun, verb, adjectival, adverbial, participial, prepositional, absolute) and clauses (independent, dependent; noun, relative, adverbial) to convey specific meanings and add variety and interest to writing or presentations.
		L.9-10.6	Acquire and use accurately general academic and domain-specific words and phrases, sufficient for reading, writing, speaking, and listening at the college and career readiness level; demonstrate independence in gathering vocabulary knowledge when considering a word or phrase important to comprehension or expression.
316	**Before Reading: Power of the Powerless**	RI.9-10.2	Determine a central idea of a text and analyze its development over the course of the text, including how it emerges and is shaped and refined by specific details; provide an objective summary of the text.
		RI.9-10.5	Analyze in detail how an author's ideas or claims are developed and refined by particular sentences, paragraphs, or larger portions of a text.
317–322	**Read Power of the Powerless**	RI.9-10.1	Cite strong and thorough textual evidence to support analysis of what the text says explicitly as well as inferences drawn from the text.

SE Pages	Lesson	Code	Standards Text
317–322	**Read Power of the Powerless** continued	RI.9-10.2	Determine a central idea of a text and analyze its development over the course of the text, including how it emerges and is shaped and refined by specific details; provide an objective summary of the text.
		RI.9-10.4	Determine the meaning of words and phrases as they are used in a text, including figurative, connotative, and technical meanings; analyze the cumulative impact of specific word choices on meaning and tone.
		RI.9-10.5	Analyze in detail how an author's ideas or claims are developed and refined by particular sentences, paragraphs, or larger portions of a text.
		RI.9-10.10	By the end of grade 10, read and comprehend literary nonfiction at the high end of the grades 9–10 text complexity band independently and proficiently.
		W.9-10.9.b	Apply grades 9–10 Reading standards to literary nonfiction.
		W.9-10.10	Write routinely over extended time frames (time for research, reflection, and revision) and shorter time frames (a single sitting or a day or two) for a range of tasks, purposes, and audiences.
		L.9-10.1.b	Use various types of phrases (noun, verb, adjectival, adverbial, participial, prepositional, absolute) and clauses (independent, dependent; noun, relative, adverbial) to convey specific meanings and add variety and interest to writing or presentations.
		L.9-10.6	Acquire and use accurately general academic and domain-specific words and phrases, sufficient for reading, writing, speaking, and listening at the college and career readiness level; demonstrate independence in gathering vocabulary knowledge when considering a word or phrase important to comprehension or expression.
323	**Reflect and Assess Critical Thinking**	RI.9-10.1	Cite strong and thorough textual evidence to support analysis of what the text says explicitly as well as inferences drawn from the text.
	Write About Literature	W.9-10.2	Write informative/explanatory texts to examine and convey complex ideas, concepts, and information clearly and accurately through the effective selection, organization, and analysis of content.
	Key Vocabulary Review	L.9-10.6	Acquire and use accurately general academic and domain-specific words and phrases, sufficient for reading, writing, speaking, and listening at the college and career readiness level; demonstrate independence in gathering vocabulary knowledge when considering a word or phrase important to comprehension or expression.
	Read with Ease: Expression	RI.9-10.10	By the end of grade 10, read and comprehend literary nonfiction at the high end of the grades 9–10 text complexity band independently and proficiently.
324	**Grammar: Use Prepositions Correctly**	L.9-10.1.b	Use various types of phrases (noun, verb, adjectival, adverbial, participial, prepositional, absolute) and clauses (independent, dependent; noun, relative, adverbial) to convey specific meanings and add variety and interest to writing or presentations.
324	**Language Development: Describe People and Places**	SL.9-10.4	Present information, findings, and supporting evidence clearly, concisely, and logically such that listeners can follow the line of reasoning and the organization, development, substance, and style are appropriate to purpose, audience, and task.
324	**Literary Analysis: Compare Literature and Film**	RI.9-10.7	Analyze various accounts of a subject told in different mediums, determining which details are emphasized in each account.
325	**Vocabulary Study: Context Clues**	L.9-10.4.a	Use context as a clue to the meaning of a word or phrase.

Common Core State Standards, continued

Cluster 2, continued

SE Pages	Lesson	Code	Standards Text
325	Research/Speaking: Slide Show	W.9-10.6	Use technology, including the Internet, to produce, publish, and update individual or shared writing products, taking advantage of technology's capacity to link to other information and to display information flexibly and dynamically.
		W.9-10.7	Conduct short as well as more sustained research projects to answer a question (including a self-generated question) or solve a problem; narrow or broaden the inquiry when appropriate; synthesize multiple sources on the subject, demonstrating understanding of the subject under investigation.
		W.9-10.8	Gather relevant information from multiple authoritative print and digital sources, using advanced searches effectively; assess the usefulness of each source in answering the research question; integrate information into the text selectively to maintain the flow of ideas, avoiding plagiarism and following a standard format for citation.
		SL.9-10.2	Integrate multiple sources of information presented in diverse media or formats evaluating the credibility and accuracy of each source.
325	Writing on Demand: Write a Personal Essay	W.9-10.1	Write arguments to support claims in an analysis of substantive topics or texts, using valid reasoning and relevant and sufficient evidence.
326–327	Listening and Speaking Workshop: Oral Report	SL.9-10.1.a	Come to discussions prepared, having read and researched material under study; explicitly draw on that preparation by referring to evidence from texts and other research on the topic or issue to stimulate a thoughtful, well-reasoned exchange of ideas.
		SL.9-10.1.c	Propel conversations by posing and responding to questions that relate the current discussion to broader themes or larger ideas; actively incorporate others into the discussion; and clarify, verify, or challenge ideas and conclusions.
		SL.9-10.2	Integrate multiple sources of information presented in diverse media or formats evaluating the credibility and accuracy of each source.
		SL.9-10.5	Make strategic use of digital media in presentations to enhance understanding of findings, reasoning, and evidence and to add interest.
		L.9-10.3	Apply knowledge of language to understand how language functions in different contexts, to make effective choices for meaning or style, and to comprehend more fully when reading or listening.

Cluster 3

SE Pages	Lesson	Code	Standards Text
328	Prepare to Read	RI.9-10.4	Determine the meaning of words and phrases as they are used in a text, including figurative, connotative, and technical meanings; analyze the cumulative impact of specific word choices on meaning and tone.
		SL.9-10.1	Initiate and participate effectively in a range of collaborative discussions (one-on-one, in groups, and teacher-led) with diverse partners on grades 9–10 topics, texts, and issues, building on others' ideas and expressing their own clearly and persuasively.
		L.9-10.6	Acquire and use accurately general academic and domain-specific words and phrases, sufficient for reading, writing, speaking, and listening at the college and career readiness level; demonstrate independence in gathering vocabulary knowledge when considering a word or phrase important to comprehension or expression.
329	Before Reading: He Was No Bum	RI.9-10.2	Determine a central idea of a text and analyze its development over the course of the text, including how it emerges and is shaped and refined by specific details; provide an objective summary of the text.

Cluster 3, continued

SE Pages	Lesson	Code	Standards Text
329	**Before Reading:** **He Was No Bum** continued	RI.9-10.5	Analyze in detail how an author's ideas or claims are developed and refined by particular sentences, paragraphs, or larger portions of a text.
330–337	**Read He Was No Bum**	RI.9-10.1	Cite strong and thorough textual evidence to support analysis of what the text says explicitly as well as inferences drawn from the text.
		RI.9-10.2	Determine a central idea of a text and analyze its development over the course of the text, including how it emerges and is shaped and refined by specific details; provide an objective summary of the text.
		RI.9-10.5	Analyze in detail how an author's ideas or claims are developed and refined by particular sentences, paragraphs, or larger portions of a text.
		RI.9-10.6	Determine an author's point of view or purpose in a text and analyze how an author uses rhetoric to advance that point of view or purpose.
		RI.9-10.10	By the end of grade 10, read and comprehend literary nonfiction at the high end of the grades 9–10 text complexity band independently and proficiently.
		W.9-10.9.b	Apply grades 9–10 Reading standards to literary nonfiction.
		L.9-10.1.b	Use various types of phrases (noun, verb, adjectival, adverbial, participial, prepositional, absolute) and clauses (independent, dependent; noun, relative, adverbial) to convey specific meanings and add variety and interest to writing or presentations.
		L.9-10.6	Acquire and use accurately general academic and domain-specific words and phrases, sufficient for reading, writing, speaking, and listening at the college and career readiness level; demonstrate independence in gathering vocabulary knowledge when considering a word or phrase important to comprehension or expression.
338	**Before Reading: miss rosie**	RL.9-10.2	Determine a theme or central idea of a text and analyze in detail its development over the course of the text, including how it emerges and is shaped and refined by specific details; provide an objective summary of the text.
		RL.9-10.4	Determine the meaning of words and phrases as they are used in the text, including figurative and connotative meanings; analyze the cumulative impact of specific word choices on meaning and tone.
339–340	**Read miss rosie**	RL.9-10.1	Cite strong and thorough textual evidence to support analysis of what the text says explicitly as well as inferences drawn from the text.
		RL.9-10.2	Determine a theme or central idea of a text and analyze in detail its development over the course of the text, including how it emerges and is shaped and refined by specific details; provide an objective summary of the text.
		RL.9-10.4	Determine the meaning of words and phrases as they are used in the text, including figurative and connotative meanings; analyze the cumulative impact of specific word choices on meaning and tone.
		RL.9-10.5	Analyze how an author's choices concerning how to structure a text, order events within it, and manipulate time create such effects as mystery, tension, or surprise.
		RL.9-10.7	Analyze the representation of a subject or a key scene in two different artistic mediums, including what is emphasized or absent in each treatment.

Common Core State Standards, continued

SE Pages	Lesson	Code	Standards Text
339–340	Read miss rosie continued	RL.9-10.10	By the end of grade 10, read and comprehend literature, including stories, dramas, and poems, at the high end of the grades 9–10 text complexity band independently and proficiently.
		W.9-10.9.a	Apply grades 9–10 Reading standards to literature.
		W.9-10.10	Write routinely over extended time frames (time for research, reflection, and revision) and shorter time frames (a single sitting or a day or two) for a range of tasks, purposes, and audiences.
		L.9-10.6	Acquire and use accurately general academic and domain-specific words and phrases, sufficient for reading, writing, speaking, and listening at the college and career readiness level; demonstrate independence in gathering vocabulary knowledge when considering a word or phrase important to comprehension or expression.
341	Reflect and Assess Critical Thinking	RL.9-10.1	Cite strong and thorough textual evidence to support analysis of what the text says explicitly as well as inferences drawn from the text.
		RI.9-10.1	Cite strong and thorough textual evidence to support analysis of what the text says explicitly as well as inferences drawn from the text.
	Write About Literature	W.9-10.1	Write arguments to support claims in an analysis of substantive topics or texts, using valid reasoning and relevant and sufficient evidence.
	Key Vocabulary Review	L.9-10.6	Acquire and use accurately general academic and domain-specific words and phrases, sufficient for reading, writing, speaking, and listening at the college and career readiness level; demonstrate independence in gathering vocabulary knowledge when considering a word or phrase important to comprehension or expression.
	Read with Ease: Intonation	RI.9-10.10	By the end of grade 10, read and comprehend literary nonfiction at the high end of the grades 9–10 text complexity band independently and proficiently.
342	Grammar: Use Correct Pronoun	L.9-10.1	Demonstrate command of the conventions of standard English grammar and usage when writing or speaking.
342	Language Development: Describe Events	SL.9-10.1.a	Come to discussions prepared, having read and researched material under study; explicitly draw on that preparation by referring to evidence from texts and other research on the topic or issue to stimulate a thoughtful, well-reasoned exchange of ideas.
342	Literary Analysis: Analyze Repetition and Alliteration	RL.9-10.4	Determine the meaning of words and phrases as they are used in the text, including figurative and connotative meanings; analyze the cumulative impact of specific word choices on meaning and tone.
343	Vocabulary Study: Multiple-Meaning Words	L.9-10.4.a	Use context as a clue to the meaning of a word or phrase.
		L.9-10.4.c	Consult general and specialized reference materials, both print and digital, to find the pronunciation of a word or determine or clarify its precise meaning, its part of speech, or its etymology.
343	Writing Trait: Trait: Voice and Style	W.9-10.5	Develop and strengthen writing as needed by planning, revising, editing, rewriting, or trying a new approach, focusing on addressing what is most significant for a specific purpose and audience.
343	Researching/Speaking: Extemporaneous Talk	W.9-10.7	Conduct short as well as more sustained research projects to answer a question (including a self-generated question) or solve a problem; narrow or broaden the inquiry when appropriate; synthesize multiple sources on the subject, demonstrating understanding of the subject under investigation.

Close Reading

SE Pages	Lesson	Code	Standards Text
344–347	Read Household Words	RI.9-10.10	By the end of grade 10, read and comprehend literary nonfiction at the high end of the grades 9–10 text complexity band independently and proficiently.

Unit Wrap-Up

SE Pages	Lesson	Code	Standards Text
348	Unit Wrap-Up Present Your Project	SL.9-10.2	Integrate multiple sources of information presented in diverse media or formats (e.g., visually, quantitatively, orally) evaluating the credibility and accuracy of each source.
		SL.9-10.5	Make strategic use of digital media in presentations to enhance understanding of findings, reasoning, and evidence and to add interest.
	Reflect on Your Reading	SL.9-10.1.a	Come to discussions prepared, having read and researched material under study; explicitly draw on that preparation by referring to evidence from texts and other research on the topic or issue to stimulate a thoughtful, well-reasoned exchange of ideas.
	Respond to the Essential Question	SL.9-10.1.a	Come to discussions prepared, having read and researched material under study; explicitly draw on that preparation by referring to evidence from texts and other research on the topic or issue to stimulate a thoughtful, well-reasoned exchange of ideas.

Unit 4 Writing Project: Problem-Solution Essay

SE Pages	Lesson	Code	Standards Text
350–353	Study Problem Solution Essays and Prewrite	W.9-10.1.a	Introduce precise claim(s), distinguish the claim(s) from alternate or opposing claims, and create an organization that establishes clear relationships among claim(s), counterclaims, reasons, and evidence.
		W.9-10.5	Develop and strengthen writing as needed by planning, revising, editing, rewriting, or trying a new approach, focusing on addressing what is most significant for a specific purpose and audience.
		W.9-10.7	Conduct short as well as more sustained research projects to answer a question (including a self-generated question) or solve a problem; narrow or broaden the inquiry when appropriate; synthesize multiple sources on the subject, demonstrating understanding of the subject under investigation.
		W.9-10.8	Gather relevant information from multiple authoritative print and digital sources, using advanced searches effectively; assess the usefulness of each source in answering the research question; integrate information into the text selectively to maintain the flow of ideas, avoiding plagiarism and following a standard format for citation.
354–355	Problem-Solution Essay: Draft	W.9-10.1	Write arguments to support claims in an analysis of substantive topics or texts, using valid reasoning and relevant and sufficient evidence.
		W.9-10.1.b	Develop claim(s) and counterclaims fairly, supplying evidence for each while pointing out the strengths and limitations of both in a manner that anticipates the audience's knowledge level and concerns.
		W.9-10.4	Produce clear and coherent writing in which the development, organization, and style are appropriate to task, purpose, and audience.
		W.9-10.5	Develop and strengthen writing as needed by planning, revising, editing, rewriting, or trying a new approach, focusing on addressing what is most significant for a specific purpose and audience.
		W.9-10.6	Use technology, including the Internet, to produce, publish, and update individual or shared writing products, taking advantage of technology's capacity to link to other information and to display information flexibly and dynamically.

Common Core State Standards, continued

Unit 4 Writing Project: Problem-Solution Essay, continued

SE Pages	Lesson	Code	Standards Text
356–359	**Problem-Solution Essay: Revise Trait: Voice and Style**	W.9-10.1.b	Develop claim(s) and counterclaims fairly, supplying evidence for each while pointing out the strengths and limitations of both in a manner that anticipates the audience's knowledge level and concerns.
		W.9-10.1.c	Use words, phrases, and clauses to link the major sections of the text, create cohesion, and clarify the relationships between claim(s) and reasons, between reasons and evidence, and between claim(s) and counterclaims.
		W.9-10.1.d	Establish and maintain a formal style and objective tone while attending to the norms and conventions of the discipline in which they are writing.
		W.9-10.1.e	Provide a concluding statement or section that follows from and supports the argument presented.
		W.9-10.5	Develop and strengthen writing as needed by planning, revising, editing, rewriting, or trying a new approach, focusing on addressing what is most significant for a specific purpose and audience.
		SL.9-10.1	Initiate and participate effectively in a range of collaborative discussions (one-on-one, in groups, and teacher-led) with diverse partners on grades 9–10 topics, texts, and issues, building on others' ideas and expressing their own clearly and persuasively.
		SL.9-10.1.d	Respond thoughtfully to diverse perspectives, summarize points of agreement and disagreement, and, when warranted, qualify or justify their own views and understanding and make new connections in light of the evidence and reasoning presented.
		L.9-10.1	Demonstrate command of the conventions of standard English grammar and usage when writing or speaking.
		L.9-10.1.b	Use various types of phrases (noun, verb, adjectival, adverbial, participial, prepositional, absolute) and clauses (independent, dependent; noun, relative, adverbial) to convey specific meanings and add variety and interest to writing or presentations.
360–362	**Problem-Solution Essay: Edit and Proofread Capitalization: Names of Places Apostrophes Spelling Parallel Structure**	L.9-10.1.a	Use parallel structure.
		L.9-10.2	Demonstrate command of the conventions of standard English capitalization, punctuation, and spelling when writing.
		L.9-10.2.c	Spell correctly.
		L.9-10.3.a	Write and edit work so that it conforms to the guidelines in a style manual appropriate for the discipline and writing type.
363	**Problem-Solution Essay: Publish and Present**	W.9-10.6	Use technology, including the Internet, to produce, publish, and update individual or shared writing products, taking advantage of technology's capacity to link to other information and to display information flexibly and dynamically.
		SL.9-10.3	Evaluate a speaker's point of view, reasoning, and use of evidence and rhetoric, identifying any fallacious reasoning or exaggerated or distorted evidence.
		SL.9-10.4	Present information, findings, and supporting evidence clearly, concisely, and logically such that listeners can follow the line of reasoning and the organization, development, substance, and style are appropriate to purpose, audience, and task.
		SL.9-10.6	Adapt speech to a variety of contexts and tasks, demonstrating command of formal English when indicated or appropriate.

UNIT 5: Fair Play

SE Pages	Lesson	Code	Standards Text
364-365	Discuss the Essential Question	SL.9-10.1.b	Work with peers to set rules for collegial discussions and decision-making, clear goals and deadlines, and individual roles as needed.
		SL.9-10.3	Evaluate a speaker's point of view, reasoning, and use of evidence and rhetoric, identifying any fallacious reasoning or exaggerated or distorted evidence.
366	Analyze and Debate	SL.9-10.4	Present information, findings, and supporting evidence clearly, concisely, and logically such that listeners can follow the line of reasoning and the organization, development, substance, and style are appropriate to purpose, audience, and task.
367	Plan a Project	SL.9-10.1.b	Work with peers to set rules for collegial discussions and decision-making, clear goals and deadlines, and individual roles as needed.
367	Choose More to Read	RL.9-10.10	By the end of grade 10, read and comprehend literature, including stories, dramas, and poems, at the high end of the grades 9–10 text complexity band independently and proficiently.
		RI.9-10.10	By the end of grade 10, read and comprehend literary nonfiction at the high end of the grades 9–10 text complexity band independently and proficiently.
368–371	How to Read Short Stories	RL.9-10.2	Determine a theme or central idea of a text and analyze in detail its development over the course of the text, including how it emerges and is shaped and refined by specific details; provide an objective summary of the text.
		RL.9-10.4	Determine the meaning of words and phrases as they are used in the text, including figurative and connotative meanings; analyze the cumulative impact of specific word choices on meaning and tone.
		RL.9-10.10	By the end of grade 10, read and comprehend literature, including stories, dramas, and poems, at the high end of the grades 9–10 text complexity band independently and proficiently.
		SL.9-10.1.b	Work with peers to set rules for collegial discussions and decision-making, clear goals and deadlines, and individual roles as needed.
		L.9-10.6	Acquire and use accurately general academic and domain-specific words and phrases, sufficient for reading, writing, speaking, and listening at the college and career readiness level; demonstrate independence in gathering vocabulary knowledge when considering a word or phrase important to comprehension or expression.

Cluster 1

SE Pages	Lesson	Code	Standards Text
372	Prepare to Read	RI.9-10.4	Determine the meaning of words and phrases as they are used in a text, including figurative, connotative, and technical meanings; analyze the cumulative impact of specific word choices on meaning and tone.
		SL.9-10.1	Initiate and participate effectively in a range of collaborative discussions (one-on-one, in groups, and teacher-led) with diverse partners on grades 9–10 topics, texts, and issues, building on others' ideas and expressing their own clearly and persuasively.
		L.9-10.6	Acquire and use accurately general academic and domain-specific words and phrases, sufficient for reading, writing, speaking, and listening at the college and career readiness level; demonstrate independence in gathering vocabulary knowledge when considering a word or phrase important to comprehension or expression.

Common Core State Standards, continued

Cluster 1, continued

SE Pages	Lesson	Code	Standards Text
373	**Before Reading: Jump Away**	RL.9-10.2	Determine a theme or central idea of a text and analyze in detail its development over the course of the text, including how it emerges and is shaped and refined by specific details; provide an objective summary of the text.
		RL.9-10.10	By the end of grade 10, read and comprehend literature, including stories, dramas, and poems, at the high end of the grades 9–10 text complexity band independently and proficiently.
374–383	**Read Jump Away**	RL.9-10.1	Cite strong and thorough textual evidence to support analysis of what the text says explicitly as well as inferences drawn from the text.
		RL.9-10.2	Determine a theme or central idea of a text and analyze in detail its development over the course of the text, including how it emerges and is shaped and refined by specific details; provide an objective summary of the text.
		RL.9-10.4	Determine the meaning of words and phrases as they are used in the text, including figurative and connotative meanings; analyze the cumulative impact of specific word choices on meaning and tone.
		RL.9-10.7	Analyze the representation of a subject or a key scene in two different artistic mediums, including what is emphasized or absent in each treatment.
		RL.9-10.10	By the end of grade 10, read and comprehend literature, including stories, dramas, and poems, at the high end of the grades 9–10 text complexity band independently and proficiently.
		W.9-10.9.a	Apply grades 9–10 Reading standards to literature.
		W.9-10.10	Write routinely over extended time frames (time for research, reflection, and revision) and shorter time frames (a single sitting or a day or two) for a range of tasks, purposes, and audiences.
		L.9-10.1.b	Use various types of phrases (noun, verb, adjectival, adverbial, participial, prepositional, absolute) and clauses (independent, dependent; noun, relative, adverbial) to convey specific meanings and add variety and interest to writing or presentations.
		L.9-10.6	Acquire and use accurately general academic and domain-specific words and phrases, sufficient for reading, writing, speaking, and listening at the college and career readiness level; demonstrate independence in gathering vocabulary knowledge when considering a word or phrase important to comprehension or expression.
384	**Before Reading: Showdown with Big Eva**	RI.9-10.2	Determine a theme or central idea of a text and analyze in detail its development over the course of the text, including how it emerges and is shaped and refined by specific details; provide an objective summary of the text.
		RI.9-10.10	By the end of grade 10, read and comprehend literature, including stories, dramas, and poems, at the high end of the grades 9–10 text complexity band independently and proficiently.
385–390	**Read Showdown with Big Eva**	RI.9-10.1	Cite strong and thorough textual evidence to support analysis of what the text says explicitly as well as inferences drawn from the text.
		RI.9-10.2	Determine a theme or central idea of a text and analyze in detail its development over the course of the text, including how it emerges and is shaped and refined by specific details; provide an objective summary of the text.

Cluster 1, continued

SE Pages	Lesson	Code	Standards Text
385–390	**Read Showdown with Big Eva** continued	RI.9-10.4	Determine the meaning of words and phrases as they are used in the text, including figurative and connotative meanings; analyze the cumulative impact of specific word choices on meaning and tone.
		RI.9-10.10	By the end of grade 10, read and comprehend literature, including stories, dramas, and poems, at the high end of the grades 9–10 text complexity band independently and proficiently.
		W.9-10.9.b	Apply grades 9–10 Reading standards to literary nonfiction.
		W.9-10.10	Write routinely over extended time frames (time for research, reflection, and revision) and shorter time frames (a single sitting or a day or two) for a range of tasks, purposes, and audiences.
		L.9-10.1.b	Use various types of phrases (noun, verb, adjectival, adverbial, participial, prepositional, absolute) and clauses (independent, dependent; noun, relative, adverbial) to convey specific meanings and add variety and interest to writing or presentations.
		L.9-10.6	Acquire and use accurately general academic and domain-specific words and phrases, sufficient for reading, writing, speaking, and listening at the college and career readiness level; demonstrate independence in gathering vocabulary knowledge when considering a word or phrase important to comprehension or expression.
391	**Reflect and Assess** **Critical Thinking**	RL.9-10.1	Cite strong and thorough textual evidence to support analysis of what the text says explicitly as well as inferences drawn from the text.
		RI.9-10.1	Cite strong and thorough textual evidence to support analysis of what the text says explicitly as well as inferences drawn from the text.
	Write About Literature	W.9-10.1	Write arguments to support claims in an analysis of substantive topics or texts, using valid reasoning and relevant and sufficient evidence.
	Key Vocabulary Review	L.9-10.6	Acquire and use accurately general academic and domain-specific words and phrases, sufficient for reading, writing, speaking, and listening at the college and career readiness level; demonstrate independence in gathering vocabulary knowledge when considering a word or phrase important to comprehension or expression.
	Read with Ease: Phrasing	RL.9-10.10	By the end of grade 10, read and comprehend literature, including stories, dramas, and poems, at the high end of the grades 9–10 text complexity band independently and proficiently.
392	**Grammar: Use Adjectives** **to Elaborate**	L.9-10.1.b	Use various types of phrases (noun, verb, adjectival, adverbial, participial, prepositional, absolute) and clauses (independent, dependent; noun, relative, adverbial) to convey specific meanings and add variety and interest to writing or presentations.
392	**Language Development:** **Ask for and** **Give Information**	SL.9-10.1.c	Propel conversations by posing and responding to questions that relate the current discussion to broader themes or larger ideas; actively incorporate others into the discussion; and clarify, verify, or challenge ideas and conclusions.
392	**Literary Analysis: Analyze** **Mood and Tone**	RL.9-10.4	Determine the meaning of words and phrases as they are used in the text, including figurative and connotative meanings; analyze the cumulative impact of specific word choices on meaning and tone.

Common Core State Standards, continued

Cluster 1, continued

SE Pages	Lesson	Code	Standards Text
393	Vocabulary Study: Relate Words	L.9-10.4.c	Consult general and specialized reference materials, both print and digital, to find the pronunciation of a word or determine or clarify its precise meaning, its part of speech, or its etymology.
		L.9-10.5.b	Analyze nuances in the meaning of words with similar denotations.
393	Writing: Write an Expressive Paragraph	W.9-10.3	Write narratives to develop real or imagined experiences or events using effective technique, well-chosen details, and well-structured event sequences.
		W.9-10.5	Develop and strengthen writing as needed by planning, revising, editing, rewriting, or trying a new approach, focusing on addressing what is most significant for a specific purpose and audience.
393	Listening/Speaking: Dramatization	SL.9-10.6	Adapt speech to a variety of contexts and tasks, demonstrating command of formal English when indicated or appropriate.
394	Workplace Workshop: Inside a School	W.9-10.4	Produce clear and coherent writing in which the development, organization, and style are appropriate to task, purpose, and audience.
		W.9-10.10	Write routinely over extended time frames (time for research, reflection, and revision) and shorter time frames (a single sitting or a day or two) for a range of tasks, purposes, and audiences.
395	Vocabulary Workshop: Make Word Connections	L.9-10.4.c	Consult general and specialized reference materials, both print and digital, to find the pronunciation of a word or determine or clarify its precise meaning, its part of speech, or its etymology.
		L.9-10.4.d	Verify the preliminary determination of the meaning of a word or phrase.
		L.9-10.5.b	Analyze nuances in the meaning of words with similar denotations.

Cluster 2

SE Pages	Lesson	Code	Standards Text
396	Prepare to Read	RI.9-10.4	Determine the meaning of words and phrases as they are used in a text, including figurative, connotative, and technical meanings; analyze the cumulative impact of specific word choices on meaning and tone.
		SL.9-10.1	Initiate and participate effectively in a range of collaborative discussions (one-on-one, in groups, and teacher-led) with diverse partners on grades 9–10 topics, texts, and issues, building on others' ideas and expressing their own clearly and persuasively.
		L.9-10.6	Acquire and use accurately general academic and domain-specific words and phrases, sufficient for reading, writing, speaking, and listening at the college and career readiness level; demonstrate independence in gathering vocabulary knowledge when considering a word or phrase important to comprehension or expression.
397	Before Reading: Fear	RL.9-10.2	Determine a theme or central idea of a text and analyze in detail its development over the course of the text, including how it emerges and is shaped and refined by specific details; provide an objective summary of the text.
		RL.9-10.10	By the end of grade 10, read and comprehend literature, including stories, dramas, and poems, at the high end of the grades 9–10 text complexity band independently and proficiently.
398–407	Read Fear	RL.9-10.1	Cite strong and thorough textual evidence to support analysis of what the text says explicitly as well as inferences drawn from the text.

SE Pages	Lesson	Code	Standards Text
398–407	**Read Fear** continued	RL.9-10.2	Determine a theme or central idea of a text and analyze in detail its development over the course of the text, including how it emerges and is shaped and refined by specific details; provide an objective summary of the text.
		RL.9-10.3	Analyze how complex characters develop over the course of a text, interact with other characters, and advance the plot or develop the theme.
		RL.9-10.4	Determine the meaning of words and phrases as they are used in the text, including figurative and connotative meanings; analyze the cumulative impact of specific word choices on meaning and tone.
		RL.9-10.7	Analyze the representation of a subject or a key scene in two different artistic mediums, including what is emphasized or absent in each treatment.
		RL.9-10.10	By the end of grade 10, read and comprehend literature, including stories, dramas, and poems, at the high end of the grades 9–10 text complexity band independently and proficiently.
		W.9-10.9.a	Apply grades 9–10 Reading standards to literature.
		W.9-10.10	Write routinely over extended time frames (time for research, reflection, and revision) and shorter time frames (a single sitting or a day or two) for a range of tasks, purposes, and audiences.
		L.9-10.1.b	Use various types of phrases (noun, verb, adjectival, adverbial, participial, prepositional, absolute) and clauses (independent, dependent; noun, relative, adverbial) to convey specific meanings and add variety and interest to writing or presentations.
		L.9-10.2.c	Spell correctly.
		L.9-10.6	Acquire and use accurately general academic and domain-specific words and phrases, sufficient for reading, writing, speaking, and listening at the college and career readiness level; demonstrate independence in gathering vocabulary knowledge when considering a word or phrase important to comprehension or expression.
408	**Before Reading: Violence Hits Home**	RI.9-10.3	Analyze how the author unfolds an analysis or series of ideas or events, including the order in which the points are made, how they are introduced and developed, and the connections that are drawn between them.
		RI.9-10.10	By the end of grade 10, read and comprehend literature, including stories, dramas, and poems, at the high end of the grades 9–10 text complexity band independently and proficiently.
409–414	**Read Violence Hits Home**	RI.9-10.1	Cite strong and thorough textual evidence to support analysis of what the text says explicitly as well as inferences drawn from the text.
		RI.9-10.2	Determine a theme or central idea of a text and analyze in detail its development over the course of the text, including how it emerges and is shaped and refined by specific details; provide an objective summary of the text.
		RI.9-10.3	Analyze how the author unfolds an analysis or series of ideas or events, including the order in which the points are made, how they are introduced and developed, and the connections that are drawn between them.
		RI.9-10.4	Determine the meaning of words and phrases as they are used in a text, including figurative, connotative, and technical meanings; analyze the cumulative impact of specific word choices on meaning and tone.

Common Core State Standards, continued

SE Pages	Lesson	Code	Standards Text
409–414	**Read Violence Hits Home** continued	RI.9-10.10	By the end of grade 10, read and comprehend literature, including stories, dramas, and poems, at the high end of the grades 9–10 text complexity band independently and proficiently.
		W.9-10.9.b	Apply grades 9–10 Reading standards to literary nonfiction.
		W.9-10.10	Write routinely over extended time frames (time for research, reflection, and revision) and shorter time frames (a single sitting or a day or two) for a range of tasks, purposes, and audiences.
		L.9-10.1.b	Use various types of phrases (noun, verb, adjectival, adverbial, participial, prepositional, absolute) and clauses (independent, dependent; noun, relative, adverbial) to convey specific meanings and add variety and interest to writing or presentations.
		L.9-10.4.a	Use context as a clue to the meaning of a word or phrase.
		L.9-10.6	Acquire and use accurately general academic and domain-specific words and phrases, sufficient for reading, writing, speaking, and listening at the college and career readiness level; demonstrate independence in gathering vocabulary knowledge when considering a word or phrase important to comprehension or expression.
415	**Reflect and Assess** **Critical Thinking**	RL.9-10.1	Cite strong and thorough textual evidence to support analysis of what the text says explicitly as well as inferences drawn from the text.
		RI.9-10.1	Cite strong and thorough textual evidence to support analysis of what the text says explicitly as well as inferences drawn from the text.
	Write About Literature	W.9-10.1	Write arguments to support claims in an analysis of substantive topics or texts, using valid reasoning and relevant and sufficient evidence.
	Key Vocabulary Review	L.9-10.6	Acquire and use accurately general academic and domain-specific words and phrases, sufficient for reading, writing, speaking, and listening at the college and career readiness level; demonstrate independence in gathering vocabulary knowledge when considering a word or phrase important to comprehension or expression.
	Read with Ease: Intonation	RL.9-10.10	By the end of grade 10, read and comprehend literature, including stories, dramas, and poems, at the high end of the grades 9–10 text complexity band independently and proficiently.
416	**Grammar: Use** **Adjectives Correctly**	L.9-10.1.b	Use various types of phrases (noun, verb, adjectival, adverbial, participial, prepositional, absolute) and clauses (independent, dependent; noun, relative, adverbial) to convey specific meanings and add variety and interest to writing or presentations.
416	**Language Development:** **Engage in Conversation**	SL.9-10.1.d	Respond thoughtfully to diverse perspectives, summarize points of agreement and disagreement, and, when warranted, qualify or justify their own views and understanding and make new connections in light of the evidence and reasoning presented.
416	**Literary Analysis:** **Analyze Suspense**	RL.9-10.4	Determine the meaning of words and phrases as they are used in the text, including figurative and connotative meanings; analyze the cumulative impact of specific word choices on meaning and tone.
		RL.9-10.5	Analyze how an author's choices concerning how to structure a text, order events within it, and manipulate time create such effects as mystery, tension, or surprise.
417	**Vocabulary Study:** **Relate Words**	L.9-10.5	Demonstrate understanding of figurative language, word relationships, and nuances in word meanings.

Cluster 2, continued

SE Pages	Lesson	Code	Standards Text
417	**Writing on Demand: Write a Character Sketch**	W.9-10.2	Write informative/explanatory texts to examine and convey complex ideas, concepts, and information clearly and accurately through the effective selection, organization, and analysis of content.
		W.9-10.5	Develop and strengthen writing as needed by planning, revising, editing, rewriting, or trying a new approach, focusing on addressing what is most significant for a specific purpose and audience.
417	**Listening/Speaking: Review**	SL.9-10.4	Present information, findings, and supporting evidence clearly, concisely, and logically such that listeners can follow the line of reasoning and the organization, development, substance, and style are appropriate to purpose, audience, and task.
418–419	**Listening and Speaking Workshop: Panel Discussion**	SL.9-10.1.a	Come to discussions prepared, having read and researched material under study; explicitly draw on that preparation by referring to evidence from texts and other research on the topic or issue to stimulate a thoughtful, well-reasoned exchange of ideas.
		SL.9-10.1.b	Work with peers to set rules for collegial discussions and decision-making, clear goals and deadlines, and individual roles as needed.
		SL.9-10.1.c	Propel conversations by posing and responding to questions that relate the current discussion to broader themes or larger ideas; actively incorporate others into the discussion; and clarify, verify, or challenge ideas and conclusions.
		SL.9-10.1.d	Respond thoughtfully to diverse perspectives, summarize points of agreement and disagreement, and, when warranted, qualify or justify their own views and understanding and make new connections in light of the evidence and reasoning presented.
		SL.9-10.4	Present information, findings, and supporting evidence clearly, concisely, and logically such that listeners can follow the line of reasoning and the organization, development, substance, and style are appropriate to purpose, audience, and task.
		L.9-10.3	Apply knowledge of language to understand how language functions in different contexts, to make effective choices for meaning or style, and to comprehend more fully when reading or listening.

Cluster 3

SE Pages	Lesson	Code	Standards Text
420	**Prepare to Read**	RI.9-10.4	Determine the meaning of words and phrases as they are used in a text, including figurative, connotative, and technical meanings; analyze the cumulative impact of specific word choices on meaning and tone.
		SL.9-10.1	Initiate and participate effectively in a range of collaborative discussions (one-on-one, in groups, and teacher-led) with diverse partners on grades 9–10 topics, texts, and issues, building on others' ideas and expressing their own clearly and persuasively.
		L.9-10.6	Acquire and use accurately general academic and domain-specific words and phrases, sufficient for reading, writing, speaking, and listening at the college and career readiness level; demonstrate independence in gathering vocabulary knowledge when considering a word or phrase important to comprehension or expression.
421	**Before Reading: Abuela Invents the Zero**	RL.9-10.2	Determine a theme or central idea of a text and analyze in detail its development over the course of the text, including how it emerges and is shaped and refined by specific details; provide an objective summary of the text.
		RL.9-10.10	By the end of grade 10, read and comprehend literature, including stories, dramas, and poems, at the high end of the grades 9–10 text complexity band independently and proficiently.

Common Core State Standards, continued

SE Pages	Lesson	Code	Standards Text
422–431	**Read Abuela Invents the Zero**	RL.9-10.1	Cite strong and thorough textual evidence to support analysis of what the text says explicitly as well as inferences drawn from the text.
		RL.9-10.2	Determine a theme or central idea of a text and analyze in detail its development over the course of the text, including how it emerges and is shaped and refined by specific details; provide an objective summary of the text.
		RL.9-10.3	Analyze how complex characters develop over the course of a text, interact with other characters, and advance the plot or develop the theme.
		RL.9-10.4	Determine the meaning of words and phrases as they are used in the text, including figurative and connotative meanings; analyze the cumulative impact of specific word choices on meaning and tone.
		RL.9-10.7	Analyze the representation of a subject or a key scene in two different artistic mediums, including what is emphasized or absent in each treatment.
		RL.9-10.10	By the end of grade 10, read and comprehend literature, including stories, dramas, and poems, at the high end of the grades 9–10 text complexity band independently and proficiently.
		W.9-10.9.a	Apply grades 9–10 Reading standards to literature.
		W.9-10.10	Write routinely over extended time frames (time for research, reflection, and revision) and shorter time frames (a single sitting or a day or two) for a range of tasks, purposes, and audiences.
		L.9-10.1	Demonstrate command of the conventions of standard English grammar and usage when writing or speaking.
		L.9-10.2.c	Spell correctly.
		L.9-10.4.c	Consult general and specialized reference materials, both print and digital, to find the pronunciation of a word or determine or clarify its precise meaning, its part of speech, or its etymology.
		L.9-10.6	Acquire and use accurately general academic and domain-specific words and phrases, sufficient for reading, writing, speaking, and listening at the college and career readiness level; demonstrate independence in gathering vocabulary knowledge when considering a word or phrase important to comprehension or expression.
432	**Before Reading: Karate**	RI.9-10.4	Determine the meaning of words and phrases as they are used in a text, including figurative, connotative, and technical meanings; analyze the cumulative impact of specific word choices on meaning and tone.
		RI.9-10.10	By the end of grade 10, read and comprehend literature, including stories, dramas, and poems, at the high end of the grades 9–10 text complexity band independently and proficiently.
433–436	**Read Karate**	RI.9-10.1	Cite strong and thorough textual evidence to support analysis of what the text says explicitly as well as inferences drawn from the text.
		RI.9-10.4	Determine the meaning of words and phrases as they are used in a text, including figurative, connotative, and technical meanings; analyze the cumulative impact of specific word choices on meaning and tone.

SE Pages	Lesson	Code	Standards Text
433–436	**Read Karate** continued	RI.9-10.10	By the end of grade 10, read and comprehend literature, including stories, dramas, and poems, at the high end of the grades 9–10 text complexity band independently and proficiently.
		W.9-10.9.b	Apply grades 9–10 Reading standards to literary nonfiction.
		W.9-10.10	Write routinely over extended time frames (time for research, reflection, and revision) and shorter time frames (a single sitting or a day or two) for a range of tasks, purposes, and audiences.
		L.9-10.1.b	Use various types of phrases (noun, verb, adjectival, adverbial, participial, prepositional, absolute) and clauses (independent, dependent; noun, relative, adverbial) to convey specific meanings and add variety and interest to writing or presentations.
		L.9-10.6	Acquire and use accurately general academic and domain-specific words and phrases, sufficient for reading, writing, speaking, and listening at the college and career readiness level; demonstrate independence in gathering vocabulary knowledge when considering a word or phrase important to comprehension or expression.
437	**Reflect and Assess** **Critical Thinking**	RL.9-10.1	Cite strong and thorough textual evidence to support analysis of what the text says explicitly as well as inferences drawn from the text.
		RI.9-10.1	Cite strong and thorough textual evidence to support analysis of what the text says explicitly as well as inferences drawn from the text.
	Write About Literature	W.9-10.2	Write informative/explanatory texts to examine and convey complex ideas, concepts, and information clearly and accurately through the effective selection, organization, and analysis of content.
	Key Vocabulary Review	L.9-10.6	Acquire and use accurately general academic and domain-specific words and phrases, sufficient for reading, writing, speaking, and listening at the college and career readiness level; demonstrate independence in gathering vocabulary knowledge when considering a word or phrase important to comprehension or expression.
	Read with Ease: Expression	RL.9-10.10	By the end of grade 10, read and comprehend literature, including stories, dramas, and poems, at the high end of the grades 9–10 text complexity band independently and proficiently.
438	**Grammar: Use** **Adverbs Correctly**	L.9-10.1.b	Use various types of phrases (noun, verb, adjectival, adverbial, participial, prepositional, absolute) and clauses (independent, dependent; noun, relative, adverbial) to convey specific meanings and add variety and interest to writing or presentations.
438	**Language Development:** **Define and Explain**	SL.9-10.1	Initiate and participate effectively in a range of collaborative discussions (one-on-one, in groups, and teacher-led) with diverse partners on grades 9–10 topics, texts, and issues, building on others' ideas and expressing their own clearly and persuasively.
438	**Listening/Speaking:** **Panel Discussion**	SL.9-10.1.b	Work with peers to set rules for collegial discussions and decision-making, clear goals and deadlines, and individual roles as needed.
		SL.9-10.1.c	Propel conversations by posing and responding to questions that relate the current discussion to broader themes or larger ideas; actively incorporate others into the discussion; and clarify, verify, or challenge ideas and conclusions.
439	**Vocabulary Study:** **Antonyms**	L.9-10.4.b	Identify and correctly use patterns of word changes that indicate different meanings or parts of speech.
		L.9-10.5	Demonstrate understanding of figurative language, word relationships, and nuances in word meanings.

Common Core State Standards, continued

	Student Handbooks, continued			
CLuster 3, continued				
SE Pages	**Lesson**	**Code**	**Standards Text**	
439	**Writing Trait:** **Trait: Organization**	W.9-10.5	Develop and strengthen writing as needed by planning, revising, editing, rewriting, or trying a new approach, focusing on addressing what is most significant for a specific purpose and audience.	
439	**Literary Analysis:** **Analyze Flashback**	RI.9-10.5	Analyze in detail how an author's ideas or claims are developed and refined by particular sentences, paragraphs, or larger portions of a text .	
Close Reading				
440–443	**Read Why We Must** **Never Forget**	RI.9-10.10	By the end of grade 10, read and comprehend literature, including stories, dramas, and poems, at the high end of the grades 9–10 text complexity band independently and proficiently.	
Unit Wrap-Up				
444	**Unit Wrap-Up** **Present Your Project**	W.9-10.3	Write narratives to develop real or imagined experiences or events using effective technique, well-chosen details, and well-structured event sequences.	
		W.9-10.4	Produce clear and coherent writing in which the development, organization, and style are appropriate to task, purpose, and audience.	
		W.9-10.10	Write routinely over extended time frames (time for research, reflection, and revision) and shorter time frames (a single sitting or a day or two) for a range of tasks, purposes, and audiences.	
	Reflect on Your Reading	SL.9-10.1.a	Come to discussions prepared, having read and researched material under study; explicitly draw on that preparation by referring to evidence from texts and other research on the topic or issue to stimulate a thoughtful, well-reasoned exchange of ideas.	
	Respond to the **Essential Question**	SL.9-10.1.a	Come to discussions prepared, having read and researched material under study; explicitly draw on that preparation by referring to evidence from texts and other research on the topic or issue to stimulate a thoughtful, well-reasoned exchange of ideas.	
Unit 5 Writing Project: Description of a Process				
446–449	**Study a Description** **of a Process and Prewrite**	W.9-10.2.a	Introduce a topic; organize complex ideas, concepts, and information to make important connections and distinctions; include formatting, graphics, and multimedia when useful to aiding comprehension.	
		W.9-10.5	Develop and strengthen writing as needed by planning, revising, editing, rewriting, or trying a new approach, focusing on addressing what is most significant for a specific purpose and audience.	
		W.9-10.6	Use technology, including the Internet, to produce, publish, and update individual or shared writing products, taking advantage of technology's capacity to link to other information and to display information flexibly and dynamically.	

Unit 5 Writing Project: Description of a Process, continued

SE Pages	Lesson	Code	Standards Text
450–451	**Description of a Process: Draft**	W.9-10.2	Write informative/explanatory texts to examine and convey complex ideas, concepts, and information clearly and accurately through the effective selection, organization, and analysis of content.
		W.9-10.4	Produce clear and coherent writing in which the development, organization, and style are appropriate to task, purpose, and audience.
452–455	**Description of a Process: Revise Trait: Organization**	W.9-10.2.a	Introduce a topic; organize complex ideas, concepts, and information to make important connections and distinctions; include formatting, graphics, and multimedia when useful to aiding comprehension.
		W.9-10.2.b	Develop the topic with well-chosen, relevant, and sufficient facts, extended definitions, concrete details, quotations, or other information and examples appropriate to the audience's knowledge of the topic.
		W.9-10.2.c	Use appropriate and varied transitions to link the major sections of the text, create cohesion, and clarify the relationships among complex ideas and concepts.
		W.9-10.2.d	Use precise language and domain-specific vocabulary to manage the complexity of the topic.
		W.9-10.2.e	Establish and maintain a formal style and objective tone while attending to the norms and conventions of the discipline in which they are writing.
		W.9-10.5	Develop and strengthen writing as needed by planning, revising, editing, rewriting, or trying a new approach, focusing on addressing what is most significant for a specific purpose and audience.
		SL.9-10.1	Initiate and participate effectively in a range of collaborative discussions (one-on-one, in groups, and teacher-led) with diverse partners on grades 9–10 topics, texts, and issues, building on others' ideas and expressing their own clearly and persuasively.
		SL.9-10.1.d	Respond thoughtfully to diverse perspectives, summarize points of agreement and disagreement, and, when warranted, qualify or justify their own views and understanding and make new connections in light of the evidence and reasoning presented.
456–458	**Description of a Process: Edit and Proofread Capitalization: Proper Nouns and Adjectives Punctuation: Introductory Words and Clauses Spelling Adjectives and Adverbs**	W.9-10.6	Use technology, including the Internet, to produce, publish, and update individual or shared writing products, taking advantage of technology's capacity to link to other information and to display information flexibly and dynamically.
		L.9-10.1	Demonstrate command of the conventions of standard English grammar and usage when writing or speaking.
		L.9-10.2	Demonstrate command of the conventions of standard English capitalization, punctuation, and spelling when writing.
		L.9-10.2.c	Spell correctly.
		L.9-10.3.a	Write and edit work so that it conforms to the guidelines in a style manual appropriate for the discipline and writing type.

Common Core State Standards, continued

Student Handbooks, continued			

Unit 5 Writing Project: Description of a Process, continued

SE Pages	Lesson	Code	Standards Text
459	**Description of a Process: Publish and Present**	W.9-10.2.a	Introduce a topic; organize complex ideas, concepts, and information to make important connections and distinctions; include formatting, graphics, and multimedia when useful to aiding comprehension.
		W.9-10.6	Use technology, including the Internet, to produce, publish, and update individual or shared writing products, taking advantage of technology's capacity to link to other information and to display information flexibly and dynamically.
		SL.9-10.4	Present information, findings, and supporting evidence clearly, concisely, and logically such that listeners can follow the line of reasoning and the organization, development, substance, and style are appropriate to purpose, audience, and task.
		SL.9-10.5	Make strategic use of digital media in presentations to enhance understanding of findings, reasoning, and evidence and to add interest.
UNIT 6: Coming of Age			
460–461	**Discuss the Essential Question**	SL.9-10.1.b	Work with peers to set rules for collegial discussions and decision-making, clear goals and deadlines, and individual roles as needed.
		SL.9-10.3	Evaluate a speaker's point of view, reasoning, and use of evidence and rhetoric, identifying any fallacious reasoning or exaggerated or distorted evidence.
462	**Take a Position**	SL.9-10.4	Present information, findings, and supporting evidence clearly, concisely, and logically such that listeners can follow the line of reasoning and the organization, development, substance, and style are appropriate to purpose, audience, and task.
463	**Plan a Project**	SL.9-10.1.b	Work with peers to set rules for collegial discussions and decision-making, clear goals and deadlines, and individual roles as needed.
463	**Choose More to Read**	RL.9-10.10	By the end of grade 10, read and comprehend literature, including stories, dramas, and poems, at the high end of the grades 9–10 text complexity band independently and proficiently.
		RI.9-10.10	By the end of grade 9, read and comprehend literary nonfiction in the grades 9–10 text complexity band proficiently, with scaffolding as needed at the high end of the range. By the end of grade 10, read and comprehend literary nonfiction at the high end of the grades 9–10 text complexity band independently and proficiently.
464–467	**How to Read Nonfiction**	RI.9-10.1	Cite strong and thorough textual evidence to support analysis of what the text says explicitly as well as inferences drawn from the text.
		RI.9-10.6	Determine an author's point of view or purpose in a text and analyze how an author uses rhetoric to advance that point of view or purpose.
		Ri.9-10.8	Delineate and evaluate the argument and specific claims in a text, assessing whether the reasoning is valid and the evidence is relevant and sufficient; identify false statements and fallacious reasoning.
		SL.9-10.1	Initiate and participate effectively in a range of collaborative discussions (one-on-one, in groups, and teacher-led) with diverse partners on grades 9–10 topics, texts, and issues, building on others' ideas and expressing their own clearly and persuasively.

UNIT 6: Coming of Age, continued

SE Pages	Lesson	Code	Standards Text
464–467	How to Read Nonfiction continued	L.9-10.6	Acquire and use accurately general academic and domain-specific words and phrases, sufficient for reading, writing, speaking, and listening at the college and career readiness level; demonstrate independence in gathering vocabulary knowledge when considering a word or phrase important to comprehension or expression.

Cluster 1

SE Pages	Lesson	Code	Standards Text
468	Prepare to Read	RI.9-10.4	Determine the meaning of words and phrases as they are used in a text, including figurative, connotative, and technical meanings; analyze the cumulative impact of specific word choices on meaning and tone.
		SL.9-10.1	Initiate and participate effectively in a range of collaborative discussions (one-on-one, in groups, and teacher-led) with diverse partners on grades 9–10 topics, texts, and issues, building on others' ideas and expressing their own clearly and persuasively.
		L.9-10.4.c	Consult general and specialized reference materials, both print and digital, to find the pronunciation of a word or determine or clarify its precise meaning, its part of speech, or its etymology.
		L.9-10.6	Acquire and use accurately general academic and domain-specific words and phrases, sufficient for reading, writing, speaking, and listening at the college and career readiness level; demonstrate independence in gathering vocabulary knowledge when considering a word or phrase important to comprehension or expression.
469	Before Reading: 16: The Right Voting Age	RI.9-10.6	Determine an author's point of view or purpose in a text and analyze how an author uses rhetoric to advance that point of view or purpose.
470–475	Read 16: The Right Voting Age	RI.9-10.1	Cite strong and thorough textual evidence to support analysis of what the text says explicitly as well as inferences drawn from the text.
		RI.9-10.2	Determine a central idea of a text and analyze its development over the course of the text, including how it emerges and is shaped and refined by specific details; provide an objective summary of the text.
		RI.9-10.6	Determine an author's point of view or purpose in a text and analyze how an author uses rhetoric to advance that point of view or purpose.
		Ri.9-10.8	Delineate and evaluate the argument and specific claims in a text, assessing whether the reasoning is valid and the evidence is relevant and sufficient; identify false statements and fallacious reasoning.
		RI.9-10.10	By the end of grade 10, read and comprehend literary nonfiction at the high end of the grades 9–10 text complexity band independently and proficiently.
		W.9-10.9.b	Apply grades 9–10 Reading standards to literary nonfiction.
		L.9-10.1.b	Use various types of phrases (noun, verb, adjectival, adverbial, participial, prepositional, absolute) and clauses (independent, dependent; noun, relative, adverbial) to convey specific meanings and add variety and interest to writing or presentations.
		L.9-10.4.c	Consult general and specialized reference materials, both print and digital, to find the pronunciation of a word or determine or clarify its precise meaning, its part of speech, or its etymology.

Common Core State Standards, continued

Cluster 1, continued

SE Pages	Lesson	Code	Standards Text
470–475	**Read 16: The Right Voting Age** continued	L.9-10.6	Acquire and use accurately general academic and domain-specific words and phrases, sufficient for reading, writing, speaking, and listening at the college and career readiness level; demonstrate independence in gathering vocabulary knowledge when considering a word or phrase important to comprehension or expression.
476	**Before Reading: Teen Brains Are Different**	RI.9-10.5	Analyze in detail how an author's ideas or claims are developed and refined by particular sentences, paragraphs, or larger portions of a text.
		RI.9-10.10	By the end of grade 10, read and comprehend literary nonfiction at the high end of the grades 9–10 text complexity band independently and proficiently.
477–480	**Read Teen Brains Are Different**	RI.9-10.1	Cite strong and thorough textual evidence to support analysis of what the text says explicitly as well as inferences drawn from the text.
		RI.9-10.5	Analyze in detail how an author's ideas or claims are developed and refined by particular sentences, paragraphs, or larger portions of a text.
		RI.9-10.7	Analyze various accounts of a subject told in different mediums, determining which details are emphasized in each account.
		RI.9-10.10	By the end of grade 10, read and comprehend literary nonfiction at the high end of the grades 9–10 text complexity band independently and proficiently.
		W.9-10.9.b	Apply grades 9–10 Reading standards to literary nonfiction.
		L.9-10.1	Demonstrate command of the conventions of standard English grammar and usage when writing or speaking.
		L.9-10.6	Acquire and use accurately general academic and domain-specific words and phrases, sufficient for reading, writing, speaking, and listening at the college and career readiness level; demonstrate independence in gathering vocabulary knowledge when considering a word or phrase important to comprehension or expression.
481	**Reflect and Assess Critical Thinking**	RI.9-10.1	Cite strong and thorough textual evidence to support analysis of what the text says explicitly as well as inferences drawn from the text.
		RI.9-10.8	Delineate and evaluate the argument and specific claims in a text, assessing whether the reasoning is valid and the evidence is relevant and sufficient; identify false statements and fallacious reasoning.
		RI.9-10.10	By the end of grade 10, read and comprehend literary nonfiction at the high end of the grades 9–10 text complexity band independently and proficiently.
	Write About Literature	W.9-10.1	Write arguments to support claims in an analysis of substantive topics or texts, using valid reasoning and relevant and sufficient evidence.
	Key Vocabulary Review	L.9-10.6	Acquire and use accurately general academic and domain-specific words and phrases, sufficient for reading, writing, speaking, and listening at the college and career readiness level; demonstrate independence in gathering vocabulary knowledge when considering a word or phrase important to comprehension or expression.
	Read with Ease: Intonation	RI.9-10.10	By the end of grade 10, read and comprehend literary nonfiction at the high end of the grades 9–10 text complexity band independently and proficiently.
482	**Grammar: Use Indefinite Pronouns**	L.9-10.1	Demonstrate command of the conventions of standard English grammar and usage when writing or speaking.

Cluster 1, continued

SE Pages	Lesson	Code	Standards Text
482	Language Development: Make Comparisons	SL.9-10.1	Initiate and participate effectively in a range of collaborative discussions (one-on-one, in groups, and teacher-led) with diverse partners on grades 9–10 topics, texts, and issues, building on others' ideas and expressing their own clearly and persuasively.
482	Literary Analysis: Evaluate the Author's Purpose and Viewpoint	RI.9-10.6	Determine an author's point of view or purpose in a text and analyze how an author uses rhetoric to advance that point of view or purpose.
483	Vocabulary Study: Specialized Vocabulary	L.9-10.4.c	Consult general and specialized reference materials, both print and digital, to find the pronunciation of a word or determine or clarify its precise meaning, its part of speech, or its etymology.
483	Writing: Write a Letter to the Editor	W.9-10.1	Write arguments to support claims in an analysis of substantive topics or texts, using valid reasoning and relevant and sufficient evidence.
		W.9-10.6	Use technology, including the Internet, to produce, publish, and update individual or shared writing products, taking advantage of technology's capacity to link to other information and to display information flexibly and dynamically.
483	Media Study: Evaluate a Public Service Announcement	SL.9-10.3	Evaluate a speaker's point of view, reasoning, and use of evidence and rhetoric, identifying any fallacious reasoning or exaggerated or distorted evidence.
484	Workplace Workshop: Inside the Postal Service	W.9-10.2	Write informative/explanatory texts to examine and convey complex ideas, concepts, and information clearly and accurately through the effective selection, organization, and analysis of content.
		W.9-10.7	Conduct short as well as more sustained research projects to answer a question (including a self-generated question) or solve a problem; narrow or broaden the inquiry when appropriate; synthesize multiple sources on the subject, demonstrating understanding of the subject under investigation.
		L.9-10.6	Acquire and use accurately general academic and domain-specific words and phrases, sufficient for reading, writing, speaking, and listening at the college and career readiness level; demonstrate independence in gathering vocabulary knowledge when considering a word or phrase important to comprehension or expression.
485	Vocabulary Workshop: Build Word Knowledge	L.9-10.4.c	Consult general and specialized reference materials, both print and digital, to find the pronunciation of a word or determine or clarify its precise meaning, its part of speech, or its etymology.

Cluster 2

SE Pages	Lesson	Code	Standards Text
486	Prepare to Read	RI.9-10.4	Determine the meaning of words and phrases as they are used in a text, including figurative, connotative, and technical meanings; analyze the cumulative impact of specific word choices on meaning and tone.
		SL.9-10.1	Initiate and participate effectively in a range of collaborative discussions (one-on-one, in groups, and teacher-led) with diverse partners on grades 9–10 topics, texts, and issues, building on others' ideas and expressing their own clearly and persuasively.
		L.9-10.4.c	Consult general and specialized reference materials, both print and digital, to find the pronunciation of a word or determine or clarify its precise meaning, its part of speech, or its etymology.

Common Core State Standards, continued

SE Pages	Lesson	Code	Standards Text
486	**Prepare to Read** continued	L.9-10.6	Acquire and use accurately general academic and domain-specific words and phrases, sufficient for reading, writing, speaking, and listening at the college and career readiness level; demonstrate independence in gathering vocabulary knowledge when considering a word or phrase important to comprehension or expression.
487	**Before Reading: Should Communities Set Teen Curfews?**	RI.9-10.8	Delineate and evaluate the argument and specific claims in a text, assessing whether the reasoning is valid and the evidence is relevant and sufficient; identify false statements and fallacious reasoning.
488–493	**Read Should Communities Set Teen Curfews?**	RI.9-10.1	Cite strong and thorough textual evidence to support analysis of what the text says explicitly as well as inferences drawn from the text.
		RI.9-10.2	Determine a central idea of a text and analyze its development over the course of the text, including how it emerges and is shaped and refined by specific details; provide an objective summary of the text.
		RI.9-10.8	Delineate and evaluate the argument and specific claims in a text, assessing whether the reasoning is valid and the evidence is relevant and sufficient; identify false statements and fallacious reasoning.
		RI.9-10.10	By the end of grade 10, read and comprehend literary nonfiction at the high end of the grades 9–10 text complexity band independently and proficiently.
		W.9-10.9.b	Apply grades 9–10 Reading standards to literary nonfiction.
		L.9-10.1	Demonstrate command of the conventions of standard English grammar and usage when writing or speaking.
		L.9-10.6	Acquire and use accurately general academic and domain-specific words and phrases, sufficient for reading, writing, speaking, and listening at the college and career readiness level; demonstrate independence in gathering vocabulary knowledge when considering a word or phrase important to comprehension or expression.
494	**Before Reading: Curfews: A National Debate**	RI.9-10.4	Determine the meaning of words and phrases as they are used in a text, including figurative, connotative, and technical meanings; analyze the cumulative impact of specific word choices on meaning and tone.
		RI.9-10.6	Determine an author's point of view or purpose in a text and analyze how an author uses rhetoric to advance that point of view or purpose.
		RI.9-10.8	Delineate and evaluate the argument and specific claims in a text, assessing whether the reasoning is valid and the evidence is relevant and sufficient; identify false statements and fallacious reasoning.
495–498	**Read Curfews: A National Debate**	RI.9-10.1	Cite strong and thorough textual evidence to support analysis of what the text says explicitly as well as inferences drawn from the text.
		RI.9-10.4	Determine the meaning of words and phrases as they are used in a text, including figurative, connotative, and technical meanings; analyze the cumulative impact of specific word choices on meaning and tone.
		RI.9-10.7	Analyze various accounts of a subject told in different mediums, determining which details are emphasized in each account.

Cluster 2, continued

SE Pages	Lesson	Code	Standards Text
495–498	**Read Curfews: A National Debate** continued	RI.9-10.8	Delineate and evaluate the argument and specific claims in a text, assessing whether the reasoning is valid and the evidence is relevant and sufficient; identify false statements and fallacious reasoning.
		RI.9-10.10	By the end of grade 10, read and comprehend literary nonfiction at the high end of the grades 9–10 text complexity band independently and proficiently.
		W.9-10.9.b	Apply grades 9–10 Reading standards to literary nonfiction.
		L.9-10.1	Demonstrate command of the conventions of standard English grammar and usage when writing or speaking.
		L.9-10.6	Acquire and use accurately general academic and domain-specific words and phrases, sufficient for reading, writing, speaking, and listening at the college and career readiness level; demonstrate independence in gathering vocabulary knowledge when considering a word or phrase important to comprehension or expression.
499	**Reflect and Assess Critical Thinking**	RI.9-10.1	Cite strong and thorough textual evidence to support analysis of what the text says explicitly as well as inferences drawn from the text.
		RI.9-10.8	Delineate and evaluate the argument and specific claims in a text, assessing whether the reasoning is valid and the evidence is relevant and sufficient; identify false statements and fallacious reasoning.
	Write About Literature	W.9-10.1	Write arguments to support claims in an analysis of substantive topics or texts, using valid reasoning and relevant and sufficient evidence.
	Key Vocabulary Review	L.9-10.6	Acquire and use accurately general academic and domain-specific words and phrases, sufficient for reading, writing, speaking, and listening at the college and career readiness level; demonstrate independence in gathering vocabulary knowledge when considering a word or phrase important to comprehension or expression.
	Read with Ease: Expression	RI.9-10.10	By the end of grade 10, read and comprehend literary nonfiction at the high end of the grades 9–10 text complexity band independently and proficiently.
500	**Grammar: Vary Your Sentences**	L.9-10.1	Demonstrate command of the conventions of standard English grammar and usage when writing or speaking.
500	**Language Development: Express Opinions**	SL.9-10.1	Initiate and participate effectively in a range of collaborative discussions (one-on-one, in groups, and teacher-led) with diverse partners on grades 9–10 topics, texts, and issues, building on others' ideas and expressing their own clearly and persuasively.
500	**Literary Analysis: Analyze Persuasive Techniques**	RI.9-10.6	Determine an author's point of view or purpose in a text and analyze how an author uses rhetoric to advance that point of view or purpose.
501	**Vocabulary Study: Analogies**	L.9-10.5	Demonstrate understanding of figurative language, word relationships, and nuances in word meanings.
501	**Writing Trait: Trait: Development of Ideas**	W.9-10.1	Write arguments to support claims in an analysis of substantive topics or texts, using valid reasoning and relevant and sufficient evidence.
501	**Research/Writing: Cause-and-Effect Essay**	W.9-10.7	Conduct short as well as more sustained research projects to answer a question (including a self-generated question) or solve a problem; narrow or broaden the inquiry when appropriate; synthesize multiple sources on the subject, demonstrating understanding of the subject under investigation.

Common Core State Standards, continued

SE Pages	Lesson	Code	Standards Text

Student Handbooks, continued

Cluster 2, continued

SE Pages	Lesson	Code	Standards Text
502–503	Listening and Speaking Workshop: Persuasive Speech	SL.9-10.3	Evaluate a speaker's point of view, reasoning, and use of evidence and rhetoric, identifying any fallacious reasoning or exaggerated or distorted evidence.
		SL.9-10.4	Present information, findings, and supporting evidence clearly, concisely, and logically such that listeners can follow the line of reasoning and the organization, development, substance, and style are appropriate to purpose, audience, and task
		SL.9-10.6	Adapt speech to a variety of contexts and tasks, demonstrating command of formal English when indicated or appropriate.
Cluster 3			
504	Prepare to Read	RI.9-10.4	Determine the meaning of words and phrases as they are used in a text, including figurative, connotative, and technical meanings; analyze the cumulative impact of specific word choices on meaning and tone.
		SL.9-10.1	Initiate and participate effectively in a range of collaborative discussions (one-on-one, in groups, and teacher-led) with diverse partners on grades 9-10 topics, texts, and issues, building on others' ideas and expressing their own clearly and persuasively.
		L.9-10.6	Acquire and use accurately general academic and domain-specific words and phrases, sufficient for reading, writing, speaking, and listening at the college and career readiness level; demonstrate independence in gathering vocabulary knowledge when considering a word or phrase important to comprehension or expression.
505	Before Reading: What Does Responsibility Look Like?	RI.9-10.8	Delineate and evaluate the argument and specific claims in a text, assessing whether the reasoning is valid and the evidence is relevant and sufficient; identify false statements and fallacious reasoning.
		RI.9-10.10	By the end of grade 10, read and comprehend literary nonfiction at the high end of the grades 9–10 text complexity band independently and proficiently.
506–511	Read What Does Responsibility Look Like?	RI.9-10.1	Cite strong and thorough textual evidence to support analysis of what the text says explicitly as well as inferences drawn from the text.
		RI.9-10.2	Determine a central idea of a text and analyze its development over the course of the text, including how it emerges and is shaped and refined by specific details; provide an objective summary of the text.
		RI.9-10.8	Delineate and evaluate the argument and specific claims in a text, assessing whether the reasoning is valid and the evidence is relevant and sufficient; identify false statements and fallacious reasoning.
		RI.9-10.10	By the end of grade 10, read and comprehend literary nonfiction at the high end of the grades 9–10 text complexity band independently and proficiently.
		W.9-10.9.b	Apply grades 9–10 Reading standards to literary nonfiction.
		L.9-10.1.b	Use various types of phrases (noun, verb, adjectival, adverbial, participial, prepositional, absolute) and clauses (independent, dependent; noun, relative, adverbial) to convey specific meanings and add variety and interest to writing or presentations.
		L.9-10.4.a	Use context as a clue to the meaning of a word or phrase.

SE Pages	Lesson	Code	Standards Text
506–511	**Read What Does Responsibility Look Like?** continued	L.9-10.6	Acquire and use accurately general academic and domain-specific words and phrases, sufficient for reading, writing, speaking, and listening at the college and career readiness level; demonstrate independence in gathering vocabulary knowledge when considering a word or phrase important to comprehension or expression.
512	**Before Reading: Getting a Job**	RI.9-10.4	Determine the meaning of words and phrases as they are used in a text, including figurative, connotative, and technical meanings; analyze the cumulative impact of specific word choices on meaning and tone.
		RI.9-10.10	By the end of grade 10, read and comprehend literary nonfiction at the high end of the grades 9–10 text complexity band independently and proficiently.
513–518	**Read Getting a Job**	RI.9-10.1	Cite strong and thorough textual evidence to support analysis of what the text says explicitly as well as inferences drawn from the text.
		RI.9-10.2	Determine a central idea of a text and analyze its development over the course of the text, including how it emerges and is shaped and refined by specific details; provide an objective summary of the text.
		RI.9-10.4	Determine the meaning of words and phrases as they are used in a text, including figurative, connotative, and technical meanings; analyze the cumulative impact of specific word choices on meaning and tone.
		RI.9-10.10	By the end of grade 10, read and comprehend literary nonfiction at the high end of the grades 9–10 text complexity band independently and proficiently.
		W.9-10.9.b	Apply grades 9–10 Reading standards to literary nonfiction.
		W.9-10.10	Write routinely over extended time frames (time for research, reflection, and revision) and shorter time frames (a single sitting or a day or two) for a range of tasks, purposes, and audiences.
		L.9-10.1.b	Use various types of phrases (noun, verb, adjectival, adverbial, participial, prepositional, absolute) and clauses (independent, dependent; noun, relative, adverbial) to convey specific meanings and add variety and interest to writing or presentations.
		L.9-10.6	Acquire and use accurately general academic and domain-specific words and phrases, sufficient for reading, writing, speaking, and listening at the college and career readiness level; demonstrate independence in gathering vocabulary knowledge when considering a word or phrase important to comprehension or expression.
519	**Reflect and Assess Critical Thinking**	RI.9-10.1	Cite strong and thorough textual evidence to support analysis of what the text says explicitly as well as inferences drawn from the text.
		RI.9-10.10	By the end of grade 10, read and comprehend literary nonfiction at the high end of the grades 9–10 text complexity band independently and proficiently.
	Write About Literature	W.9-10.1	Write arguments to support claims in an analysis of substantive topics or texts, using valid reasoning and relevant and sufficient evidence.
	Key Vocabulary Review	L.9-10.6	Acquire and use accurately general academic and domain-specific words and phrases, sufficient for reading, writing, speaking, and listening at the college and career readiness level; demonstrate independence in gathering vocabulary knowledge when considering a word or phrase important to comprehension or expression.

Common Core State Standards, continued

Student Handbooks, continued

Cluster 3, continued

SE Pages	Lesson	Code	Standards Text
519	**Reflect and Assess Critical Thinking** continued **Read with Ease: Phrasing**	RI.9-10.10	By the end of grade 10, read and comprehend literary nonfiction at the high end of the grades 9–10 text complexity band independently and proficiently.
520	**Grammar: Use Compound Sentences**	L.9-10.1.b	Use various types of phrases (noun, verb, adjectival, adverbial, participial, prepositional, absolute) and clauses (independent, dependent; noun, relative, adverbial) to convey specific meanings and add variety and interest to writing or presentations.
520	**Language Development: Persuade**	SL.9-10.4	Present information, findings, and supporting evidence clearly, concisely, and logically such that listeners can follow the line of reasoning and the organization, development, substance, and style are appropriate to purpose, audience, and task.
520	**Literary Analysis: Evaluate Functional Documents**	RI.9-10.5	Analyze in detail how an author's ideas or claims are developed and refined by particular sentences, paragraphs, or larger portions of a text.
521	**Vocabulary Study: Multiple-Meaning Words**	L.9-10.4.a	Use context as a clue to the meaning of a word or phrase.
		L.9-10.4.c	Consult general and specialized reference materials, both print and digital, to find the pronunciation of a word or determine or clarify its precise meaning, its part of speech, or its etymology.
521	**Writing on Demand: Write an Expository Essay**	W.9-10.2	Write informative/explanatory texts to examine and convey complex ideas, concepts, and information clearly and accurately through the effective selection, organization, and analysis of content.
		W.9-10.4	Produce clear and coherent writing in which the development, organization, and style are appropriate to task, purpose, and audience.
521	**Reading: Technical Documents**	RI.9-10.2	Determine a central idea of a text and analyze its development over the course of the text, including how it emerges and is shaped and refined by specific details; provide an objective summary of the text.

Close Reading

SE Pages	Lesson	Code	Standards Text
522–525	**Read Trashing Teens**	RI.9-10.10	By the end of grade 10, read and comprehend literary nonfiction at the high end of the grades 9–10 text complexity band independently and proficiently.

Unit Wrap-Up

SE Pages	Lesson	Code	Standards Text
526	**Unit Wrap-Up Present Your Project**	SL.9-10.3	Evaluate a speaker's point of view, reasoning, and use of evidence and rhetoric, identifying any fallacious reasoning or exaggerated or distorted evidence.
		SL.9-10.4	Present information, findings, and supporting evidence clearly, concisely, and logically such that listeners can follow the line of reasoning and the organization, development, substance, and style are appropriate to purpose, audience, and task.
	Reflect on Your Reading	SL.9-10.1.a	Come to discussions prepared, having read and researched material under study; explicitly draw on that preparation by referring to evidence from texts and other research on the topic or issue to stimulate a thoughtful, well-reasoned exchange of ideas.
	Respond to the Essential Question	SL.9-10.1.a	Come to discussions prepared, having read and researched material under study; explicitly draw on that preparation by referring to evidence from texts and other research on the topic or issue to stimulate a thoughtful, well-reasoned exchange of ideas.

Unit 6 Writing Project: Persuasive Essay

SE Pages	Lesson	Code	Standards Text
528–531	**Study Persuasive Essays and Prewrite**	W.9-10.1.a	Introduce precise claim(s), distinguish the claim(s) from alternate or opposing claims, and create an organization that establishes clear relationships among claim(s), counterclaims, reasons, and evidence.
		W.9-10.1.b	Develop claim(s) and counterclaims fairly, supplying evidence for each while pointing out the strengths and limitations of both in a manner that anticipates the audience's knowledge level and concerns.
		W.9-10.5	Develop and strengthen writing as needed by planning, revising, editing, rewriting, or trying a new approach, focusing on addressing what is most significant for a specific purpose and audience.
		W.9-10.7	Conduct short as well as more sustained research projects to answer a question (including a self-generated question) or solve a problem; narrow or broaden the inquiry when appropriate; synthesize multiple sources on the subject, demonstrating understanding of the subject under investigation.
		W.9-10.8	Gather relevant information from multiple authoritative print and digital sources, using advanced searches effectively; assess the usefulness of each source in answering the research question; integrate information into the text selectively to maintain the flow of ideas, avoiding plagiarism and following a standard format for citation.
532–533	**Persuasive Essay: Draft**	W.9-10.1	Write arguments to support claims in an analysis of substantive topics or texts, using valid reasoning and relevant and sufficient evidence.
		W.9-10.4	Produce clear and coherent writing in which the development, organization, and style are appropriate to task, purpose, and audience.
		W.9-10.6	Use technology, including the Internet, to produce, publish, and update individual or shared writing products, taking advantage of technology's capacity to link to other information and to display information flexibly and dynamically.
534–537	**Persuasive Essay: Revise Trait: Development of Ideas**	W.9-10.1.a	Introduce precise claim(s), distinguish the claim(s) from alternate or opposing claims, and create an organization that establishes clear relationships among claim(s), counterclaims, reasons, and evidence.
		W.9-10.1.b	Develop claim(s) and counterclaims fairly, supplying evidence for each while pointing out the strengths and limitations of both in a manner that anticipates the audience's knowledge level and concerns.
		W.9-10.1.e	Provide a concluding statement or section that follows from and supports the argument presented.
		W.9-10.5	Develop and strengthen writing as needed by planning, revising, editing, rewriting, or trying a new approach, focusing on addressing what is most significant for a specific purpose and audience.
		W.9-10.7	Conduct short as well as more sustained research projects to answer a question (including a self-generated question) or solve a problem; narrow or broaden the inquiry when appropriate; synthesize multiple sources on the subject, demonstrating understanding of the subject under investigation.
		SL.9-10.1	Initiate and participate effectively in a range of collaborative discussions (one-on-one, in groups, and teacher-led) with diverse partners on grades 9–10 topics, texts, and issues, building on others' ideas and expressing their own clearly and persuasively.

Common Core State Standards, continued

Unit 6 Writing Project: Persuasive Essay, continued

SE Pages	Lesson	Code	Standards Text
534–537	**Persuasive Essay: Revise Trait: Development of Ideas** continued	SL.9-10.1.d	Respond thoughtfully to diverse perspectives, summarize points of agreement and disagreement, and, when warranted, qualify or justify their own views and understanding and make new connections in light of the evidence and reasoning presented.
538–540	**Persuasive Essay: Edit and Proofread Capitalization: Titles of Publications Italics and Underlining Spelling Compound Sentences**	W.9-10.6	Use technology, including the Internet, to produce, publish, and update individual or shared writing products, taking advantage of technology's capacity to link to other information and to display information flexibly and dynamically.
		L.9-10.1.b	Use various types of phrases (noun, verb, adjectival, adverbial, participial, prepositional, absolute) and clauses (independent, dependent; noun, relative, adverbial) to convey specific meanings and add variety and interest to writing or presentations.
		L.9-10.2	Demonstrate command of the conventions of standard English capitalization, punctuation, and spelling when writing.
		L.9-10.2.c	Spell correctly.
		L.9-10.3.a	Write and edit work so that it conforms to the guidelines in a style manual appropriate for the discipline and writing type.
541	**Persuasive Essay: Publish and Present**	W.9-10.6	Use technology, including the Internet, to produce, publish, and update individual or shared writing products, taking advantage of technology's capacity to link to other information and to display information flexibly and dynamically.
		SL.9-10.1	Initiate and participate effectively in a range of collaborative discussions (one-on-one, in groups, and teacher-led) with diverse partners on grades 9–10 topics, texts, and issues, building on others' ideas and expressing their own clearly and persuasively.
		SL.9-10.5	Make strategic use of digital media in presentations to enhance understanding of findings, reasoning, and evidence and to add interest.
		SL.9-10.6	Adapt speech to a variety of contexts and tasks, demonstrating command of formal English when indicated or appropriate.

UNIT 7: Making Impressions

SE Pages	Lesson	Code	Standards Text
542–543	**Discuss the Essential Question**	SL.9-10.1.b	Work with peers to set rules for collegial discussions and decision-making, clear goals and deadlines, and individual roles as needed.
		SL.9-10.3	Evaluate a speaker's point of view, reasoning, and use of evidence and rhetoric, identifying any fallacious reasoning or exaggerated or distorted evidence.
544	**Analyze and Discuss**	SL.9-10.4	Present information, findings, and supporting evidence clearly, concisely, and logically such that listeners can follow the line of reasoning and the organization, development, substance, and style are appropriate to purpose, audience, and task.
545	**Plan a Project**	SL.9-10.1.b	Work with peers to set rules for collegial discussions and decision-making, clear goals and deadlines, and individual roles as needed.
545	**Choose More to Read**	RL.9-10.10	By the end of grade 10, read and comprehend literature, including stories, dramas, and poems, at the high end of the grades 9–10 text complexity band independently and proficiently.
		RI.9-10.10	By the end of grade 10, read and comprehend literary nonfiction at the high end of the grades 9–10 text complexity band independently and proficiently.

UNIT 7: Making Impressions, continued

SE Pages	Lesson	Code	Standards Text
546–549	**How to Read Drama**	RL.9-10.4	Determine the meaning of words and phrases as they are used in the text, including figurative and connotative meanings; analyze the cumulative impact of specific word choices on meaning and tone.
		RL.9-10.10	By the end of grade 10, read and comprehend literature, including stories, dramas, and poems, at the high end of the grades 9–10 text complexity band independently and proficiently.
550–551	**How to Read Poetry**	RL.9-10.4	Determine the meaning of words and phrases as they are used in the text, including figurative and connotative meanings; analyze the cumulative impact of specific word choices on meaning and tone.
		RL.9-10.7	Analyze the representation of a subject or a key scene in two different artistic mediums, including what is emphasized or absent in each treatment.
		SL.9-10.1.b	Work with peers to set rules for collegial discussions and decision-making, clear goals and deadlines, and individual roles as needed
		SL.9-10.4	Present information, findings, and supporting evidence clearly, concisely, and logically such that listeners can follow the line of reasoning and the organization, development, substance, and style are appropriate to purpose, audience, and task.

Cluster 1

SE Pages	Lesson	Code	Standards Text
552	**Prepare to Read**	RI.9-10.4	Determine the meaning of words and phrases as they are used in a text, including figurative, connotative, and technical meanings; analyze the cumulative impact of specific word choices on meaning and tone.
		SL.9-10.1	Initiate and participate effectively in a range of collaborative discussions (one-on-one, in groups, and teacher-led) with diverse partners on grades 9–10 topics, texts, and issues, building on others' ideas and expressing their own clearly and persuasively.
		L.9-10.6	Acquire and use accurately general academic and domain-specific words and phrases, sufficient for reading, writing, speaking, and listening at the college and career readiness level; demonstrate independence in gathering vocabulary knowledge when considering a word or phrase important to comprehension or expression.
553	**Before Reading: Novio Boy: Scene 7, Part 1**	RL.9-10.4	Determine the meaning of words and phrases as they are used in the text, including figurative and connotative meanings; analyze the cumulative impact of specific word choices on meaning and tone.
		RL.9-10.7	Analyze the representation of a subject or a key scene in two different artistic mediums, including what is emphasized or absent in each treatment.
554–566	**Read Novio Boy: Scene 7, Part 1**	RL.9-10.1	Cite strong and thorough textual evidence to support analysis of what the text says explicitly as well as inferences drawn from the text.
		RL.9-10.2	Determine a theme or central idea of a text and analyze in detail its development over the course of the text, including how it emerges and is shaped and refined by specific details; provide an objective summary of the text.
		RL.9-10.3	Analyze how complex characters develop over the course of a text, interact with other characters, and advance the plot or develop the theme.

Common Core State Standards, continued

Cluster 1, continued

SE Pages	Lesson	Code	Standards Text
554–566	**Read Novio Boy: Scene 7, Part 1** continued	RL.9-10.4	Determine the meaning of words and phrases as they are used in the text, including figurative and connotative meanings; analyze the cumulative impact of specific word choices on meaning and tone.
		RL.9-10.7	Analyze the representation of a subject or a key scene in two different artistic mediums, including what is emphasized or absent in each treatment.
		RL.9-10.10	By the end of grade 10, read and comprehend literature, including stories, dramas, and poems, at the high end of the grades 9–10 text complexity band independently and proficiently.
		W.9-10.9.a	Apply grades 9-10 Reading standards to literature.
		W.9-10.10	Write routinely over extended time frames (time for research, reflection, and revision) and shorter time frames (a single sitting or a day or two) for a range of tasks, purposes, and audiences.
		L.9-10.1.b	Use various types of phrases (noun, verb, adjectival, adverbial, participial, prepositional, absolute) and clauses (independent, dependent; noun, relative, adverbial) to convey specific meanings and add variety and interest to writing or presentations.
		L.9-10.4.a	Use context as a clue to the meaning of a word or phrase.
		L.9-10.6	Acquire and use accurately general academic and domain-specific words and phrases, sufficient for reading, writing, speaking, and listening at the college and career readiness level; demonstrate independence in gathering vocabulary knowledge when considering a word or phrase important to comprehension or expression.
567	**Before Reading: Oranges**	RL.9-10.3	Analyze how complex characters develop over the course of a text, interact with other characters, and advance the plot or develop the theme.
		RL.9-10.4	Determine the meaning of words and phrases as they are used in the text, including figurative and connotative meanings; analyze the cumulative impact of specific word choices on meaning and tone.
568–570	**Read Oranges**	RL.9-10.1	Cite strong and thorough textual evidence to support analysis of what the text says explicitly as well as inferences drawn from the text.
		RL.9-10.3	Analyze how complex characters develop over the course of a text, interact with other characters, and advance the plot or develop the theme.
		RL.9-10.4	Determine the meaning of words and phrases as they are used in the text, including figurative and connotative meanings; analyze the cumulative impact of specific word choices on meaning and tone.
		RL.9-10.7	Analyze the representation of a subject or a key scene in two different artistic mediums, including what is emphasized or absent in each treatment.
		RL.9-10.10	By the end of grade 10, read and comprehend literature, including stories, dramas, and poems, at the high end of the grades 9–10 text complexity band independently and proficiently.
		W.9-10.9.a	Apply grades 9-10 Reading standards to literature.

Cluster 1, continued

SE Pages	Lesson	Code	Standards Text
568–570	**Read Oranges** continued	W.9-10.10	Write routinely over extended time frames (time for research, reflection, and revision) and shorter time frames (a single sitting or a day or two) for a range of tasks, purposes, and audiences.
		L.9-10.6	Acquire and use accurately general academic and domain-specific words and phrases, sufficient for reading, writing, speaking, and listening at the college and career readiness level; demonstrate independence in gathering vocabulary knowledge when considering a word or phrase important to comprehension or expression.
571	**Reflect and Assess Critical Thinking**	RL.9-10.1	Cite strong and thorough textual evidence to support analysis of what the text says explicitly as well as inferences drawn from the text.
	Write About Literature	W.9-10.1	Write arguments to support claims in an analysis of substantive topics or texts, using valid reasoning and relevant and sufficient evidence.
	Key Vocabulary Review	L.9-10.6	Acquire and use accurately general academic and domain-specific words and phrases, sufficient for reading, writing, speaking, and listening at the college and career readiness level; demonstrate independence in gathering vocabulary knowledge when considering a word or phrase important to comprehension or expression.
	Read with Ease: Expression	RL.9-10.10	By the end of grade 10, read and comprehend literature, including stories, dramas, and poems, at the high end of the grades 9–10 text complexity band independently and proficiently.
572	**Grammar: Use Complex Sentences**	L.9-10.1.b	Use various types of phrases (noun, verb, adjectival, adverbial, participial, prepositional, absolute) and clauses (independent, dependent; noun, relative, adverbial) to convey specific meanings and add variety and interest to writing or presentations.
572	**Language Development: Engage in Discussion**	SL.9-10.1.c	Propel conversations by posing and responding to questions that relate the current discussion to broader themes or larger ideas; actively incorporate others into the discussion; and clarify, verify, or challenge ideas and conclusions.
		SL.9-10.1.d	Respond thoughtfully to diverse perspectives, summarize points of agreement and disagreement, and, when warranted, qualify or justify their own views and understanding and make new connections in light of the evidence and reasoning presented.
572	**Literary Analysis: Compare Themes**	RL.9-10.2	Determine a theme or central idea of a text and analyze in detail its development over the course of the text, including how it emerges and is shaped and refined by specific details; provide an objective summary of the text.
573	**Vocabulary Study: Idioms**	L.9-10.5.a	Interpret figures of speech in context and analyze their role in the text.
573	**Writing: Write a Script**	W.9-10.3	Write narratives to develop real or imagined experiences or events using effective technique, well-chosen details, and well-structured event sequences.
573	**Listening/Speaking: Choral Reading**	L.9-10.6	Acquire and use accurately general academic and domain-specific words and phrases, sufficient for reading, writing, speaking, and listening at the college and career readiness level; demonstrate independence in gathering vocabulary knowledge when considering a word or phrase important to comprehension or expression.
574	**Workplace Workshop: Inside a Restaurant**	W.9-10.4	Produce clear and coherent writing in which the development, organization, and style are appropriate to task, purpose, and audience.
		W.9-10.10	Write routinely over extended time frames (time for research, reflection, and revision) and shorter time frames (a single sitting or a day or two) for a range of tasks, purposes, and audiences.

Common Core State Standards, continued

Cluster 1, continued

SE Pages	Lesson	Code	Standards Text
575	Vocabulary Workshop: Interpret Non-Literal Language	L.9-10.4.a	Use context as a clue to the meaning of a word or phrase.
		L.9-10.4.c	Consult general and specialized reference materials, both print and digital, to find the pronunciation of a word or determine or clarify its precise meaning, its part of speech, or its etymology.
		L.9-10.4.d	Verify the preliminary determination of the meaning of a word or phrase.
		L.9-10.5.a	Interpret figures of speech in context and analyze their role in the text.

Cluster 2

SE Pages	Lesson	Code	Standards Text
576	Prepare to Read	RI.9-10.4	Determine the meaning of words and phrases as they are used in a text, including figurative, connotative, and technical meanings; analyze the cumulative impact of specific word choices on meaning and tone.
		SL.9-10.1	Initiate and participate effectively in a range of collaborative discussions (one-on-one, in groups, and teacher-led) with diverse partners on grades 9–10 topics, texts, and issues, building on others' ideas and expressing their own clearly and persuasively.
		L.9-10.6	Acquire and use accurately general academic and domain-specific words and phrases, sufficient for reading, writing, speaking, and listening at the college and career readiness level; demonstrate independence in gathering vocabulary knowledge when considering a word or phrase important to comprehension or expression.
577	Before Reading: Novio Boy: Scene 7, Part 2	RL.9-10.4	Determine the meaning of words and phrases as they are used in the text, including figurative and connotative meanings; analyze the cumulative impact of specific word choices on meaning and tone.
		RL.9-10.5	Analyze how an author's choices concerning how to structure a text, order events within it, and manipulate time create such effects as mystery, tension, or surprise.
578–587	Read Novio Boy: Scene 7, Part 2	RL.9-10.1	Cite strong and thorough textual evidence to support analysis of what the text says explicitly as well as inferences drawn from the text.
		RL.9-10.2	Determine a theme or central idea of a text and analyze in detail its development over the course of the text, including how it emerges and is shaped and refined by specific details; provide an objective summary of the text.
		RL.9-10.4	Determine the meaning of words and phrases as they are used in the text, including figurative and connotative meanings; analyze the cumulative impact of specific word choices on meaning and tone.
		RL.9-10.5	Analyze how an author's choices concerning how to structure a text, order events within it, and manipulate time create such effects as mystery, tension, or surprise.
		RL.9-10.7	Analyze the representation of a subject or a key scene in two different artistic mediums, including what is emphasized or absent in each treatment.
		RL.9-10.10	By the end of grade 10, read and comprehend literature, including stories, dramas, and poems, at the high end of the grades 9–10 text complexity band independently and proficiently.
		W.9-10.9.a	Apply grades 9–10 Reading standards to literature.

Cluster 2, continued

SE Pages	Lesson	Code	Standards Text
578–587	**Read Novio Boy: Scene 7, Part 2** continued	L.9-10.1.b	Use various types of phrases (noun, verb, adjectival, adverbial, participial, prepositional, absolute) and clauses (independent, dependent; noun, relative, adverbial) to convey specific meanings and add variety and interest to writing or presentations.
		L.9-10.2.c	Spell correctly.
		L.9-10.6	Acquire and use accurately general academic and domain-specific words and phrases, sufficient for reading, writing, speaking, and listening at the college and career readiness level; demonstrate independence in gathering vocabulary knowledge when considering a word or phrase important to comprehension or expression.
588 Before Reading: Your World		RL.9-10.4	Determine the meaning of words and phrases as they are used in the text, including figurative and connotative meanings; analyze the cumulative impact of specific word choices on meaning and tone.
		RL.9-10.5	Analyze how an author's choices concerning how to structure a text, order events within it, and manipulate time create such effects as mystery, tension, or surprise.
589–590	**Read Your World**	RL.9-10.1	Cite strong and thorough textual evidence to support analysis of what the text says explicitly as well as inferences drawn from the text.
		RL.9-10.2	Determine a theme or central idea of a text and analyze in detail its development over the course of the text, including how it emerges and is shaped and refined by specific details; provide an objective summary of the text.
		RL.9-10.4	Determine the meaning of words and phrases as they are used in the text, including figurative and connotative meanings; analyze the cumulative impact of specific word choices on meaning and tone.
		RL.9-10.5	Analyze how an author's choices concerning how to structure a text, order events within it, and manipulate time create such effects as mystery, tension, or surprise.
		RL.9-10.7	Analyze the representation of a subject or a key scene in two different artistic mediums, including what is emphasized or absent in each treatment.
		RL.9-10.10	By the end of grade 10, read and comprehend literature, including stories, dramas, and poems, at the high end of the grades 9–10 text complexity band independently and proficiently.
		W.9-10.9.a	Apply grades 9–10 Reading standards to literature.
		W.9-10.10	Write routinely over extended time frames (time for research, reflection, and revision) and shorter time frames (a single sitting or a day or two) for a range of tasks, purposes, and audiences.
		L.9-10.6	Acquire and use accurately general academic and domain-specific words and phrases, sufficient for reading, writing, speaking, and listening at the college and career readiness level; demonstrate independence in gathering vocabulary knowledge when considering a word or phrase important to comprehension or expression.

Common Core State Standards, continued

SE Pages	Lesson	Code	Standards Text
591	Reflect and Assess Critical Thinking	RL.9-10.1	Cite strong and thorough textual evidence to support analysis of what the text says explicitly as well as inferences drawn from the text.
	Write About Literature	W.9-10.2	Write informative/explanatory texts to examine and convey complex ideas, concepts, and information clearly and accurately through the effective selection, organization, and analysis of content.
	Key Vocabulary Review	L.9-10.6	Acquire and use accurately general academic and domain-specific words and phrases, sufficient for reading, writing, speaking, and listening at the college and career readiness level; demonstrate independence in gathering vocabulary knowledge when considering a word or phrase important to comprehension or expression.
	Read with Ease: Intonation	RL.9-10.10	By the end of grade 10, read and comprehend literature, including stories, dramas, and poems, at the high end of the grades 9–10 text complexity band independently and proficiently.
592	Grammar: Use the Present Perfect Tense	L.9-10.1.b	Use various types of phrases (noun, verb, adjectival, adverbial, participial, prepositional, absolute) and clauses (independent, dependent; noun, relative, adverbial) to convey specific meanings and add variety and interest to writing or presentations.
592	Language Development: Use Appropriate Language	SL.9-10.6	Adapt speech to a variety of contexts and tasks, demonstrating command of formal English when indicated or appropriate.
592	Literary Analysis: Rhythm and Meter	RL.9-10.5	Analyze how an author's choices concerning how to structure a text, order events within it, and manipulate time create such effects as mystery, tension, or surprise.
592	Research/Speaking: Oral Report	W.9-10.7	Conduct short as well as more sustained research projects to answer a question (including a self-generated question) or solve a problem; narrow or broaden the inquiry when appropriate; synthesize multiple sources on the subject, demonstrating understanding of the subject under investigation.
		W.9-10.8	Gather relevant information from multiple authoritative print and digital sources, using advanced searches effectively; assess the usefulness of each source in answering the research question; integrate information into the text selectively to maintain the flow of ideas, avoiding plagiarism and following a standard format for citation.
		W.9-10.9.a	Apply grades 9–10 Reading standards to literature.
593	Vocabulary Study: Idioms	L.9-10.5.a	Interpret figures of speech in context and analyze their role in the text.
593	Writing on Demand: Write a Theme Analysis	W.9-10.2	Write informative/explanatory texts to examine and convey complex ideas, concepts, and information clearly and accurately through the effective selection, organization, and analysis of content.
		W.9-10.5	Develop and strengthen writing as needed by planning, revising, editing, rewriting, or trying a new approach, focusing on addressing what is most significant for a specific purpose and audience.
594–595	Listening and Speaking Workshop: Poetry Slam	SL.9-10.6	Adapt speech to a variety of contexts and tasks, demonstrating command of formal English when indicated or appropriate.
		L.9-10.3	Apply knowledge of language to understand how language functions in different contexts, to make effective choices for meaning or style, and to comprehend more fully when reading or listening.

SE Pages	Lesson	Code	Standards Text
596	**Prepare to Read**	RI.9-10.4	Determine the meaning of words and phrases as they are used in a text, including figurative, connotative, and technical meanings; analyze the cumulative impact of specific word choices on meaning and tone.
		SL.9-10.1	Initiate and participate effectively in a range of collaborative discussions (one-on-one, in groups, and teacher-led) with diverse partners on grades 9–10 topics, texts, and issues, building on others' ideas and expressing their own clearly and persuasively.
		L.9-10.6	Acquire and use accurately general academic and domain-specific words and phrases, sufficient for reading, writing, speaking, and listening at the college and career readiness level; demonstrate independence in gathering vocabulary knowledge when considering a word or phrase important to comprehension or expression.
597	**Before Reading: To Helen Keller**	RL.9-10.4	Determine the meaning of words and phrases as they are used in the text, including figurative and connotative meanings; analyze the cumulative impact of specific word choices on meaning and tone.
598–603	**Read To Helen Keller**	RL.9-10.1	Cite strong and thorough textual evidence to support analysis of what the text says explicitly as well as inferences drawn from the text.
		RL.9-10.4	Determine the meaning of words and phrases as they are used in the text, including figurative and connotative meanings; analyze the cumulative impact of specific word choices on meaning and tone.
		RL.9-10.10	By the end of grade 10, read and comprehend literature, including stories, dramas, and poems, at the high end of the grades 9–10 text complexity band independently and proficiently.
		L.9-10.1.b	Use various types of phrases (noun, verb, adjectival, adverbial, participial, prepositional, absolute) and clauses (independent, dependent; noun, relative, adverbial) to convey specific meanings and add variety and interest to writing or presentations.
		W.9-10.9.a	Apply grades 9–10 Reading standards to literature.
		L.9-10.6	Acquire and use accurately general academic and domain-specific words and phrases, sufficient for reading, writing, speaking, and listening at the college and career readiness level; demonstrate independence in gathering vocabulary knowledge when considering a word or phrase important to comprehension or expression.
604	**Before Reading: Marked and Dusting**	RL.9-10.4	Determine the meaning of words and phrases as they are used in the text, including figurative and connotative meanings; analyze the cumulative impact of specific word choices on meaning and tone.
605–608	**Read Marked and Dusting**	RL.9-10.1	Cite strong and thorough textual evidence to support analysis of what the text says explicitly as well as inferences drawn from the text.
		RL.9-10.4	Determine the meaning of words and phrases as they are used in the text, including figurative and connotative meanings; analyze the cumulative impact of specific word choices on meaning and tone.
		RL.9-10.7	Analyze the representation of a subject or a key scene in two different artistic mediums, including what is emphasized or absent in each treatment.
		RL.9-10.10	By the end of grade 10, read and comprehend literature, including stories, dramas, and poems, at the high end of the grades 9–10 text complexity band independently and proficiently.

Common Core State Standards, continued

Cluster 3, continued

SE Pages	Lesson	Code	Standards Text
605–608	**Read Marked and Dusting** continued	W.9-10.9.a	Apply grades 9–10 Reading standards to literature.
		W.9-10.10	Write routinely over extended time frames (time for research, reflection, and revision) and shorter time frames (a single sitting or a day or two) for a range of tasks, purposes, and audiences.
		L.9-10.1.b	Use various types of phrases (noun, verb, adjectival, adverbial, participial, prepositional, absolute) and clauses (independent, dependent; noun, relative, adverbial) to convey specific meanings and add variety and interest to writing or presentations.
		RL.9-10.10	By the end of grade 10, read and comprehend literature, including stories, dramas, and poems, at the high end of the grades 9–10 text complexity band independently and proficiently.
609	**Reflect and Assess Critical Thinking**	RL.9-10.1	Cite strong and thorough textual evidence to support analysis of what the text says explicitly as well as inferences drawn from the text.
	Write About Literature	W.9-10.3	Write narratives to develop real or imagined experiences or events using effective technique, well-chosen details, and well-structured event sequences.
	Key Vocabulary Review	RL.9-10.10	By the end of grade 10, read and comprehend literature, including stories, dramas, and poems, at the high end of the grades 9–10 text complexity band independently and proficiently.
609	**Read with Ease: Phrasing**	RL.9-10.10	By the end of grade 10, read and comprehend literature, including stories, dramas, and poems, at the high end of the grades 9–10 text complexity band independently and proficiently.
610	**Grammar: Use Compound and Complex Sentences**	L.9-10.1.b	Use various types of phrases (noun, verb, adjectival, adverbial, participial, prepositional, absolute) and clauses (independent, dependent; noun, relative, adverbial) to convey specific meanings and add variety and interest to writing or presentations.
610	**Literary Analysis: Analyze Alliteration and Consonance**	RL.9-10.4	Determine the meaning of words and phrases as they are used in the text, including figurative and connotative meanings; analyze the cumulative impact of specific word choices on meaning and tone.
610	**Language Development: Elaborate During a Discussion**	SL.9-10.1.a	Come to discussions prepared, having read and researched material under study; explicitly draw on that preparation by referring to evidence from texts and other research on the topic or issue to stimulate a thoughtful, well-reasoned exchange of ideas.
611	**Vocabulary Study: Connotation and Denotation**	L.9-10.5.b	Analyze nuances in the meaning of words with similar denotations.
611	**Writing Trait: Trait: Voice and Style**	W.9-10.5	Develop and strengthen writing as needed by planning, revising, editing, rewriting, or trying a new approach, focusing on addressing what is most significant for a specific purpose and audience.
611	**Listening/Speaking: Recite Song Lyrics**	SL.9-10.6	Adapt speech to a variety of contexts and tasks, demonstrating command of formal English when indicated or appropriate.
		L.9-10.5.a	Interpret figures of speech in context and analyze their role in the text.
612–613	**I Believe in All That Has Never Yet Been Spoken**	RL.9-10.10	By the end of grade 10, read and comprehend literature, including stories, dramas, and poems, at the high end of the grades 9–10 text complexity band independently and proficiently.

Unit Wrap

SE Pages	Lesson	Code	Standards Text
614	**Unit Wrap-Up** **Present Your Project**	SL.9-10.6	Adapt speech to a variety of contexts and tasks, demonstrating command of formal English when indicated or appropriate.
	Reflect on Your Reading	SL.9-10.1.a	Come to discussions prepared, having read and researched material under study; explicitly draw on that preparation by referring to evidence from texts and other research on the topic or issue to stimulate a thoughtful, well-reasoned exchange of ideas.
	Respond to the Essential Question	SL.9-10.1.a	Come to discussions prepared, having read and researched material under study; explicitly draw on that preparation by referring to evidence from texts and other research on the topic or issue to stimulate a thoughtful, well-reasoned exchange of ideas.

Language and Learning Handbook

SE Pages	Lesson	Code	Standards Text
617–626	**Strategies for Learning and Developing Language**	SL.9-10.1.c	Propel conversations by posing and responding to questions that relate the current discussion to broader themes or larger ideas; actively incorporate others into the discussion; and clarify, verify, or challenge ideas and conclusions.
		SL.9-10.3	Evaluate a speaker's point of view, reasoning, and use of evidence and rhetoric, identifying any fallacious reasoning or exaggerated or distorted evidence.
		SL.9-10.4	Present information, findings, and supporting evidence clearly, concisely, and logically such that listeners can follow the line of reasoning and the organization, development, substance, and style are appropriate to purpose, audience, and task.
		SL.9-10.6	Adapt speech to a variety of contexts and tasks, demonstrating command of formal English when indicated or appropriate.
		L.9-10.1	Demonstrate command of the conventions of standard English grammar and usage when writing or speaking.
		L.9-10.4	Determine or clarify the meaning of unknown and multiple-meaning words and phrases based on grades 9–10 reading and content, choosing flexibly from a range of strategies.
		L.9-10.4.c	Consult general and specialized reference materials, both print and digital, to find the pronunciation of a word or determine or clarify its precise meaning, its part of speech, or its etymology.
		L.9-10.5.a	Interpret figures of speech in context and analyze their role in the text.
		L.9-10.6	Acquire and use accurately general academic and domain-specific words and phrases, sufficient for reading, writing, speaking, and listening at the college and career readiness level; demonstrate independence in gathering vocabulary knowledge when considering a word or phrase important to comprehension or expression.
627–630	**Listening and Speaking**	SL.9-10.1	Initiate and participate effectively in a range of collaborative discussions (one-on-one, in groups, and teacher-led) with diverse partners on grades 9–10 topics, texts, and issues, building on others' ideas and expressing their own clearly and persuasively.
		SL.9-10.1.c	Propel conversations by posing and responding to questions that relate the current discussion to broader themes or larger ideas; actively incorporate others into the discussion; and clarify, verify, or challenge ideas and conclusions.

Common Core State Standards, continued

Student Handbooks, continued

Language and Learning Handbook, continued

SE Pages	Lesson	Code	Standards Text
627–630	Listening and Speaking continued	SL.9-10.1.d	Respond thoughtfully to diverse perspectives, summarize points of agreement and disagreement, and, when warranted, qualify or justify their own views and understanding and make new connections in light of the evidence and reasoning presented.
		L.9-10.1.a	Use parallel structure.
		L.9-10.5	Demonstrate understanding of figurative language, word relationships, and nuances in word meanings.
631–634	Viewing and Representing	RI.9-10.7	Analyze various accounts of a subject told in different mediums, determining which details are emphasized in each account.
		W.9-10.8	Gather relevant information from multiple authoritative print and digital sources, using advanced searches effectively; assess the usefulness of each source in answering the research question; integrate information into the text selectively to maintain the flow of ideas, avoiding plagiarism and following a standard format for citation.
		SL.9-10.2	Integrate multiple sources of information presented in diverse media or formats evaluating the credibility and accuracy of each source.
		SL.9-10.5	Make strategic use of digital media in presentations to enhance understanding of findings, reasoning, and evidence and to add interest.
635–638	Technology and Media	W.9-10.6	Use technology, including the Internet, to produce, publish, and update individual or shared writing products, taking advantage of technology's capacity to link to other information and to display information flexibly and dynamically.
		SL.9-10.5	Make strategic use of digital media in presentations to enhance understanding of findings, reasoning, and evidence and to add interest.
639–644	Research	W.9-10.7	Conduct short as well as more sustained research projects to answer a question (including a self-generated question) or solve a problem; narrow or broaden the inquiry when appropriate; synthesize multiple sources on the subject, demonstrating understanding of the subject under investigation.
		W.9-10.8	Gather relevant information from multiple authoritative print and digital sources, using advanced searches effectively; assess the usefulness of each source in answering the research question; integrate information into the text selectively to maintain the flow of ideas, avoiding plagiarism and following a standard format for citation.
		L.9-10.3.a	Write and edit work so that it conforms to the guidelines in a style manual appropriate for the discipline and writing type.

Reading Handbook

SE Pages	Lesson	Code	Standards Text
648–660	Reading Strategies	RL.9-10.1	Cite strong and thorough textual evidence to support analysis of what the text says explicitly as well as inferences drawn from the text.
		RL.9-10.10	By the end of grade 10, read and comprehend literature, including stories, dramas, and poems, at the high end of the grades 9–10 text complexity band independently and proficiently.
		RI.9-10.1	Cite strong and thorough textual evidence to support analysis of what the text says explicitly as well as inferences drawn from the text.

Reading Handbook, continued

SE Pages	Lesson	Code	Standards Text
661–685	Reading Fluency	RL.9-10.10	By the end of grade 10, read and comprehend literature, including stories, dramas, and poems, at the high end of the grades 9–10 text complexity band independently and proficiently.
		RI.9-10.10	By the end of grade 10, read and comprehend literary nonfiction at the high end of the grades 9–10 text complexity band independently and proficiently.
686–689	Study Skills and Strategies	SL.9-10.1.a	Come to discussions prepared, having read and researched material under study; explicitly draw on that preparation by referring to evidence from texts and other research on the topic or issue to stimulate a thoughtful, well-reasoned exchange of ideas.
		SL.9-10.2	Integrate multiple sources of information presented in diverse media or formats evaluating the credibility and accuracy of each source.
690–697	Vocabulary	L.9-10.4	Determine or clarify the meaning of unknown and multiple-meaning words and phrases based on grades 9–10 reading and content, choosing flexibly from a range of strategies.
		L.9-10.4.a	Use context as a clue to the meaning of a word or phrase.
		L.9-10.4.b	Identify and correctly use patterns of word changes that indicate different meanings or parts of speech.
		L.9-10.4.c	Consult general and specialized reference materials, both print and digital, to find the pronunciation of a word or determine or clarify its precise meaning, its part of speech, or its etymology.
		L.9-10.4.d	Verify the preliminary determination of the meaning of a word or phrase.
		L.9-10.5	Demonstrate understanding of figurative language, word relationships, and nuances in word meanings.
		L.9-10.6	Acquire and use accurately general academic and domain-specific words and phrases, sufficient for reading, writing, speaking, and listening at the college and career readiness level; demonstrate independence in gathering vocabulary knowledge when considering a word or phrase important to comprehension or expression.

Writing Handbook

SE Pages	Lesson	Code	Standards Text
699–705	The Writing Process	W.9-10.4	Produce clear and coherent writing in which the development, organization, and style are appropriate to task, purpose, and audience.
		W.9-10.6	Use technology, including the Internet, to produce, publish, and update individual or shared writing products, taking advantage of technology's capacity to link to other information and to display information flexibly and dynamically.
706–715	Writing Traits	RI.9-10.10	By the end of grade 10, read and comprehend literary nonfiction at the high end of the grades 9–10 text complexity band independently and proficiently.
		W.9-10.1.c	Use words, phrases, and clauses to link the major sections of the text, create cohesion, and clarify the relationships between claim(s) and reasons, between reasons and evidence, and between claim(s) and counterclaims.
		W.9-10.2.c	Use appropriate and varied transitions to link the major sections of the text, create cohesion, and clarify the relationships among complex ideas and concepts.

Common Core State Standards, continued

Writing Handbook, continued

SE Pages	Lesson	Code	Standards Text
706–715	**Writing Traits** continued	W.9-10.2.e	Establish and maintain a formal style and objective tone while attending to the norms and conventions of the discipline in which they are writing.
		W.9-10.2.f	Provide a concluding statement or section that follows from and supports the information or explanation presented.
		W.9-10.3.d	Use precise words and phrases, telling details, and sensory language to convey a vivid picture of the experiences, events, setting, and/or characters.
		W.9-10.4	Produce clear and coherent writing in which the development, organization, and style are appropriate to task, purpose, and audience.
		L.9-10.1	Demonstrate command of the conventions of standard English grammar and usage when writing or speaking.
716–737	**Writing Purposes, Modes, and Forms**	W.9-10.1	Write arguments to support claims in an analysis of substantive topics or texts, using valid reasoning and relevant and sufficient evidence.
		W.9-10.4	Produce clear and coherent writing in which the development, organization, and style are appropriate to task, purpose, and audience.
		W.9-10.5	Develop and strengthen writing as needed by planning, revising, editing, rewriting, or trying a new approach, focusing on addressing what is most significant for a specific purpose and audience.
		W.9-10.6	Use technology, including the Internet, to produce, publish, and update individual or shared writing products, taking advantage of technology's capacity to link to other information and to display information flexibly and dynamically.
		SL.9-10.2	Integrate multiple sources of information presented in diverse media or formats evaluating the credibility and accuracy of each source.
		L.9-10.3.a	Write and edit work so that it conforms to the guidelines in a style manual appropriate for the discipline and writing type.
738–772	**Grammar, Usage, Mechanics, and Spelling**	L.9-10.1	Demonstrate command of the conventions of standard English grammar and usage when writing or speaking.
		L.9-10.1.a	Use parallel structure.
		L.9-10.1.b	Use various types of phrases (noun, verb, adjectival, adverbial, participial, prepositional, absolute) and clauses (independent, dependent; noun, relative, adverbial) to convey specific meanings and add variety and interest to writing or presentations.
		L.9-10.2	Demonstrate command of the conventions of standard English capitalization, punctuation, and spelling when writing.
		L.9-10.2.a	Use a semicolon (and perhaps a conjunctive adverb) to link two or more closely related independent clauses.
		L.9-10.2.b	Use a colon to introduce a list or quotation.

Writing Handbook, continued

SE Pages	Lesson	Code	Standards Text
738–772	**Grammar, Usage, Mechanics, and Spelling** continued	L.9-10.2.c	Spell correctly.
		L.9-10.3	Apply knowledge of language to understand how language functions in different contexts, to make effective choices for meaning or style, and to comprehend more fully when reading or listening.
773–781 Troubleshooting Guide		L.9-10.1	Demonstrate command of the conventions of standard English grammar and usage when writing or speaking.
		L.9-10.3	Apply knowledge of language to understand how language functions in different contexts, to make effective choices for meaning or style, and to comprehend more fully when reading or listening.

Index of Skills

A

Absolutes 756

Academic vocabulary 7, 8, 9, 10, 30, 54, 96, 97, 98, 120, 140, 185, 186, 188, 210, 211, 234, 284, 285, 286, 306, 328, 370, 372, 396, 420, 465, 468, 486, 504, 547, 548, 551, 552, 576, 596

Academic writing forms *see Writing forms*

Adjectives 302, 416, 456, 458, 457, 746, 762, 766-767, 776

Adverbs 438, 757, 738, 759, 761, 762, 771

Alliteration 342, 610, 630, 782

Allusion 630, 693, 782

Analogy 501, 630, 693, 723, 782

Anecdote 130-134

Antagonist 782

Antecedent 745

Antonyms 395, 417, 439, 696

Apostrophe

  contractions 360, 362, 750, 768

  possessive nouns 360, 741, 768

Appositive 117, 763, 769

Argument 469, 471-475, 782

  claim and supporting evidence 350, 466, 469, 528, 529, 783

  compare 487, 490, 491, 492, 493, 494, 496, 497, 498

  evaluate 505, 511

  purpose 97

  reasons supporting 509, 510

  viewpoint 469

  see also Writing forms; Writing modes

Article 782

  feature article 735

  informative 200-204, 477-480

  magazine 20-24, 408-414

  news 165-179

  persuasive 472-475, 495-498

  science 99, 101-109, 164

  science procedure 110-114

Articles (part of speech) 741

Ask questions 4, 5, 95, 164, 621, 649, 657

  of the author 141, 144, 146, 149, 150, 151, 152, 153, 154, 155, 657

  question-answer relationships 121, 124, 125, 126, 129, 130, 132, 133, 134, 657

  self-question 99, 102, 103, 108, 109, 110, 112, 114, 657

Audience 78, 168, 266, 352, 448, 530, 700, 712-713

Author's purpose 96, 97, 99, 103, 105, 106, 109, 110, 111, 113, 114, 121, 126, 127, 129, 132, 133, 134, 141, 144, 145, 146, 149, 150, 151, 329, 336, 482, 512, 514, 515, 517, 518

Author's tone 512, 514, 515, 517, 518

Author's use of language 41, 196, 221, 376

  see also Rhetorical devices

Author's viewpoint *see Viewpoint*

Autobiographical narratives 75-89, 307, 309-315, 782

B

Base words 29, 275

Bias 631

Biography 598, 782

Blank verse 782

C

Capitalization

  abbreviations 767-768

  direct quotations 274, 276, 766

  first word of a sentence 86, 766

  greeting and closing in letters 766

  months, days, special days, holidays 767

  names of groups 176, 178, 767

  names of places 360, 362, 767

  pronoun *I* 86, 766

  proper nouns and adjectives 456, 458, 739, 766

  titles of publications 538, 540, 766

  visual clue for reading 662

Characters/characterization 782

  actions of 55, 397, 553

  analyze 43, 55, 63

  antagonist 782

  critical viewing 35, 36, 41, 58, 61, 219, 220, 246, 319, 423, 429, 581

  dialogue 55

  dynamic character 784

  motives 787

  plays 548, 553, 559, 562, 573, 577

  poems 567

  protagonist 789

  short stories 8, 31, 34, 35, 36, 37, 39, 40, 43, 42, 58, 59, 60, 62, 64, 216, 265, 370, 404, 421, 424, 428

  static character 790

  traits 783

Chronological order 270, 285, 307, 310, 311, 313, 315, 316, 318, 321, 322, 329, 332, 333, 334, 335, 336, 337, 439, 708

Citing sources 643, 703

Claim 350, 466, 469, 528, 529, 783

Clarify ideas 31, 35, 37, 39, 42, 43, 44, 47, 48, 624, 650

Clauses 520, 572, 610, 746, 757, 759, 761, 763, 771

Climax 26, 264, 265, 783

  see also Plot diagram

Close reading 70-73, 160-163, 258-261, 344-347, 440-443, 522-525, 612-613

Cognates 694

Colon 663, 771

Commas 119, 456, 458, 520, 539, 610, 663, 756, 761, 762, 769

Communication 483, 626, 635, 734-737

  see also Language development; Letters; Listening and speaking workshop; Nonverbal communication

Comparison 482, 624, 718

  of arguments 487, 490, 491, 492, 493, 494, 496, 497, 498

  of images and poetry 589

  of literature and film 325

  of plays and short stories 549

  of responses to literature 592

  of script and performance 553, 557, 558, 565, 566

  of themes of plays and poetry 572

Complications in plot 264, 265, 783

  see also Plot diagram

Compound words 693, 770

Conclusion 166, 167, 350, 532, 642

Conflict 8, 264, 265, 370, 548, 783

  see also Plot diagram

Conjunctions 520, 539, 572, 610, 738, 759, 761, 769

Connections, make (activity) 30, 54, 98, 120, 140, 188, 234, 286, 306, 328, 372, 396, 420, 468, 486, 504, 552, 576, 596

  reading to life 7, 95, 185, 283, 465, 547, 550

  writing to life 76, 166, 264, 350, 446, 528

Connections, make (reading strategy) 380, 381, 401, 403, 421, 425, 432, 436, 444

  text to self 369, 373, 376, 377, 378, 379, 382, 383, 384, 386, 388, 390, 397, 408, 409, 412, 414, 427, 430, 431, 434, 654 text to text 369, 373, 377, 382, 383, 384, 387, 397, 407, 408, 413, 654

text to world 369, 373, 377, 382, 383, 384, 388, 397, 408, 435, 654

Connections, make (vocabulary strategy) 207, 209, 257, 393, 395, 417, 439, 690, 694

Connotation 117, 140, 611, 692, 783

Consonance 610, 783

Context clues 55, 325, 650

analogy 693

appositive definition 117, 119

connotation and denotation 117, 692, 783

definition 117

examples 137

figurative language 691–692

idioms 573, 575, 593, 691

multiple-meaning words 303, 343, 691

simile and metaphor 692

technical and specialized language 483, 692

unfamiliar words 691

Contractions 360, 750, 768

Controlling idea 78, 352, 448, 528, 530, 700, 706

Counterclaims 350, 505, 528, 529, 723

Cover letter 512, 513

Critical thinking

analyze 25, 67, 115, 135, 157, 229, 255, 301, 323, 341, 391, 415, 437, 481, 499, 519, 571, 591, 609

assess 135, 157, 205, 229, 255, 499, 519, 571

compare 25, 49, 67, 115, 135, 157, 205, 229, 255, 301, 323, 391, 415, 437, 481, 499, 519, 571, 591, 609

compare across texts 341

see also Connect across texts; Connections, make (reading strategy)

draw conclusions 229, 391, 481

see also Draw conclusions; Synthesize

evaluate 25, 49, 591, 609

generalize 115, 205, 415, 571

see also Generalizations, form; Synthesize

imagine 49, 67, 135, 205, 255

infer 115

see also Inferences, make

interpret 25, 49, 67, 157, 205, 255, 301, 323, 391, 415, 437, 481, 499, 571

judge 157, 301, 323, 341, 437, 591, 609

speculate 25, 49, 67, 115, 135, 229, 323, 341, 391, 415, 437, 519

synthesize 301, 341, 481, 499, 519, 591

see also Draw conclusions; Generalizations, form; Synthesize

Critical viewing

character 35, 36, 41, 58, 61, 216, 219, 220, 246, 319, 423, 429, 581

design 33, 38, 214, 237, 320, 381, 406, 424, 427

effect 17, 71, 73, 213, 240, 345, 347, 382, 399, 404, 569, 582

images 589

observations 248

photographs 0–1, 89, 90–91, 180, 278–279, 364–365, 460–461, 542–543

plot 18

setting 14, 57, 239, 376, 402

symbol 605

theme 13

Cultural background 66, 128, 146, 149, 335, 427, 478, 513, 514, 558, 601, 613

D

Dangling modifier 762

Dash 119, 662, 770

Definition map 30, 188, 286, 468, 486, 651

Denotation 140, 611, 692, 783

Description 719, 783

Descriptive language 130, 136

Details 265, 515, 517, 642

see also Main idea; Supporting details

Determine importance 4, 5, 283, 287, 295, 296, 300, 307, 315, 316, 322, 329, 332, 334, 336, 337, 338, 339, 340, 348, 652

see also Main idea: details and; Summarize

Development of ideas

essay 298, 299, 300

informational text 287, 291, 292, 293, 294, 295, 296

magazine article 408, 411, 413, 414

see also Writing traits

Diagram 103, 104, 202, 203, 447, 478, 479

Dialect 50, 698, 783

Dialogue 783

in plays 548, 553, 558, 572, 573, 577

in short stories 8, 31, 55

Dictionary 257, 303, 395, 485, 619, 695, 703

Direct object 751

Double negatives 760

Draft *see Writing process*

Drafting tips 268, 450

Drama 545, 555–566, 579–587, 614, 783

characters 548, 553, 572, 577

conflict 548

conventions 572, 784

dialogue 548, 553, 572, 577

how to read 546–549

playwright 548

plot 548, 577

scenes/acts 553

script 577, 587

script and performance, compare 553, 557, 558, 565, 566

setting 548

short story compared to 549

stage direction 548, 553, 577

theme 572

Draw conclusions 229, 391, 469, 473, 474, 475, 476, 478, 480, 481, 526, 644, 658

see also Synthesize

E

Edit and proofread *see Writing process*

Editing tip 745, 765

Editorial 735, 784

Ellipsis 770

Elliptical clause 763

E-mail 208, 512, 734

Emotional appeal 532, 723

Emotional responses, identify 597, 600, 603, 604, 606, 608, 660

End marks 86, 662, 663, 759, 760, 768

Essay 258–261, 296–300, 344–347, 784

compare-contrast 718

development of ideas 296, 300

entrance essay 717–718

how-to 719–720

literary response 720–721

persuasive 505, 508–511, 527–541, 723

photo-essay 788

problem-solution 349–363, 725, 726

reflective 717–718

panel discussion 418–419

persuasive speech 502–503

poetry slam 594–595

retell a story 232–233

role-play 52–53

Listening strategies 617–620

actively and respectfully 363, 419, 627

clarify meaning 419

note taking 363

overcome barriers 627

self-monitor 630

Literary criticism 786

Literary response essay 720–721

Literary terms 782–790

Literature, film compared to 324

see also Genre

Loaded words 494, 496

Logical appeal 532, 723

M

Magazine article 20–24, 408–414

Magazine opinion piece 489–493

Main idea

details and 296, 298, 300, 313

implied 653

in nonfiction 287, 291, 292, 294, 295, 296, 318

stated 652

see also Text structure: main idea and details

Map 147, 310, 473, 632

Media

evaluate a public service announcement 483

feature writing and 735–736

as information source 636–637

interpret and analyze 634

interpret information from 637

Memoir 44–48, 141, 143–151, 316–322, 787

Mental images, form

see Visualize

Metaphor 251, 338, 339, 340, 551, 604, 692, 787

Meter 592, 787

Modifiers *see Adjectives; Adverbs*

Mood 392, 630, 634, 787

Multimedia presentation 281, 348, 459, 483, 633, 638, 643

Multiple-meaning words 303, 343, 521, 691

Myth 787

N

Narration 787

Narrative writing *see Genre; Writing forms; Writing modes*

Narrator 185, 787

Narrator's point of view

first-person 185, 186, 199, 211, 235, 238, 244, 247, 250

omniscient 256

third-person 200, 214, 217, 218, 220, 223, 224, 241

see also Viewpoint

Negative words 760

News article 165–179, 285, 735

News commentary 152–155

Nonfiction *see Genre*

Non-literal language 575

Nonverbal communication 626

Note cards 640

Note taking 620, 640

Nouns 361, 362, 456, 458, 738, 739, 740, 766–767, 768

Novel 3, 74, 93, 164, 183, 262, 281, 348, 367, 417, 444, 463, 526, 545, 614, 787

O

Object 751, 758

Onomatopoeia 787

Opinions, express 188, 500, 621

Opinion statement 25, 67, 723

Oral report 27, 137, 326–327, 592

Order of importance 708

Organization *see Writing traits*

P

Paradox 788

Parallel structure 361, 630, 765

Paraphrase 47, 109, 133, 291, 299, 426, 473

Parentheses 119, 770

Parody 733, 788

Participles 592

Parts of speech *see Adjectives; Adverbs; Articles; Conjunctions; Interjections; Nouns; Prepositions; Pronouns; Verbs*

Peer conference 85, 175, 273, 359, 455, 537, 702

Performance 553, 557, 558, 565, 566

Period 86, 663, 760, 768

Personal anecdote 723

Personal narrative 44–48, 75–89, 141, 142, 143–151, 160–163, 316–322, 384–390, 433–436, 788

Personification 604, 788

Perspective *see Viewpoint*

Persuasion 520, 625

see also Argument; Genre; Writing forms; Writing modes

Photo-essay 788

Photographs 462, 477, 632

see also Text features

Phrases 324, 738, 742, 746, 756, 757, 761, 763, 769,

Phrasing *see Reading fluency*

Plagiarism 640, 703

Plan and monitor 4, 7, 9, 11, 20, 31, 44, 55, 64, 648–651

see also Clarify ideas; Predictions, confirm; Predictions, make; Preview; Set a purpose

Play *see Drama*

Playwright 548

Plot 11, 19, 55, 63, 788

climax (turning point) 26, 264, 265, 783

complications 264, 265, 783

exposition 264

falling action 26, 783

organization of 267

problem 26

resolution 26, 264, 789

rising action 26, 783, 790

see also Plot diagram

Plot diagram 26, 264, 722

Poems/poetry 225–228, 250, 251–254, 254, 338–340, 550–551, 570, 588–590, 602, 605–608, 612–614, 788

haiku 785

meter 592, 787

narrative poem 567–570

repetition 550

rhyme 251, 253, 550, 588, 590

rhythm 225, 227, 251, 254, 588, 590, 592

see also Writing forms

Point of view *see Author's viewpoint; Narrator's point of view; Viewpoint*

Position in argument *see Argument*

Position statement 700

Possessives 302, 360, 741, 743, 768

Predicate 26, 68, 87, 714, 761, 764

Predictions

confirm 19, 39, 42, 61, 150, 199, 219, 224, 249, 337, 382, 407, 431, 586, 649

make 7, 11, 15, 16, 18, 19, 37, 40, 60, 62, 148, 195, 217, 220, 242, 247, 313, 334, 379, 403, 427, 584, 649

Prefixes 27, 29, 51, 275, 694

Prepositions/prepositional phrases 324, 738, 742, 758

Presentation strategies

answer questions 348

ask for feedback 89, 363, 459

bring the right materials 459

eye contact 89, 232, 326, 363, 419, 503, 594

facial expressions 232, 502, 594

gestures 232

good posture 502

look around the room 594

look at notes 232, 326

manage discussions and presentations 628–629

overcome anxiety 629

pacing 89, 363

position 348

practice in front of a someone 459

read slowly 459

read with expression 89, 363, 541

relaxed position 502

self-monitor 630

speak clearly and loudly 232, 326, 348, 503, 594

speak with emotion and energy 419

stay on topic 503

tone of voice 232

use rhetorical devices 630

use visuals 459

see also Speaking skills

Presenting tip 277, 459

Preview 11, 19, 20, 22, 24, 648, 649

Prewrite *see Writing process*

Prewriting tip 78, 169, 266, 352, 448, 530

Primary sources 641

Problem 26

see also Plot Diagram

Problem-and-solution text structure 708

Problem-solution essay 349–363, 725

Problem-solution essay planner 725

Procedural text 97, 110–114, 204, 719–720

Pronouns 86, 116, 177, 178, 189, 200, 211, 235, 256, 342, 482, 738, 742, 743, 744, 745, 763, 773–774

Proofreader's marks 86, 176, 274, 360, 456, 538, 703

Proofreading tips 86, 176, 274, 360, 456, 538

Protagonist 789

Publish and present *see Writing process*

Publishing tips 89, 179, 363, 541

Pun 630, 789

Punctuation *see Apostrophe; Colon; Commas; Dash; Ellipsis; End marks; Exclamation point; Hyphen, Italics, Parentheses, Period, Question mark, Quotation marks, Semicolon, Underlining*

Purpose for writing 78, 168, 266, 352, 447, 448, 530, 700

see also Author's purpose

Q

Question 351, 700

Question mark 86, 662, 760, 768

Quickwrite 30, 49, 140, 234, 306, 396, 415, 468, 596

Quotation marks 274, 276, 432, 771

Quotations 168, 200, 274, 275, 276, 487, 500, 630, 643, 700, 766, 771

R

Reading fluency

accuracy and rate 13, 25, 33, 49, 57, 67, 101, 115, 123, 135, 143, 157, 191, 205, 213, 229, 237, 255, 289, 301, 309, 323, 331, 341, 375, 391, 399, 415, 423, 437, 471, 481, 489, 499, 507, 519, 555, 571, 578, 591, 599, 609, 650, 661, 665–685

expression 25, 157, 255, 323, 437, 499, 571, 664–665, 670, 673, 675, 679, 681, 683

intonation 67, 135, 205, 341, 415, 481, 591, 662, 667, 669, 671, 676, 678, 680, 684

phrasing 49, 115, 229, 301, 391, 519, 609, 663, 666, 668, 672, 674, 677, 682, 685

Reading handbook 678–697

Reading selections *see Index of Authors and Titles*

Reading strategies

use 4–5, 74, 648

use graphic organizers 651

see also Ask questions; Connections, make (reading strategy); Determine importance; Draw conclusions; Emotional responses, identify; Generalizations, form; Inferences, make; Monitor reading; Plan and monitor; Sensory images, identify; Summarize; Synthesize; Visualize

Reasons 505, 509, 510, 511, 528, 530–531, 723, 789

Rebuttal 528

Reference tools 619, 695, 703

see also Dictionary; Style guide (manual); Thesaurus

Reflect and assess 25, 49, 67, 115, 135, 157, 205, 229, 255, 301, 323, 341, 391, 415, 437, 481, 499, 519, 571, 591, 609

Reflective essay 717–718

Relate words 393, 417, 690

Repetition 342, 550, 630, 789

Research 27, 28, 69, 51, 116, 118, 137, 303, 304, 325, 343, 484, 501, 592, 636, 639–644, 700

Research report 121, 123–129, 642–644, 726

Resolution 26, 264, 789

see also Plot diagram

Resources 640, 689

Résumé 514, 731

Reviewing strategies 688

Revise *see Writing process*

Revision checklists 84, 174, 272, 358, 454, 536

Rhetorical devices 789

Rhyme 251, 253, 550, 588, 589, 590, 789

Rhyme scheme 588, 790

Rhythm 225, 251, 254, 588, 589, 590, 592, 790

heads 20, 99, 121, 284, 287, 408, 469, 487

information graphic 284

key terms 99

map 147, 310, 473, 632

paragraphs 284, 287

photo 20, 21, 22, 24, 284, 408

title 284, 287, 384, 421

Text structure 708

see also Chronological order; Main Idea and details; Procedural text

Theme 370, 791

critical viewing 13

of personal narrative 384, 387, 388, 389, 390

of plays 572

of poems 567, 570, 572

of short stories 266, 373, 377, 378, 379, 380, 381, 382, 383, 397, 400, 401, 403, 404, 405, 407, 421, 424, 428, 430, 431

Thesaurus 695, 703

Think, pair, share 9, 286, 371, 467

Time-order words 27, 307, 316

Title

capitalization 538, 540, 766

italic or underlining of 538, 770

quotation marks 771

of short stories 421

Tone 158, 630, 791

of functional documents 512, 514, 515, 517, 518

in problem-solution essays 356

of short stories 392

word choice 302

Topic 78, 168, 352, 373, 448, 530, 639, 699, 791

Topic sentence 69, 642, T642, 700

Tragedy 791

Transition words and phrases 270, 362, 439, 447, 450, 458

Trickster tales 69

Troubleshooting guide 773–780

U

Underlining 538, 770

Unfamiliar words 691

Unit project

ad campaign 463, 526

children's book 3, 74

comic book or graphic novel 367, 444

documentary 93, 164

gallery walk 183, 262

multimedia presentation 281, 348

skit 545, 614

Unit wrap-up 74, 164, 262, 348, 444, 526, 614

V

Verbal irony 432

Verbal phrase 756

Verbals 756

Verbs 50, 136, 158, 206, 230, 275, 276, 457, 482, 500, 592, 747, 748, 749, 751, 752-755, 756, 760, 765, 775

Verses 550, 791

Viewing and representing 631, 632, 634

see also Critical viewing

Viewpoint 788

author's 152, 153, 154, 155, 202, 204, 482

first-person narrator 185, 186, 187, 189, 199, 211, 235, 238, 244, 247, 250

omniscient 256

in persuasive argument 469, 475

in short stories 194

third-person author 204

third-person limited 206

third-person narrator 200, 214, 217, 218, 220, 223, 224, 241

word choice 494, 498

see also Author's viewpoint; Narrator's point of view

Visualize 4, 5, 547, 553, 556, 560, 562, 563, 564, 566, 567, 569, 570, 577, 588, 597, 600, 604, 614, 660

see also Emotional responses, identify; Mental images, form; Sensory images, identify

Visuals 447, 459, 643

analysis of 433

construct and clarify meaning 620

effects of 633–634

graphic displays 632

map 632

monitor understanding of 631

photos, illustrations, videos, artwork 632

respond to and interpret 631

self-correcting thoughts concerning 631

use in writing and presentations 483, 500, 502, 633, 643

Vocabulary 19, 24, 43, 48, 63, 66, 109, 114, 129, 134, 151, 155, 199, 204, 224, 228, 250, 254, 295, 300, 315, 322, 337, 340, 383, 390, 407, 414, 431, 436, 475, 480, 493, 498, 511, 518, 566, 570, 587, 590, 603, 608

access vocabulary 16, 105, 107, 124, 133, 192, 241, 290, 294, 305, 311, 312, 377, 410, 426, 428, 430, 474, 508, 585

clarify vocabulary 55, 58, 60, 63, 64, 65, 66, 650

see also Academic vocabulary; Key vocabulary; Vocabulary workshop

Vocabulary note 433

Vocabulary routine 690, 696

Vocabulary workshop

access vocabulary 305

build word knowledge 485

context clues 119

interpret non-literal language 575

relate words 395

word families 209

word parts 29

Voice 158, 302, 791

active and passive 752

see also Writing traits

W

W/H questions 166, 167, 169, 170, 699

Word choice 302, 356, 597

for functional documents 513

in persuasive argument 496, 498

in poetry 572

Word families 207, 209, 257, 694

Word origins

Greek, Latin 51, 209, 231

Old English 51, 257

other languages 209

Word parts 29

base/root words 209, 231, 257, 275

compound words 693

inflected forms 694

prefixes 27, 29, 51, 275, 694

suffixes 29, 69, 275, 539, 694

Index of Authors and Titles

INDEX OF ART AND ARTISTS

Photo Credits

Acknowledgments, continued

collection. **237** Siete Leguas, 1991, Alfredo Arreguin, Oil on Canvas, Private collection; ChromaCome/PhotoDisc/Getty Images. **239** Curbside Culture, 2005, Wayne Healy, Acrylic on canvas, 48 x48, Courtesy of Patricia Correla Gallery, Santa Monica, California; Mark Garlick/Science Source. **240** Phoenix Rising, 2004, Paul Botello, Acryllic on canvas, 72 x36, courtesy Patrica Correia Gallery, Santa Monica, California. **243** The Art Archive/SuperStock. **244** There is Such a Place #62, 2002. Armand Vallee. Oil 12x16, collection of the artist. **245** DLILLC/CORBIS. **246** Carmen, 1994, Angeline Kyba. Oil on Canvas, Angeline Kyba Studio, Puerto Vallarte, Mexico. **248** Sol y Sombra, 2003, John Farnsworth, Oil on canvas, private collection. **249** DLILLC/CORBIS. **250** Tom Brakefield/CORBIS. **252** Potapov Alexander/Shutterstock; Galushko Sergey/Shutterstock; Steve Lewis/Getty Images; Mel Curtis/Getty Images. **253** Charles Klein/Getty Images; Silvestre Machado/Getty Images; Digital Stock/CORBIS. **254** Digital Stock/CORBIS; Chester Higgins Jr./Photo Researchers, Inc.; Paul Vozdic/Getty Images. **256** Ocean/CORBIS. **262** Laurel Leaf; Scholastic; Hampton-Brown. **263** Jeff Greenberg/PhotoEdit, Inc. **264** Frank Wing/PhotoDisc/Getty Images. **268** Ryan McVay/PhotoDisc/Getty Images. **270** Ron Watts/Getty Images. **278–279** Martin Puddy/CORBIS. **279** Comforters, Ron Waddams 1993, Acrylic on board/The Bridgeman Art Library. **281** stockelements/Shutterstock. **282** Exactostock/Superstock. **283** bikeriderlondon/Shutterstock. **286** FXQuadro/Shutterstock. **287** Liz Garza Williams. **289** Liz Garza Williams. **290** Mark Richards/PhotoEdit, Inc. **291** A.B./Getty Images; 2013 PictureQuest/Jupiterimages Corporation. **293** Stockbyte/Getty Images. **294** Michael Newman/PhotoEdit, Inc.; Image Source/Getty Images. **296** William C. Gordon. **297** Penni Gladstone/CORBIS. **298** William C. Gordon. **299** VICTOR ROJAS/AFP/Getty Image. **300** VICTOR ROJAS/AFP/Getty Image. **302** Fran, Reproduction rights obtainable from www.CartoonsStock.com. **304** Ronnie Kaufman/Larry Hirshowitz/Blend Images LLC/CORBIS. **305** Leonello Calvetti/Shutterstock. **306** Peter Turnley/CORBIS. **306** Bob Daemmrich/CORBIS. **307** JazzSign/Lebrecht/The Image Works. **307** JazzSign/Lebrecht/The Image Works. **308** JazzSign/Lebrecht/The Image Works. **309** JazzSign/Lebrecht/The Image Works; 2004 Universal Pictures. Courtesy of Universal Studios Licensing LLLP. **310** George Marks/Getty Images; Bryan Mullennix/Getty Images. **311** 2004 Universal Pictures. Courtesy of Universal Studios Licensing LLLP. **313** Bryan Mullennix/Getty Images; Underwood Photo Archives/SuperStock. **314** AP Photo/John Hayes, File. **315** JazzSign/Lebrecht/The Image Works. **317** Philippe Reichert/Getty Images. **319** Mother and Child, 2003 (oil on board), Rothenstein, Anne (b.1949)/Private Collection/The Bridgeman Art Library. **320** Patterned Landscape, 1999 (oil on canvas), Rothenstein, Anne (b.1949)/Private Collection/The Bridgeman Art Library. **322** Karen de Vinck/Christopher de Vinck. **324** Universal/courtesy Everett Collection. **328** Mike Baldwin, Reproduction rights obtainable from www.CartoonStock.com; Nik Wheeler/CORBIS. **329** Mitch Kezar/Getty Images; Carl Mydans/Time & Life Pictures/Getty Images. **330** Mitch Kezar/Getty Images; Carl Mydans/Time & Life Pictures/Getty Images. **332** Chicago Fire Department; Mike B. **335** Richard Hutchings/PhotoEdit, Inc.; Hansel Mieth//Time Life Pictures/Getty Images. **336** EFF HAYNES/

AFP/Getty Images; AP Photo/Bebeto Matthews. Marion Ettlinger. **339** Steve Collier; Collier Studio/CORBIS; Old Woman, 2005, Maia Stefana Oprea. Acrylics, watercolor and ink, private collection of Ortsana Van Der Wateren, London. **340** St. Mary's College of Maryland. **344** ianmcdonnell/Shutterstock. **345** plainpicture/neuebildanstalt/Dott. **347** Graham Dean/CORBIS. **349** Mary Kate Denny/PhotoEdit, Inc. **350** Ariel Skelley/Getty Images. **354** SW Productions/Getty Images. **356** Davis Barber/PhotoEdit, Inc. **364–365** David Alan Harvey/Magnum Photos. **365** Cooool Papa Bell, Kadir Nelson 1985, Oil on Canvas, collection of the artist. **366** William Steig/The New Yorker Collection/www.cartoonbank.com. **367** Capstone Press(MN); Perfection Learning; Random House; stockelemets/Shutterstock. **368** Ocean/CORBIS. **369** Francis Wong Chee Yen/Shutterstock. **370** ifong/Shutterstock; MetaTools. **371** Ocean/CORBIS. **372** Najlah Feanny/CORBIS; Mika/CORBIS. **373** Lewis Mulatero/CORBIS; Lewis Mulatero/CORBIS. **374–375** Lewis Mulatero/CORBIS. **374** Dr. Rene Saldana, Jr. **375** BS_Lexx/Shutterstock; Ingram Publishing/Alamy. **376** Oglethorpe Bridge, 2005, Rani Garner. Oil on canvas, collection of the artist. **378** CORBIS/Fotosearch. **381** Kari Van Tine/Illustration Source. **382** Wrestlers (oil on canvas), Harrap, Peter (Contemporary Artist)/Private Collection/The Bridgeman Art Library. **383** Frank Krahmer/Getty Images. **385** JILL CONNELLY/CORBIS SYGMA. **386** Gregg DeGuire/WireImage/Getty Images. **389** Reuters/CORBIS. **390** Bettmann/CORBIS; Michael Brennan/CORBIS. **392** Edward Koren/The New Yorker Collection/www.cartoonbank.com. **394** Mike Kemp/Getty Images; Lisa F. Young/Shutterstock; Comstock/Getty Images. **395** ben bryant/Shutterstock. **396** L. Clarke/CORBIS; Carla Donofrio/Shutterstock. **397** 2013 Artists Rights Society (ARS), New York. Scala/Art Resource, NY. **398** Sadie Weger/Terry Trueman. **399** 2013 Artists Rights Society (ARS), New York. Scala/Art Resource, NY. **400** Ingram Publishing/Fotosearch. **402** Melanie Acevedo/Getty Images. **404** Le Crieur, 2002, Steven Spazuk, Soot on paper, collection of the artist. **406** Yo Oura/Getty Images. **409** Saul Bromberger & Sandra Hoover Photography. **410** Saul Bromberger & Sandra Hoover Photography. **411** Saul Bromberger & Sandra Hoover Photography. **412** Saul Bromberger & Sandra Hoover Photography. **416** Flash Parker/Getty Images. **418** PunchStock. **420** Darren Robb/The Image Bank/Getty Images; Studio Peggy/Getty Images. **421** 2013 Banco de México Diego Rivera Frida Kahlo Museums Trust, Mexico, D.F./Artists Rights Society (ARS), New York. Schalkwijk/Art Resource, NY. **422** University of Georgia, Peter Frey. **423** 2013 Banco de México Diego Rivera Frida Kahlo Museums Trust, Mexico, D.F./Artists Rights Society (ARS), New York. Schalkwijk/Art Resource, NY. **424** Rafael Lopez/theispot.com. **427** Grandmother, 1983, James E. Corley. Oil Painting, collection of the artist; CORBIS. **429** Portrait with Eyes closed, 2004, Yolanda Gonzalez. Acrylic on canvas, Private collection. **433** Walter Bibikow/Getty Images. **434** PhotoDisc/Getty Images; Lynn James/Getty Images; Image Source/Getty Images. **435** Catherine Karnow/CORBIS; PhotoLink/PhotoDisc/Getty images. **428** Charles Barsotti/The New Yorker Collection/www.cartoonbank.com. **440** Diana Walters/Shutterstock. **441** Bill Manbo. **442** Dorothea Lange/UC Berkeley, Bancroft Library; Paul Kitagaki Jr. 2012. **443** Manzanar National Historic

Site/Park and Recreation; Museum of History and Industry; Paul Kitagaki Jr. 2012. **444** Capstone Press(MN); Perfection Learning; Random House. **445** Stockpile Collection/PunchStock. **450** ImageGap/Alamy. **452** Aflo Foto Agency/Alamy. **458** ImageGap/Alamy. **460–461** Kitra Cahana/National Geographic Stock. **461** Gilbert Mayers/SuperStock. **462** ZUMA Wire Service/Alamy. **463** stockelements/Shutterstock; Viking Childrens Book; Laurel Leaf; Speak. **465** Hill Street Studios/Getty Images; Jason Stitt/Shutterstock. **468** Ariel Skelley/CORBIS; ericsphotography/Getty Images. **469** Carl & Ann Purcell/CORBIS. **470** Carl & Ann Purcell/CORBIS. **472** David R. Frazier Photolibrary, Inc./Alamy. **473** Source: Federal Highway Adinistration, U.S. Department of Transportation, 2004. **474** Library of Congress. **477** SW Productions/Photodisc/Getty Images; Michael Freeman/CORBIS; 2013 Steve Allen/Jupiterimages Corporation. **482** Harley Schwadron; Reproduction rights obtainable from www.cartoonstock.com. **484** Kevork Djansezian/Getty Images; Henry Diltz/CORBIS; MANNIE GARCIA/CORBIS. **486** Kevin C. Downs/Getty Images. **487** Nadia M.B. Hughes/Getty Images; John Terence Turner/Getty Images. **488** Nadia M.B. Hughes/National Geographic Stock. **489** John Terence Turner/Getty Images. **490** Nadia M.B. Hughes/National Geographic Stock; 2013 Comstock/JupiterImages Corporation. **491** Journal-Courier/Steve Warmowski/The Image Works. **493** Nadia M.B. Hughes/National Geographic Stock. **495** Plush Studios/Getty Images. **497** Jeremy Woodhouse/Getty Images; altrendo travel/Getty Images. **500** Jerry King; Reproduction rights obtainable from www.CartoonStock.com. **502** Cleve Bryant/PhotoEdit Inc. **504** Jose Luis Pelaez; Inc./Getty Images; Yuriy Nedopekin/Getty Images. **505** Jeff Greenberg/PhotoEdit, Inc. **506** Jeff Greenberg/PhotoEdit, Inc. **508** Jeff Greenberg/PhotoEdit, Inc. **510** Gary Null/NBC/NBCU Photo Bank/Getty Images. **511** Jeff Greenberg/PhotoEdit, Inc. **513** Push/Getty Images. **520** Anna Gawrys; Reproduction rights obtainable from www.CartoonStock.com. **522** Hara Estroff Marano; Patrick McCarthy; PRAKASH SINGH/Getty Images. **523** KEENPRESS/National Geographic Stock. **524** See Li/Demotix/CORBIS. **525** JUSTIN GUARIGLIA/National Geographic Stock. **526** Viking Childrens Book; Laurel Leaf; Speak. **527** Stockdisc/Getty Images; Stuart Gregory/Photodisc/Getty Images; David Young-Wolff/PhotoEdit, Inc.; Ron Levine/Getty Images. **528** Michael Newman/PhotoEdit, Inc. **533** Stockdisc/Getty Images. **534** Dennis MacDonald/PhotoEdit, Inc. **542–545** Diana Cook & Len Jenshel/National Geographic Stock. **542** Ingine/Digital Vision/Getty Images. **545** stockelements/Shutterstock; Little, Brown Books for Young Readers; Laurel Leaf; Graphia. **546** Phil Boorman/Getty Images. **547** Dean Berry/Getty Images; Tina Chang/CORBIS. **548** takayuki/Shutterstock; John Henley/CORBIS. **550** William Manning/CORBIS. **552** Gary Houlder/CORBIS; Tres Besos, 2005, Joe Ray. Acrylic on Canvas Board. Private Collection. **553** National Geographic Learning. **554** Batista Moon; Tres Besos, 2005, Joe Ray. Acrylic on Canvas Board. Private Collection. **557** Liz Garza Williams. **558** Liz Garza Williams. **561** Liz Garza Williams. **563** Liz Garza Williams. **565** Liz Garza Williams. **568** Ger Stallenberg/Het Ware Huis. **572** Tim Pannell/CORBIS. **574** Chuck Savage/CORBIS; Jeff Greenberg/PhotoEdit, Inc.; erwinova/Shutterstock. **576** National Geographic Library. **577**

Tres Besos, 2005, Joe Ray. Acrylic on Canvas Board. Private Collection. **579** Tres Besos, 2005, Joe Ray. Acrylic on Canvas Board. Private Collection. **581** Liz Garza Williams. **582** Liz Garza Williams. **584** Liz Garza Williams. **586** Liz Garza Williams. **589** 2013 Colin Anderson/JupiterImages Corporations; Digital Vision/iStockphoto.com. **590** 2013 Colin Anderson/JupiterImages Corporations; Schomburg Center for Research in Black Culture. **595** Brian Cahn/CORBIS; Vladitto/Shutterstock. **596** Katja Zimmermann/Getty Images. **597** Courtesy of the Library of Congress, LC-USZ62-78987. 598 Courtesy of the Library of Congress, LC-USZ62-78987. **601** Bettmann/CORBIS; American Foundation for the Blind, Helen Keller Archives. **602** PAL/Topham/The Image Works. **603** Bettmann/CORBIS. **605** Clearing the bark from sticks and arranging it in swirling patterns, 2003, Strijdom van der Merwe. Land art/photo documentation, Kamiyama, Tokushima, Japan; Carmen Tafolla. **606** CORBIS. **607** Erika Larsen 2004/Redux. **612** Elena Blokhina/Shutterstock. **613** Elena Blokhina/Shutterstock; Carla Golembe/Getty Images. **614** Little, Brown Books for Young Readers; Laurel Leaf; Graphia. **618** Barna Tanko/Shutterstock; Jose Luis Pelaez Inc./CORBIS. **622** Tim O'Hara/CORBIS. **623** Zero Creatives/Getty Images. **626** OLJ Studio/Shutterstock. **631** Steve Mason/Getty Images. **632** Jennifer Thermes/Getty Images; Scala/Art Resource, NY; The Bridgeman Art Library. **633** Terry Warner; Reproduction rights obtainable from www.Cartoonstock.com; Jeff Rotman/Getty Images; Darwin Wiggett/AllCanadaPhotos.com/CORBIS. **634** Skylines/Shutterstock; Flying Colours/Getty Images; Hiroshi Higuchi/Getty Images. **635** Maksim Kabadou/Shutterstock; Igor Klimov/Shutterstock; EDHAR/Shutterstock. **638** 2013 Microsoft; 2013 Microsoft; 2013 Microsoft. **793** Arthur Tilley/Getty Images; Peter Turnley/CORBIS. **794** Bob Daemmrich/CORBIS. **796** L. Clarke/CORBIS.

ILLUSTRATION CREDITS

Annie Bissett: **156** (youth sports charts), **492** (curfew chart), **495** (curfew pie chart); Dale Glasgow: **124** (family meals graph), **127** (teen meals graph); Christy Krames: **202** (muscle fiber), **203** (steroids/teen), **478** (teen brain), **479** (nerve fiber); National Geographic Maps: **147** (U.S./Mexico map), **310** (Florida map), **473** (U.S. driver's license age map)